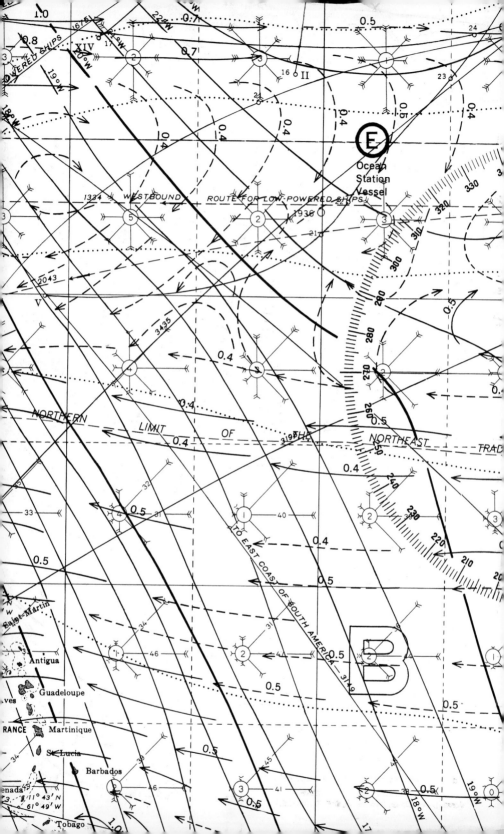

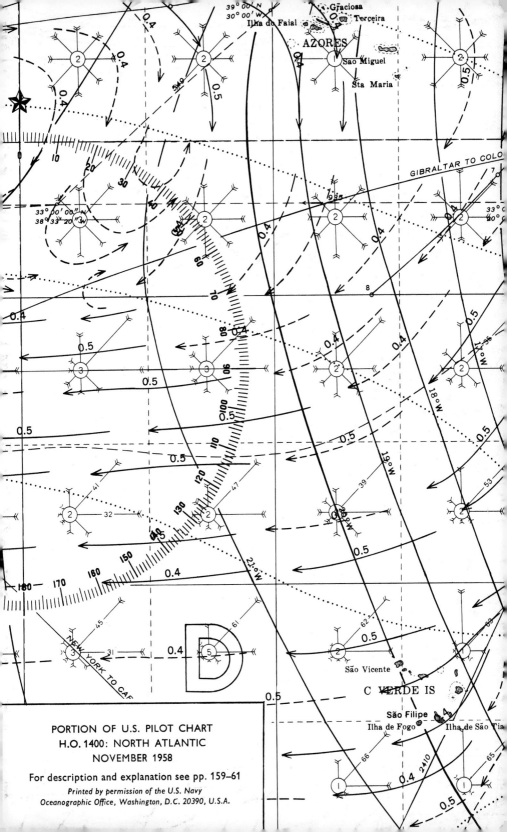

PORTION OF U.S. PILOT CHART
H.O. 1400: NORTH ATLANTIC
NOVEMBER 1958

For description and explanation see pp. 159–61

Printed by permission of the U.S. Navy
Oceanographic Office, Washington, D.C. 20390, U.S.A.

CRUISING UNDER SAIL

Incorporating

VOYAGING UNDER SAIL

By

ERIC HISCOCK

Author of

Around the World in Wanderer III, Beyond the West Horizon
Sou'west in Wanderer IV, Come Aboard, etc.

WITH 251 PHOTOGRAPHS BY
THE AUTHOR
AND 102 DIAGRAMS

THIRD EDITION

ADLARD COLES LIMITED
8 Grafton Street, London W1

Adlard Coles Ltd
William Collins Sons & Co. Ltd
8 Grafton Street, London W1X 3LA

First published in Great Britain in
hardback by Oxford University Press 1981
Published in paperback by
Adlard Coles Ltd 1985

British Library Cataloguing in Publication Data
Hiscock, Eric Charles
Cruising under sail: incorporating 'Voyaging under Sail'.—3rd ed.
1. Yachts and yachting
2. Seamanship
I. Title   II. Hiscock, Eric.   Voyaging under sail
623.88′223   GV813

ISBN 0–229–11765–1

Printed in Great Britain at the
University Press, Cambridge

To

ROGER A P PINCKNEY

ONE-TIME COMMODORE OF THE

ROYAL CRUISING CLUB

*who taught me and many others
how to cruise without fuss*

and

TOM & ANN WORTH

able and courageous voyagers

PREFACE TO
THE THIRD EDITION

TODAY there is no hard dividing line between cruising and voyaging, for even the smallest seaworthy cruisers can, and often do, make outstanding ocean crossings, and the two branches of sailing are closely inter-woven. When, therefore, with wider experience and a sense of the changing scene, I came to revise and rewrite the greater part of this book for a third edition, it seemed best to combine it with its companion book, *Voyaging Under Sail*, which also needed revision. This has the advantage that repetition is avoided, and that the information on both types of sailing may be found in a single volume.

Yacht *Wanderer IV*   ECH
Bay of Islands, New Zealand
December 1980

FROM THE PREFACE
TO THE FIRST EDITION

CRUISING under sail is one of the finest sports. Those who take
part in it pit their knowledge and skill not against a human
opponent for kudos or gain, but against the sea in all its moods.
Their ventures therefore receive little or no publicity, and that is
as they would wish, for they know that only those who love and
respect the sea as they do can appreciate their reasons for cruising
– the spice that a suggestion of danger lends to it; the satisfaction
of working the winds and tides to the best advantage; the
confidence which is acquired when a good landfall is made after a
rough passage or a difficult piece of pilotage has been successfully
carried out; the feeling of achievement when a strange coast or
harbour has been reached under sail; and the never-ending fasci-
nation of handling and looking after a seaworthy yacht and her
gear. Cruising teaches one to rely on one's judgement and skill,
and it is one of the few worthwhile things that can still be enjoyed
today by a man or woman of independent spirit, for there are no
restrictions, no organizing body is needed, and the sea is open and
free for all who have the inclination to sail on it and a suitable
vessel for the purpose. It may cost as much or as little as one is
prepared to spend, for an old and cheap yacht, provided she is
sound, may be just as suitable for cruising, though perhaps not
quite so convenient or such fun to sail, as an expensive one of
modern design and build, and a small yacht, though not so
comfortable, may be just as seaworthy as a large one.

There are many different forms of the sport. One man gets his
pleasure by making short day sails along the coast, spending each
night at anchor, sharing with his wife and family the peace of the
creeks and the novelty of life in their compact and mobile floating
home. Another, who can spare the time, gets his satisfaction by
making long passages in the open sea, taking the weather as it
comes, and driving his yacht day and night until she fetches up in
some foreign land. The cruising done by the majority, whose
numbers are swelling steadily year by year, probably lies between
these two extremes. Nevertheless, the basic knowledge required is
identical for all kinds of cruising, and it is one of the fascinations of
the sport that the most modest ditch-crawler must in some part
equip himself with the same knowledge and experience that would

serve to take his yacht (if she were of a suitable type and well found) across the oceans of the world.

Several admirable guides to cruising, which are of very great value to yachtsmen, have been published in the past, and my reason for writing yet another book on this subject is that I believe there is a need for a new assessment, in the light of changing conditions and modern knowledge, of many matters which have been taken for granted by several generations of yachtsmen. This work is not, therefore, simply a recapitulation of previously published matter, but aims, in addition to providing briefly the best of the earlier knowledge, at making available to the cruising man the most up-to-date information on all matters likely to be of interest to him, and in a volume that is not too large for any yacht's bookshelf.

I have made this book as complete as my knowledge will allow, stressing the practical side of rigging work and seamanship, and using my own photographs where possible to make each point clearer and more interesting. Many of the matters covered are controversial, and where I have expressed an opinion this has been based on my own experience at sea. In recent years improvements have been made to fittings and gear above and below decks, increasing the seaworthiness, ease of handling, and efficiency of old yachts as well as new; I have described those which tests at sea have shown to be sound, and of which the cost is not excessive.

So that any desired information may be found quickly and easily, a comprehensive index, which also includes plate references, has been compiled, and as a definition of each nautical word as it appears in the text would be tiresome for the more advanced reader, these have been placed in a glossary which should be consulted by the newcomer who is in doubt.

Yarmouth, I.W.   E C H
December 1949

ACKNOWLEDGEMENTS

I WISH to take this opportunity of expressing my gratitude to my wife for so neatly interpreting my rough sketches, and to my friends Richard Gatehouse (of Brookes & Gatehouse) for checking what I wrote about radio and echo-sounders, and Michael Handford (of Cranfield Sails) who corrected the chapter on working sails. I also wish to thank M G Duff & Partners for valuable information on galvanic action, and the following, who allowed the plans of yachts designed by them to appear in Chapter 11: Rodney Warington Smyth, Maurice Griffiths, Laurent Giles & Partners, John G Alden, and Arthur C Robb. I am also grateful to many sailing friends who have given me help and allowed me to photograph their yachts and their gear.

A WORD TO FEMALE READERS

I WELL understand that many of you are quicker to learn and are more skilful in the arts of sailing and navigation than are your male counterparts, and that you do not normally make such a fuss about it; I also know that without your company seafaring for males would be a savourless occupation. Nevertheless it does seem to me to be clumsy, tiresome, and rather absurd to insert the words 'she' or 'her' each time after 'he' or 'his' is used, and surely even the most feministic of you would not wish me to change 'seamanship' to 'seapersonship'. I therefore hope that you will not regard me as a chauvinist, and will appreciate that although they are couched in traditional masculine terms, my remarks are addressed equally to you.

ECH

CONTENTS

Part I

THE YACHT AND HER GEAR

PART II

SEAMANSHIP

Part III
VOYAGING

Part IV
MISCELLANEA

LIST OF PLATES

LIST OF DIAGRAMS

PART I

The Yacht and her Gear

1

HULL FORM

Definitions – Tonnage and displacement – The lines – Stability – Multi-hulls – Bows, sterns, rudders, and balance – Shoal draught – Speed – Size

THERE is no need for the newcomer to cruising to understand much about yacht designing, which is a specialized and complex subject calling for a high degree of skill, attention to detail, a sense of proportion, a knowledge of mathematics, and an artistic eye. But he should acquire some knowledge of hull form so that he may be able to compare one yacht with another, and judge which kind is most likely to suit his purpose; also he will find that a study of hull form in relation to performance at sea is fascinating, for there are so many factors to be taken into account, each having a possible bearing on the others, and there is no finality.

Definitions (Fig 1)[1]

Length over all (LOA) is the extreme length of the hull measured in a straight line between bow and stern; but in advertising the term is sometimes used misleadingly to include projections such as a bowsprit.

Length between perpendiculars (LBP) is measured on deck from the fore side of the stem to the after side of the sternpost (on which the rudder is hung) and therefore does not include a counter or canoe stern. LBP is one of the factors used in the formula for computing the Thames Measurement (which is defined below).

Load waterline (LWL) is the line on the hull which is reached by the water when the yacht is trimmed to float where the designer intended her to. It is measured not round the body of the yacht but along her fore-and-aft centre line between the points where the stem and the stern enter the water.

Beam is the extreme width measured to the outside of the skin at the yacht's broadest part.

Depth is an internal measurement taken from the under side of the deck amidships to the top of the main keel.

Draught is the depth of water needed to float the hull.

---

[1]A glossary of the nautical terms used in this book will be found on pages 520 ff.

Overhangs are those parts of the hull above the water at bow and stern which project beyond the ends of the LWL.

Flare is the outward curve of the sides above water which makes the hull wider on deck than it is on the LWL at that station.

Tumble-home is the opposite of flare, being the inward curve of the sides above the water, making the beam at deck level less than it is at the LWL or at some other point on the side at that particular station.

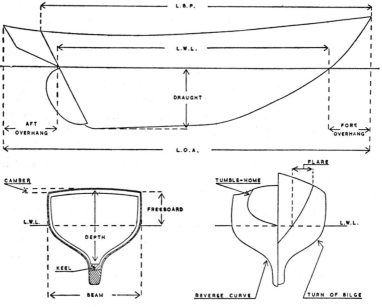

Fig 1   Definitions

Camber is the athwartships curve of the deck so that water will drain off instead of lying on it, and it adds strength.

Freeboard is the height from the waterline to the edge of the deck.

Sheer is the fore-and-aft curve of the deck or the top of the rail which gives a hull greater freeboard at bow and stern than amidships.

Reverse sheer is the fore-and-aft curve of the deck or top of the rail which gives a hull greater freeboard amidships than at bow and stern. Yachts having this feature are sometimes referred to as hog-backed.

Tonnage and displacement

The word ton is derived from tun, a cask used in the wine trade, and the size of a ship used to be judged by the number of tuns that could be stowed in her holds. Today there are three kinds of tonnage with which the yachtsman may be concerned. The one most commonly used in the UK until recently was devised by members of the Royal Thames Yacht Club in the nineteenth century for handicapping racing yachts and is known as Thames measurement. Only beam and LBP are used when calculating it (LBP – beam × beam × ½ beam, all in feet, divided by 94); draught therefore has no bearing on it so that a raft 7 metres (23 feet) long and 2 metres (7 feet) wide would have the same Thames measurement as a deep-bodied cruising yacht of the same dimensions but drawing perhaps 1·5 metres (5 feet) of water – just over 4 tons. So it would appear to be an absurd form of measurement, but when used for comparing the sizes of yachts of similar type it served fairly well. It is rarely used outside the UK, and even there LOA alone is being increasingly used as an indication of size, but it continued to appear in *Lloyds' Register of Yachts* until the demise of that publication in 1980.

Net register tonnage, which is required when a yacht is being registered as a British vessel, is found by calculating the capacity of the hull and then making certain deductions for engine space, bosun's stores, chartroom, etc, each figure being carved in its appropriate compartment. The figure finally arrived at by the Department of Trade surveyor is carved on the main beam along with the official number.

As a floating object displaces its own weight of water, the displacement of a yacht is her actual weight. This figure will probably be needed by the owner only if he is arranging to have his yacht slipped (hauled out), lifted by crane, or transported by road or rail. It will have been calculated by the designer and listed with the other particulars, such as the weight of ballast, and unless the yacht is large will be in kilograms or pounds.

For some years the general trend has been towards lighter displacement for a given waterline length and beam, and this has been achieved largely by more scientific methods of construction. In its extreme form the hull of light-displacement type has a round or flat bottom, and as there is not a lot of it in the water, freeboard has to be high to provide space in the accommodation. It probably has a short but deep fin keel to provide lateral resistance, and with ballast at its lower end to give stability; such a keel may make hauling out difficult and taking the ground dangerous. It should be noted that the bottom of any keel ought to be a U or V in section, so that on grounding on a falling tide the yacht may be given a list to port or starboard as desired. If the bottom of the keel is wide and flat the yacht will tend to sit squarely on it, and if she grounds sideways on to a slope she will, as the water level falls, assume the same angle as the slope and may eventually tumble over downhill. Also, when hauled out or dried out it will be impossible to scrub and paint the whole of the underside of a flat keel. The light-displacement yacht is, of course, more easily driven and therefore requires less sail area, and she will reach her maximum speed quicker. It has often been said that she is wet, but all that makes a properly designed yacht wet is her speed through the water, and if she is snugged down so as to travel at the same speed as a yacht of heavier displacement, she should be just as dry provided she has adequate freeboard. But the heavier displacement yacht of the same waterline length may have more room below, and she should be able to accommodate the stores and water for a long cruise without being put noticeably below her designed LWL, whereas the performance of many a light-displacement yacht has been spoilt and her freeboard reduced by putting aboard the necessary cruising equipment. The yacht of heavier displacement may be stronger and have a longer life, though this is not necessarily so, for the strength of a yacht depends largely on the workmanship and materials which have gone into her construction. Whether or not her motion will be more comfortable will depend not so much on her displacement as on her hull form.

The heavy-displacement yacht of today is frequently a motor-sailer, ie she is designed to sail reasonably well and yet have an engine of sufficient power and a propeller large enough to push her effectively to windward. The term 'motor-sailer' (an improvement on the term 'fifty-fifty' which it supersedes) is often used in a derogatory sense; but it should not be, for a good motor-sailer does what her owner requires, carrying him efficiently and in some comfort from one place to another.

The lines

Pilot cutters and fishing vessels, many of which have in the past been successfully converted for use as yachts, and some of the older yachts themselves, were not designed on paper. A would-be owner would explain to the builder of his choice what he wanted and in what respects the new vessel should differ from others of her kind. The builder then constructed a model for the approval of the owner and, according to the latter's wishes, cut away a little wood forward or aft or fined down the sections until the model pleased the owner and incorporated such points as he considered desirable. Careful measurements were then taken from the model so that the profile and sections could be drawn full size in chalk on the mould-loft floor, thus allowing the various members controlling the vessel's size and shape to be cut or formed correctly. The method was a little rough, but many a fine vessel was modelled in that manner, and some adjustment of inside ballast frequently had to be made to enable her to float in the desired trim when she was launched.

The designing of yachts on paper has now entirely superseded the model method, though models floating in tanks are sometimes used for testing purposes, and so precise are the calculations that nearly every modern yacht is designed with all her ballast on the keel, leaving no margin for errors. From careful measurements taken from the drawings, the designer prepares a table of offsets from which the builder can make his full-size drawings in the mould loft.

One used to be able to learn much about the shape of yachts in relation to the purpose for which they were designed by studying the reproductions of the lines drawings which appeared in yachting magazines and books together with the comments of designers, editors, and other knowledgeable people. But today, unfortunately, very few designers are willing to allow the lines of their creations to be published, because there is a risk of them being copied by unscrupulous people who wish to avoid paying the architect's just fees; so it is rare to see a set of lines, and often even the underwater profile has to be guessed at. Incidently, when published lines are copied the resulting yacht is unlikely to be a success, for the reproductions are too small to allow them to be enlarged to a size from which accurate working measurements can be taken without going through a complete refairing of them.

Stability

The pressure of the wind on a yacht's sails, gear, and freeboard tends to capsize her, and she relies on her ballast and initial stability to keep her more or less upright.

Ballast is additional weight, pigs of iron or lead placed low down in the hull, or cast in the form of a ballast keel and bolted on beneath the structural keel, or with steel construction the lead may be melted and poured into the keel cavity. With some glass reinforced plastic (GRP) yachts a similar cavity is filled with scrap lead, or a cast keel may be encapsulated in GRP, but with all GRP yachts a bolted-on ballast keel is to be preferred. The lower the ballast can be placed the greater is its righting moment, and that is one of the reasons why lead is preferred to iron for ballast keels in spite of its greater cost, for, weight for weight, lead takes less space, and its centre of gravity can therefore be placed lower without increasing the draught. Lead also has the advantage that it does not rust, and that a piece can be removed from it if necessary without much trouble; but it has not the strength of iron and it is more susceptible to damage in the event of the yacht striking a rock. The modern practice is to place all the ballast on the keel, but a little of a cruising yacht's ballast may with advantage be inside so that it can be moved to trim her correctly on the occasions when she takes aboard stores and water for a long passage.

Initial stability has nothing to do with ballast; it depends on the shape of the sections and on the proportion of beam to length. The more beam a yacht has in proportion to her length, the greater will be her initial stability; a shallow-draught yacht will need greater beam than another of the same length but with deeper draught, and of two yachts of similar type but different size, the smaller will require relatively greater beam; for that reason a large yacht cannot successfully be scaled down to make a small one, and vice versa. No precise figures can be given, but the beam of a normal 10·5 metre (35 foot) cruiser might be approximately one-third of

---

PLATE 1 (*facing*). A. A moderately rounded forefoot. B. A typical Laurent Giles bow with a fair amount of overhang. C. Short overhangs and plenty of sheer. D. The lean lines of a rather extreme clipper bow, and beyond, the long forward overhang of an old racing yacht. E. A counter on the left and a canoe stern on the right. F. A sawn-off counter terminating in a pleasing transom with some tumble-home. G. A transom stern with good proportions and little of it submerged. H. A typical Norwegian stern.

PLATE 2 (*overleaf*). Stages in traditional wood construction. A. The backbone – keel, stem, and sternpost – has been assembled. B. The ballast keel has been added, and the ten moulds have been erected at their stations. C. Ribbands have been fastened temporarily outside the moulds, and the fitting of steam-bent timbers against them has been started at the bow. D. All the timbers are now in position, every third one being doubled. E. Growing from top and bottom the skin planking replaces the ribbands. F. With planking completed the moulds are removed and stringers fitted. G. Coachroof coamings and deck beams are in position. H. The deck has been laid and the bulwarks fitted.

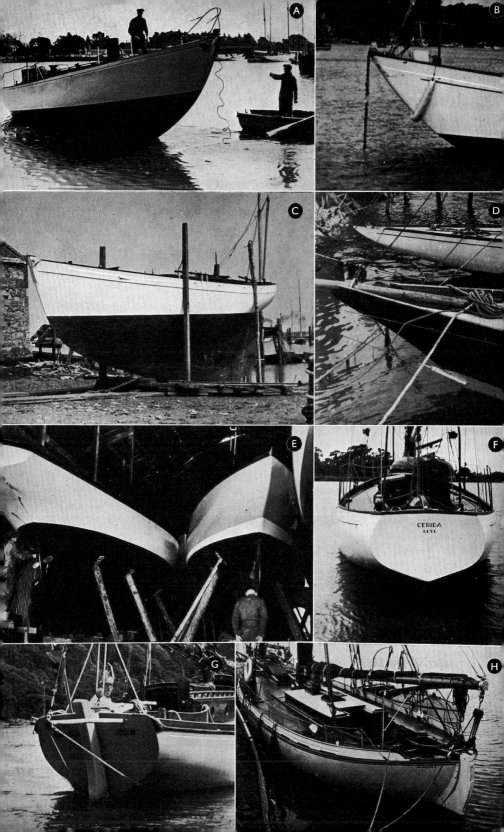

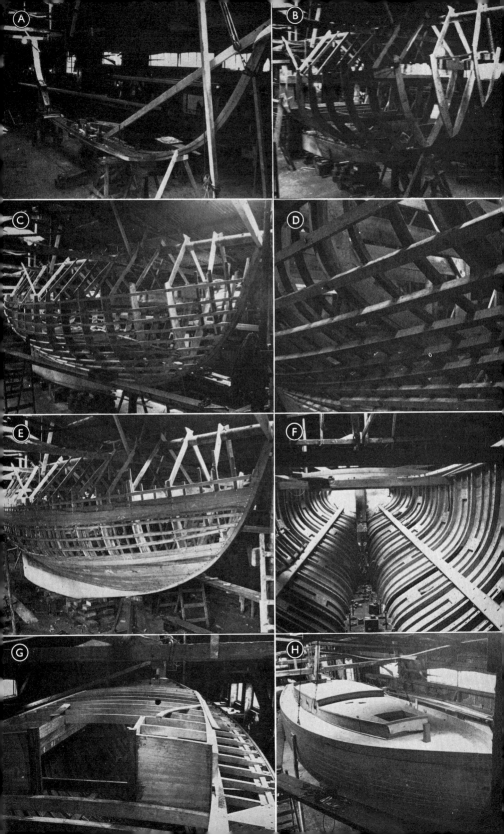

her waterline. A smaller yacht might need to have it increased to as much as $2\frac{1}{2}$ beams to the waterline.

A yacht which has weak or slack sections sloping easily from LWL to keel, without any very pronounced turn to the bilge, will be crank or tender, ie she will heel over too readily to the pressure of the wind; but a yacht with fuller sections having a firm turn at the bilge will be stiff, ie she will stand up better to the pressure of the wind. One is apt to judge the stability of a yacht by her midship section as that is the one most readily seen, but all her sections will have a bearing on her stability, and of two yachts of the same size with similar midship sections, the one that is fuller in the ends, carrying her beam farther fore and aft, and having in consequence more rounded waterlines, will be the stiffer. The stiffest section of all is the square one such as is possessed by the Thames spritsail barge, and it takes a very great pressure of wind to heel such a craft over far; but should she heel beyond a certain angle she will suddenly lose all her stability and will capsize. That cannot happen to a yacht with ballast, for the greater her angle of heel the greater will be the righting-moment of her ballast and the less the pressure on her sails. Only in exceptional circumstances is it possible for a ballasted yacht to capsize, and then, provided the inside ballast (if she has any) does not get adrift, she will right herself; but one without ballast relying entirely on initial stability could not do so.

To sail on a long passage at a steep angle of heel is tiring for the ship's company and bad for their morale, and when close to a lee shore in a strong wind the safety of the yacht may depend on her ability to stand up to her canvas. Ample stability is therefore very necessary for a cruising yacht, but it is a matter which needs careful consideration by the designer, for it is possible to make a yacht too stiff so that her motion is violent and she will then be hard on her crew and her gear. A yacht need not necessarily have rounded sections, for, like the barge, her bottom may be flat and join the topsides at an angle, the intersection being known as a chine. But her sections will not be square, like those of the barge (unless she is that rare thing, a barge yacht); her bottom will have some rise of floor (upward slope of the bottom from keel to chine) and some flare to her sides; in fact she is often known not by the term 'hard-chine' but 'V-bottom'. It is generally considered that such a craft is easier for the amateur shipwright to build, particularly if he is building in steel, when she may have not one but several chines each side. Sometimes it is possible to fit more spacious accommodation into a yacht of this type, or at least to give her a wider cabin sole, but her performance under sail will depend on her shape; if she is too flat-floored forward she will pound badly in a headsea, but if her rise of floor is too steep she will be tender; so it will be understood that the angle the bottom makes with the sides at the chines is an important matter.

Multi-hulls

Vessels having more than one hull have been in use in the Indian Ocean and the Pacific for many hundreds of years, and the word catamaran, which comes from the Tamil *katṭa-maram* meaning tied tree, has been used to describe all such native craft. Today, however, in English-speaking countries the word is used only for a vessel having two hulls of similar size and shape parallel to one another, while a vessel which has a float at each side of the main hull is known as a trimaran. The object of such designs is chiefly to obtain stability with the minimum weight, and therefore an increase of speed for a given sail area. Indeed, a multi-hull is a completely unballasted craft. The speed/length formula given on page 19 does not apply to such craft, in which speeds in excess of 20 knots have been attained in favourable conditions with waterline lengths of less than 6 metres (20 feet).

Many fine cruises and ocean passages have been made in catamaran and trimaran yachts, but that is not necessarily proof of their superiority as cruisers, and compared with yachts of traditional type they have certain disadvantages.

The possibility of a capsize must be regarded as the most serious of these. In a strong puff of wind the weather hull of a catamaran may lift out of the water, and if it lifts beyond a certain point the vessel will lose all stability and will capsize; to prevent her turning upside down a float is sometimes fitted at the masthead, but to right a capsized cruising catamaran would be impossible for her crew without help. The trimaran is less likely to capsize, partly because the helmsman will notice the lee float becoming depressed in time to luff or ease sheets, but if driven too hard she can bury her bows and pilchpole, ie turn stern over bows, and both she and the catamaran are subject to considerable stresses in a seaway. Sound engineering principles coupled with first-class materials and workmanship should be able to withstand these; nevertheless structural failures do occur. With a fresh wind abeam or forward of the beam catamarans and trimarans are faster than conventional yachts; their acceleration is remarkable and they are great fun to sail. But as their speed depends on their light displacement, performance can be ruined (and seaworthiness impaired) by taking aboard the gear and stores generally considered necessary for cruising. The well-designed catamaran's windward ability appears to be comparable with that of most other sailing craft in moderate or fresh winds, but in light winds she is slow because of her low sail-area/wetted-surface ratio. The trimaran, with greater wetted surface, is a poorer performer to windward, and may be difficult to put about in certain circumstances.

To summarize, the advantages of the multi-hull are: high speed; easy motion in some circumstances as she is not subject to rhythmic or accumulative rolling; small angle of heel, perhaps only 5 to 10 degrees as against 15 to 20 degrees of the mono-hull in similar strengths of wind, and because of the smaller angle of heel the sails are more efficient; shoal draught, which enables her to make use of shallow anchorages and to be beached easily for bottom painting or repair; comparatively easy for an amateur to build. The disadvantages are: risk of capsize, which for some owners is a constant anxiety; structural weakness where the cross-members are secured to the hulls, though, as noted above, it should be possible to overcome this; if much weight of stores and water, or elaborate accommodation, is aboard performance will be spoilt and seaworthiness possibly impaired; the multi-hull does not lie steadily at anchor in a breeze, and because of her great beam a berth for her at a marina may not easily be found, the tri taking more room than the cat. Nevertheless both types of multi-hull offer remarkable opportunity for the designer and builder, and with the improvements that time no doubt will bring could possibly be the popular cruisers of the future.

Bows, sterns, rudders and balance

It is desirable for a cruising yacht to have some overhang at bow and stern. Not only do overhangs provide a reserve of buoyancy to prevent the yacht from pitching too deeply when sailing against a head sea, or from being pooped when running, but when she is heeled a part of them becomes submerged, thus increasing the waterline length and making the lines easier for the water to flow along.

The straight stem bow is rarely seen today. Usually, but not always, it is lean and combined with a square deep forefoot so that the keel is long and straight; a bow of that kind lacks reserve buoyancy and is inclined to plunge deeply in a seaway, but it gives the yacht an easy pitching motion. The deep forefoot and long keel offer considerable lateral resistance when the yacht alters course, so a straight-stemmer will be slow to answer her helm, and instead of turning in a small space will make a wide sweep. She will, however, usually heave-to well and lie more steadily to her anchor.

The clipper bow, of which the stem has a forward curve sometimes known as a fiddle head, has, particularly when it is adorned with trailboards and bowsprit, a certain grace and swagger about it. It is a seakindly bow for a vessel of 12 metres (40 feet) or more, but in small sizes is not always satisfactory, for if the forward waterlines are fine the yacht will pitch quickly into a short headsea only to be brought up with a jerk by the flare above the LWL, the water being thrown clear away each side; the energy thus used retards forward progress.

The spoon bow, which has U-shape sections and generally a very long overhang (Plate 1D), is normally considered unsuitable for a cruising yacht as the flat part of the U tends to pound and may even damage itself in heavy weather; it is rarely seen today. The good modern bow has a moderate overhang with a sweeping upward curve to the stem and a gently rounded forefoot (Plate 1A and B); the water- and level-lines come to it in fair, easy curves and the sections are rounded V-shape; this form of bow is not lean enough to plunge deeply, nor flat enough to pound.

There are four types of stern: transom, sharp or lifeboat, counter, and canoe. Of these the transom (Plate 1G) is the easiest to build and is therefore cheaper than the others. It looks more pleasing if the topsides are given some tumble-home, and if it is raked aft so that the yacht has a small overhang at the stern. It has often been said that a transom stern may cause an overtaking sea to break; but any vessel if driven too hard in heavy weather could cause that to happen no matter what type of stern she has, and a well-proportioned transom stern is probably as seaworthy as any other kind; but it is not the best where speed is concerned, for the level lines are cut off suddenly by it instead of curving sweetly to their natural termination. The lower part of a transom should be in the form of a broad V, not a flat-bottomed U, with its point on or just above the waterline so that no part of it can become submerged and cause drag; but it must be admitted that nearly every transom does drag to some extent when the yacht is travelling fast and is heeled, for the lee-quarter wave produced by her progress through the water then rises well above the designed LWL.

The sharp stern is often thought to be the most seaworthy because it is the type with which lifeboats are provided. But there it is used because it is less easily damaged than any other kind of stern, and because lifeboats sometimes have to manœuvre stern first in broken water. Unless it is fairly full like the Norwegian stern (Plate 1*H*) a sharp stern is apt to lack buoyancy. Both transom and sharp sterns have a common advantage over other types in that the rudder can easily be inspected or removed for repairs.

In a counter stern (Plate 1*E* left) the topsides extend beyond the sternpost and terminate at a flat or curved archboard so that the deck retains a considerable width, tapering though it does, right to its end. Sawn-off counters are similar except that they are not so long and that they finish at a small transom tucked up well above the water (Plate 1*F*). A counter allows the level lines to be longer and better shaped, which is important as they are submerged when the yacht is heeled; but for cruising the counter must not be too long or too flat or it will pound in a seaway just as a spoon bow will. A well-tucked-up sawn-off counter is probably the best of all types of stern for the cruiser as it provides plenty of reserve buoyancy so that the yacht will lift readily to an overtaking sea, and it gives good deck space aft.

Because the measurement rules for racing yachts encouraged it, the forward-sloping transom was widely adopted in the mid-1970s, and unfortunately this then became fashionable for cruising yachts, in which it should have found no place. With this type of stern the sharp edge where topsides meet the transom is vulnerable to damage against which it is not easily protected, and deck space aft (where the cruiser needs it for the stowage of items such as lifebuoys, outboard motor, fishing tackle, and perhaps for the installation of a wind-vane gear or davits for a dinghy) is restricted, as also is the size of the stern locker where space is needed for lines, fenders, etc.

With the canoe stern the topsides extend beyond the sternpost as they do with a counter, but instead of terminating at an arch-board or small transom, they come together on the curved stern timber so that the deck ends at a point. A well-proportioned canoe stern with easy U-shape sections and well drawn out, is a sea-kindly end for a yacht, and it can be very attractive but it lacks deck space. When a yacht with too chubby a canoe stern is heeled, the curve of the submerged side is rather sharp for the water to flow round easily, so she is unlikely to be fast.

Counter and canoe sterns have the disadvantage that the stock of the rudder, where it passes through the yacht from LWL to deck, has to be enclosed in a watertight trunk, so the rudder cannot be removed easily for examination or repair.

A yacht with a long keel has her rudder hung on the sternpost with its lower pintle on the keel – a good and strong arrangement (Fig 2A). It used to be thought that for a yacht to be steady on the

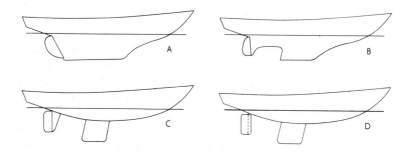

Fig 2   Keels and rudders
A long keel; B deadwood cut away; C fin with rudder on skeg; D fin with spade rudder semi-balanced.

helm, and to be capable of steering herself, a long, straight keel was needed, and to make the keel as long as possible the sternpost must be vertical. But to judge by the performance of many modern yachts with comparatively short keels, a long keel would not appear to be necessary, and almost all conventional sternposts are now raked with the top aft so as to reduce the area of wetted surface. But if too much rake is given the yacht may be difficult to steer, for some of the effort of the rudder will then be wasted in an attempt to drag the stern down instead of turning it sideways; also the rudder blade, if of wood, will tend to float upwards when the yacht heels, but that can be cured by letting a piece of lead into its trailing edge. A rake of 30 degrees is reasonable.

However, the long keel and its associated deadwood offers a lot of wetted area, and the skin friction caused by this reduces speed, especially in light winds; therefore it is now customary to dispense with part or the whole of the deadwood, so that the underwater profile line rises more or less vertically from the after end of the keel, and comes down farther aft to make a support and protection for the rudder, which usually will have no rake (Fig 2*B*). The fin-keel yacht has her rudder quite separate from the keel, possibly on a skeg (a vertical fore-and-aft member, Fig 2*C*), or it may be a simple, unsupported spade, perhaps of the semi-balanced type, ie with a portion of the blade forward of the rudder's line of rotation (Fig 2*D*); as the fin-keel yacht tends to lack directional stability, her rudder is usually placed as far aft as possible to increase the steering moment. Sometimes such rudders are raked with the top forward, but this is not a good arrangement because such a rudder loses power as the yacht heels, and at excessive angles of heel may stall and lose all control. With no support outside the hull, a spade rudder imposes a great bending strain on the stock where it emerges from the hull; and, as has been known for a long time, it is important for the rudder of any sailing vessel to have immediately ahead of and almost in contact with it a fore-and-aft member – deadwood, rudder post, or skeg – to direct a smooth flow of water to both sides of the rudder. Without this the yacht may be difficult or impossible to steer unless big angles of rudder are applied, and of course the greater the angle the greater will be the drag and the harder the work for the helmsman. A semi-balanced rudder cannot effectively be used in conjunction with a rudder post or skeg, so it should have no place in a sailing vessel, but in a power-driven vessel it is efficient because of the propeller race acting on it, and then not only gives good control but reduces the power needed to turn it.

A properly balanced yacht is one which will not alter her fore-and-aft trim at any angle of heel when sailing in smooth water. In the early days of this century it was the fashion to build yachts with lean bows and heavy quarters, and to induce them to float on the designed waterline when at rest or when sailing upright by the distribution of the inside ballast. But as soon as a yacht of that type heeled the tendency was for the stern to lift and the bow to drop, so that she griped or bored, and much helm was required to prevent her from rounding up into the wind. To ease the helmsman's labours most of such craft were fitted with long bowsprits and big jibs, but it was not unheard of for large unbalanced yachts to get completely out of control in strong winds. A great improvement to an unbalanced yacht can often be made by shifting weights (inside ballast or heavy items such as the chain cable) from forward to aft.

Today the designer sees carefully to the matter of balance on his drawing-board, and he designs a yacht so that the immersed areas of any two sections equidistant from the midship section are equal whether she is upright or heeled; in smooth water she cannot therefore alter her fore-and-aft trim. The shape of the hull has much more effect on the amount of helm a yacht will carry than has the shape or disposition of her sail plan, and a well-balanced yacht may even be made to turn to windward with any one sail set.

Thanks largely to the publicity which Admiral Turner and T Harrison Butler gave to the subject in the yachting magazines, everyone is now aware of the importance of balance in yachts; as a result we have more easily handled craft which do not drag about with them the steep quarter waves which were the inseparable companions of their lean-bow, heavy-quarter predecessors. It is possible to design a yacht with such perfect balance that she carries neither weather nor lee helm, but such a state of perfection is best avoided or the helm will feel dead, and all yachts for safety should carry a modicum of weather helm.

In yachts without much overhang at each end, with little or no flare in the bow sections, and with fine quarters, plenty of sheer is necessary to provide reserve buoyancy at bow and stern when beating into or running before a heavy sea, and to avoid excessive windage when heeled. The majority of cruising men consider that a bold and lively concave sheer-line is a pleasing thing which it is desirable for any vessel to have no matter what her function may be, but during recent years eyes have had to grow accustomed to yachts without any sheer, or with reverse sheer.

Shoal draught

An owner may wish to keep his yacht in a creek or harbour where there is little water, or he may have to do most of his sailing in a shoal-encumbered area such as the Thames Estuary, or Chesapeake Bay. His needs will best be met by a shoal-draught cruiser, and provided such a yacht has been designed by a man who thoroughly understands that type, she should be just as safe and seaworthy as one with deeper draught; but she may not perform so well when sailing close-hauled, especially in light winds, for her lateral grip on the water will not be so firm and she will therefore make more leeway (sag away to leeward of the course). To reduce the amount of leeway which a shoal-draught yacht would otherwise make, she may be provided with a centre-board, which can be lowered down through a slot in the keel for sailing, and hauled up in shallow water or when she is about to take the ground, or she may have bilge keels.

The old conception of a centreboard in this country was that the board should be a sort of drop keel, which by its weight would give the yacht additional stability. It was therefore made of iron and in some instances even had a lead bulb attached to its lower end. When lowered, a heavy centreboard of that type placed a great strain on the yacht, causing her to leak; also it was easily bent so that it could not be drawn up into its case, and it required powerful lifting gear.

The shoal-draught cruiser should have sufficient initial stability in her hull and/or enough ballast on her keel to prevent her from capsizing, and her centreboard should be regarded purely as a device to increase her lateral resistance and enable her to sail to windward without making excessive leeway. It should therefore be of wood or GRP and have only enough metal in the form of a band or tip to make certain that it will drop down through the slot in the keel when the lifting gear is released, and it should be of such a shape and so arranged that when lowered to its full extent there will still be sufficient of it in the keel slot to take all the lateral strains (Fig 3).

It is important that the centreboard cruiser should have a small amount of fixed keel projecting below her bottom to give some grip on the water when it is so shallow that the centreboard cannot be used, otherwise she will make so much leeway as to be unmanageable.

In shoal-draught yachts bilge keels have three advantages over the centreboard: they are simpler, and therefore cheaper, to construct, they do not interfere with the internal arrangements of the yacht, and when the yacht takes the ground they enable her to sit upright (Plate 27). Such keels are usually angled at about 20 degrees from the vertical, so that when the yacht is heeled the lee keel is more or less perpendicular, thus offering greater lateral resistance than a fixed keel or centreboard of similar area, while the windward keel becomes increasingly less efficient as the angle of heel increases. If the keels are set not parallel to the keel line but are given a toe-in forward of 2 or 3 degrees, the lateral resistance efficiency of the lee keel is increased; but experiments have shown this to be a theoretical rather than a practical consideration, and it is outweighed by the unwanted drag which may be created on every point of sailing.

A distinction should be drawn between the bilge-keel yacht and the twin-keel yacht. Whereas the former is of normal shallow-draught type with her outside ballast-keel on the centre line and a fin of wood, GRP, or steel fastened on each side at the turn of the bilge, the latter has no keel on the centre line of the hull, but instead is built with two large fins which carry all the ballast and on which she sits when taking the ground. Her rudder may be hung on a skeg on the centre line, or she may be fitted with twin

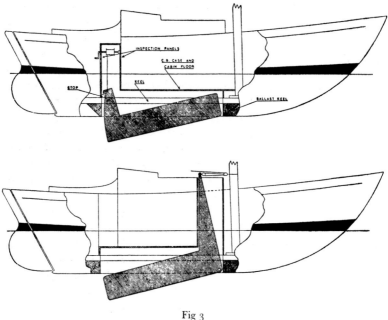

Fig 3

Top: A centreboard housed beneath the cabin sole with lifting gear and inspection panels under the bridge deck. *Bottom*: An alternative arrangement with the lifting gear on deck.

linked rudders, one on each of her fin keels. In the UK the Hon R A Balfour, now Lord Riverdale, was the originator of this type of craft and produced the first of his line of *Bluebirds* in 1923.

There is one other type, or, more properly, group of types, of vessel used for sailing in shallow water – the Dutchman. A number of these attractive craft with their bluff bows, great beam, and pleasing curves, are to be found cruising round the coasts of Europe. All of them have flat bottoms and carry leeboards, but they vary in other respects just as our own local fishing-boats did. In the larger sizes these vessels make excellent floating homes, but they are indifferent performers to windward so that the majority of them are fitted with powerful engines.

Speed

As a yacht moves forward she has to push away from her the water her hull displaces, and when she does this at slow speed she parts the water gently with her stem, and allows it to slip easily along her sides and bottom and come together again without any fuss at her stern. But as her speed increases the water has to be displaced faster, and waves are then formed which will vary in shape according to the shape of the yacht. If her lines are long and easy they will not cause so much disturbance as they would if short and sharply curved, and less energy will be used up in wave-making; so it will be seen that the longer a yacht is the faster should she sail. Sooner or later, however, every yacht reaches a speed which she cannot exceed under sail; then increased wind or extra sail area will be more than she can stand up to, so that she will drag her lee deck, rail, and some of her rigging through the water; the additional resistance will slow her up, the awkward shape of her hard-pressed and steeply heeled hull will create steeper waves, and not until sail has been reduced enough to allow her rail to lift clear of the water will she increase her speed to the maximum again. Although it is possible for a tender yacht to put her lee rail under before reaching her maximum speed, the majority of yachts sail at their best speed with the lee rail just clear of the water.

The highest speed is usually attained with the wind on or just abaft the beam, and as the yacht will then be heeled she will create a different set of waves each side of her. On her windward side there will be two waves, the weather bow-wave and the rather larger quarter-wave, separated from one another by a deep trough. On the lee side will be the lee bow-wave topped with spray, a second and smaller wave amidships (with some yachts this is so small as hardly to be seen), and the lee quarter-wave. Astern will be a number of following waves each an equal distance apart. The size and shape of all the waves a yacht makes depend on her shape; if, for example, she possesses an easy run with fine quarters, the largest waves will be those at the bow, while if she has heavy quarters the quarter and following waves will be the larger.

As speed is related to waterline length, it is possible to work out what the speed of a yacht should be. For a good type of cruiser with easy flowing lines the formula is

$$\text{speed in knots} = \sqrt{(\text{LWL in feet})} \times 1.4;$$

so that if her LWL is 25 feet her maximum speed will be 7 knots. But some adjustment has to be made to the multiplier according to the type of yacht. For a full-bodied, short-ended cruiser with rounded rather than flowing lines, the figure might be as low as 1·25; for a large racing yacht it may be increased to 1·5. The above formula does not apply to multi-hull craft.

The speed of yachts is deceptive. When sailing at or near their maximum speed they appear, because of the closeness of the water and the roaring of the bow wave, to be going very fast indeed, and then a reading of the patent log or speed indicator, or a timed run over a measured distance, is enlightening – and often disappointing.

Some long, flat-floored yachts of very light displacement may for short periods considerably exceed their theoretical maximum speed by planing. To do so they have to lift themselves bodily higher in the water and skim along on the surface, thus reducing their displacement and becoming easier to drive. Racing dinghies will often plane in strong winds, and some larger craft also manage to do so for short periods on being helped to rise by an overtaking sea; but a moderate type of cruising yacht cannot plane, though she may appear to do so when she is running before a strong wind and is carried forward at high speed on the breaking crest of a sea.

Size

With a few notable exceptions a yacht of about 7 metres (23 feet) is the smallest in which it is convenient to do much extended cruising. Though a yacht smaller than that may be a good sea boat, her motion in a seaway will be quick and tiring, her accommodation is of necessity cramped, and she may be unable to make satisfactory progress to windward in heavy weather. But the newcomer would be well advised to learn to handle a small yacht before attempting to take charge of a large one; she will not be so likely to lead him into serious trouble, and he will be able to do all the fitting out and maintenance work himself, thus saving expense; and learning from the start by practical experience how everything should be done.

The very small, light-displacement yacht of around 5·5 to 6·5 metres (18 to 21 feet) has opened up a new concept of cruising; on a suitable trailer she, the 'trailer-sailer', can be towed by a car of sufficient power from the owner's home, where she may be kept in garage or garden, to the cruising ground of his choice. Although this way of cruising lacks the satisfaction of passage-making from one cruising ground to another, it does have the advantage that the ever-increasing problem and expense of having a convenient permanent berth afloat on a mooring or at a marina is avoided. There are limits to the size of yacht that may be towed on the highway, and for these the police should be consulted.

Once the handling of a small craft has been mastered the owner nearly always wants something larger; her size may depend on the number of companions he wishes to take cruising, the degree of comfort he desires, the amount of money that he can afford for first cost and maintenance, and to some extent on the kind of cruising he intends to do. It should be remembered that a yacht need not be of large size to be able to make open-water passages in safety, for countless quite tiny ones have done that; but the larger the yacht the faster and more weatherly she should be. No yacht is comfortable at sea, though some are less uncomfortable than others, and a long vessel will probably have a less violent motion. However, for coastwise cruising the smaller yacht has the advantage of being able to work her way into and out of rivers and harbours which might be too small or shallow for a larger craft, and the smaller places are often the most desirable. There is also this point to be considered: a yacht which requires several people to man her may be held up in port if one of her crew is unable to join her and a replacement cannot be found.

2

CONSTRUCTION

*Wood – Metal – Ferro-cement – Glass-reinforced plastics – Corrosion,
galvanic action and electrolysis – Fouling and worm*

THE building of yachts is a highly skilled craft no matter what materials are used, and here it is intended to touch only on the broader aspects of construction so that the reader may understand the purpose served by the various parts of a yacht and the advantages and disadvantages of different methods and materials. The strength of a yacht and the length of her life mainly depend on the quality and nature of the materials of which she is built and the methods and workmanship used in knitting them together. Bulk does not necessarily mean strength, and with the popularity of light displacement that is just as well, for if a yacht is to be light her scantlings (the width and thickness of the various items used in her construction) must be kept within reasonable bounds.

Wood (Figs 4 and 5, and Plate 2)
From time immemorial vessels have been built of wood, and although today the majority of small yachts are of glass-reinforced plastic, wood is still regarded by many as the most trustworthy material, probably because it is more widely understood. The amateur builder likes it because it is clean and pleasant to work and is sweet smelling.

With traditional wood construction the keel, stem, sternpost, and deadwood are erected and joined together, wood plugs, known as stopwaters, being driven in to prevent leaks at joins which cannot otherwise be made watertight. On this backbone frames (ribs which are sawn to shape) or timbers (steam-bent to shape), conforming to the yacht's athwartship sections, are erected, and each pair is bound together and to the keel by floors of wood or metal. The timbers are strengthened part way up inboard by longitudinal members known as stringers, and at the top by similar members known as shelves. The beams supporting the deck are fastened to the shelves. Longitudinal planks are laid over the timbers from stem to stern, and are fastened to them usually with copper spikes clenched over rooves (washers), the ends of the planks (the hoodends) fitting into grooves (rabbets) cut in stem

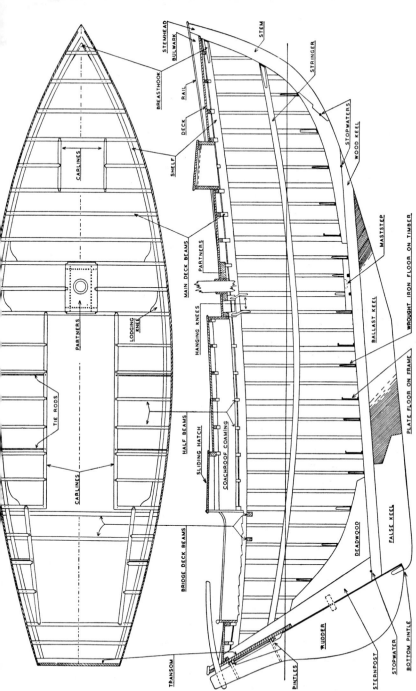

Fig 4   Deck and profile construction drawings of a 7 metre (23 foot) yacht built of wood in the traditional manner, giving the terms used.

and sternpost, and the lower edges of the lowest planks each side (the garboard strakes), lie in rabbets cut in the keel. The planking is carvel laid, ie edge to edge, except in some very small craft such as dinghies, where it may be clinker laid, ie with each plank slightly overlapping the next, like shingles on a roof. The seams of carvel-laid planks, which should be Y-shape, not V-shape, are

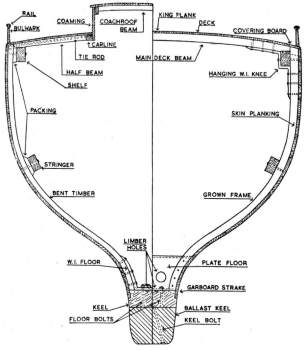

Fig 5   Sections showing construction details and terms used.

made watertight by caulking (driving in a strand of cotton) and paying (filling with putty). The deck may also be laid in planks, caulked, and payed with glue, or, more often, with a rubber compound, or for lightness the deck might be of plywood covered with GRP.

To gain extra headroom below deck a coachroof may be provided, half beams being fitted between shelves and carlines, and vertical coamings erected on the carlines to take the coachroof beams and decking. With no full length beams a coachroof in conjunction with a cockpit may create a weakness, so a narrow bridgedeck with two full-length beams is often built at the forward end of the cockpit. However, to gain headroom without the complication and possible weakness of a coachroof, some yachts have the topsides built up higher in way of the cabin; as all deck beams are then full length this is a strong arrangement, and it provides some reserve buoyancy in the event of the yacht being hove far over in a squall; yet it has never become popular.

The construction plans of a small yacht I once owned, built in the above manner, are shown on pages 23 and 24, for although this method of construction is not widely used today, the drawings do show the various parts of the structure with their names, and these serve similar purposes and retain the same names in yachts built of other materials. The scantlings, which appeared on the original drawings, have been omitted.

Strip planking, in which a large number of narrow planks is used, each one edge-nailed and glued to its neighbour, is popular with amateur builders because it eliminates the need for steam-bending, heavy cramping, and caulking, and it calls for less skill; but the cost of materials is higher. The double diagonal skin, which consists of two layers of thinner short planks laid at an angle to one another, is also popular with amateurs, especially in New Zealand. There is a similar form of planking in which strips of hardwood perhaps only 3 millimetres ($\frac{1}{8}$th inch) thick are laid on top of one another on a matrix (a hull built specially for this purpose), each with the grain running in a different direction – there may be as many as nine layers – and all are glued together. After the glue has set the shell is lifted off the matrix, and the timbers, etc, are fitted. This light and very strong form of construction is known as cold-moulded, and is suitable when several hulls are to be built to one design and the same matrix can be used for all. Many of the members of a wood hull, stem, sternmost, timbers, etc, are not necessarily cut or bent to shape, but are built up of many thin laminations glued together; this gives increased strength, but it has to be remembered that glue is one of the more costly items.

A wood yacht well built of good and suitable materials, is strong and elastic (I once had the misfortune to put such a one on a reef where she pounded for 48 hours but came to no harm) and is easy to repair, but there are two drawbacks which do not apply to yachts built of other materials; these are rot and damage caused by worm. Rot may be caused by the presence of sapwood and/or fresh water, coupled with lack of ventilation, and elm and pine are particularly susceptible. If at the time of building all the timber is well seasoned and is free of sapwood, and it is treated with a preservative such as Cuprinol, if ventilation is thorough throughout with no dead pockets, and if rain does not get in or condensed water get trapped, rot should not occur. Salt water is a preventative, so it is a good plan to flush the bilge with sea water occasionally, and leave a little standing so that the adverse effects of rain or condensation will be nullified. Trawlermen, knowing that one of the most likely places for rot to start was in the unventilated counter, used to toss handfuls of salt into the counter of a new trawler to 'pickle 'er'. Some remarks on worm will be found on page 37.

Metal

Of the materials commonly used for yacht construction steel is the strongest and most elastic. A stranding on a reef with a sea running (something that should never happen, but does occasionally) which would probably hole a yacht of wood or GRP construction, or even one of ferro-cement, may do little more than dent or buckle the plating, and this could probably be hammered out from inboard without sacrificing much strength. Professionally built by a yard which has the skill and the equipment to form plates to compound curves, and assembled entirely by welding, a one-off hull can be built in steel at less cost than in any other material. Because of the thin plating and the small scantling of frames and other members, the metal hull has, size for size, more space inside than has a hull constructed in any other material, and tanks as separate units for water and fuel do not have to be provided, for use is made of double-bottom tanks, ie the tanks are formed by bulkheading off and covering sections of the bilge.

Steel is heavy, weighing 7,285 kilograms per cubic metre (450 pounds per cubic foot) compared with 1,600 kilograms per cubic metre (100 pounds per cubic foot) of GRP and 642 kilograms (41 pounds) for the same volume of teak, but of course the steel skin will be very much thinner than skins of other materials. Although plating less than 2·5 millimetres ($\frac{1}{10}$ inch) thick would be amply strong for a small yacht it would not provide a sufficient margin for corrosion, and it could not be welded without buckling; plating of 3·1 millimetres (0·125 inch) is generally preferred, and one square metre of this weighs 22·8 kilograms (4·7 pounds per square foot) which is approximately the same as the weight of a square metre of 12 millimetre ($\frac{1}{2}$-inch) GRP, which would serve as skin for a 15-metre (50-foot) yacht, or a square metre of 38 millimetre (1½-inch) teak, which would be adequate for a conventional 18-metre (60-foot) yacht. Therefore weight for weight steel is not competitive with GRP or teak for the skin of a small yacht, but probably starts to be so at 12 to 14 metres (40 to 45 feet) LOA. However, there are certain savings in weight that should be considered before condemning it for the building of a small yacht; for instance, the steel yacht does not call for the solid masses of keel, deadwood, stringers, etc, which are required by the conventional wood yacht and to some extent by the GRP yacht.

Because of her welded construction the steel yacht is all in one piece, so she will retain her shape properly with no working seams and therefore no leaks, and if her decks, coachroof-coamings and cockpit are all of steel there will be no leaks there either; it is no exaggeration when an owner says he has been brushing the dust and cobwebs out of his steel yacht's bilge.

The amateur steel worker can build his own steel yacht if he is prepared to accept a multi-chine design so as to avoid the compound curving of plates, and it should be noted that the multi-chine hull – double, triple or even quadruple – is to be preferred to the single chine as it reduces turbulence and noise and improves performance, though it will still offer greater resistance than a round bilge hull.

A point often mentioned in favour of steel construction is that repairs and alterations can easily, quickly, and cheaply be made by cutting and welding. This may be so, but one has to remember that welding is a heat process, and that not only will it destroy the paint on both sides of a plate over a wide area, but unless internal insulation, joinery work, and electric wiring is removed in the vicinity of the welding operation, damage will result and the fire risk will be great.

With so much in its favour one may wonder why the steel yacht is not more popular than it is in Britain and the USA. One reason no doubt is that those countries have few yards capable of or willing to undertake such work, unlike Holland where small steel vessels of high quality have been built for many years. There is also a fear of condensation and galvanic action and electrolysis.

Condensation need present no problem if, after meticulous painting, the inside of the hull including deck and coachroof is provided with insulating material, either glued or sprayed on before the joinery work is started. Such insulation will be found of particular value in extremes of temperature, and will help to deaden much of the noise which is inseparable from a metal hull. Galvanic action and electrolysis need pose no greater risks than they do in yachts built of other materials. However, the hull below the LWL will need to be insulated as well as possible against action by the copper content of the anti-fouling paint, and is usually done by means of epoxy paints, while sacrificial plates will be fitted, see page 35.

Having owned jointly with my wife and lived aboard a steel yacht for eleven years, I am convinced that the major drawback of the material is the time and/or expense of maintaining the vessel to a reasonably high standard. The unfortunate fact is that salt-water causes steel to rust, and no matter what protective coating is used (new ones often come on the market to highlight the imperfections of the old) sooner or later water will get through or in behind it; rust will then form and lift the coating. When that happens, chipping, wire-brushing, grinding, or if the area is large, sand- or shot-blasting will have to be done to remove the rust and etch the steel before it is recoated. This is such a filthy job that many yacht yards do not permit it and it is harmful to bare decks, brightwork and paint still in good condition. It therefore seems that one must be prepared to live with a more plebeian kind of yacht which has no exterior woodwork and so can more easily be sand-blasted and spray-painted (preferably all in one colour to avoid the need for cutting-in) and by eliminating woodwork on deck the inevitable rust-producing areas where steel meets wet wood will be avoided. Chainplates, pinrails, male fittings for guardrail stanchions, and other deck equipment will no doubt all be of stainless steel welded in position, but a wider use of that material might be made with advantage by, for example, welding on a narrow strip of it along all sharp edges and corners where paint is most likely to give way.

Some builders use filler to hide imperfections and conceal the slightly wavy surface of the plating. But this should never be done, for in time the filler will lift in small or large blisters, or will crack or fall away or have to be removed; then, unless it is replaced and faired up, unsightly depressions will be left, and water will leach into the adjoining filler.

Although, as has already been said, a steel yacht should not leak, inevitably she will at some time or another take water aboard through a door or hatch, through a propeller-shaft gland, or when the anchor cable carries it into the locker, so it is desirable at the time of building to fill any spaces where water might lodge, and to make a clear runway for it to the bilge-pump suction. Cement is a good protection for steel and is generally used for the above purpose, yet it is not uncommon for a hair-crack to open where the cement stops, and if water enters there the plating will eventually rust through from inboard. Such cracks should be filled with soft sealant, or perhaps pitch might be used instead of cement.

If we are prepared to accept less 'yachty-looking' yachts steel, which has much to recommend it, may well achieve greater popularity.

Aluminium alloy at about 2,570 kilograms per cubic metre (160 pounds per cubic foot) produces a strong but very light hull, and in its marine form, when it contains a small percentage of magnesium, is not subject to corrosion, but may be quickly damaged or destroyed by electrolysis. Though it is used for some large one-off racing yachts because the resulting ballast/displacement ratio can be favourable, it appears to be little used for the building of cruising yachts, probably because of its high cost and the special welding technique needed. The only alloy cruising yachts with which I am familiar are Tom and Ann Worth's cutter *Beyond* (British), and Don and Cassy Boots' cutter *Spencerian* (American), and both have circumnavigations to their credit. *Beyond* did have some galvanic troubles, notably with rivets and through-hull fittings, but *Spencerian*, in which more modern techniques were used, did not.

Cupronickel (70 per cent copper and 30 per cent nickel) would appear to be the ideal metal for yacht construction were its cost not so high – probably nearly twice that of steel. It is strong, electrically almost inert, and it was reported of the 15·8-metre (52-foot) *Asperida*, the only yacht I know of built in cupronickel, that she never had any paint on her bottom and never needed any because of itself the alloy had sufficient antifouling properties, and any slight fouling that formed in port got washed off when she moved.

Ferro-cement

The first ferro-cement boats were built in France in 1855, and at least one of them was said to be still afloat 120 years later, but the material did not come into wide use for the building of yachts until the 1970s, when there was considerable disagreement among promoters and builders over the details of construction, and ten years later some of these had still not been resolved.

Although several firms build yachts in ferro-cement the labour costs are high, and the material appears to lend itself more readily to amateur use. A male plug, a female mould, or temporary wooden sections may be employed, but the open frame method is the most widely used. In brief this consists of bending 12-millimetre (½-inch) mild steel pipes and/or mild steel rods to conform to the profile of the yacht and her sections. When these have been set up in their correct relation to one another, high-tensile steel rods are fastened longitudinally like stringers, trans-verse rods are fitted, and the whole framework is then covered with from four to eight layers of wire netting; finally a mortar of cement and sand is forced in through the netting, usually from inboard, and smoothed off on the other side, and the plastered hull is left in a wet environment for several weeks to cure and gather strength which continues to increase over some years.

Apart from an ability to weld, not a lot of skill is required, for the pipes and rods are not difficult to bend to the desired form, and little expertise, though a lot of time and patience, is needed to lace on the wire netting so that the final matrix is taut and smooth. A team is required for mixing the mortar and doing the plastering, for it is important (as most builders agree) that the operation once started should be completed without a break. Some skill and perseverance is needed to ensure that no air pockets, which would be a source of weakness, are left, that the mortar covers the wire mesh everywhere, but by no more than 3 millimetres (⅛th inch) or extra and highly undesirable weight will be added, and to get a smooth finish on the outside.

At 731 kilograms per square metre (150 pounds per square foot) ferro-cement is a comparatively heavy material and, like steel, is not best suited to a vessel of less than about 12 metres (40 feet). It lends itself very well to compound curves but not to flat areas which, if they are present, will need special strengthening inside, and failure to do this may have been the reason why serious damage has been done to some yachts when stranding, for of itself the material has great strength. For these reasons alone it is not wise to build to a design originally intended for construction in some other material, and in doing so some enthusiastic amateur builders have produced hulls so heavy that they floated much below their designed waterlines, making them crank, wet, and poor performers. In an attempt to popularize the material many exaggerated statements have been made about cost, some claim-ing that a ferro-cement yacht will be 50 per cent cheaper than if built in any other material. But of course it is only the material used in the hull that will be cheaper, and the hull accounts for no more than one-third of the total cost of a yacht, the remainder going to the accommodation, tanks, masts, rigging, sails, engine, etc, and these remain the same no matter of what material the hull may be built. Some people have been so misguided as to build yachts that were much too large for their pockets, and then had to finish them cheaply and badly, while others abandoned their projects at an early stage.

Nevertheless success can be achieved by the amateur if he builds in ferro-cement to a design by a specialist in that field, and follows that designer's recommendations to the best of his ability. The popularity of the material may be judged by what Richard Hartley, New Zealand's eminent ferro-cement designer and builder, told me: in 1976 1,400 of his designs of between 9·8 and 17·4 metres (32 and 57 feet) were under construction, and that figure did not include designs sold by his world-wide agents.

That an amateur-built ferro-cement hull can withstand the rigours of ocean voyaging was shown by the 16-metre (52-foot) cutter *Awahnee*, in which Bob and Nancy Griffith, who built her themselves, not only circumnavigated the world twice (once by way of the Horn) but later made a circuit of Antarctica in 60 degrees South.

Glass-reinforced plastics (GRP)

The first commercially built GRP yachts appeared in the USA in the late 1950s; since then GRP has become the most widely used of all yacht-building materials in the country and in the UK, for it lends itself readily to mass production. Some of the earlier yachts moulded in this material were of unsuitable design, were produced by upstart firms which had no knowledge of the sea, and as the material was new and not fully understood, were badly moulded and poorly finished. Today many of the old-established yacht builders and some specialist firms mould GRP yachts of high integrity.

Reinforced plastics all combine a low-strength resin reinforced with a high-strength filler, which is bonded to the resin. The most commonly used resin is of the polyester group, which can be moulded without pressure and cured without heat, and during curing becomes hard and rigid. The reinforcement used is fibrous glass, hence the commonly applied term 'fibreglass'; but Fiberglass is a registered trade name for a particular brand of material in the USA. The fibres are laid up in various ways to form a mat or cloth so that its greatest tensile strength may be in one or more directions according to the job it has to do, much as the grain of timber is used, and strengthening members can be built up where needed.

As with other building materials there are several ways of doing the job, and from time to time new ones are evolved, but at present the most widely used commercial method is, briefly, as follows: the hull is built full size in wood, usually strip-planked, and the outside is given the highest possible finish, for on this will depend the finish of the GRP hull. The wood hull is known as the plug, and after being turned upside down a female mould is laid up on the outside of it. As there is then no further use for the plug, it is usually completed, fitted out and sold as a high-quality wood yacht. The inside of the female mould is coated with wax, or other substance, to ease eventual removal, and the gel coat, which will form the glossy, protective finish to the outside of the GRP hull, is sprayed on. This is followed by layers of resin-impregnated glass-fibre mat, rolled to expel all air pockets; the process is continued until the skin has been built up to the intended thickness, which will vary in different parts of the hull according to the stresses it must take, eg thick near the keel, thin at the topsides. In the same manner strengthening and stiffening members, such as floors, frames, and bulkheads, are built up where required with layers of epoxy-impregnated glass mat, and this is done while the shell is still in the mould so that there may be no deformation of it on removal. As a mould is an elaborate and expensive production, its cost needs to be spread over as many hulls as possible, and for this reason, among others such as the need for humidity- and temperature-control, the method is not economical for the production of a one-off hull, and therefore has little appeal for the amateur builder who, if he does wish to use GRP, will probably adopt the sandwich system. This consists of putting a layer of balsa (a very light timber) or closed-cell foam on a wooden plug, covering it with a layer of epoxy, and after removal from the plug coating the inside with epoxy; this results in a light, strong, and well-insulated hull.

The deck and superstructure will be one or more separate mouldings which later are bonded to the hull, and in some earlier yachts these bonds were a source of leaks, but this weakness has been overcome. However, so as to make it easy to withdraw the moulding from the mould, commonly a number of undesirable shapes are incorporated. Coachroof coamings, for example, may be given excessive tumble-home and so may the forward end of the cockpit; then to prevent rain falling straight into the cabin through open ports or companionway, the openings must be kept closed, thus much reducing ventilation in wet weather.

High-pressure salesmanship has claimed the most remarkable advantages for GRP, some of which are not justified. The material, which is expensive and not fire resistant, has great flexibility but little elasticity, so that although it may survive great shocks from being dropped, it does not seem so well suited to the normal stresses of seagoing and harbour use unless, as with ferro-cement, any flat areas are strongly reinforced; and it is harmed by chafe. Colour impregnation in the gel coat, which would be so valuable if it were durable, does not last indefinitely, and the plastic is affected by dirt in the water and atmosphere, so that eventually it must be painted for the sake of appearance; and contrary to a common belief it has no antifouling properties, except those inherent in a smooth surface. The process of moulding (or repairing) GRP is a sticky, smelly business which does not attract the best class of labour, and the work is not easy to oversee. A common occurrence is the blistering of the gel coat, particularly on the underwater body; this is known as osmosis. The blisters, on being burst, are found to contain water, which has either percolated in from outside or was present at the time of moulding. This is a cause of great concern, for if allowed to remain, delamination of the layers of mat may result, so some builders have discontinued using a gel coat and rely instead for protection entirely on paint. Certainly it would appear that the GRP yacht should not be left permanently afloat, but should occasionally be taken out of the water so that she may dry out to some extent, and if a moulded hull is to be comfortable to live aboard it needs to be insulated.

The advantages of this form of construction are great, and among them we can list: lighter displacement in suitable design and execution than is possible with orthodox wood construction, little likelihood of leaks, no risk of attack by gribble, teredo or rot, ease of repair in the event of damage (though some deny this), and greatly reduced maintenance.

Corrosion, galvanic action, and electrolysis

Rust is a nuisance in spoiling the appearance of a yacht, and is difficult to stop once it has got properly started; it could be a cause of weakness if allowed to continue unchecked for a long time, although a great deal of rust is produced by a very small wastage of metal, and of itself, so long as it is not being constantly rubbed off, rust provides some measure of protection to the steel beneath. Steel is more prone to rust than is iron, but the latter is not now much used for yacht fittings because, for a given scantling, it is not so strong. The best protection for iron or steel fittings exposed to seawater is galvanizing, whereby, after a bath in acid to remove all foreign matter, a coat of zinc is bonded to the metal; if this is well done it will form a protective coat which is serviceable for several years. However, fittings of stainless steel are now widely used, and although a brown discoloration often occurs on them it seems to have no ill effect, and can usually be rubbed off with metal polish or a plastic saucepan scourer.

It is common knowledge that if two dissimilar metals (eg copper and steel) close to or touching one another are immersed in an electrolyte such as seawater, a current will flow between them and the less noble of the metals will be attacked and perhaps destroyed. Alkali is formed round the nobler metal, and under certain circumstances acid round the other. Both acid and alkali are harmful to any adjacent timber, and electrochemical decay of the timber may be caused. The usual symptoms are the destruction of the paint and stopping round and over a fastening, and a local softening of the timber. All timbers may be attacked, but spruce, teak, iroko, and pitchpine offer good resistance, while oak, elm, and mahogany have poor resistance. But far more serious than this may be the result of the corrosion of one metal through galvanic action with another.

The following list of metals commonly found in yachts is arranged with the most noble metal first and the basest metal last. The farther apart in this list any two metals may be the greater will be the galvanic action between them to the detriment of the latter one:

stainless steel; copper; admiralty bronze; manganese bronze; tin; lead; cast iron; mild steel; aluminium; galvanized steel; zinc.

Clearly the ideal yacht would have all her underwater fittings of the same metal. This is not practicable, though in theory it should be possible with a steel yacht, but then the sea-cocks guarding her through-hull fittings would need to be of steel as well as her propeller and its shaft, and steel cocks in small sizes are not easy to come by. Stainless steel is a much more suitable material for a shaft, and bronze for a propeller, so these different metals are used, and at once there is a risk of galvanic action between them and/or the steel fabric of the hull. Perfect insulation in the form of non-metallic paint or a rubber compound might solve the problem, but in practice such coatings are subject to damage or blistering and peeling. The wood yacht will probably be fastened with copper, but physically that is not a suitable material for rudder pintles and keel bolts, for which bronze and steel are likely to be used; so here again galvanic action could take place. Even a GRP hull with plastic through-hull fittings needs some underwater metal parts.

In days now past when bronze fittings were cast and machined in the yard where the yacht was being built, it is probable that all would have exactly the same metal composition, but today such parts are usually provided by several firms using materials sufficiently different in composition to create a galvanic couple. Some alloys are subject to self-destruction when immersed for a period of time in seawater; common yellow brass, for example, loses its zinc content so that the interior of a fitting turns crystalline and weak although the surface, which may have become pink, appears to be in good condition. Therefore, yellow brass should not be used for marine purposes.

Designers and builders of integrity do their best to avoid the use of unsuitable or incompatible metals, but as we have seen this is not entirely possible, and the subject is a complex one; so other steps are usually taken to minimize the risk. In its more advanced form a protective system comprises a piece of inert metal through which is fed a suitable electric current; but in yachts we are mostly concerned with anodes of a metal low in the order of electric potential, secured on or near the fitting which is to be protected, and with which it must be in perfect electrical contact. Such anodes are known as sacrificial plates, for they are corroded away instead of the fittings or plating they are placed to protect, and they can be renewed when necessary. Zinc, and by this is meant not commercial zinc, which is soon rendered useless by the formation on its surface of an inert substance, but an alloy of zinc specially prepared for the purpose, is the most widely used type of anode. Advice on the size, number, and the positioning of sacrificial plates can be had from a firm, such as M G Duff & Partners, which specializes in anodic protection. A steel yacht might call for three zincs each side, one amidships and two in way of the propeller. The best way of attaching a zinc to a metal hull is not to weld it, for renewal would then be difficult, but to have two holes in it to fit easily over two steel studs; the studs are welded to the plating and the zinc is slipped on and held by a nut on each stud, as with Duff's Guardian zincs. Fitted in that manner a zinc has perfect electrical contact with the hull and is easy to replace. Zincs must not be painted. Their active life depends on many factors, and normally should be several years, but if the zincs waste away rapidly, or more rapidly than they have in the past, the cause should be investigated.

But no matter what metals were used in a yacht's construction, or what protective measures taken, the prudent owner will from time to time examine underwater fastenings and fittings, and will withdraw one of any set of bolts, particularly those holding a ballast keel, and subject it to twisting and bending strains to determine its condition, and if it is found to be defective he would be wise to renew the whole of that set of bolts. But the withdrawal of keel bolts is often awkward, and other things such as watertanks may first have to be removed, so it might be more satisfactory in the first place to enlist the services of a firm that specializes in the radiography of keelbolts, such as X-ray Marine Ltd, so that only those seen to require replacement need be withdrawn.

Electrolysis differs from galvanic action in that it is a form of corrosion caused by stray electric currents seeking an earth, and it can be highly destructive. It is aggravated by the proliferation of electric equipment in the modern yacht, or even aboard her neighbour. Yachts of metal construction are most at risk, but one of any material can sink if electrolysis destroys a through-hull fitting or the pipe it guards. The yacht's wiring should therefore be a two-wire system and should not be earthed (grounded), and the introduction into the system of any additional electric equipment should only be undertaken with caution and a knowledge of what is involved. All insulation should be perfect, and all connections clean and tight, so that there may be no stray currents; however, most yachts have engines, and with the majority of these the electric equipment – not only the starter motor, but instruments such as oil-pressure and water-temperature gauges – is fed by a single wire and earth return, when faulty insulation may, unnoticed, cause serious damage; unless this can be changed to the two-wire system, it is important to install a switch or switches to isolate the engine and its equipment from the battery at all times when the engine is not running.

Fouling and worm

Floating in the sea, more especially in harbours and near the coasts, are many organisms, both marine and vegetable, which in the young state will adhere to and grow on the underwater body of any craft afloat, and even on the topsides during a passage lasting for several weeks (Plate 64A). The first sign of the vegetable growth is often a thin slimy film which can easily be rubbed off, but if it is left a thick growth of weed will develop, green in colour on and just below the waterline and brown or red further down, the green kind needing more light than the other. In addition, several types of soft branching animal growths will appear together with barnacles, mussels, and jelly bags; the latter are primitive relations of the higher vertebrate animals. As the animal growths are not directly dependent on light, they usually abound on the lower parts of the hull.

All these fouling growths, and they grow more readily on a vessel in port than on one that is under way, tend, by the extra friction they offer, to reduce her speed; even the first thin coating of slime will take the edge of the performance, and it is possible for a sailing vessel to become so slow as to be unmanageable. This happened to *Wanderer IV* on a 38-day passage from Panama to the Marquesas islands. Her bottom was clean and freshly painted when she left Panama, but on arrival at the islands her entire bottom was covered with goose barnacles between 2·5 and 10 centimetres (1 and 4 inches) long. As a result she was difficult to handle and a speed of about 3 knots was all that she could manage.

But there are in addition two forms of creature, the teredo (or shipworm) and the gribble, which can and do cause very severe damage to wooden yachts. The first of these is almost invisible when it attaches itself to the planking and looks for a suitable spot at which to start operations. It bores straight into the wood for a short distance; there it grows and becomes worm-shaped with a shell at one end fitted with cutting teeth; it then proceeds to bore lengthways along the plank, lining its tunnel with a shelly substance, and rarely breaking surface, so that the damage caused is not visible though it may be extensive. In British waters the teredo seldom grows to more than 23 centimetres (9 inches) in length, but in the warm waters of the tropics it may be as long as 1·8 metres (6 feet). It may remain alive in wood which is out of water for three weeks, and is much less affected than most marine organisms by fresh water.

The gribble is not unlike a small woodlouse, about 3 millimetres ($\frac{1}{8}$ inch) long, and though it prefers the brackish waters of tidal rivers it is active out at sea. It bores into the wood to a depth of about 5 centimetres (2 inches) and then returns to the surface, repeating the operation again and again, converting the wood into a pulpy mass which gets washed away, thus exposing a deeper layer to attack. The parts most often attacked by the gribble are the undersides of the keel and false keel, and the after side of the sternpost. It can survive in wood out of water for up to a fortnight.

No matter how hard or how sound timber may be, all kinds generally used in yacht construction are, to a greater or lesser extent, subject to attack by worm and gribble. An infallible protection is metal sheathing, and for this copper, which also has powerful antifouling properties especially when new, was commonly used in the past but is rarely seen today. Sheathing with GRP or nylon also provides protection, but neither has any antifouling properties. Good paint will keep worm out of a wooden hull, but it must be in perfect condition, for the worm can enter through a tiny crack or hole. New yachts, the bottoms of which have had perhaps only a few coats of paint, are sometimes attacked, while older neighbouring yachts with a thick accumulation of paint on their bottoms remain unscathed.

For many years antifouling compositions have been in use containing among their ingredients poisons of one kind or another – usually copper or mercury – but as the weeds and creatures which foul a vessel's bottom obtain their food from the sea, the composition must be so made that the poison is slowly liberated in order to make a toxic solution in the near neighbourhood and thus arrest the growth of the organisms in their embryonic state. These work more or less successfully, but in the summer months when the warm water encourages rapid growth the effects of the paint often do not last more than 6 or 8 weeks, nor are the more expensive brands necessarily the most effective, for local conditions vary, and it might be wise to enquire which paint has been found to be the most effective in one's home port. There are two distinct types of antifouling paint: contact leaching and soluble matrix. The former contains a high concentration of copper and other toxic compounds in a hard, insoluble binder, which is durable and will withstand repeated scrubbing. The soluble matrix type is not so costly and works by the washing away of the surface at a controlled rate; on being scrubbed much of the paint is removed so recoating will be necessary more often, thus probably costing just as much in the end as if contact leaching paint had been used.

In the mid-1970s a new system of deterring fouling was evolved in the USA, and soon after became available overseas. Under the trade name Aqua Sonic this consists of providing the hull below the LWL with one or more internal transducers each side, each transducer protecting an area of about 5 metres (16 feet) in diameter, depending on the thickness of the hull and the material of which it is made; the transducers, fed by a common oscillator, induce a sonic condition in the hull, and this, it is claimed, inhibits the growth of marine organisms, thus much increasing the periods between bottom scrubbing and painting. The system, which works off the yacht's battery or a shore supply of electricity, emits a continuous buzzing noise, and if this is found to be objectionable it is suggested that music from a radio or tape player may be used instead (if that can be tolerated) and it is reported to be just as effective.

3

ACCOMMODATION

Sleeping-berths – Galley, cooking stoves, and refrigerators – Freshwater – Saloon and chart tables – Cockpit and steering arrangements – Lighting, heating, and ventilation – Sanitation

EXCEPT in a large yacht the layout below deck will be a compromise, but as one may sometimes be cold, wet, or tired when cruising, a warm, dry saloon in which to seek shelter when under way or at anchor is desirable. Although the accommodation need not be expensive or elaborate, there is no reason for it to be spartan or unpleasing to the eye; it is not effeminate to have a tidy, attractive, and comfortable saloon, as a visit paid to many a yacht which has made a good cruise or voyage will show.

Accommodation arrangements vary considerably even in yachts of similar size and hull form, for each owner or designer has his own ideas, but there are certain essentials which merit consideration in every yacht. One of less than 9 metres (30 feet) LOA is generally divided into three parts. Aft is the cockpit or steering well (but see page 58); amidships is the main cabin or saloon, which is entered from the cockpit or deck through doors and/or a sliding hatch by a ladder or flight of steps, the whole entry being known as the companionway; and forward is the forecastle (pronounced fo'c'sle), sometimes known as the forepeak. Except in a very small yacht the forecastle is usually separated from the saloon by a bulkhead (athwartships partition) with a door in it or

---

PLATE 3 (*facing*). *A.* The navigator's space in *Alano* has a table and drawers for charts and stowage for books and instruments (see plan on p. 196). *B.* Aboard *Cardhu* the galley is separated from the saloon by a sideboard, and from the central alleyway by a flat-topped oak bar over which the cook may swing his legs and sit while attending to his pots. *C.* Plenty of teak and fine craftsmanship show in this corner of the saloon in *Chinita*, one of the Hong Kong-built Vertue class. *D.* I took this photograph aboard the New Zealand yacht *White Squall* at Tahiti a few minutes after Ross Norgrove had sailed her there direct from Auckland, to show that dirt and disorder need play no part in cruising.

PLATE 4 (*overleaf*). *A.* The galley aboard *Widgee*, one of the 9-metre (29½-foot) Wanderer class, is situated in the best place close to the companionway where there is plenty of air and headroom. *B.* *Svea*'s galley with its decorative tiles and knife stowage. *C.* *Outward Bound*, built by John and Mary Caldwell, also has the galley aft on the traditional port side; the paraffin-burning refrigerator can be seen behind Mary. *D.* To keep the cook in place the best shape for a galley is a narrow U with its arms fore-and-aft, as in *Wanderer IV*; note the safety bar in front of the cooker.

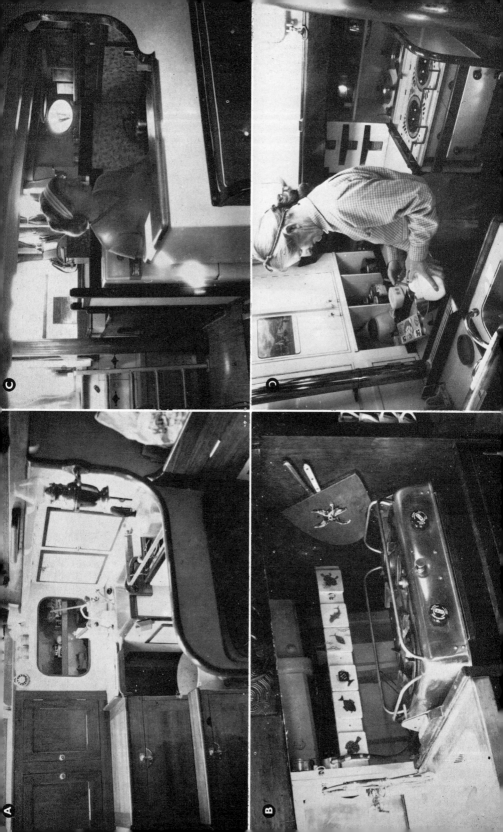

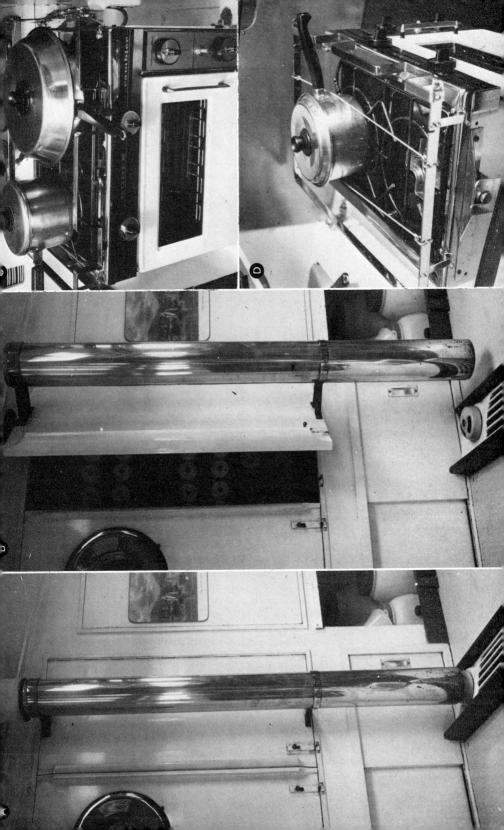

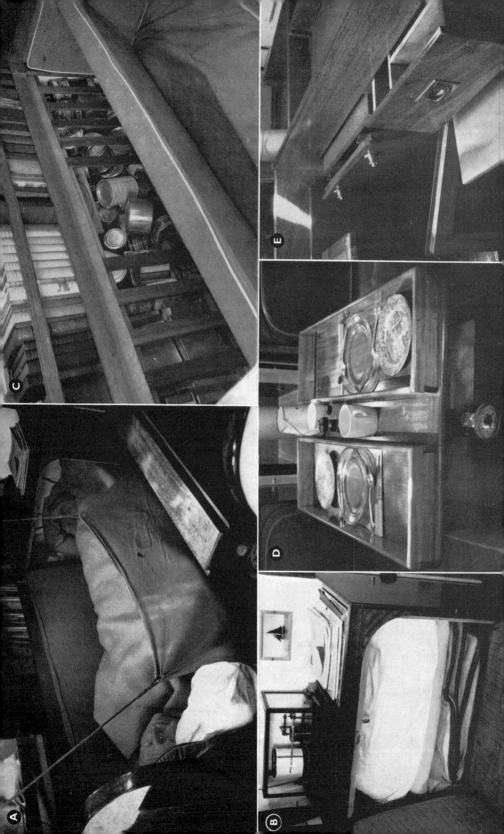

an opening fitted with a curtain, and it can also be entered from the foredeck or forward coachroof by way of the forehatch; this should have coamings built up above deck level, but some modern metal hatches are fitted flush with the deck, which is a bad arrangement as they must be kept closed when there is any water on the deck. The hatch invented by Maurice Griffiths, GM (Fig 6) is superior to the ordinary type as it is leak-proof. The inner

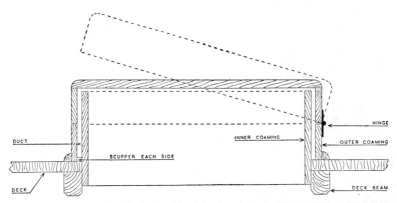

Fig 6   The leak-proof hatch designed by Maurice Griffiths, GM, ARINA. The same principle may be used for skylights

coaming, which should be at least 2·5 centimetres (1 inch) higher than the outer coaming, directs any water that may get in between the hatch and the coaming into a duct which lies between.

PLATE 5 (overleaf). A. If the flue of a paraffin-burning refrigerator is not a close fit at top and bottom condensation will not occur, and B, if it is secured to a locker door the door can be opened. C. The nearest fiddle of a cooker should have gaps or dips to accommodate the handles of low utensils. The oven door should be hinged at the bottom, not at the side like this one. D. Spring curtain wire, from which the plastic covering has been removed, in use as a temporary means of stopping pots from slipping. This swinging stove is correctly pivoted at hot-plate level.

PLATE 6 (facing). A. A canvas bunk-board is comfortable, and when not in use stows flat beneath the mattress. To economize in space, the foot of a bunk may be recessed beneath a sideboard: by day the bedding is stowed there, B, and the recess covered with an upholstered panel, as in C; this picture also shows a locker for canned food made with vertical slats behind the hinged settee back. D. Each leaf of this table is fitted with its own removable fiddles, and a hand bearing-compass is shipped on a bracket on the table leg to act as a tell-tale. E. High fiddles on the galley bench, and beneath it a self-locking drawer, lockers, and sliding bread and meat boards (Wanderer III).

Scuppers at the corners of the outer coaming allow the water to escape from the duct to the deck. The tops of hatches are often made of clear acrylic, a translucent material sold under the trade names Perspex and Plexiglass.

A larger yacht will probably be divided into a greater number of compartments, having in addition to the above a separate galley, heads (wc), and one or more sleeping cabins; but the greatest impression of space and airiness is obtained by having the minimum number of bulkheads.

Though it is natural for an owner to wish to take with him his wife, his family, or his friends, overcrowding should be avoided or tempers will fray and pleasure be spoilt. The necessity for a full-length sleeping-berth for every member of the party will be the first factor deciding how many people a yacht of a given size can accommodate, but in addition there must be sufficient locker space not only for the sails, gear, and navigation equipment, but also for the personal belongings of everyone. There are many 7·3 metre (24 foot) yachts with sleeping berths for four people, but I would regard that as overcrowding for anything more than a week-end, and a yacht of 9 metres (30 feet) or more will be needed for such accommodation to be comfortably arranged.

To increase the headroom, a raised coachroof is usually built above the saloon sole (floor). Sitting headroom is essential in any yacht, and for that a minimum distance of 0·9 metres (3 feet) from the top of the cushion on the seat to the underside of the deck is needed by a person of average height. In a small yacht it may be impossible to obtain that height under the side decks if the seats are the correct distance of 36 centimetres (14 inches) above the sole, and unless the space beneath the side decks is filled out with a backrest (which may make the seats too narrow) the back of one's head will rest uncomfortably against the coachroof coaming. If the needed headroom beneath the side decks cannot be obtained, it is preferable to dispense with a coachroof and have built-up topsides in way of the saloon, giving a raised deck amidships (page 209).

Full standing headroom below is often insisted on, but if that is to be obtained in a yacht of less than 9 metres (30 feet) LOA, either she must have excessive freeboard, a high and unsightly coachroof, or the sole must be placed so low that it is too narrow; but as there is rarely room for walking about in a small yacht, full headroom is of little real advantage except in the galley and at the aft end of the saloon, where it can be provided by means of a doghouse, ie a raised part of the coachroof or deck. Today the coachroof is nearly always carried through forward of the mast to give headroom in the forecastle, heads, or sleeping cabin.

In arranging and furnishing the accommodation it is best to avoid unusual or complicated ideas, for generally they do not work well at sea. Simplicity with strength and reasonable lightness should be the aim everywhere. There will need to be near the companionway a space where oilskins (foul weather gear) can be hung and sea-boots stowed, with drainage to the bilge. There should be proper lockers for all the stores and equipment that will be carried, their shelves fitted with high fiddles, and their doors with fastenings that do not permit them to burst open if anything should chance to touch the release catches; in this respect there is much to be said for common bolts or old fashioned turn-buttons. A large number of moderate-size lockers is better than a few big ones because it is then not necessary to remove many articles to reach the one sought. There is often some wasted space between the settee backrests and the yacht's side, because anything stowed there is apt to fall out when the backrest is opened; but if vertical slats 6·5 centimetres (2½ inches) apart are fitted with a larger gap here and there, a good stowage place for canned goods will be made (Plate 6C). All sideboards, galley working areas, etc, should be provided with vertical fiddles at least 4 centimetres (1½ inches) high, and there should be adequate hand-holds and grab-rails, and nothing so flimsy that it will give way when a body is flung against it in a seaway.

Sleeping-berths

Unless it is intended for a child, a sleeping-berth should be not less than 2 metres (6¼ feet) long; it should not be narrower than 51 centimetres (20 inches), and if it is to be used at sea not wider than 71 centimetres (28 inches), but that is too wide to be comfortable when used as a settee. It will need to be provided with a thick mattress (usually of sponge rubber), and some arrangement must be made to keep the occupant and bedding in place when the yacht is under way. That may be done with a wooden bunkboard 30 centimetres (12 inches) or so high, but a bunkboard made of sailcloth or netting, arranged to be hooked or lashed in a vertical position at night, is much to be preferred as it is more comfortable and takes hardly any room when stowed under the mattress. There must be a stowage place for the bedding in the daytime when settees are used as sleeping-berths; sometimes this is outboard of the settee backrest, but then the vessel's side must be lined to protect the bedding from leaks or condensation. An alternative arrangement is to have a sideboard over one end of a settee; the sleeper's feet go into the recess beneath it by night and the bedding stows there by day (Plate 6, *A* and *B*). The backrest· for a settee should have a slope of about 1 in 6.

A yacht of 9 metres (30 feet) or more will probably have a sleeping cabin separate from the saloon, with built-in bunks on which the bedding may remain at all times; but the settees in the saloon may also be needed as sleeping-berths, and an additional berth, known as a pilot berth, is sometimes provided outboard of, and higher than, one of the settees, or a quarter berth, part of which may be under a cockpit seat. The plans of most production yachts show a **V**-shape double-berth in the forecastle, but this can rarely be used at sea because of the noise and motion in that part of the vessel, and even at anchor it has the drawback that it occupies space that could better be used for sails or other gear, and it makes stowing the anchor cable difficult. If there must be a double-berth there its mattress should be in two parts so that the area may be divided by a bunk-board for use at sea; but as with all berths that are not parallel to the fore-and-aft line – and they are found too often because of the common desire to cram in the maximum number of sleeping-berths which look all right on paper – it will be uncomfortable when the yacht is heeled, for the sleeper on one side will have his head lower than his heels, and vice versa. A cot, made usually of galvanized pipe across which sailcloth is laced, hinged to the yacht's side is sometimes arranged for occasional use in the forecastle. The Root berth also is of canvas, one edge being attached to the yacht's side and the other to a wood or metal bar which ships into sockets at each end. Either of these types of berth may be comfortable enough, but they need thick mattresses to guard against the cold which otherwise will strike up at the sleeper from below.

Except perhaps in a permanent bunk a sleeping-bag may be preferred to separate sheets and blankets. One can be made by sewing or buttoning several blankets together, the occupant getting in under as many layers as are needed, a second bag made of sheets first being inserted. One side of the bag should be left open for about 1 metre (3 feet) from the head, or it may be difficult to get into and may split. My editor, Neil Curtis, who has wide experience of sleeping bags, has kindly contributed the following: there is a very wide range of manufactured sleeping bags available to suit almost every need and at a variety of prices. The choice is between down (duck, or even better, goose) and synthetic fibres. There is no doubt that down still offers the best insulation for a given weight but it is now very expensive and does not retain its insulation properties if it is wetted. Man-made fibres are heavier and may cause some condensation but they are very much cheaper and have excellent wet-cold properties. The best synthetic filling currently available is Holofil made by the Dupont Company. Shape, covering material, zipped or unzipped (a zip forms a cold spot) should all be considered before making a decision.

Galley, cooking-stoves, and refrigerators

In some old yachts the galley is situated in the forecastle, an unsuitable position which is a relic from the days when yachts carried paid hands who lived forward and were responsible for the cooking. Today the owner, his wife, or one of his friends will do the cooking, and that occupation should be made as pleasant as possible by placing the galley where the motion is least violent, the maximum light and fresh air are obtainable, and where the cook can converse with the rest of the ship's company and perhaps see something of what is happening outside. For these reasons the best position from the cook's point of view will be at the aft end of the saloon adjacent to the companionway. But that situation does have drawbacks; in a very small yacht the cook will obstruct the companionway, and as the direction of the draught below is nearly always from aft forward, cooking fumes will be carried through the yacht before going out of the forehatch, and may condense on the deckhead and bulkheads. Therefore a compromise is occasionally made by placing the galley at the fore end of the saloon. The traditional side for the galley is to port ie the lee side when the vessel is on the starboard (right of way) tack, and the ideal shape is a narrow U with its arms fore-and-aft to give the cook security in any weather (Plate 4*D*).

There are five types of fuel used in cooking-stoves; solid fuel (coal, charcoal, or wood), commercial alcohol (methylated spirit), diesel, paraffin (kerosene), and gas. Solid fuel is rarely used because of its bulk and the time needed to get a hot fire going, but in large yachts the Esse or Aga heat-storage, anthracite-burning stoves are almost ideal for continuous living aboard, particularly in high latitudes, but they are heavy. Alcohol is popular in the USA because an alcohol fire can be extinguished with water, but a point often overlooked is that because the flash point of its vapour is only 345 °C (653 °F) the vapour can be ignited without a flame; therefore if a stove with its tank close to a burner is refilled a few seconds after the burner has been turned off, a serious explosion and fire may result. Pressure alcohol stoves need to be preheated, the fuel is expensive, prohibitively so in some countries where it may be cheaper to burn duty-free rum, and is less efficient than other fuels, 65,000 Bthu per 4·5 litres (1 gallon) as against 100,000 for gas and 129,000 for paraffin.

Diesel is a cheap, safe fuel, and if the yacht has a diesel auxiliary engine it would seem logical to use the same fuel for cooking. But to work efficiently and cleanly the diesel stove may need a fan to be run, more or less depending on the quality of the fuel which varies widely, to get it to vaporize in the pot burner, and a big diameter chimney probably 12·5 centimetres (5 inches) is required. Where warmth is needed as well as cooking heat such a stove may serve well, but unless it is kept burning fast, some time will elapse before cooking temperature is obtained, and no matter how well it is burning some oily soot will be deposited on a pot when cooking on an open flame.

Paraffin also is a safe, low-cost fuel and is available everywhere. Cookers burning this fuel by way of a wick are now rarely seen, the clean and much more efficient vaporizing (Primus type) burner being used instead; this may be of the silent or roarer type, and the only advantage of the latter, which as its name implies makes a lot of noise, is that it is less susceptible to draughts. In its simplest form such a stove comprises a burner mounted on top of a fuel tank which is provided with a filler cap, a release valve, and a hand pump. Below the burner is a cup into which, when the stove is to be started, is poured a small quantity of alcohol; this is lighted to preheat the burner, and when all of it has burnt the release valve is closed and a few strokes of the pump are given to force fuel up through the burner and nipple where it appears as a white, strong-smelling vapour, and when this is ignited it burns with a clean, odourless, blue flame. To extinguish the flame the release valve is opened to let the compressed air out. Depending on the quality of the fuel, carbon will form in the nipple, and this must be removed with the pricker provided. If, on lighting, the paraffin flares up with a smoky, yellow flame, insufficient priming alcohol was used (a can dispensing at each tip precisely the amount required is available), or fuel was pumped into the burner before all the alcohol had burnt, or an attempt was made to light the stove in a draught. If the release valve is opened the flare-up will quickly die down. Although such a stove might be carried as a complete spare unit, it is not often employed as the main source of cooking in the yacht of today, where a more sophisticated, multi-burner stove is preferred. This, for example, might be provided with two or three burners at the hot-plate level and a separate burner in the oven, each burner being of the self-pricking type, ie having a knob on a spindle which when turned anti-clockwise pricks the nipple, and when turned the other way reduces the flame and finally turns it off; but if such a burner is run for long periods with a very low flame it will carbon up. The fuel tank, which may be remote from the stove and served by a separate pump, can be left with the pressure in it at all times when serving self-pricking burners, but if the tank is more than a few inches from the burners, each of the latter must have an additional nipple installed immediately beneath it, otherwise the burner will 'breathe', and may do so to such a degree that it blows itself out. Unless the stove is free to swing (see below) alcohol may be thrown by the motion out of the preheating cup; this can be overcome by packing the cup with asbestos string, or the cup may be removed and a clip-on asbestos preheating wick, such as is provided with the Tilley and other pressure lamps, used in its place. Paraffin varies widely in quality, and on one cruise in US waters I found it so poor that I used instead mineral spirit, paint reducer, or even cleaning fluid, all of which I was told are refined forms of paraffin. Sometimes paraffin is contaminated with water from condensation or other sources, and a drop of this in a hot burner will be converted into steam; the flame then goes out, and a match applied to the burner may be blown out several times before fuel comes through again. The cure for this is to install a bowl filter, preferably with a paper cartridge, in the pipeline between tank and burner.

Liquified petroleum gas (butane, propane, or a mixture of the two, commonly known as LPG) continues to increase in popularity for cooking in yachts. Its advantages are: no preheating, pumping, pricking or forced draught is needed, and it lends itself readily to use with oven and grill. However, it is not everywhere so readily available as is paraffin. In the UK it is supplied by the Calor Gas Co, and empty cylinders are exchanged for full ones; in mainland Europe Boto Gas offers a similar service, but in other parts of the world exchange facilities do not exist, and empty cylinders have to be refilled, which may present difficulties as cylinder connections vary in type and thread, though all are left-handed. The big drawback to LPG is that in the event of a leak the gas, being nearly twice as heavy as air, will accumulate in the bilge where a chance spark, as from an engine's self-starter, will ignite it and a devastating explosion result; many yachts and their people have been badly damaged by such explosions, and some have been lost. Stringent precautions must therefore be taken. The cylinder – ideally there should be two of these in tandem connected by cocks so that when one runs out (this is bound to happen while the stove is in use) the other can at once be brought into operation – should be carried on deck or in a special locker with a drain, the exit of which must of course be above the LWL so that any leakage will go overboard. The cylinder, in which the gas is held under pressure as a liquid, is connected by high pressure pipe to a regulator which reduces the pressure to the working pressure of about 0·35 kilograms per square centimetre. Most cylinders are designed to be mounted in the upright position, and must be so mounted to prevent liquid gas from entering the pipe and regulator; but cylinders that may be mounted in a horizontal position are available for a stowage position which dictates their use, and on these the side that must be uppermost is marked; they should be mounted with their axes for-and-aft rather than athwartships. The connection between regulator and stove should be of copper tube with no break or union in it, and if the stove swings, its flexible pipe should be of approved material (BS 3213) and a cock should be fitted where this joins the copper pipe; this cock should be kept closed, as also should the cock on the cylinder, at all times when the stove is not in use. When lighting a burner the match should be lit before the burner is turned on, and when cooking is finished the cock at the flexible pipe connection should be turned off before the burner is turned off, so that no gas remains in the flexible pipe. If the above recommendations are followed the chance of a leak will be minimized, and as the gas is provided with a strong artificial odour, one would need to have a very bad cold not to notice it. Additional protection might be provided by a gas-detector installed in the bilge; if gas should accumulate there the detector will sound an alarm, and some sophisticated units will also turn the gas off, electrically, at the cylinder; I regard this last as an undesirable complication. Incidentally, any gas stove with an oven should be provided, as most are, with a temperature-actuated flame failure device, to shut off the flow of gas if the oven burner should for some reason go out. This might happen if the oven is insufficiently ventilated, for the average oven burner requires up to 5·6 cubic metres (200 cubic feet) of air per hour to ensure proper and efficient use of the fuel.

Gas cylinders can be had in a variety of sizes. One holding 9 kilograms (20 pounds) weighs when full about 18 kilograms (40 pounds), and this is the largest size that can be conveniently transported by hand to a filling station; even with this a two-wheel shopping trolley is a help. My wife and I find that 9 kilograms (20 pounds) of gas lasts us between thirty and forty days with simple cooking, which includes two hot meals a day with a weekly roast and perhaps a baking of bread. It is not practicable to weigh a gas cylinder on board to determine how much gas remains in it; but if a little hot water is poured down the side of the cylinder and is closely followed by a finger, a point will be reached where the cylinder is found to be cold – that will be the level of the gas remaining. It is wise now and then to check the gas system from cylinder to burner by nose and/or soapy water, to see if there are any leaks, and examine the piping for abrasion. The flame of a gas burner should be blue; if it is yellow tipped and makes pans sooty, the aeration screw on the burner's stem probably needs adjustment, or the wrong type of gas is being used, eg butane with a stove intended for propane.

Compressed natural gas (CNG) which at present is available to yachts only in some parts of the USA, has the great safety factor of being lighter than air, and therefore cannot accumulate in the bilge.

Opinion is divided as to whether it is best to have the cooking-stove fixed or swinging. If it is fixed it should be arranged so that the cook is never to leeward of it or he will be in danger of being scalded if hot liquid is flung out of a pot. If the stove burns alcohol or paraffin, the tank should be so arranged that the pressure release valve is never below the level of the fuel on either tack. Long and successful voyages have been made with fixed stoves, but my wife and I prefer the stove to swing on pivots arranged fore and aft; it is important that these pivots are at hot-plate or burner-top level (Plate 5D), for if they are above that level the hot-plate will act not as a sea-saw but as a swing, then pots and their contents may be flung off by centrifugal force. A shallow swinging stove will need ballast at its lower side to counteract the weight of filled pots on the hot-plate. A safety bar should be provided to stop the cook from being thrown against the stove (Plate 4D).

Whether it is fixed or swinging any seagoing stove needs fiddles, ie an arrangement of rails round the hot-plate to keep pots and pans from sliding off; most of such fiddles are the same height, about 5 centimetres (2 inches) all round, but if a utensil with a low handle, such as a frying-pan, is to be used, it is important to have a gap or dip in the front fiddle beside a burner to accommodate the handle (Plate 5C). Intermediate fiddles can be arranged to be moved and locked to hold pots over their respective burners; a cheaper arrangement is to have two or more lengths of spring curtain wire, from which the plastic covering has been removed, stretched between opposite fiddles (Plate 5D) but their life is very short. The oven door should have its hinges not at the side but at the bottom, then when it is being opened one has some control of the sliding shelves and their contents.

A small number of yachts, mostly American, use electricity for cooking. No doubt this is convenient when plugged in to the mains at a marina, but since at other times a generator giving 110 or 220 volts must be started up and run if only a kettle of water is to be boiled, I would regard it as unsuitable, and the exhaust noise is an irritation to the neighbours.

A galley sink is a convenience only if it can be arranged to drain overboard; it should be arranged as nearly as possible on the centre fore-and-aft line, and will need a cock to be closed when sailing closehauled or dirty water will squirt back up it; if it has to be fitted near or below the LWL, either it must drain into a container which will have to be emptied over the side, or be provided with a pump, which is likely to be put out of action by tea-leaves and other scraps which inevitably find their way into a sink sooner or later. A plastic bowl is easier to keep clean, may use less water, and takes little room when not in use, but it should have vertical, not sloping sides. Nevertheless, nearly every modern yacht does have a galley sink, often two of them provided with fresh- and saltwater pumps. Incidentally, saltwater is almost as efficient as fresh for washing-up purposes, provided it is really hot and a detergent is used, but it makes the dishcloth sticky. Stowage for crockery, cooking-pots, etc, should be arranged so that these articles cannot get adrift in a seaway, and yet will be accessible on either tack. With a little ingenuity the galley and pantry can be made models of tidy efficiency (Plate 4). A piece of elastic stretched diagonally across a pantry locker will stop odd-shaped items pushed in behind it from rattling.

For the stowage of fresh food a cool, ventilated locker is desirable but is difficult to arrange, and in a temperate climate the bilge may serve well enough if it has a grating each end to let air circulate; but many yachts are provided with ice-boxes or refrigerators, and some with deep-freeze chambers. If in the chosen cruising area one knows where ice can conveniently be obtained, the ice-box has much to recommend it on the grounds of simplicity, but like a refrigerated chamber it needs to be well insulated. For this purpose polyurethane, a closed-cell foam, has taken the place of cork and glass-wool, but it should be not less than 5 centimetres (2 inches) thick; all corners and joins in the box must be airtight, and the inside lined with a smooth, easily wash-able material such as GRP. To avoid loss of cold air when being opened, the box ought to be of the top-opening kind, and its lid provided with a gasket. Arrangement must be made to catch the water formed as the ice melts, for this will contain organic matter, and if allowed into the bilge will cause the latter to stink; if the drain pipe is S-shape, like that of a wash-basin, the water held in it will prevent loss of cold air.

A unique way of using an ice-box was that employed by Bob Kittredge on his world voyage in *Svea*. When loading the box for a passage he did not buy ice; instead he bought a quantity of canned beer (to which he was partial) and had it frozen at the local ice-plant. He then lined the sides and bottom of the ice-box with several layers of the cans, and put his supply of meat in the remaining central space. Thus no space was wasted and there was no water to dispose of.

For coastwise cruising in a warm climate a refrigerator may be regarded as something more than a luxury, for it will enable the crew to live more off fresh food than would otherwise be possible and will help to prevent waste; but unless room can be found for one with a capacity of 0·06 cubic metres (2 cubic feet) or more, its value on a long passage will not be great.

If a liquid under pressure is permitted to expand it will absorb heat from its surroundings, and this is the principle of refrigera-tion. In a mechanical refrigerator the refrigerant (Freon 21, a non-inflammable, non-toxic gas) is compressed by a compressor driven either by a thermostatically-controlled electric motor, as is used in most household models, but which inevitably puts a considerable drain on a yacht's battery, or by the auxiliary engine. The running time needed will depend on the outside temperature, the required inside temperature, the frequency with which the cold chamber is opened, and on the efficiency of the installation.

Remarkable claims for efficiency are often made, but from my own observations in many tropical anchorages it seems that at least two hours of battery charging or compressing in the morning and another half hour or so in the evening are needed, and it seems that more delays in port are due to refrigeration problems than any other cause.

The absorbtion-type refrigerator has no moving parts, and the refrigerant, in a coiled pipe, is caused to expand by the direct application of heat, the source of which may be LPG or paraffin. The former should be regarded as dangerous in a yacht, for the gas cylinder cock has to be left open at all times. For eleven years my wife and I have been using a paraffin-burning, absorbtion-type refrigerator in port with success, and the only troubles we had were due to poor-quality fuel. A unit of this kind should not be too closely built in with joinery-work as it requires a good supply of air to condense the refrigerant, and the circular wick needs careful trimming. The heat from this is best vented through the deck; if this is done as in Plate 5 there will be no condensation. Consumption of fuel is less that 4·5 litres (1 gallon) a week. We never attempt to use the unit at sea, for it is a household model and unsuitable, but John Guzzwell altered his so that the fuel was gravity-fed through a float chamber, and in *Treasure* used it with success all the way from England to New Zealand.

Freshwater

Two and a quarter litres (½ gallon) of freshwater per person per day is sufficient for drinking, but allows nothing for washing, and except when on an ocean passage few people would attempt to keep their water consumption down to that uncomfortable minimum. In ordinary coastal cruising the average consumption is about 9 litres (2 gallons) per person per day, but it is possible to manage on 4·5 to 7 litres (1 to 1½ gallons) without hardship; 4·5 litres (1 gallon) of water weighs 4·6 kilograms (10 pounds), one cubic foot contains 28 litres (6¼ gallons), and a ton, 1,018 litres (224 gallons) will occupy 1 cubic metre (36 cubic feet). So it will be understood that the quantity of freshwater a yacht will carry depends not on the wishes of her owner but on the space available for tanks, and the weight she can comfortably accommodate.

If possible the tanks should be arranged more or less amidships, either in the bilge or under the settees, where the weight of water will not affect the fore-and-aft trim. The metal, GRP or ferro-cement, yacht will probably have double-bottom tanks, ie tanks of which the yacht's skin forms one side, but the wood yacht will need individual tanks of galvanized or stainless steel (never copper) to be installed. Tanks should be capable of being made independent of one another in case of a leak or if water from a doubtful source has to be put into one of them and used, perhaps, for washing purposes only. This does not necessarily mean a lot of piping, for one deck-filler and pipe can serve two tanks through a 3-way cock, and one pump can suck from either tank through another 3-way cock. In addition each tank will need an air-vent, which usually takes the form of a pipe leading from the highest part of the tank to a position high up under the deck, with its upper end bent over to prevent dirt from entering; the pipe should be of large diameter to relieve the tank of pressure when water is taken from a high-pressure source. A plastic pipe might be connected temporarily to the air-vent when a tank is being filled to carry any overflow to a cockpit drain. To avoid galvanic action and save weight, the entire plumbing system is often of plastic instead of metal piping. Any tank needs an inspection hole large enough for every part of the tank to be reached through it for cleaning.

In the very small yacht with no room for a tank, water is sometimes carried in plastic bottles, which can be stowed away in all manner of odd corners, or she might have several plastic containers each holding 9 litres (2 gallons) or more to stow in the cockpit or elsewhere, but if water containers of translucent material are left for any length of time in daylight a green mould may grow in them; however, this appears to be harmless.In any cruising yacht some easily handled containers will be useful for ferrying off water from the shore, but a 15-metre (50-foot) length of 2·5-centimetre (1-inch) internal diameter hose with a screw adaptor to fit a 2·5-centimetre (1-inch) tap should also be carried for use when lying alongside near a water supply. Newly galvanized tanks need several 24-hour soakings before being put into service, or the water will be cloudy. The same applies to plastic containers and GRP tanks to eradicate taste and smell, but some GRP tanks continue to impart a taste to the water which no soaking will remove; it is said that a cartridge-type water-filter at the tap or pump will remove this, but I have had no experience with it. However, it would appear that if osmosis occurs in a GRP tank (and this is not uncommon) styrene, which smells of pear-drops and is a poison, will be liberated into the water, causing headaches and nausea. The only solution then might be to cut out the top of the tank and install a flexible tank or one of metal, remembering that a flexible tank as well as calling for support at its sides and bottom also needs its top to be held down firmly. If in some remote place water must be taken from an unclean or doubtful source, it can be purified by adding a quarter of a teaspoonful of hypochlorate of lime to every 227 litres (50 gallons); this will not affect the taste. Alternatively purifying tablets, such as Halazone, may be used; a small bottle contains 1,000 tablets, enough for 1,136·5 litres (250 gallons). The length of time water will remain sweet depends on its purity and the condition of the tanks, but in 40 years of cruising I have never known tank water to become undrinkable.

When no water supply is available, or the water is of doubtful quality, or perhaps on a long ocean passage, we pray for rain, and in a tropical downpour a surprisingly large quantity may be caught in a very short time. Perhaps the harbour awning or a special sailcloth catchment will be used, but at sea these do not always work well because heavy rain is often accompanied by a strong wind. Then a sail may serve the purpose well if its foot is in a groove on the boom, or the track on the boom is recessed, for this will serve as a gutter to catch and carry the water to the fore end of the boom where it may be collected by the bucket and transferred to a tank. But at the start plenty of water should be let go to waste, for unless the sail is clean and free from salt the water will be brackish, and if put in a tank part filled with good water may contaminate it. Sometimes a coachroof or doghouse is provided along its edges with solid coamings instead of the more usual open grab-rails, and its lower corners with scuppers, for the purpose of collecting rain; but again the area must first be clean.

Aboard the larger yacht water is often pumped by electricity. One arrangement is to have a small electric, motor-driven pump which is switched on by the opening of a tap; it runs all the time the tap is open and stops when the tap is turned off; this seems to have little to recommend it over the small, hand-operated pump, which in any event will be provided as a back-up for use if the electric system fails. The other arrangement is a complete pressure system in which an electric pump puts water under pressure into a tank which may hold a large quantity; the pump is activated by a pressure switch, and runs only when most of the water in the tank has been drawn off. If there are several taps serving several basins and sinks the system has much to recommend it, but it is bulky and heavy, and to prevent it working too often air must occasionally be bled into the system to replace air absorbed by the water. The system encourages waste (washing hands under a running tap) but is ideal in connection with a shower. If the shower rose is a small bore and water is used only for wetting and rinsing, 9 litres (2 gallons) of water is plenty for one shower bath; the hand-held rose on a flexible pipe (telephone type) is the most ecconomical. However, some may well consider it a lot less bother and a good deal cheaper to go on deck with a cake of soap during a shower of rain, or to use a bucket and sponge.

Saloon and chart tables

The saloon table, which may have one or two drop leaves so as not to obstruct the passage through to the forecastle, needs to be of robust construction and strongly supported, for it will often be grabbed or lurched against at sea. A comfortable height above the settee cushion top is 25 centimetres (10 inches). It is best fitted with an arrangement of fiddles 4 centimetres ($1\frac{1}{2}$ inches) high, spaced according to the size of the plates and other utensils to keep a meal securely in position (Plate 6D), but the fiddles need to be easily removable (perhaps being held by metal pegs shipping into metal-bushed holes) otherwise the table cannot be used for writing or chart work. If the table is to swing (an arrangement I do not care for) it must have a very heavy balance weight close to the fulcrum pins, and will then adapt itself to any period of roll. If the weight is too low it will assert its own natural period, and if this nearly coincides with the vessel's roll, the table can get out of hand and throw everything off. The pins, hooks, or bolts used for securing the table when in port ought to be as far as possible from the fulcrums to avoid an unfair strain, and to ensure that the table is rigid. A damp cloth or sponge mat will do much to prevent articles sliding about.

The dinette arrangement, where the table is to one side of the saloon and the seats each side of it face fore and aft, is not suitable for a small yacht unless she is very flat-floored, or for any yacht which is tender, attractive though it may appear on paper, for leg-room is limited by the curve of the bilge, and it is difficult to remain on the seats when the yacht is heeled. A portable table for use in the cockpit is of particular value when in port in the tropics where meals will often be taken and guests entertained under the awning there.

Charts are an essential part of a cruising yacht's equipment, and they ought not to be kept rolled up or they will curl and be difficult to handle. A British Admiralty chart (the former Admiralty, including the Hydrographic Department, is now incorporated in the Ministry of Defence, but the term 'Admiralty chart' and the like continue) folded once as it comes from the printer measures 70 by 50 centimetres (28 by 20 inches) and somewhere a stowage space of that size must be found as well as a flat area on which a chart may be laid while being worked on. 100 of such charts will need a space 5 centimetres (2 inches) deep. But when planning this, charts published by other countries may need to be considered; those made in the USA and Canada, for example, come in a variety of shapes and sizes, and are mostly larger than British Admiralty (BA) charts and have to be folded more than once, thus requiring a greater depth of stowage space. The ideal arrangement is to have a table measuring 1 metre by 70 centimetres (40 by 28 inches) so that a chart may be spread out open on it, but only a very few yachts can afford so much space, and most make do with a table on which the chart, folded once, can be laid, and often this has to be the saloon table, though a folding table over part of a sleeping-berth can sometimes be arranged. The best stowage plan is to have drawers beneath the chart table, and these may with advantage be of the self-locking type, ie with a piece cut from the front edge of both runners, so that when pushed in the drawer drops and cannot be opened again without first being lifted; a wedge glued to the under side of the front of the drawer will also serve the purpose. If space cannot be found for drawers, it may be possible to stow the charts on battens close up under the deck, or under a berth or settee mattress.

The trend in modern designs is to give the navigator and his gear a space to themselves near the foot of the companionway; then the table is usually arranged in such a way that the navigator sits at it facing fore or aft, and the area may be shielded from spray by a sheet of clear acrylic. Here the navigator does not obstruct the way through, and is spared the discomfort of having on occasions to work with his head downhill over a leeward-sloping table, but since his knees have to go under the table charts cannot be stowed there. For use at night the chart table will need a light, and if this is electric it may be provided with a little cover made of red nylon with elastic in its hem, so that it can be slipped on to the lamp to preserve night vision. However, there is now some doubt as to whether a red light is effective, and as it makes almost invisible anything printed in red on the chart, it may be better to use a well-shaded white light of very low power and narrow beam. An effective shade for a reading or other electric light below deck can be made from a strip of stout paper glued in position (Plate 7D), and can be embellished with postage stamps or other small and colourful items.

Cockpit and steering arrangements

Aboard a sailing vessel the traditional position for the helmsman is right aft, chiefly because from there he gets the best view of the sails and can more readily feel the direction of the apparent wind. Most yachts therefore have the cockpit (where the helmsman sits or stands) near the stern, and today it is usually self-draining, ie drains into the sea, not into the bilge, even though it may then be so shallow that it offers little comfort or shelter, but a folding canvas hood at the forward end and weathercloths laced to the guardrails each side will help. A common arrangement for the drains is to have one each side at the fore or after end of the cockpit sole, which is sloped a little towards the drain, the drain pipes being crossed so that the port side of the cockpit discharges on the starboard side, and vice versa, so that water will not readily flood back up the leeward drain. Drains are rarely large enough, and the biggest possible size should be used. An alternative in a craft with a transom stern is to slope the sole aft and have one large drain on the centre line. Like all other underwater holes the through-hull fittings for the drains must be provided with sea-cocks. If the cockpit does not drain overboard, I feel there should be some means of preventing it from draining into the bilge in heavy weather, perhaps with a portable canvas lining such as I made for the 7-metre (24-foot) *Wanderer II* for her voyage to the Azores, otherwise much pumping will be needed to keep the bilge free of water. Whether the cockpit self-drains or not it ought to be sealed off from saloon or cabin by a seat-high bridge deck, or well-fitting washboards (Plate 7E); hinged doors are not sufficiently strong or watertight in the event – and in my experience it is a rare one – of the cockpit filling, and a strongback (also seen in Plate 7E) might be provided for use if this seems likely. In the sort of weather in which this might happen, the motion will be such that much of the water will be flung out immediately (unless the cockpit is unusually deep) leaving only a few bucketfuls swilling about in the well.

Usually the fore-and-aft cockpit seats are hinged to give access to the lockers beneath them, and the gutters and drains with which they are provided do not prevent some water entering on the lee side in heavy weather unless the lids can be dogged down on gaskets. It may therefore be better, if it can be arranged, to have the only access to the lockers from inside the saloon or cabin. But fore-and-aft seats the full length of a cockpit are a mixed blessing, for to haul effectively on a sheet, or work a winch mounted on the lee coaming, one has to kneel on the seat and lean to leeward. So it is worth considering terminating the seats before they reach one end or the other of the cockpit; then sheets and winches can be worked from a standing position right up against the cockpit coaming, enabling greater power to be applied more comfortably and efficiently.

An increasing number of yachts have the cockpit not aft but more or less amidships, particularly those with heavy engines or large fuel tanks, which are also best placed amidships. Such a position avoids some of the troubles associated with stern cockpits, provides a dry and more accessible position for machinery, and permits a welcome break from the traditional accommodation plan, especially in a large vessel. The saloon will then usually be forward of the cockpit, and the sleeping-cabin aft, but if access to the latter is by way of a forward-facing companionway it will be vulnerable to rain and spray, and in port in rainy weather one will often get wet feet on the way to one's bunk. So in a yacht large enough to accommodate it there may be a passage below deck to one side of the cockpit well, connecting saloon and sleeping-cabin, sufficient headroom being provided under a cockpit seat. The passage will lead through the engine-room, or be separated from it by a plywood or plastic partition which can be removed for access to the engine. But like so many things connected with yacht accommodation, this is a compromise, and some contend that it is preferable to have the engine-room completely isolated, so that heat, odour, and noise are confined and do not permeate the rest of the yacht. A centre cockpit is often a wet place, for there freeboard is at its lowest, and when the wind is forward of the beam spray from the bow-wave is blown aboard in that area, sails and masthead windsock or burgèe are not so easily seen as they are from aft, and wheel steering, instead of being an option, becomes mandatory. However, one of the advantages of a centre cockpit in a large yacht, perhaps in one of 15 metres (50 feet) or so, is that it may permit the inclusion of a great cabin aft. Often this is attempted in a craft too small to accept it, when it appears as no more than a top-heavy caricature of the real thing, with insufficient space for anything except a double bunk; but when space permits and the designer is an artist, the great cabin can be a gracious, spacious apartment well lighted by a span of stern windows; though it may be used solely as a sleeping-cabin, it is more often the main living and dining saloon, when the galley will be situated in or near it; usually the deck over the great cabin is raised a little above the level of the main deck to become the poop. One of the best great cabins I have seen was that aboard Irving Johnson's *Yankee*, a steel 15·4-metre (50·5-foot) ketch designed for crossing oceans and climbing mountains – by way of canals (Plate 46).

Only when the cockpit is aft is there a choice between tiller and wheel steering. The tiller has the great merit of simplicity, and short of the tiller breaking there is nothing that can go wrong; also the helmsman gets a better 'feel' and knows at all times how much helm and in which direction it is applied, but his position is very restricted. The length of the tiller depends partly on the size of yacht and on her steering characteristics – the greater the strain on the helm and the greater the angle of rudder rake the longer the tiller need be to give leverage – but even a short tiller takes much space, for it must have swinging room from amidships to about 30 degrees each side. For this reason even very small yachts are often steered by wheel, though it scarcely seems logical for one of less than 10·5 metres (35 feet) LOA.

There are several ways in which the mechanics of wheel steering may be arranged. If the wheel can be placed almost directly over the rudder stock a rack and pinion may be used, but if the wheel is remote from the rudder, as it will be with a centre cockpit, some form of linkage must be provided. With many gears this is arranged as follows: the horizontal wheel shaft is fitted with a sprocket which engages a short length of roller chain; each end of the chain is secured to a flexible wire rope, and these ropes are led through fairlead sheaves to a quadrant on the rudder stock. Alternatively, as with the Mathway gear, the wheel may be connected by a train of torque tubes or rods, bevel boxes, and universal joints, to a short tiller on the rudder stock; this may appear to be a complication, but in practice such a linkage is remarkably free from friction and wear, but it takes a little more room than the wire rope linkage and is more expensive; however, apart from checking the oil level in the bevel boxes occasionally, and applying a grease-gun to the nipples, no maintenance or adjustment is required. Another means of connecting wheel and rudder is by an hydraulic system filled with oil; movement of the wheel works a pump which is connected by two small-bore pipes to a steering cylinder, the piston of which is linked to a tiller on the rudder stock. But with most of these systems the helm has no 'feel', ie if the wheel is left free, pressure of water on the rudder will not return the rudder to the amidships position, so hydraulic steering is little used for sailing vessels.

No matter how excellent a steering gear may be, arrangements should be made so that in the event of failure of some part of it, or something fouling and jamming it, it can be quickly disconnected and an emergency tiller shipped. The best arrangement is to have the top of the rudder stock made square in section and brought almost to deck level, where it may be covered by a flush-fitting screw-in plate. The emergency tiller has a square socket to fit the rudder stock, so it can be shipped in a moment. Incidentally, such an arrangement will be found ideal if the yacht is to be steered by a pendulum-type wind-vane gear, but is difficult to fit if the yacht has a great cabin.

The most suitable number of turns of the wheel from hard over to hard over will be dictated by the size of the yacht and her steering characteristics, one that is hard to steer calling for more turns (greater mechanical advantage); 2 turns should be enough for a well-balanced yacht of up to about 17 metres (55 feet), but the greater the diameter of the wheel the easier will steering be. The king-spoke of the wheel, the spoke that will be uppermost when the rudder is amidships, traditionally has a turk's head worked on it so it can be felt in the dark. The brass-bound, varnished teak wheel, with six or eight spokes has largely gone out of fashion, to be replaced by the 'destroyer-type' wheel, which is entirely of metal, or metal and wood, with a smooth rim. The choice is of course a personal one, and though it should be said that the smooth wheel will not foul the helmsman's clothes and tear them, the helmsman cannot drop a bowline over a spoke when he wishes to leave the wheel for a moment to light his pipe or take a look at the chart.

Lighting, heating, and ventilation

Daylight may reach the inside of a yacht by way of skylights, hatches with translucent tops, windows in a doghouse, portlights in topsides or coachroof coamings, or through decklights, and as all but the last of these can be arranged to open they may also play some part in the ventilation system. A skylight of the old type, ie with its opening panels hinged on the fore-and-aft line, will let in rain and spray if left open, but if built to the Maurice Griffith pattern, and provided with hinged side-flaps, it may be left part open on the flaps in most weather conditions when head to wind, then it will also serve as an extracting ventilator; but if it is of translucent material the flaps must also be of translucent material or they will exclude light when the skylight is fully closed. Port-lights (sometimes known as scuttles) in the topsides are pleasant as they give a sea-level view and one may see out without standing up; but if they are made to open there will be a risk that they may be forgotten and left open when the yacht gets under way. They ought to be provided with hinged metal covers, known as dead-lights, for use in the event of the glass being broken, though with toughened glass that is unlikely to happen except perhaps when lying alongside a wharf or another vessel which has some protru-sion. Fitted in the coamings of a coachroof, portlights are excel-lent, and it may often be possible to keep those on the lee side open for ventilation even in bad weather. However, there are bound to be drips while being opened after rain or spray has wetted them, or due to condensation, so a drip-catcher should be provided. This may take the form of a trough-shaped grabrail running the full length of each coaming (Plate 37 *bottom*), accumulated water being mopped out with a sponge, or a drain provided, but this should not lead out through the coaming, for if a sea is shipped water will be forced in through it; it should be piped to the bilge or to some suitable container. Additional light in dark corners can be provided by flush-fitting glass decklights; the prismatic, radial, and lens types provide more light than plain ones, but as the radial light projects below the deck it cannot well be used where head-room is limited, and there could be a risk of fire with the lens type if anything inflammable is at the focal point when the yacht is quite still, ie tied up alongside in quiet weather. Glass is slippery to walk on.

Most yachts are wired for electric light, the current for which is provided by a battery which is charged by the auxiliary engine or a separate generating plant. If the installation is well done and the components are of good quality, this is certainly the most con-venient form of lighting, and it has the merit that it is not affected by draughts and does not appreciably raise the temperature. However, battery charging will be a frequent necessity, and this should be done with some thought for others: the running of an engine in a quiet anchorage should be avoided as far as possible, and if it must be done the forenoon should be chosen rather than disturb the peace of the evening.

As good lights and sufficient of them are necessary if the saloon is to be the cheerful, comfortable place at night that it should be, paraffin-burning lamps have much to recommend them, even if only as supplementary to electric lights. If they are of the wick type no defect can put them out of action for more than a few moments so long as a spare chimney is held in reserve, but they are susceptible to draughts and of course must be slung in gimbals to keep them upright. Once the flame has been got to burn level – and for that the wick should be slightly concave if it is a wide one, and slightly convex if it is narrow – the wick will not need trimming with scissors; wiping off the carbon with a rag is all that should be needed. A screw of newspaper makes an excellent cleaner for glass chimneys.

A more powerful light which is not affected by draughts can be made from a paraffin-vapourizing lamp such as the Tilley. This works on the Primus principle, having to be preheated with alcohol; the blue flame from the burner plays on a mantle (which is fragile) and gives an intense white light and a good deal of heat. It is wind- rain- and spray-proof and serves well as an emergency light on deck. Another type of mantle lamp, such as the Aladdin, requires no preheating or pressure, and is silent, heat for the mantle being provided by a wick, but it is susceptible to draughts. LPG can be used for lighting; here again a mantle is employed and the light is a bright one with a green tinge, but the safety factor is low, for the gas cylinder will have to be left open for long periods so that all gas pipes aboard are full and under pressure.

Accommodation which is finished in the traditional yacht style with lots of polished or varnished teak or mahogany, is serviceable and attractive in a somewhat gloomy way; but a saloon finished in white enamel is lighter and gives an impression of greater space. However, grab rails, door jambs, and the fiddles on sideboards, indeed anything that will be frequently handled, is best of varnished hardwood, otherwise it will quickly show finger-prints and signs of wear. If an exception is taken to the glossy finish of enamel, egg-shell paint with a mat finish can be used. Since cooking and smoking causes white paint to turn yellow, a non-staining material such as Formica might be used as a ceiling under deck and coachroof; an occasional wipe with a damp cloth will keep it clean.

Except in tropical waters some means of heating the accommodation and drying clothes will be needed, especially in autumn and winter, but no heating stove other than an electric one (which is not practical unless lying alongside and shore power is available) should be used in the confined space of a yacht's accommodation without adequate ventilation and a chimney, for it will take oxygen from the air, probably produce lethal carbon-monoxide, and if it burns liquid fuel will cause condensation; the consumption of oxygen may be such that without proper ventilation a wick lamp or a candle will flicker and eventually go out, and asphyxiation of people on board follows.

All solid fuels are bulky; smoke from household coal will soon coat sails and rigging with soot; anthracite and charcoal are clean, but the latter is expensive and often hard to find. Nothing on board could look more cheerful and cosy on a damp, chilly evening than an open fire burning wood, and beachcombing for it can be fun, but because the firebox must be small, frequent stoking is needed. A stove with doors is best for it will burn a variety of fuels, and with doors closed and damper adjusted may be persuaded to remain alight all night without attention. A blow-lamp or a gas-poker is often the quickest way to get a fire going.

Several types of stove burning liquid fuel are available. Taylors make one running on paraffin with which a Primus burner heats ceramic elements, and its chimney need be only 2·5 centimetres (1 inch) in diameter. The Kempsafe stove (Plate 7A) burns diesel fuel and is fed from a header tank through a drip-feed; for use at sea the tank needs to be well above the level of the drip-feed on both tacks. This stove calls for a long chimney preferably with no kinks in it and with a diameter of about 10 centimetres (4 inches). No pressure or preheating is required, for the vapourized fuel should burn with a reasonably clean flame round the rim of the pot burner. Once it is going a heater such as this requires little attention, and while spending a winter in British Columbia my wife and I had one going day and night for several months, the only requirement being to pump fuel up into the header tank and to drain condensation from the sump at the base of the chimney occasionally. But like all drip-fed heaters, should the flame blow out the pot will fill with fuel, and unless this is removed a serious flare-up will result when the heater is relighted. Since hot air rises, any heating stove should be installed as low down as possible.

Stainless steel or copper are the best materials from which to make a chimney, though with some stoves the chimney may have to be lagged or made of asbestos to keep it hot enough to induce a draught; but this is best avoided below deck for there one wishes the chimney to radiate as much heat as possible. Good insulation will be needed where the chimney passes through the deck, but obviously the type of fitting which relies on a water trough is useless when the vessel is heeled under sail. There is a variety of cowls of which the Charlie Noble (like a squat H Plate 7C) is probably the best, but many stoves burn best without a cowl except when there is a down-draught such as may be caused by a sail or when lying alongside a high wall. The type of heater which supplies hot air through ducts to various points in the accommodation calls for the continuous running of an electric fan.

To obtain a small quantity of warm water for washing one's face, or doing the dishes, most people are satisfied with a kettle heated on cooker or stove, but if there is a shower on board something more than this will be required. A small geyser burning LPG seems the obvious solution, but it will call for a pressurized water system or a header tank. Some yachts use a calorifier, in which hot water from the cooling system of the auxiliary engine is diverted to run through a coil of pipe in a lagged tank to heat the water in that tank, and here again a pressurized water system is needed; calorifies have caused damage to engines through galvanic action.

Good ventilation is essential not only for the wellbeing of the yacht (particularly if she is of wood construction) but, as has already been seen, for her people also. Natural ventilation, as opposed to forced ventilation by fans, depends on the following facts: warm air rises, cold air falls, and if an orifice is shielded on its windward side, the wind rushing past will create a partial vacuum and suck air out of it. The partly open forehatch will therefore act as an extractor if the yacht is lying head to wind or nearly so, and fresh air will therefore be drawn through the yacht from aft where it can enter through the companionway, though a hood over the companionway may interfere with it. When the wind is blowing from astern the direction of the air current inside the yacht may be reversed, but rarely is. If a hatch or skylight is provided with removable hinge-pins or other suitable fittings it can be turned 180 degrees at will to suck or blow (Plate 14 *bottom*). So that they and their contents may remain sweet and free from mildew, all lockers and drawers should have plenty of ventilation holes at top and bottom, and in a wood yacht the ceiling (the lining near the yacht's sides) should have a small gap at top and bottom so that changes of temperature, or a difference of temperature between sea and air, may cause air currents to flow. But in addition adequate provision should be made for ventilation in bad weather and when the yacht is left unattended and her hatches and ports must be closed. The common cowl ventilator is very efficient, and if one is fitted at the fore end of the deck and another right aft, and they are turned with their mouths in opposite directions, one will act as an extractor and the other as an intake. Such cowls used to be of metal but are now more often of plastic which will not dent when knocked, but with most of these the mouth is not large enough – it should be at least twice the diameter of the neck. However, a cowl is worthless if it has to be plugged up in bad weather, for it is under such conditions that it is most needed by the people on board.

The simple water-trap ventilator shown in Fig 7, left, and Plate 8 D, is probably as efficient as any other, and is generally known as the *Dorade* type because the American yacht of that name was the first to give it wide publicity. The cowl is mounted at one end of a box on deck or coachroof, and the box is provided with 2·5 cm (1 in) scuppers at each side to let water escape; at the other end and inside the box is an upstanding pipe to conduct air through the deck to or from the accommodation. Such a box is best mounted in a fore-and-aft attitude, and is often incorporated as part of a hatch, skylight, or other erection, and should be not less than 15 centimetres (6 inches) high. As some air may short-circuit through the scuppers, these may be closed with flaps or plugs in fine weather. To make the ventilator more efficient in fine weather the box may be provided with a second position for the cowl immediately over the hole through the deck; with this second position covered by a cap the vent works in the usual manner, but in fine weather the positions of cap and cowl are reversed, then the cowl will blow straight below so that the air does not have to take a circuitous route. Instead of an upstanding pipe a baffle between cowl and deck opening can be, and often is, used.

The mushroom (or dome-top) ventilator (Fig 7, *right*) is rain- and spray-proof provided it is not opened too far, but when open it will not keep heavy water out. Its main use is at bow and stern, and for additional fine weather ventilation of heads and galley, but this will be in addition to the through ventilation which should be capable of working on a definite system under all weather conditions by way of the water-trap vents; smoke may be used for testing its efficiency. There are several patent ventilators on the market which are spray- and rain-proof, and some have electric fans incorporated. In the tropics a silent table fan is a help in

keeping air on the move when there is no wind, but when there is
wind a windsail (Plate 16) will send a steady stream of air down
below, enough to blow papers off the table and discourage flies.
Owners have their own ideas on these, and one sees many vari-
eties; the kind shown in Plate 16*D* is more effective than some, for
as it embraces three sides of the hatch it scoops well, and all it does
scoop goes below. However, as a windsail will gather not only
wind but rain, it needs to be so arranged that it can instantly be let
go or collapsed when a shower is imminent.

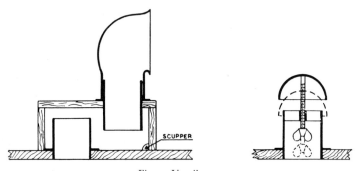

Fig 7   Ventilators
Left, water-trap or Dorade type; *right*, mushroom.

Although an awning (sometimes called a canopy in the US)
plays no part in the ventilation system, it does much to keep the
accommodation cool by shading the deck against the sun, and
enables pleasant use to be made of the cockpit in port. Incidentally, a light colour for deck and topsides is cooler than a dark one.
If the awning is made of light material, especially nylon or
terylene, it will let through too much light and be noisy in a breeze.
I have found Vivitex, and American proofed-cotton material and
grey-green in colour, ideal. Many awnings are tent-shape, the
ridge being stretched between mast and backstay, or between two
masts, and held just above the boom by a halyard (Plate 14, *top*),
although I believe a flat awning a little wider than the yacht's
beam, and extended athwartships by long battens in pockets, is
better, for it can be tilted a little one way or the other to guard
against a low morning or evening sun, and its sagging centre could
be provided with a spout and pipe for the collection of rain. But if
an awning is too complicated one will hesitate to spread it, and if it
is too large or flimsy one will worry for it in every puff of wind.
Though many yachts on charter in the West Indies do so, it is

unseamanlike to put to sea with a harbour awning spread, for it interferes with the working of sails and gear. However, a small rectangle of sailcloth, perhaps measuring 2 metres (about a fathom) each way and provided with a line at each corner, might with advantage be rigged to protect the helmsman when long spells of steering have to be undertaken in sunshine – even a golfing umbrella has been pressed into service on occasions.

Sanitation

In the days of sail the seaman's latrine was known as the heads (*Concise Oxford Dictionary*) because the part of the ship used for the purpose was a grating in the heads (or bows) near the heel of the bowsprit, and the term is widely used today.

Although a bucket half-filled with sea-water before use, and fitted in its own little locker with a hinged seat, is quite satisfactory in uncrowded waters, nearly every yacht, even the smallest, has a mechanical heads in which effluent is pumped out and sea-water pumped in by one or separate pumps; the two-pump kind is the more reliable though a little more complicated to use; to prevent water syphoning back inboard, especially when heeled, the soil pipe should be taken as high up as possible under the deck before discharging overboard below the LWL. Sea-water is a good disinfectant, and provided the heads are flushed through several times after each use, and the pump glands and sea-cocks are correctly adjusted so that there are no leaks, the unit should give many years of clean, trouble-free service, but foreign bodies, such as hair, matches, and string are liable to put the discharge pump out of action by holding the valves open. Over a period of time a hard deposit will form inside the discharge pipe; Blakes of Gosport, makers of the famous Baby Blake heads, reckon this reduces the bore of the pipe by 3 millimetres ($\frac{1}{8}$ inch) a year. Attempts to remove the deposit are not usually successful, so it may be best to have the pipe of plastic instead of metal, then it can easily be removed by slackening off two hose-clips and be replaced cheaply.

It seems wasteful to place the heads, which is probably used only a few minutes each day, amidships where the motion is least and the beam greatest, but in a yacht where both saloon and cabin are used for sleeping, a position between them clearly has advantages. Many owners prefer to have the heads not in a small compartment of its own, which may be difficult to ventilate and keep clean, but in the forecastle where the forehatch can provide the required 1 metre (3 feet) of headroom even in a very small yacht. For the average person a comfortable height for the seat above the sole is 35 centimetres (14 inches).

Obviously some discretion needs to be exercised, and heads should not be pumped out in tideless harbours or close to bathing beaches; some countries, notably the USA, are legislating against the discharging of raw sewage by yachts anywhere in their coastal waters. Since most environmentalists are agreed that such pollution of the water by yachts is very small and is quickly converted into harmless but useful matter, such legislation might be of greater value if directed first at industrial and municipal concerns which continue to discharge large volumes of harmful material. Nevertheless, thought should be given to the matter when a new yacht is being planned or built, otherwise access to some waters may be denied her. There are several ways in which the requirements can be met, such as the recycling system with which a chemically-treated water supply of small volume is used to flush the heads repeatedly, or the installation of a holding tank into which the discharge from the heads goes to be sucked out later at a disposal station, or pumped out at sea clear of the land. As at least 4·5 litres (1 gallon) of water is needed to flush the heads after use, a holding tank needs to be of large capacity, impossibly large if there are several people aboard a small yacht for more than one day, and even in the busy waters of Long Island Sound sewage disposal stations are few and far between. The air-vent from a holding tank needs to be carried well up the mast, or the stink will permeate the vessel.

The drains from galley-sink and wash-basins will need some attention, for soaps and detergents build up strong-smelling slime which will need cleaning out occasionally. A bottle-brush on a flexible wire followed by some work with a rubber suction cup, and lots of sea-water, are the best things to use.

4

RIGS

Gaff and bermudian – Sloop – Cutter – Yawl – Ketch – Schooner – Some other
rigs – Choice of rig for voyaging

IT is obvious that the wind blowing on a sail from astern will overcome the retarding effect of the water on the hull and drive a vessel forward, but how a sailing vessel can make forward progress with the wind blowing from abeam or forward of the beam is not quite so clear.

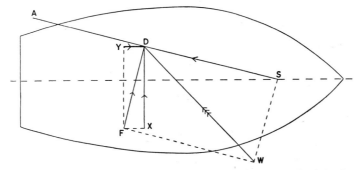

Fig 8   Parallelograms of forces applied to the wind on a close-hauled sail

Let us assume for a moment that a sail is flat, not curved fore-and-aft as it really is. Fig 8 shows a small boat with a single sail close-hauled on the starboard tack; SA represents the sail and WD the force and direction of the wind which is blowing at an angle of 45° to the fore-and-aft line of the boat. By applying the parallelogram of forces, the wind force WD can be resolved into two forces FD and SD. SD, running aft along the sail, is useless and we will disregard it (though it may be said to retard forward progress slightly by its friction on the sail) and we are left with the force FD acting at 90° to the sail. If we resolve that force into its component parts relative to the midship line of the boat, we have XD, which expends its energy in heeling the boat and driving her to leeward, and the much smaller force YD which is all that is left of the original wind force to drive the boat forward. If the boat had no lateral grip on the water she would be pushed further to

leeward by force *FD* than forward by force *YD*; but as a sailing
boat or yacht is designed to offer great resistance to lateral movement and the minimum resistance to forward movement, she will
move forward and make only a small amount of leeway.

Fortunately a yacht close-hauled does not have to rely only on
the pressure of the wind on the windward side of her sails, for the
propelling force of that is small. A well-cut sail has a curve
fore-and-aft, fairly steep at the luff (the forward edge), and gradually flattening out towards the leech (the after edge), and therefore
resembles the curve of the upper surface of the wing of a bird or
aeroplane. Knowledge gained in the designing and building of

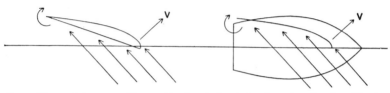

Fig 9   The partial vacuum, *V*, caused by the wind at the leading edge of an aircraft's wing
(*left*) and a close-hauled sail (*right*)

aircraft has shown that when the airstream meets a wing at a small
angle, by flowing up over the hump at the forward or leading edge
it creates a partial vacuum there, as shown by the arrow marked *V*
on the left of Fig 9; this tends to draw the wing upwards and
forwards. A similar vacuum is formed by the wind at the luff of a
correctly shaped sail, as is shown at the right of Fig 9; but as the
sail is not in a horizontal but a vertical plane, the vacuum tends
not to lift the yacht but to pull her forward. It is stated that this
force is very much greater than the force acting on the windward
side of the sail; but it is worth noting that most of the research
work has been done on double-surface aerofoils, which are rigid,
whereas the curve of a sail is not rigid, and it varies according to
the manner in which it is set and the direction of the wind.
Nevertheless, certain important facts which can be applied to sails
have emerged from aircraft research.

Most of these centre round the leading edge, the luff of the sail.
It is there that the greatest suction on the lee side is produced, but
some of that power is lost by eddies created by the mast. Therefore
a sail which is set flying or on a stay is more efficient than one set
close abaft a mast.

If the speed of the air flowing past the leeward side of the luff can be increased, the suction there will also be increased. In a yacht this is achieved by setting a headsail forward of the mast; a headsail also increases the efficiency of the mainsail by smoothing out some of the eddies on its lee side, but care has to be taken that it is not sheeted in too flat or it will backwind the mainsail instead of assisting it, and cause it to shake. To obtain the best effect it appears to be desirable that the headsail should overlap the mainsail to some extent, but a large overlap is not necessarily an advantage and in a cruising yacht should be avoided as it causes sheeting difficulties which may lead to an undesirable reduction in the length of the crosstrees. An overlap one-sixth of the length of the foot of the headsail is large enough.

The middle part of a sail, the bunt, is less efficient than the luff (except when running before the wind) because there is less suction on its lee side, and the angle it makes with the fore-and-aft line of the yacht is less advantageous; the leech is even less efficient, for the above points are aggravated, and there are always some eddies behind it to interfere with the smooth wind flow, no matter how well the sail has been made.

An efficiently rigged yacht of good hull form is able to sail within 45° to 50° of the true wind in smooth water, and if her destination lies to windward she will reach it by tacking, beating, turning, or working to windward, ie sailing with the wind for a time on one bow, and then for a time with it on the other bow. The angle between her tacks will therefore be between 90° and 100°, but she will, of course, make some leeway, the amount depending on the shape of her hull and its area of lateral resistance, and on the strength of the wind. A further complication arises in that as the yacht moves forward the force and direction of the true wind will alter according to her speed, so that her sails will have to be trimmed for the apparent wind which comes from more ahead and with greater velocity (page 236).

The area of sail required to give the best performance close-hauled in a whole-sail breeze will clearly depend on the type of yacht and her rig, but an approximate idea can be obtained by squaring the LWL in metres or feet, calling the answer square metres or square feet of sail, and taking three-quarters of it. The area of a triangular sail, HTC in Fig 10, is found by ruling a perpendicular XT from one side to the opposite corner; then multiply CH by half of XT. To find the area of a quadrilateral sail, divide it into two triangles by joining any two opposite corners; find the area of each of the triangles and add them together. When measuring the area of a fore-and-aft sail it is usual to disregard any curve the leech may have, and consider the leech as being a straight line.

The centre of lateral resistance of a yacht (CLR) is the centre of gravity of a plane figure the outline of which corresponds to her underwater profile, ie the point at which lateral pressure would

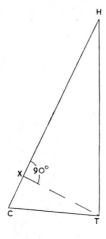

have to be applied to move the plane figure sideways with no tendency for it to pivot. In the sail plan the CLR is projected upwards and is marked on the LWL. It can be found quite simply by cutting out the shape of the underwater profile from a piece of stiff paper and balancing it on a knife edge.

The centre of effort (CE) is the centre of gravity of the whole sail plan regarded as a plane figure; on the sail plan it is projected downwards and is also marked on the LWL, where practice has shown that it should always be forward of the CLR. The distance apart of these two points is called the lead and is usually expressed as a percentage of the LWL.

Fig 10   Finding the
area of a sail

Many yachtsmen regard the CE and CLR as having an important influence on the balance of a yacht under sail. They do indeed appear to be important, but it should be realized that as soon as a yacht starts to move through the water, the position of the CLR moves to an unknown extent and varies its position according to the speed. Also, as the sails are

PLATE 7 (*facing*). *A*. A diesel-burning cabin heater; the drip-feed control and sight glass are well protected by the table. *B* and *C*. Two types of chimney cowl; that at *C*, called a Charlie Noble, is probably the better as it offers no obstruction yet prevents a downdraught, but it takes more stowage space. *D*. An effective shade for a cabin light can be made from stiff paper glued on; this one is decorated with a tortoiseshell brooch. *E*. When there is no bridge deck between cockpit and companionway, a washboard slid into grooves will help to stop water from getting below in heavy weather. Here a temporary strongback to strengthen the door in storm conditions is also shown.

PLATE 8 (*overleaf*). *A*. Mosquito screens shipped in a companionway and fitted with a cat flap. *B*. A double coaming forehatch provided with side-flaps to form an extractor. *C*. The side-flaps are hinged and can be folded flat and secured with turn-buttons when the hatch has to be completely closed. *D*. A water-trap ventilator installed at the break of a coachroof; a winch handle stows on the side of the box. *E*. A simple form of portlight screen; the netting is sewn to a frame of stiff wire and is sprung into place.

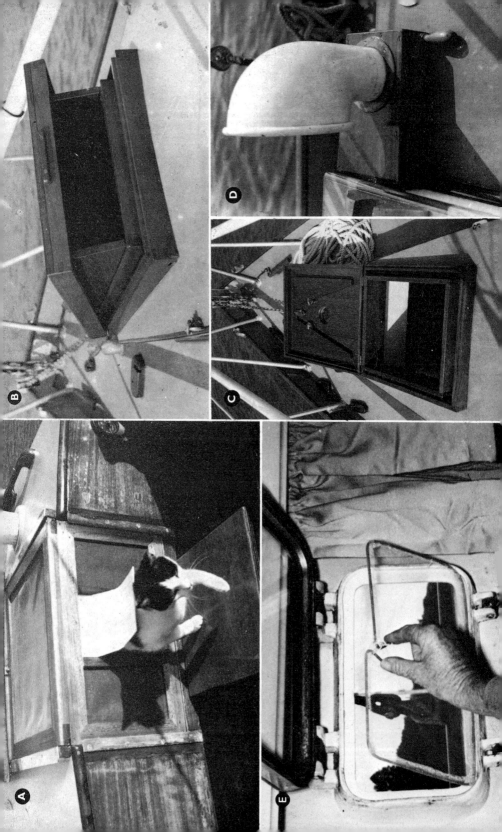

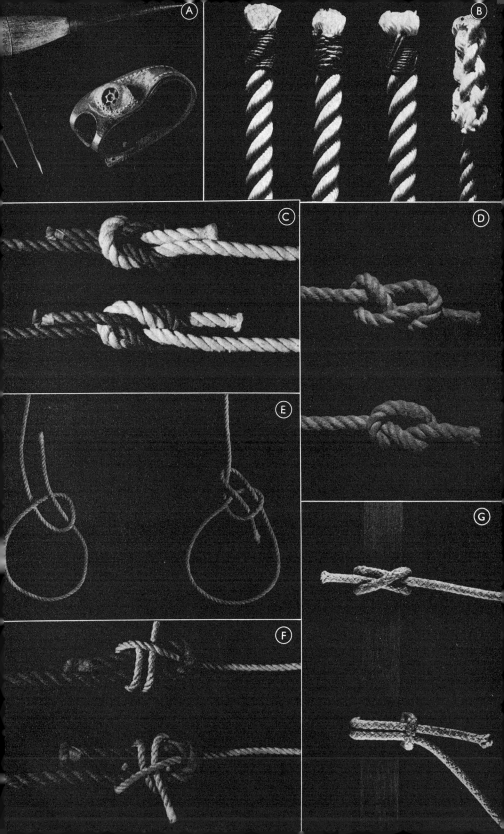

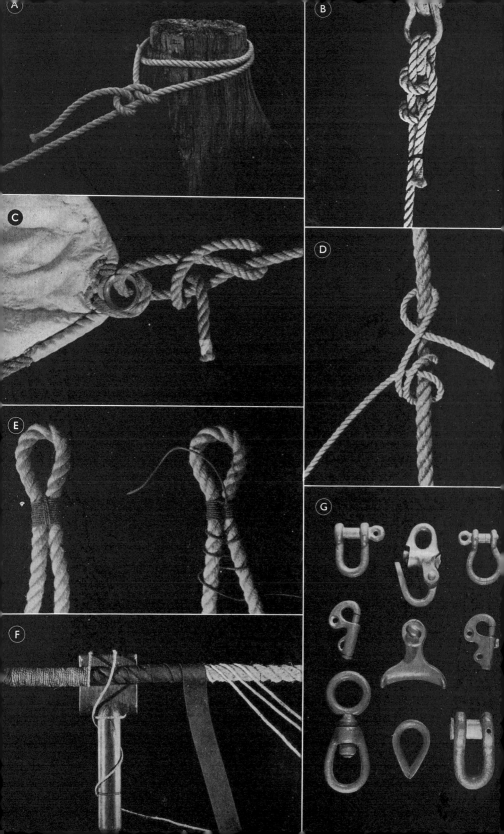

not flat and are not trimmed exactly fore-and-aft, their real centre of dynamic energy cannot possibly coincide with the CE which is merely a geometric convention.

Gaff and bermudian

All headsails commonly used aboard cruising yachts are triangular, but mainsails, mizzens, and the foresails of schooners may be quadrilateral or triangular. The quadrilateral or gaff sail takes its name from the spar by which its head is extended from the mast; the triangular sail has no gaff and is known as jib-headed, leg-o'-mutton, Marconi, or bermudian, the latter term being the one most frequently used in Britain. The foot (lower edge) of either type of sail is nearly always extended by a boom, but there are a few instances of boomless mainsails and mizzens being used in yachts.

Whether the gaff or the bermudian rig is best for a cruising yacht has been one of the most controversial subjects among yachtsmen, but that the argument has now been almost settled in favour of the bermudian rig is shown by the fact that not one yacht in a thousand built today is given gaff rig, and that more and more gaffers are being converted to the bermudian rig. Nevertheless as the gaff rig will no doubt continue to lend an air of grace and character to the coastal scene for many years to come, we should examine briefly the advantages and disadvantages of both rigs.

The bermudian sail is the most efficient for sailing to windward chiefly because, areas being equal, it has a longer luff. Also it is generally agreed that for a sail to work to the best advantage on the wind the mast should be kept straight, and this can be done with a bermudian sail which, sliding on a track, allows the rigging to be attached to any part of the mast without interfering with the

---

PLATE 9 (*overleaf*). *A*. Sail needles, spike, and seaming palm. *B*. Whippings. *From left to right*: common, west country, and palm-and-needle. *Extreme right*: a back splice. *C*. Reef knot, and below it a granny. *D*. Figure-of-eight knot, and below it a thumb knot. *E*. Bowline. The first step is shown on the left, and the completed knot on the right, but the parts have not been hove taut. *F*. Double sheet bend, and below it the bend incorrectly made. *G*. Clove hitch at the top, and cow hitch below.

PLATE 10 (*facing*). *A*. Round turn and two half-hitches. *B*. Fisherman's bend. *C*. Topsail sheet bend. *D*. Rolling hitch. *E*. Round seizing on the left, racking seizing in process of being made on the right, showing figure-of-eight turns. *F*. Worming, parcelling, and serving a rope. *G*. *From left to right, top row*: U-shackle, snap shackle, and bow shackle. *Middle row*: Hank with end pull, span shackle, and hank with side pull. *Bottom row*: Swivel, heart-shaped thimble, and chain-joining shackle.

hoisting or lowering of the sail; with a gaff sail no rigging can be attached to the mast below the gaff jaws, for it would prevent the jaws from sliding up or down unless they are on a track, but this has never proved popular. With the bermudian sail the top of the mast can be stayed against forward pull by a permanent backstay leading down to the stern or to a boomkin projecting from the stern; such a stay cannot be fitted permanently with gaff rig because it would prevent the gaff from swinging across when tacking or gybing; so a pair of running backstays, commonly known as runners although they now have no connection with the single-block purchase of that name, are used instead, the weather one having to be set up and the lee one let go each time the yacht tacks or gybes. Requiring only one halyard instead of two, and having no gaff, the bermudian rig has less weight and windage aloft in spite of the necessarily taller mast, and is not so prone to trouble with chafe.

If a well-cut and properly rigged topsail is set above the mainsail, the gaff rig can be quite efficient to windward; but when the topsail has been taken in the gaff rig becomes inefficient, for then a large reduction has been made to the total leading edge, so if an owner is not prepared to make use of a topsail, the gaff rig has little to recommend it so far as sailing to windward is concerned; but the cruiser is not always close-hauled. With the wind free the gaff rig should not be less and may be more efficient than the bermudian, for it appears to possess more drive, probably because, having a shorter hoist, the head of the sail does not sag to leeward so much for a given length of sheet. In this connection it should be mentioned that the all-round performance under sail of many an able, heavy-displacement yacht has been spoilt when converting her from gaff to bermudian rig, chiefly because a considerable reduction to the total area of sail was made at the same time, an inevitable corollary unless the height of the mast was increased.

An outstanding advantage of the gaff sail is that it can nearly always be set or lowered with the wind in any direction. This is not so with the bermudian sail. Badly designed tracks and slides, and lack of lubrication of them, are contributory causes, but even when they do work properly the sail is still difficult to handle when it is full of wind, for its headboard is liable to get jammed beneath one of the lower shrouds when being hoisted.

Some of the ways in which yachts are rigged are shown in Fig 11, and before condemning any of them it is worth remembering that outstanding cruises and voyages have successfully been made under all these rigs.

Sloop

The sloop has only two sails, mainsail, and headsail, and if the latter sets to the masthead, as it usually does, the rig is the simplest of the orthodox rigs, but the mast will need to be stiff in the fore-and-aft plane because it will be properly stayed fore-and-aft only at the top, and yet must withstand considerable compression. Because of its simplicity and the minimum weight and windage aloft, the sloop rig is particularly suitable for a small yacht. Owing to the increased leverage, a pound aloft is equal to many pounds on the keel, and all weight above the LWL tends to make a yacht heel. Small craft are more easily heeled than large ones, and they should be given every chance to remain as upright as possible, for when heeled to a steep angle the sails lose some of their efficiency and the hull assumes an awkward shape for moving ahead through the water.

The sloop rig is efficient so long as a large headsail is set, but when an increase of wind calls for a smaller headsail to be set, some efficiency is lost because the gap between mainsail and headsail is too great and the slot effect is lost. If the headsail is set not to the masthead but to some point lower down (three-quarter rig), and this seems to me to have little to commend it, a pair of runners, or jumper stays (page 117), will probably be needed to counteract its forward pull. If the single headsail of the sloop is too large to be handled comfortably by the available crew, cutter rig will be more suitable.

Cutter

Like the sloop, the cutter has a single mast, but carries two working headsails instead of one. The outer sail is known as the jib, and the inner one as the forestaysail, which is usually abbreviated to staysail; I prefer to reserve the word foresail for the fore-and-aft sail set on the aft side of a schooner's foremast. As with the sloop, the jib will probably set to the masthead; a lower position has no merit, but will be called for with gaff rig, in which the top of the mast cannot be permanently stayed aft. The staysail will be hanked to a stay lower down (the forestay or inner forestay), and unless it is very small or the mast is very stiff, will require runners, otherwise it will pull the mast forward and its luff will sag to leeward instead of being straight, as it should be. A cutter with little or no forward overhang may need a bowsprit to allow a sufficiently large area of head canvas to be set without the jib overlapping the staysail too much.

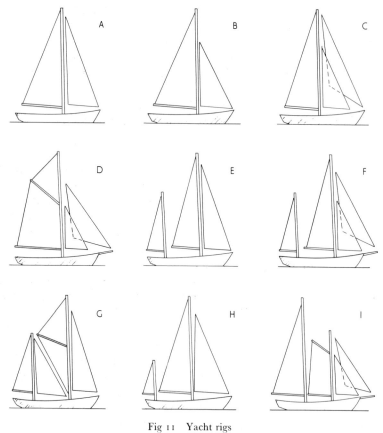

Fig 11   Yacht rigs

A sloop; *B* three-quarter sloop; *C* cutter; *D* gaff cutter; *E* ketch; *F* double headsail ketch; *G* wishbone ketch; *H* yawl; *I* schooner, gaff rigged on the fore, bermudian on the main.

Cutter rig has the advantage over the sloop that the two smaller headsails may be easier to handle than one large one, and that a reduction of head canvas can be made quickly by taking in either the jib or the staysail, while aboard a sloop in similar circumstances the headsail would have to be reefed or changed for a smaller one, as no yacht will sail well without a headsail of some kind; incidentally, the cutter will sail better under mainsail and staysail than she will under mainsail and jib. As her staysail is a powerful sail and is easy to handle it should be of ample size, so her mast will need to be well into her; two fifths of the LWL aft of the forward end of the LWL is considered to be the correct position for it; there its weight will be kept out of the bow, and being in the most beamy part of her it can be more easily supported by its shrouds.

A trend among the racing yachts of the late seventies was to have very narrow mainsails and enormous overlapping headsails. This example should not be followed by the cruiser, for next to a cutter's staysail the mainsail will be the easiest sail to handle, and it needs to be of a good size for reaching and running.

Yawl

It has often been said than an able-bodied man can handle a sail of 46·5 square metres (500 square feet), but many people consider this is at least 9·3 square metres (100 square feet) too much; so, unless a sloop or cutter can always be sure of having a crew of not less than three, one to steer and two to handle the mainsail, that sail, like all others, should be limited in area to 37–46·5 square metres (400–500 square feet).

The yawl rig, which has two masts, main and mizzen, the mizzen mast being stepped abaft the rudder post, may be adopted where the mainsail of a cutter or sloop would be too large to be handled by the available crew. The rig is nearly as efficient as the cutter, but when close-hauled the mainsail may backwind the mizzen, and it has to be admitted that more than one yawl has been found to sail to windward better on being converted to cutter rig by the simple expedient of removing the mizzen mast, even though the total sail area was then reduced. The rig has the advantages that a quick reduction of after canvas can be made by stowing the mizzen, and that off the wind a mizzen staysail can be set; this term is misleading, for the sail is not hanked to a stay (except in the wishbone ketch) but is set flying from the mizzen masthead to some point on deck, usually abreast the mainmast. Very few yawls will handle under jib and mizzen as is commonly supposed.

Ketch

The ketch, also a two-masted rig with one or two working headsails, differs from the yawl in having a taller mizzen mast stepped forward of the rudder post, so that the mizzen is larger and the mainsail is smaller than those sails would be in a yawl of the same size. The mizzen is therefore of some real use, and a ketch should handle under jib and mizzen or mainsail and staysail, the latter being the better combination. As the rig splits up the sail area into more nearly equal areas than do any of the other rigs, with the possible exception of the schooner, the ketch is often considered a good rig for a large yacht which is to be sailed short-handed; but, after the schooner, it is also the least efficient to windward because of the multiplicity of its gear and the lack of drive given by one large sail. It cannot point so high as a sloop, cutter, or yawl, and the mainsail will usually back-wind the mizzen when close-hauled unless the main boom is short with a consequent reduction in mainsail area. When running, the mizzen will take some of the wind from the mainsail unless the mainsail and mizzen are wing and wing, ie squared out on opposite sides, and it is not easy to keep them like that except in smooth water. But, as with the yawl, the ketch can set a mizzen staysail when off the wind.

The bermudian ketch rig is most suited to an easily driven craft, as the narrow sails lack area and power. However, the effective area of sail between the masts can be increased if the wishbone ketch rig is used. The triangular mainsail is then extended by a divided spar known as a wishbone; each half of this spar has a parabolic curve so that the sail set within it may take up a natural curve on any point of sailing. The spar is pivoted some distance up the mainmast, and is controlled by a sheet leading through a block on the mizzen mast and down to the deck. The triangular space below the mainsail is filled by the mizzen staysail which in this instance is smaller than the usual mizzen staysail, is hanked to the mizzen stay, and is a working sail.

Schooner

The schooner may have two or three masts; if there are three they are usually all the same height, but if only two, though they may be the same height, it is more common for the foremast to be the shorter. The rig may be gaff, bermudian, staysail or wishbone, or a combination of these, and because a variety of light-weather sails can be set between the masts, the schooner excels on a reach, but she is an indifferent performer to windward and, except for some jury-rigged motor-sailers, the rig is rarely seen in British waters. This is unfortunate because there is something attractive and romantic about it, a point which is apt to be overlooked in the modern pursuit of efficiency at all costs.

Some other rigs

The cat or una rig enjoys a considerable popularity in the USA where it is usually placed in a very beamy, shoal-draught, centre-board hull with a huge rudder, a type indigenous to the waters round Cape Cod. The rig consists of a single gaff or bermudian sail fitted with a boom and set on a mast which is placed right in the bow. The lack of a headsail is a great handicap, and because of its forward position the mast is difficult to stay efficiently. The rig is rarely seen in Britain except in dinghies and a few craft on the Norfolk Broads.

The sliding gunter sail is similar to the bermudian sail but, instead of being set on a track on a tall mast, the mast is kept short and the lower part of the luff of the sail is attached to it either by a lacing or mast hoops. The upper part of the luff is laced to a yard which is sent aloft on a halyard to lie close alongside and extend well above the upper part of the mast. Jaws at the heel of the yard embrace the mast and help to keep the yard upright. This rig has the advantage of a long leading edge, and that when the sail is reefed the weight and windage aloft is brought lower down with it; but because it is impossible to stay the gunter yard or to set a headsail to the top of it, the rig is suitable only for boats and very small yachts.

The standing lug is a quadrilateral sail which is usually fitted with a boom, its head being laced to a yard which projects a short distance forward of the mast. The tack of the sail is secured either to the mast or to the forward end of the boom. It is a simple rig, all its spars are short, and it is suitable for sailing dinghies.

The spritsail is also quadrilateral and is crossed from tack to peak by a spar known as a sprit, which replaces both boom and gaff. The heel of the sprit is slung on the lower part of the mast and the spar is kept standing; the angle of the sail to the fore-and-aft line is controlled by two vangs from the peak end of the sprit set up at the deck each side by tackles or winches. The sail is not lowered when stowed but is brailed in to the mast (drawn in like a curtain), by brails which pass round it and through several cringles. This was the rig of the Thames barge and it was most suitable for her as it enabled a large vessel to be handled by a small crew, and when brailed up the sail was clear of the cargo hatch; but the long, heavy sprit cannot be regarded as safe for a seagoing vessel and the rig is therefore hardly ever used in yachts, though the system of brailing up is employed aboard a few yachts which have boomless gaff mainsails.

Although the Chinese have been using fully battened lugsails on unstayed masts for thousands of years very few yachts carry such a rig, but one of the most famous to do so was the engineless folkboat *Jester*, in which first Colonel H G (Blondie) Hasler and later Michael Richey, MBE, made a number of seamanlike and trouble-free crossings of the North Atlantic both ways, taking part in the single-handed races. Another famous yacht with Chinese rig is the 13-metres (42-foot) two-masted *Galway Blazer II*, in which Bill King circumnavigated single-handed by way of the three stormy capes, Agulhas, Leeuwin, and Horn. The advantages of the rig are that there is no standing rigging, and no sail changing is required, while reefing and stowing the sail is extremely simple. The disadvantages are that no extra sails can conveniently be set in light weather, and that there is likely to be considerable chafe in way of the parrels which hold each of the battens to the mast.

Choice of rig for voyaging

The following brief list of yachts which have made great voyages shows that no rig has a monopoly, and that the choice is not dictated by the peculiar conditions of long-distance voyaging; but it is probable that some of the owners made do with the rigs their vessels already possessed when they acquired them.

Macpherson's *Driac*, Pye's *Moonraker*, Casper's *Elsie*, Worth's *Beyond*, Le Toumelin's *Kurun*, and Davenport's *Waltzing Matilda* were cutters; Slocum's *Spray* started as a cutter but was converted to yawl rig. Clark's *Solace*, Robinson's *Svaap*, Van de Wiele's *Omoo*, O'Brien's *Saoirse*, and Smeeton's *Tzu Hang* were ketches; Pidgeon's *Islander*, Muhlhauser's *Amaryllis*, and Franklen Evans's *Kochab* were yawls, while Fahnestock's *Director* and Crowe's *Lang Syne* were schooners. Many of the smaller yachts, including Nance's *Cardinal Vertue*, Ann Davison's *Felicity Ann*, and my *Wanderer III* were sloops; Roth's *Whisper* started as a sloop but was converted to cutter; and, as mentioned above, Hasler's and later Richey's little Folkboat *Jester*, and King's *Galway Blazer II* were junk rigged.

My present yacht, *Wanderer IV*, is a ketch, for she was a stock design (a matter of cost) and arranged for that rig. I was interested to try it, and my experience after some 60,000 miles with it confirms the opinions expressed below. My preference for voyaging is a single-masted rig, and I would not choose two masts unless my vessel were of such a size that with one mast any sail would be too large to be handled by one person, ie in excess of 37 square metres (400 square feet). As noted earlier in the chapter, the single mast will be well inboard, where its weight and the drive of the sails set on it will not tend to depress the bows, and there it can be more efficiently stayed both fore-and-aft and athwartships. Also as noted above, when running dead with the ketch or yawl the mizzen will partly blanket the mainsail unless the sails are spread wing and wing, but they will not remain comfortably like that for long in the open sea. Therefore, on that point of sailing, unless tacking to leeward is resorted to, the mizzen will usually be taken in and that much sail area be lost. Robinson believed that the ketch was the ideal rig for the ocean-going yacht, and that was how his *Svaap* was rigged for her splendid circumnavigation. But at Durban I met the Driscoll brothers from Australia; they had built *Walkabout*, a replica of *Svaap*, and had just crossed the Indian Ocean in her. They had found the mizzen such a nuisance, blanketing the mainsail when running and causing so much weather helm when the wind was on the quarter – this appears to be a common failing of the rig – that they eventually gave up using it and were planning to convert the yacht to cutter rig. An argument in favour of the ketch or yawl is that sail can be reduced quickly and easily by handing the mizzen, but it should not be a long or difficult job to reef the mainsail of a cutter or sloop provided the gear for that purpose is efficient, and such a reduction of sail will be less likely to interfere with the balance of the yacht and her steering than will a big reduction of sail at one end of her. But when on a reach the ability to set a mizzen staysail, thus much increasing the sail area, may be of some value, and in light winds when the swell may throw the wind out of the heavy working sails, it may be possible to make satisfactory and chafe-free progress under genoa and mizzen staysail alone, as Franklen-Evans in *Kochab* often did on his several voyages between England and New Zealand. A fisherman's staysail (sometimes known as a mule) may be set between the masts of a ketch, and will help to steady her; but it is not an efficient sail because its sheet must lead to the head of the mizzen mast, which is too far to windward no matter what the course may be, and the sail therefore creates more heeling influence than forward drive.

The ketch, as has already been said, is not so efficient to windward as the sloop or cutter, and although I would not hold that against the rig because not a lot of windward sailing is normally involved when voyaging, there may be occasions when ability to windward is important. The Holmdahls in *Viking* took 51 days for the 4,000-mile passage from Balboa (Panama Canal Zone) to the Marquesas, and on arrival there they tried to beat into Taiohae Bay, a place which is bedevilled with calms and catspaws. For many hours they struggled to reach water shallow enough to anchor in, but *Viking* was a heavy vessel with a very snug ketch rig, and they failed. Trader Bob Mckitterick watched from his veranda with surprise and dismay as towards evening the Holmdahls gave up the struggle and headed away for another island in the group, where they anchored precariously for a short time in a heavy swell, and then, still weary with their long voyage, sailed on for another seventeen days to reach Tahiti. I think the moral of this story, and others of the same sort, is that if you intend to rig a heavy-displacement vessel as a ketch you must see to it that she can carry plenty of sail, or else install an engine of reasonable power, as indeed almost everyone does today. One final remark about ketch or yawl rig is that because of the mizzen boom and sheet it may be difficult, perhaps impossible, to use a wind-vane steering gear.

The sight of a schooner delights me. There is something glamorous and rakish about that rig, something redolent of palm-fringed anchorages sweet with the scent of vanilla and the heady aroma of copra. I have often thought that I would like to own a gaff-rigged schooner with a poop, a great cabin, and a fiddle-head, a couple of graceful squaresail yards crossed on the fore, and a merry Polynesian crew to work her; but she would need a powerful motor to make up for her inefficiency to windward in narrow waters. It is true that not so very long ago sailing vessels which were not polished performers to windward used to make their way into difficult places; but labour was cheap then, and they carried large crews which were capable of towing or kedging, and the mortality among them was high.

No matter whether they have one or two masts, the tendency among yachts today is to set a single headsail to the top of the mainmast. This is a pleasant simplification in that only one pair of headsheets has to be attended to, and that so long as the mast is sufficiently stiff it need have only a single pair of crosstrees, and no runners are required. But I question if this is the best rig for a short-handed voyaging yacht of any size, as the No 1 headsail may be too large to be handed comfortably by one person when a freshening wind calls for it to come in, and when it is in a smaller sail will have to be set in its place, and the slot effect will then be lost. With the two-headsail rig a freshening wind will call for only one of the headsails, preferably the outer one, to be handed, and it may then be unnecessary to set another sail in its place – a considerable saving of physical effort. With this rig a bowsprit may be desirable because it will enable a greater area of sail to be carried without increasing the height of the mast, and this is of value in light winds with the usual ocean swell, for the lower a sail is the less will the motion affect it. Also, when the yacht is close-hauled or is reaching, and she is required to steer herself or to be reasonably well-balanced to assist a vane gear to do its work properly, there will be a better chance of achieving this if there are two pairs of headsail sheets to adjust instead of one; and with the outer headsail, the jib, set from a bowsprit, its extra leverage, coupled with the fact that it is less likely to be interfered with by the mainsail, may make it possible for the yacht to steer herself with the wind on the quarter, a difficult feat, but one which the yawl *Spray*, the ketch *Saoirse*, and the cutter *Kurun* – all with bowsprits – managed to perform.

5

ROPE AND ROPE WORK

*Fibre rope – Tools and fittings – Whippings – Knots, bends, and hitches –
Seizings – Worming, parcelling, and serving – Splicing fibre rope – Wire rope
– Making eyes in wire rope – Joining wire to fibre rope – Terminals for wire
rope – Belaying ropes – Blocks, tackles, and winches*

BEFORE considering in detail the standing and running rigging of
the individual spars and sails, it is desirable that the reader should
have some knowledge of the various kinds of ropes used aboard a
yacht, and the methods employed for fastening one to another or
to some other object. Indeed, it is essential that he should be able
to make the commoner knots, bends, hitches, and splices, for the
rigging of any yacht will need attention if it is to be kept in a
seaworthy and efficient condition, and he will not always be
within reach of a professional rigger.

Fibre rope

The traditional type of rope can be made from any fibre that is
capable of being twisted into strands; the longer the individual
fibres are the greater will be the friction between them and the
better will the rope hold together. The fibres are spun with a
right-handed twist into yarn, which is varied in size according to
the size and type of rope being made. A number of yarns are then
twisted left-handed to form a strand, and three strands are laid up
to form a right-handed, or hawser-laid, rope. The spiral spaces
between the strands of a rope are known as contlines.

Natural fibres, such as hemp, manilla, cotton, and sisal, which
were used in the past for rope-making, have been almost entirely
superseded by synthetic materials, of which the following are the
most important: nylon is a polyamide filament derived from coal;
it is the strongest of the synthetic materials used in rope-making,
though it absorbs a little water and loses a little of its strength
when wet; it is unsuitable, for halyards and sheets because of its
great elasticity, which may reach 40 per cent of the rope's length
before the rope breaks; but it serves well for topping-lifts and
anchor cables, and is sometimes used for towing, but for that
purpose it is unsafe because if it should part the broken ends may
fly back with sufficient force to cause injury. Terylene (dacron in

the USA) is a polyester filament derived from oil; it does not absorb water, and if it has been 'pre-stretched' in the rope-making process it will have so little elasticity that it will serve well for most running rigging purposes, and often takes the place of flexible wire for halyards. Polypropylene and polythene are also derived from oil; the former is soft, the latter is hard and slippery and is not trustworthy in continual sunshine; both float, but except for certain purposes connected with commercial fishing, this seems to me to be a disadvantage, as a floating rope is likely to be damaged by passing craft and may foul their propellers, and in a dirty harbour will get fouled with floating oil.

As continuous filaments can be produced from the above materials, the ropes made from them are much stronger than were even the best of the natural-fibre ropes, and they have enabled a new type of rope, known as braided rope, to be evolved. This consists of a core of three strands or filaments laid up parallel or plaited together (this core may provide as much as 90 per cent of the rope's total strength) and the core is encased in a protective outer plaited sleeve of the same material. Such a rope is more supple than a 3-strand rope, and is commonly used for sheets, especially if they are to be handled by winches, on the barrels or drums of which it has a good grip. However, the interstices of the plait will hold water, and such a rope may take a long time to drain and dry.

Synthetic ropes do not swell or become stiff when wet, and they are not subject to damage by bacterial growth or insects, but after considerable exposure to sunlight 3-strand rope in particular hardens and becomes less tractable, and probably loses some of its strength; nylon rope stretches when wet and shrinks when dry. Although the outer surface quickly becomes fluffy when chafed, this acts as a protection and the rope will then withstand considerable further chafe without much harm, and it does have a remarkably long life; nevertheless, the normal precautions against chafe should be taken.

Synthetic cordage can be had in sizes suitable for all seagoing requirements, and in the smaller sizes is used for lashings, lacings, seizings, flag halyards, etc, and the smallest of all is sail- and whipping-twine, which is sometimes ready dressed with wax to help it render more easily. Marline consists of two loosely laid up strands of hemp dressed with Stockholm tar, and every seaman likes to have a ball or two of this on board because of its pungent nautical smell and splices served with it look so good. But, unlike synthetic materials, it is subject to rot, and for most purposes where it might be used terylene is to be preferred.

Until 1973 it was customary in the UK to describe the size of a rope by its circumference in inches, but now the diameter in millimetres is used instead, and the traditional coil of 120 fathoms has been changed to one of 220 metres. In the USA the size is also the diameter, but is still measured in inches. The following conversion table may be of use.

Circumference in inches	Diameter in inches	Diameter in millimetres	Strength, 3-strand terylene (dacron)	
			pounds	kilograms
3/4	1/4	6	1,250	565
1	5/16	8	2,240	1,016
1 1/4	3/8	10	3,500	1,587
1 1/2	1/2	12	5,000	2,267
1 3/4	9/16	14	7,000	3,175
2	5/8	16	8,960	4,064
2 1/2	13/16	20	12,320	5,590
3	1	24	17,920	8,120

Although the strength of the ropes has been given in the above table, this is more of academic than practical value where small sizes are concerned, for since one cannot get a good grip or haul without damage to the hands on a rope less than about 12 millimetres ($\frac{1}{2}$ inch) in diameter, that will probably be the smallest size used for running rigging no matter how small the yacht may be.

If synthetic rope is over loaded heat will be generated; not only will this weaken it but will tend to make the strands or filaments stick together and the rope become stiff. When a rope is being coiled a start must be made close to the standing part (the part of the rope that is fixed or made fast), thus leaving the free end to turn and twist as it may to rid itself of any superfluous turns; right-hand 3-strand rope should be coiled clockwise. Braided rope is best flaked down in a figure-of-eight, otherwise undesirable turns will be put into it and it may twist or kink when running out.

Tools and fittings (Plate 9A and 10G)

The tools needed for rope work are simple and few; a marlinespike for opening up the strands and a sharp knife are the essentials, and the seaman carries these on his person either in a pocket, on a lanyard round his neck, or in a sheath on his belt. A spike is frequently used for doing up or undoing shackles, and for that purpose one with a gentle taper is needed; the banana-shaped spike with a sudden taper near the end, as found on many clasp-knives, will not get a secure grip in the eye of a shackle pin, and some sailors therefore carry a special key for use on shackles, or even a small adjustable spanner. A large wooden spike, known as a fid, may be useful when working with a thick rope, but as the strands of synthetic rope are prone to kink if opened too much (this seriously weakens them) a hollow metal spike, known as a Swedish fid, into which a strand may be laid while being passed between strands of the standing part, is a much better tool to use. For wire splicing a special spike is desirable, one with a very gentle taper and with its point ground to the form of a small screwdriver blade for levering the strands apart. A palm and some sailmaker's needles and a reel of insulating tape will also be found useful. In order to serve a rope (ie bind it tightly with twine or seizing wire) a serving board will be required, for it is impossible to get the turns on tight enough by hand. This is wooden tool (sometimes in the form of a mallet) with a half-round score in it to take the rope, and a handle around which the twine is held. An improved kind of serving board has a reel on the handle to hold the twine so as to avoid the necessity for passing the ball of twine round the rope each time a turn is taken. In addition to the above tools a vice, a hammer, a chisel or hacksaw, and a pair of wire-cutters (pliers) will be needed for wire work.

A thimble is a round or heart-shaped metal fitting grooved for a rope, so that a rope spliced round it will be protected against distortion and chafe. An eye fitted with a thimble is known as a hard eye as opposed to a soft eye, which has no thimble.

A shackle is a metal link, often U-shape, with holes at the ends of its arms into which a pin is screwed. The pin has at one end an eye for a spike, a square for a spanner, or a slot for a screwdriver, so that it may be tightened properly. A shackle is used for joining together in a non-permanent manner items of rigging, such as two ropes with eyes at their ends, or a block to a rope or some other fitting. A snap-shackle is also used for joining in a non-permanent manner; it is closed by a hinged bar which is held in the closed position by a spring-loaded plunger, and is therefore quicker in use than a common shackle.

A hank is a metal clip fitting, the jaw of which is also closed by a spring-loaded plunger. It is sewn or seized, or cramped to the luff of a sail which is to be hanked on to a stay, up and down which it must be free to slide.

Whippings (Plate 9B)

Made up as it is of a number of yarns and strands twisted together, a rope will quickly become unlaid and frayed in use unless its end is whipped, ie bound with turns of twine to hold its parts together. There are several kinds of whippings but only three need concern us: common, west-country, and palm-and-needle. To make a common whipping, lay one end of a length of twine lengthways along the rope near the end which is to be whipped, and then take half a dozen tight turns with the twine round the rope and its own laid-back end, working towards the end of the rope; next lay the other end of the twine back along the rope (with the lay) and take another half-dozen turns with the loop of twine round the rope and the laid-back end. The two ends of twine will therefore emerge together in the middle of the whipping; haul them taut and cut them off short. A common whipping is quickly made, but does not last long. The west-country whipping is made by middling a piece of twine round the rope and then half-reef-knotting it at each turn; when a dozen turns have been made the ends are reef-knotted together. This will hold more securely than a common whipping and it is sometimes more convenient to use when the end to be whipped is very short or in an awkward position.

The palm-and-needle whipping is much more secure and may last the life of the rope. Pass the threaded needle through the rope between two strands and draw nearly all the twine through; then take the necessary number of turns tightly round the rope with the twine and finish off by following up and down each contline with the needle to make two turns, known as frapping turns, with the lay of the rope. Most people then cut the ends off short, but I prefer to knot them together with a reef knot concealed between the strands. In Plate 9B marline, which is much too thick, has been used instead of whipping twine so that the turns can be more clearly seen. The end of a small size synthetic line can be prevented from unlaying by heat-sealing instead of whipping. Hold the extreme end in the flame of a match for a moment then press the melted strands together with a well-wetted thumb and finger. The strands of larger synthetic ropes may also be heat-sealed before or after whipping to give a neat appearance. This may be done by pressing the square-cut end of the rope for a moment on a piece of hot metal – not the hotplate of the galley stove as it makes a stain which is difficult to remove.

Knots, bends, and hitches (Plates 9 and 10)

A large number of knots, bends, and hitches can be made with a rope's end, with the strands of a rope, or with two ropes (the *Ashley Book of Knots* shows nearly 4,000), but all that the cruising yachtsman will need to meet any contingency are three knots, three bends, and three hitches. He should be so familiar with them that he can tie or untie any of them right- or left-handed in daylight or on the darkest night, but as any knot, bend, or hitch weakens a rope to some extent where one part bites into the other, an eye splice or a short splice should always be used when possible for its strength is greater – perhaps 90 per cent of the full strength of a new rope. A rope should never be untwisted in the making of a knot, or for any other purpose, for that would weaken it even more.

The *figure-of-eight knot* (Plate 9*D*) is used for preventing the end of a rope from running out through a block or fairlead and is usually put on the ends of sheets. It can be loosened by bending back the standing part until the first loop of the knot is eased. The thumb or overhand knot (shown below it) should not be used as it can jam so tight as to be impossible to undo.

The *reef knot* (Plate 9*C*), as its name implies, is used for tying together the reef points of a sail, and it is used in any similar instance where it is necessary to tie together the ends of a rope tightly round some object. As will be seen in the illustration, each standing part lies alongside its own end, and care must be taken not to tie a granny knot (shown below it) where the standing part and its own end are separated from one another, for it may slip when a strain is put on it and is difficult to undo. The reef knot may be loosened by pulling one of the ends sharply back against the direction in which it normally lies, or it can be made with one end looped to form half a bow, and a sharp pull on this end will undo the knot. The reef knot should not be used for joining two ropes together as in that capacity it gives only 45 per cent of the full strength of the rope and is liable to slip.

The *double sheet bend* (Plate 9*F*) is used for joining together two ropes of similar or different sizes. A loop is made with the larger rope by doubling back its end, then the smaller rope is passed through the loop and round the outside of the *short* end of the thick rope before being tucked twice under its own standing part, *not* round the standing part of the thick rope first as shown in the lower part of the illustration. This bend gives 55 to 60 per cent of the strength of the rope.

A *bowline* (Plate 9*E*) is the knot used to make a temporary loop at the end of a rope. Holding the rope with the standing part away from you, form a small loop in it a convenient distance from its end and in such a manner that the standing part lies behind; then, having made a loop of the desired size, bring the end of the rope up through the small loop as shown on the left of the illustration, pass it round behind the standing part and down through the small loop again as shown on the right. To undo a bowline one breaks its back, ie the standing part is bent downwards towards the large loop and the small loop of the knot can then be rolled over to loosen the whole structure. A bowline gives 50 to 60 per cent of the strength of the rope.

A *round turn and two half-hitches* (Plate 10*A*) is used for making a rope fast to a post or ring, but it should not be used when the strain is likely to be great as it is inclined to jam. It gives 70 to 75 per cent of the strength of the rope.

The *fisherman's bend* (Plate 10*B*) is generally to be preferred to a round turn and two half-hitches as it is less inclined to jam. As will be seen in the illustration, it differs from the round turn and two half-hitches in that the first of the half-hitches is made through the round turn and round the standing part instead of round the standing part only. This is the recognized method of bending a rope cable to an anchor, but it is then usual to seize the end to the standing part with a length of twine as an additional safety measure.

The *clove hitch* (Plate 9*G*) is a favourite for making fast a dinghy's painter to a bollard as it can be made quickly by dropping the two loops of the hitch over the bollard; but the bowline is to be preferred for that purpose, for the clove hitch may jam itself very tight and be difficult to undo when there is a strain on the standing part. It is frequently used where a small rope has to be made fast to the standing part of a larger one and at the end has to be kept free for further purposes, eg ratlines and temporary guardrails. Note that a clove hitch is not made as shown lower down in the same illustration, for here the two ends come out in the same direction whereas they should come out in opposite directions. This incorrect kind of clove hitch is known as a cow hitch and was used in the days when shrouds were set up with deadeyes and lanyards. The clove hitch gives 60 per cent of the strength of the rope.

The *rolling hitch* (Plate 10D) is similar to the clove hitch, but it has an additional turn and is used where one rope has to be made fast to the standing part of another so that it will not slip in the longitudinal direction of the pull, eg for holding a rope which is under strain while something is being done with that rope's end. With a strain on the standing part it will not slip, but if the strain is released the hitch can be slid along the other rope to any desired position. When making this hitch it is important to see that the additional round-turn embraces not only the large rope but also its own standing part.

A *topsail sheet bend* (Plate 10C), also known as a buntline hitch, is used for making fast a single sheet to the clew of a sail, and the flogging of the sail will not shake it loose. The sheet is passed through the cringle (the eye in the corner of the sail) and is then clove hitched to its own standing part in such a manner that the second loop of the clove hitch is in between the first loop and the cringle.

As synthetic ropes are more slippery than natural fibre ropes, precautions may need to be taken when using some of the above knots, bends, and hitches, all of which were evolved for use with natural fibre ropes. These might consist of putting on an extra half-hitch, or seizing the ends to the standing parts; and although a bowline weakens a rope considerably, two important lines which must be joined temporarily may best be secured one to the other by two bowlines instead of using a double sheet bend.

Seizing (Plate 10E)

A seizing is a lashing of a more or less permanent character employed to hold two ropes side by side, or to hold two parts of a rope together so as to form an eye, eg jib-sheets in small craft are sometimes seized together round a thimble which is shackled to the clew cringle of the sail.

To make a round seizing bring the parts of the rope close together, clove-hitch a length of twine to one of the parts and with its long end take a dozen or so turns tightly round both parts of rope; finish off with two or three frapping turns up and down over the round turns and reef knot the ends together so that the knot is concealed between the parts of the ropes as shown on the left of Plate 10E.

Such a seizing is adequate if an equal strain is to be placed on both parts of the rope, but where the strain will be taken only by one part at a time, a racking seizing should be used for it will not slip. This is shown in process of being made on the right of the illustration, and it will be seen that figure-of-eight turns are taken round the parts which are to be held together; if the rope is being seized round a thimble, the seizing should be commenced close to the thimble. The seizing is finished off with frapping turns, but sometimes a complete set of round turns is put on over the racking turns for additional strength before finishing.

Worming, parcelling, and serving (Plate 10*F*)

To worm a rope is to fill in the contlines with small stuff so as to make a smooth suface before parcelling and serving, but this is rarely done today.

Parcelling consists of wrapping a strip of waterproof material round a rope (usually one of galvanized wire to keep out damp) in a spiral overlapping manner with the lay; insulating tape is excellent for the purpose as each turn will stick to the next.

To serve a rope is to bind it tightly with twine or seizing wire to protect it from chafe, to hold the parcelling firmly in place, or to make a neat finish to a splice and lend it strength by holding the interlaced strands in close contact with one another. The process is commenced like a common whipping by laying the end back and binding round it and the rope. The serving must be put on tightly and for this a serving board is essential, the rope being stretched horizontally by means of a tackle or winch. The twine leads round the board as shown in Plate 10*F* and one or two turns are taken round the handle to give the right tension. Unless the board is provided with a spool to hold the twine, the ball of twine will have to be passed round the rope as each turn is made, and then it is a help to have a second person to pass the ball and to take any turns out of the twine. The serving is finished off like a common whipping by laying back the end, serving over it, and then pulling taut. The life of a marline serving can be much prolonged by giving it several coats of varnish.

Splicing fibre rope (Plate 11)

A splice is made by interlacing the strands and is used to join together two ropes permanently or to make a permanent eye at the end of a rope; it is much to be preferred to any knot or bend because of its greater strength.

To make an *eye splice* unlay the rope for a distance equal to at least four times its circumference and put a whipping on it at that point, or bind with insulating tape. To prevent the individual strands from unlaying, I prefer not to heat-seal or whip them but to bind the end of each with thin adhesive tape to stiffen it, and make it pointed so that it is easy to interlace with the strands of the standing part without having to force the latter widely apart with a risk of kinking them. With the standing part leading away from you horizontally, form an eye of the desired size (small eyes are usually made round a metal or nylon heart-shaped thimble) and bring the unlaid part of the rope close alongside and to the right of the standing part. With your fingers or with a spike lift the uppermost strand of the standing part where the beginning or neck of the splice is to be, and pass the middle unlaid strand, marked A in the illustrations, under it from right to left against the lay. Pull it through as far as it will comfortably go (Plate 11A). Then take the left-hand strand B and pass it under the next strand to the left of the one A is under (Plate 11B), and pull it tight. Lastly, turn the rope over and tuck the third strand C under the remaining unoccupied strand of the standing part (Plate 11C). The standing part of the rope will now have a strand of the end coming out between each of its strands, and it is important to see that each bears an equal strain or the splice will not be strong. Continue tucking each strand in turn over one and under one until all of them have made four complete tucks; the splice will now look as in Plate 11D. To make a neat finish it is usual to taper the splice after the fourth tuck, and I find the most convenient way of doing so is to remove a third of the yarns in each strand before making the next tuck, and then to remove half of the remaining yarns before making the final tuck. Roll the splice well beneath your foot on the deck, or hammer it gently, and it will become round and smooth as in Plate 11E and the strands will bind more tightly one to another.

Although braided (or plaited) rope cannot be spliced in the above manner it can have an eye worked in its end by a much more complicated method known as the Knight's splice. This calls for a special splicing tool and some expertise, and anyone wishing to try it would do well to apply to one of the makers of braided rope, such as Marlow Ropes Ltd, for an illustrated pamphlet on the subject which is too involved to be included here. Various other ways of forming eyes in braided rope have been tried, including terminal attachments, but a common and quite satisfactory method is to sew the two parts together with heavy twine of the same material, taper by cutting out some of the yarns and then put on a strong serving. At least 30 centimetres (11·8 inches) of overlap should be allowed for a 1-centimetre (0·4-inch) rope, and this may rule it out for certain purposes, eg as the halyard for a sail which will be chock-a-block when set.

Ropemakers often incorporate a coloured yarn to indicate a certain type of rope, and some make braided ropes with the outer protective sleeve entirely coloured for the benefit of crew members who are not familiar with the yacht and her gear. It appears to be generally agreed that white rope should be used for the main-sheet, yellow for the jib, blue for the genoa, and red for the spinnaker, but such a colour code will be of little value on a dark night.

The *short splice* is used for joining permanently two 3-strand ropes which will not have to pass through a block or fairlead. The end of each rope is unlaid, a short whipping is put on at that point and the ropes are clutched together so that each strand of one rope lies between two strands of the other. Three complete tucks are then made with the strands of each rope against the lay of the other, over one and under one, and the splice is then tapered in the usual way.

A *long splice* (Plate 11, *F* to *I*) is used for joining two 3-strand ropes of the same size which have to pass through a block and must not therefore have an increased circumference at the splice.

Unlay the end of each rope to a distance equal to twelve times its circumference, then clutch the ropes together as for a short splice (Plate 11*F*). Unlay one strand of one of the ropes and at the same time lay into its place the complementary strand from the other rope and continue until all but 7·6 centimetres (3 inches) of the strand has been laid. (Plate 11*G* shows this having been done to the right-hand rope.) Next unlay a strand from the left-hand rope and lay in its place a strand from the right-hand rope. The third pair of strands are left where they are in the middle of the splice, which will then appear as in Plate 11*H*, with three pairs of strands sticking out. These should be slightly reduced in size by removing a few yarns before being knotted together with an overhand knot, ie a half reef knot (see Plate 11*I*). All the ends, having been cut off a short distance from their respective knots, are tapered and tucked into the rope beneath the adjacent strands, and if the splice is well rolled these joins will hardly show.

Though the long splice may be useful in the event of a sheet or halyard becoming stranded, it should be replaced by a new rope at the first opportunity, for the ends of the strands will almost certainly work out of the spliced rope if it is much used through a block. Incidentally the strength of this splice depends entirely on its length, and the one shown in the illustrations has intentionally been kept much shorter than it ought to be in order to get it into the pictures on a sufficiently large scale.

The *back splice* (Plate 9B, right) is a lazy man's method (being quick and easy) of preventing a 3-strand rope from unlaying, and it is often a cause of irritation as it may not pass through a block or eyelet. Unlay a little of the rope, 8 centimetres (3 inches) should be sufficient for an 8-millimetre (0·3-inch) rope, and pass each strand over the next strand and tuck it, working anti-clockwise. When that has been done the ends of all the strands will be lying down alongside the rope. Pull them taut and tuck each strand twice over and under the strands of the rope, just as the second and third tucks of a splice are made. Roll the splice under foot and cut the ends of the strands off close.

Wire rope

Wire rope is used extensively in the rigging of yachts because it is stronger than fibre rope, so that a smaller size can be used with a saving of windage; it does not stretch appreciably, and it is not prone to damage by chafe. It may be made of stainless steel or galvanized steel and varies in flexibility according to its construction. The strongest but least flexible form of wire rigging is a solid rod, but unless the fittings at its ends have several degrees of freedom in all directions, metal fatigue is likely to occur, and it is easily bent or kinked which weakens it. It is rarely used in cruising yachts except sometimes for the bobstays of bowsprits and boomkins.

In the manufacture of ordinary wire rope a number of solid-drawn wires are twisted together to form strands, and six strands are laid up right-handed round a centre heart, which may be a similar steel strand or a core of oil-impregnated hemp or non-absorbent plastic. The individual strands may also have hearts of either steel or fibre. The thicker the individual wires are, and therefore the fewer, the stronger and stiffer will be the rope, and if it is of galvanized steel, the longer will its life be because thicker wires can have a thicker coat of protective zinc. But the smaller the wires are, and therefore the greater their number, the more flexible will the rope be, and flexibility is increased if the hearts of the strands and of the rope are of fibre instead of wire.

Increased flexibility brings with it reduced strength and increased stretch. In Britain wire ropes are measured by their diameter in millimetres, and their construction is described by figures thus: $7 \times 7, 6 \times 19, 6 \times 24$. The first figure refers to the number of strands and the second figure to the number of wires in each strand; 7×7 rope therefore has seven strands (six laid up round a centre strand) and seven wires in each strand; it contains no fibre. A 6×19 rope has six strands laid up round a fibre heart, and nineteen wires in each strand; the strands contain no fibre. A 6×24 rope consists of six strands round a fibre heart, each strand containing twenty-four wires round a fibre heart; this is the most flexible of the three constructions mentioned, and the weakest. The purist might say that 1×19 rope is not a rope at all, for it consists of only one strand made up of nineteen thick wires; but as this is (apart from rod) the strongest and smoothest of all types used for standing rigging and has the least stretch, it is the most popular; but it cannot be spliced, and must be used with special fittings (page 100).

If first cost is not a matter of great importance I would recommend the use of stainless steel for the standing rigging because it requires no protection unless it is in contact with another metal. It is subject to a form of brown discoloration which, however, can be rubbed off; but after a number of years in use it may deteriorate, the first sign of this being the snapping of an individual wire, the ends of which stick out to snag sails or hands. This may not happen for ten years or more, but when it does happen no further reliance should be placed on that rope. Galvanized steel rope is only about one third the cost of stainless, but if it is neglected its life may be no more than a third of that of stainless. However, it can be given a long life if, while new, the lower 1·5 to 2 metres (5 or 6 feet), which are much exposed to spray, are parcelled with insulating tape, served and varnished, and all remaining exposed parts are dressed once or twice a year with boiled linseed oil. In that manner I made the standing rigging of one yacht last for eleven years and 70,000 miles of cruising. Stainless wire should, however, be used for any stay to which a sail is hanked, for hanks quickly rub off zinc or any other protective coating.

Flexible wire rope is more easily handled than the stiffer and stronger kind used for standing rigging, but both kinds need treating with care to avoid kinks, which permanently weaken them. Only pre-formed wire rope should be used; in this the wires of the strands and the strands themselves are set to the linear shape they will assume in the finished rope before being laid up; they are therefore not under tension and do not so readily unlay themselves as do those of non-pre-formed rope, and are much easier to handle while being spliced. The best way of taking wire from a coil is to use the outer end and roll the coil along the deck, or let it rotate while suspended on an oar or boathook. It may be cut with a cold-chisel or hacksaw, a whipping first being put on each side of the point where the cut is to be made.

Wire rope in some small sizes can be had sheathed in plastic, and this is commonly used in the luffs of headsails and for guard-rails.

The following table gives the construction and breaking strain of a variety of wire ropes.

The breaking strain of wire rope in tons

					Diameter in millimetres						
	Con-st'n	3	4	5	6	7	8	10	12	14	16
For standing rigging											
Stainless steel	Rod	1·2	1·9	2·7							
,,	1 × 19	0·9	1·5	2·1	3·6	4·6	5·6				
,,	7 × 7	0·8	1·1	1·65	2·7	3·4	4·05				
Galvanized steel	1 × 19	0·85	1·45	2·25	3·4	4·45					
,,	7 × 7	0·7	1·0	1·5	2·7	3·3	3·4	5·1	7·4	10·1	13·4
For running rigging											
Stainless steel	7 × 19	0·85	1·1	1·7	2·95	3·5	4·2				
Galvanized steel	6 × 19	0·6	0·9	1·3	2·3	2·9	3·1	4·7	6·7	9·1	12·4
,,	6 × 24		0·8	1·1	1·9	2·4	2·7	4·4	6·1	8·7	11·2

Seizing wire, which is made of seven galvanized or stainless wires laid up left-handed as a single strand, can be had in various sizes. It is used for making wire seizings and servings just as twine is used for fibre ropes. In its galvanized form this wire has no spring and shows no tendency to unlay.

Making eyes in wire rope

Since terminal fittings swaged to wire ropes (page 100) are now so widely used in the rigging of yachts, it is unlikely that the owner will need to make eye splices in wire rope except in the event of some part of the rigging failing; but even then, as the making of a splice takes a considerable time and some skill, he might do better to make do with bulldog grips (Fig 12), of which a stock of suitable sizes should be carried on board. A bulldog grip is a U-shape clamp with a sliding bar grooved on its inside to fit the lay of the rope, and is held in position on the U with nuts. As the U tends to crush the wire the grip should be put on with the U part round the short end, not round the standing part of the rope; the grips should be the correct size to fit the rope, and three of them be used for each eye. An eye can also be made by seizing the end to the standing part with a racking seizing of wire after the parts have been parcelled and served to prevent slip. This method was used for the lower eyes in the shrouds of large square-riggers, there being four seizings for each eye.

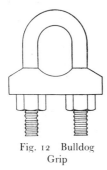

The modern development of this arrangement is to use not seizings but compressed ferrules (Talurit or Nicropress Plate 12*E*). After the eye has been formed round a thimble the end of the rope is laid back alongside the standing part, the ferrule is slipped on to embrace both parts and is squeezed by an hydraulic press so as to grip the rope. To reduce the risk of galvanic action, ferrules of copper are used with stainless steel wire and alloy with galvanized wire, and with 1 × 19 rope it is safest to use two ferrules for each eye. Of course the operation can only be performed by a yard or rigger with the necessary press.

Fig. 12   Bulldog
Grip

There are several ways of making eye splices in wire rope, and the simplest, known as the Admiralty splice, is described briefly here (Plate 12). Put a whipping of twine or adhesive tape on the rope at the point to which it is to be unlaid, then separate the strands, binding the end of each with tape, or giving it a sharp twist with a pair of pliers, to stop it unlaying, and then cut out the centre strand or core. Form an eye of the desired size, and seize a thimble in it if the eye is to be a hard eye. Then proceed much as when splicing fibre rope, ie tuck each strand under one strand of the standing part. If the rope is of stiff 7 × 7 construction an unsightly lump will be produced at the base of strand No 4, but this can be avoided in the following manner. After tucking No 4 miss No 5 and tuck No 6 under two strands; then return to No 5 and tuck it between the two strands under which No 6 passed. This refinement is not essential. Having finished the first complete set of tucks, hammer gently to get them to bed down comfortably, then continue tucking each strand under one and over one until three full tucks have been completed. A splice weakens a rope at the point where the final tuck is made, but tapering the splice in much the same way as a fibre rope splice is tapered lessens this effect, and a well-made splice in wire rope should give 85–90 per cent of the full strength. Finally parcel and serve. Incidentally, the Admiralty splice is much shorter than, for example, the Liverpool splice, in which each strand is twisted round and round one of the strands of the standing part.

A *strop* is a ring made of fibre or wire and is sometimes used for the slinging of a block or other gear from mast or spar. It may be made by short-splicing together the ends of a piece of fibre or wire rope, but if the increased circumference of the splice is a disadvantage, a salvagee strop can be used. This is made by driving two nails the right distance apart into a board and putting turns of twine or seizing wire round and round them until the strop is sufficiently thick. The turns are then marled, ie a round turn and half-hitch is taken at frequent intervals with a length of twine to hold the strands together while the strop is removed from the board and is parcelled and served.

Joining wire to fibre rope (Fig. 13)

As a wire rope cannot be belayed on a cleat or pin, a fibre rope tail must be attached to the end of it when it is to be used as a halyard or sheet, unless it leads direct to a closed drum winch. If the join between wire and fibre does not have to pass through a block, the wire may have an eye spliced in its end, and the fibre rope can be spliced to that.

Wire rope may, however, be spliced direct to fibre rope in such a manner that the circumference of the splice is not materially increased and will be able to pass through a block or round a winch drum. Unlay the wire rope for a distance equal to thirty times its circumference, having first put a whipping on it at that point. Cut out the fibre heart and the heart of every strand, no matter whether it is of fibre or wire, so as to reduce the size of the strands; then take three alternate strands, lay them up right-handed to form a three-strand rope for half of their length and put a whipping on at that point. Unlay the fibre rope for a few centimetres and clutch it and the three unlaid strands of the wire rope together, lay up a few centimetres of the fibre rope and put a whipping on it. Then introduce the three-strand wire rope into the centre of the fibre rope as far as its whipping by working it in with the lay; bring its strands out one between each pair of fibre strands and tuck them against the lay of the fibre rope over and under one until they have been used up, and put a whipping round their last tuck, where their ends should be buried in the rope. (This stage of the splice is shown in the upper part of Fig 13.) Tuck in the same way the other three strands of the wire rope for a half of their length, cut off, bury the ends, and whip. Finally, taper the strands of the fibre rope and serve them down firmly round the standing part of the wire rope. (The completed splice is shown in the lower part of Fig 13.)

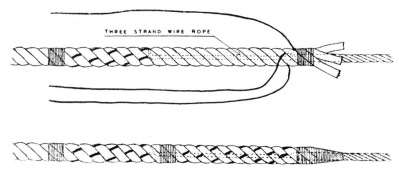

THREE STRAND WIRE ROPE

Fig 13   Wire to fibre rope splice

Terminals for wire rope

It was stated earlier in this chapter that a 1 × 19 wire rope cannot be spliced and that terminal fittings must be used with it; some of these can also be used with any other kind of wire rope; they may cost more than splices, and are stronger when new, but some may lose their strength over a period of time. There are three types: swaged, swageless (for want of a better term), and zinc-socketed.

The swaged terminal is the most widely used. It consists of a sleeve to fit the wire closely, and its end may be an eye, a fork, a threaded stud (to fit direct into a rigging screw), or some other connection. The sleeve is squeezed onto the wire under enormous pressure in a big, rotary-hammer machine, and thereafter cannot be removed. There are standard dimensions for before and after swaging, and if these are exactly followed by the operator, and his machine is in good order, the fitting will have the full strength of the rope. In time such fittings sometimes develop hair-cracks which weaken them, and it is thought that these may be due to exposure to saltwater. I therefore protect the lower swages of my rigging with insulating tape covered with a varnished serving; but some people regard this as wrong because, they say, stainless steel should never have the air excluded from it. However, the protected swages in my present yacht are still in good condition after eleven years of use.

The swageless terminal is an excellent but more expensive alternative; it can be fitted in a few minutes ashore or afloat, and no tools except a couple of spanners are needed. Just as with the swaged terminal it can be had with an eye, a fork, or a stud end, and provided it is properly assembled it has a strength in excess of the rope to which it is attached. The terminal consists of four parts – sleeve, olive, end-fitting, and locknut. The rope is pushed through the sleeve and its strands opened out to embrace the olive, which is a narrow, cone-shaped fitting. (For a 1 × 19 rope the olive is bored to take the core through its centre.) The strands are then brought together again and the rope is inserted into the end-fitting; sleeve and end-fitting are screwed tightly together to clamp the rope, and the locknut is hardened up. A swageless terminal made by Norseman Ropes is shown in Plate 12E.

The zinc socket terminal has a cone-shaped socket made in one with an eye or fork, and its narrow end fits the rope closely. Having been threaded, the rope's end is splayed out in the socket, which is then filled with molten zinc. Flexible wire rope cannot be held securely in this manner, and even with standing rigging wire there have been failures possibly because of galvanic action between the filler and the wire, overheating of the wire, or because solder was used instead of zinc.

Belaying ropes

To belay or turn up a rope is to make it fast to a cleat, belaying pin, etc, in such a manner that it can be cast off (let go) under any conditions. A round turn should first be taken (this also gives control when letting the rope go), then a sufficient number of figure-of-eight turns to prevent the rope from slipping back, and finally one or two more round turns as shown in Plate 13A.

No matter whether cleats are made of wood, metal, or plastic, all corners and edges should be well rounded and there should be no sharp angles in which a rope might jam. There are several types of cleat on the market, and they include some of the jamming kind, which will hold a rope without the need to take a turn, so that it can be quickly belayed or cast off; but my experience of jamming cleats is that they damage the rope, for they concentrate their pinching action on one small part of it. The wood cleat designed by E G Martin is far superior to the common cleat (Fig 14) and its long base allows two additional fastenings to be used.

Where possible a cleat should be through bolted or riveted and so arranged that its centre line is at 15° to the direct pull of the rope.

Many of the cleats and pins in yachts are too small to allow a sufficient number of turns to be taken round them; then to ensure that the rope will not slip, one should make a back hitch with it over one end of the cleat or pin, as in Plate 13*B*. This used to be frowned upon by old hands because if done with a natural fibre rope, which would shrink when wet, it could set up so tightly as to be impossible to undo; but that will not happen with synthetic rope.

Halyards are sometimes belayed on pins in a pinrail or fiferail fastened to the deck near the mast, and some yachts have been damaged in strong winds by the upward pull of the halyards lifting the deck. Such pinrails should be bolted to tie-rods below deck to brace them either to the keel or the mast, but it is much better, and this is current practice, to belay the halyards on winches and cleats on the mast. Pinrails arranged outboard through the covering boards of a wood yacht should be side-bolted to the frames.

A samson post to which a rope has to be belayed may have a pin through it (Plate 30*F*) so that the usual figure-of-eight turns can be taken, but if it is to be used for the anchor cable or a large size rope it is best without a pin, the chain or rope being made fast in the following manner. Take two turns round the post, then form a bight and pass this under the standing part, drop it over the post and pull tight. But any vessel needs a strong bollard, cleat, or samson post not only forward, but on each quarter, and at least one each side amidships, for use when securing alongside; indeed, she could scarcely have too many of them.

68 kilograms (150 pounds) is about the maximum pull that a man can exert provided he has a firm foothold and the rope is large enough to afford a good grip; but he can, of course, exert a downward pull equal to his own weight. A more powerful pull can be got by swigging. This consists of taking a turn with the rope round a pin or cleat, and, while holding the end with one hand to prevent it slipping, grasp the standing part well above the pin and pull it out at right angles; then ease it back to its original position, keeping a downward pull on it, and at the same time haul the slack gained round the pin. With one man swigging and another taking up the slack, a rope may be set up very tightly.

The coil of rope left over beneath a cleat or pin ought not to be left lying on deck where it may get tangled or washed overboard; it may be hung on the cleat or pushed in between the standing part and the mast (Plate 13C); a neat and effective way of hanging it up is to pass your hand through the coil, grasp the rope where it leaves the cleat, form a small loop by twisting it once, pull it through and drop it over the top of the cleat (Plate 13 D, E, and F).

Care is needed when veering out a rope which is under strain, and this should be done handsomely, ie gradually and carefully. A sufficient number of turns should be kept on the cleat or pin so that the rope is fully under control, otherwise it will be pulled through one's hands, and burn or skin them.

Blocks, tackles, and winches

A block (the landlubber knows it as a pulley) is a mechanical device for changing the direction of the lead of a rope with the minimum of friction; it consists of a shell containing one or more sheaves which are free to revolve on a pin, each having a score on its circumference to hold the rope. A metal hook, eye, becket, swivel, or other fitting is attached to one or both ends of the block so that it may be secured to some object. Until about 1950 the shells of most yacht blocks were made of ash usually with internal strops of iron to strengthen them, and the metal sheaves were often patent, ie fitted with roller races to reduce friction. For wire running rigging the blocks were usually entirely of steel. Since then improvements have been made in the design and manufacture of blocks, and today most of them, whether for use with fibre or wire rope, have their shells and sheaves made of laminated plastic, which has great strength and is impervious to corrosion. Their strops, fastenings, and fittings are of stainless steel or manganese bronze. Such blocks need no lubrication or other maintenance and are light in weight. However, their cost is high, and it should be remembered that although such fittings may be considered necessary in an ocean racer, many a cruiser has got along very well with plain ash, rope-stropped blocks costing less than a quarter of the price.

When choosing a block the most important consideration is the size of sheave. This must be of sufficient width to accommodate the rope comfortably, and the greater its diameter the more easily will the rope render round it and the less will be the wear and tear. A sheave to accommodate wire rope needs to be of greater diameter than one for fibre rope of the same size, about six times the circumference of the rope.

Of the several fittings available for blocks, the oval eye and shackle has the widest use, and as this allows up to 150° of twisting movement, it may often be used where the weaker and more expensive swivel eye had been thought essential.

Where a temporary change of lead for a rope is needed a snatch-block is a convenience. This has a piece of the shell and strop cut away at one side so that the rope can be dropped into the block without having to pass its end through. The gap is usually closed with a hasp and pin to prevent the rope jumping out.

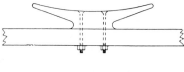

Fig 14   Common cleat (*upper*) and
E G Martin's improved cleat (*lower*)

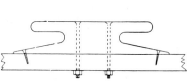

A fiddle block has two sheaves, but instead of being mounted side by side they are placed in the same plane, each having a separate pin; the block is therefore kept thin, and so that the ropes shall lead clear of each other one sheave is greater in diameter than the other. A sister block is similar, but both sheaves are of

---

PLATE 11 (*facing*). *A.* Making an eye splice. First (middle) strand tucked. *B.* Second strand tucked. *C.* Third strand tucked. *D.* All strands have been tucked three times (four tucks are safer with synthetic rope) and the splice is now ready for tapering. *E.* The tapered and rolled splice. *F.* The first step in the making of a long splice; the ropes are clutched together. *G.* A strand has been unlaid from the right-hand rope and a strand from the left-hand rope has been laid into its place. *H.* A strand has been unlaid from the left-hand rope and a strand from the right-hand rope has been laid into its place. The splice is now ready to be finished by knotting each pair of strands together. *I.* A pair of strands joined with an overhand knot.

PLATE 12 (*overleaf*). *A.* Making an eye splice with wire rope; the first strand being tucked alongside the spike against the lay of the standing part. *B.* Strands 1 and 2 have been tucked and hove taut. *C.* All six strands have been tucked once, but strand 6 has been passed under two strands of the standing part to avoid the lump that it would make if tucked under one strand only. *D.* An eye splice completed, tapered, and hammered. This has been made round a heart-shaped thimble, and the seizings holding the rope to the thimble have not yet been removed. *E.* A Norseman Ropes swageless terminal fitting with fork end, and below it a similar terminal with eye end fitted to a 1 × 19 rope. *F.* A Talurit splice, and above it the collar, flatter and shorter, before compression.

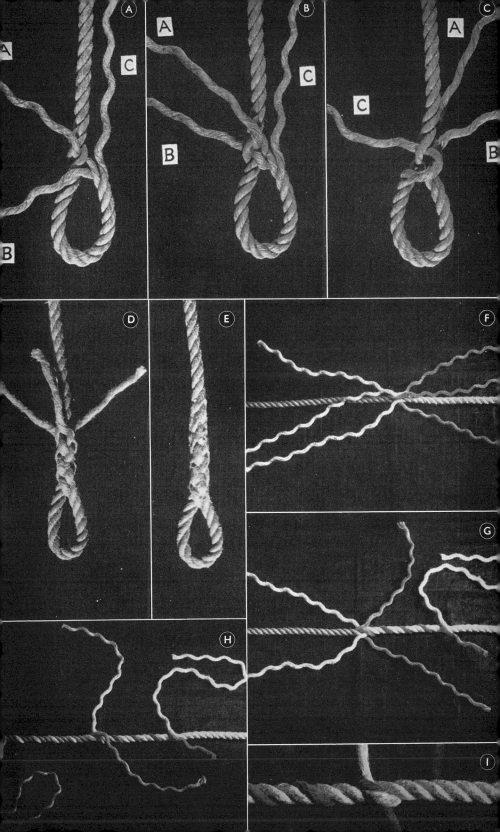

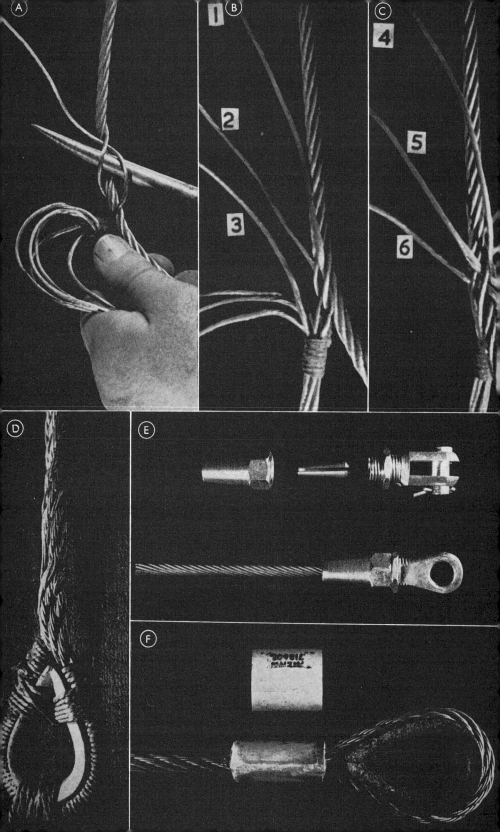

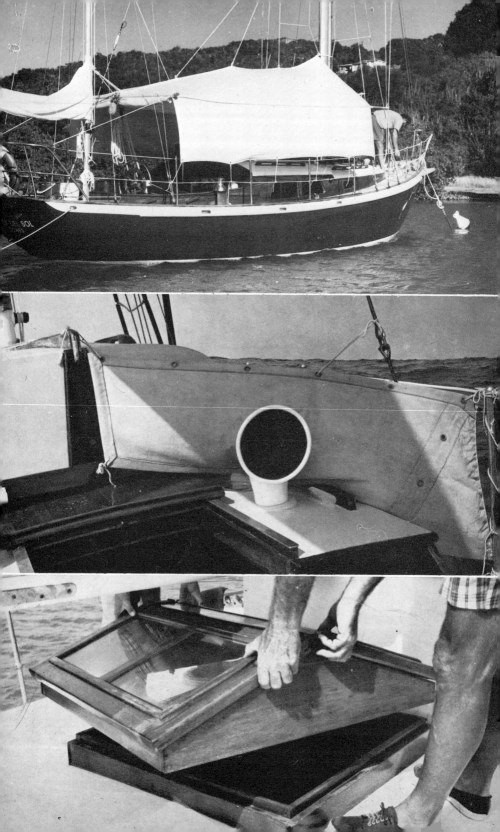

the same diameter. Neither of these types of block is much used today.

A purchase or tackle (pronounced tay-kle) is used to multiply power at the expense of time, and consists of two blocks, one fixed and the other movable; the power gained is equal to the number of parts of rope leading from the movable block, less the loss caused by friction; so, to obtain the maximum power from a tackle, the block with the most parts of rope should be attached to the weight which is to be moved. The fixed block does not increase the power; it merely changes the lead. Friction varies according to the size of the sheave and the flexibility of the rope; it may be taken as one-tenth of the load for every sheave the rope passes over. When one tackle is applied to the hauling part of another tackle the total power, less friction, is the power of the one multiplied by the power of the other.

Fig 15 shows diagrammatically the tackles most likely to concern the yachtsman. When a weight has to be lifted, eg hoisting a sail, the upper block will be fixed so as to give a downward lead for the rope which is to be hauled on, and one of the proportions of the power of that tackle will therefore be lost. A single whip, for example, gives no extra power when used in that way. But when a single whip is used for sheeting a sail, setting up a runner, or hauling on a rope, the block becomes movable and a theoretical advantage of 1 to 2 is gained. In order to show this each tackle in Fig 15 has been drawn right way up first and then inverted, and the power required to lift the weight of one unit has been given as a fraction of that unit. Friction has not been considered.

The purposes for which these tackles are used will be discussed in subsequent chapters, but it should be mentioned here that an

---

PLATE 13 (*overleaf*). A. Belaying a rope on a cleat. B. Belaying a rope on a cleat and finishing off with a back hitch. C. The fall of the halyard coiled up and pushed in between the standing part and the mast. D. An alternative way of hanging up the fall of a halyard. Pass your hand through the coil, grasp the rope where it leaves the cleat, and form a small loop by twisting it once. E. Then pull the loop through the coil and drop it over the top of the cleat. F. The coil hung up.

PLATE 14 (*facing*). Top: Provided with flaps that can be raised or lowered at its sides and after end, this awning gives excellent protection from the sun, but would be of little use for collecting rainwater. *Middle:* A weathercloth rigged to shelter the cockpit when the wind is forward of the beam and the yacht has no cockpit hood; here it is secured to the stern of the upturned dinghy and to the weather runner. *Bottom:* This skylight can be lifted from its coamings and placed with its hinges fore-and-aft or athwartships so as to extract or blow as desired with the wind from any direction.

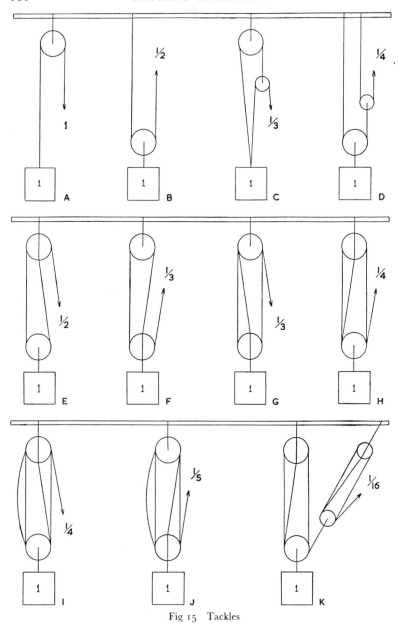

Fig 15   Tackles

A whip; *B* inverted whip; *C* Spanish burton; *D* inverted whip upon whip; *E* gun tackle; *F* inverted gun tackle; *G* luff tackle; *H* inverted luff tackle or handy billy; *I* double purchase; *J* inverted double purchase; *K* luff upon luff. The power required to lift one unit, friction excluded, is expressed as a fraction of that unit.

inverted whip upon whip gives the same theoretical advantage as an inverted luff tackle, 1 to 4; but as the whip upon whip has only two sheaves against the luff tackle's three, less power is wasted in friction and it is therefore more efficient.

A handy billy is an inverted luff tackle, the 2-sheave movable block having a short rope tail which can be fastened with a rolling hitch to any rope on which extra power may be needed temporarily, and the fixed single-sheave block may also have a tail, or perhaps a loop or a hook for securing it to some fixed object.

Winches have, to a large extent, taken the place of tackles, with a consequent simplification of rigging and reduction in weight and windage aloft. In its simplest form a winch consists of a drum or barrel turned on a spindle by a handle, and the longer the handle is in relation to the diameter of the drum the greater is the mechanical advantage gained. As many turns as are necessary to prevent the rope from slipping are taken round the drum, which is then rotated by the handle; the drum is held from running back when the strain is taken off the handle by pawls, often spring-loaded, which fall in between the teeth which are formed at one end of the drum. This is the kind of winch generally used aboard yachts for hauling in the sheets and setting up the halyards, and some, known as self-tailing, automatically keep tension on the drum and cleating of the rope is not then necessary.

More powerful winches, of which there are several kinds, have the power transmitted from the handle to the drum through a train of gearwheels. Although this kind is sometimes used for hoisting sails, it is more commonly employed for handling head-sail sheets, and for weighing anchor; in the latter capacity it is known as a windlass, and is fitted with a gipsy wheel having shaped recesses to grip the chain cable; (in the USA this is known as a wildcat); it may or may not also have a drum for handling rope; some gipsys are able to handle both chain and fibre rope.

A capstan, which offers an alternative means of weighing anchor, has a vertical drum, and in its old form was worked by handspikes thrust into holes round its head, the crew walking round and round; but later the handspikes were replaced by crank-handles which drove the drum through worm or bevel gearing. Much of the power applied to such capstans is wasted in overcoming friction.

Some further remarks on winches and windlasses will be found in Chapters 8 and 9.

6

MASTS AND STANDING RIGGING

Wood and metal masts – Mast steps – Standing rigging for bermudian masts –
The staying of two-masted rigs – Standing rigging for gaff masts – Mast
bands, tangs, and chainplates – Size of standing rigging – Setting up the
rigging – Setting up the runners – Lightning protection

For many years it was believed that for a yacht to give her best performance there should be a little slack in her standing rigging so that the mast might bend athwartships, and that to set the rigging up taut 'took the life out of her' especially when sailing close-hauled. Today that belief has almost died, though some people still hold firmly to it. In this as in other things we should respect the opinions of experienced sailors, remembering that sailing vessels do indeed have their individual likes and dislikes which cannot always be accounted for. However, the majority is now agreed that a bermudian mast should be kept as straight as possible so as to act as a strut. The performance of racing craft has shown the need for this, and if the cruising man wants sailing efficiency he will follow racing practice as far as is compatible with convenience, safety, and cost.

Although the dismasting of an inshore racing yacht will cause inconvenience and expense, the fact that she is generally racing in more or less sheltered water and in company with others will mitigate any more serious consequences. But the loss of her mast by a cruising yacht out of sight of other vessels might be disastrous. Even the carrying away of her rudder is not so serious, for a jury rudder of some kind could probably be improvised; but to rig a jury mast capable of carrying sufficient sail to enable her to keep off a lee shore or to complete an ocean crossing before the stores of food and water are exhausted, might well prove to be impossible, though it is truly remarkable what pluck and determination can achieve. Voss rigged a jury mast in *Sea Queen* after she had been rolled over and dismasted in a typhoon near Japan, but an even more remarkable feat was performed aboard the 14-metre (46-foot) ketch *Tzu Hang*, which Miles and Beryl Smeeton and John Guzzwell were attempting to sail from Melbourne to the Falkland Islands by way of Cape Horn in 1957. In latitude 52°S, longitude

98°W, about 1,150 miles west by north of the Horn, after fifty days at sea and while running before a great gale, the yacht capsized and lost both her masts and suffered other extensive damage, including the loss of skylights, hatches, and rudder. After the water had been baled out, two hollow masts were built from woodwork taken from the saloon, they were stepped, a jury rudder was made and shipped, and *Tzu Hang* was then sailed 1,350 miles to Coronel in Chile, her best day's run being 77 miles. On her second attempt to round the Horn she was again capsized and dismasted, and once again she returned to Chile under jury rig; but her third attempt, this time by the more difficult route from east to west, was successful, and she sailed from 50°S to 50°S in the remarkably fast time of fourteen days.

Clearly the masts of voyaging yachts, and the standing rigging which supports them, should be strong and sound beyond any possibility of doubt, and while following closely the efficient design and arrangement of the racing yacht, should not be reduced, as her's so often are, to the minimum size in order to cut down weight and windage.[1]

Wood and metal masts

With very few exceptions solid masts of wood are not used in yachts now chiefly because of their weight. The idea of using hollow spars is not new; bamboos have been in use in the Far East from the earliest times, and in this country attempts were being made in the 1860s to lighten spars by boring longitudinal holes through them; but soon afterwards that was abandoned in favour of cutting them in half lengthways, hollowing out the two pieces, and binding them together again with iron bands, or, at a later date, glueing the halves together. Today hollow wood spars are built up in a variety of shapes and constructions from selected pieces of timber, usually spruce, varying in number from two to eight at any one section and held together entirely by glue. In some of the earlier ones the glue failed, and with this in mind I have always painted glued-up masts white to keep them cooler and provide better protection than is offered by varnish; one of these masts was still in perfect condition after twenty-seven years of voyaging including much time spent in the tropics; it was re-painted every second year or so after rubbing down, but was never burnt off. Apart from the appearance, which some may

[1] The names given to the standing and running rigging of a yacht will be found inside the cover at the end of the book.

prefer, the only advantage of varnishing a mast is that the glue lines may be seen and any decay might therefore be noticed. The wood mast has the advantage that the positions of fittings can be altered or new ones attached with little difficulty.

Fig 16 shows sections of four typical hollow wood masts. The round mast, shown at *A*, offers the least total disturbance to the flow of wind on the luff of the close-hauled sail, but an oval mast, as shown at *B*, is more rigid fore-and-aft, and is the more widely used, particularly with masthead rig. The rectangular mast, at *C*,

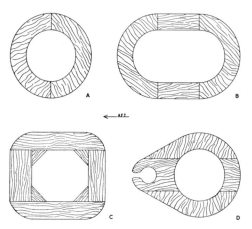

Fig 16 Sections of hollow wooden masts

A round; *B* oval; *C* rectangular with extra thickness at aft side; *D* streamlined with groove for luff rope of sail.

is easier and therefore cheaper to build, it wastes less wood, and is said to be the strongest section of all. A streamlined, or pear-shaped, mast is shown at *D*, and this offers the least disturbance to the wind reaching the *windward* side of the sail set on it; in theory such a mast should be free to pivot and line itself up with the sail, and in some small craft it is so arranged, but this is believed to have little advantage. Here the mast is shown with a groove for the luff rope of the sail instead of a track, but although often used in sailing dinghies this has some serious disadvantages aboard a cruiser.

In the late 1940s hollow masts made of aluminium alloy started coming into use, and their popularity has increased ever since. Fig 17 shows some examples of sections of alloy mast extrusions. Such masts can be, and often are, tapered in the upper part by cutting out narrow wedges and welding the remaining parts together, but a mast intended for masthead rig should retain its full section throughout even though it may look clumsy. The advantages of an alloy mast are that it can be stronger than a hollow wood mast for

a given weight, and is less easily compressed, or it can be lighter
for an equal strength. Also it needs little maintenance because it
will have been anodized by its maker; this is an electro-chemical
process which produces a hard corrosion resistant oxide film (it
can be coloured) integral with the surface of the aluminium.
However, care must be taken to insulate all fittings, particularly

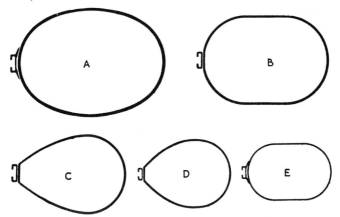

Fig 17   Sections of alloy masts
(Approximately to same scale)

	For yachts up to	1 wl	walls
A	45 ft (13·7 m)	10½ × 7½ in (26·7 × 19 cm)	4·5 mm (0·17 in)
B	35 ft (10·7 m)	9½ × 6 in (22·8 × 15 cm)	4·1 mm (0·16 in)
C	30 ft (9 m)	7¾ × 5½ in (19·6 × 14 cm)	4·1 mm (0·16 in)
D	26 ft (8 m)	6¼ × 4¾ in (16 × 12·06 cm)	3.2 mm (0·12 in)
E	22 ft (6·70 m)	6 × 3½ in (15 × 9 cm)	2·6 mm (0·10 in)

Because of its great fore-and-aft dimension the section
shown at *E* is particularly suitable for masthead rig.

winches made of bronze, or damage to the spar will be caused by
galvanic action. If the mast wall is thick enough, fittings can best
be attached by machine screws of stainless steel in tapped holes,
otherwise by self-tapping screws or aluminium pop-rivets; a large
number of small fastenings is preferable to a small number of large
ones. A metal mast should be lined with a layer of foam plastic on
its inside surface during construction so as to reduce the noise of
tapping halyards, but see page 166.

Mast steps

A mast may have its heel (lower end) stepped low down in the
yacht, or on the deck or coachroof, but with either arrangement

consideration must be given to the very great downward thrust caused by the modern rig in which the standing and running rigging is set up with considerable tension and large headsails are used. A mast on a step low down and wedged where it passes through deck or coachroof is stronger than a similar mast stepped on deck, and its only drawbacks are that it needs to be a little longer, is more difficult to step or unstep, and its presence below may interfere with the accommodation, particularly in a small craft. In a wood yacht the step for it needs to be strong and long so as to distribute the load over as many floors as possible, otherwise leaks may occur at the garboard strakes. In the GRP yacht the step should be of metal or GRP construction incorporating wide webs, and be solidly glassed to the hull. If the mast is stepped on the coachroof that area will call for special strengthening, and except perhaps in a very small yacht should be supported from immediately beneath by a pillar; but then little would be gained by having the mast so stepped. With both arrangements the step will have a section to match the mast heel so that the mast cannot be stepped with a twist in it, and ideally the under side of the heel should be radiused slightly fore-and-aft so that the mast may take up any angle of rake without placing its entire load on one end of its heel; but this might rule out the old tradition of placing a coin (preferably one of gold) under the heel. In the event of the yacht being knocked down or shipping a sea on the beam, the mast stepped on the coachroof will impose a great athwartships strain on that erection, and in some instances this has resulted in the splitting of the coamings. Strengthening beams should therefore be incorporated, but not just under the coachroof only, for they should continue down the coamings, out under the side decks and well down the topsides. It is common to provide the mast where it passes through the partners (the strengthening pad on deck or coachroof) with a set of well-fitting wedges to hold it firmly, but some people contend that wood wedges caulked and payed are too rigid and set up undesirable stresses, and that wedges of rubber are preferable. If the wedges leak they can be covered with a canvas collar, but this should not be tacked to a wood mast because the holes made by the tacks will injure the wood; it should be fastened with a lashing round the mast, its lower edge being held by a wood or metal ring screwed to the deck. The leathering of an oar can be taken as a simple example of the harm that can be done to a spar by breaking the outer fibres; some people, having fastened on the leather, trim off the ends with a sharp knife, which makes a tiny cut in the wood, and in almost every instance where such oars break they do so at one or other of these cuts.

The rake of a mast is its cant out of the perpendicular so that the masthead is forward or aft of the heel; rake should not be confused with a bent mast such as is seen in a few racing classes. In the majority of rigs the mast is raked aft, so that the centre of gravity of the mast and the theoretical centre of effort of the sail plan is brought further aft and has some effect on the amount of helm the yacht carries; it also enables the after staying of the mast to be more efficient, and it certainly looks right.

Yachts intended for sailing on inland waterways, such as the Norfolk Broads, where they will have to pass beneath bridges, have their masts stepped in tabernacles. A tabernacle consists of two stout members rising from either the top of the keel or the deck; the heel of the mast fits between them and is free to pivot on a pin which passes through them, so that by slackening up the forestay, which is fitted with a tackle, the mast can be lowered. When in the erect position the after side of the heel of the mast presses against a stop which is usually a cross member binding the uprights of the tabernacle to one another; this prevents the mast from falling forward. The raising or lowering of a tall or heavy mast is not something to be undertaken lightly, and should not be attempted except in quiet water and with little wind, for the mast will be unsupported athwartships throughout the operation because the shrouds will be slack except when the mast is in the vertical position, and a severe twisting strain might be placed on the tabernacle. With the mast in or near the horizontal position the strain on the tackle controlling it from forward will be considerable, and if the mast is to be handled often, it will be best to provide a pair of temporary sheerlegs pivoted one at each side of the deck abeam of the mast tabernacle, and secure the forestay and the tackle to their apex. With the mast in the horizontal position the sheerlegs will be vertical, and they will gradually come down to the horizontal position as the mast is raised (Fig 18). Incidentally, this is probably the only way in which a jury mast of useful height could be stepped aboard a dismasted yacht at sea, but I would be sorry to have to attempt it.

Standing rigging for bermudian masts

Standing rigging comprises the fixed stays and shrouds which hold a mast up straight; running rigging comprises the flexible cordage, blocks, etc, used for the setting, trimming, and general handling of the sails.

The theory of standing rigging is simple. Wherever a mast would show signs of bending under the pull or thrust of the sails, there a shroud or stay should be attached to hold it straight. (Fore-and-aft supports are known as stays, athwartships supports as shrouds.) The greater the angle made by the support and the mast the more efficient will that support be and the less will be the compression on the mast. Let us consider for a moment only the

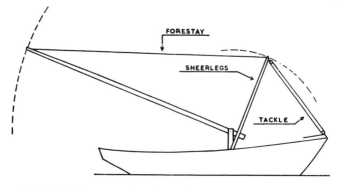

Fig 18   Raising a mast in a tabernacle with the help of sheerlegs

athwartships pressure, and from one side only, ie the windward side. If we have a craft with a beam of 3 metres (10 feet) and a mast measuring only 6 metres (20 feet) from deck to head, a single shroud from the edge of the deck to the masthead will make an angle with the mast of 14°, which is large enough to be reasonably efficient (Fig 19A). But if we double the height of the mast, the angle the shroud makes with the mast will be reduced to 7° (Fig 19B), so that the shroud is less efficient and we should need to set it up tighter, which would increase the compression on the mast and the strain on the hull. That can, however, be overcome by fixing a crosstree or spreader half-way up the mast and passing the shroud over the end of it; then if the crosstree has a length equal to half the beam, the angle the shroud makes with the mast will be increased again to 14° (Fig 19C). But the shroud will tend to press the end of the crosstree downwards, as shown by the vertical arrow, and to counteract that pressure the crosstree should be cocked up a little at its outer end so as to bisect the angle made by the shroud passing over it (Fig 19D); it thus becomes a strut. The longitudinal pressure placed on the crosstree by the shroud will tend to bend the mast at that point, as shown by the horizontal arrow, so a second shroud will have to be fitted there to hold the mast straight.

If we now increase the height of the mast by another 6 metres (20 feet) we shall have to fit a second crosstree at the 12-metre (40-foot) point and lead a third shroud over it to the masthead.

Fig 19   Development of shrouds

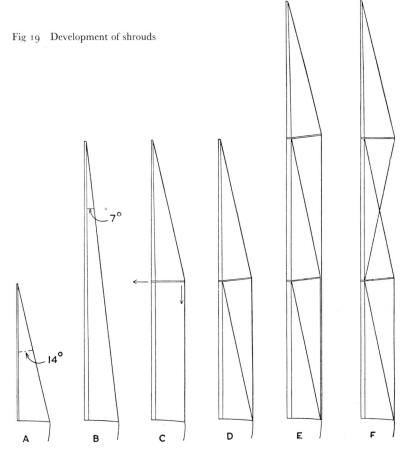

This topmast (masthead) shroud may come down to the edge of the deck alongside the lower and intermediate shrouds (Fig 19*E* and Plate 15*B*), or it may be secured to the mast at the root of the lower crosstree (Fig 19*F* and Plate 15*D*), when it is known as a diamond shroud. The first arrangement is best for a cruising yacht because the shroud may be adjusted when necessary without anyone having to go aloft, but as it employs a greater length of wire there will be a little more stretch and windage, and it will increase the compression on the lower part of the mast. There is a third method, known as linked rigging, in which the topmast shroud and intermediate shroud are joined together at the lower crosstree end, from which point a single wire rope of greater strength leads to the deck (Plate 15C). But then, as with the diamond shroud arrangement, it is necessary to have a rigging screw aloft. In the above description the lee rigging, which is of course identical in every way, has been disregarded because it is always a little slack when sailing and therefore gives no support to the mast; also it is unlikely in practice that the crosstrees will be evenly spaced as shown in the figure, for the position of the upper ones may depend upon the point of attachment of a headsail or some other factor.

To give the best possible spread to the shroud passing over it, the crosstree should be as long as possible, though it should not exceed, and ought to be a little less than half the vessel's beam, or it might get damaged when lying alongside another vessel or a high quay. Provision should be made for holding the shroud in the slot at the crosstree end, or it might drop out when on the lee side. This may be done with a small bolt or pin, or a wire seizing through holes near the extremity of the crosstree, and as a spinnaker or a large headsail may at times foul the end of a crosstree, and when running the mainsail will press on it, some form of protection should be provided to prevent damage to the sail. Sometimes this is a rounded guard of strip metal, or a parcelling of canvas, leather, or baggywrinkle, or a rubber ball or disc of wood might be threaded on the shroud so as to lie on top of the crosstree, though this could only be done at the time the rigging was made up.

The fore-and-aft supports (stays) for the masthead sloop will be simple: (Fig 20A) a forestay (sometimes known as the jibstay, headstay, or topmast stay), leading from masthead to stemhead, will support it forward, and a backstay will support it aft. From about its centre, where the (usually) single pair of crosstrees is positioned, the lower shrouds, of which there are two each side, will have their lower ends spread forward and aft a little along the vessel's side to give some fore-and-aft support to the middle of the mast. But when the rig is one with two working headsails (such as the cutter Fig 20B), the inner headsail (the staysail) will be set hanked to a stay lower down the mast. Although it is not always

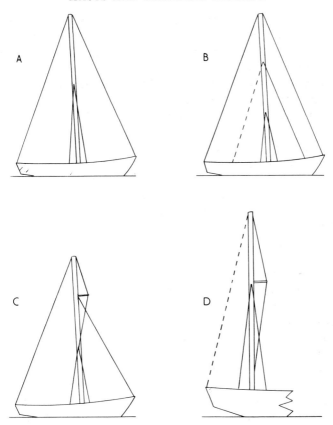

Fig 20   Staying of masts

done, I am sure that the mast at the point to which the staysail sets
calls for a pair of shrouds to take the athwartships strain, and a
pair of runners to take the forward pull of the sail, otherwise the
mast will bow and the luff of the sail will sag to leeward. The rig
will probably call also for a second pair of crosstrees. So in any rig
where two headsails are set, we must be prepared to put up with
the inconvenience of runners. Since these are movable, some
people include them with the running rigging, but as they support
the mast I regard them as part of the standing rigging. Ideally
they should be led so far aft that the angle they make with the mast
is equal to the angle the luff of the staysail makes with the mast;
the farther forward they are the harder will they be to set up
properly.

Usually the backstay is a single wire rope set up between masthead and stern, or to a boomkin projecting from the stern if needed to carry the stay clear of the end of the boom; ample clearance must be provided, for during a gybe all-standing the boom end will lift and get closer to the backstay as it slams across. Sometimes two backstays are provided, one to each quarter; this provides slightly better mast support, but should be avoided with ketch or yawl rig as it complicates the setting of a mizzen staysail. With these two-masted rigs the single backstay usually terminates before nearing the mizzen mast, and is there provided with two legs to pass one each side of the lower part of the mizzen mast; the backstay thus enables the main boom to be longer than it might otherwise be. Screw or hydraulic adjusters, by means of which the tension on the backstay can be increased when sailing to windward, though common in racing yachts, are out of place in a cruiser.

A jumper stay, passing over its own spreader (which is usually called a jumper strut) is sometimes used for the fore-and-aft stiffening of some part of a mast. For example, the forward pull of the headsail of a 'three-quarter' sloop (one in which the headsail sets not to the top of the mast but to a position lower down) could be taken by fitting a jumper strut there, and leading a jumper stay from the masthead over the strut and down to a point half way up the mast, thus triangulating the upper part of the mast (Fig 20*C*); in this situation a pair of jumper stays passing over jumper struts each at an angle of 45° to the fore-and-aft line is commonly used (Plate 15*A*). Such an arrangement, though it may dispense with runners, does not do the job so well, and in my view is an undesirable complication in this instance.

The staying of two-masted rigs

The masts of a ketch or yawl should be stayed independently, yet it is quite common for the main and mizzen mastheads to be linked with a triatic stay, the intention being that the mainmast will support the mizzen. With no sail set from its forward side the mizzen mast will not call for a backstay, but runners from the masthead will be required on the occasions when a mizzen staysail is set, though some people use the mizzen topping lift for the purpose. However, the mizzen mast will need staying forward, otherwise when the mizzen is hard-sheeted the mast will be pulled aft. Unless the main boom is very short there will be no possibility of fitting a mizzen stay at a sufficiently advantageous angle, and to overcome this problem the rigging may be arranged as follows (Fig 20D), and this concerns the tall mizzen mast of a ketch more than the short mizzen mast of a yawl, which will probably be stiff enough to require no forward staying. The mast has a pair of crosstrees at about its middle point to spread the topmast shrouds; from that point a pair of lower shrouds each side lead down and are spread fore and aft at their lower ends in the usual manner to provide some fore-and-aft support, the forward positions of the forward shrouds being limited only by the swing of the main boom. A jumper strut pointing forward is fitted at the root of the crosstrees, and a jumper stay from the masthead is taken over it and brought down to a position on the mast close to the deck. A common mistake made by some designers is to place the jumper strut half way between masthead and crosstrees, and to terminate the jumper stay at the root of the crosstrees; then, although the lower half of the mast is supported fore-and-aft by the spread-out lower shrouds, and the upper half is triangulated by jumper strut and stay, there is nothing to prevent the mast bending or even breaking in way of the crosstrees.

The mastheads of a schooner are joined one to the other by a triatic stay, and if the foresail is gaff-rigged a second stay, known as the mainstay, may be provided to join the head of the foremast to the point on the mainmast to which the runners are secured. Therefore the efficiency of the rig to windward, and perhaps its very safety, will depend on the weather runner, for unless the main boom is shortened so much as to be absurd, a permanent backstay cannot be fitted.

Standing rigging for gaff masts

The principles involved when arranging the standing rigging for gaff rig are similar to those for bermudian rig, but because the jaws of the gaff must be free to slide, no rigging can be attached to the mast below the point reached by the jaws when the sail is fully set. The lower shrouds, usually two a side, are attached to the mast close above the upper position of the gaff jaws, and in the usual manner their lower ends are set up to the vessel's sides a little forward and aft of the mast to provide some fore-and-aft support. If the mast is short a third shroud each side will support the masthead adequately without the need for crosstrees, but if a gaff topsail is to be set, the mast will be taller and crosstrees will almost certainly be needed to give the topmast shrouds sufficient spread. When the distance between crosstrees and masthead is considerable, a fourth shroud each side, known as a cap shroud, may be fitted half way between the root of the crosstrees and the masthead. This shroud will be spread part way out along the crosstree, where it will pass over a thumb cleat or through a slot.

It is unlikely that the jib will be set to the masthead because of the impossibility of rigging a permanent backstay, and instead will be in way of (near or in the neighbourhood of) the peak halyard blocks; if its forward pull overcomes the pull of the peak halyard when close-hauled a pair of runners will be needed at that point; but in a large vessel they may be needed more urgently to counteract the forward thrust of the gaff jaws, and so keep the luff of the staysail straight. If a light-weather headsail is to be set from the masthead, a pair of temporary backstays set up by tackles may be needed.

Mast bands, tangs, and chain plates

There are three methods of attaching the upper ends of the standing rigging to a wood mast. They may have soft eyes spliced in them to be dropped over the masthead to rest on hounds (wooden chocks) or thumb cleats screwed and glued to the mast. This is the usual arrangement for the lower shrouds of gaff-rigged yachts; it saves some expense as no special metal-work need be made and the use of shackles aloft is avoided; but the eyes are liable to damage the mast unless it is protected by a metal collar. The traditional order of placing the shrouds on the mast when soft eyes are used is the forward starboard one underneath, then the forward port one followed by the aft starboard and finally aft port.

But soft eyes cannot conveniently be used with bermudian rig, except at the masthead, because the mainsail track has to pass over them. If they are used the track is usually on a wooden batten which is cut away for each soft eye so that the track will run straight, and of course a section of the track will have to be removed each time the mast is dressed or undressed, which is bad practice because it will encourage the screws to work loose. In some older bermudian- and in many gaff-rigged yachts metal bands in two halves bolted together and having eyes for the attachment of the rigging are used. But unless these have a large bearing surface they tend to crush the outer fibres of the mast, and pull down under load, and unless the rigging is spliced direct to the eyes, which means that it cannot be removed when laying up, shackles have to be used. A shackle is frequently the weakest link, and modern practice is to avoid its use entirely in the standing rigging by using tangs and clevis pins (see below). If, however, a shackle has to be used it should be the narrow **D**-type, not the weaker bow type (Plate 10*G*); it should be of a size larger than the wire with which it is to be used, and its pin should be screwed right home or it may break at the thread long before the breaking load of the shackle itself is reached. To ensure that the pin cannot work loose, it is common practice to secure its eye to the main part of the shackle with seizing wire. Shackles may be had in stainless or galvanized steel, the former being the stronger, and the size of a shackle is given as the diameter of the metal used in the **D** or bow, the pin sometimes being of a greater diameter than this.

The best way of securing rigging to the mast, and this is the method now used with all metal masts and some wood masts, is by means of double tangs and clevis pins. A double tang consists of two strips or plates of steel welded face to face for a portion of their length, the plates being spaced from one another at the end which is to accept the item of rigging, and these are drilled to take a pin. The hard eye or terminal fitting of the rigging wire is thrust into the space and held by a clevis pin, ie a large-diameter pin kept in position by a small head at one end and a split pin at the other. The tangs may be through-bolted to a wood mast or welded or riveted to a metal mast, and are often made in one piece with plates bearing sockets for the attachment of crosstrees or other items of gear. Tangs at the masthead are usually incorporated in a cap to fit over the top of the mast, and the aftermost tang may project a short distance and be supported from below to form a crane, so that the backstay secured to it may clear the headboard and leech of the sail when tacking or gybing.

The chainplates (or shroudplates) to which the lower ends of the standing rigging are attached must of course be well secured to strong or specially strengthened parts of the hull, bolted or riveted in wood or GRP yachts and welded in metal yachts; but a point sometimes overlooked is that the longitudinal axis of a chainplate should continue the line of the item of rigging which is attached to it so as to avoid bending or breaking strains, and that the hole in its upper end should, like the hole in a double tang, exactly fit the pin of the toggle or rigging screw to which it is attached; if the hole is too large only a small part of the circumference of the pin will be in contact with it, and the pin will be weakened.

Additional spread may be given to the shrouds of a narrow

vessel or one with a very tall rig by means of channels. These are wood or metal ledges built out from the topsides at deck level to keep the eyes of the chainplates away from the sides, the lower parts of the plates being fastened to the hull in the usual way. They are awkward when lying alongside and are rarely seen today.

Size of standing rigging

Clearly the size of wire rope and fittings used for the standing rigging will depend not only on the size of yacht but on her type and rig, a stiff one requiring stronger rigging than a tender one, and a yacht with only three shrouds a side needing stronger wire than one with four or five. The matter would be difficult enough to decide if one had only to consider the strains imposed on the rigging by the sails in smooth water, but it is probable that in a seaway strains exceeding the yacht's displacement can be imposed momentarily on the rigging. It is generally considered that the combined breaking strain of all the shrouds on one side should be one-third greater than the yacht's displacement, but a designer of experience is needed to judge how that load should be divided. However, the safety of the mast is of such vital importance when cruising, that one will probably decide on a greater margin of safety, for the few extra pounds aloft will be a small price to pay for one's peace of mind.

Setting up the rigging

Obviously some powerful form of adjustment must be provided at the lower ends of shrouds and stays so that they may be set up to the desired tension. In days now past this was done with deadeyes and lanyards. A deadeye (a thick disk of hardwood, often lignum vitae, with three holes in it) was spliced in at the lower end of the shroud and a matching deadeye was secured to the chainplate. A lanyard of greased rope, with a Mathew Walker stopper knot at its end, was rove through the six holes to form a purchase; it was hove taut by one of the halyards and secured at the neck of the splice with a cow hitch and seizing. The method had the merit of simplicity and low cost, but it was a long operation. Today rigging screws (sometimes known as turnbuckles or bottle screws) are used. A rigging screw (Plate 17D and E) comprises an open or closed body with a right-handed internal thread at one end and a left-handed thread at the other; screw bolts having eye, fork, or stud ends screw into the body, and when the body is turned (it may have a hexagon for a spanner or a hole for a spike) the ends are drawn together or thrust apart. Under strain the body will have a tendency to unscrew itself, and this must be prevented by a locking device. With the closed body type of screw this will be a locknut on each bolt, and as these may work loose they should be checked frequently. With the open body type the ends of the bolts are sometimes squared to take square washers which are held in place by small split pins; this is a positive and safe device. If no arrangement for locking is provided, the bolts should be secured to the body or to one another with seizing wire. Rigging screws are made of stainless steel, bronze, or galvanized mild steel; there is no galvanic action between stainless steel and bronze, but if the wire rope is of galvanized steel only galvanized steel rigging screws should be used with it.

When making a choice between stainless steel or bronze rigging screws the following point may be of interest. I have experienced stainless steel screws becoming immovable and useless while being set up under load. I was told that this was because the swarf, the burr left after cutting the threads, had not been removed; but the more likely cause was the galling between threads, almost a welding, which can occur when stainless steel surfaces are brought together and moved under high load. This never happened to the bronze screws with which I replaced the defective stainless steel screws, but admittedly they were made of a special bronze called Superstron which Lewmar Marine Ltd use for this purpose. Another reason for my preference for bronze is that it is not subject to metal fatigue to the same degree as stainless steel. A rigging screw must, of course, be as strong as the wire rope it is to set up. To be absolutely safe in this respect the diameter of the threaded bolts (this is the dimension used when stating the size of a rigging screw) should be twice the diameter of the wire rope, and of course the pins in forks, eyes, and tangs should all be of that same diameter. As the rigging screws aboard a cruising yacht are nearly always at deck level where their weight and windage will have no appreciable effect on her performance, one can afford to have them of large size to provide a good safety margin. However, the failure of a tested rigging screw machined from the solid by a reputable maker will almost certainly be due not to a fault but to fatigue; this may be caused, as mentioned above, by the holes in chainplate and/or terminal fitting being larger than the pins engaging with them, or to the rigging screw being too rigidly connected to the chainplate or other fitting, so that it is unable to give to lateral strains, notably those imposed by slack rigging.

There should be at least 5° of freedom laterally at the fork or eye, and more than that if a sail is to be hanked to the stay which the rigging screw sets up; the only way of obtaining that freedom without having oversize holes and a consequent weakening of pins, is to insert a toggle, which gives the effect of a universal joint, between rigging screw and chainplate. Although toggles are available for use with all high-quality rigging screws, they are often sold as an option at extra cost.

The threads of galvanized steel rigging screws need some form of protection if rusting is to be prevented. For many years I used anhydrous lanoline for the purpose, and I parcelled with insulating tape the exposed parts of the bolt threads, covered this with a west country whipping of marline, and varnished; after long periods of sailing I found on removing the covering that the threads were as clean and bright as the day they were cut. Anhydrous lanoline is also an excellent protection for shackle pins and bolts of all descriptions, but it is not a lubricant.

A wire rope may be shortened slightly by twisting its end in the direction of the lay, a fact that may sometimes be found of use in small craft if, for example, the forestay is shackled direct to the stemhead fitting without a rigging screw; but a wire rope should never be lengthened by untwisting it as that would reduce its strength.

Only by experiment can one discover the correct tension to be put on shrouds and stays when setting up the rigging. The aim should be to keep the mast as straight as possible, both fore-and-aft and athwartships, on all points of sailing, and this can best be judged by looking up the track with one's eye close to its bottom end. The tension needed will vary according to the length, size, and construction of the wire rope, the area of sail, and the spread of the rigging, and, because long wire ropes stretch more than short ones, the topmast rigging will require to be set up harder than the lower rigging, and the shrouds which lead to the point of attachment of a headsail hardest of all. The individuals of a pair of shrouds should be set up equally, and this can sometimes be judged by the note given when the wire is struck. Only a trial sail can show whether the work has been done correctly, and one ought not to be able to see any slackness in the lee rigging of a bermuda-rigged yacht, though it should feel a little slack when the yacht is close-hauled and heeled 10° or more. Many trials and adjustments will probably be needed to get everything just right in a new yacht or one with a new rig.

Setting up the runners

Rigging screws cannot, of course, be used for setting up the runners as those ropes have to be let go and set up quickly when tacking or gybing, yet it is essential that they be set up properly if the headsails are to stand with straight luffs.

A tackle, such as a Spanish burton, may be used, but it is not easy to get a runner set up sufficiently tight by such means as some strength and skill is needed, though this will depend to some extent on the drift of the runner, ie the distance abaft the mast of the point at which it leaves the deck; the greater the drift the easier will it be to get the runner taut, with the exception mentioned below.

An arrangement sometimes used in small craft is to have two eyebolts fastened through covering board and shelf and connected to one another with a wire span; the lower end of the runner has a span shackle (Plate 10*G*) sliding on the wire and can be hauled aft by a rope tail belayed within reach of the helmsman, or a tackle or winch may be used if additional power is needed. The act of hauling the runner aft along the span gives a mechanical advantage, though the greater the drift the less will this be, and the span can be marked by a whipping at the point to which the runner must be hauled to set it up properly. As the runner puts a powerful swigging strain on the span, the whole affair must be strong. Sometimes a length of track is used instead of a wire span, the lower end of the runner then having a slide to fit the track.

The simplest, most efficient, and now almost universal method of setting up a runner is by means of a lever on deck which is locked by passing a little way over its own dead centre. The original lever, the Highfield, can let go only a short length of the runner, an amount equal to twice the distance between the point of attachment on the lever and the pivot of the lever; but even so it is possible to arrange for the lee runner to be given sufficient slack to permit the boom to be squared right off. Plate 18*A* shows the arrangement. The runner, the lower part of which must be of flexible wire, leads down through the fairlead block in the foreground, then aft to a snatch block on deck, then forward to the lever. When sailing close-hauled sufficient slack is provided by lifting the lever and pivoting it through 180°. To obtain more slack for reaching or running, the bight of the wire is lifted out of the snatch block, when the runner will be free to go forward to the rigging, where it may be secured by a hook on a length of shock cord, though if it is to remain there for any length of time it will be best lashed securely to prevent it swinging and chafing the sail. However, there are other types of lever, such as the Lewmar shown in Plate 18B and C, which when released give more slack than the Highfield lever. Instead of the pin or bolt holding the runner to the lever being fixed, it is free to slide on or within the lever to the stop near the handle end. When the runner is set up the pin is near the pivot end of the lever, but when the lever is released the pin slides towards the other end, thus giving more slack.

When a large single headsail is to be set in a yacht which has a forestay and a topmast-stay, arrangements are sometimes made for releasing the lower stay so as to make the handling of the sail easier when tacking. This can be done by ending the stay a short distance above deck and connecting it by means of a hook or Senhouse slip to a short length of flexible wire which passes through a block on deck to a Highfield lever. To cast off the forestay one has only to release the lever and unhook the stay from the short wire.

Lightning protection

Anyone who is at sea near one of the great thunderstorms which are common in many parts of the world – when one flash of lightning rapidly follows another, when there is no noticeable pause between the flash and the peal of thunder, and the mast is the only upstanding thing in all that part of the ocean – may feel apprehensive. However, he should gain some comfort by remembering that since lightning will take the shortest electrical path to earth, his yacht's mast will not attract a lightning discharge unless it is almost immediately beneath the area of the cloud in which the maximum potential is being built up; in other words the chance of being struck is small.

A lightning conductor fitted to a mast is intended to conduct the electric charge harmlessly to earth by providing a straight path of low resistance from truck to sea. Ideally there should be at the masthead a sharp copper spike projecting at least 20 centimetres (8 inches) above any masthead fittings. If the mast is of wood the spike should be earthed by a stranded copper wire of large cross-section, taking the most direct route to a copper plate not less than 0·093 square metre (1 square foot) in area below the waterline, and all mast fittings should be earthed to this wire. An alloy mast is of itself a sufficient conductor, but again it must be properly earthed. A conductor is said to provide a safety cone of 60° at its apex, and if the second mast of a ketch or schooner projects beyond that cone it must be provided with its own lightning conductor.

Some people, however, contend that this is the wrong approach, for, they say, the function of the earthed spike is not to conduct lightning but to emit a stream of charged particles under the conditions of a strong electrical field, such as exists in a thunderstorm, and that this will neutralize the air around it, making a lightning strike less likely by diverting it elsewhere. In this instance earthing may be achieved by way of a stay or shroud, for high voltages are not involved, but the termination of the stay or shroud at the deck must be continued to the sea by, for example, a chainplate, a chain anchor cable, or a temporary length of trailing wire. This will not be required with a metal hull, but is particularly important with one of GRP, for that material has high insulating properties.

Unfortunately, and in spite of such precautions, the occasional yacht is struck by lightning; but the damage is usually minor and may be confined to electric and electronic equipment; so far as is possible such equipment should be disconnected in a thunderstorm, and the aerial of a radio set unplugged. Probably the risk of a strike will be reduced once the rain has started, but this may be late in coming and often marks the end of the storm. St Elmo's fire, a blurred ball, or balls, of greenish light which may rest on the truck or other parts of the mast or rigging, is harmless, and usually indicates that the worst of the storm is over.

7

WORKING SAILS

*Sailcloth – Sailmaking – Lacings, tracks, and slides – The care and repair of
sails – Preventing chafe*

PROBABLY everyone realizes that the sailing qualities of a yacht
depend largely on the shape of her sails, and that the art of
sailmaking has now become a science. It is of course not difficult to
stitch together a number of cloths so that they lie flat, but a sail
must have a belly, or draught, in the right place so that it may
assume the desired curve when filled with wind. This is obtained
by varying the amount of overlap at the seams, and providing
curved edges at luff and foot; also the manner in which the
boltropes (the ropes that take the strain along the edges of a sail)
are attached to the cloth has some bearing on the set of the finished
sail. Although practically every sail made today has machine-
sewn seams, skilled handwork is needed for the making of grommets, and the sewing on of boltropes, headboards, etc, and good
sails therefore cannot be cheap. Every care should be taken of
them, not only on account of the initial cost, but because their
efficiency will depend to some extent on the manner in which they
are subsequently treated.

Sailcloth

The material from which sails are made is woven in cloths of
different weights. The threads which run the long way of the cloth
are known as the warp, or ends, and those which run across it are
called the weft, or picks; there is more stretch in the warp than
there is in the weft. As cotton cloth comes off the loom it has at
each side a smooth, non-fraying edge known as a selvedge; but in
terylene the selvedge tends to be wavy and useless, and if so is
removed by the sailmaker before the cloth is used.

Up to the late 1950s the sailcloth most widely used in yachts
was woven from cotton, but the place of that material has now
been almost entirely taken by terylene (known as dacron in the
USA) and for some light-weather sails by nylon. A cotton sail
needed careful stretching when new; as it absorbed water its
weight increased when wet, and the shrinking that then took place

had to be attended to by slacking off halyard and outhaul if the shape of the sail was not to be permanently spoilt; also cotton sails were subject to rot. A terylene sail suffers from none of these drawbacks, and has the additional merit of being smoother, thus offering less friction to the wind blowing over it, and of being less permeable, thus the pressure difference between the windward and leeward sides is increased with a probable increase in efficiency. These properties, however, vary according to the finishing process, which includes heat relaxing to knit the fabric together. Terylene has little elasticity, it does not stretch appreciably under load, and as it is very much stronger than cotton one might well think that a much lighter cloth could be used for a sail of the same area; but this is not so where small sails are concerned because in strong winds lightweight terylene tends to vibrate and will not hold its shape; on average it can be about 10 per cent lighter than cotton for a given sail. It is however, bad practice to have a sail made of unnecessarily heavy cloth, for it will not so readily assume the all-important curve or free itself of wrinkles in a light wind; and as the motion of a yacht throws the sails about, the heavier they are the more easily will the wind be knocked out of them by their inertia in light weather. Many small cruisers have been handicapped by sails which were much too heavy, but with the advent of terylene this mistake has become less common.

The disadvantages of terylene are few. Prolonged exposure to sunlight causes it to harden and lose some of its strength, when a sail needle thrust through it will break the fibres, instead of parting them, and will leave a ragged hole; for continuous use in the tropics I would regard a working life of three or four years as normal. It is not easy to sew terylene, though this is being overcome by the introduction of machines of improved design; and because it is not so soft as cotton, the stitching of the seams stands proud instead of sinking in, and is therefore more susceptible to chafe. I believe, however, that this matter has been much exaggerated, and that it is not so serious as was at first supposed is, I think, shown by the following facts. When my 9-metre (30-foot) sloop *Wanderer III* made her first 3-year circumnavigation she had a hand-sewn cotton mainsail, and the seams of this needed a little attention from time to time, particularly near the head where they chafed on the topmast shrouds. During her second circumnavigation she had a terylene mainsail. This was machine-sewn in the normal way, but each seam was reinforced with a row of hand-made stitches. This sail required no more attention to the seams than did the cotton sail, but it should be borne in mind that on both voyages all possible precautions were taken to minimize chafe.

When choosing the weight of cloth for a sail, the deciding factor is not so much the size of yacht as the area of that particular sail, the purpose for which it is to be used, and the strength of wind in which it will be set; also the type of yacht and the kind of cruising she is to do may have some bearing on it. The following table of suggested weights of terylene has been provided (like much else in this section) by my friend Michael Handford of the well-known firm of sailmakers, Cranfield Sails, of Burnham-on-Crouch, Essex, which has made sails for me for more than 20 years; but the table is not intended to replace the discussion which every owner ought to have with his own sailmaker before ordering a new sail. The weights given in the table are in ounces per square yard, the measure commonly used by British sailmakers.

SIZE	LOA		LWL		MAIN	MIZZEN KETCH
	Feet	Metres	Feet	Metres		
A	25	7·6	22	6·7	5·5	
B	28	8·5	24	7·3	7·5	
C	33	10·1	26	7·9	8·5	7·5
D	40	12·2	30	9·1	9·25–10	8·5
E	46	14·0	35	10·7	10	9·25
F	50–60	15·2–18·3	35–45	10·7–13·7	11·75	9·25
G	60–65	18·3–19·8	45–55	13·7–16·8	11·75	11·75
H	70	21·3	55–60	16·8–18·3	13	13
I	80–100	24·4–30·5	70–85	21·3–25·9	13–17	13–15

SIZE	LIGHT GENOA	HEAVY GENOA	No 1 JIB	No 2 JIB	TRYSAIL & STORM JIB	MIZZEN STAYS'L	SPINNAKER
A	4	4·6	7	7	8	1·5 N	1 N
B	4	6	7·5	7·5	8	1·5 N	1·2 N
C	4·6	7	8·5	10	10	2 N	1·2 N
D	4·6	7·5	10	10	10	2 N	1·5 N
E	4·6–6	8·5	10	10	10	3	1·5 N
F	4·6–6	8·5	11·75	11·75	13	3–4·6	1·5 N
G	6–7·5	8·5–10	11·75	13	13	4–4·6	2 N
H	7·5	8·5–10	13	15	15	4·6–7·5	2 N
I	7·5	8·5–10	13–17	15–17	17	7·5	2 N

Cloth is terylene except where N for nylon is shown

The above table is of necessity approximate; for instance it does not follow that waterline length and overall length will tally, but both are included as a guide. The US standard yard is a smaller measure than the Imperial square yard as it is only 28·5 inches (71 centimetres instead of 36 inches (91·4 centimetres) wide; so the US weight will be less for a similar sail, eg if 10-ounce cloth is specified in the UK, the equivalent in the USA would be about 8-ounce.

Nylon is stronger than cotton and has many of the advantages of terylene, but it is too elastic to be used for sails which are carried on the wind, and if a nylon sail is used for any length of time in strong winds, it pulls out of shape and becomes baggy at the leech. Nylon is, however, widely used for spinnakers. Both terylene and nylon can be coloured, but the former, especially in the heavier weights, is more difficult to dye, and this has resulted in a poor range of colours and availability with cloth heavier than about 8 ounces per square yard. The process involves applying both temperature and pressure in an autoclave. A reasonable rating of fastness has been obtained, which appears to stand up satisfactorily to the small amount of sunshine experienced in British waters, but fading (particularly of red and brown) is usual in the tropics. I have no proof, but I suspect that coloured sailcloth has a shorter life than white sailcloth, for the colour holds more heat, though it may repel ultraviolet light. However, dark coloured sails are easier on the eyes than white sails and, contrary to common belief, are more readily seen from another vessel.

Sailmaking

The bermudian mainsail (Fig 21) has in racing yachts a high aspect ratio, ie a short foot and long luff, the luff being sometimes as much as three times the length of the foot, for most races are won by ability to windward, and a long leading edge has the advantage on that point of sailing. But in a cruising yacht a very tall mast is not desirable, and if she is rigged as a bermudian sloop or cutter, she will have a mainsail of such a length on the foot that the boom will clear the back-stay when gybing or tacking. Manifestly the height of the mast will then be dictated by the desired size of the sail, the usual ratio of foot to luff being between $1\frac{3}{4}$ and $2\frac{1}{4}$ to 1. In two-masted rigs the aspect ratio of each of the sails will be greater to provide sufficient area. If roller reefing is to be used, the angle the boom makes with the mast should not be less than 85°; but the smaller the angle there the less risk will there be of the end of the boom dipping into the sea when running or reaching in heavy weather.

The gaff sail (Fig 21, *top left*) admits of more variation in its proportions because its head and the angle the gaff makes with the mast can be varied as well as the length of luff and foot. The late Claud Worth gave the ideal proportions in his classic *Yacht Cruising* (Potter) as follows: luff between two-thirds and four-fifths of the length of the foot, and the gaff to be at 90° to a line drawn from throat to clew. In a sail of the above proportions the gaff will make an angle of about 35° with the mast. Although the length of the boom is not limited by a permanent backstay, it should not project much beyond the stern or complications will arise in the lead of the sheet, and reefing might be difficult.

As the shapes of headsails vary from one yacht to another according to the shape of the fore triangle (which depends on the position of the mast) and whether one sail or two together are to be used, little can be said about their proportions here; but it is important that there should be a sufficient distance between the head of the staysail and the luff of the mainsail, so that the mainsail is not back-winded there, for the leech of the staysail will be nearer the yacht's centre line at that point than elsewhere, while the mainsail will be at a broad angle. It is also important that a masthead sail should stop well short of the masthead, and that the heads of jib and staysail be kept well apart. If the luff of a headsail makes an angle with the mast of less than 15°, difficulty will be experienced in keeping it straight.

The cut of a sail is the manner in which the cloths are arranged, and the variety of cuts is limited only by the fact that a sail should have the cloths lying parallel, or at right-angles, to any side which is not supported by a spar or a boltrope. The reason for this is that if a cloth is cut diagonally that edge will have abnormal stretch, but modern cloth is so stable that this, particularly with genoas, can sometimes be ignored. The leech of a mainsail or mizzen is the unsupported side, and in Fig 21 the cloths are laid at right-angles to it; this is known as horizontal cut, and is the most widely used arrangement. The cloths could be laid parallel to the leech (vertical cut), as was often done with gaff sails, but the seams would then reduce efficiency by lying across the flow of the wind. Also, bermudian sails commonly have round, or roach, to the leech, and this might not be wise with vertical cloths. Admittedly, if a horizontal-cut sail does have any roach the cloths will not come to the leech exactly at right-angles, but the amount of curve is so small that this can be disregarded. However, roach is of more interest to racing than cruising people for it is only a means of obtaining extra, unmeasured, sail area for a given height of mast

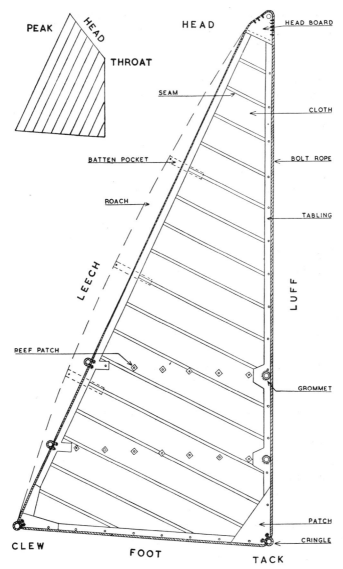

PEAK HEAD HEAD HEAD BOARD

THROAT SEAM CLOTH

BATTEN POCKET BOLT ROPE

ROACH TABLING

LEECH LUFF

REEF PATCH

GROMMET

PATCH
CLEW FOOT TACK CRINGLE

Fig 21   The parts of a mainsail or mizzen
Top-left a vertical-cut gaff sail.

and length of boom. To prevent such a leech from curling or flapping it is essential to fit flexible wood or GRP battens in pockets spaced along it; but these are often a nuisance and some-times a danger, for they can get foul of the rigging, and they make the setting and handing of the sail more difficult. The cruising man would do better to have his sail made with a straight leech, as is shown in the figure, so that battens should not be needed, though in fact they often are to make the leech set well. If battens must be used, the pocket for the lower one should be parallel to the foot of the sail so that the batten does not have to be removed when reefing, and all battens should be thinner at their forward than at their after ends. Pockets of the drop-in type in which the batten does not rely on a lashing to keep it in place, and usually with a piece of elastic at the forward end to keep the batten firmly up against the leech, are widely used, but a couple of stitches across the entry of a normal pocket will serve just as well provided the battens do not often have to be removed.

With the majority of mainsails and mizzens the foot is secured to the boom at intervals along it, or for its full length, but occasionally sails are made loose-footed, ie they are secured to the boom only at tack and clew. The advantages claimed for this are that a lighter boom can be used, for as no bending load is imposed on it, it acts purely as a strut, and that such a sail is more efficient because its foot can assume a natural curve fore-and-aft instead of being held flat; but a loose foot also permits a sail to curve the other way, from head to foot, which is not efficient; also roller reefing gear cannot be used with it.

Working headsails are usually diagonal-cut, ie with cloths at right-angles to the leech and to the foot (the unsupported edges); the seam where they join one another is known as the mitre (Fig 22). Quite a lot of mainsails and mizzens have also been made like that, and owners have spoken highly of them.

Normally the seams where the cloths of a sail are overlapped and joined to one another are made with two rows of machine-sewn zigzag stitches, the zigzag permitting more elasticity than the straight stitch. However, it is common practice to put in a third row of stitches between the other two to guard against the risk of chafe (Plate 20C). It might be thought that three rows of stitches would get chafed just as quickly as two, but that is not always so, for in some sail lofts the normal two rows of stitches are made 'on and off', ie part in the double cloth and part in the single to prevent the edges of the cloths from curling outward; since these stitches cross a heat-cut and sometimes very sharp edge, they are particularly vulnerable. A centre row of stitches, being made entirely in the double cloth, is therefore less easily chafed than 'on and off' seams. Because of the thicker twine that can be used, the third row of stitches might with advantage be made by hand, were it not for the high cost and the unfortunate fact that hand-seaming tends to pucker terylene, and the puckers never flatten out.

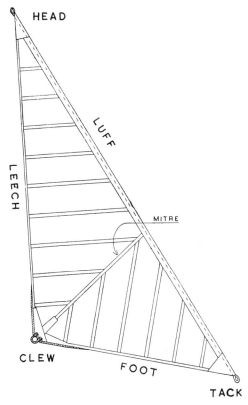

Fig 22   The parts of a diagonal-cut headsail

A wide hem, known as the tabling, is made right round the sail, the corners having additional strengthening, known as patches, and it is to the tabling that the boltropes are sewn, the needle passing between, not through, the strands. A mainsail or mizzen should have terylene boltropes, and I know of no good reason for providing them with luff ropes of wire. But for a headsail to stand with a straight luff it is best fitted with a flexible wire rope as fibre rope has too much elasticity for the purpose, but for light weather 'stretch-luff' genoas luff ropes of terylene are becoming increasingly popular. For a storm staysail or spitfire jib (small, heavy-weather sails) I would certainly prefer terylene boltropes because of the ease with which the sails can then be folded up. After thimbles have been spliced or cramped into its ends, the luff wire is sewn tightly into a pocket formed by the tabling (Plate 20A). Some grades of stainless wire, when sewn into polyester cloth exposed to salt water, may be liable to destruction by a chemical action, and galvanized steel wire quickly rusts at its lower end where spray reaches it; however, plastic-coated galvanized wire appears to have overcome the problem and may well last the life of the sail if the Talurit ferrule forming the eye is cramped on over the plastic coating so that water cannot enter, and the bared bitter end of the wire is turned back under the ferrule.

The taped sail, in which all boltropes of wire or fibre are dispensed with, and their place taken by a tape made of several thicknesses of terylene, appeared with a lot of publicity in the USA in the late 1950s. For a variety of reasons it did not then become popular with British sailmakers or their clients, but it is making a comeback for use with slotted headsail foils in combination with small-section lines to locate the sail in the groove of the foil.

The leech of a sail is normally unsupported, but it will have, running through the tabling, a light line which can be adjusted to correct any tendency to curl or flap. For offshore cruising some people have a boltrope sewn to the leech to guard against the risk of the sail splitting right across; but this would seem unnecessary, and such a rope is likely to make the sail set badly and will cause

---

PLATE 15 (*facing*). A. The upper part of the mast of this three-quarter sloop is stiffened by a pair of jumper struts and stays, the headstay going to the root of the jumper struts. B. Conventional rigging with two pairs of crosstrees with separate topmast, intermediate, and lower shrouds. C. The same arrangement as in B except that to reduce weight and windage the intermediate and topmast shrouds are linked to one another at the lower crosstrees, so there is only a single wire from each lower crosstree to the deck. D. Here the topmast shrouds are rigged as diamonds, which is undesirable for a cruiser as they call for rigging screws aloft.

PLATE 16 (*overleaf*). A. A simple form of roll-damping gear aboard *Widgee*. The spinnaker boom is held out one side by topping lift and guys, and takes a line which is secured to a 3-legged span made fast, B, to a triangular piece of wood weighted at one corner. C. A windsail hoisted on the staysail halyard with its tube passing down through the forehatch. D. A windsail enclosing three sides of the forehatch is more effective, and will probably reverse the normal aft-to-forward circulation of air below deck. This hatch has removable hinge pins, and its top has been removed.

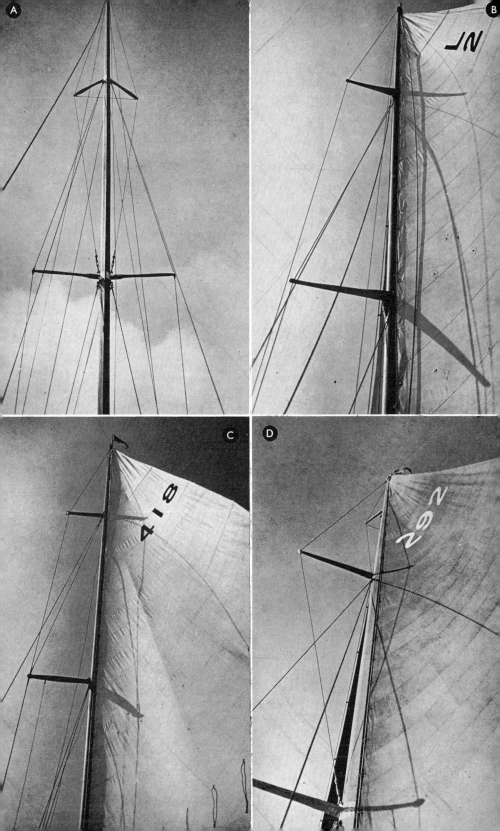

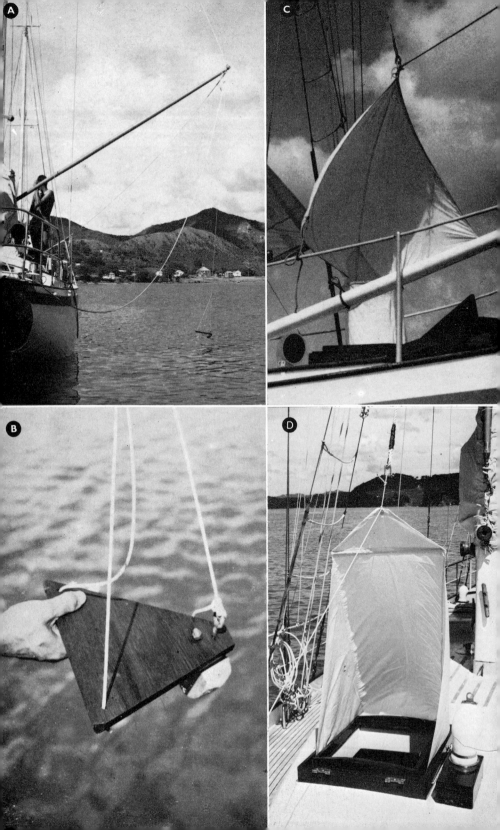

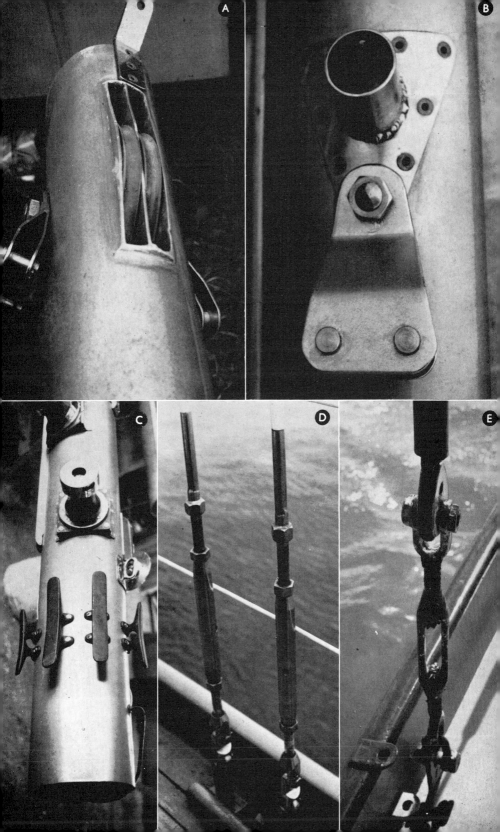

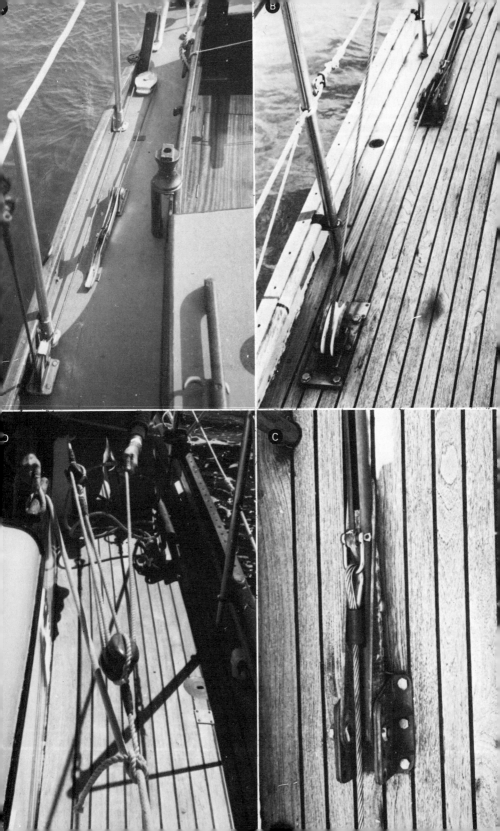

extra eddies at the leech. However, it is wise to have storm sails roped all round. Where a boltrope terminates it is not cut off abruptly but is rat-tailed, ie gradually reduced to a point by unlaying the strands, tapering by scraping with a knife, and laying them up again.

A cringle is a strong rope eye formed outside the boltrope at the corner of a sail, and sometimes on the luff and leech for reefing purposes; it is fitted with a thimble to take the halyard, sheet, reef pendant, or lashing. But as a cringle cannot successfully be made on a terylene sail, grommets are widely used instead; a grommet (Plate 20B) is made by cutting a hole in the sailcloth, fitting it with a sewn-in metal ring, and lining it with a brass eyelet. In recent years sailmakers have adopted hydraulically pressed grommets in which a stainless steel turnover is used to secure two toothed plastic rings, one on each side of the sail, to form an eye; pressure of 30 tons or more is used. The resulting eye is strong and durable but is not amenable to repair at sea. Brass eyelets are fitted where needed in the tabling along the luff and foot of a mainsail, mizzen, schooner's foresail, and along the foot of a boom staysail, to take the slides, lacing, or stops which hold it to mast and boom, also in the head of a gaff sail and along the luffs of headsails which hank to stays. Bermudian sails have headboards of wood or alloy to give them extra spread, to prevent wrinkles, and to distribute the load more fairly.

Lacings, tracks, and slides

The traditional method of securing the luff of a gaff sail to the mast is by means of mast loops seized to eyelets in the sail, but they make additional work when fitting out and they are apt to chafe

---

PLATE 17 (*overleaf*). A. The head of an alloy mast fitted with sheaves for two halyards, and tangs with clevis pins to take the eyes of the standing rigging. B. A crosstree socket and tangs bolted and riveted to an alloy mast. C. The heel of a metal mast, which is to be stepped on deck, with cleats and winches in position. D. Rigging screws fitted with locknuts and with toggles at their lower ends to permit freedom of lateral movement. E. An open body rigging screw which is locked by square washers and split pins, but it should, of course, be provided with a toggle.

PLATE 18 (*facing*). A. A runner led through a snatch block and set up with an old-style Highfield lever; by releasing the lever and lifting the wire out of the snatch block ample slack is provided. B. Alternatively a more expensive type of lever incorporating a slide (close-up at C) may be used. D. Using a handy-billy (a 4-part tackle) instead of a winch to harden in the staysail sheet, on which it is made fast with a rolling hitch (in the foreground).

the mast; also, if roller reefing gear is used, the hoops on the lower part of the sail have to be cast off before a reef can be taken in. It is much better to use a lacing, and the eyelets should then be of such a size as to take 8-millimetre (0·3-inch) rope. When reefing with roller gear it will then only be necessary to unreeve some of the lacing, and if the lacing is correctly rove, not round and round the mast but round and back the same side (Plate 19*B*), it will not jam and will automatically adjust itself evenly. A lacing has the additional advantage of reducing the total number of slides (see below) so that the sail is easier to set or hand when full of wind, and when stowed takes less height on the mast. I have been shipmates with luff lacings in yachts of from 7 to 15 metres (23 to 50 feet LOA) and they all worked perfectly. The only merit of hoops is that they enable one to climb aloft more easily; but ratlines are in every way more convenient when one wishes to go aloft to examine or attend to gear, look for land, or pilot among coral reefs. Ratlines are lengths of rope with an eye spliced in each end seized to each pair of lower shrouds at intervals of about 46 centimetres (18 inches) to form the rungs of a ladder (Plate 19*B*); where three lower shrouds a side are fitted the ratlines are clove-hitched to the middle one. Racking seizings are used to hold the ratlines to the shrouds over short parcellings of insulating tape to prevent them from slipping down. Wooden ratlines are more comfortable to use, but it is difficult to prevent them from chafing the sail when the sheet is eased. Instead of ratlines some yachts have mast-climbing stairs (Plate 19*A*), metal brackets fastened by screws to the sides of a wood mast, or by pop rivets to an alloy mast, each with a strut from its outer edge to the mast. The strut is intended not only for strength but to prevent one's foot from slipping off, and should therefore slope up to form a stirrup. Care will be needed to ensure that halyards and other gear are so led that chafe on the stairs cannot occur.

Neither hoops nor a lacing can be used for the luff of a bermudian sail above the lower shrouds, so slides running on a metal track are used. The two common types of track are shown in Fig 23; in the one the slides fit externally, in the other internally. The first is the lighter and cheaper of the two, but is the more easily damaged, and the internal type is much to be preferred. On a metal mast the track is riveted, or embodied in the extrusion, on a wooden mast it is screwed at 7·5-centimetre (3-inch) intervals, the ideal length of screw being 6·3 centimetres (2·5 inches) for silver spruce; but many hollow masts have not walls of such a thickness.

The screws should be checked occasionally and their holes re-plugged if necessary, for if a screw works loose it will prevent movement of the slides and make it impossible to set or lower the sail. A reinforced track, which has an extension each side to take the screws or rivets, avoids this trouble, but because of its extra weight and cost its use is confined to certain positions where extra strains are imposed, eg sliding goosenecks. The slide attachments must be free to swing athwartships, otherwise the sideways pull of

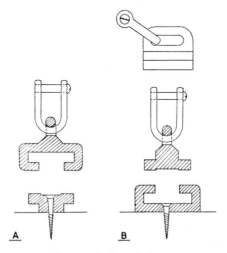

Fig 23   Tracks and slides
A external slide; *B* internal slide.

the sail when it is full of wind will cause the slides to bind on the track, making setting and handing the sail difficult. Long D shackles, with pins countersunk and slotted for a screwdriver, serve well provided the boltrope is protected by a piece of leather or plastic at each shackle. However, nearly all slides are now made of plastic – the black ones appear to have a longer life than the white ones, but both suffer from fatigue in the tropics – and shackles eat into and weaken them. The excellent method of attachment used by Cranfield and some other sailmakers is to be preferred. A length of terylene tape, perhaps 40·6 centimetres (16 inches) is sewn to the slide and is passed through the eyelet and the slide several times until all of it has been used up. The tape is then sewn to itself with figure-of-eight stitches between slide and boltrope, a hole for the needle first being punched with a bradawl through the several layers of tape; if the tape is not too tight it will permit athwartships movement of the sail on the slide. I have never known one of these tape fastenings to chafe or let go. It is often said that plastic slides need no lubrication, but they do benefit from it, and a few drops of light oil applied occasionally help them to run easily and sweetly; track and slides need cleaning with a little paraffin on a rag now and then.

A stop will be needed at the lower end of the track to prevent the slides from dropping out when the sail is lowered; a simple turn-button serves well and allows the sail to be taken off the track (unbent) when necessary. But it is common to have, in addition and just above the point where the upper slide will be when the sail is lowered, a gate in the track (Plate 23C); this allows one to drop the slides into the lower part of the track when bending on the sail, instead of having to push each one up and hold it until the next has been inserted. A gate is also an advantage when a trysail has to be hoisted on the same track, for the mainsail slides can be left in the lower part, but see page 379.

The arrangement whereby the track is dispensed with and the boltrope of the sail runs in a groove formed on the after side of the mast, is neat and widely used in very small craft, but it is not suitable for a cruiser because the sail unthreads from the groove as it is lowered and must be re-threaded each time the sail is set, which is no easy matter in a fresh breeze; it also creates much friction. However, such an arrangement is quite satisfactory on the foot, and with jib furling gears.

The care and repair of sails

The advent of terylene has greatly simplified the care of sails. In the days of cotton a new sail needed careful and gradual stretching, and throughout its life the slacking of halyard and outhaul whenever it became wet, if its shape was not to be permanently spoilt; also frequent airing was necessary to prevent rot or the growth of mildew. A terylene sail does not need these attentions, and when bending on a new one for the first time it can, and should, be pulled right out to its made length on luff and foot straight away; but it will probably need some adjustment thereafter. It can be stowed away while wet without much harm, though this is not to be recommended because such treatment will encourage the growth of black mildew spots, which are hard to remove and are particularly noticeable if the sail is not coloured. This, however, is more often caused by stowing a sail in a cotton bag; so terylene bags should be used, each having the name of its sail stencilled on it, and/or each bag being of a different colour. It is as well to bear in mind that a sail which has been exposed to spray will dry on a fine day, but when damp or foggy weather sets in the salt will absorb moisture and the sail will become damp. The cure for this is to hang the sail up in the rain or wash it with freshwater, and this is particularly important when stowing sails away for the winter. Terylene sails can be cleaned, but this should not be done before first consulting one's sailmaker. I think it is best not to fold them but to leave them loose with plenty of newspaper among them if there is any risk of rats or mice getting into the store, for although these rodents prefer cotton to terylene or nylon, they like newspaper best of all when making their nests.

As ultraviolet light has a harmful effect on terylene and nylon, headsails when not in use should be stowed below, and the mainsail (and mizzen, if there is one), should be coated. A gaff mainsail or mizzen can be stowed neatly in the following manner. Place the tiers, under the foot of the sail and over the boom, each in its right place equidistant from its neighbours. Get the sail all to one side of the boom, pick up the middle of the leech, draw it as far forward as it will go and hold it against the boom. Work the bulk of the sail forward, then pick it up fold by fold and, placing each along the boom, hold it there. The last fold to be lifted will be the foot of the sail; this should be pulled tightly over all the previous folds to form an outer skin, which will help to shed rain. Stowed like this the sail will have a neat taper from mast to boom-end. Make fast the bunt tier (the one in the middle); then, starting with the aftermost, tie each one in turn, passing its ends round the sail and over the gaff and haul taut before passing them beneath the boom and reef-knotting them together. A bermudian sail with the full length of its luff on a track cannot be stowed in this way; it will have to be flaked down on top of the boom in a series of folds so that the luff rope makes a succession of S-bends; but if a lacing is used for the lower part of the luff, the foot of the sail can still be used as a skin. It may be as well to remove all battens before stowing a sail for any length of time to avoid getting them bent.

As the purpose of a sail coat is to protect the sail from sun and rain, and to keep it clean, it can be one of the many plastic-coated materials, a close-woven proofed cotton (unproofed cotton will grow mildew rapidly) or an acrylic cloth. As lacing the coat round the mast and beneath the boom is a tedious business, it is best to have eyelets on one edge and hooks on the other, so that the lacing line, which can with advantage be of shock cord, is kept permanently rove through the eyelets and is dropped over the hooks on the other edge. A wet sail should not be coated unless there is dirt in the air, and then should be dried at the earliest opportunity.

Before putting sails away for the winter they should be examined for damage. Any large repairs, such as the fitting of a new luff wire or a large patch, or the resewing of chafed seams, are best entrusted to a sailmaker who will make a far better job of them than the amateur, and if they are given to him in the autumn, not only will the spring rush be avoided, but the work may not cost so much. Do not send tiers or battens to the sail loft, as they may get mislaid.

However, the owner can easily repair small tears or chafed places himself, and the experience gained may be useful one day when at sea or on some distant coast. Hand-sewing sail needles are numbered 8 to 19, according to size, No 8 being the largest, and this was used in the past for sewing boltropes to large cotton sails; but a needle bigger than No 15 is hardly ever used with synthetic materials, partly because terylene twine is so much stronger than natural fibre twine that a smaller size can be used. The needle is thrust through the cloth by means of a leather seaming palm (Plate 9A) which is worn on the sailmaker's hand, and has an iron (a disk with indentations) to press against the eye of the needle. A roping palm is similar but its iron has larger indentations to accommodate the bigger needle, and it has a leather guard projecting a short way over the thumb across which the twine leads when a pull on a stitch is being taken. The amateur is inclinded to use too large a needle; but it is equally wrong to use the smallest needle into which the twine can be crammed, for the triangular part of a small needle may not open a sufficiently large hole in the cloth, which may then be torn by the twine. The twine, which should have a right-handed lay (machine twine is laid up left-handed and will kink if used for hand sewing) is rubbed with beeswax to make it render easily, or twine can be bought ready treated with paraffin wax.

The round seam (Plate 20F) may be used for repairing a small tear; it is made by pinching together the two sides of the tear and sewing over and over, starting and finishing with a knot, but the stitches must be of even length and should not be pulled tight or they will tear the cloth. Although this could be used with cotton cloth, for the slight pucker formed soon flattens out when rubbed,

with terylene the herringbone stitch (Plate 20*D* and *E*) is the one
to use as it does not pucker the cloth, and each stitch is interlocked
with its neighbours. It should be started 0·6 centimetre ($\frac{1}{4}$inch) or
so beyond the tear, and if the cloth is very old the length of the
stitches should be varied to spread the load. It is best not to start
with a knot, but to tuck the end of the twine under the first few
stitches, which will hold it, and to finish in a like manner. A very
small hole may be darned just as one would darn a sock, but a
large hole, or an area which has been weakened by chafe, will need
a patch of approximately the same weight of cloth as the sail, and
it should be fitted with its warp lying in the same direction as the
warp of the sail. A patch stronger than the sail may tear the cloth
surrounding it, so when patching an old sail use a piece of old
material. Turn in the edges of the patch 1·3 centimetres ($\frac{1}{2}$inch)
and crease them well, cutting a mitre at each corner of the turn-in
so that there will be only two, not three, thicknesses of cloth there;
alternatively cut the patch with a very hot knife to seal its edges,
then no turn-in will be necessary. Place the patch in position and
draw a pencil line round it. Keeping the edge of the patch on the
line, sew it to the sail with the flat seam. Then turn over and cut
out the damaged part of the sail; make a small cut at each corner
so that the edges can be folded under to make a hem, or as before
use a hot knife, and sew them to the patch from that side with the
flat seam. After sewing has been finished, rub the seams well to
make them lie flat.

It sometimes happens that a seam or part of a seam needs to be
restitched when the yacht is out of reach of a sail loft, and this is
not a job to be undertaken lightly. Hold one end of the seam in a
clamp or vice, and arrange it in such a way that you can get the
part of the seam to be stitched across your knees when sitting on
deck. Tack, or pin, the edges of the cloths together every handspan
or so to make sure that they keep level, or stick them with adhesive
tape, and sew away from the clamp, which should be to the right
of you, using the flat seam, and make the stitches run not with
the warp but diagonally across it. The most difficult part of the
business is to hold the cloths together while passing the needle
through them, but if the sail is not too heavy you should be able
to get your left hand beneath it and hold it up with your thumb
in a bight of the canvas. If the cloth is in good condition the old
needle holes of the original machine-made stitches should be
used.

Some ocean voyaging people have made major repairs to

terylene sails with contact glue. After the glue has been applied and the surfaces brought together, I understand that if the area is well hammered the repair will last indefinitely, but I never had occasion to try it. However, double-sided adhesive tape is widely used to hold seams together prior to stitching, and sailmakers refer to this as 'glueing', but the tape is not strong enough to hold the cloths together permanently.

Preventing chafe

A sail ought not to be allowed to rub against anything hard or rough when at sea, or the constant movement may cause the stitches of the seams or the cloth itself to be damaged. It is when running that a sail set abaft a mast is most likely to get chafed, for part of it will press against the shrouds if the sheet is paid out sufficiently for the sail to do its work properly. Because of its greater hoist, a bermudian sail takes on more twist than a gaff sail, and its upper part is therefore more subject to chafe. Careful lead of the gear, preventing the lee runner from swinging about, and keeping the boom from lifting by means of a boom guy or a martingale will do much to reduce chafe; but if in spite of all precautions the sail still rubs on a wire rope, a type of chafing gear known as baggy-wrinkle may be fitted to the wire to provide a soft cushion. Naturally this is more often seen in ocean-going yachts than in those confined to coastwise cruising, and it is frequently carried to excess.

To make a length of baggy-wrinkle (Plate 21), hitch two lengths of terylene twine side by side in a convenient horizontal position, and knot them together near one end. Cut some old rope, such as a condemned halyard, into 10-centimetre (4-inch) lengths, and unlay the strands. Put one of the 10-centimetre (4-inch) strands across beneath the double twine, bring its ends up outside the twine and turn them down beyond the standing part of the strand and between the two lengths of twine; then slide the strand along until it reaches the knot. Do the same with the second strand, sliding it along hard up against the first one, and continue until a sufficient length has been made; then reef knot the two lengths of twine together against the final strand. A short wooden spreader to keep the two parts of twine apart a little makes the work easier.

The finished length of baggy-wrinkle is served tightly round the wire rope, strand ends outward, and is secured with the short lengths of twine left over at each end. About 1 metre (3 feet) is required to serve 0·3 metre (1 foot) of 8-millimetre (0·3-inch) rope, but this will depend somewhat on the size of the strands from which it was made. It is not necessary to serve the whole of the wire rope with baggy-wrinkle; 0·3-metre (1-foot) lengths at 0·6-metre (2-foot) intervals should be sufficient to hold the sail away.

8

SPARS AND RUNNING RIGGING

Boom and gooseneck – Gaff and jaws – Main and mizzen running rigging –
Crutches and gallows – Reefing – Headsail running rigging – Bowsprit –
Headsail furling/reefing gear – The lead of the gear

ALTHOUGH the racing yacht displays a wealth of costly gear for
the handling of her sails, the cruising man need not feel he must
buy similar equipment, for a few seconds longer taken to change
sails or trim their sheets, or a little extra weight and windage, are
of no real importance to him. Winches, for example, are needed
for getting in the headsail sheets during a race when course is
altered or the wind changes direction, for every second counts
then; but they are expensive, and although a few are an undoubted advantage aboard the cruiser they are not essential, for
she can usually be luffed to spill some of the wind from a sail while
its sheet is being hardened in, or a tackle with a little human power
may be used.

Boom and gooseneck

Like masts, booms may be of wood or alloy. The only advantage of
the former, which is now little used, is that alterations and additions can more readily be made, and that if the spar is solid it can
easily be tapered, which is an advantage when roller reefing gear
is used, but because of its weight a solid boom is harder on the sail
and on the crew. For roller reefing the middle of the boom needs to
be of greater diameter than the ends to prevent the rolled-up sail
becoming increasingly baggy; but its after end should then have a
greater diameter than its forward end, for when the sail is rolled on
the boom, the luff rope, which is vertical, will roll up on top of its
previous turns, while the leech of the sail, which is not vertical,
will roll up in a spiral; so if the boom has the same diameter at each
end, more of the sail will be rolled up forward than aft, and the
after end of the boom will droop. It is not uncommon for the after
end of the boom to droop so far when reefed as to make further
reefing impossible unless the topping lift is used to hold the boom
up, when so much wind will be spilt from the sail as to make it
inefficient. If the boom is of the same diameter throughout, and

with one of alloy it usually is because of the cost of tapering, tapered battens of wood may be rolled up with the sail experimentally; these can be altered until the after end of the boom shows no tendency to droop and the sail does not have too much belly in the middle, after which they may be secured permanently with pop rivets or glue. When roller reefing is not used, a wood boom sometimes has a rectangular section, its depth being greater than its width, to stiffen it against the bending strain imposed by the foot of the sail.

The tack of the sail is usually shackled to an eye at the forward end of the boom; it is important to ensure that when so secured it is in line with the eyelets on the luff to which the slides are attached, otherwise an unfair strain will be placed on the adjacent eyelets; if it is not in line the trouble may be cured by fitting a slightly curved batten to the after side of the lower part of the mast to carry the track and so bring the eyelets above the tack into line with it.

The gooseneck, the fitting which holds the forward end of the boom to the mast, has to allow the boom freedom to swing athwartships and, to a limited degree, up and down, and since great strains are imposed on it at times, it needs to be strong and well engineered. In its early form it comprised a pair of wood jaws embracing the mast, but today it is entirely of metal and incorporates two pins, one in a vertical, the other in a horizontal plane, to form a trunion or universal joint. The fitting is held to a wood mast by one or two bands tightly clamped round the mast, but with a metal mast it will be bolted or riveted. An alternative arrangement for either type of mast is to have the gooseneck sliding on a short length of reinforced track, and this has certain advantages when the sail is being set, see page 149.

The foot of a sail may be secured to the boom by stops or a lacing (rarely used now), or by slides on a track; but if roller reefing is used the track should be recessed into the boom so that the slides do not girt the sail too badly when it is rolled over them. Alternatively the foot may be secured by having its boltrope held in a groove along the boom; this is a neat arrangement, and its only disadvantages are that a martingale cannot so conveniently be used with it (see page 153) and that reef points and tiers cannot be passed between boom and sail. The racing man likes to be able to adjust the tension on the foot of a sail – tightening it when close-hauled and easing it when sailing free – and will employ a worm gear, a tackle, or a winch for the purpose; but the ability to adjust the tension is of very little value for cruising, when the foot will usually be hauled out to its made length and permanently secured to an eye at the boom end with a lashing of small line.

Gaff and jaws

The gaff of a gaff-headed sail should be as light as possible, so one of alloy is to be preferred. The saddle of the jaws, which used to be of wood but now is of steel, may be kept to the mast by a parrel of line or wire on which lignum vitae beads are threaded to reduce friction when the sail is being set or taken in; but the parrel needs to be strong, for a sudden momentary strain is liable to be put on it during a gybe, and a better form consists of a curved bar held in position by bolts. This and the saddle should be covered with white hide or PVC and kept well greased. When running, the gaff will bear heavily on the lower after shroud, so it is as well to protect it there, especially if it is a hollow wood spar, with a strip of hardwood at each side. The attachment for the throat block should be at the point where the gaff is hinged to the saddle; if it is placed aft of the hinge, as it sometimes is to keep it clear of the mast, the throat will drop a little and slacken the luff when the sail is peaked up, or if the peak is dropped without first easing the throat halyard, a severe strain will be placed on the luff rope.

Main and mizzen running rigging

Because of the weight of the gaff, all manner of complicated arrangements were evolved for rigging the halyards of gaff-headed sails, but with few exceptions the halyard for a bermudian sail is a single rope passing over a sheave at the masthead. For this purpose flexible wire rope is widely used, and since this is awkward to handle and impossible to belay on a cleat, it is sometimes provided with a tail of fibre rope; but as it is impossible to get any but a very small sail properly set without some additional help, the fibre rope tail might be rigged as a whip or as a more powerful purchase if required, but such arrangements have now given way almost entirely to winches. With the fibre tail the sail can be got most of the way up by hand, then a few turns are taken round a top-action, open-drum winch on the mast (Plate 23A) and the winch used for the final part of the work to get the luff tight. For a sail of 46·5 square metres (500 square feet) a power of 6 to 1 is sufficient, such as would be provided by a 15-centimetre (6-inch) handle on a winch with a drum 5 centimetres (2 inches) in diameter; but a drum of greater diameter than that will be required if the halyard is to grip it, and this will of course call for a longer handle; a 30-centimetre (12-inch) handle is about as long as is convenient. If the halyard is all of wire, ie has no fibre rope tail, it will have to be handled by a closed-drum winch (Plate 23*B*) on which the wire is spooled as the sail goes aloft. This has the disadvantage that as hoisting the sail can only be done by turning the handle the operation is slow, and power is steadily lost as the turns of wire build up and increase the diameter of the drum; to lower the sail a brake on the winch is released, and it is then that any overriding turns of wire on the drum are likely to jam.

However, as was mentioned in Chapter 5, halyards of pre-stretched 3-strand terylene are preferred by many people, and I would strongly recommend anyone with a wire main or mizzen halyard to change to one of terylene. With a wood mast it should not be difficult to enlarge the hole at the masthead and fit the necessarily wider sheave, but a metal mast might have to be returned to its maker for this to be done. A fibre rope is easy to splice and handle, and it has a longer life than has wire; for example I had a terylene jib halyard in use for a circumnavigation, and when it was tested by its maker it was found at its weakest point (where it had worked in a block) still to have 68 per cent of its original strength; in similar use a wire halyard would have needed replacing at least twice.

No doubt the most sensible way of getting the luff of a mainsail tight is not to strain it upwards, when one is pulling against the weight of the sail and wasting energy at the masthead sheave, but to haul the sail nearly up and then heave its tack down. For this purpose the sliding gooseneck mentioned earlier will be required, and the boom will be hauled down the track by a tackle rigged from its under side to the deck. With this method the weight of sail and boom assists in tightening the luff.

Bearing in mind that the pin on which the masthead sheave revolves has to carry a load twice that applied by the winch or tackle, it needs to be strong and well supported. With the metal mast the box in which the sheave is shipped will ensure this; but with a wood mast a cheek plate attached each side to the mast cap and extended downward will take the strain and distribute it more fairly. To prevent the halyard from binding on the mast or pulling the headboard of the sail in against the track, the diameter of the sheave should exceed the fore-and-aft dimension of the mast at that point by a total of about 5 centimetres (2 inches). Clearly the sheave should be a close (but free) fit in its hole or box. Stainless steel is the best material for the pin, and tuffnol or glass-filled nylon for the sheave, then lubrication should not be needed.

There is something to be said in favour of having more than one sheave at the masthead. A second sheave will serve to carry the topping-lift, and if the main halyard should ever part or its end go aloft, the topping-lift could serve temporarily as a halyard. In *Wanderer III* I had three masthead sheaves fitted, the third one being for the genoa halyard; but to avoid weakening the mast at that point, only one sheave hole was cut in the wood, the other sheaves being fitted in chocks glued and screwed on either side. No doubt when the genoa was set its halyard imposed a twisting strain on the masthead, but no ill effects were noticed. The arrangement eliminated all masthead blocks.

To reduce windage aloft it is common for racing yachts to have internal halyards, the falls of which pass down through the mast and come out over sheaves at deck level. I feel that the cruiser should avoid this practice, which involves using wire instead of fibre rope and makes replacement difficult, and the noise and wear caused by the halyards tapping the inside of the mast cannot be stopped.

The above halyard arrangement cannot be used for the throat halyard of a gaff sail because a sheave in the mast close above the gaff jaws would be a cause of weakness, and side sheaves would restrict the movement of the jaws. Therefore the halyard will need to be rigged as a gun tackle, luff tackle, or double purchase, according to the size of the sail and the weight of the gaff. It is convenient to have the same power on throat and peak halyards so that the gaff may be hoisted or lowered horizontally, and this is particularly important in a small yacht where both halyards may be handled simultaneously by one person. The gaff usually has one or more wire spans to which the blocks are attached, thus distributing the load along it and enabling a lighter spar to be used than would be possible if the pull of the peak halyard was concentrated at one point.

The topping lift, which supports the after end of the boom while the sail is being set, reefed, or lowered, may be rigged in one of two ways. It can be shackled to an eye at the end of the boom and led over a sheave or through a block at the masthead (not at some lower point where it could chafe the sail); its fall, which may with advantage be belayed not at the mast but out near the shrouds, should pass through one or more thimbles so placed as to prevent it from swinging about and fouling the crosstrees when there happens to be no strain on it (Plate 64C). Alternatively it can be secured at the masthead and led over a sheave in the end of the boom to a tackle lying along the underside of the boom; the moving block of that tackle may be fitted with a slide running on a track to prevent it slamming about when the weight is off the topping lift. The latter arrangement reduces weight and windage aloft, but it cannot be fitted when roller reefing is employed.

Often the topping lift is of wire rope, and if it is used at sea, as it should be to take some of the strain off the leech of the sail when a guy or a martingale in combination with the mainsheet is holding the boom down, it will be liable to fatigue at the masthead sheave. If a boom guy or a martingale is not employed, the topping lift will fall slack and perhaps chafe the sail each time the boom-end lifts as a puff of wind catches the sail or the yacht rolls; but this can be prevented by seizing a length of shock-cord (elastic rope) to it a short distance above the boom-end, and making this fast to the eye on the boom where the lift is shackled on; this will hold the wire taut except for its lower end, which will be in a bight and will straighten out to take the strain only when a load comes on it. However, I prefer to have the entire topping lift of fibre rope, preferably nylon, which has so much elasticity that it may need no shock-cord to take up the slack, and its life is much longer than that of wire. Nevertheless, it should be remembered that when wet a nylon rope increases its length, and when dry contracts.

One of the advantages of bermudian rig is that the topping lift can be taken (as indeed it should be) to the masthead so that the sail may be set or taken in clear of it on either tack. But a gaff sail must be guided up the correct side of the topping lift, and if the lift is to leeward the sail will press against it and be difficult to handle. Two topping lifts are therefore sometimes used in gaff-rigged yachts so that the weather one may be set up and the lee one eased off, but for coastwise cruising they are a nuisance because the sail must be guided into the narrow space between them when being set. Lazy jacks (lines which run from one lift down beneath the boom and up to the other lift) may be fitted to gather in the sail as it is lowered, but they can cause chafe, are a nuisance when reefing, and have little to recommend them except in a large craft or one with a very heavy sail.

Braided terylene rope serves excellently for a mainsheet, or indeed for any sheet, as it is flexible and easy to handle, and it takes a good grip on the drum of a winch; but it should not be less than 12 millimetres ($\frac{3}{4}$ inch) or it will not be comfortable to pull on. At the time of writing I am still using as mainsheet a rope of the above type made by Marlow Ropes, which has been in use for eleven years and about 60,000 miles. If the sheet is rigged as an inverted luff tackle, ie with a double block or two single blocks on the boom and one block on deck (an additional block will be needed to give a fair lead to the cleat), it will have a power of 4 to 1, which is enough for a sail of 28 square metres (300 square feet), provided the blocks are large, the rope leads fairly through them, and one can effectively put one's weight on it. Rather than increase the purchase for a larger sail with the added complication and friction that will create, I feel it is better to employ a winch at the end of the existing purchase. When no winch is required, I prefer the sheet to be double-ended instead of single-ended, so that each end may pass through a fairlead block to its own cleat within reach of the helmsman; the sheet can then be tended from either side of the cockpit. When roller reefing is employed the double block will be shackled to a lug or bail on a swivel fitting at the extreme end of the boom; this fitting will also have a lug or eye for the topping lift, and should as well have one each side for the boom guy. If such a fitting is of bronze, and if the shackles securing the sheet block and topping lift are of stainless steel, the bronze will in time get worn away by the harder metal – a snap shackle worn in this manner is shown in Plate 19D. To overcome this on long voyages I coat the bronze with a hard two-part filler such as Marinetex, renewing it from time to time as necessary. If the boom much overhangs the stern, or the existence of a wind-vane steering gear prevents the block being at the end of the boom, the block will have to be attached to the boom by a claw ring. This fitting has rollers between which the sail will feed while being roller-reefed, and in the days of cotton sails it invariably damaged the sail; but with sails of tough terylene the risk should be small. The claw ring must be secured to the swivel fitting at the boom-end by a line or bar, otherwise it will work itself forward along the boom when the sheet is eased.

When roller reefing is not employed it is possible to have several single blocks on the boom instead of one multi-sheave block, and to spread them out to distribute the load and counteract the tendency of the boom to bend with the upward pull of the sail. With such an arrangement the end of the sheet is commonly led from the last (foremost) block on the boom down through a fairlead block on coachroof or bridgedeck to a cleat, or, if required, to a winch.

Often the lower block of a mainsheet tackle is arranged to slide athwartships on a metal horse, or on a track. This may be necessary to carry it over the tiller or some other obstruction, but its primary purpose is to give the sheet a lead from the lee side, which will help in keeping the boom from lifting without pinning it in too hard amidships. Sometimes the position of the lower block can be adjusted and held at any desired point on the horse or track. Occasionally the horse is very high, or the metal guardrail at the stern is employed as a horse, and this has the merit of keeping the mainsheet, when eased, clear above the guardrails so that it cannot chafe on them.

A boom guy will prevent the boom from slamming about in a seaway when the sheet is eased and the wind is light, thus assisting the sail to remain asleep and preventing an involuntary gybe. But, in conjunction with the mainsheet, it serves another important purpose, that of restricting the boom's tendency to lift, thus reducing the twist in the upper part of the sail, and by stopping the sail from moving up and down against the lee rigging, minimizes chafe. The guy's efficiency in this capacity will, however, depend on the height of the boom; within reason the higher it is the better, and this enables the helmsman to see more readily under the sail, the boom is less likely to dip in the sea, and the stowing of a dinghy amidships is simplified.

A boom guy need not be elaborate. A single rope made fast, preferably with a snap shackle, to the fitting at the boom-end, led forward outside the lee rigging and brought through a fairlead to a cleat or bollard on the foredeck, will serve. It may be set up by the simple expedient of paying out a little more sheet than is required, making the guy fast, and then hardening in the sheet. To save a journey forward each time the sheet is trimmed, or when gybing, the guy can be taken through a snatch block forward and brought aft outside the weather rigging to be made fast near the helmsman, where it may with advantage be set up on an idle headsail sheet winch. But the guy will bear so heavily on the weather guardrail stanchions and rigging that I would not care to use the method except in a very small vessel.

However, in preventing the boom from lifting, a martingale (I prefer the seaman's old term rather than the modern one 'kicking strap') is more effective. This comprises a tackle leading from the boom to the deck or the foot of the mast. The latter position has the merit that the tackle need not be adjusted when the sheet is trimmed, but because of the small triangle involved it imposes a considerable thrust on the gooseneck; this will be eliminated if the tackle leads to a position on the deck further aft, but then it will require adjustment each time the sheet is trimmed unless its lower block travels on an athwartships track. If the foot of the sail is held to the boom with slides, a good way of securing the martingale to the boom is by means of a length of strong, flat rubber, having a little elasticity, with a stout ring at each end (Plate 19*E*); Simpson Lawrence makes such a fitting, and calls it a snubber. But if the foot of the sail is in a groove, and/or the sail is roller reefed, a claw made of sheet metal will have to be used instead, and this may need to be held by a line taken to the swivel fitting at the boom-end to stop it slipping forward.

Crutches and gallows (Plate 24)

The old form of scissors crutch used for supporting the after end of the boom when the sail is stowed is inconvenient, as it has to be held in position while the boom is being lowered into it, and it may be capsized and lost if the mainsheet is not set up taut; but if there is room, it can be improved by securing its feet to the deck with hinges and it will lie flat when not in use. The single crutch which ships into sockets in the cockpit is more satisfactory and allows the boom to be offset so that it does not obstruct the companionway in a small yacht; it may be of wood or metal tubing. A gallows, with two or three alternative notches for the boom, is much to be preferred; it presents a larger target when lowering the boom, and will hold it steady on the lee side while the sail is being reefed or stowed. But to make sure that the boom, which may droop when roller reefing gear is used, can clear it when tacking or gybing, its supports may be made of telescoping tubes held in the extended position by removable pins.

Reefing

A mainsail, mizzen, or schooner's foresail may be reefed (reduced in area) by rotating the boom, which will roll the sail up on it like a blind, or by pulling the reef cringles down to the boom, securing them there, and gathering up the cloth between them with reef points or a lacing.

Roller reefing has so many advantages that I would prefer to have it in any yacht. It is simple and quick in operation, all the work is done from a comparatively safe position beside the mast, and it can be done on any point of sailing without the need to bring the boom inboard. Its disadvantages are that a stiffer, and therefore heavier, boom may be needed, for the mainsheet can be attached only at its end, unless a claw ring is employed; if the boom is not correctly proportioned its outer end will droop as the sail is rolled; and the final result does not always produce a perfectly setting sail, as the leech has a tendency to creep forward. Also, as has already been mentioned, a tackle for adjusting the topping lift cannot be used along the boom, and a martingale can only be used with a claw. It is often said that a reef cannot be taken in while at anchor without first setting the sail, but Colin McMullen (one-time commodore of the Royal Cruising Club) overcame that problem aboard his 10·6-metre (35-foot) sloop *Saecwen* in the following manner. He passed a line through the halyard shackle at the head of the sail, took it round and under the bunch of stowed sail close to the mast, omitting the lower slides which were going to be rolled up, and secured it to its other end at the head of the sail. He then released the lower slides from the track, hoisted the bunched-up sail about a metre (say 3 feet), removed the tiers and took in the rolls one at a time, going aft after each roll to pull the leech of the sail aft to eliminate wrinkles.

The gear for roller reefing consists at the gooseneck end of a fitting on which the boom can revolve, and mechanism for turning it and holding it from unrolling. There are two types: in one the boom is revolved with a ratchet handle and is held by a pawl (Turner's gear Plate 25*A*); this is fast in action but is suitable only for a small sail. In the other, more widely used type, the boom is revolved by a worm gear, a handle being shipped on either end of the worm shaft (Plate 25*B*, *C*, and *D*). This is powerful but slower, and as it is essential for its proper working that the worm gear be well lubricated, the most suitable kind is one which is totally enclosed, and it is an advantage if it is provided with a disk guard to stop the luff of the sail from creeping forward onto the gear. A common failing with some of these gears is that the boss of the handle is not long enough so that the handle fouls the sail as soon as a few rolls have been taken in; also the crank of the handle is often too short to give adequate power. The type in which a square recess in the handle ships on the squared end of the worm shaft is to be preferred to the bayonet fitting, as it is less likely to slip off.

For use with small sails there is a type of gear with which the spindle passes through the mast and the handle ships on its forward end. This can be used only with a metal mast, must be installed when the mast is made, and cannot be used with a sliding gooseneck. A more recent development is to have the luff of the sail within the hollow mast with means for rotating it, so that when the clew is slacked away the sail may be rolled up inside the mast as far as necessary for reefing, or completely for furling. Of course this calls for a special mast and a sail made specially or adapted to fit it. Because of the mechanical complications and the fact that reefing will move the centre of effort of the sail further forward than will the usual methods of reefing, I regard it as a questionable seagoing arrangement.

When reefing a bermudian sail with roller gear the topping lift should be used with caution; it should no more than just take the weight of the boom, or the leech will become slack, creep forward, and roll up with wrinkles in it. The sail should be kept full all the time, otherwise a hand may have to be stationed aft to pull the leech out along the boom, and this could well be impossible at sea. The halyard should be eased handsomely at the same time as the boom is rotated, the pull of the reefing gear hauling the sail down against the pull of the halyard; if the luff is allowed to become slack the sail will roll up unevenly, especially if it is of light cloth. As the sail comes down the lacing must be unrove or the slides removed from the track. If the gooseneck slides on a track, the halyard should be eased until the gooseneck reaches its lowest point. The boom is then revolved until the gooseneck has risen to its highest point. This is repeated until a sufficiently deep reef has been rolled down. When reefing a gaff sail with roller gear it should be kept well peaked to ensure that the leech does not become slack, and it may not be necessary to ease the peak halyard at all, as lowering the throat may drop the peak sufficiently; but this will depend on the angle of the gaff and the lead of the peak halyard. As accidents do sometimes happen to roller reefing gears, a sail intended for roller reefing is usually provided with cringles and a row of lacing eyelets to be used in an emergency.

Reefing in the old-fashioned manner with cringles and points or a lacing (Plate 26) is now often called slab or jiffy reefing, and it has been given so much publicity in yachting magazines that one might be forgiven for believing it had only recently been invented. A sail intended for this kind of reefing is provided with a grommet or a cringle on the luff and leech at the height above the foot to which the reef is to extend. The line between the grommets is provided with a row of reef points, short lengths of line in pairs, one each side of the sail, or with eyelets for a lacing. A sail may have one or several reefs.

When tucking in a reef a permanent boom gallows will be found convenient, for the boom can be got down and held steady on it while the work is being done; if there is no gallows, take the weight on the topping lift. Then proceed as follows. Ease the halyard, and pull the reef cringle on the luff down to the boom and secure it there with a shackle or snap shackle, one shackle for each reef being permanently seized to the gooseneck. Alternatively a length of rope with a figure-of-eight knot in one end may be rove through the reef cringle, then through the tack cringle and back to a cleat on the boom.

The next step is to haul the reef cringle on the leech down to the boom, which is done with a pendant and tackle or with a pendant and winch. There are two common ways of reeving the pendant; it may be spliced to the cringle and led down round a side sheave on the boom to a tackle lying along the boom; or it may have a stopper knot at its end and will then be rove through a wooden chock with a suitable-size hole in it (bee-block) on the opposite side of the boom to the sheave, up through the cringle, and down round the sheave to the tackle. The advantages of the latter method are that the cringle is hove down to the centre instead of the side of the boom (that may be important with a boom of large diameter), and two parts of the pendant take the strain instead of one; also there is in theory a mechanical advantage of 2 to 1 as the pendant is in the form of a whip, but most of that is lost in friction at the cringle. Against the double pendant are the facts that the sail is likely to get nipped and chafed between the two parts, and because the pendant is twice as long as a single one, the tackle has to be twice as long also and there may not be sufficient length for it on the boom if the boom is short or the reef a deep one. As in any except the smallest craft the leech cringles will be out of reach from the deck when the sail is set, the pendants should be kept ready rove when at sea.

It is common to have only one reef tackle. This is hooked into an eye in the end of the reef pendant, the cringle is hauled down and lashed to the boom, the tackle then being unhooked ready for the next reef. This economizes in gear and saves some congestion on the boom, but it means that the boom has to be hauled right inboard for the lashing to be passed and for the tackle to be hooked into the next pendant. Obviously the simplest method is to have a single pendant for each reef leading to its own small winch on the boom.

After the cringles on luff and leech have been hauled down and secured, a big bag of sailcloth will be left hanging between them. It is unseamanlike to leave this flogging in the wind and it might fill with water, so the reef points must be tied or the lacing rove to gather it up. This takes some time, particularly in a large vessel where part of the boom may be almost out of reach; a crew member has to leave the safety of the mast and stand perhaps on tiptoe on a cockpit coaming reaching overhead, and as he will need both hands he cannot obey the old axiom: 'one hand for the ship and one for yourself'. This is one of the reasons why I, like the Bristol Channel pilots in their short-handed cutters with their Appledore worm gear, prefer roller reefing. But a possible advantage of the old method is that the reef, instead of being parallel to the boom, may be arranged with the cringle on the leech higher than the cringle on the luff, so that when the sail is reefed the outboard end of the boom will be higher than normal, and thus less likely to bury itself in the sea as the yacht rolls. This is known as a rolling reef, and I have never seen a sail with it, but Moitessier had it in *Joshua* and considered it essential when sailing in a stormy area. It takes longer to reeve a lacing than to tie points – one can scarcely keep the latter rove at all times since it will be likely to foul the pendants and tackle – but a lacing can be undone quicker than reef points and it distributes the load evenly over all the eyelets, automatically adjusting itself. It matters little whether the points are tied or the lacing taken under the boom or between boom and sail; the latter makes a neater job and calls for shorter reef points, but of course cannot be done if the footrope is in a groove. It now remains only to set up the halyard and ease off the topping lift.

If, with a sudden increase in the strength of the wind, or when starting from an anchorage in a strong wind, the second reef has to be taken in, it is seamanlike to tuck in the first reef also so that sail may be increased gradually by shaking out the reefs one by one as the wind moderates.

To shake out a reef, take the weight of the boom on the topping lift, or secure the boom in the gallows; ease the halyard a little, and unreeve the lacing, or untie the points, taking care that none are missed or the sail may tear when being set. Slack up the reef tackle if each reef has a tackle to itself; otherwise hook the tackle into the pendant and take the strain while the lashing is cast off, then slack away. Finally, unlash or unshackle the luff cringle, hoist away on the halyard to set the sail, inserting the slides in the track or reeving the lacing as it goes up, and then ease the topping lift.

Headsail running rigging

Little effort is required to haul a headsail up its stay, so a single part halyard passing through a block on the fore side of the mast (or maybe a side sheave if the sail sets to the masthead) will serve. Some extra power will, however, be needed to get the luff taut so that it does not sag between the hanks. For this purpose a short tackle between the tack of the sail and the deck fitting may be used, but it is more convenient to have a winch on the mast for the halyard. The closed-drum winch, on which the halyard stows itself, is too slow in action, for a headsail often needs to be set smartly when getting away from a congested berth.

The correct positioning both fore-and-aft and athwartships of the fairleads through which the headsail sheets must pass on their way aft will depend on the size and shape of the sail, and to some extent on the speed of the yacht to windward – the faster she sails the farther inboard will they need to be. The aim should be to sheet the sail in such a way that it does not backwind the sail set abaft it or shake too soon, and that its leech does not curl to windward of a fore-and-aft line. I suggest that it be tried on a line which makes an angle of about 15° with the centre fore-and-aft line on the deck at the point where the luff of the sail would come if continued downward. It is often thought that the fore-and-aft position of the lead should be where the mitre of the sail, if projected, would touch the deck. But that is not often so, though it might be correct for a sail with a low clew; a more likely position will be where a line from a position two-fifths up the luff and drawn through the clew would touch the deck. If, on coming to the wind, the leech of the sail shakes before the foot, the lead is too far aft; if the foot shakes first the lead is too far forward. Headsail sheet leads are commonly on slides on tracks, each held in position by a pin engaging one of a number of holes in the track for ease of adjustment. As smaller headsails should be sheeted farther inboard than large ones each may call for its own sheet leads, but this is rarely arranged except in racing yachts. In a small yacht the fairlead itself might be a lignum vitae bull's-eye, though of course the sheet will render better through a block, and this should be of the non-tumbling kind otherwise it will beat persistently on the deck in light weather.

The ideal headsail sheets are single parts of braided terylene. They may have eyes at their ends to be secured to the clew of the sail with a jib sheet shackle, ie one in which the pin has a counter-sunk head slotted for a screwdriver instead of the usual eye for a spike, and is therefore less likely to hitch up on the falls of halyards when passing round the mast during a tack. However, if it has to pass round an inner forestay it may still hitch up, and then it will be better to secure each sheet with a bowline. Snap shackles should not be used, for when the sail flogs in stays centrifugal force may cause them to open.

The sheets are most conveniently hardened in by means of an open-drum sheet winch on the deck or coaming each side of the cockpit or at the aft end of the coachroof. With two or more turns on the winch the slack can be rattled quickly in, and the handle need be used only for the final hardening. If the winch is of the top action kind, ie having the handle at the top of the drum, the turns will be put on before the handle is shipped; if it is of the bottom action type, the handle will remain in place, but can only be used with a ratchet action, and a stop may need to be provided to prevent it whirling round while the slack is being pulled in. I must repeat that winches are expensive items, particularly if they are of the geared variety, but this pair will sometimes have other uses such as the setting up of boom and spinnaker guys and the trimming of trysail sheets, and even though they may not be essential, they will be much appreciated when handling a large genoa in a breeze. An economy can sometimes be made by having one winch only, placing it on the yacht's centre line, and leading the sheets to it through blocks; in large yachts this is often a powerful, two handled, geared affair commonly known as a coffee grinder. The loading on a headsail sheet winch may be as much as 15 kilograms per square metre (3 pounds for each square foot) of the sail's area. Some consider that self-tailing winches are worth their extra cost because they hold the sheet on the drum leaving the operator free to use both hands on the handle.

When a yacht has no sheet winches, or the existing pair is reserved for use with a second headsail, a common way of rigging a sheet is as a whip (Fig 24A); but in light winds the weight of a pair of blocks at the clew may spoil the set of the sail, or they may be a danger to anyone working on the foredeck. Bull's-eyes, being lighter, are sometimes used instead, but the friction in them is so great that most of the mechanical advantage of the whip is lost. If there is sufficient distance on deck between the fairlead and the

point where the sheet is made fast, the arrangement shown in Fig
24*B* is to be preferred, for here the block travels along the deck and
can be of proper size, and if need be a handy billy can be clapped
on to the fall of the whip for the final haul when the greatest power
is required.

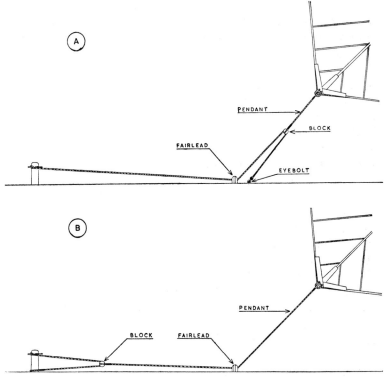

Fig 24   *A* A common way of rigging a headsail sheet; *B* A better method with the block of
the whip travelling along the deck

Some consider that it is worth while to rig a headsail in such a
way that it will look after itself when tacking or gybing. The sheet
for such a sail, and there will be only one, is arranged to slide
athwartships on a horse or track forward of the mast. The lead is
then so vertical that to make the sail draw properly its foot must be
extended by a boom, and the end of the sheet must go forward to a
block under the forward end of the boom before going aft, otherwise its pull will prevent athwartships movement on the horse.
There are several ways of arranging a staysail boom, the best

being for it to extend the full length of the foot, its forward end being pivoted on the forestay. Another method, which has had its period of popularity, is to have the boom a little shorter than the foot, and to pivot it on some deck fitting, such as the windlass or samson post, a little abaft the forestay. The argument in favour of this is that with the sheet hardened in the sail will be flat for windward work, but on the sheet being eased, it will assume a fuller and more efficient curve. Experience has shown that it does nothing of the sort; the belly coming too far aft and the upper part of the sail growing inefficient as the boom-end lifts.

With a two-headsail rig it is undoubtedly an advantage to have the staysail look after itself when tacking, and to perform as a small spinnaker when running dead before the wind, but the price one has to pay for this is, in my opinion, too high. As the boomed sail has to stop short of the mast, it is smaller in area and less efficient than a boomless sail; the boom restricts the space on the foredeck, it may prevent the forehatch opening, and is much in the way when light-weather sails or ground tackle are being handled. If the sail is hanked to the stay in the normal way it will not slide right down when the halyard is let go unless the boom is topped up or the outhaul slackened. This can, however, be overcome in the following manner. Use hanks for the upper three-quarters of the luff only, and rings, not fastened to the sail, for the lower quarter. Splice a piece of line to an eyelet one-quarter of the way up the luff, and lead it down through two thimbles seized to the luff and through one of the rings at each point of attachment, and secure it to the tack so that when the sail is set the line will be taut. As soon as the sail starts to come down, the line will slacken and allow the lower part of the luff to pull away from the stay and drop easily. A lacing will serve equally well, but will quickly get chafed.

Bowsprit

It may be considered retrograde in these days of high aspect rigs to consider having a bowsprit, but for quite some time American designers have been alert to its advantages (often in conjunction with a clipper bow) for the ocean-going yacht, in which it is preferable to spread the sail plan out fore-and-aft rather than carry it up high, for the yacht's motion will often throw the wind out of tall sails.

The modern bowsprit is not the single round and naked spar of the past, difficult and dangerous to get out along, and requiring shrouds and a net between them to keep the jib out of the water while it is being set or handed, but is usually a sturdy platform, or sometimes a bipod with a grating across it, and the whole fitted with guardrails 75 centimetres (29·5 inches) high to provide a safe position for working and to hold the lowered jib inboard. It calls for no shrouds, but a bobstay to withstand the upward pull of the jib will almost certainly be required. In that capacity wire rope is not ideal as the chafe of the chain anchor cable on it may cause stranding unless it is fitted with plastic hose, which of a suitable size may be impossible to force over the terminal fittings. Sometimes a rod is used, but this is liable to become bent and lose strength. Galvanized chain serves very well, but see page 178. If the bowsprit is long, or the bow has much overhang, a strut known as a dolphin-striker projecting downward from the stem, may be employed to give greater spread to the bobstay in the same way as a crosstree gives extra spread to a shroud; but it is an undesirable complication and is liable to get damaged by the anchor cable when the yacht sheers. To look well and help to keep the tack of the jib out of the water when punching into a headsea, the bowsprit should be steeved up so as to continue the line of the forward sheer, but not so high as to obstruct the helmsman's forward view.

Many a bowsprit has been lost (sometimes together with the mast in single headstay rigs) through failure of the bobstay fitting at the stem. A simple eye-bolt is not good enough, and in a wood or GRP yacht the fitting should be made with the eye in one with a plate, which is held by two bolts passing through the stem with nuts set up over a second plate inboard. The inner plate will strengthen the stem at the point where it has been weakened by the holes for the bolts. The steel yacht will have a plate welded to the stem.

Headsail furling/reefing gear

The earliest gear for rolling up on its own luff a headsail set flying (not hanked to a stay) was invented by R F Wykeham-Martin, and in the UK this was widely used with the jibs of small cruisers in the 1920s and 1930s. It consisted of a swivel at the head of the sail, and a drum at the tack on which a furling line was spooled. This gear is still made: 1 × 19 wire is used for the luff rope of the sail, and the sail is rolled up with the lay of the rope to overcome any tendency for the rope to unlay. To set the rolled-up sail, the furling line is eased away as the sheet is hauled on and as the sail unrolls it puts turns of line on the drum; to furl the sail the sheet is eased handsomely while the furling line is hauled on. The rolled-up sail can be lowered, but it is difficult to stow because of the stiffness of the wire and the sail rolled round it.

Although the ability to unroll the jib when getting under way, and to roll it up instead of lowering it when coming to a berth, were undoubted advantages, what the cruiser really wanted was a quick and simple means of reefing the sail so as to avoid the need to take in one sail and set another when the strength of the wind changed.

Today under various trade names arrangements for doing this are available, and the most suitable one for cruising is the type in which an alloy extrusion is slipped on the existing headstay around which it is free to rotate. The headstay need not be altered, and will continue to serve its original purpose, but its condition cannot be examined without dismantling the extrusion. The lower end of the extrusion is provided with a drum and furling line, and the sail is hauled up a slot in the extrusion. The greater the diameter of the drum in relation to the diameter of the extrusion, the easier will the work be, but a large sail will best be handled if the furling line is taken to a winch.

The disadvantages of this and any other kind of headsail reefing gear are that if the sail is to set properly in strong winds it will need to be made of sufficiently heavy cloth and will then be too heavy in light winds, and, when reefed, the athwartships positions of the sheet fairleads should be moved further inboard if the sail is to set properly close-hauled. It would also appear that an existing head-sail cannot successfully be used with the gear because when partly rolled up it will have too much belly; so a flatter sail will be required and this will lack efficiency when fully set. It is probably for this reason that although some makers say that the sail can be reefed with their gear, they recommend changing to a smaller sail in heavy weather, which of course defeats the object.

A headsail for use with roller gear will need to be cut high in the clew so that the line the sheet makes with it in the vertical plane does not alter as the sail is reefed. Another point to consider is that when the sail is completely rolled up a strip of it all along the leech and foot will remain exposed to sunlight; to avoid the degradation of the sailcloth that might otherwise result, a broad strip of acrylic material should be sewn along leech and foot to protect the sail against ultraviolet light, for it is difficult to coat a rolled-up headsail, and the only attempt I have seen was not a success.

It is probable that the advantages of roller furling/reefing gears far outweigh the disadvantages aboard a short-handed cruising yacht, particularly if she is to make long passages, and many experienced owners, including Irving Johnson in *Yankee* and Bob Kittredge in *Svea*, spoke highly of them.

The essential points about such gears are these: the safety of the mast must never depend for support on a furling gear with swivels; it must have a permanent stay set up in a proper manner, though as mentioned above, an alloy extrusion may safely revolve on it; and no matter what may happen, it must be possible in any circumstances to get the sail down on deck.

A modern tendency is to employ expensive and sometimes complicated equipment for doing simple jobs, and a point often overlooked is that if the lower part of a headsail is provided with reef cringles and a row of reef points, the sail can be lowered while tack and sheet are shifted to the reefing positions, the foot rolled up and tied and the sail re-set, all in a very short time.

It is not often that one needs to make a headsail up in stops, but occasions may arise when this sail will be needed immediately the anchor has been broken out or the mooring dropped in a crowded anchorage when there may not be time to set it in the usual way; then, if it is not fitted with furling gear, it can be set in stops. To do this lay the sail on deck with its luff straight, fold it once lengthways so that the clew cringle lies just outside the luff, then roll up the folded sail tightly to the luff and tie it with stops of easily broken cotton string at 60-centimetre (2-foot) intervals. Bend on the sheets and, making sure that they are quite slack, hoist the sail on its halyard. It will then be ready for use and, when it is required, a sharp pull on a sheet will break the stops and make it instantly available.

The lead of the gear

The running rigging of a full-rigged ship required more than 200 belaying pins; each rope had its own pin, and the layout was standard so that a seaman might know where everything was to be found aboard any ship. But there is little systematic about the arrangement of pins and cleats in yachts, and often they are too small and insufficient in number. Single part halyards should normally be brought to the mast or to a position very close to it, but to avoid congestion there, it is sometimes desirable, and particularly with gaff rig, to take each fall of a double-ended halyard out to pinrails on opposite sides near the shrouds; the topping lift and possibly the spinnaker gear may also go there.

   Much can be done to prolong the life of fibre ropes by arranging their lead so that they cannot touch one another, but it is not always possible to prevent them from touching the standing rigging; where that happens the rope should be led through a large smooth thimble seized to the wire. Lengths of plastic tube threaded on the lower parts of the shrouds will do much to prevent the chafing of sheets and will reduce friction when they are being handled; even a piece of old sailcloth wrapped round a rope and held with line or a couple of clothes-pegs will serve temporarily to prevent chafe. Each yacht presents her own problems and some experiment will be needed in a new yacht, or in one in which the rig has been altered, before the best lead for the gear is found; even then frequent inspections should be made during a passage, especially when sails are reefed, to make sure that the lead of ropes in blocks and over sheaves is fair and that there is nothing to cause chafe on any point of sailing.

   Mention has already been made of the noise of the falls of idle halyards beating against the mast. Not only is this an irritation to anyone within earshot, but it destroys the anodizing of an alloy mast and may cause fatigue of a wire rope. The problem is not difficult to overcome. If there are pins or cleats near the rails by the shrouds, the falls of the idle halyards can be taken to them, thus keeping them away from the mast. But if the halyards must be kept belayed on the mast, there are two ways in which they can be kept clear of it. Thumb cleats may be fastened to the crosstrees a short way out from the mast, and the falls of the halyards flipped into them before being made fast (Plate 64C); alternatively short lengths of line or shock-cord (known as catharpings) may be used to pull the falls out towards the shrouds as high up as one can reach. The matter needs to be dealt with for, other considerations apart, the noise made usually by unattended craft in a large marina on a windy day, is such as to disturb the whole neighbourhood.

9

GROUND TACKLE

Types of anchor – Cables – Windlasses and riding gear – Anchor work –
Buoying the anchor – Moorings

WITH the intention of reducing weight in yachts of light-displacement type, or with considerations of labour saving and convenience of stowing in mind, some builders and owners equip their yachts with inadequate ground tackle. This is a great mistake, for every yacht should be capable of riding out a gale in sheltered water without dragging her anchors, and there may come a time when, owing to the failure of some part of her gear, only her anchors and cables stand between her and destruction on a lee shore. Her ground tackle should therefore be of good design and of adequate weight and strength.

Types of anchor

Although the traditional fisherman anchor is not now widely used, it is an excellent standby, for its sharp fluke will often take a hold on a rock or coral bottom where modern patent anchors may not, and as the names of its several parts have been handed down to the modern anchors, they are shown in Fig 25.

As the stock is longer than the chord, when lying on its side the anchor is unstable, and as soon as a horizontal pull comes on the ring, the anchor turns over and one of its flukes starts to bite into the ground. The angle the fluke makes with the ground causes it to dig deeper as the pull is increased (Plate 29*A*, *B*, and *C*). Obviously a vertical pull on the ring will cause the anchor to break out, and for that reason it is essential always to ride to a sufficient scope of cable so that the pull may be in a horizontal direction. Once the anchor has got a hold, a sideways pull on the ring, such as a yacht will give when sheering about, will not break it out, for the stock lying on the ground will prevent it from capsizing.

The disadvantage of the fisherman-type anchor is that its upper fluke may be fouled when the yacht swings at the turn of the tide or to a change in the direction of the wind and drags a bight of the cable round it; then as soon as a strain comes on the chain the fluke will be lifted and the anchor will drag (Plate 29*D*). An anchor can

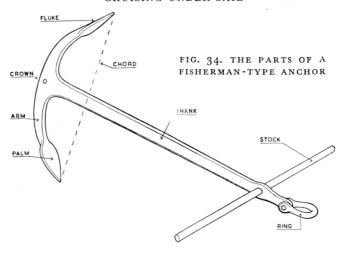

FIG. 34. THE PARTS OF A
FISHERMAN-TYPE ANCHOR

Fig 25   The parts of a fisherman-type anchor

also be fouled by the chain taking a turn round the stock; that kind of fouling is not always so serious though it may cause the anchor to tilt over and drag. These troubles can only be prevented by mooring the yacht between two anchors laid out in opposite directions so that she can never swing over either of them; that is the correct procedure in any anchorage where there is a tidal stream or little room, but it entails much extra work and is undesirable when bringing up in an open anchorage from which a

---

PLATE 19 (*facing*). *A*. Mast-climbing stairs are more comfortable and convenient than ratlines of rope; each is arranged with its strap uppermost to provide a stirrup for the foot. *B*. A lacing on the lower part of the luff is better than slides when roller reefing is employed; it should be rove not round and round but back the same side after passing through each eyelet. Seen here also are rope ratlines and a spinnaker boom stowed up-and-down the fore side of the mast. *C*. Sheet winches at a convenient working height and a well-arranged pinrail. *D*. If bronze fittings are used in conjunction with stainless steel they are liable to get worn, as happened to this snap shackle which secured a spinnaker boom guy to a stainless eye during a long passage. *E*. A martingale held to the boom with a snubber, a tough rubber strap.

PLATE 20 (*overleaf*). *A*. An oval thimble fitted to the tack of a headsail; a fine example of the sailmaker's art. *B*. A grommet at the clew of a sail, which here is protected by sewn-on plastic. *C*. For a terylene sail three rows of machine-made stitches at each seam are better than two, for the outer rows may be susceptible to chafe where they pass over the edge of the cloth, as can be seen here with the upper row. *D* and *E*. With the herring-bone stitch the sides of a tear are held flat and edge to edge, and each stitch is interlocked with the next. *F*. The round seam is a quick method of repairing a small tear in a light sail, but should not be pulled tight or the cloth will always remain puckered.

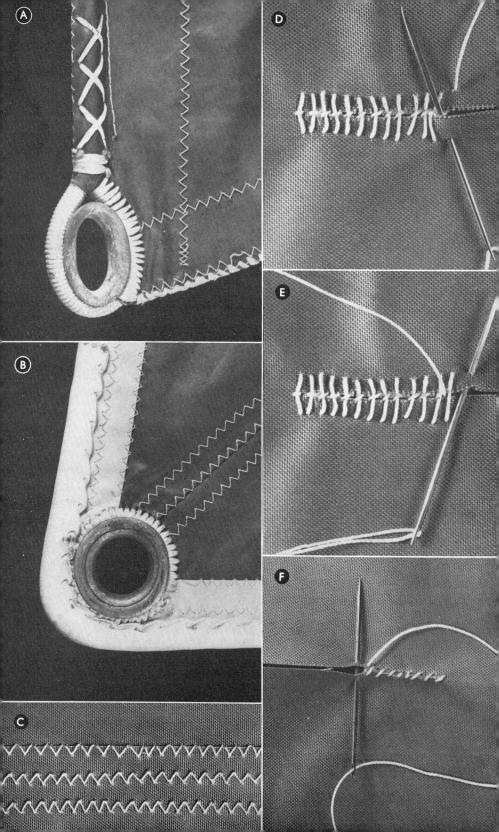

change in the direction of the wind might compel one to make a quick departure.

A number of patent anchors have been devised to prevent fouling without the need of mooring, and of these the CQR (secure) and the Danforth are the most widely used and trusted. The CQR consists of a single fluke in the form of two handed ploughshares back to back and held to the shank by a pin on which it is free to pivot within certain limits; it has no stock. When the anchor falls to the bottom it lies on its side because it is unstable in any other position, and its weighted point is tilted downwards a little. As soon as a horizontal pull comes on the ring the fluke starts to dig in, and as it does so the anchor turns over on to a level keel, and if the pull is great enough it will bury itself completely (Plate 30A, B, and C). Once it has dug in it is almost impossible for the cable to foul it. Weight for weight the holding power is at least one third greater than that of the best type of fisherman anchor, and the ratio increases with the size. But no matter how small a yacht may be, I do not consider it is wise to use any type of patent anchor weighing less than 13·5 kilograms (30 pounds) for although it might well have ample holding power once it had dug in, it may not be heavy enough to force its way through a layer of weed to reach the holding ground, and if it does not bite in quickly, its fluke may become so foul with weed as it slides along that it will not bite in at all. As a CQR of 13·5 kilograms (30 pounds) is not made, I would use the 15·8-kilogram (35-pound) rather than the 11·3-kilogram (25-pound) model. In larger yachts the higher cost of the CQR over the fisherman is to some extent offset by the saving in weight. From time to time attempts have been made to 'improve' the CQR, which in its original form was the most

---

PLATE 21 (*overleaf*). A. To make a length of baggy-wrinkle, place a 10-centimetre (4-inch) strand of old rope beneath the two strands of twine which are held apart by a small spreader. B. Bring its ends up outside and pass them down between the strands of twine beyond the strand's standing part. C. Then slide the strand along until it is hard up against the last one. D. Serving a shroud with baggy-wrinkle. E. The baggy-wrinkle in position, held at top and bottom by the short ends of twine which are fastened to the shroud with clove hitches.

PLATE 22 (*facing*). The 13.7-metre (45-foot) gaff cutter *Dyarchy*, one of the most loved and admired cruising yachts of her time, was designed by the late Jack Laurent Giles for Roger Pinckney, who has here left the ship to sail herself for a moment while he brings aft the lee backstay before tacking in the narrow entrance of Newtown Creek. Under her new owner, W H Batten, she made a North Atlantic circuit in 1975–6, and a voyage to the Azores and back in 1979.

scientific and sophisticated anchor ever to have been devised, and sometimes with disastrous results, as may be seen in the table below where the German version is shown as the least efficient of all types tested. Also in some other versions the shank is so short that the anchor is difficult to break out. For these reasons it is wise when buying an anchor to specify a genuine CQR (as made by Simpson Lawrence) rather than a 'plough' anchor, a term which can cover a multitude of bastards.

The American-designed Danforth anchor (Plate 31A) has two flat pivoting flukes of large area placed close together with the shank between them; the stock lies across the crown, and the crown is so shaped that it tilts the points of the flukes downward. This anchor also cannot be fouled by its cable once it has dug in; it is neater than the CQR when stowed on deck as it lies almost flat, and on the bottom it bites in more quickly; its holding power is said to be a trifle less than that of the CQR, but one two-thirds the weight of a fisherman can safely be used in small sizes and one half the weight in large sizes. However, for the reason given above, I would recommend the 13·5 kilogram (30 pound) size as the minimum.

The Tri-grip anchor, a stockless type with three pivoting flukes, is a French invention. It is reported to dig in quickly, but I have had no experience with it, and some tests made with a prototype do not appear to have been very satisfactory.

The only advantage of the Admiralty stockless anchor, such as is carried by most naval and merchant ships, is that it will stow itself neatly in a hawsepipe, but since it relies largely on its weight it is of little interest to the yachtsman.

A new design of anchor, known as the Bruce, was developed for the purpose of anchoring oil rigs, and after some years of service in the North Sea came on the market in sizes suitable for yachts. At a glance it has a similarity to the CQR, but it has no moving parts, and it is not a plough. There are three flukes, the outer ones curving upwards (Plate 30E). Reports speak highly of it, and compare it favourably with the CQR; it is claimed that a shorter scope of cable may be used with it, but so far I have had no experience with this newcomer.

Tables showing the comparative holding power of different types of anchor can be misleading because so much depends on the nature of the holding ground, and for a cruising yacht's anchor to be reliable it must perform well on a variety of sea-beds. However, the following table, which was compiled from tests made by the staff of *L'Auto Journal*, gives the holding power in three types of bottom, and is therefore more reliable than most. The efficiency factor of each anchor, shown in the right-hand column, was arrived at by dividing the total resistance by the weight of the anchor, and this seems as fair a comparison as any.

Anchor	Weight		Distance anchor dragged before holding			Resistance in sand and mud		Resistance in sand and shingle	
	kg	lb	m	ft	in	kg	lb	kg	lb
Genuine CQR	7·3	16	1·4	3	5	425·0	937	327·5	722
Danforth	7·3	16	0·5	1	9	370·1	816	259·9	573
French Plough	10·4	23	1·6	5	3	524·8	1,157	29·9	66
Fisherman	11·8	26	1·0	3	3	249·9	551	210·0	463
Fisherman	8·6	19	1·4	3	5	130·2	287	59·9	132
Tri-grip	10·0	22	0·3	0	11	170·1	375	54·9	121
German Plough	10·0	22	Did not hold			24·9	55	10·0	22

Anchor	Resistance in clay		Total resistance		Efficiency factor
	kg	lb	kg	lb	
Genuine CQR	519·9	1,146	1,295·0	2,855	178
Danforth	445·4	982	1,075·0	2,370	148
French Plough	529·8	1,168	1,084·5	2,391	104
Fisherman	300·3	662	760·2	1,676	64
Fisherman	175·1	386	365·1	805	42
Tri-grip	140·2	309	365·1	805	36·5
German Plough	10·0	22	44·9	99	4·5

Every yacht should carry at least two anchors; a bower, which is the main anchor, and a kedge of about two-thirds the weight of the bower. A third anchor of the same weight as the bower may be carried as a standby in case the bower should get lost or a second heavy anchor be needed in an emergency. Some large yachts carry two bower anchors each on a chain cable of its own, and where the kedge anchor would exceed 27 kilograms (60 pounds) this is probably the best arrangement.

Cables

An anchor cable should be sufficiently strong yet easy to handle and stow, and preferably heavy enough to hang in a deep curve (catenary) from the bow of the yacht to the anchor, so that it will pull on the anchor ring in a horizontal direction and act as a spring; if there is no catenary the pull on the anchor will not be horizontal, and unless the cable has some elasticity the yacht may snub (jerk) on it each time a strong puff of wind catches her or each time she rises to a sea, and will put a severe momentary strain on the anchor and cable. Chain, flexible wire, or fibre rope can be used, but of these I consider chain is much the best, not only because of the above mentioned catenary, which it will provide, but because it will stow itself in the cable locker, and will take only a small space; it cannot be damaged by chafe, has a very long life, and because of the effort required to drag a bight of chain over the sea bed, a yacht will lie more quietly and take less room than one lying to a fibre rope cable. Chain should be galvanized and have short oval links, or stud links. If the links are too long, as they sometimes are in cheap chain, it is possible for one of them to get jammed across, and then a small strain may break it. When an excessive strain is put on a chain, the links lengthen a little and the sides pull in towards one another before breaking. With stud-link chain, where each link has a crossbar, the sides cannot pull together, so size for size it is stronger than short-link chain, but it is also heavier and is not available in sizes smaller than 11 milli-metres ($\frac{7}{16}$ inch).

Chain is measured by the diameter of the metal of the link, and is usually supplied in lengths of 27 metres (15 fathoms), each length is known as a shackle and is usually fitted with a large link at each end for joining purposes. However, chain can be provided in any length to order, and this obviates the need for joining shackles. It is advisable always to buy chain from a reputable firm, and for an additional charge the makers will arrange for a few links of the chain to be tested. Calibrated chain should be specified if it is to be handled by a windlass with a gipsy (known in the USA as a wildcat), for the links of uncalibrated chain some-times vary in length and will then not fit the recesses on the gipsy; to ensure a good fit it is best to buy both chain and windlass from the same firm. High tensile chain is not to be recommended, for although it has a high breaking load it may ultimately fail without previous signs of stretch. The following table gives the weight of various sizes of short-link galvanized steel chain together with the proof load, ie the strain that can be applied without distortion of the chain.

| Diameter of metal in link | | Weight | | Proof load | |
mm	in	kg/m	lb/15 fathoms	kg	lb
6·5	¼	1·1	67	725	1,598
8	5⁄16	1·5	97	1,190	2,623
9·5	⅜	2·2	135	1,700	3,748
11	7⁄16	2·8	168	2,280	5,026
12·5	½	3·5	223	3,000	6,614
14	9⁄16	5·0		3,800	8,377
16	⅝	6·0		4,700	10,362
20	¾	8·4		6,800	14,991

Chain should be stowed as low as possible so that its weight may act as ballast; to save space the chain locker, which should be immediately under the navel pipe, need not be built right up to the deck, and the chain may reach it by way of a wooden chute (Plate 31C) or plastic tube of a size in which it is impossible for the chain to jam. The locker should be easily get-at-able and its bottom be provided with a grating or drainage holes to let water escape into the bilge. If two bower anchors are carried and each has its own chain, the chains should be kept apart by a partition in the locker and each have its own chute. The navel pipe (the fitting in the deck through which the chain passes to the locker) should also be of ample size so that twisted links cannot get jammed in it. The metal cover provided will not make it watertight, and in heavy weather a small yacht can take aboard a lot of water through her navel pipe unless it is blocked with a rubber or cork bung split along its diameter and with a recess to fit the chain carved in each half of it. An alternative is to unshackle the cable from the anchor and tie to its end a rubber ball of slightly larger diameter than that of the navel pipe; the weight of the chain will hold the ball in position.

The inboard or bitter end of the chain will need to be secured in such a way and in such a position that it can easily be cast off in the event of the cable having to be slipped. All too often a shackle is used to secure the end to an eyebolt at the bottom of the locker where it is awkward to get at and its pin may be difficult to remove. It is safer to secure it with a synthetic fibre rope of such a length that the end link can reach the deck to be cut free there in an emergency.

Lengths of chain can be joined to one another either by a split link, which has two symmetrical halves to be riveted together, or by a chain-joining shackle (Plate 10G); the latter is much to be preferred as it is stronger and easier to do up or undo; it should be fitted with its bow forward. The pin of a chain shackle is oval and its head is countersunk so that it cannot get hitched up when the chain is running out; it is held by a wooden peg driven through a hole in one arm of the shackle which registers with a hole in the pin; elm is the best material to use as it swells quickly when wet and remains firmly in position. The shackle can be undone instantly by driving out its pin with a hammer and punch, the wooden peg being broken in the process. A D-shackle of a size a little larger than the chain is used for securing the chain to the anchor ring, its pin passing through the end link of the chain, not through the anchor ring. But as the CQR anchor has no ring the shackle must be reversed so that its pin will go through the hole in the shank made to fit it; since the shackle will probably not pass through the end link of the chain, two shackles back to back may have to be employed.

Insufficient scope of cable is the most common cause of anchors dragging; when using chain, three times the depth of water at high water should be veered, and more in strong winds or when there is a sea running. However, in depths exceeding 18 metres (10 fathoms) the proportion of chain may be less. Some means of marking the chain is necessary so that one may know how much has been veered. A common method is to paint a few links a different colour at, say, each 9-metre (5-fathom) point, but as this cannot be seen at night, and soon gets chafed off, I have found it better in a yacht without a windlass to mark each chosen point with a short piece of small line with one figure-of-eight knot in it at the first point, two knots at the second, and so on. These marks can be felt in the dark as the chain runs out. Some windlasses are fitted with meters which show how much cable is out.

Flexible wire rope is unsuitable as an anchor cable. Its only merit is that it is lighter than chain of equal strength, but it provides little catenary, its life is short, and as it needs to be wound on a drum of large diameter no space is saved. If, therefore, it is decided not to use chain because of its weight and/or high cost, one cannot do better than choose a nylon rope. Of course this provides no catenary, so to get a near horizontal pull on the anchor a greater length will have to be veered (at least five times the depth of water at high water), and to help with this matter and to avoid some chafe, the first 9 metres (5 fathoms) of cable adjoining the anchor should be of chain, and the nylon is best spliced round a thimble so that it may be shackled to the chain; the inboard end, where it passes over the stemhead roller, will need to be protected against chafe, possibly with plastic hose if it is in use for any length of time; in this connection it should be remembered that many yachts have become total losses, particularly in coral waters, due to nylon cables chafing through.

A nylon cable (in the USA it is often called a rode) has, in addition to lack of catenary and susceptibility to chafe, the following disadvantages: as it is not self-stowing, when anchor is being weighed the cable will have to be coiled or flaked down or wound on a drum; if it is of the braided type and is stowed below it will carry a lot of water down with it, and if it is handled by a windlass it will call for a hand to keep turns on the drum all the time. Because of the greater scope needed, a yacht lying to a nylon cable will require more swinging room and will sheer about more than one lying to chain because, even if there is a bight of the cable lying on the sea-bed it will offer little resistance through friction. Its merits are: great strength and elasticity, light weight, and low first cost. Every yacht requires a nylon cable for use when a kedge anchor has to be taken away by dinghy, or when anchoring in a great depth, when the length of chain hanging up and down would be hard to get aboard again because of its weight and the friction at the stemhead roller. When chain is being hauled in over the small-diameter stemhead roller such as is often fitted in production yachts, the loss through friction may be as much as half the power applied as against only 19 per cent when rope is used. The roller should therefore be as large as possible and probably glass-filled nylon on a stainless shaft are the best materials. The cheeks of the fitting should be carried well above the roller so that there can be no possibility of the cable jumping off, which is most likely to happen when at anchor in a strong wind in shallow water.

The following table gives suggested weights of CQR anchors for yachts of different LWL, together with appropriate chain cable sizes for sloop- or cutter-rigged yachts of normal type; a yacht which has more than one mast, or has high freeboard or considerable displacement, will probably need heavier ground tackle; this also applies to shoal-draught yachts, including multi-hulls, which tend to sheer about more and are therefore hard on their anchors.

LWL		Anchor		Chain	
metres	feet	kilograms	pounds	millimetres	inches
8·5	28	15·8	35	6–8	$\frac{1}{4}$–$\frac{5}{16}$
10·6	35	20·4	45	9	$\frac{3}{8}$
12	40	27	60	11	$\frac{7}{16}$
13·7	45	34	75	12	$\frac{1}{2}$

With Danforth anchors similar sizes are suitable, but these anchors are not made in exactly the same weights as CQR anchors, differing from them by about 2·3 kilograms (5 pounds). I repeat that, for the reason given earlier, I do not recommend the use of an anchor of less than 13·5 kilograms (30 pounds), no matter how small the yacht may be. The length of cable is not given in the table because this will depend not on the size of yacht but on the depth of water in which she will anchor, and except in a very small craft, where considerations of weight may make it undesirable, I would regard 55 metres (30 fathoms) as the minimum.

Windlasses and riding gear

Although it is possible to fit a windlass of sufficient power to make the handling of any weight of ground tackle easy, one has to remember that the more powerful a manually worked windlass is, the slower will it deliver the cable; speed is important, for once the anchor has been broken out the yacht will not be under complete control until it has been brought to the surface, and if she is got under way while it is still near the sea bed it might foul some obstruction.

A yacht of up to about 9 metres (30 feet) LOA will not require a windlass unless her crew is weak, and because of its weight and the space it needs she will be better without one, but she could with advantage be fitted with a chain pawl. This simple fitting consists of a strong pawl arranged immediately over the stemhead roller so as to hold the chain link by link as it is hauled in (Plate 31B); there is therefore no need to belay the chain at moments when the strain becomes excessive, and risk getting one's fingers hurt. When chain is to be veered the pawl is thrown over on its back and the cable paid out hand over hand.

In yachts exceeding 9 metres (30 feet) some mechanical assistance is generally considered to be desirable for weighing anchor. A handy-billy, or other form of tackle, may be clapped on to the cable with a rolling hitch when the strain is extra heavy in a strong wind or tide, or when breaking the anchor out; this has the merit that the foredeck is kept clear; but unless a chain pawl is fitted, the chain will have to be stopped off after each haul while the tail of the handy-billy is moved along it.

There are many models of windlass from which to choose (Plate 31), from the simple hand-operated type to the powerful hydraulic or electric kind which in the larger sizes may have two gipsies and two warping drums; for vessels of 15 metres (49 feet) or more these last are ideal except that an engine must be run to work the pump for the hydraulic type, and the electric type will put a heavy drain on the batteries unless a generator is kept running. Of hand-operated windlasses there are two distinct kinds; one is worked by turning a crank handle to rotate the gipsy through a train of gearwheels, the other by moving a lever fore-and-aft. The former usually delivers the chain more rapidly, but unless the spindle on which the handle is shipped is at least 0·6 metre (2 feet) above the deck a man cannot use his full strength on it. The ratchet type worked by lever is the best for small craft, for the windlass itself need be no more than 30 centimetres (1 foot) high, and the lever, which allows the work to be done in a standing position, is unshipped after use; in some models the lever is arranged to deliver chain only on one stroke, in others on both strokes and this is the best. A capstan, in which the drum and gipsy are mounted with their common axis vertical to the deck, and is rotated by worm or bevel gears, is heavy and inefficient and has little to recommend it.

Most windlass gipsies are fitted with a foot- or hand-operated clutch or brake to control the gipsy so that when the pawl(s) have been thrown back chain can be veered under complete control; but if the windlass has no clutch or brake the chain should pass through a compressor; this consists of an eccentrically-mounted roller moved by a lever; movement of the lever forces the chain down on to a bed and slows or stops it by friction. When sufficient cable has been veered, and there is no compressor, the clutch is engaged to stop the gipsy rotating, and the yacht is usually left riding to the chain on the gipsy. But there is a possibility that in heavy weather this might damage the windlass or cause the chain to jump. Rather than remove the chain and belay it on a samson post or other strongpoint, one can proceed as follows: make fast a length of nylon rope to the cable with a rolling hitch and belay its other end to a strong point; then ease the clutch so that the strain of the cable is transferred from the gipsy to the rope, then re-engage the clutch. If the nylon rope is of small size and is long enough it will by its elasticity act as a spring and prevent snubbing. An alternative way of preventing snubbing is to provide some additional catenary by lowering a weight down the cable, then before the yacht could snub she would have to pull back enough to lift the weight to a position directly in line between her stemhead and the anchor. But when riding out a gale in shallow water I have found a nylon spring more effective than a weight and a lot easier to rig.

When a vessel with a bowsprit is lying at anchor in a breeze the cable will grind against the bobstay each time she sheers in one direction. R R Vancil showed me how he overcame this with his *Rena*, and I have successfully used a modification of his method with *Wanderer IV*. The bobstay plate at the stem has a second hole in it just below the hole for the bobstay shackle, and into this I shackle a piece of nylon rope of about the same length as the bobstay. After the anchor has been let go and cable veered, the nylon rope is secured with a rolling hitch to the cable outboard of the stemhead roller; a little more cable is then veered until the yacht lies to the nylon rope with the chain above it quite slack. Like that the chain cannot touch the bobstay, and because the yacht is held by the low-down bobstay plate instead of the high-up stemhead roller, she sheers about less and lies more steadily. The arrangement has only one drawback: if one wishes to veer more cable, some cable has first to be hove in so that the rolling hitch may be reached and released. A devil's claw, a two-pronged hook to engage over a link of chain, may of course be used instead of a rolling hitch, but it is a tricky thing to make as it must be able to slip on or off the cable only when required to do so and not at other times.

A multi-hull at anchor tends to sheer about more than a mono-hull, but this can be reduced if she lies to a bridle. In the catamaran, having veered almost enough cable, a spring from the other hull is bent on to the cable with a rolling hitch, and cable is then veered until the strain is shared by cable and spring. The trimaran will need a spring from each float made fast to the cable at the same point.

Anchor work

In the days when we all used heavy and unwieldy fisherman-type anchors, the anchor was not left at the bows when under way except perhaps temporarily when, Brightlingsea fashion, it lay with its ring at the stemhead and its crown hauled up and aft and lashed to lie against the rail. Usually, and with the cable still secured to it, the anchor was brought aft as far as the rigging where it was secured with its flukes inboard and its stock outboard up-and-down a shroud. A man of average strength and ability could manage that with an anchor not exceeding about 22·5 kilograms (50 pounds). But for a larger anchor with its heavier chain a second hand might be needed as well as the assistance of the staysail halyard or an anchor burton, if the anchor was to be manœuvred aft and got partly inboard without damage to the topside. But the lighter and neater anchor of today is frequently left forward to rest partly on the stemhead roller, a position to which the CQR and the Bruce readily lend themselves (Plate 30D and E), and there it is lashed or wedged securely. The Danforth is not easy to stow in that manner, though it can be done (Plate 31A) and is usually brought inboard and lashed on chocks on the foredeck, or it may be stowed just below the deck in the covered anchor well with which some yachts are provided. If the anchor has to be lifted inboard, a short length of rope spliced to the ring or eye at the crown is a help; when the anchor has been brought to the stemhead one has only to catch up the short rope with the boathook and, hauling on it at the same time as a little cable is paid out, lift the anchor crown-first up over the rail and onto the deck. The procedure is, of course, reversed when preparing to let go, and a person of average strength and ability should be able to handle a CQR or Danforth of about 27 kilograms (60 pounds) in that manner provided there is sufficient space to pass it between or below the forward guardrails or pulpit. Methods of handling a kedge anchor will be found on pages 248 ff.

Buoying the anchor

The bottoms of many rivers and harbours are foul with the anchors and chains of moorings, some of them long since abandoned, and if his anchor should chance to hook on to one of these the owner may be put to considerable trouble or expense in recovering it, or the anchor and a length of cable may be lost. If the chain on which the anchor has hooked is a light one, it may be possible to heave it up within reach by means of the yacht's windlass so that a line can be passed beneath it to hold it up while the anchor is lowered away and cleared. But if it is too heavy, or is tightly stretched between two anchors, assistance may have to be sought from a boatyard which will probably have a barge capable of lifting the mooring. First, however, it will be worthwhile to try to clear the anchor by sailing or motoring over it from various directions with plenty of cable out.

To prevent such troubles an anchor should be buoyed before being let go in a place where the sea bed is suspected of being foul. To do this, bend one end of a light rope to the crown of the anchor and make the other end fast to a buoy of some kind with the words 'anchor buoy' painted on it so that it shall not be mistaken for a mooring. The length of the line should equal about twice the depth of water at high water, otherwise the buoy might get dragged under if the stream runs fast. A floating line should not be used as it might foul the propeller of a passing craft. If the anchor fouls an obstruction the buoy is taken aboard and its rope hauled on while cable is veered, and the anchor should come clear.

Moorings

A permanent mooring at the yacht's home port is a great convenience, for it saves the labour of weighing and cleaning two anchors and cables before every sail and of relaying them again afterwards; also, in a crowded yachting centre a mooring may enable the yacht to lie within reasonable distance of a landing-place where space would be too restricted to permit anchoring. If, however, there is room and cost is a consideration, a yacht may lie unattended on her own anchors quite safely, provided her ground tackle is good and is properly laid. For six years I kept a yacht on her own anchors in the Beaulieu River, weighing and relaying them every time I went sailing, and she came to no harm. But as the bottom there is mud they and their cables needed much cleaning. This was easy with the kedge, for I recovered it by under-running its rope cable with the dinghy, and scrubbed as I went. Since the yacht had no windlass I was able to leave the bower's chain cable on deck to be sluiced with bucketsful of sea-water after getting under way. Today in a larger vessel I have the luxury of a hose coupled to a sea-water pump, so the cable can be washed link by link before it reaches the stemhead roller, but to work the pump the auxiliary engine has to be run.

The simplest kind of mooring, and a satisfactory one provided that the bottom is soft and there is sufficient swinging room, is a single concrete block with a slightly concave bottom, and weighing about 22·5 kilograms (50 pounds) for every ton of the yacht it is to hold. Once this has sunk in, suction will hold it against a strong pull. The block must have a stout steel eye in its upper side to which the chain is shackled, and the total length of the chain should be not less than three times the depth at high water. It is usual to have the chain in two or three lengths, the lower piece being of considerable size so as to have a good catenary and leave a large margin for corrosion; it should be of such a length that its upper end can be reached at low water so that the swivel joining it to the next piece of chain can be examined for wear and corrosion and replaced if necessary. If no swivel is fitted, the chain will become twisted and shortened by the yacht swinging round the mooring; it would then be subject to an unfair strain, and in an extreme instance could hold the yacht's bow down as the tide rose. The riding chain, the upper piece which is to be made fast aboard the yacht, should be of a size larger than the yacht's bower anchor cable. A rope with a buoy at its end will be attached to the upper end of the riding chain so that the latter may be hauled up when the mooring is to be used; although it is not intended that the yacht shall ride to this rope, it should be of ample strength, for conditions are sometimes such that the buoy has to be picked up when the yacht is still making headway, thus subjecting the rope to a considerable strain before the chain can be hauled up and made fast. Its length should be at least $1\frac{1}{2}$ times the depth at high water.

A single mooring such as this cannot often be used at a yachting centre, for the yacht would take up more than her fair share of room, so a double mooring will be used. This consists of two weights or anchors joined to one another by a heavy ground chain of a length equal to six times the depth at high water. In the middle of the ground chain is a swivel to which the riding chain with its rope and buoy is shackled. If anchors are used instead of concrete blocks, each should be at least twice the weight of the yacht's bower anchor. Fisherman-type anchors with the upper arm cut off or bent down so that the fluke touches the shank, serve well and are cheap, but when being laid they must be lowered horizontally by ropes to make sure that they reach the bottom right way up. The pins of all shackles used in a mooring should be wired (not with copper wire) or better still have their ends burred over, so that they cannot work loose.

If space allows, the ground chain of a double mooring should be laid up and down stream so that the yacht pulls on one anchor on the flood and the other on the ebb, and a stranger anchoring near by is less likely to get his anchor foul of a mooring laid that way. But in a crowded place the local custom should be followed.

The most satisfactory kind of mooring buoy is one of plastic with a large upstanding eye or loop on top. Such a buoy is light and floats high, and its smooth surface is easy to clean. The yacht's name and size, under- rather than over-estimated, should be painted on the buoy.

It is sometimes difficult to get the thimble and shackle where the buoy rope joins the riding chain over the roller at the stem, and in some yachts it is necessary to take the chain through an enclosed lead or hawse-hole in the bulwarks. Rather, therefore, than shackle the rope to the extreme end of the riding chain, it is better to shackle it on 3·6 metres (2 fathoms) from the end; then, when the point of attachment has been brought within reach, the short end of chain can be led inboard and made fast, after which the buoy rope can be eased off. To simplify belaying, the end may be shackled back to form a loop which can be dropped over the samson post or bitts. It is customary to hang the buoy on the forestay; this is not only to give it a chance to dry out but to proclaim to any newcomer that the yacht is lying on a mooring.

A boathook is more often used for picking up a mooring buoy than for any other purpose, and for that a head with a double hook is convenient; but there are occasions when one has to push off from a slippery weed-covered quay on which the smooth curved back of the hook may slip; a head with a spike is then better, and the type which has a short spike projecting from between the double hooks is probably the best for all-round use; it should be securely fastened to the shaft not just with the usual screw but with glue. The other end of the shaft should be shod with rubber so that it may be used to push against another yacht's topside without causing damage.

The man who buys and lays a mooring is the owner of it; all the gear belongs to him and no one has any right to use it without his permission. This point does not appear to be clearly understood by everyone, for some people regard a vacant mooring as public property to be used by anyone who cannot find a convenient berth or wishes to avoid the bother of anchoring. It is an unfortunate fact that such people often disregard the tonnage figure painted on the buoy, and use a mooring which is too small for their craft, with the result that the anchors are dragged if the wind is strong, and the owner is put to the inconvenience of relaying them; others fail to get the riding chain aboard and therefore chafe the buoy rope. Generally an owner does not object to his mooring being used in his absence, provided it is not abused, for use will keep the buoy and buoy rope clean and free from weed; but the borrower should not leave his yacht unattended on it unless he has ascertained from a reliable source that the owner will be away for some time, and he must, of course, relinquish it immediately the owner requests him to do so, no matter how inconvenient that may be.

However he would be wiser to trust to his own ground tackle

than rely on a mooring the condition of which he cannot possibly know.

By laying a mooring the owner does not necessarily secure any prior right to that particular piece of ground or area of water; if, in his yacht's absence, another vessel should bring up so close to his mooring as to prevent him from picking it up or lying on it without a risk of collision, he has no right to order the other vessel to move, though a polite request will usually produce the desired result. But if his yacht is lying on her mooring (or her anchor), any other vessel bringing up afterwards must keep clear of her and not give her a foul berth, ie bring up so close as to touch her or any part of her gear under any conditions of wind and tide.

Nearly every yacht, with the possible exception of one with the owner living permanently aboard and continually moving from place to place, will have a berth at a marina or a mooring in her home port. In my view it is selfish in these days of overcrowding for an owner to have another mooring in, perhaps, his favourite or most frequently used anchorage, for that mooring will be obstructing an anchorage which others may wish to use.

In some places, harbour authorities have laid down moorings with large steel or wooden buoys, or have driven in piles, to which yachts may secure on payment of a mooring fee. They then lie moored stem and stern, and when in a river it is best to lie with the bow upstream because the ebb usually runs harder than the flood, and a yacht does not sheer about so much when lying head to tide. But if it is necessary to moor to a single large buoy, a bull-rope should be used to prevent the yacht from bumping into it and damaging herself when wind and tide are opposed. This consists of a line made fast to the ring of the buoy (in addition to the cable), rove through a block at the end of the bowsprit, and brought inboard where it is made fast with sufficient tension to keep the yacht away from the buoy. If she has no bowsprit, a spinnaker boom or other spar may be rigged out temporarily over the bow.

10

ENGINE AND BATTERY

The engine and its needs – The propeller – Outboard engine and sweep –
The battery

A RELIABLE auxiliary engine enables a yacht to maintain a
reasonable average speed in light winds and calms, and to enter or
leave harbour under almost any conditions of wind and tide; it will
assist her to get away from a lee shore, a tide race, or any other
dangerous situation, and it will allow her cruising range to be
extended with the certainty of being able to return to her home
port at the desired time. If, then, we consider that the main objects
of cruising are to visit a large number of places or cover many
miles in the shortest possible time and with the least physical and
mental effort, the engine must be regarded as the most important
item.

But much of the pleasure of cruising is to be had by getting the
best possible performance out of the yacht under sail in all conditions, and by overcoming any difficulties that are met by skilful
seamanship. Certainly the cruises most worth reading about, and
therefore most worth doing, are those which were undertaken by
yachts without engines, or during which the engines were used
only in calms when time was running short, for in cruising, as in
mountaineering (to which it is much akin) the easy way is not
always the most satisfying. Nevertheless the engine, and there are
very few yachts without one now, is a valuable part of the equipment, for it enables one to visit harbours which are too small or too
congested to permit manœuvring under sail without risk to one's
own vessel or others, and to berth at marinas which might otherwise be inaccessible, while even on an ocean passage it can be a
great help. I am glad to have had the opportunity of sailing
through the doldrums, those areas of calms and squalls, heat and
rain, which lie between the trade wind belts, for I feel it is an
experience every sailorman should have at least once in his
lifetime, so that he may learn to be patient and to appreciate some
of the difficulties with which his forefathers had to contend. But
having had that experience on several occasions, I now do not
hesitate to use the engine there, and on a recent crossing made
good in thirty-six hours of motoring what on an earlier voyage

under sail alone had taken two weeks to accomplish. Engines which can be relied upon have also enabled yachts to call at islands which have no sheltered anchorages, and which in the past sailing vessels visited only with considerable risk.

The engine and its needs

For normal cruising purposes one horsepower per ton of displacement should be sufficient – *Wanderer IV* (22 tons) requires no more than 18 horsepower to give her a speed of $5\frac{1}{2}$ knots in quiet weather. But if the yacht is to be capable of making good progress against a headwind and sea, or to reach her maximum hull speed under power (some owners feel this is essential) at least 3 horsepower per ton will be required. However, in this matter the size and pitch of the propeller have to be considered, for unless the propeller matches the engine (a decision made by designer or engine-maker) it cannot use the rated horsepower. One often hears proud owners making claims of remarkable fuel economy for their engines. These are unjustified, for any engine in good condition will consume almost exactly the same quantity of fuel for a given horsepower as any other engine of similar type. A diesel engine consumes approximately 225 millilitres (0·4 pints) of fuel per brake horsepower per hour, and it is by the quantity of fuel consumed (if this can be measured with sufficient accuracy) that one can discover how much horsepower the engine is providing; for example, a 40-horsepower engine burns something very close to 9 litres (2 gallons) per hour when it is delivering its full power; but if it burns only 4·5 litres (1 gallon) per hour at the same revolutions per minute it is providing only 20 horsepower; so either it is not running at full acceleration or, if it is, the propeller is too small or has insufficient pitch to absorb the full horsepower.

Power for power the petrol (gasoline) engine is lighter than the diesel engine, but the fire/explosion risk is very much greater; the cost of fuel and the consumption of fuel are higher, and since it depends on a spark for combustion, electricity is essential for its running, whereas the diesel depends for combustion on the heat generated by compression. However, it has to be admitted that because of its higher compression ratio the diesel (unless it is fitted with decompressors, and many are not) is impossible to start by hand and requires electricity for the purpose. In this connection we have to bear in mind that a battery in a partly exhausted condition can cause damage to the starter motor, which is not a continuously-rated machine, and may burn out if it has to crank slowly and excessively; so an hydraulic starter, or a hand-wound impact starter, if it can be fitted, might be preferable. The two-stroke petrol engine has the merits of light weight and mechanical simplicity, but as the lubricating oil has to be mixed with the fuel in a proportion suitable for full load conditions – usually 190 millilitres ($\frac{1}{3}$ pint) to 9 litres (2 gallons) – there is apt to be too much of it when running light, and this, combined with the fact that the operating temperature is then lower, tends to oil up the sparking plugs.

Since the engine is such an important item it should be looked after with the same consideration as any other part of the yacht's equipment, and no doubt the majority of engine failures are due to lack of this attention. Obviously the maker's instructions should be followed, but it may be worth noting here the major needs of any internal-combustion engine. They are: a sufficient supply of air and clean fuel, adequate lubrication, proper cooling, and an unobstructed exhaust. Given these requirements most engines will run indefinitely.

Provided the air filter is clean sufficient air is easy to arrange, for one has only to ensure that there is a proper vent to the engine compartment. Fuel supplied by a service station pump is normally filtered, but I would not bank on that in some countries, for example Mexico; it might therefore be wise always to fill the tank through a funnel provided with a waterproof gauze, and this is essential when fuel is taken, as it sometimes must be overseas, from steel drums, for these may contain rust and water. The tank should have a clear air-vent, and a sump where condensed water may collect, and a means of draining or sucking it out. But even with these precautions fuel may still be contaminated, so on its way to carburettor or fuel-pump it should pass through a primary filter consisting of a gauze and a sediment bowl, and then through a second filter bowl containing a paper element; these filters should be serviced and the element replaced with a new one at the intervals specified by the engine-maker, and when replacing the filter bowls, or any other part of the fuel system which may have been disturbed, it is essential that they seat properly, for if they leak an air-lock may form and the engine will be starved. With petrol, a fuel pipe led too close to a hot part of the engine can cause an air-lock.

Proper lubrication may seem obvious enough (topping up to the maximum mark on the dipstick with oil of the correct grade), but it is equally important to drain the sump and replenish with fresh oil at the specified periods. As the sump drain plug will almost certainly be out of convenient reach, a hand pump to suck the old oil out should be provided. At the same time the element in the oil filter should be changed. Although the oil in a diesel engine quickly turns black this is not necessarily a sign that it needs renewing.

Except with an air-cooled engine, which calls for proper ducting of an adequate air supply, the marine engine is cooled either by sea-water, or by freshwater which in turn is cooled in a heat exchanger. The former arrangement, in which a pump draws sea-water in and circulates it through the jacket, has the merit of simplicity, but saltwater is corrosive. With the normal heat exchanger two pumps are required, one for circulating the freshwater round the engine and through the heat exchanger coil, the other for pumping sea-water through the heat exchanger tank. But with a yacht of metal construction simple keel cooling can be employed. With this the hot water is circulated through a baffled tank, the sides of which are formed by the skin plating, where the heat is removed by convection. It is usual with freshwater cooling to mix drill oil or anti-freeze with the water to inhibit rusting.

Many an engine with its exhaust manifold below the LWL has been damaged by sea-water flooding back through the exhaust system, or even by water injected into the system for cooling and silencing purposes. To prevent this happening, the exhaust pipe should be carried in an inverted U as close up under the deck amidships as possible and then sloped down to the outlet at the stern; if water is injected into the system it should enter at the side of the inverted U farthest from the engine. Even with this, or one of the several variations, it is a wise precaution to fit a cock at the outlet and keep it closed when the engine is not operating. Alternatively an Aquavalve (as is used by boats towing water-skiers in Australia) might be fitted at the outboard end of the exhaust pipe (Plate 64D). It consists of a cage holding a light plastic ball which, when the engine is not running, is held against the outlet by a coil spring; but the spring must be of light gauge or it will create undesirable back-pressure when the engine is running.

As with most mechanical things an engine is all the better for being used, and even though its services may not be needed it is a good plan to run it for a short time at least once a week. This will dry out the electrical system, circulate the oil to prevent corrosion, and will ensure that when the engine is needed it will start readily. It is worth noting that the engines of the Royal National Lifeboat Institute lifeboats are run for a short time every day, a precaution taken to guard against the risk of the engines not starting instantly when urgently needed.

The propeller

A propeller is described by its diameter and its pitch, ie the distance it would move forward in one complete revolution if it had a solid grip on the water. Its direction of rotation is said to be right-handed if it turns clockwise when viewed from aft, and left-handed if it rotates anti-clockwise; the latter is the most usual direction of rotation for a marine engine, but some types of reduction gear may cause the propeller to turn in the opposite direction. A small propeller causes less drag than a large one when the yacht is under sail, so for purely auxiliary purposes, and if the highest possible performance under sail is desired, it is better to have a small propeller working at high speed rather than a large, slow-turning one, in spite of the fact that better driving power would be had by fitting a reduction gear and a large propeller.

In the past it was common to have the propeller shaft emerging from one quarter or the other, so as to avoid the need to cut a hole in the sternpost. But today this is rarely done, the shaft being on the centre line with the propeller in the space between keel and rudder, above the rudder, or in an aperture cut in the sternpost or deadwood. The aperture should not be cut in the rudder or steering will be difficult.

A major consideration is that the propeller should not cause unnecessary drag when the yacht is under sail and the engine is not in use. A two-blade propeller causes less drag than one with three blades if it is in an aperture or abaft some hull member and is held with its blades up and down, while it (and a three-blade propeller) will cause more drag if allowed to spin than if locked. But few people will choose to leave a propeller spinning because of the rumble of the shaft and the wear on it and its bearings, and with some hydraulic gearboxes damage may result if the propeller and its shaft are left free-spinning for any length of time. With the hydraulic gearbox the shaft will be stopped from turning by a brake, a mark on the shaft indicating when the blades of the two-blade propeller are up and down, but with other types of gearbox the shaft may be held from turning by putting the engine in gear.

To reduce drag to a minimum, a folding two-blade propeller is sometimes fitted; the blades are hinged on the boss so as to fold flat together, clam-like, when the yacht is under sail, centrifugal force throwing them out to the working position when the engine revolutions build up. There are also variable-pitch propellers with which the blades, when not in use, are swivelled on the boss into the fore-and-aft (feathering) position, which is at 90° to the neutral position, when the yacht is under sail; no clutch is required, but the shaft has to be bored longitudinally to accept the control rod. A disadvantage of a two-blade propeller is that it may cause vibration when in use owing to both the blades passing at the same time through the dead water immediately abaft the keel or sternpost, unless the latter is well streamlined.

Outboard engine and sweep

For a very small yacht the outboard has some advantages over the inboard engine. There will be no installation costs and no drag from aperture and/or propeller when under sail, for then the engine will be tilted with its propeller out of the water or be taken on board, and there will be great saving in weight. But the outboard will need to have a long shaft and it will take up just as much room as an inboard when stowed below, perhaps more, and it is liable to make a mess. Occasionally arrangements are made for using an outboard over the side amidships, where it will be less affected by pitching, but the special brackets needed to hold it there are a nuisance, and a danger to another yacht lying alongside. Sometimes it is placed in a well, but the drag caused by this is too great to be tolerated, and the most generally accepted position is over the stern.

No great effort is needed to keep a little yacht moving along by means of a sweep at 1 to 1½ knots in a calm and smooth water. It may be used over the side, the oarsman standing facing forward and leaning his weight on the loom of the sweep, the yacht being steered with the helm; the sweep should be well balanced so that little effort is needed to lift its blade out of the water. But if the cockpit is too small to allow the sweep to be used comfortably, one may scull with it over the stern (page 502) a rowlock being shipped in the taffrail for the purpose.

The Chinese yuloh is more efficient than a sweep for sculling provided that its proportions are correct for the yacht in which it is to be used, and they can only be arrived at by experiment. In effect the yuloh is a long sweep, curved or bent in the middle so that the part from blade to taffrail is at a steeper angle to the water than is the part from taffrail to loom. At the point where it is bent it is shipped on a pin, on the taffrail, on which it is free to pivot. Its inboard end is controlled by a lanyard to the deck. Its loom has only to be pulled and pushed to and fro athwartships, when the blade will automatically turn from one stroke to the next, and most of the energy applied to the handle will be utilized in driving the yacht forward.

When towing a yacht by dinghy the tow-rope should be as long as is reasonable, otherwise the dinghy will only jerk at it, but if the dinghy is small and light not much progress will be made; so if there is an outboard motor for the dinghy it will be better to use that, but not for towing; secure the dinghy alongside the quarter, run the motor and steer with the yacht's rudder.

The battery

For her navigation lights, if for no other purpose, the yacht will need electricity, and for this she must have a battery. Unless she will make only a very occasional night passage, when dry cells or a battery to be recharged ashore might serve, she will need some means of charging the battery on board.

There are two main types of storage battery, lead/acid and alkaline. Each cell of the former provides about 2 volts, and this does not drop appreciably until the battery is nearly discharged; but such batteries have a comparatively short life, perhaps something between two and eight years. As they give off hydrogen while on charge they should be stowed in a well-ventilated place. The alkaline cell provides only 1·2 volts, so a greater number of cells is required to provide a given voltage, also first cost is much higher; it is rarely used in yachts except those of large size.

If the current consumed by some item of equipment is known (this is usually marked on it in watts) together with the capacity of the battery in ampere-hours, it is possible to tell for approximately how long the battery will keep that item of equipment working. In theory a battery with a capacity of 100 ampere-hours could provide a current of 1 ampere for 100 hours, or 2 amperes for fifty hours, etc.

As one volt × one amp. = one watt,

$$\frac{\text{watts}}{\text{volts}} = \text{amps.}$$

Suppose, for example, the yacht has three navigation lights, each 12 watts, running off her 90 ampere-hour 12-volt battery. The total consumption will be 36 watts.

$$\frac{36 \text{ watts}}{12 \text{ volts}} = 3 \text{ amps.}$$

$$\frac{90 \text{ a/h}}{3 \text{ amps.}} = 30 \text{ hours.}$$

If, then, the lights are switched on for a total of 30 hours they will discharge the battery completely.

But it must be realized that no battery has an efficiency of 100 per cent, and that ageing reduces the capacity. A 100 ampere-hour battery will in fact not give 1 ampere for 100 hours even when new, and it will be found that when recharging the 100 ampere-hour battery a charge of at least 140 ampere hours will be needed. A battery slowly loses its charge when not in use, and the higher the temperature the greater is the loss; at 18 °C (65 °F) the loss is approximately 1 per cent per day, but at 38 °C (100 °F) it is as much as 3 per cent per day. If the battery remains uncharged for two or three months sulphation of the plates will result, thereby reducing efficiency; regular charging is therefore essential. The level of electrolyte (sulphuric acid 30 per cent and water 70 per cent) must not be allowed to fall below the plate separators, being topped up with distilled water or rainwater as necessary. The only satisfactory way of determining the state of charge of the battery is to test the specific gravity of each cell with a hydrometer. With most of these instruments the float is marked in three colours, perhaps red at the top, white in the middle, and green at the bottom. If the level of the sample of electrolyte, when drawn into the pipette, is in the red zone the cell is discharged, or nearly so; if it is in the white zone the cell is at half charge, and if in the green zone the cell is fully charged; the reading should be approximately the same for all the cells of one battery. If the hydrometer is marked with specific gravity figures, 1·280 indicates fully charged, 1·200 indicates half charged, and 1·113 indicates that the battery is in a fully discharged condition. However, these figures are valid only at 16 °C (60 °F) and require adjustment at higher temperatures.

There are two types of generator: dynamo and alternator. Both generate alternating current, which has to be rectified (converted to direct current) for the purpose of charging batteries; the dynamo does this mechanically by means of its commutator and brushes, while the alternator uses diodes (one-way electric valves) for the purpose. For use afloat the alternator appears to have every advantage: it is smaller and weighs less than a dynamo of similar output, it requires hardly any maintenance, and as it is effective over a wide speed range, a high output can be obtained at low engine speeds.

To avoid over-charging, the generator fitted to the marine engine is invariably provided with a control box or panel which, like that fitted in a car, automatically regulates the charge, high to start with, then tapering off so that the battery shall not be over-charged, for if the charging rate is too high the battery temperature will rise above the safe limit of 43 °C (110 °F) and harm will be done.

I am not convinced that this is the best way to charge a yacht's battery unless the engine is used for long periods of propulsion, for after the control has reduced the charging rate it is scarcely worthwhile to continue running the engine purely for the purpose of battery-charging, and if the engine is a diesel it will not when running with so small a load reach its proper working temperature, and that will do it no good. I therefore believe that if space can be found for it a separate charging plant, with which the charging rate can be controlled by hand, is desirable; this will enable the battery to be charged more quickly and without the need to run the auxiliary engine with a small load. But with such a plant it is important to know what the proper charging rate for the battery is because if this is exceeded the temperature of the battery will rise beyond the safe limit. Lucas/CAV, in their excellent booklet *Marine Electrical Systems*, give the formula, based on the 10-hour rate, as follows: Divide the capacity of the battery (in ampere-hours) by 10, and multiply by 1·4 (the battery efficiency factor); for example, the charging rate for a 100 ampere-hour battery is 14 amperes. During charging the specific gravity of the electrolyte will slowly rise, and will have reached its maximum when no further increase is detectable for three successive hourly readings, after which charging must cease.

Other means of charging batteries have been tried with varying degrees of success, among them solar cells, windmills, and free-spinning propellers. Solar cells are expensive, and large panels of them are required if they are to provide more than an ampere or so. I have met several yachts with windmills, but their owners reported that at the best they provided only 2 or 3 amperes on average. Charging by means of a free-spinning propeller would appear to be the most satisfactory of these methods. Aboard *Williwaw* the large three-blade propeller was connected by belts by way of a lay shaft (to get the required revolutions per minute) to an alternator, and this gave a charge of 25 amperes when the yacht was sailing at 6 knots. But, whereas a large three-blade propeller with its shaft locked may increase a vessel's resistance by 20 per cent, if it is allowed to spin but is not able to rotate at a sufficiently high speed – that might be the result of coupling a generator to it – the resistance could be increased by as much as a further 25 per cent. The maximum drag appears to be caused with a propeller speed of around 100 rpm. It would therefore seem that this method of charging a battery might have a considerable effect on the performance of a yacht under sail, and, as was noted earlier, could cause wear on shaft and bearings and damage to the gearbox, though *Williwaw* experienced no such troubles on her long voyages, which included a circumnavigation and a transit of the North West Passage.

The majority of yachts have 12-volt systems, and because of this there is a wider selection of electric equipment available to run on 12 volts than there is for the 24-volt system. Advantages of the 24-volt system are that a drop in voltage due to a long run of cable is a smaller proportion of the whole, and that equipment for the higher voltage – though often difficult to obtain – tends to be more robust.

At most marinas shore power of 110 or 240 volts alternating current is available, and many yachts make use of this through a suitable converter to keep their batteries fully charged.

Some notes on wiring, and on the risks of electrolysis will be found on page 36.

11

SOME NOTABLE YACHTS

Alano – Beyond – Kochab – Lone Gull II – Rena – Trekka – Tryste II – Wanderer III

In this chapter will be found the plans and some description of several cruising yachts which have made notable voyages, and with which I am personally familiar; some of them have provided the basis for considerable fleets of similar type. No stock design or mass-produced yacht has been included because of designers' reluctance to permit plans to be published, as was noted in Chapter 1. Even among this selection of older yachts it will be seen that in two instances perspective drawings (from which a yacht cannot be built) are shown instead of sets of lines to avoid the risk of plagiarism. However, a perspective drawing provides a very good likeness, indeed it may even give a better idea of the shape of the hull to those who are not accustomed to the reading of lines, because of its three-dimensional quality. Can you resist taking a second look at the fascinating view of *Beyond* as seen by a fish low down on the starboard quarter, to enjoy again the harmonious curves that speak so eloquently of sea-kindliness, buoyancy, and power, and visualize her forging her way across some wide ocean with the trade wind in her sails? I may be accused of partisanship because I have included in so small a selection three designs from the board of one architect; but these three are of widely different types, and I believe that more small yachts built to plans by the late Jack Laurent Giles have crossed oceans than have those from the board of any other British designer. The selection may serve to show that it is not so much the size and type of vessel that contributes to the success of a voyage as the seamanship, ability and staying power of the people who sail her.

Alano (Figs 26–8 and Plate 32)

When Fred Georgeson from the USA decided to dispose of his property there and live afloat, he came to England for a yacht chiefly because the cost of building here was less; he asked Rodney Warington Smyth, ARINA, to design for him the 10·8 metre (35½-foot) cutter *Alano* and had her built of wood by Falmouth

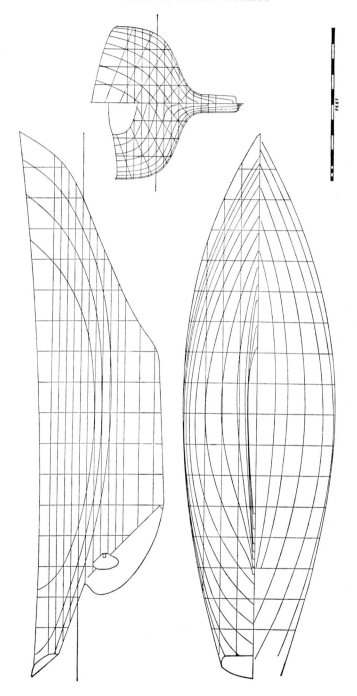

Fig 26 *Alamo*, Lines

LOA 10·8 metres (35·5 feet); LWL (8 metres (26·4 feet); beam 3 metres (10 feet); draught 1·7 metres (5·8 feet); displacement 7¼ tons.

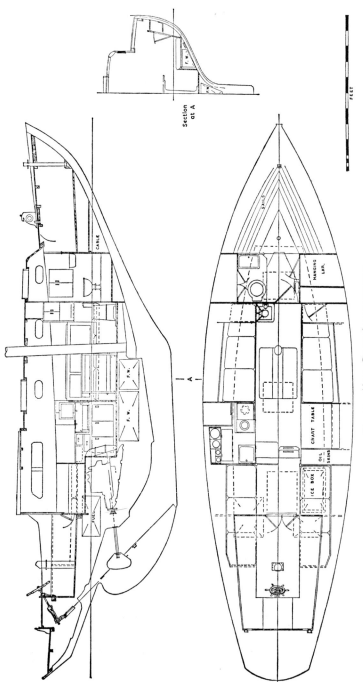

Fig 27 *Alano*, General arrangement

Boat Construction Company. I saw her while she was building and met her three years later at Gibraltar. In the meantime Fred and his wife, sometimes with a crew, sometimes alone, had sailed her from Falmouth to the Mediterranean and had cruised the full length of that sea, covering some 15,000 miles. They were delighted with her and had looked after her well.

Fig 28 *Alano*, Sail plan

With a beam of 3 metres (10 feet) on a waterline length of 8 metres (26 feet) her displacement of $7\frac{1}{4}$ tons is comparatively light, and her working sail area of 51 square metres (550 square feet) (maximum 665 square feet, 61·8 square metres) gives her a good turn of speed; but, as is inevitable with any yacht which is a floating home, and must therefore contain all manner of things beyond a yacht's normal equipment, she floats a little low on her marks when she has to carry in addition the stores and water needed for a long voyage; and that was her condition when I saw her, for she was just about to start on her first crossing of the North Atlantic.

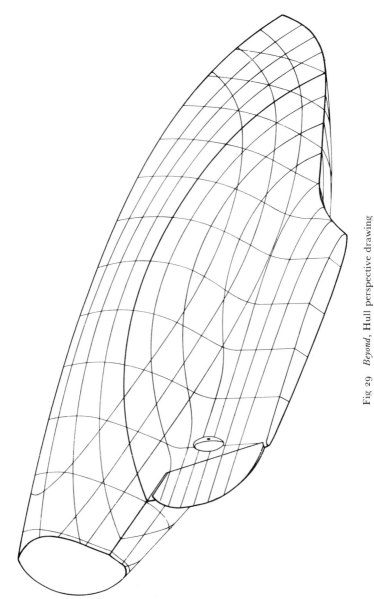

Fig 29 *Beyond*, Hull perspective drawing

LOA 13 metres (43 feet); LWL 9·7 metres (32 feet); beam 3·2 metres (10·6 feet); draught 2·1 metres (7 feet)

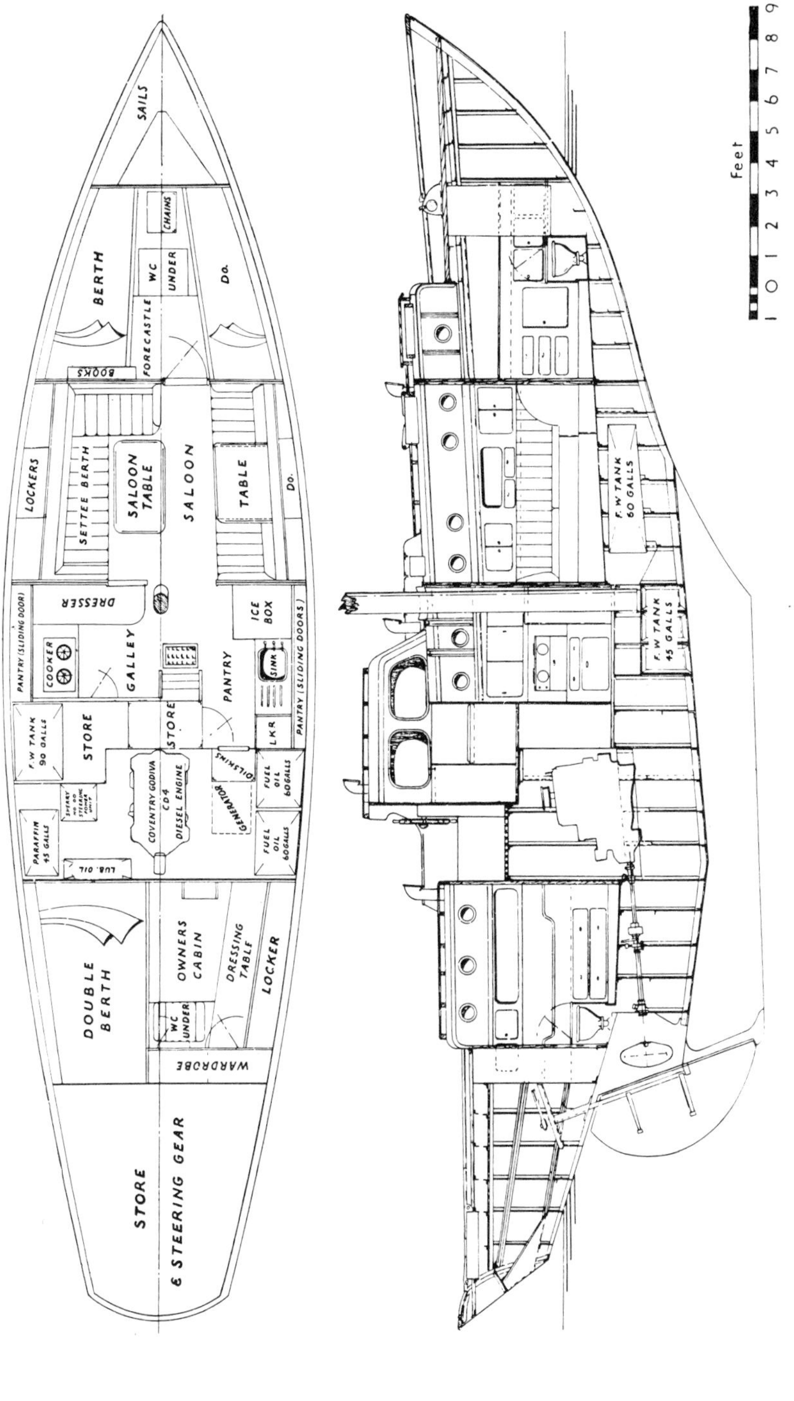

Fig 30 *Beyond*, General arrangement

There can be little doubt that in a yacht of this size the cutter rig is more suitable than the sloop for short-handed cruising; and with roller reefing for the mainsail, and the staysail on a boom, *Alano* proved to be easy on her crew even in the Mediterranean, where calms alternating with strong winds are common. She has a range of 400 miles at 6 knots under her 35-horsepower Perkins diesel engine.

For some time the Georgesons did charter work in the West Indies, and for this *Alano*'s general arrangement proved to be suitable, the charterers having the saloon with its two berths and direct access to the heads, while the owners occupied the quarter berths, which are separated from the saloon by galley and chart space and a curtain if desired. The large self-draining cockpit is an asset when day sailing in the tropics, for when at anchor meals may be eaten there at the portable table beneath the awning, and two people can sleep on the seats, which, like those in many American yachts, are fitted with portable cushions.

Beyond (Figs 29–32 and Plates 33 and 49)

An outstanding voyage of the early 1950s was that of the 13-metre (43-foot) auxiliary cutter *Beyond*. In her the late Tom Worth and his wife Ann made an efficient and seamanlike voyage round the world in two years and two months. For the first half, by way of Panama to New Zealand, they were accompanied by Peter Taylor and his wife; but the Taylors decided to settle in New Zealand, and the Worths were alone for the arduous homeward voyage by way of the Great Barrier Reef, Torres Strait, and Suez. This received little publicity, which is, perhaps, as the Worths would

---

PLATE 23 (*facing*). *A*. Open drum halyard winches in use with fibre ropes. *B*. A wire halyard needs a winch provided with a brake, and it loses power as the sail is hauled aloft because the turns of wire building up on the drum increase its diameter. *C*. The gate in a mast track should be just high enough to permit all the mainsail slides to be accommodated below it. *D*. A short length of duplicate track on the lower part of the mast permits the trysail slides to be inserted before the mainsail is lowered, a switch leading them into the main track after the mainsail is down.

PLATE 24 (*overleaf*). *A*. A hinged boom gallows which will lie down on the counter when not in use. *B*. Where the boom is comparatively short, as in this yawl, the top of the doghouse may be the best position for the gallows. *C*. A single crutch which ships into sockets in the cockpit. *D*. This gallows has telescopic legs which are extended when in port and held in position by pins. *E*. Under way the pins are withdrawn and the crossbar drops to half its height so that the boom is well clear of it. The high mainsheet horse provides a good anchorage for the guardrails and keeps the sheet clear of them.

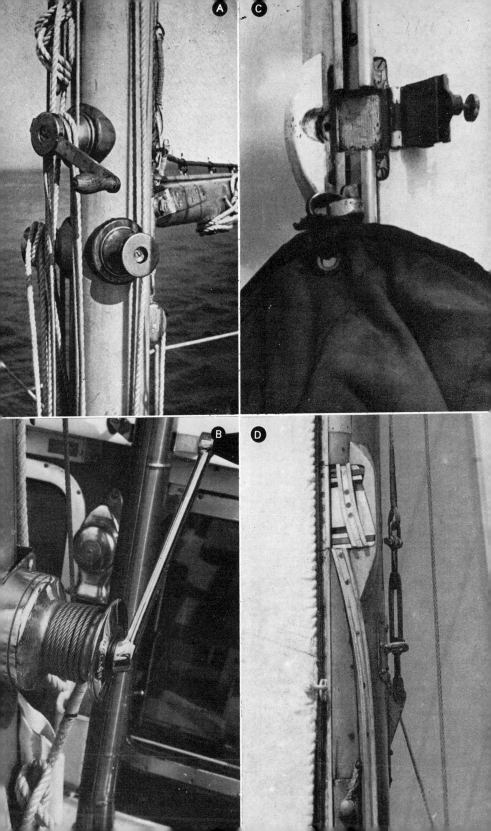

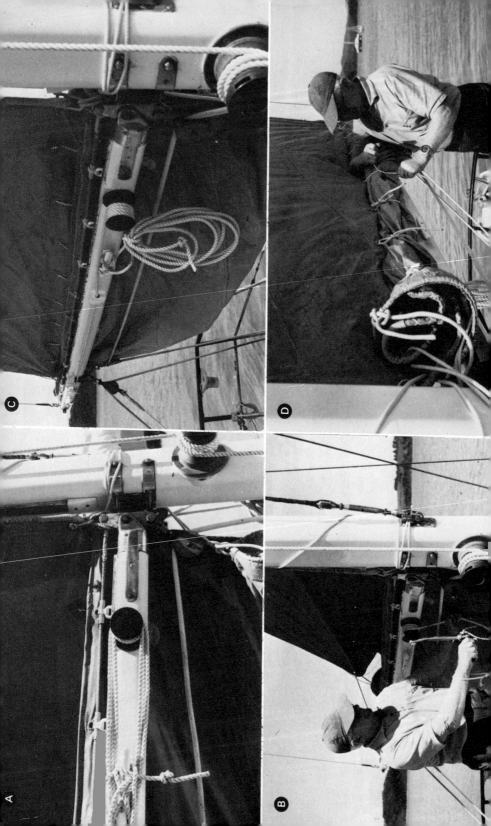

wish, but for it they were awarded the premier British cruising trophy, the challenge cup of the Royal Cruising Club, which had previously been awarded to Muhlhauser in *Amaryllis* and O'Brien in *Saoirse* for their circumnavigations. Everything went according to plan, the ship equalled every expectation, and the Worths obtained the utmost pleasure and satisfaction from the whole great enterprise.

Beyond was designed to incorporate her owners' special requirements by Laurent Giles & Partners of Lymington, as a fast, medium-displacement type of vessel, safety and sea-kindliness being the first considerations, and she was built by the Sussex Shipbuilding Company at Shoreham, the hull entirely of Birmabright light alloy, and the main deck and internal joinery work of Burma teak. She was insulated below deck with an asbestos spray.

At the time she was built it was unusual for a sailing yacht to have a central cockpit; but this position was partly dictated by the fact that she was to have a diesel motor and big-capacity tanks for fuel and water, and it permitted these heavy weights to be placed in the best of all positions, amidships. One might suppose the central position to be wetter than the aft position when the wind is forward of the beam, but here the doghouse (Plate 33 *top*), in which are the compass, automatic helmsman, and chart table, gives good protection to the helmsman on that point of sailing, and the only time that water was shipped in the cockpit was when running before a gale off Portland Bill at the very end of the circumnavigation. Tom was an engineer, so naturally his ship had a good share of gadgets and mechanical devices, but the principle

---

PLATE 25 (*overleaf*). A. Turner's ratchet reefing gear. B. Here the mast track is carried aft on a tapered pad to lead the lower slides fairly to the boom when the sail is rolled down. C. This gooseneck is on a track and can be hove down by the tackle beneath it. D. The foot of this sail is held in a groove in the boom, which helps the sail roll down neatly. The gears shown at B, C, and D are of the powerful enclosed worm type, and in the two lower pictures have guards to stop the sails creeping forward while being rolled.

PLATE 26 (*facing*). Reefing. A. The halyard has been eased away while the reef cringle on the luff of the sail was secured to the boom, and then set up taut again. B. The reef cringle on the leech is being hove down by its pendant, which leads to a small winch, and as the handle has no locking device a safety line round the wrist is used (after one handle had been lost overboard). C. The leech cringle has now been hove right down to the boom, and the pendant made fast round winch and cleat. D. Tying the reef points to gather up the foot of the sail, which otherwise would blow about and possibly fill with rain or spray.

was that these were for added comfort, ease, or convenience, and
should they all go wrong he would still have a normal, well-found
ship.

The plans show how well the accommodation was arranged for
a complement of four to live in comfortably in the tropics or in
home waters, with its large stowage space for all the stores needed
for a long voyage, together with tanks to hold 682 litres (150

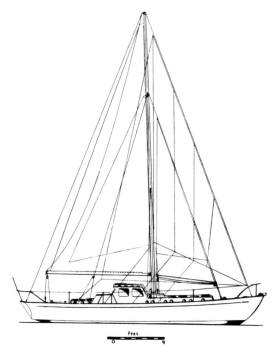

Fig 31   *Beyond*, Sail plan

gallons) of fresh water, 546 litres (120 gallons) of diesel oil – giving
the yacht with her 22 horsepower Coventry Godiva engine a range
of 1,400 miles at an economical cruising speed of 4·5 knots – 204·5
litres (45 gallons) of paraffin and 91 litres (20 gallons) of lubricating oil, as well as 0·07 cubic metres (2½ cubic feet) of refrigerated
space. And all this was done on the comparatively moderate
displacement of 11¾ tons, thanks to the powerful lines of the hull
and the light-alloy construction.

The all-inboard cutter rig with mainsail, staysail, and No 1 jib
has an area of 70 square metres (750 square feet), and there is no
sail larger than can conveniently be handled by one man or

woman. For running in the trade winds she carried twin sails with a combined area of 70 square metres (750 square feet) (Plate 49).

In this fine little ship there are many brilliantly conceived and carefully worked-out details, such as the combined boom gallows, mainsheet horse, and after bollards; the projecting fairlead forward to keep the anchor cable clear of the stem; the closing lifeboat-type fairleads for warps; the double coachroof and wheelhouse tops with air spaces to keep the accommodation cool; the motor-cycle saddle for the helmsman; these and many others have now been widely adopted.

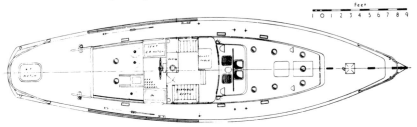

Fig 32 *Beyond*, Deck plan

From the original *Beyond* design Laurent Giles & Partners developed the popular centre cockpit *Salar* class, of which many have been built in Britain, Australia and New Zealand.

Kochab (Figs 33–5)

It is not uncommon for yachts to be specially designed and built for people who intend to make ocean passages, but it is rare for a yacht to be designed and built for a person who has already gained wide experience in blue-water sailing and who intends to make further voyages. When that does happen the resulting plans and the yacht that materializes from them are of particular interest and value.

In 1949–50 Dr I J Franklen-Evans with one companion sailed the 10-metre (33-foot) yawl *Stortebecker III* from England to New Zealand. Two years later and with two companions, he sailed the same yacht from New Zealand north-east across the Pacific to British Columbia. By then he had come to the conclusion that *Stortebecker* was too small for a complement of three to live in comfortably, and that passage-making with only two people in a yacht which would not readily self-steer, except under twin running sails (this was before vane steering gear had been perfected),

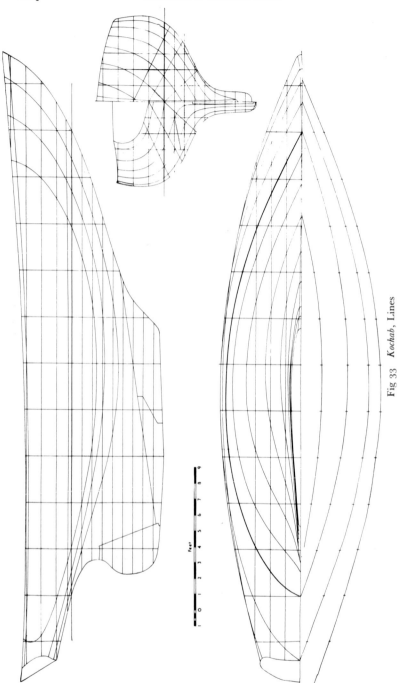

Fig 33　*Kochab*, Lines

LOA 12 metres (39·4 feet); LWL 8·8 metres (29 feet); beam 3·2 metres (10·5 feet); draught 1·8 metres (6 feet).

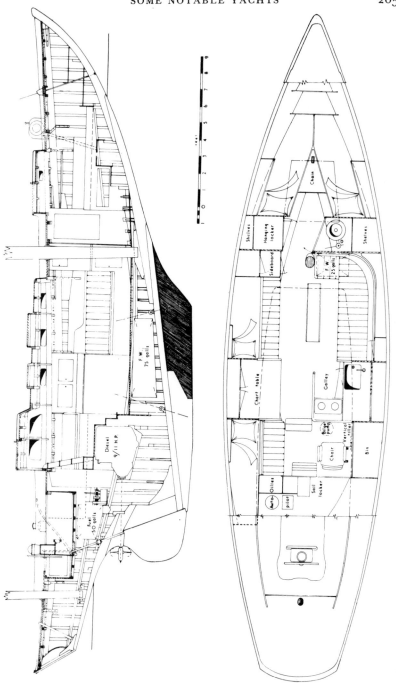

Fig 34 *Kochab*, General arrangement

was too exhausting. So he decided to have a larger yacht built, not only to permit a crew of three to live aboard and cruise in comfort, but also to enable passages to be made more quickly, and to carry the stores needed without being overloaded. The length of the new yacht was not to exceed 12 metres (40 feet), and she was to be capable of being sailed single-handed if necessary; she was to have

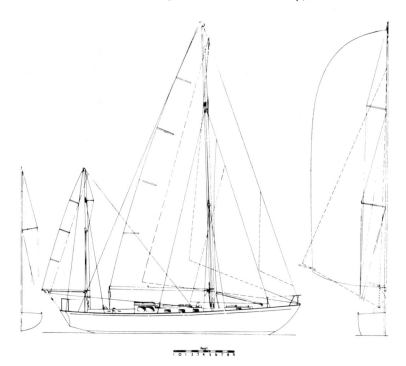

Fig 35   *Kochab*, Sail plan

a comfortable motion, and be able to steer herself. Additional requirements were that she should be absolutely watertight when battened down, and that she should go well to windward on a moderate draught, so as to be able to beat through narrow passes. An unusual feature is that two sling bolts are fitted to the keel so that the yacht may be lifted by crane or ship's derrick for scrubbing and painting in places where there is insufficient range of tide and no slip is available, the two parts of the sling passing out through the skylights.

For the design he went to Arthur Robb, a New Zealander who came to England in 1936, and until his death in 1969 was one of the foremost yacht designers. The yacht was built by Herbert Woods at Potter Heigham, Norfolk, in 1956, was christened *Kochab* (a star of the constellation Ursa Minor), and in the autumn of that year set out straight from her builder's yard on a voyage to New Zealand. She took part in the Honolulu race on the way, and after some fast passages arrived safely at her destination. She subsequently returned to England and again sailed out to New Zealand.

To keep the mainsail of a manageable size for single-handed sailing, and to permit the use of a mizzen staysail, yawl rig was chosen. It will be noticed that the mizzen mast, unlike so many of its kind, is not pushed right aft but is in a position where it can be properly and independently stayed. Both main and mizzen backstays are set up by levers close to the helmsman. With a light wind on the beam, when working sails are inclined to flog and do no work, they can be taken in and the yacht sailed under genoa and mizzen staysail only, a combined area of more than 46·5 square metres (500 square feet) of light sailcloth. On a reach a total sail area of 123·6 square metres (1,330 square feet) can be set, and for running there is a masthead spinnaker of 93 square metres (1,000 square feet). In addition there is a pair of twin running sails with a total area of 41·8 square metres (450 square feet).

Kochab's owner commented:

Her motion is never violent, and I would say she is dry, but close-hauled in a seaway plenty of spray comes aboard, and with a quartering sea we get an occasional crest that strikes just aft of amidships and sometimes fills the cockpit. In bad weather she has always been well behaved, and I think we could keep her sailing in most conditions. She heaves-to in moderate winds, force 3–4, quite well, but in strong winds we have always taken all sail down. She lies a-hull in force 6–7 with the wind abeam, or with her head slightly down wind; in force 7–9 she is reasonably comfortable and lies with her head slightly up into the wind. We have had a staysail set in these conditions but it was of no real advantage. The yacht herself is admirable and is just the right size for two to handle; with a good, steady wind she will easily log 160 miles a day, and is capable of 180.

Lone Gull II (Figs 36–9)

Besides being well known and respected as editor of *Yachting Monthly* for many years, Maurice Griffiths, GM, ARINA, has made a great name for himself as a designer of shoal-draught yachts. *Lone Gull II* is of particular interest as he designed her for

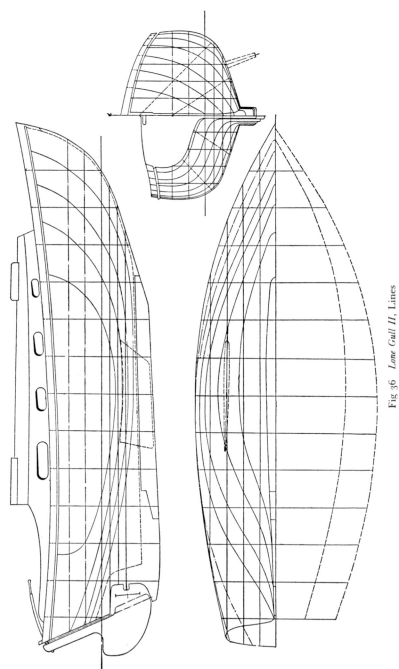

Fig 36 *Lone Gull II*, Lines

LOA 8·5 metres (28 feet); LWL 7·3 metres (24 feet); beam 2·7 metres (9 feet); draught 1 metre (3·3 feet); displacement 4½ tons.

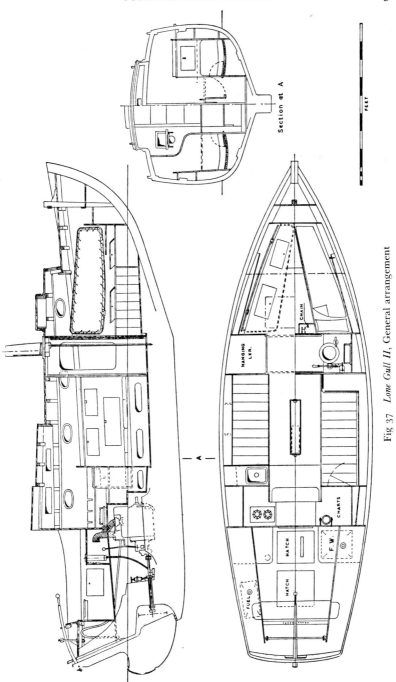

Fig 37 *Lone Gull II*, General arrangement

his own use, and gave her bilge keels instead of a centreboard so that she might sit upright when taking the ground in the shallow creeks which he loves so well. She was built of teak and mahogany on rock elm timbers by Harry Feltham, Ltd, at Portsmouth.

The yacht quickly exhibited two characteristics which are of particular value to the cruiser. The first is an almost uncanny ability to hold her course unattended for long periods even when

Fig 38   *Lone Gull II*, Sail plan

running, and this is something which one does not usually associate with shoal-draught vessels. The second was a refusal to build up a rhythmic roll under any conditions of wind and sea. Commenting on the latter quality, Maurice says that although the bilge keels undoubtedly help as roll-dampers, just as did the anti-roll chocks fitted to some steamships in the past, he believes that the deliberately flattened parts in the bow and stern sections (much larger in area than the bilge keels) are chiefly responsible.

Each bilge keel is formed of three streamlined planks, 11·4 centimetres ($4\frac{1}{2}$ inches) wide at the top and tapering to a fine trailing edge. The bottom plank of greenheart is fastened with socket bolts to the middle plank so as to be easy to replace should it become damaged. The upper two planks are through-bolted to heavy bilge stringers with oak partners, which cover three adjacent planks beneath the stringers and between the frames, making a very strong assembly to withstand the shocks of grounding. The bilge keels are not weighted, the ballast of 2 tons being carried on the main keel in the orthodox manner, with 226·8 kilograms (500 lb.) of inside ballast for trimming.

The mast is in a tabernacle, and a winch on the mast has a gipsy for handling the chain, which stows itself in a locker at the after end of the forecastle. The built-up topsides amidships (another

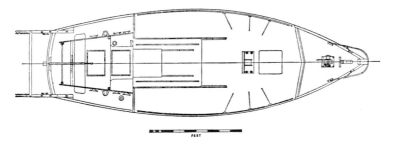

Fig 39   *Lone Gull II*, Deck plan

characteristic of MG's designs) and the wide cabin sole permitted by the flat floor, help to make her a remarkably spacious and comfortable vessel in which to live and cruise.

The stowing of a dinghy on deck always presents something of a problem in small yachts but the designer has overcome the difficulty in a manner which, although common among the trading vessels of the Baltic and elsewhere, is unusual in small yachts: he arranged for a pair of stout wooden davits to be built out over the stern (Fig 39), and carried the dinghy athwartships in them. These davits also provide good anchorage for the twin backstays and guardrails.

Although *Lone Gull II* was designed expressly for shoal-water cruising, some replicas have made extensive cruises, and I have met several of them voyaging happily in the South Pacific.

Rena (Figs 40–2 and Plates 34 and 35)

I first saw this 14-metre (46-foot) ketch moored fore-and-aft in the Pontinha at Madeira, rolling very gently in the swell; but the next time we met she was lying absolutely still above her own reflection in a tiny tree-shaded Florida lagoon, with a gangway rigged to the

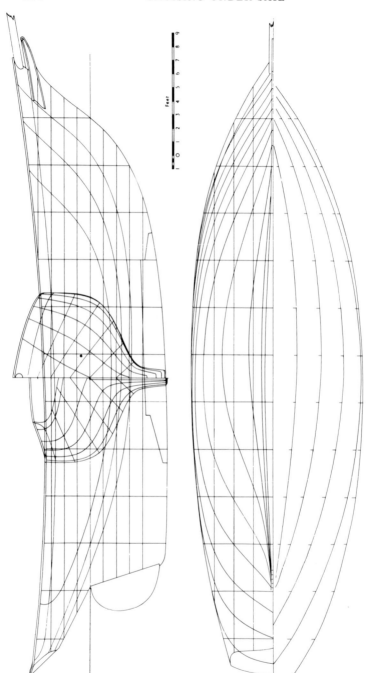

Fig 40   *Rena*, Lines

LOA 13·8 metres (45·6 feet); LWL 10·6 metres (34·8 feet); beam 3·8 metres (12·7 feet); draught 1·8 metres (5·9 feet); displacement 18 tons.

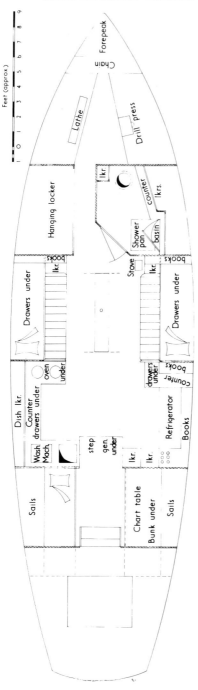

Fig 41 *Rena*, General arrangement

near-by lawn; on our third meeting she was at anchor in the lee of
a low, scrub-covered Bahama island. On each occasion I considered her to be one of the most beautiful yachts I had ever seen.
As beauty lies in the eye of the beholder, I know that everyone will
not agree with my perhaps old-fashioned opinion, but to me that
clipper bow with its carved trailboards and upthrust bowsprit, the

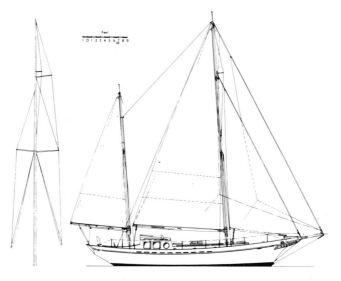

Fig 42   *Rena*, Sail plan

bold sheer, and the neatly tucked-up counter stern, are quite
perfect in their sea-kindly grace and harmony. I noticed, too, the
smaller details of rig, gear, and hull: the rake of the masts, the
snug-fitting sailcoats, the immaculate deck and sides, the golden
shine of the brightwork; all combined to make what the American
press might call a 'million-dollar luxury yacht'. But *Rena* was
nothing of the sort, she was the practical, floating, cruising home
of Commander Vancil and his wife, and the whole of her hull and
accommodation, all her sails, and most of her fittings, including
even the barometer and washing machine, and the automatic
helmsman, were fashioned by the Vancils with their own hands
and no outside help. After Vancil, a pilot and engineer, had
retired from the US Navy he and his wife Jo vanished for a time
from social life; they rented a field beside the intracoastal
Waterway at Great Bridge, Virginia, threw up a shed, and for four

years, seven days a week from 6 am to 10 pm, they worked to make their dream come true.

The design comes from John G Alden & Co of Boston, Massachusetts, a firm which understands so well the need for a cruising yacht to possess some character. Here we may see how a clipper bow, which in Britain is almost forgotten, but in America shows signs of increasing popularity, should be drawn. It makes not only an attractive but a good, practical end for a cruising yacht of this size, and with its bowsprit permits 99 square metres (1,064 square feet) of sail to be carried without unduly tall masts or excessive overlap; how well the stern matches it, and how firm are the sections to enable the yacht to stand up to her canvas with a draught of less than 1·8 metres (6 feet).

After the hull had been completed it was sheathed all over, including deck and coachroof, with GRP to reduce maintenance, and the masts and booms were treated in a like manner. A handsome curved bipod was built instead of the single spar bowsprit shown on the sail plan. The Vancils worked out their own general arrangement plan, and some may criticize this because of the large area of 'wasted' space at the after end of the saloon; but often something which may look wrong on paper proves to be correct in reality, and so it is here, and a wonderfully generous impression of space and comfort has been achieved. The engine is a Sheppard 50 horse-power diesel.

Trekka (Figs 43–5)

In the early 1950s a number of very small yachts were built to take part in coastal races. A few of these made notable voyages; the Laurent Giles-designed 6·1-metre (20-foot) cutter *Sopranino*, for example, crossed the North Atlantic in 1951 by the southern route, sailing from the Canary Islands to Barbados, a distance of 2,700 miles, in 28 days. But it would not be correct to assume that only then did very small craft start making such long passages; between 1877 and 1903, for instance, the North Atlantic was crossed from west to east by at least ten craft with an overall length of 6·1 metres (20 feet) or less.

The 6·4-metre (21-foot) *Trekka* is of the same type as *Sopranino*, and in hull form is little more than a large sailing dinghy with a fin keel added after construction; she is a particularly interesting example of what one might presume to be the smallest practical ocean cruiser; indeed, many people might consider her to be a lot too small. She also was designed by Laurent Giles, and was built at Victoria, BC by her owner, John Guzzwell.

Although she is very little longer than *Sopranino*, her displacement is just double that of the earlier boat; this is largely because she was given thicker planking to withstand possible collision with floating logs in Canadian waters. An essential feature of both

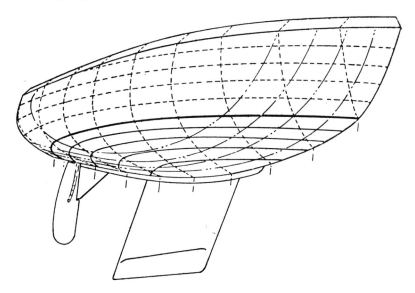

Fig 43   *Trekka*, Hull perspective drawing

LOA 6·3 metres (20·8 feet); LWL 5·6 metres (18·5 feet); beam 2 metres (6·5 feet); draught 1·4 metres (4·5 feet). (Drawing by courtesy of the editor of *Yachts and Yachting*.)

craft, and one to which their designer attached great importance, was that they should be, so far as possible, unsinkable; this was achieved by having watertight compartments at bow and stern capable of floating the little vessels even if their central portions should become flooded. Reverse sheer, which can sometimes be hideous, and in a larger yacht often has little to commend it, is the only practicable method of making habitable so small a vessel as *Trekka* without resorting to excessive freeboard at stem and stern, but, as may be seen here, when reverse sheer is drawn by an artist it can be pleasing to the eye. An unusual feature is that the upper few inches of the topsides are canted inboard to minimize a boxy appearance, but at the same time, of course, reducing the deck area a little.

In such a craft it is of the first importance to keep the weight down to the minimum, and here the construction has been cleverly devised to that end. Permanent plywood bulkheads act as moulds and are tied together with the bunks and other internal parts to make a light, rigid, and strong framework. The laminated keel and the steam-bent timbers are of oak, and the skin planking is of 1·4 centimetre ($\frac{9}{16}$-inch) red cedar, edge-glued. The hull and

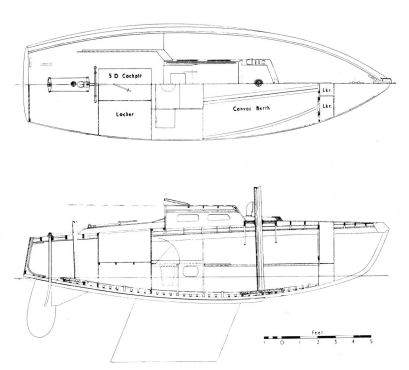

Fig 44   *Trekka*, General arrangement

plywood deck are covered with GRP. The fin keel and rudder skeg are of 1-centimetre ($\frac{3}{8}$-inch) steel plate through-bolted to two lengths of angle-iron bolted to the wood keel; the angle irons run from the forward end of the fin to the after end of the rudder skeg, and no doubt help to stiffen the yacht longitudinally. The fin with its bulb weighs 589·7 kilograms (1,300 pounds) and can easily be removed without touching any bolts through the hull if the yacht is to be transported overland. *Trekka* was rigged as a ketch to make her more readily steer herself in the days before vane gear was available. The working area is 17 square metres (184 square feet), but with the masthead genoa and mizzen staysail set, the area can be increased to 31·6 square metres (340 square feet).

In September 1955 this miniature cruiser, deeply laden with provisions for 60 days and 109 litres (24 gallons) of water in plastic

Fig 45   *Trekka*, Sail plan

bottles, left Vancouver Island with her owner/builder as sole crew, and made a perfectly executed and trouble-free voyage around the world by way of the Cape and Panama, and was the smallest vessel ever to have done so. Since then, under new ownership, she has made a second circumnavigation.

Other yachts have been built to the *Trekka* design, notable among them the sloop-rigged *Tarema* (Plate 38 *left*) and the slightly larger ketch-rigged *Manuiti II* (Plate 38 *right*). The former was built in Tasmania, the latter in New Zealand, and both have wide-ranging Pacific voyages to their credit.

Tryste II (Figs 46 and 47 and Plates 36 *left* and 51 *bottom*)

As was mentioned in Chapter 1, many fine voyages have been made in multi-hulls, but few have been so far-ranging or carried out in such an efficient and trouble-free manner as those of the 12-metre (39-foot) trimaran *Tryste II*. While lying at San Diego, California, in 1969 my wife and I had the good fortune to meet her

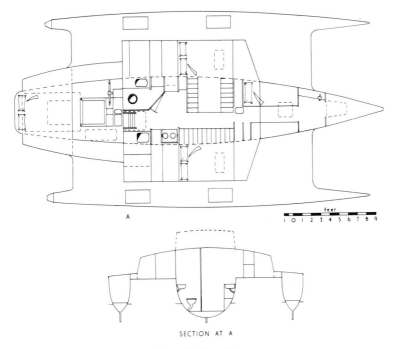

SECTION AT A

Fig 46   *Tryste II*, General arrangement

LOA 12 metres (39·3 feet); beam 6·2 metres (20·4 feet); draught 0·6 metre (2 feet).

and her owners, Ernie and Val Haigh, who were sailing with four of their five school-age daughters. They had built the yacht, a modification of Hadley Nicol's *Cavalier*, in a barn on Saltspring Island BC, taking two years over it. My wife and I were impressed by the space in her homely saloon and the modesty of her owners, but we had no idea of the great voyage about to be started; this proved to be a circumnavigation of the globe by way of New Zealand, Torres Strait, the Cape, and Panama; it took five years, including much time spent in Australian and South Pacific waters, one trip from New Zealand to New Caledonia being carried out by Ernie single-handed. In 1977 Ernie and Val once more left Canada and made an 18,000-mile one year to the day circuit of the Pacific, again calling at New Zealand, where again we met them.

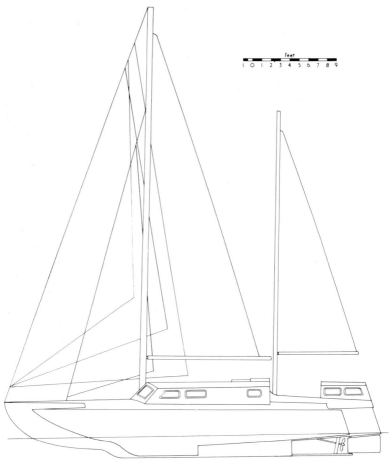

Fig 47   *Tryste II*, Sail plan
Working sail area 59·5 square metres (640 square feet).

Apparently the lines were never fully drawn, and the hulls (three diagonal skins of 5-millimetre ($\frac{3}{16}$-inch) fir) were built on moulds provided by the designer. Laden for a voyage with, among much else, 455 litres (100 gallons) of water, the yacht drew 13 centimetres (5 inches) more than the designed 61 centimetres (2 feet); nevertheless her passage times were by no means slow, eg Cocos Keeling to Rodriguez, almost 2,000 miles in 12 days, and her best day's run was 205 miles. No great use was made of the 36-horsepower Perkins engine, but running slow this could give a range of 240 miles on the 136 litres (30 gallons) of diesel fuel carried. In early days the common weakness of trimarans showed up: working at the joins where cross-members and floats were married, but after Ernie had strengthened these in New Zealand the trouble did not occur again.

It is common for people to put all they have into just one voyage and then swallow the anchor, but not so with the Haighs. Just as I was about to write this in a Canadian marina Ernie and Val came to call, and on being pressed they admitted that they were planning yet another long voyage in their well-proved *Tryste II*, but unlike some other planners they preferred to talk about it not in advance but when it is a *fait accompli*.

Wanderer III (Figs 48–50 and Plate 37)

When my wife and I decided to have a yacht built in which to attempt a voyage round the world, we went for plans to Laurent Giles & Partners, the designers of our previous yacht, *Wanderer II*, and of the 7·6-metre (25-foot) Vertue class, which I regard as one of the finest of small cruisers. A number of outstanding blue-water voyages have been made in these little yachts, notable among them being Humphrey Barton's crossing of the Atlantic by the intermediate route in *Vertue XXXV* (Plate 36 *right*), Hamilton's voyage from Hong Kong to England by way of the Cape of Good Hope in *Speedwell of Hong Kong*, John Goodwin's voyage in the same little vessel from England to the West Indies and Cape Town, and Bill Nance's wonderful single-handed voyage in *Cardinal Vertue* round the world east-about by way of Cape Horn. We wanted an overall length of 9 metres (30 feet), and it so happened that Jack Giles had already drawn the plans of a yacht of that size which we all agreed would most nearly suit our purpose. So, after some modifications and a different general arrangement plan had been made, we got William King of Burnham-on-Crouch, Essex, to build to that design.

The hull is of heavy displacement type (7 tons) with all the ballast (3 tons of lead) on the keel. Apart from size, the most obvious differences between it and that of the Vertue class are that the latter has a greater proportion of beam to waterline length,

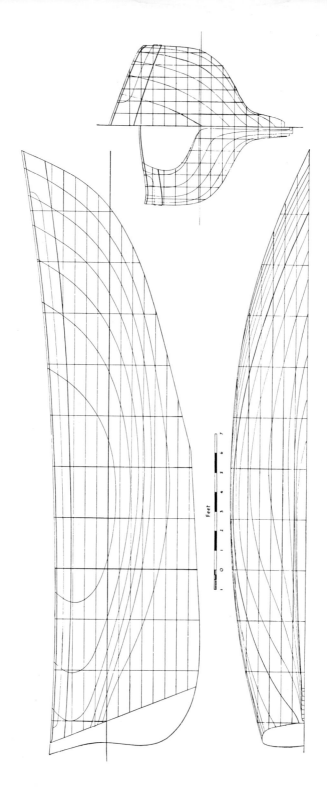

Feet

Fig 48 *Wanderer III*, Lines

LOA 9·2 metres (30·3 feet); LWL 8 metres (26·3 feet); beam 2·5 metres (8·4 feet); draught 1·5 metres (5 feet).

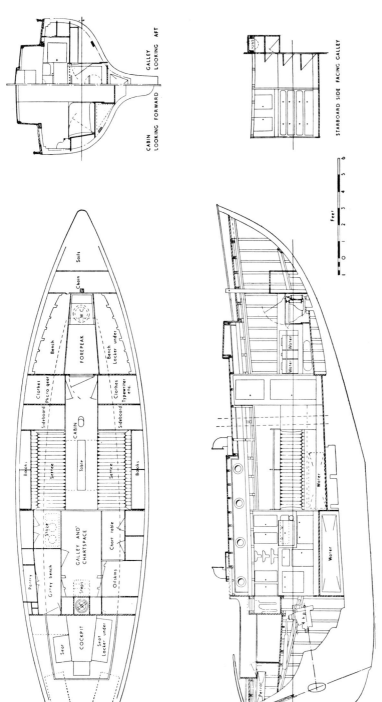

GALLEY
LOOKING AFT

CABIN
LOOKING FORWARD

STARBOARD SIDE FACING GALLEY

Sails

Chain

WC

FOREPEAK

Bench

Clothes

Sideboard Photo gear

Locker under

Bench

Clothes Typewriter etc.

Sideboard

CABIN

Settee

Books

Table

Settee

Books

Pantry

Stove

GALLEY AND CHARTSPACE

Galley bench

Chart table

Oilskins

Seat

COCKPIT

Seat Locker under

Step

Water

Water

Water

Water

Feet

0 1 2 3 4 5 6

Fig 49 *Wanderer III*, General arrangement

exactly one-third, and greater rake to the sternpost. It was hoped that *Wanderer*'s more vertical sternpost might assist her to steer herself, but I now realize that this has little bearing on the matter, while it has the disadvantage of increasing the wetted surface.

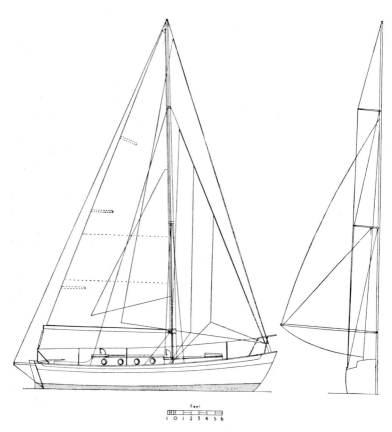

Fig 50   *Wanderer III*, Sail plan

As the new yacht would have to carry a considerable weight of stores, water, and gear, the freeboard of the original design was increased, and this proved to be a fortunate precaution, for when she was launched she was 15 centimetres (6 inches) down on her marks, due to the fact that the available West African mahogany – a light timber which had been specified for planking – was of such poor quality that iroko, a heavy timber, was used instead. Fortunately the increased displacement had no effect on performance beyond making her a little slow, and in light winds she could do with more sail than her maximum of 55·8 square metres (600 square feet).

The coachroof provides sufficient headroom in the galley/chartroom, so that there is no need for a doghouse, and it is therefore possible to carry a 2·3-metre (7½-foot) dinghy in the best of all places, amidships abaft the mast, where, as there is no skylight, it steals neither light nor air from the accommodation. The cockpit is self-draining, and the only water to get below enters through the hinged lid of the lee cockpit locker.

Below deck the arrangement is unusual in having only two berths; there is a large amount of locker space, and the galley/chartroom, where the most important work is done when at sea, is of considerable size. It may not be obvious from the plan that the chart table extends right out to the ship's side beneath lockers which are arranged above it, or that there is stowage space beneath it in drawers and lockers for 400 Admiralty charts. Forward of the sideboards over the feet of the settee-berths, lockers extend out to the side of the ship and up to the deck; they are fitted with shelves for clothes, typewriter, photographic equipment, etc, and ventilation holes enable them to share in the natural forward-moving flow of air. In the forecastle are the heads, chain locker, rack for water cans, a bin locker, and room for all sails.

The yacht was launched in March 1952, and, after a trial cruise in Irish waters, my wife and I set out in July of that year on a west-bound voyage round the world. We sailed by way of Panama, New Zealand, Australia, Torres Strait, and the Cape of Good Hope, and returned home within three years, having made good some 32,000 miles. In the summer of 1959 we set out on a second circumnavigation by a route which differed from the earlier one in many respects, and again took three years over it. In 1965–7 we made a two-year trip to the East Coast of America, bringing *Wanderer*'s total sea mileage up to about 110,000. In 1978 she completed her third circumnavigation (there cannot be many yachts of her size to have done that) in the capable and loving hands of Giselher Ahlers from Germany. She is a fine small cruiser, and never caused us any anxiety, but I formed the opinion that greater beam and more spread-out ballast might have made her motion easier. Apparently Laurent Giles & Partners thought so too, for they subsequently produced such a design with a beam of 2·8 metres (9·3 feet) on a 7·5-metre (24·5-foot) waterline, and a number of yachts, known as the Wanderer class, have been built to this.

PART II

Seamanship

12

MANŒUVRING

Getting under way – Reaching – Running – Sailing close-hauled – Turning to windward – Running aground and getting off – Bringing up – Mooring – Manœuvring under power

MANY people have learnt to sail in dinghies, and there is some truth in the saying that if you can sail a dinghy you can sail anything. But this method of approach can be discouraging, especially for the not-so-young, because of the physical difficulties of sailing small open boats which, in the hands of the inexperienced, may easily ship water or capsize. I consider that the beginner will learn to sail more quickly in a larger craft with a deck to keep the water out, a ballast keel to prevent capsizing, and a cockpit in which to be secure while he concentrates on what he is doing. From the very first he will be able to cook his meals, sleep aboard, and be independent of the shore, thus starting his cruising career straight away.

If possible the first few outings should be made with an experienced sailor – for the gregarious there is a plethora of sailing schools – but before going afloat for the first time he would be well advised to read something about the handling of sailing craft, and this chapter is written in an attempt to give the basic information. It should, however, be understood that seamanship cannot be learnt from books or lectures alone; it is an art that can always be improved upon, with something fresh to learn each time one goes afloat. That is one of the fascinating things about sailing; there is no finality, for conditions are never quite the same, and the older we become the more clearly do we realize the limitations of our skill and knowledge. But that should not deter anyone from taking up sailing late in life, for with a little concentration and in a comparatively short period of practical handling, the novice can acquire sufficient knowledge to enable him to keep off the mud, avoid collisions, and make reasonably good progress in the desired direction; it is on the finer points of helmsmanship and seamanship that a lifetime can be spent attempting to reach perfection, and in learning the peculiarities of different vessels, for few perform alike.

Getting under way

For the sake of simplicity it will here be assumed that the yacht is rigged as a sloop, ie with a mainsail and single headsail and no runners, and that she is steered with a tiller; the mizzen of a ketch or yawl, or the foresail of a schooner would be treated in much the same way as a sloop's mainsail.

Any yacht which is free to swing by the bow to an anchor or a mooring will lie head to wind so long as there is no tidal stream; but if there is a tidal stream running past the yacht it will have more effect upon her than the wind has, unless the wind is strong and the tide is very weak. A yacht with normal or deep draught will tend to lie head to tide, or nearly so, no matter from which direction the wind is blowing, though the wind on her hull and rigging may cause her to sheer about, especially if it is blowing directly against the run of the tide. A yacht with shallow draught or a fin keel will sheer about more wildly and will swing to the wind when the tide starts to ease earlier than one with a long keel or deeper draught.

The way the yacht lies in relation to the wind will decide the procedure for getting under way. If she is lying with the wind ahead or forward of the beam, set the mainsail first and ease its sheet if necessary so that the wind will be spilt from it. Then set the headsail, and if you wish to get away on, say, the port tack, ie to sail with the wind on the port side, put the rudder to starboard (helm or tiller to port) so that the tide, acting on it, will sheer the yacht's head to starboard; immediately it does so back the headsail, ie sheet it to windward by hauling in its port sheet, and slip the mooring. Finally, sheet the headsail to leeward, letting go its port sheet and hardening in the starboard one; also harden in the mainsheet if that has been eased, so as to get the yacht sailing. If there is no tide running, the rudder cannot be used to give the initial sheer in the desired direction unless the mooring is dropped and the yacht is allowed to gather sternway, when the rudder will have to be reversed; but by setting the headsail and holding its clew out to port (if you are going off on the port tack) the bow of a modern type of yacht can nearly always be made to pay off. A yacht with a long straight keel may, however, show some reluctance to pay off, and if there is not enough room to make use of sternway she may have to be assisted to do so by taking the mooring buoy outside the rigging to what is to be the weather quarter (the port one in this instance); then, with the clew of the headsail held out to port, cast off the mooring chain from forward and haul on the buoy rope from aft; this will cant her head the right way, and as soon as the headsail has filled the buoy can be let go.

When getting under way from an anchor with the wind ahead or forward of the beam, set the mainsail first, as before. Should the presence of nearby craft or some other obstruction make it essential to go off on a particular tack, heave in the anchor cable until it is up-and-down (vertical). Then set the headsail and back it. When the yacht's head begins to pay off in the appropriate direction, the anchor must be broken out smartly and got up to the stemhead without delay. Sometimes the anchor, having a good hold, will not leave the bottom at the desired moment, and before it has been made to do so the yacht may have come round on to the wrong tack. In that case stop heaving as soon as it is obvious that she is going about, and if necessary veer a little cable to ensure that she does not lift the anchor herself on the wrong tack. If the anchor is buoyed (see page 179) and the buoy can be reached with the boathook, the anchor may be broken out at the right moment by heaving on the buoy rope.

If it does not matter on which tack the anchor breaks out, the easiest method of getting under way, and certainly the best if there is a lee shore close astern, is to sail the anchor out. To do this, set the mainsail and headsail before hauling in any cable. Back the headsail so that the yacht pays off on either tack, then haul in its lee sheet and keep the helm up (tiller to windward) a little so that she begins to sail, and as she forges ahead haul in the slack of the cable. Very soon it will come taut; catch a turn with it round the samson post and it will pull her head round on to the other tack. Sheet the headsail to leeward, keep the helm up a little, and as she forges ahead on that tack the cable will slacken again and you will be able to haul some more of it in before it becomes taut once more and pulls her bow round again. Continue in that manner, and as the yacht approaches her anchor the tacks will grow shorter until eventually she will sail right over her anchor and, provided you catch a turn with the cable the moment she does so, she will break it out of the ground. There are two points to recommend this procedure: the yacht does most of the work and all the time she is sailing farther away from the lee shore. If she is fitted with a windlass or a chain pawl, there will, of course, be no need to take a turn with the cable at the end of each short tack; all you will have to do is haul in the slack and let the pawl hold it.

When the wind is abeam or abaft the beam, the mooring must be slipped or the anchor weighed before any sail is set; if a sail were to be set first, it would fill with wind and drive the yacht over and round her cable, making it extremely difficult to cast off the mooring or weigh the anchor. Get the mainsail ready for setting in advance with the topping lift set up, the halyard shackled on, and all but one of the tiers cast off; bend on the headsail and have it ready for setting, or set it in stops (p. 165); then let go the mooring or break out the anchor. If the mainsail is needed to extricate the yacht from some awkward position it may have to be set the instant she is under way, but if there is room to leeward, it will be best to run clear of the other craft in the anchorage under headsail only and find a clear space before setting the mainsail.

It is a mistake to think that if the wind is abeam the mainsail can be set before getting under way, for the lower aftermost shroud will prevent the sail from going right out at 180° to the wind, and that is the only position in which the wind can be spilt completely from it. But if necessary an exception may be made for a gaff sail in a light or moderate wind, and it can then be set with the boom topped up and the peak lowered so that it will not hold much wind.

It sometimes happens that though one may have picked up a mooring or anchored in a clear berth, later arrivals have brought up so close that there is not room in which to manœuvre under sail and get clear. One of the following suggestions may then be of use. If there is a clear way out astern, but no room in which to turn under sail, the yacht may be swung on her mooring by casting it off from the bow and hauling it in aft before setting any sail; but except in a very small craft or one which is riding to a fibre cable, an attempt to weigh anchor over the stern is likely to be difficult or impossible without damaging the rail, for there is unlikely to be a

---

PLATE 27 (*facing*). Maurice Griffiths has made a great reputation for himself as a designer of shoal-draught yachts. *A. Barcarole*, one of his bilge keel designs, on the hard at Burnham-on-Crouch, and *B, Gooney Bird*, built in Fiji for John Harrison, here seen sailing in her tropical home waters. *C.* A small Rayner-designed bilge-keeler squats happily on the beach at Yarmouth, IW.

PLATE 28 (*overleaf*). Two famous yachts, both built of steel. *Top:* The 16-metre (53-foot) ketch *Williwaw* was designed by Louis Van de Wiele, and in her Willy de Roos circumnavigated the Americas by way of the North-west Passage (the first yacht to thread that icy waterway) and the Horn. *Bottom: Joshua* in which Bernard Moitessier made many fine voyages, including one from Moorea to Alicante (14,216 miles in 126 days) during which he developed his special heavy-weather technique (page 375).

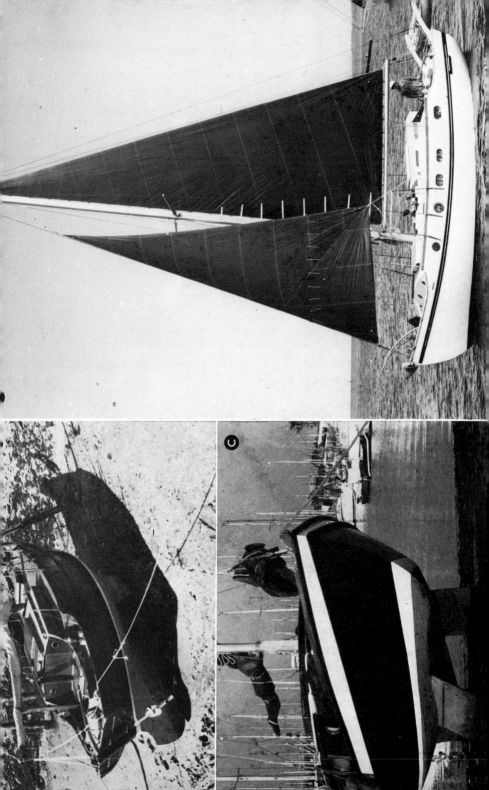

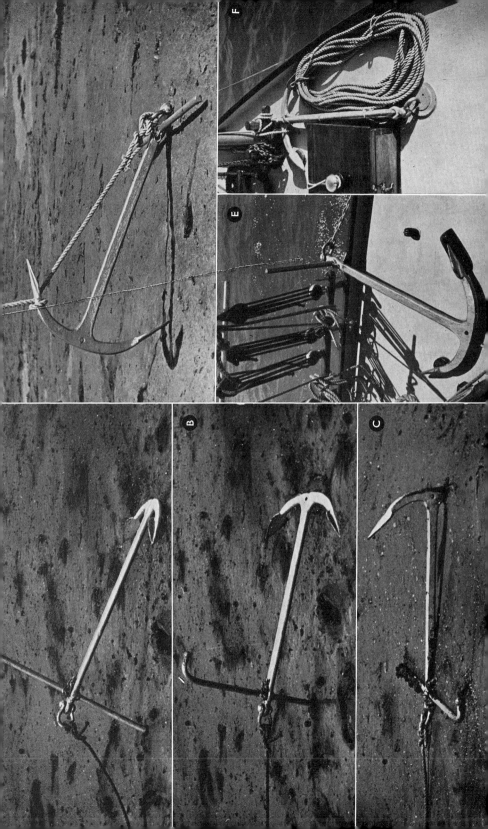

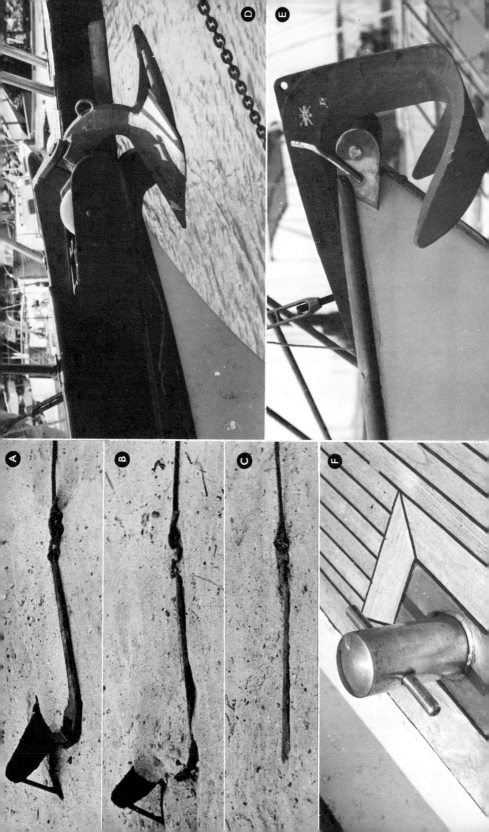

suitable lead for the chain. An alternative would be to ask permission to run a line off to one of your neighbours; then you can weigh the anchor or slip the mooring, drop astern of your neighbour, set what sail you need, and slip from her. This, however, is a situation in which most people would prefer to use the auxiliary engine.

Reaching

A vessel is said to be reaching when she is sailing with the wind abeam or forward of the beam, but not so far forward as to compel her to sail close-hauled with the sheets hard in. If she is nearly close-hauled but with her sheets just started (eased off a trifle), she is said to be on a close reach, but if the wind is abeam or nearly abeam she is said to be on a broad reach, and such a wind is often known as a soldier's wind.

Steering on a reach requires little skill, for one has only to keep the yacht on her course, steering either by some landmark or by the compass. For most yachts it is the fastest point of sailing, each sail drawing to the best advantage and none backwinding or being blanketed by another, but the sails must be properly trimmed. If their sheets are eased too much, the sails will shake and fail to do their full work, but if they are hardened in too much, some of their forward drive will be lost and the yacht will make excessive leeway. The correct trim can be found approximately by easing the sheets until the luffs of the sails start to lift or shake and then hardening them in just a little more than is necessary to fill them properly and put them to sleep. The yacht should carry a little weather helm, ie the tiller should have to be held slightly up to

---

PLATE 29 (*overleaf*). *A.* A fisherman-type anchor lying on its side. *B.* As the stock is longer than the chord, the anchor is unstable when lying on its side and a horizontal pull on the ring will cause it to turn over so that *C* one of its flukes bites into the ground. *D.* A foul anchor. If this happens, a pull on the cable will lift the lower fluke from the ground and cause the anchor to drag. *E.* An anchor stowed abreast the main rigging with its flukes in wooden chocks on deck and its stock in a vertical position outside the rail. *F.* An unstocked kedge anchor stowed on chocks alongside the fore hatch. The kedge cable is lashed beside it.

PLATE 30 (*facing*). *A.* A CQR anchor lies on its side when it drops to the bottom. *B.* As soon as a strain comes on the cable the anchor, which has a weighted tip to its fluke, starts to dig in and turns over on to an even keel until *C*, nothing is visible except the shank, and it is therefore impossible for the cable to foul the anchor. *D.* A CQR anchor stowed at the stemhead; a large-diameter roller for the cable (here it is of white nylon and the upper part of it can just be seen) much reduces the power needed to weigh anchor. *E.* The Bruce anchor has no moving parts and was developed for use with oil rigs. *F.* This stainless steel bollard is welded to the steel deck on which the teak planking is laid; for use with a chain cable it would be better without the pin.

windward to keep her on her course; but if she carries excessive weather helm (assuming that her hull is balanced), either the mainsheet has been hardened in too much or the headsheet has not been hardened in enough. If she carries lee helm the reverse is probably the cause.

A little weather helm is a desirable feature in any sailing vessel; it gives life to the tiller, enables the helmsman to feel how his craft is sailing, and if caught in a squall she will tend to come head to wind (luff) and thus ease herself. A yacht which carries lee helm is dangerous, for in a squall she will tend to turn away from the wind (bear away), thus increasing the pressure on her sails, and may even become unmanageable in heavy weather. A few yachts are so perfectly balanced that they carry neither weather nor lee helm, and may hold their course unattended for long periods; but they are more difficult to steer to windward owing to lack of life in the tiller.

Running

A vessel is said to be running when she is sailing with the wind abaft the beam. With the wind between abeam and 45° abaft the beam, running is much the same as reaching from the helmsman's point of view; he will only have to steer a course by landmark or by compass and the mainsail and headsail will continue to draw. But if the wind is further aft, the headsail will be blanketed by the mainsail, with a consequent reduction in speed, and it will flap uselessly from side to side as the yacht rolls. Running dead (dead before the wind) is the one point of sailing on which the fore-and-aft rigged vessel compares unfavourably with her square-rigged predecessor, for (unless a spinnaker is set) the only effective sail will be to one side of the centre line, tending to push her round into the wind, and the sail, being abaft the mast, will chafe on the lee shrouds if it is squared right off. In smooth water the foresail of a schooner or the mizzen of a ketch or yawl may be squared off on the opposite side to the mainsail, but sailing wing and wing, as that is called, will not be possible if the yacht rolls much, and all sailing vessels do roll when running before a fresh wind and sea. By fighting against it in an attempt to steer an exact course, the helmsman may only succeed in making such rhythmic rolling worse; but by allowing the yacht to wander a little off her course as she may wish, but not to the extent of making her gybe, the rolling can sometimes be reduced.

When the yacht is running dead before the wind, the helmsman can no longer sit complacently and steer the desired course by compass or landmark; he must watch the wind and the behaviour of the yacht, for if he were to allow the wind to come much on what should be the lee quarter (running by the lee) it might get round to the forward side of the mainsail and cause that sail to swing suddenly across to the other side. This is known as gybing all standing and is dangerous if there is much weight in the wind, for the sail and boom will gather considerable momentum during the gybe and the sudden check as they are stopped by the sheet coming taut may carry something away or cause the sail to split; if the runner of a two-headsail rig is set up at the time, the boom will strike it and may be broken, or the runner itself may be carried away. The prudent helmsman will therefore never allow the yacht to run by the lee, for, although the true wind could be permitted to come a long way round on the lee side before it could reach the fore side of the sail and cause a gybe, it is the apparent wind with which he is concerned, and the rolling of the yacht will cause this to change direction considerably and rapidly, while the force of gravity acting on the boom when the yacht rolls in the opposite direction to that on which the boom is extended will also be conducive to a gybe. The burgee, or masthead sock, although helpful, cannot be relied upon to indicate the true direction of the wind because of the rolling, neither can the run of the sea, for it does not always run true with the wind. The most reliable guide is the feel of the wind on the back of one's neck and ears, so if a sou'wester is worn the back of its brim should be turned up and the ear-flaps tucked away or a hood should be removed; I have noticed that women with hair covering their ears are not quite happy when steering before the wind. Running by the lee, incidentally, causes a reduction of speed.

An alteration in the direction of the wind or a change of course may make a gybe necessary, but a properly executed gybe is not dangerous. Haul in the mainsheet until the boom is as near amidships as it is possible to get it, and belay. In order to avoid a premature gybe it is as well to luff a little to bring the wind fine on the quarter while that is being done. Then put the helm up, and as the wind passes from one quarter to the other the sail will gybe across with very little force. The yacht will show a strong inclination to luff immediately after the gybe, so the mainsheet should be paid out smartly. Even though you may have taken a turn with the sheet round a cleat or pin, do not keep it in your hand during a gybe, for you might be unable to hold it and there would be a risk of your hand being skinned. Finally, sheet the headsail across so that it will be ready if the yacht has to come on the wind.

Sailing close-hauled

A yacht is said to be close-hauled when the wind is forward of the beam and she is sailing as close to it as possible with the sheets hardened in until the sails lie more nearly fore-and-aft than on any other point of sailing. This is also known as sailing on a wind or 'full and by' (ie keeping the sails full of wind and steering by the wind, not by a mark or compass). Only by practice can you learn how to get the best out of your vessel when she is close-hauled, for you will have to strike the happy medium between sailing her so close to the wind that her sails begin to shake and she loses way, or so far off the wind that although she moves fast through the water she does not make good the desired course.

Yachts vary in their performance close-hauled. A weatherly type of cruiser with bermudian rig should sail within 45° to 50°, and one with gaff rig within 50° to 55° of the true wind. It should, however, be understood that, except when running dead before the wind, it is the apparent and not the true wind for which the sails have to be trimmed; the direction of the apparent wind when the yacht is on a given course will depend upon her speed and on the strength of the wind. It is a simple matter to draw a diagram to show what the angle of the apparent wind will be in any given set of circumstances. In the upper drawing of Fig 51, Y indicates the position of a yacht close-hauled on the starboard tack, and YC her course. We will assume that she is sailing at an angle of 45° to the true wind which is blowing at 6 knots and that her speed is 5 knots. (These unlikely figures have been chosen to exaggerate the diagrams.) Draw TY at 45° to YC to indicate the direction of the true wind, and using any convenient scale make it 6 units in length to represent its speed of 6 knots. From T draw TA parallel to YC and make it 5 units in length to represent the yacht's speed. Then AY is the direction of the apparent wind, and if we measure the angle AYC with a protractor we will find that the apparent wind is at 25° to the yacht's course. In the centre of Fig 51 is a similar diagram drawn for a slower yacht sailing at only 3 knots with a 6-knot wind, and it will be seen that the apparent wind makes a larger angle with her course (30°) than it did with the faster yacht. The lower drawing shows that in a stronger wind (10 knots) the apparent wind reaching a yacht travelling close-hauled at 5 knots makes a larger angle with her course than did the lighter wind, 30°

as compared with 25°. Such diagrams, though of little practical value, do show that the sheets of a fast yacht need to be hardened in more than those of a slow yacht on the same course, and they also show why it is that slow boats are sometimes able to sail closer to the wind than fast ones. The length of AY, measured with the same scale as was used when drawing TY and TA, is the strength of the apparent wind in knots.

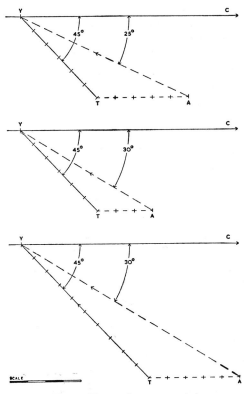

Fig 51   True and apparent wind

Y is the position of the yacht, and YC her course; TY is the direction of the true wind, and AY the direction of the apparent wind. The direction of the apparent wind changes according to the speed of the yacht and/or speed of the true wind.

The usual fault the beginner makes when sailing close-hauled is to sheet his sails in too flat and then to point up too close to the wind, so that although his yacht may head in the desired direction she does not move fast enough through the water. The average cruising yacht when treated in this manner will become lifeless and drift away to leeward; her sheets should be eased a little to get her moving even though she will then not point so high. If the sails are correctly sheeted there ought, in most yachts, to be no sign of any sail backwinding another, though some yachts with large headsails appear to go best on a wind with the luff of the mainsail just lifting. It is a good plan as a beginner to sheet your sails in such a way that the headsail (the jib in a two-headsail rig) will be the first sail to shake when you luff; that can then be your guide, and the moment it shows any sign of lifting you will know you are sailing too close to the wind and that you must bear away a little. If you accustom your eye to the angle the burgee makes with the yacht's fore-and-aft line, you will soon find yourself using that as your guide and your headsail will not shake so often. Later, when you have got used to your yacht you will discover that you can sail her close-hauled fairly well with your eyes shut, judging her performance by the feel of the tiller and the brush of the wind on your cheek; you will also find that you can luff with advantage when the wind strengthens (the apparent wind is then at a broader angle to your course) but that to keep the yacht going properly you will have to bear away a little when it eases. Remember the old doggerel:

> In a puff spring a luff,
> In a lull keep her full.

The set of the sails is more important when close-hauled than on any other point of sailing; the luffs of the headsails must be kept as straight as possible, and that can only be done if the runner and/or backstay is set up properly. The topping lift and the lee runner must not be allowed to girt the mainsail and spoil its belly.

Most helmsmen prefer to keep to the windward side of the tiller. One can judge the direction of the wind better from there, and it is less tiring to hold the tiller up by pulling than it is to push it up from a position to leeward. But the steering position is a personal matter and some prefer to steer from the leeward side in light airs in order the better to watch the headsail. However, as was noted in an earlier chapter, wheel steering allows the helmsman a wider choice of position.

Turning to windward

If you are unable to fetch your destination or lay your course by sailing close-hauled, you will have to beat, turn, or work to windward by sailing as close as you can to the wind first on one tack then on the other.

To come about (or stay) you will put the helm down (to leeward) so that the yacht shoots up head to wind and pays off on the other tack, and as she does so sheet the headsail across to the other side. If the headsail is sheeted across too soon and backed, it may prevent the yacht from coming about, causing her to miss stays and fall back on the original tack; but if the sheeting of the headsail is left until too late the work will be harder.

Never at any time use the rudder violently or it will reduce the yacht's speed by the resistance it offers to the water flowing past it. Your aim should be to sail the yacht round from one tack to the other, not to force her round by jamming the helm hard down, but of course a small yacht with a fin keel and a rudder well aft will spin round much quicker than one of heavy displacement or long keel type. Do not let fly the headsail sheet too soon or the driving power of the headsail will be lost and the unnecessary flapping will do it no good. If there is much sea running, or if you know the yacht to be a little reluctant in staying, sail her extra full for a few moments just before you stay so that she may have every chance of gathering plenty of speed. Warn your crew by the words 'ready about', then with the cry 'lee oh' put the helm down gently and she will start to round up, but remember that so long as her sails are full they will be helping her to move through the water. When the sails start to shake the helm may be put over a little farther, but at no time should it be put over more than 30°, for the rudder would then tend to act too much as a brake. If she is very slow in coming about, and some short, beamy yachts with long straight keels are, she may almost have lost way by the time she is head to wind, and it will then be necessary to keep the headsail backed to make sure that she pays off on the other tack. If, while she is in stays, she pitches heavily into a particularly steep sea, she may lose all way and remain in stays until the wind causes her to gather sternway. When a vessel is going astern her rudder has the opposite effect to that which it has when she is moving ahead, so she can be made to pay off on the new tack by reversing the position of the tiller. This is known as making a sternboard and was a recognized and much-used manœuvre in the days of square-rig, but it should not normally be necessary with a fore-and-aft-rigged craft. Remember that if your yacht does gather sternway when in stays, and you omit to reverse the helm, she will fall back on her original tack. One may, of course, wear her round instead of staying her, ie put the helm up and turn her round away from the wind, gybe, and continue turning her until she is close-hauled on the new tack. But unless the wind is very strong or the sea is very heavy, wearing has nothing to recommend it and it loses one some ground.

Except when she is running, a sailing vessel besides moving forward will be pushed sideways through the water by the pressure of the wind on her sails, gear, and hull. This sideways movement is known as leeway and is expressed as an angle in degrees or compass points measured between the course that she is pointing and the real course made good. The amount of leeway made will depend on the type of yacht, the point of sailing, the weight of the wind, and the size of the sea; a yacht with shallow draught or high freeboard will make more leeway than one with deep draught or moderate freeboard; more leeway is made close-hauled than when reaching and more in heavy weather than in light; the speed of the yacht and the state of her bottom, whether it is clean or foul, also have a bearing on it. A well-designed cruiser when carrying full sail close-hauled in moderate weather should not make more than 5° (about half a point) of leeway.

Running aground and getting off

Anyone who sails much in rivers and creeks or in shoal-encumbered waterways, is certain to run aground sooner or later owing to an error in pilotage, lack of local knowledge, or by trying to take a short cut across a shoal where there is insufficient water. Many of us, especially when we first started sailing, have spent a good deal of time stuck firmly on the mud.

If the bottom is hard and comparatively flat you will feel a series of bumps as the keel touches it; if you alter course instantly towards deep water and send your companions forward where their weight may depress the bow enough to enable the after end of the keel which is touching to lift clear, the yacht may sail off. But if the bottom is of soft mud, as it frequently is in rivers and creeks, the keel will cut into it, and probably the first indication you will have that your yacht is aground is a lack of life in the tiller and a bump as the dinghy (if it was being towed) runs up and hits the stern. Immediate action may get her afloat again even though the tide is falling, but panic, delay, or the wrong procedure will allow the tide time to drop a little, and as soon as there is the slightest sign of the yacht being sewed (left by the tide) it will probably be useless to make any further attempt to refloat her until the next flood. The action to be taken will depend on how, in relation to the wind and tide, she has gone aground, and to a lesser degree upon the shape of her underwater profile. Whenever possible the aim should be to make her sails do the work, but in some instances it will be necessary to lay out an anchor and haul her off.

One runs aground most often when beating up or down a river, for there is then a temptation to make the tacks too long. If the grounding takes place when the yacht is in the act of staying with, say, the deep water on her port side, no matter whether the flood is making or the ebb is running, back the headsail by hauling in its starboard sheet, and it should then push her head round so that the mainsail will fill on the other tack and she will sail off into deep water. If that fails, go forward and push from the starboard bow with a spar (the spinnaker boom, perhaps), or even jump overboard and push if she is a very small craft, for relieving her of your weight will help; but be prepared to scramble aboard again the moment she starts to sail.

In this, as in all instances where a yacht may be swung round to get her off the mud, one with a deep heel and cut-away forefoot, or with a well-rockered keel, will be easier to handle; a yacht with a long straight keel and deep forefoot will generally have to be hauled off by the same route as she went on, as any attempt to swing her round will only result in piling up a mound of mud against the side of her forefoot.

If, when beating to windward with the flood, you run aground with the sails full and drawing, let fly all the sheets immediately and get the sails down or they will drive the yacht further on. Then lay the kedge out on the weather bow, and as soon as the bow has been hauled round, the sails can be set on the other tack to help her off. There is no need to strain on the warp; be patient and let the tide float the yacht before you start to haul. But if she has run aground in similar circumstances on the ebb, there will not be much chance of getting her off until the next flood, for by the time you have lowered the sails and run out the kedge she may have sewed and nothing will move her then.

When reaching, if you run aground on the windward side of the river, the mainsail will tend to drive the yacht more firmly on. If the wind is forward of the beam, pay out the mainsheet until the mainsail holds no wind, back the headsail and, if necessary, push off with a spar from the weather bow. But if the wind is so nearly abeam that it cannot be spilled from the mainsail by paying out the sheet, get that sail down without delay and she should blow off under the backed headsail.

There is not much excuse for running aground on the lee side of a river, for it is an axiom that a sailing vessel should always be kept well to windward so as to have something in hand if the wind should head her off. But if this does happen when reaching, no matter whether the flood or the ebb is running, get the sails down at once, for if they are left up they will only drive her on farther. Then lay out the kedge either off the weather bow or directly astern. The longer the cable used the better, otherwise when she floats off she will be so close to the lee shore that you may have difficulty in getting under way without blowing ashore again. Indeed, the mistake commonly made when laying out a kedge is to give insufficient scope of cable, so that when the cable is hauled on the anchor pulls home. Of course the kedge will have a much better chance of holding if the first few fathoms of its cable are of chain.

If the yacht is running with the mainsail out to starboard and she grounds with the deep water to port, get the headsail down, and as the mainsail will tend to push her round towards deep water, she should sail off even though the tide may be ebbing. But if, with her mainsail to starboard she should go aground when running with the deep water to starboard of her you will have to act quickly if the tide is ebbing. The mainsail will be driving her harder on, so get it down at once, swing it across to the port side and reset it, then she should sail off into deep water. Unless she is still dragging her keel through the mud and so has steerage way, or unless at the time of grounding you were running by the lee (which you should not have been doing), it will be a sheer waste of time to attempt to make the mainsail gybe while it is set.

Should the yacht run aground with shoal water on both sides of her, no matter what point of sailing she is on, get all sail off her and lay out the kedge aft; but there will not be much chance of hauling her off if the ebb is running unless you work very fast.

In any of the above circumstances, if it is found impossible to get the yacht afloat on the ebb, make sure that she lists towards the bank, otherwise if the bank is steep or the yacht has deep draught and narrow beam, there might be some risk of her failing to rise on the flood before the water had reached the cockpit or hatches. Swing the boom with the stowed mainsail on it out towards the bank, or range the cable and any other heavy weights on that side of the deck. If the yacht has already listed the wrong way, it is risky to attempt to prop her up with a leg, for as the tide falls there will be a great strain on it and it might break. A better plan is to lay out an anchor abeam, bend its cable to a halyard, and by heaving on that it may be possible to roll a small yacht over so that she lists the right way. Then, having ensured her safety, you must wait as patiently as you can for the next flood, and some of the time might be used to advantage by giving the exposed side of the bottom a scrub.

Sometimes a small yacht which has gone aground on the ebb may be got free by rolling her from side to side to make the keel loosen its hold while the kedge cable is being hauled on, or the wash from a passing vessel may lift her so that she can be pulled off.

The situation of a yacht which has run aground on an exposed lee shore may be dangerous, especially if the bottom is hard and there is any sea running. If this should happen and you are unable to sail her off, get the sails down without delay and run out your kedge on the longest line you have and do your utmost to haul her off; but if you do not succeed bear in mind that as the yacht will be there for some hours it is possible that the wind may freshen and the sea increase before next she floats, so at low water make your preparations for the worst. Lay out the bower anchor to seaward on its full scope of cable, and if you have the slightest doubt as to its holding power, back it up with the kedge. To do this lay the kedge out beyond and directly in line with the bower, and make fast the end of its cable to the chain 9 metres (5 fathoms) or so from the bower anchor, using a rolling hitch with the end seized back so that it cannot slip or work loose. Should there be any sea running when the flood makes, the yacht will start to bump before she floats properly. Begin hauling on the chain as soon as there is the slightest chance of moving her, for the less she bumps the better. Provided that conditions are not bad you will be able to haul out to the bower and weigh it, and then sail out the kedge. But if it is blowing hard you might be wise to buoy the anchor chain and slip it (hoping to reclaim it at some later date) and then sail out the kedge; even if you lose the bower and a shackle of cable you will consider that a small price to have paid for extricating your vessel from a dangerous situation which might have become disastrous.

Backing up the bower with the kedge may also be of use in sheltered water when the bower, dropped on very soft mud, cannot get a sufficiently good hold to enable a grounded yacht to be pulled off in a strong wind.

One speaks or writes glibly enough of laying out the bower and chain cable; but that is by no means an easy thing to do in the average yacht's dinghy, and may be impossible if there is any sea running at the time, for the chain has to be taken in the dinghy (if it is paid out from the yacht one cannot drag it more than a short way along the bottom) and its weight will make the dinghy unseaworthy and difficult to row. The only satisfactory way of laying it out the necessary distance is first to run out the kedge well beyond where the bower is to be dropped, then to sling the bower from the dinghy's stem, load the chain into her and pull her out along the kedge warp paying out the chain as you go.

When sailing in the neighbourhood of shoals at high water, spring tides, or when the tides are taking off, every care must be taken to avoid running aground, for the yacht might then get beneaped and have to remain ashore for anything up to a fortnight if the succeeding tide does not rise high enough to float her. So if you are navigating in some place that you do not know well or which is indifferently marked, it would be wise to stand on and off or anchor until the tide has dropped a little before proceeding. If you should have the misfortune to run your yacht ashore at high water when tides are taking off and fail to get her afloat at once, do everything you can to ensure that she comes off on the next tide. Your preparations will consist of laying out one or two anchors astern and digging a trench along that line to take the yacht's keel when the time comes to haul her off; heavy weights may be removed and the water tanks emptied to lighten her, or a line from her masthead to an anchor laid out abeam may enable her to be heeled to reduce her draught.

Unless it is powerful and has a large propeller, an auxiliary engine may not of itself refloat a grounded yacht unless she has gone ashore gently, but if she has grounded on the flood it will in most circumstances save the need for laying out an anchor, and in any event its help can be enlisted to reduce the labour of hauling off.

Bringing up

Because of the almost universal installation of engines in cruising yachts, and the grossly overcrowded conditions of many yacht harbours, anchoring or picking up a mooring is today largely done under power, the sailor thereby sacrificing one of the most satisfying acts of seamanship. Under power a mooring should always be picked up with the yacht as nearly head to tide as possible, but in the hope of encouraging a stronger interest in seamanship, and to cover those occasions when there is ample room, or the engine fails to start, I give below in some detail the procedure for doing this under sail. However, it should never be attempted as an exhibition, and if there is the slightest risk of fouling other craft or causing anxiety to their owners, it will be far more seamanlike to hand all sail and proceed under power.

The same two basic rules which apply when getting under way are also applicable when picking up a mooring: if, when the mooring has been picked up, the yacht will lie with the wind forward of the beam, it may be approached with the sails set, but if the yacht will lie with the wind abeam or abaft the beam, the sails must be lowered before attempting to secure the mooring. How she will lie in relation to the wind can best be judged by other craft of similar type brought up near by; but if there is none you will have to judge by the angle the wind makes with the tide, and unless the tide is nearly slack you should be able to see from the ripples it makes round the buoy which way it is running. There is also a third rule to be remembered: the buoy should only be picked up when the yacht is head to tide and with her way over the ground almost stopped, never when she is moving with the tide. If there is no tide she will, of course, come to her buoy head to wind.

Before attempting to pick up a mooring you must learn how much room your yacht takes to turn and how far she will shoot head to wind in winds of different strength before she loses way. At the first opportunity, therefore, when you have reached open water, throw a lifebuoy overboard and practise picking it up. You will not have to bother about the tide because both yacht and buoy will be equally affected by it, and the skill you will attain may one day stand you in good stead if you have to pick up a man who has fallen or been washed overboard. When you can pick up the lifebuoy with a fair degree of certainty, practise approaching a mooring in a tideway so that you may learn how much to allow for tides of different strength when manœuvring.

The easiest condition for picking up a mooring is at slack water, when there is no tide running. When the yacht has reached a position to leeward of the buoy and such a distance from it that, without further assistance from her sails, she will just be able to carry her way to it, put the helm down and luff for the buoy with sails shaking. If you misjudge the distance and shoot up to the buoy with too much way, do not attempt to pick it up but act as you would if you had failed to reach it; bear away, run down to leeward, and make another attempt.

If the yacht is beating up to her mooring against the tide, act as in the previous case, but get a little closer to the buoy before luffing for it so as to allow for the run of the tide. As the buoy and its rope will be streamed down towards the yacht by the tide, it will be just as well if she has a little headway over the ground when she reaches it so that when you have picked it up you will be able to haul the riding chain aboard without much effort. If the yacht has lost all way by the time she reaches the buoy, you will have to haul her up against the wind and tide to get the chain aboard.

If the yacht is beating up to the mooring with a fair tide under her, or is running down to it against the tide, luff head to wind a short distance to windward of the buoy and take the mainsail down. Bear right away and run back over the tide under the headsail until the yacht is within such a distance of the buoy that she will reach it without further assistance; then hand the headsail. Here again it will save labour if the yacht still carries a little way when she reaches the buoy. If the wind is so light that the headsail alone is insufficient to enable her to run back over the tide to the mooring, you will have to reset a little of the mainsail.

When running up to the mooring with a fair wind and tide, you may sail past the buoy and then beat back to it. But a quicker and more seamanlike method, and the only one that can be used if the wind is not strong enough to enable the yacht to beat back against the tide, is to steer a little to leeward of the buoy and begin to luff when it is abeam or nearly abeam, so that by the time the yacht has rounded up head to wind and reached the buoy she will almost have lost way. This calls for skilful judgement which can only be gained by practice, but the speed of the yacht as she rounds up can be controlled to some extent by hardening in or easing out the mainsheet.

When the wind is blowing at 90° to the tide, the mooring may be reached in one of two ways: you may sail up to windward of the buoy, lower the mainsail, and run back to the buoy under headsail only; or you may sail to leeward of the buoy, luff, and pick it up head to wind with sails set, but then the sails must be lowered the instant the buoy has been got aboard or the yacht will sail wildly round the mooring. When rounding up with the tide on the beam, head a little to tideward of the buoy so as to allow for the tide carrying the yacht down to it. When executing this manœuvre in a narrow creek the chief difficulty is to make the yacht sail slowly so that she does not overshoot the buoy when rounding up to it. It should be possible to make a handy and well-balanced yacht sail under headsail only, but if she will not do so and the mainsail has to be kept set, harden the sheet right in so that the sail is as nearly flat amidships as you can get it; paying out all the sheet, hoping that the sail will lift, usually results in the yacht sailing faster than ever.

Should there be some other vessels lying near your mooring, and you do not know your own craft well or are not quite sure of your ability to handle her, have an anchor ready to let go at once if you miss the buoy and the tide sets you down towards them. This is a seamanlike precaution, and if you do have to anchor you can run a line off to your mooring, weigh, and haul up to it at your leisure. But if you have omitted to get an anchor ready and feel that you have lost control of your vessel, do not hesitate to run her ashore while you think out the next manœuvre; it is far better to do that than to risk damaging her or some other craft by collision.

Anchoring is much easier than picking up a mooring. But here again the two basic rules apply: if, when the yacht has brought up to her anchor, the wind will be forward of the beam, one may anchor with the mainsail set; but if the wind will be abeam or abaft the beam when she has brought up, the sails should be lowered before letting go the anchor. The same procedure will be followed as when picking up a mooring but with this one important difference: whereas one plans to make the yacht reach her mooring buoy with headway almost lost, an anchor should be let go while the yacht is moving over the ground, for even the CQR or the Danforth can be fouled if cable is dropped on top of it before it has dug in. She may have headway or sternway, but before letting go ascertain from the chart or a cast of the lead, or from the echo-sounder, that there will be sufficient water there to float the yacht at low tide. If you let go with headway, give the yacht a sheer with the tiller as you do so in order that she may make a wide sweep to one side of the anchor as she drops back, and so run no risk of dragging the bight of the cable over the anchor. Less judgement is needed when letting go with headway than with sternway, for one can sail up to the berth and drop the anchor in the chosen place with certainty, and the strain as the cable comes taut will ensure that the anchor bites in hard and gets a good hold at once. The CQR or the Danforth should be given plenty of cable straight away so that when the pull comes on the anchor it will be in a horizontal direction and the anchor will immediately dig in.

Finally, if the cable is of chain, veer a length equal to three times the depth at high water; if a rope cable is used veer five times that depth. If the anchor is to be buoyed, the buoy should be streamed before the anchor is let go.

Mooring

In normal weather a yacht lying in an anchorage where there is plenty of room and no tidal stream should be quite safe on one anchor with a proper scope of cable out, but in a river or estuary

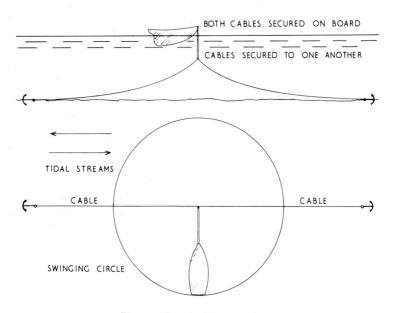

Fig 52   Moored with two anchors

where there are tidal streams, or when lying close to another vessel which is moored, she should be moored between two anchors placed, for preference, up and down stream (Fig 52); in the USA this is often called a 'Bahamian moor'. There are three ways in which this may be accomplished. The most common is to anchor with the bower and then take the kedge out in the dinghy and drop it where required, and that will be done most easily if a time is chosen when the tide is running in the direction in which the kedge is to be laid. Make fast one end of the cable to the kedge, lower it overboard, and sling it outside the stern of the dinghy with a short piece of line rove through its ring and secured inboard in such a way that it can be cast off easily; then coil or flake down the cable in the dinghy and make fast its upper end aboard the yacht. Row off in the direction in which the kedge is to be laid, allowing the cable to run out over the stern of the dinghy (a second hand will be a help in preventing kinks); when all the cable has gone, cast off the lashing so that the anchor will drop. The common practice of carrying the kedge in the dinghy and throwing it overboard is unseamanlike, for the dinghy might capsize or the anchor catch in one's clothes. If the kedge has to be laid out against the tide, make the end of its cable fast in the dinghy, row off to the chosen spot, drop the kedge, and row back to the yacht, paying out the cable as you do so. On arriving back at the yacht haul the cable as taut as you can get it and secure it to the bower cable with a rolling hitch outboard of the stemhead roller; then pay out some cable so as to drop the hitch well below the keel where the yacht will clear it when she swings and passing craft will not foul it. If the kedge cable is long enough, make the rolling hitch with a bight of itself and bring its end aboard, then a new arrival will be able to see that you are moored. A tighter moor can be made if the operation is carried out at low water, and if the kedge cable is held taut by a short length of rope while the rolling hitch is being made.

Do not attempt to moor fore-and-aft with the bower cable at the stemhead roller and the kedge cable through a fairlead at the stern, for no yacht will lie comfortably stern to tide; she will sheer about and probably lie with the tide on her beam, thus putting a great strain on her anchors and obstructing the passage of other craft. However, if other yachts are moored in that fashion, or one wishes to lie end-on to the swell in an open anchorage to minimize rolling, there may be no alternative.

There are two ways of mooring which do not require the use of a dinghy: the dropping moor consists of letting go the bower up-tide in the usual manner, and as the yacht drops back on the tide a length of cable equal to six times the depth at high water is paid out. The kedge is then let go and half of the bower cable is hauled in while the kedge cable is paid out until there is an equal scope of cable on each anchor. As before, the cables are secured to one another and the hitch is dropped under foot.

The running moor is similar except that it is done under sail or power, and that the first anchor is let go down-stream of the chosen berth. The first anchor having been dropped, the yacht is sailed or motored on against the tide past her berth while cable is paid out generously; then, just before a length equal to six times the depth at high water has been veered, sail is got off her or the motor is stopped, and the second anchor is let go; its cable is then paid out while the other cable is hauled in until, as before, there is an equal scope of cable on each anchor. The tide will assist in this part of the manœuvre. A running moor is a satisfactory thing to accomplish, but the skipper and his crew will need to know the yacht and her gear intimately, for any hitch in the running of the cables or in the handing of the sails might cause the operation to have to be abandoned.

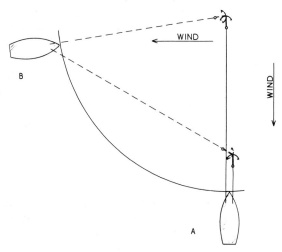

Fig 53   Lying to two anchors

A kedge is sometimes of use in an anchorage where there is little or no tidal stream. If, for example, the yacht is lying too close to another vessel or to the shore, the kedge may be laid out from the other bow to hold her away, and possibly this could be done by setting a headsail and getting the yacht to sheer in the desired direction, but this is more likely to succeed if done under power. Or it might be that the wind is freshening and bad weather is expected and one has some doubt about the holding power of the bower. The kedge can then be dropped under foot and both cables veered so that the strain is shared by bower and kedge (Fig 53). If the wind is expected to veer, as it usually does in the southern half of a depression in the northern hemisphere, and if there is any choice in the matter, the first anchor should be let go from the port bow and the second from the starboard bow, so that as the yacht swings with the veering wind the cables will not cross and the yacht will ride with open hawse, nor will there be any risk of the first anchor's cable fouling the second anchor.

A kedge which has been let go on a dropping or running moor or on a sheer, can of course be weighed from the yacht by veering bower cable and hauling on the other cable until she is over the kedge, but a kedge which has been laid out by dinghy may have to be weighed from the dinghy. First haul in a little chain to lift the rolling hitch clear of the water; then, if the kedge is buoyed, you can row out to it and weigh it by its buoy rope and haul yourself back to the yacht, cleaning the cable as you go and coiling it down in the dinghy. But if the kedge is not buoyed you will underrun its cable, pulling it through the sculling notch in the dinghy's transom. If the anchor has a good hold, you may not be able to break it out even though you heave the dinghy's stern down level with the water. If that is so get the cable as tight as you can, belay it in the stern of the dinghy, and then move forward where your weight depressing the bows may lift the stern enough to break the anchor out.

Manœuvring under power

The behaviour of a sailing yacht under power depends on her windage, the shape of her underwater profile, the position of the propeller, and its size and direction of rotation. Before attempting to handle a yacht under power in a confined space, the owner will be well advised to practise laying her alongside a buoy where there is ample room in various conditions of wind and tide; he will then discover the size of her turning circle both to port and to starboard, for it will not be the same both ways, and will find out by experiment what she will do when the astern gear is engaged when she has headway, sternway, or no way on her. There are, however, a few fundamental facts with which he should first be acquainted.

Any propeller has a turning effect on a vessel owing to its lower half working in denser water than its upper half. The resulting paddle-wheel effect (known as transverse thrust) tends to move the shaft, and therefore the stern of the vessel, in the direction in which the upper half of the propeller is turning. A left-handed propeller (turning anti-clockwise when viewed from astern while driving ahead) will swing the stern to port; a right-handed (clockwise-turning) propeller will swing the stern to starboard. A large propeller naturally produces a greater transverse thrust than a small one; the turning effect is greatest when the vessel is stationary, and may almost disappear when she has gathered headway. The screw race, sent aft by the propeller when it is turning to drive the vessel ahead, will impinge on the rudder, making some control possible even when the vessel has no way on her. As already noted, a left-handed propeller turning ahead will move the stern to port, but if the rudder is put over to port the pressure of the screw race on it will overcome this and swing the stern to starboard. So it should be possible to turn a vessel with a left-handed propeller round to port in her own length by giving short bursts of power alternatively ahead and astern, leaving the rudder all the time over to port, for when the propeller is running astern it will be turning right-handed and so will carry the stern to starboard, and the screw race, now flowing forward, will have no effect on the rudder. The vessel should not be allowed to gather sternway, but if she does the rudder must of course at once be put to starboard.

These are the basic facts to be considered when manœuvring a yacht under power, but the effect of the wind on her must not be disregarded. The bow of the average yacht will tend to blow away to leeward, and unless she is moving forward fairly fast the rudder may have insufficient control to hold her head into a strong wind. Once her head has paid off it cannot be brought back to the wind without running the engine long enough and fast enough for her to gather good headway, and a low-power engine may be incapable of doing that. If there is room, a sternboard could of course be used to get her head to wind, but her bow will certainly blow off again before she can gather headway. In such conditions it might pay to approach the mooring or the berth more or less stern to wind, for the yacht should then lie quietly with her stern or her quarter to the wind and be under proper control, but the behaviour of a long-keel yacht when going astern is likely to be unpredictable.

When going alongside a quay, pontoon, or another vessel, if there is any choice in the matter the yacht with a left-handed propeller should do so starboard side to. If she approaches at a small angle and is given a kick astern as her bows near the quay, this will not only stop her headway, but the transverse thrust of the propeller will push her stern neatly in so that she will lie close alongside and one can step ashore to make fast. Obviously the yacht with a right-handed propeller will find it easier to berth port side to. But to perform such manœuvres competently in the varying conditions that prevail (slack water and calm are rare) calls for good judgement, skill, a knowledge of the yacht's peculiarities, and some luck, particularly if there is nobody ashore to handle lines, and even if there is one must beware, for the willing helper is not always able to make fast a line quickly and securely, or even to let one go.

The use of springs when lying alongside is described on page 359, and such lines can often be of help when coming to or leaving a berth alongside. For example, if the yacht with a left-handed propeller has to berth port side to, there will be difficulty in getting her stern to come in, for the kick astern needed to stop her will swing her stern out. But if a line from her port quarter can be got ashore and made fast abreast the bow (ie an aft spring) the kick astern will put a strain on it, and that will pull the stern in to the quay. Or suppose the yacht with a left-handed propeller is lying starboard side to with a vessel ahead and another astern of her and she wishes to leave by going ahead. The boathook might be used to push the bows out far enough; but if that is not possible an after spring should be rigged from the starboard quarter; a kick astern will put a strain on this, pulling the stern in to the quay and swinging the bows out, and when the bows are clear of the vessel ahead the spring can be cast off (if there is nobody ashore to let it go it should be rigged as a slip, ie with both ends on board) and the yacht can go ahead. If in the above circumstances the yacht wishes to leave stern-first, a fore spring should be rigged from her starboard bow to a point ashore; a kick ahead with the engine will then swing her stern out.

13

LIGHT-WEATHER SAILS AND THEIR HANDLING

Headsails and mizzen staysails – Topsails – Running sails

IF a sail is to draw well in light winds it needs to be made of suitably light cloth, otherwise it will hang wrinkled and lifeless, and its own inertia will fling the wind out of it as the yacht rolls. So every yacht should be provided with a genoa and/or a yankee jib of light material, and of large size so that her total sail area may in light weather be increased beyond what she normally sets in her working sails. In addition she should have some form of running sail for use when the wind is aft and the headsail(s), blanketed by the mainsail, will not draw; the gaff-rigged yacht should have a topsail, and a ketch or yawl a mizzen staysail.

Headsails and mizzen staysails

Broadly speaking a genoa may be regarded as a headsail which fills the whole fore triangle and perhaps overlaps the mainsail to some extent. The yankee, which is a development of the old jib-topsail (a light sail set above the working jib), is a narrower sail but with its luff, like that of a genoa, hanked to the topmast stay and usually extending the full length of it; it is used in conjunction with the working staysail in the two-headsail rig, and is easier to handle than a genoa because of its smaller area. Of course a genoa can be, and often is, used in a yacht which has a two-headsail working rig, but it then has to be passed round the inner forestay each time a tack or gybe is made, unless the forestay is rigged in such a manner that it can be cast off and taken aft to the mast when the genoa is to be used (Page 126). Unlike the racing yacht, the cruiser will not need to fill her sail locker with a variety of headsails for use in different weights of wind, and unless she has a large crew, she will be unable to make proper use of them. She will probably do very well with just one large light headsail for winds up to, say, force 4; but for use in light airs a similar sail of much lighter cloth (a ghoster) will be an undoubted advantage, but it should not be kept set if the wind exceeds force 3 or its shape might be permanently spoilt.

The size and proportions of such sails will no doubt be decided by designer and sailmaker, but the following points merit consideration: much overlap of the mainsail by the genoa should be avoided or chafe of the leech of the latter may occur unless the crosstrees are short, thus weakening the integrity of the topmast shrouds; and, unlike the sail intended for racing, its foot should not be parallel to the water but should have a high clew, then the helmsman will have a clear view under it and it will not scoop up water. If the clew of the yankee is too high, the sheet will lead up to it at a steep angle and prevent the main boom from being eased out sufficiently when reaching.

The same halyard as is used for a working headsail will probably be used for the light-weather sail, though some yachts do have a separate halyard and twin headstays, the intention being that when changing headsails the second one can be hanked on before the first one is lowered. I am not impressed by such an arrangement, for the extra halyard is a complication at the masthead, the sail will chafe on the lee stay, and unless the stays are widely separated there will be a risk that hanks high up may grab both stays. So that a headsail shall not be hanked on and set upside down, it is the custom of most sailmakers to sew their trademark in cloth of a different colour near the tack of each sail, and this can be felt with the fingers in the dark. As the sheets for big headsails usually have to pass outside the shrouds, the rail cappings are generally provided with tracks on which fairlead blocks slide for adjustment and are held each by a pin engaging with a hole in the track. The load on the sheets is considerable, and the load on such a fairlead block and its attachment may be as much as twice the load on the winch which handles the sheet.

Special sails intended for reaching only: balloon jib and reaching staysail, are little used in cruising yachts today, for the genoa and the yankee, which of course can be carried close-hauled are also efficient sails for reaching.

A light-weather headsail is usually set in easy conditions, but when it has to be changed for something smaller and heavier the wind will have freshened and no doubt the sea will have got up. With a full crew the big sail can be handed without the course having to be altered, one man being stationed at the halyard, one forward to pull the sail down its stay, and the remainder along the foot to gather the sail inboard; and the usual result is that both crew and sail get wet. Where searoom permits I therefore prefer to sacrifice a little of the distance made good when changing head-sails, and for a few moments bear right away so that they may be dealt with in the lee of the mainsail – and on a deck which is not at a steep angle or being swept by spray. Before attempting to lower a sail, particularly one that is full of wind, take the coil of halyard off the cleat and flake it down on deck all clear for running; also make sure that the bitter end is fast so that it cannot fly aloft. Some people make use of a downhaul when handing a headsail. This is a line made fast at the head of the sail and led down through several hanks to a fairlead at the tack, then along the deck to a cleat near the mast; as the halyard is slacked away the sail may be hauled down its stay without the need for someone to go right forward, but unless the foot of the sail is grabbed as soon as it is within reach it will probably go overboard unless the sail is empty of wind. However, this is not necessarily a disaster; indeed, when taking in the genoa in strong winds aboard *Express Crusader*, Naomi James while making her efficient and courageous single-handed voyage round the world by way of the Stormy Capes, nearly always dropped the sail into the sea.

As mentioned earlier, the term mizzen staysail (Plate 39) is misleading, for aboard the normal ketch or yawl there is no mizzen stay, and the sail is set flying from the mizzen masthead to some point on the weather deck in the vicinity of the mainmast – the taller the mizzen mast the farther outboard will the tack need to be, the intention being that the sail should interfere as little as possible with the mainsail; the sail must be set to leeward of the main backstay – a single backstay is in this instance preferable to twin backstays. Normally the sheet, having passed to leeward of the mizzen shrouds, will lead through a block at the end of the mizzen boom and then to a cleat on that spar. To set the sail, make fast the tack, belay the sheet, bend on the halyard and hoist away. Hardening in the sheet may need some strength, for there is likely to be a heavy load on it; but if there are reefing winches on the boom one of them will of course be used. To take the sail in, let go the sheet first, then the halyard and haul the sail down by its luff. With the wind on the beam a mizzen staysail pulls well, but in my experience it is more or less limited to that point of sailing, for if the wind is a little forward of the beam the sail will backwind the mizzen, and if the wind is abaft the beam it will interfere with the flow of wind into the mainsail. Nevertheless, it will be of value in a light wind and a swell when the heavier working sails will not draw.

Topsails (Plate 40)

With gaff rig I would regard the topsail more as a working than a light-weather sail, and the handing of it equivalent to taking in the first reef of a bermudian sail; however, it is convenient to include it here. It should be of lighter cloth than the mainsail, and to set well be of such a shape that its head and foot are of equal length. It is best made with the mitre running horizontally from clew to luff, and a thimble to take a single leader (a rope spliced round the mast at the point where the thimble will be when the sail is set) should be seized to the luff at the mitre, and the leader be rove through it and secured before the sail is sent aloft. The sail must be a little smaller than the space available so that it can be sheeted flat for sailing close-hauled. If the mast is not tall enough to permit the correct proportions, part of the luff can be bent to a light wood or alloy yard; then the thimble should be seized to the heel of the yard, and the leader rove through it will ensure that the yard is kept under control as it goes up, and is held vertical when aloft. The halyard should pass over a sheave at the masthead rather than through a block, which would allow too much drift; the sheet will pass over a side-sheave at the end of the gaff on the opposite side to that on which the main topping lift is rigged, then through a block or bull's-eye slung from the gaff jaws, and down to a cleat on the mast; the tack will be set taut by winch or tackle. Although these three ropes should come down to the mast or the deck close to it, the leader may with advantage be belayed out by the shrouds so as to hold the sail clear to one side while being set or handed. If these suggestions are followed, the gaff topsail will prove to be a valuable and easily handled sail.

Running sails

Purely for the purpose of running, a squaresail with all the gear it needs is not really worth having in a small vessel. Among others who have tried it was Bill Leng, to whom Macpherson presented *Driac II* when he gave up sailing. He told me that during his passage from the Cape to England he became convinced that the squaresail was not worth its locker space, and the ship ran faster and much more steadily under mainsail and spinnaker. But a squaresail does, of course, reduce the work when gybing.

To make a squaresail worthwhile it must be of ample area, the yard on which it is set being at least twice the beam of the vessel, and it should be possible to set a raffee (a triangular sail with its lower corners hauled out to the yardarms) above the squaresail to increase the area in light winds; also the standing rigging needs to be so arranged that it is possible to brace the yard sharp up to enable the square canvas to be carried with the wind on the beam or even forward of the beam. This means that the lower shrouds will have to be led well aft, and the crosstrees pivoted so that the lee topmast shroud can be pushed back out of the way by the yard as it is braced up. Although this can be done aboard a gaff-rigged vessel without jeopardizing the mast or seriously interfering with the working of the fore-and-aft sails, it cannot be done safely when the mast is tall and is intended for bermudian rig. However, in large vessels making long passages, some square canvas may have advantages, as was shown by the 29-metre (96-foot) brigantine *Yankee* during the four 18-month voyages that she made round the world in ten years; she even set studding sails. *Yankee* carried a crew of about twenty amateurs, but that squaresails do not necessarily require large crews was demonstrated by Robinson, who modernized the brigantine rig for his 21-metre (70-foot) *Varua* so that she could be handled by two men, as he describes in his book *To the Great Southern Sea* (Peter Davies). Conor O'Brien, who circumnavigated in his 12·8-metre (42-foot) ketch *Saoirse* (Plate 58 *bottom*) in 1922–5, and was the second to do so, was also a staunch advocate of squaresails in yachts, and anyone who is interested in the subject, which revives some of the difficulties and delights of the great days of sail, and is seeking sound, practical advice, may find what he needs in O'Brien's *The Small Ocean-going Yacht* (Oxford University Press).

Today nearly everyone prefers to use a spinnaker, which is set forward of the mast on a boom of its own rigged out from the mast on the side opposite to that on which the mainsail is carried. The name is said to have originated from the yacht *Sphinx*, one of the first vessels to boom out a balloon jib in that way, hence sphinxaker, later corrupted to spinnaker. The sail can be carried with the wind from astern to abeam, providing increased sail area at a time when the headsail(s) may be blanketed by the mainsail. Tending as it does to balance the mainsail, it makes steering easier. But it is the least seaworthy of all of a yacht's sails, for it can only be controlled by its three corners, and unless care is exercised it can easily get out of control while being set or handed.

We have to consider two distinct types of spinnaker, the triangular, and the symmetrical or parachute, for although the names given to their parts and their gear are the same, they are rigged and handled in different ways. The spinnaker boom, which is sometimes known as the pole, has a topping lift and is trimmed by the after-guy, a rope leading from its outboard end to a cleat or winch aft; the boom's tendency to lift is restricted by a fore-guy which is made fast forward. The boomed-out corner of the sail is the tack, the inboard corner, to which the sheet is attached, is the clew.

The triangular spinnaker is the type most widely used in voyaging yachts, indeed, it is often no more than a headsail boomed out on the windward side; it is much the safer and easier to deal with, and aboard a yacht fitted with a bowsprit is probably the only kind that can conveniently be used. It is best set from the masthead, otherwise it will bear heavily on the headstay(s) on which it will chafe in a seaway, and it will be sheeted to some point on the deck or on the mast. It may have its own double-ended halyard rove through a swivel block aloft, its parts being led down one each side of the headstay(s) so that the sail may be hoisted on either side, and if they are belayed near the shrouds each side they will be clear of other gear and not be likely to become twisted; alternatively an existing headsail halyard may be used.

To avoid having to manhandle the boom, I find it is best to keep it shipped permanently in its gooseneck so that when it is not in use it may be stowed up-and-down the fore side of the mast (Plate 19 B), its upper end being held by its taut topping lift in a shaped wooden chock or metal crutch on the mast. For this arrangement the boom must be of such a length that it will pass under the inner forestay if the yacht has double headsail rig. The boom will have a sheave or block for the outhaul at its outboard end, and except with a very small sail the tack is best hooked to a traveller on the boom.

To set the sail, lower the boom by its topping lift to a horizontal position, and trim it to the correct angle (90° to the apparent wind) by means of its after-guy, and set up the fore-guy. Make fast the sheet, and secure the tack to the outhaul. Run dead before the wind and hoist the sail, then haul its tack out to the end of the boom. Aboard a small yacht, where there may be no topping lift or outhaul, and the boom is stowed on deck, lay the boom fore-and-aft with its outboard end at the stemhead; bend on the guys and the tack of the sail and make fast the sheet; run the boom forward until its inboard end can be shipped in its gooseneck on the mast, then hoist the sail and trim it with the guys. To avoid chafe when the wind is on the quarter or the beam, it is necessary to pass the sheet round forward of the inner forestay to the lee side; but except in the lightest of airs it is best to hand the spinnaker and set the headsail(s) when the wind comes on the beam.

To hand the spinnaker, bear away and ease the after guy to let the boom go forward; take the sheet round the inner forestay if there is one, and make fast, then run the sail in and lower it in the lee of the mainsail. When gybing, the sail will have to be lowered and unbent while the boom is lifted by its topping lift and dropped the other side. The natural tendency for the boom to lift in a fresh wind can be reduced by raising its inboard end; the gooseneck is therefore often fitted on a short length of track on the mast so that it may be moved up and held by a clamp, or a pin engaging one of a number of holes. Open jaws to fit on the mast are simple and cheap and serve quite well in very small craft, but need to be secured in position with a line.

The symmetrical (or parachute) spinnaker, as its name suggests, has luff and leech of equal length, and enormous belly, its effective area far exceeding the area calculated from the usual measurements, and it is largely due to this sail, which sometimes is of fantastic size, that racing yachts make such fast down-wind passages. But it is a difficult sail to handle, and when it is set calls for constant vigilance on the part of the helmsman; so unless the cruising yacht has an adequate and competent crew she will, in my opinion, best do without it. However, it does have the advantages that a shorter boom than would be needed for a triangular spinnaker of equal size can be used; the sail does not require a low foot, which obstructs the helmsman's view, and because of the fullness at its head it is a lifting rather than a pressing sail; also as both halves of it are identical, there is in a small craft no need to lower it when gybing, for what was the tack on the old gybe becomes the clew on the new gybe, and vice versa. The sail is set forward of the headstay(s), its halyard block being placed above the topmast stay; its sheet leads to the lee side of the yacht. If the sail is to be carried with the wind on the beam, it is important to take the sheet right aft to the lee quarter, otherwise the sail will set in a bag and cause excessive leeway. Provided this spinnaker remains full it cannot chafe on anything, but its weakness is that the rolling of the yacht, or an indifferent helmsman, may cause it to collapse; also during setting and handing it is liable to twist itself round one of the headstays unless a sail or net is set on that stay.

The gear for this sail is a little different from that used with a triangular spinnaker. The boom must be fitted with a topping lift at the point of balance, for the sail has no boltropes and should not be allowed to take the weight of the boom. Both ends of the boom are identical, and although special fittings are available for use on them the following simple arrangement will be found to work well in a small yacht with a solid wood boom, and is considered to be in use here because it much simplifies the description of how to set, gybe, and hand the parachute spinnaker. Taper both ends of the boom so that either will fit into the common cone-shaped cup on the gooseneck. Take two lengths of fibre rope and splice a snap-shackle to one end of each, but make the eye of the splice of such a size that it will jam on the tapered end of the boom. These two identical ropes will serve as sheet and after-guy as required. The fore-guy is a length of rope with a snap-shackle spliced into one end.

Suppose the spinnaker is to be set to port. Clip the snap-shackle of the rope that is to act as sheet to the starboard lower cringle of the sail. Pass it round the forestay, outside the starboard shrouds, and belay it on the quarter. Snap the shackle on the rope that is to act as the after-guy on the port lower cringle of the sail, and slip the eye of that rope over the outboard end of the spinnaker boom; lead the guy outside the port shrouds and belay it on the quarter. Lift the boom, which should be lying on deck in a more or less fore-and-aft direction, with the topping lift and ship its inboard end in the gooseneck cup. Hoist the sail in the lee of the mainsail, then trim the boom to the correct angle by means of the after-guy. Finally go aft and snap the shackle of the fore-guy on to the after-guy and slide it forward until it reaches the end of the boom; then belay the fore-guy forward.

To gybe (Fig 54), ease the after-guy to allow the boom to go forward; unship the inboard end of the boom from the gooseneck cup and slip on to it the eye of what has been the sheet but will now be the guy. Gybe the mainsail. Unshackle the fore-guy and push the eye of what has been the after-guy but will now be the sheet off the port end of the spinnaker boom. Run the boom athwartships and ship its port end into the gooseneck cup. Trim sheet and after-guy correctly and finally clip the fore-guy snap-shackle on to the new after-guy, slide it forward, and set it up.

To hand the sail, ease the after-guy to let the boom go right

forward so that all the wind is spilt from the sail; disengage the
guy from the end of the boom, ease away handsomely on the
halyard and gather the sail inboard in the lee of the mainsail.

Before any attempt is made to set a parachute spinnaker the sail
must be packed in its bag in such a way that its two long sides,

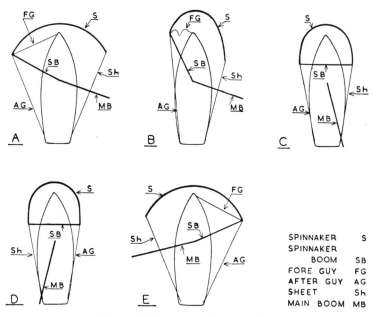

Fig 54   Gybing a parachute spinnaker

A Yacht running with spinnaker boom to port. *B* The after-guy is eased, allowing the
spinnaker boom to go forward. *C* Boom is unshipped from the mast, and the eye of the sheet
(which is now to become the after-guy) is slipped on to it. The fore-guy is unclipped. *D* The
main boom is gybed. *E* The port end of the spinnaker boom is unshipped from the eye of
what has been the after-guy but is now to be the sheet, and is shipped in the cup on the
mast. Sheet and after-guy are trimmed; fore-guy is clipped on and set taut.

which are usually marked with tapes of different colours, do not
cross one another, and with its three cringles at the opening of the
bag; this is a job which is best done down below out of the wind.
To make the setting and handing of the sail easier, a device known
as the Spinnaker Sally was developed by Jack Fretwell. It consists
of a series of plastic rings which hold the spinnaker in stops, as it
were, while it is being hoisted or lowered. The rings are strung
together on a light endless line rove through the thimble at the end
of the halyard, and when one of its parts is pulled on, slips the

rings up and off the head of the sail where they lie in a pile as the sail bellies out beneath them. When the sail is to be handed, the other part of the endless line is hauled on to pull the rings down over the sail to gather it in and collapse it. As the rings remain in place when the sail is bagged, the sail does not need to be repacked after each use.

14

AVOIDING COLLISION

Navigation lights – Steering and sailing rules – Anchor lights – Procedure in fog

THE International Regulations for Preventing Collision at Sea were revised in 1972 and came into force in 1977. The helmsman of even the smallest vessel should make himself familiar with the relevant parts of them before going afloat, otherwise he will be a danger to himself and others. The more important rules, from the yachtsman's point of view, are discussed in this chapter.

Navigation lights (Fig 55)

When under way a power vessel exceeding 7 metres (23 feet) in length must carry on her port side a red light arranged in such a manner as to show over an arc of $112\frac{1}{2}°$ from ahead to $22\frac{1}{2}°$ abaft the beam, and on her starboard side a similar green light. These lights are known as sidelights. From her foremast, or other forward position well above the sidelights, she must carry a white light (the Regulations call this a masthead light, but it is not necessarily at the masthead) so arranged as to show from ahead to $22\frac{1}{2}°$ abaft the beam on both sides, thus covering the same arc as is covered by the combined red and green lights, ie $225°$. If she exceeds 50 metres (164 feet) in length she must carry a second identical white masthead light abaft and higher than the first white light, and this must be visible over the same arc; if she is less than 50 metres (164 feet) this second light is optional. Right aft she must show a lower white light visible over the remainder of the

---

PLATE 31 (*facing*). *A.* A Danforth anchor stowed at the stemhead. *B.* In a small yacht a chain pawl fitted above the stemhead roller is better than a windlass; it weighs little and takes no space, and cable can be hauled in quickly when the work is light; when a strain comes on the cable the pawl holds it. *C.* An open chute between navel pipe and locker has the merit that the chain cannot jam. *D.* An electric windlass which in an emergency can be worked, though slowly, by hand lever. *E.* The double-acting lever windlass is to be preferred to one worked by crank-handle as the operator can use his full weight on it. *F.* A capstan is heavier and not so effective as a windlass.

PLATE 32 (*overleaf*). After a 5,000-mile cruise in the Mediterranean, the 10·8-metre (35·5-foot) cutter *Alano* sets out deeply laden from Gibraltar on her first crossing of the North Atlantic by the trade wind route. A description of her, together with her lines and plans, appears on pages 194 ff.

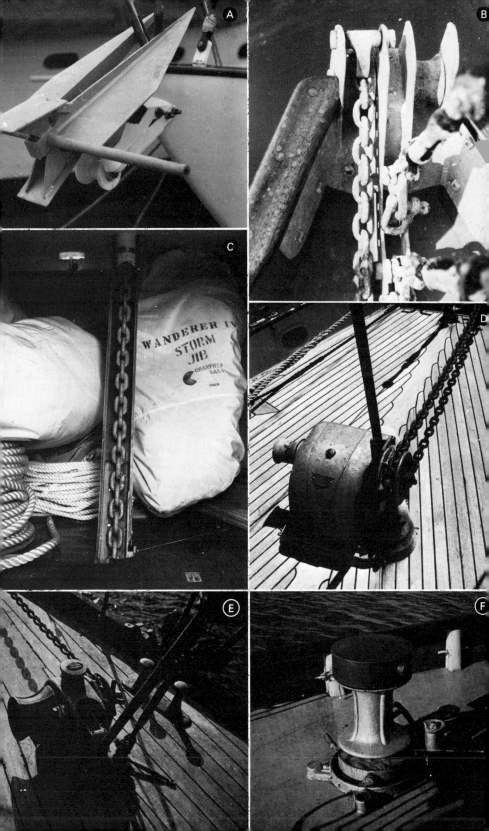

circle, ie 135°, from aft to 22½° abaft the beam on either side (Fig 55 *right*). It may be wondered why the arcs of visibility are not specified in round numbers; this is because they were originally based on compass points, a compass point being 11¼°.

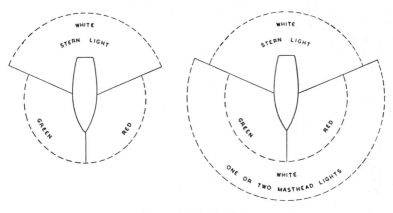

Fig 55   Navigation lights

Left: Sailing vessel (the red and green masthead lights which she may carry in addition are not shown here). *Right*: Power-driven vessel.

A sailing vessel exceeding 7 metres (23 feet) in length must carry red and green sidelights similar to those of a power-driven vessel (but see below), and she may in addition, though she hardly ever does, carry a red all-round light over a green all-round light near the top of the foremast. This pair of red and green lights gives no indication of the vessel's heading, but might be of value in showing her whereabouts before her lower lights become visible;

PLATE 33 (*overleaf*). *Top*: *Beyond*'s central cockpit is well protected by the doghouse, in which is the chart table and compass. The port cockpit seat lifts for access to the engine-room, and the hatch in the foreground leads to the after cabin. There is a saddle for the helmsman. *Bottom right*: The ship has all manner of brilliantly conceived and carefully worked-out details, such as the combined mainsheet horse, boom gallows, and bollards seen here, and forward, *bottom left*, the projecting lead for the anchor chain, and the lifeboat type fairleads for warps. Some of these ideas have been incorporated in more recent examples of this type of yacht.

PLATE 34 (*facing*). *Top*: With her clipper bow and trailboards, sweeping sheer, and graceful counter, the 14-metre (46-foot) ketch *Rena* (see pages 211 ff.) must surely be one of the most lovely yachts ever to come from the board of the American designer John Alden. *Bottom*: This view from the bipod bowsprit gives some idea of the fine workmanship the Vancils, her owners, put into her building, which they did entirely with their own hands.

in common with most people I regard them as confusing and unnecessary. A sailing vessel must also carry the same stern light as a power-driven vessel, but she must not carry a masthead light unless her engine is running, when she of course becomes a power-driven vessel. If she is less than 7 metres (23 feet) and is unable to carry the prescribed lights, she should have a white light handy (a torch) to show if a risk of collision should arise.

From the above it will be understood that when at night a red light over a green light (very rare) is seen the vessel is under sail; if a single red or a single green light is seen the vessel to which it belongs is also under sail, but if in addition one or two white lights are visible, the vessel is under power. If both red and green lights (excluding the rare red over green arrangement) can be seen together the vessel is bows on, and if she is showing two white masthead lights they will be in line; this is a dangerous situation one endeavours to avoid. If a single white light is seen, but no red or green light, it may belong to a small power vessel hull-down; however, it may be a vessel's stern light, and if so we must be at least $22\frac{1}{2}°$ abaft her beam, and although there will be nothing to tell us whether she is under sail or power, ours will be the overtaking vessel and it will be our duty to keep clear of her.

All this may seem simple enough, but there are some other arrangements of navigation lights which should be understood, and the more common of these are listed below:

A vessel towing another vessel when the length of the tow does not exceed 201 metres (660 feet): two vertical white lights on the mast of the tug in addition to sidelights and sternlights. Three vertical white lights are carried if the tow exceeds 201 metres (660 feet). A yellow light is carried above the sternlight and covers the same (135°) arc. The vessel being towed must show sidelights and a sternlight. If tug and tow are restricted in their ability to manœuvre, the tug will, in addition to the above lights, show a red over a white over a red.

A vessel constrained by her draught and unable to alter course: in addition to her usual lights, three red lights in a vertical line. By day a black cylinder.

A vessel aground: two red lights visible all round, vertically one over the other as well as anchor lights. By day three black balls.

A pilot vessel: at the masthead a white light over a red light, both visible all round. Side and sternlights are also shown if she has way on her.

A trawler with her trawl down: a green light over a white light, visible all round, in addition to the usual navigation lights. By day two black cones with apexes together.

A fishing vessel other than a trawler: a red over a white light visible all round, in addition to the usual side and sternlights.

A dredger: in addition to a red over white over red, two red lights to be shown if passage is restricted to one side; two green lights at the side that may be passed close-to.

As, however, fishing vessels and dredgers sometimes do not observe the rules where lights are concerned, and often have such brilliant working lights that their navigation or identification lights are difficult to make out, it is wise to keep well clear of them when possible, and not pass between two fishing vessels which are in continuous close company, for they are probably pair-trawling.

Although sailing vessels of less than 7 metres (23 feet) do not have to carry permanent navigation lights, the prudent owner will see that his vessel does, for although it might be argued that he could take avoiding action on identifying the lights of another craft, he might have the misfortune to meet another yacht sailing without lights, or, particularly in foreign waters, unlit fishing vessels.

If paraffin-burning lanterns are to be used, they must be of the internal cone windproof type, and should be as large as possible, preferably with 19-millimetre (¾-inch) wicks. But as electricity is so much more convenient and efficient – as anyone will know who has struggled to light paraffin lanterns on the cabin floor and carry them forward on deck, and ship them without their being knocked or shaken out – it is well worth using for this purpose if for no other.

When sailing vessels carried only narrow headsails and rarely set spinnakers at night, the sidelights were usually arranged on lightboards (or screens) secured to the shrouds and just within reach of the deck. But with the increased use of spinnakers and the advent of genoas, such a position became useless as those sails masked one or both lights, and many yachts then took to carrying their sidelights on coachroof or doghouse, where they were often cleverly incorporated with ventilators or other fittings. But placed so low the lights were frequently hidden from other ships by intervening seas, and the lee one could still be masked by a low-cut genoa when the yacht was heeled. Today nearly every yacht has guardrails round her bows (a pulpit) and this provides a more suitable position for the sidelight lanterns where they will be a reasonable height above the sea and cannot be masked by any sail. They should be properly lined up and preferably screened so that neither can be seen on the wrong bow, and (a dreary bureaucratic ruling) the screens may no longer be painted gay red and green, but must be matt black. However, in that situation the lanterns will be so close to one another that there is no good reason for having them separate when a single bi-colour lantern, which is permitted by the regulations for vessels up to 20 metres (66 feet) will serve just as well, and if electricity is used will economize in current or permit a more powerful light to be shown for the same consumption. The height of this lantern can be increased by mounting it on a short staff projecting upward from the pulpit. Such an arrangement was used by Bernard Hayman, editor of *Yachting World*, in his *Barbican*; he did much to investigate and solve the difficulties of showing efficient lights in yachts, and I have used with appreciation some of his findings and suggestions in this section.

An even better arrangement is to mount at the masthead a tri-colour lantern, which incorporates not only the red and green sidelights but also the white sternlight, all supplied by a single bulb; but at present (1981) such a tri-colour lantern is not permitted in yachts exceeding 12 metres (40 feet).

Originally a bi-colour lantern had a wide sector of ambiguity or low power, caused partly by the vertical pillar which separated the glasses of different colours; but now this appears to have been overcome by using acrylic colour screens edge-glued together so that a vertical pillar is not needed, and by employing a bulb with a vertical filament. I have observed such lanterns at sea, and have been impressed by the quick, clear change from one colour to another as course or bearing changed, and because of its height such a light is visible farther than one mounted on the pulpit. The only disadvantage of the vertical-filament bulb is that replacements are not always readily available, and a normal bulb cannot be used as a temporary measure because it will not fit the bayonet-holder employed with a vertical-filament bulb. Any navigation lantern using electricity should have very small ventilation holes drilled in its bottom, otherwise fogging of the glass and/or corrosion of the bulb-holder will occur.

Many lanterns made for yachts are fitted with dioptric lenses. These much intensify the power of the light by concentrating it into a narrow horizontal plane; but, except for riding lights (page 276), dioptric lenses are unsuitable for sailing craft because when heeled the light is directed down into the sea on one side and up to the sky on the other. But the fresnel lense, such as is fitted in some of the lanterns approved by the Department of Trade for use in British-registered yachts, has the property of making a light appear larger than its source of illumination, and this increases to some extent the distance the light can be seen.

For a sailing vessel of less than 12 metres (40 feet) the sidelights must be visible for 1 mile and the sternlight for 2 miles. Between 12 metres (40 feet) and 20 metres (66 feet) both side and sternlights must have a visibility of 2 miles. Much of its power is lost when a light shines through a colour glass; the following table gives the approximate distances at which light bulbs of various powers can be seen through clear and coloured glass, assuming that the visibility is good, the glass is clean, the bulb is new, and the voltage is the same as is marked on the bulb; this last may be difficult to achieve, for not only does the voltage of a battery drop while it is in use, but there will be a voltage loss if the bulb is remote from the battery and the cable feeding it is not of adequate size – the lower the voltage the larger is the gauge of copper wire needed.

Bulb	*Clear glass*	*Red or green glass*
6 watts	2 miles	$\frac{3}{4}$ mile
12 watts	3 miles	1 mile
24 watts	5 miles	2 miles

When a sailing vessel is proceeding under power she must, of course, show the lights of a power vessel, so she will need to be fitted with a power vessel's masthead light (this used to be called a steaming light). If she is less than 12 metres (40 feet) this must have a visibility of 2 miles, if she is between 12 and 20 metres (40 and 66 feet) it must be visible for 3 miles. But when this light is switched on the yacht may not continue to use a tri-colour lantern at her masthead, but rather must show normal side and stern-lights, thus having to run three bulbs (four if she has separate sidelights) instead of one, but since her engine will be charging the battery, the drain of current will not be so serious. Incidentally, the low side and sternlights may be of value even when under sail, for should the bulb in the masthead tri-colour lantern fail there will be little possibility of replacing it at sea. Such failures are not uncommon but I have found that bulbs with large glass envelopes last longer than the more usual kind with small envelopes.

Instead of the prescribed lights, some yachts, especially those making ocean passages, show only a single all-round white masthead light. Its merit is that it can be seen from a much greater distance than can a red or green light, and unlike the tri-colour lantern it may serve to illuminate the burgee or masthead windsock. If its bulb fails, a paraffin-burning riding light lashed somewhere low down (perhaps to the boom gallows) where it may show beneath the sails, could serve, though it might dazzle the watchkeeper. Some yachts on the western seaboard of North America make use of all-round masthead strobe lights; for a low consumption of current these give a high-intensity flashing light which can be seen a long way off. As this type of light is not mentioned in the Regulations one must presume it to be illegal, but having spent nights in company with salmon trollers (all with strobe lights) off the coast of British Columbia, I am convinced of its suitability for attracting attention – and the important thing is to be seen.

A ship travelling at 15 knots, and many are faster than that, covers 2 miles in 8 minutes, so if she sights the 2-mile red or green light of a sailing vessel at extreme range, she has only that time to assess the situation and alter course; but if the sailing vessel is less than 12 metres (40 feet) long and carries the prescribed 1-mile sidelights, 4 minutes is all the time the big ship has. This is not long enough for a VLCC (very large crude carrier) to answer her helm; so even the smallest yacht should show the most powerful lights she can.

If the ship has her radar working, and many do not use radar when well clear of the land, the situation is not much better. A yacht is a small target for radar to pick up, but she will show up better on the radar PPI (plan position indicator, the map-like display) if she carries a radar reflector to act like a mirror and return the radar beam to the sender. In its more usual form this comprises a set of metal plates nested accurately together to provide eight reflective right-angle triangular spaces. Size is very important, and the measurement from any corner into the right-angle in the centre should be not less than 25 centimetres (10 inches); it should be carried at a minimum height of 4 metres (14 feet) above the sea, and be fixed in such a way that the uppermost triangular space is in the catchwater position. Given these conditions one *might* be visible at a distance of 2 miles. The plain fact is that we are not very visible by eye or by radar, so we must be prepared to take avoiding action ourselves; but before doing so we should look astern to make sure that no ship is approaching from that direction to complicate matters. If in extreme circumstances we are compelled to draw attention to ourselves, this can be done with a white or green hand-held flare (a red flare should not be used as it is a distress signal), or perhaps by directing a powerful light, such as that from an Aldis signalling lamp, at the bridge of the ship, though this might result in the watchkeeper aboard her losing his night vision, and so make matters worse.

Steering and sailing rules (Figs 56 and 57)

    Rule 12 (a) When two sailing vessels are approaching one another, so as to involve risk of collision, one of them shall keep out of the way of the other as follows:

        (i) When each has the wind on a different side, the vessel which has the wind on the port side shall keep out of the way of the other.

        (ii) When both have the wind on the same side, the vessel which is to windward shall keep out of the way of the vessel which is to leeward.

        (iii) If a vessel with the wind on the port side sees a vessel to windward and cannot determine with certainty whether the other vessel has the wind on the port or on the starbord side, she shall keep out of the way of the other (Fig 57).

    (b) For the purpose of this rule the windward side shall be deemed to be the side opposite to that on which the mainsail is carried or, in the case of a square-rigged vessel, the side opposite to that on which the largest fore-and-aft sail is carried.

    Rule 13 (a) Not withstanding anything contained in the Rules of this Section any vessel overtaking any other shall keep out of the way of the vessel being overtaken.

    (b) A vessel shall be deemed to be overtaking when coming up with another vessel from a direction more than 22·5 degrees abaft her beam, that is, in such a position with reference to the vessel she is overtaking, that at night she would be able to see only the sternlight of that vessel but neither of her sidelights.

A certain method of ascertaining whether risk of collision exists is to watch the compass bearing of the converging vessel; if the bearing changes she will pass clear (provided she does not alter course), but if it does not change, a risk of collision should be deemed to exist. By night, if the sky is clear, it will be found much easier to watch the other vessel in relation to a star close above her; if she moves in relation to the star she will go clear. The fact that some landmark is opening out ahead or astern of the other vessel is no indication that she will go clear.

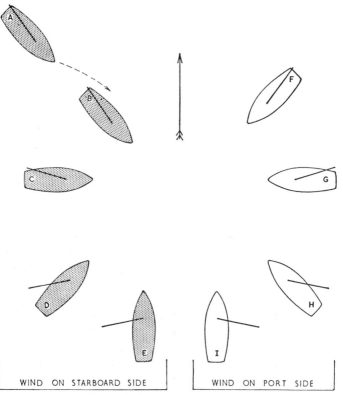

WIND ON STARBOARD SIDE   WIND ON PORT SIDE

Fig 56   Right of way, sailing vessels

(The arrow indicates the direction of the wind.)

All vessels with the wind on the starboard side (*A–E*, shaded) have right of way over all those with the wind on the port side (*F–I*, unshaded). *B* has right of way over *C*, *D*, and *E*, because she is to leeward of them; *C* has right of way over *D* and *E*, and *D* over *E* for the same reason. *A* keeps clear of *B* because she is overtaking. *F* has right of way over the other vessels with the wind on the port side because she is to leeward of them, and for the same reason *G* has right of way over *H* and *I*, and *H* over *I*.

Rule 18 states that when a power-driven vessel and a sailing vessel are proceeding in such directions as to involve a risk of collision, the power-driven vessel must give way; but this does not give the sailing vessel the right to impede a power-driven vessel which is restricted in her ability to manœuvre because of size, draught, width of channel, etc. Indeed, such action is expressly forbidden by the rule, and in a narrow channel (Rule 9) all vessels must keep as close as possible to the starboard side.

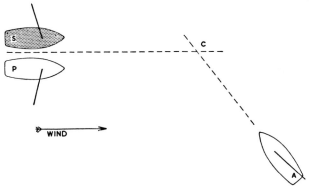

Fig 57   Rule 12 iii
A has right of way over *P* but not over *S*.

The term 'power-driven vessel' includes a yacht which is under both sail and power at the same time; to let others know that her engine is running she is supposed to carry (but rarely does) a shape in the form of a cone 2 feet in diameter point up in some prominent position. If she has no such shape, her helmsman should remember that those aboard the other vessel may not know that his is under power, so he should make his alteration of course to keep clear in good time. By night she should, of course, carry the lights prescribed for power-driven vessels.

The steering rules for power-driven vessels have no connection with the wind, and are as follows (Fig 58):

Rule 14 When two power-driven vessels are meeting on reciprocal or nearly reciprocal courses so as to involve risk of
collision, each shall alter her course to starboard so that each
shall pass on the port side of the other.

Rule 15 When two power-driven vessels are crossing so as to
involve risk of collision, the vessel which has the other on her

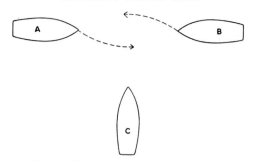

Fig 58   Right of way, power-driven vessels

A and *B* are meeting end on, so both must alter course to starboard, but *A* must give way to *C*, for *C* is on her starboard side. *B*, having *C* on her port side, has right of way over her.

own starboard side shall keep out of the way and shall, if the circumstances of the case permit, avoid crossing ahead of the other vessel.

A power-driven vessel may make the following signals on her whistle or siren:

One short blast: 'I am altering my course to starboard.'
Two short blasts: 'I am altering my course to port.'
Three short blasts: 'I am operating astern propulsion.'

A short blast is one of about one second's duration; a prolonged blast is one of 4 to 6 seconds duration.

The following rhymes may assist the helmsman of a yacht under power by night to remember the steering rules when meeting other vessels under power.

Meeting steamers do not dread.
When you see three lights ahead
Starboard wheel and show your red.
Green to green or red to red,
Perfect safety, go ahead.
If to starboard red appear,
'Tis your duty to keep clear;
Act as judgement says is proper,
Port or starboard, back or stop her.
But when upon your port is seen
A steamer's starboard light of green,
There's not so much for you to do
For green to port keeps clear of you.

As the rules were made to prevent collisions, not to cause them, some judgement and common sense must be applied in construing them. Although Rule 17 states that the vessel with right of way should hold her speed and course, it adds that if the other vessel fails to give way, she herself should take such action as may be necessary to avoid collision. You will see, therefore, that if your vessel has the wind on the starboard side, and some other vessel with the wind on her port side cuts across your bows instead of giving way as she should, no matter how indignant you may feel you have no right to carry away her ensign staff or ram her dingy if she is towing one, but must take the best action you can to avoid collision; if you fail to take such action you may be legally to blame for any damage done; the other vessel may or may not be to blame. Your action will probably be taken at the last moment, for you will have been expecting the other vessel to get out of your way; as by then it might be dangerous to bear away in an attempt to pass under her stern, for if you collided with her you would be travelling fast, the best action will be to luff up alongside her when you may strike her only a glancing blow. An experienced seaman will never place you in such a situation if he can possibly avoid it, and when it is his duty to give way he will alter course in good time, for he will understand the doubt in your mind. But there may be occasions when, as mentioned earlier, a big ship cannot give way to a yacht because of lack of water or some obstruction to navigation, or she may not have seen you, for even in daylight a yacht is not easily seen from high up on a ship's bridge unless her sails stand out against the sky. So you might bear in mind the following epitaph which, I think, is not so well known as it should be.

> Here lies the body of Michael O'Day
> Who died maintaining the right of way;
> He was right, dead right, as he sailed along,
> But he's just as dead as if he'd been wrong.

Yachts taking part in a race obey some different rules; for example, one racing yacht may luff to prevent another racing yacht from overtaking her to windward, a manœuvre which is not permitted by the International Regulations. To show that she is racing she will fly at her main masthead or in the rigging a square flag instead of a burgee; some put this up long before the race is due to start and omit to exchange it for a burgee after the race is over. When a yacht which is racing and one that is cruising converge so that there is a risk of collision, the International Regulations apply to both yachts, but most cruising yachts will give way if possible and allow the other a wide berth so that her wind is not interfered with; unfortunately this courtesy is often abused by racing dinghies.

In some areas, such as the Straits of Dover, where traffic is particularly heavy, separation schemes have been established to reduce the risk of collision. In these areas, which are shown on the charts, there are two lanes; ships bound in one direction have to keep in one lane, and those bound the other way keep in the other lane; a separation zone lies between the lanes. Crossing such an area should be avoided, but if it must be done (Rule 10 (c)), the crossing must be made as nearly as practicable at right angles to the general direction of traffic flow. Yachts may navigate in either direction inshore of the traffic lanes if they wish.

Anchor lights

A vessel of between 7 and 50 metres (23 and 164 feet) in length when at anchor must carry forward where it can best be seen a lantern so constructed as to show an all-round white light, or by day one black ball. Larger vessels show an additional similar white light lower down at the stern. Failure to comply with this regulation might mean that compensation would not be paid in the event of a yacht being run into and damaged; but it is not customary for yachts to show anchor lights (often known as riding lights) when lying on their moorings or at anchor in recognized yachting centres, unless such places are frequented by fishing or trading vessels. A vessel of less than 7 metres (23 feet) is not called on by the Rules to show an anchor light unless she is in or near a navigable channel.

The anchor light may with advantage have a dioptric lens to concentrate its power, and if of the paraffin-burning type it should have a windproof cone interior. In a small yacht the simplest way of hanging up the riding light is to have a short length of line spliced to its top, and to fasten this with a rolling hitch to the forestay as far up as one can reach; hemp line is preferable to synthetic as it is less likely to slip on the stay; the lantern is steadied by two lanyards from its bottom hitched to the guard-rails. In a larger vessel the lantern may be hoisted by a headsail halyard, a hank seized to some part of it being clipped to the forestay to prevent it from swinging about; the lower lanyards will be secured as before. To save trouble many yachts use a masthead light as a riding light, but at close quarters this is often unnoticed or misleading and I do not recommend it. The traditional time for setting the riding light is immediately after flags have been lowered at sunset, and it should be taken in (or switched off) before making colours in the morning, preferably some time before, as few things look more slovenly than a riding light left burning after the anchorage is astir. For lie-a-beds there are electric riding lights which by means of a photo-electric cell switch themselves off at daybreak. By day a vessel at anchor should (as noted above) exhibit a black ball shape forward, and if at anchor in busy waters this is a wise precaution, for a large vessel may need to take avoiding action at a considerable distance when she may not be able to tell if the yacht is at anchor or is moving under engine. Such a shape can be made by slotting together two disks of plywood.

Procedure in fog

One of the most dangerous situations for a sailing yacht is to be caught in a busy shipping lane in fog. After hoisting a radar reflector (page 270), if it is not carried permanently aloft as it should be, the best action her skipper can take is to move as quickly as possible to less crowded waters, or get into shallow water and anchor until the fog clears; but when acting on the latter suggestion he should bear in mind that fog is often accompanied or followed by a fresh wind.

In fog or poor visibility vessels should make the following signals on their whistles, sirens, or horns:

A power-driven vessel under way and moving through the water: One prolonged blast at intervals of not more than 2 minutes.

A power-driven vessel under way but not moving through the water: Two prolonged blasts at intervals of not more than 2 minutes.

A sailing vessel, no matter what her point of sailing may be, gives one prolonged blast followed by two short blasts, but this same signal is also made by a vessel not under command, a vessel restricted in her ability to manœuvre, a vessel constrained by her draught, and a vessel engaged in fishing.

All vessels when at anchor in fog should ring their bells rapidly for about 5 seconds at intervals of not more than one minute. But in fog sound can be very misleading, and no great reliance as to distance or direction should be placed on it.

Vessels of·less than 12 metres (40 feet) in length are not obliged to give the above signals, but are supposed to make some other suitable noise. Probably the best kind of foghorn for a sailing yacht is the hand-operated plunger type; I have heard that the aerosol type is liable to freeze up in operation.

15

WEATHER

An accurate forecast of the strength and direction of the wind is of great value, enabling one to judge whether it is prudent to start out on a passage, or if at sea to decide what course to steer to place the yacht in the safest or most advantageous position before the arrival of bad weather. Meteorology is a complex subject still far from being an exact science, and even the experts at meteorological offices with a wealth of information at their disposal frequently make inaccurate forecasts. So the yachtsman, whose observations are limited to the small area of sky within his view and to readings of only one barometer, can hardly expect to become a very reliable weather prophet. But his chief concern will be to know if the wind is likely to become strong or reach gale force, and by combining the readings of his barometer with a little rudimentary weather lore he may be able to forecast that.

Instruments

It is common knowledge that warm air rises and cold air moves in to take its place; the atmospheric pressure at sea-level therefore varies within narrow limits. One of the chief causes of wind is air moving from an area of high pressure to a low-pressure area. The pressure is measured by the height of a column of mercury that it will support in a tube, the upper end of which is sealed and the lower end left open to the atmosphere. The average height at sea-level is 76 centimetres (29·9 inches) or 1,013 millibars (3·4 millibars equal 0·25 centimetres ($\frac{1}{10}$ inch)).

Because of its weight and size and the need for it to be kept upright, a mercurial barometer is quite unsuitable for use in small craft, so in yachts an aneroid barometer is used instead. This consists of a thin metal chamber partly exhausted of air and hermetically sealed so that it is susceptible to the slightest change in external pressure; its top is connected by an arrangement of levers and springs to a pointer in such a way that its movements are greatly magnified. The dial over which the pointer moves may be marked in millibars or inches, but millibars are used almost exclusively today. A small screw at the back of the instrument enables the pointer to be set in agreement with a mercurial barometer, and although this should be done occasionally, for the metal chamber cannot be relied upon to hold its form indefinitely, the yachtsman will be concerned with the up and down movements more than the actual height.

The barograph is an aneroid barometer in which the variations of pressure are recorded in ink on a chart mounted on a revolving clockwork- or battery-driven drum which takes a week to make a complete revolution. It therefore gives a continuous record of the pressure, and although a similar result can be obtained by plotting the readings of an ordinary barometer, taken every two hours or so, on a piece of squared paper and sweeping a line through the dots, few people have the time or inclination for this. The pictorial record provided by a barograph is valuable when attempting to make a weather forecast, and the instrument is therefore to be preferred to an ordinary aneroid. It should be secured in an athwartships position so that the pen will be less likely to leave the chart when the yacht rolls, but in rough weather the motion may cause the ink line to be rather thick. (The barograph seen in Plate 6B has given trouble-free service at sea for 25 years.)

Most of us can judge with sufficient accuracy for weather forecasting whether the temperature is rising or falling, but if a thermometer is used it should be remembered that it is the outside air temperature that is required, not the temperature in the cabin. A wet-and-dry bulb thermometer for recording humidity, and an anemometer for measuring the force of the wind, are not needed for the rough forecasting which is all that most sailing people attempt, but the latter is of considerable interest in checking one's estimates of strong winds; if it is hand-held the results are likely to be disappointing unless we remember that official measurements are taken at a height of 10 metres (33 feet) above the ground or the sea, where the wind may be approximately one-third stronger than at ground- or sea-level. But many yachts have anemometers and wind-direction sensors at the masthead with dials in the cockpit. We must also take into consideration the speed of our vessel in relation to the direction of the true wind. There are two types of hand-held wind-measuring instruments. The anemometer proper (Plate 42E) has a number of wind-driven cups which rotate a vertical spindle; this in turn moves a pointer on a scale marked in knots or in kilometres or miles per hour. In the ventimeter (Plate 42F) wind enters at the bottom of a transparent cylinder and pushes a disk up a vertical rod against the force of gravity; the cylinder has wind strengths engraved on it, and the reading is taken at the point reached by the disk. The anemometer is the steadier and more accurate, and is not affected by damp, but it is more expensive.

Weather systems

There are two main weather systems, anticyclones and depressions. An anticyclone is a high-pressure system which moves very slowly, or may remain stationary for some time, and often covers a huge area. In the northern hemisphere the wind circulates in a clockwise direction around and a little out from the high-pressure centre, where there is sometimes a large area of calm. The anticyclone – for which the barometer rises slowly, remains high perhaps for several days, and then just as gradually falls – is normally associated with fine settled weather, though the wind may blow with considerable force on the outskirts. In summer in European waters an anticyclone is usually accompanied by a clear sky, but in the winter, particularly in the southern half of the system, the sky is often uniformly overcast. Fog may be experienced, forming at night and dispersing when the sun gains strength.

A depression is a fast-moving, low-pressure system, the lowest pressure being in the centre. In the northern hemisphere the wind blows in an anti-clockwise direction around and a little inwards towards the centre, increasing in strength as the centre is approached. A depression is caused in the following manner. When cold air from the polar region meets warm air from the equatorial region a bulge is produced in the polar front (the line where they meet). The warm air rises, causing an area of low pressure to develop, and this in turn causes the air to circulate anti-clockwise around the area (in the southern hemisphere it circulates clockwise). The cold air is thus deflected round, and coming in behind the bulge forces its way beneath the warm air; the line where that occurs is called the cold front. On the opposite side of the bulge the warm air rises over the cold air; the line where that occurs is called the warm front. The cold front, travelling faster, eventually catches up the warm front; all the air in the original warm front is then lifted up and occluded. When that happens the source of energy is removed, the depression expends itself and is said to have filled up.

Fig 59 shows a depression with warm and cold fronts before occlusion. The concentric lines are isobars, ie lines of equal barometric pressure, and the height of the barometer in millibars is written against each. The long thick arrow shows the direction in which the depression is travelling; over the British Isles this is usually between east and north-east; the speed varies within wide limits, but averages about 25 miles per hour. The small arrows show the direction of the wind; from these it will be seen that the low-pressure centre always lies a little abaft the starboard beam of a vessel which is heading into the wind; the abrupt change in the

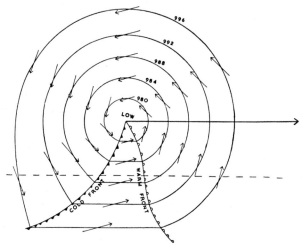

Fig 59   A depression with warm and cold fronts before occlusion

direction of the wind at the warm and cold fronts will also be noticed. An observer situated on the centre line of approach will experience a south-east wind with a falling barometer; the wind will remain constant in direction but will increase in strength until the centre has reached him. There may then be a short uneasy calm followed by a strong wind from the opposite direction, north-west, and the barometer will begin to rise. An observer situated in the southern half of the depression (on the dotted line in Fig 59) will experience a south or south-east wind with a falling barometer. As the barometer continues to fall the wind will veer (shift clockwise) to south-west and west, and as the warm front passes over him the temperature will rise and there will be drizzle or rain. Then when the cold front passes over him there will be a drop in the temperature, the barometer will begin to rise and the wind will veer suddenly to north-west, blowing hard for a time in squalls, and then moderating as the outer isobars pass over. It often happens that the cold front has caught up with the warm front and occlusion has taken place by the time the depression reaches the British Isles. There will then be only one very rapid change in the direction of the wind at the occluded front, though the wind will, of course, veer as the depression passes over, and the period of warm damp weather which occurs between a warm and cold front will be short and quickly over. The centres of many depressions pass north of the British Isles, but if the centre should pass south of an observer he will experience a backing wind, ie one which shifts anti-clockwise, starting at east and finishing at north, but no warm or cold fronts will pass over him.

Weather lore

Sailors will agree, I think, that the information afforded by the barometer is of value provided that it is interpreted correctly; but this is not always easy. Able as he is to obtain readings of a barometer at only one place, he might be unable to tell whether a fall indicated the approach of a depression or merely the dispersion of an anticyclone, were it not for the fact that depressions are nearly always preceded by certain signs in the sky. The first of these will be the appearance of mares' tails, the long wisps of whitish cloud (cirrus) seen radiating high up in the western sky. These may sometimes be seen 300 miles away, so if the depression is approaching at 25 miles per hour one may have warning of it 12 hours in advance and before the barometer starts to fall. In some instances the sky will give as much as 24 hours' notice of the approach of a depression. But it should be remembered that cirrus also appears quite often in fine settled weather giving the sky a wild torn look, and it is only when these clouds have some semblance of cohesion that they are associated with bad weather. As the depression approaches, the mares' tails gradually increase until the sky is covered with a whitish film (cirro-stratus) through which the sun or moon may appear dimly surrounded by a solar or lunar halo, and one can usually reckon that a halo in temperate regions presages bad weather, possibly within 48 hours. (A halo, incidentally, may appear on the other side of a depression when the bad weather has passed, though this is rare.) Meanwhile the wind, if it has been blowing from west or south-west, will lose strength for a time and will back temporarily to the south or south-east before starting to blow hard, and the barometer will begin to fall.

> When the wind shifts against the sun
> Trust it not, for back it will run.

The sequence of weather that will follow has already been described, but how long the bad weather will last will depend on the area of the depression and the speed of its advance; generally the longer the preliminary symptoms are seen before the arrival of the depression the longer will the bad weather last.

> Long foretold, long last,
> Short warning, soon past.

From time to time rules have been published by observers giving results by which it is claimed that weather may be forecast by fluctuations of the barometer combined with thermometer readings; but space forbids their inclusion here, and from the yachtsman's point of view it will probably be sufficient if he learns the main rules which are more or less well established and are easily remembered by the old rhymes.

A marked and rapid fall foretells stormy weather and rain:

> At sea with low and falling glass,
> The greenhorn sleeps like a careless ass.
> But when the glass is high and rising
> May soundly sleep the careful wise one.

Instances of fine weather with a low glass sometimes occur, but a period of wind or rain usually follows.

Severe gales, usually from the north-west, frequently occur after the barometer begins to rise suddenly from a very low point.

> Quick rise after low,
> Foretells a stronger blow

or

> While rise begins after low,
> Squalls expect and a clear blow.

In general, unsteadiness or a rapid rise of the barometer indicates unsettled weather, while steadiness or a slow rise foretells fine weather.

From the earliest times sailors have been accustomed to study the sky, the winds, the waves, and other signs of nature from which they might forecast coming changes in the weather.

Perhaps one of the best set of rules is that compiled by Admiral Fitzroy, and I quote some of them here as they form a sound foundation on which the yachtsman can base his own investigations into the fascinating subject of weather lore.

'A rosy sky at sunset presages fine weather; a red sky in the morning bad weather, or much wind – if not rain.

> A red sky in the morning is a sailor's warning;
> But a red sky at night is a sailor's delight.

'A grey sky in the morning, fine weather; a high dawn (when the first light in the sky is some distance above the horizon), wind; a low dawn, fair weather.

'A dark, gloomy blue sky is windy; but a light bright blue sky indicates fine weather.

'A bright yellow sky at sunset presages wind; a pale yellow sky, wet.

'Small inky-looking clouds foretell rain; a light scud driving across heavy clouds presages wind and rain.

'Soft-looking or delicate clouds foretell fine weather with moderate or light breezes; hard-edged, oily looking clouds, wind.

'Generally speaking natural, quiet, delicate tints or colours, with soft undefined forms of clouds, foretell fine weather but gaudy colours or unusual lines, with hard definite outlines presage wind or rain.'

And here are a few more of the old rhymes which most sailors know.

> If the rain before the wind, tops'l sheets and halyards mind.
> If the wind before the rain, soon you may make sail again.
>
> Mackerel sky and mares' tails.
> Make lofty ships carry low sails.

The bar or ribbed cirrus (mackerel sky) is a clear danger signal.

> When clouds appear like rocks and towers,
> The earth's refreshed by frequent showers.
>
> If clouds look as though scratched by a hen,
> Get ready to reef your topsails then.

It is said that in European waters a sure sign of stormy weather is the presence of porpoises playing close inshore, or when they venture up harbours and rivers. I regard this theory as debatable, though it has been handed down in the old rhyme:

> When the sea-hog jumps,
> Look out for your pumps.

Brilliant phosphorescence at sea can usually be relied on to indicate a period of fine weather with sunshine and light breezes.

Remarkable clearness of atmosphere when distant objects appear very clear cut and distinct is nearly always a sign of approaching rain.

High clouds travelling in a different direction to the wind indicate a shift of wind.

These are but a few of the many weather signs; the observant mariner who looks about him instead of believing without question everything that was broadcast in the latest forecast will discover many others for himself.

Except when a depression is passing over, the wind in the neighbourhood of the land usually lulls at night. In warm weather the land heats up in the daytime more than the sea, the air over it rises and air comes in from off the sea to take its place, so an on-shore breeze blows. But at night the reverse happens; the land cools more rapidly and becomes colder than the sea so that an off-shore breeze blows. Such land and sea breezes do not extend far from the shore, so it may pay in such weather to keep close to the coast even though one may have to deviate some distance from the direct course.

Each volume of the Admiralty *Pilot* (page 330) contains notes on the pecularities of the weather found in the area covered, and climatic tables showing what weather has been experienced over a period of years at certain points in the area.

Forecasts

Unfortunately for the amateur weather forecaster the weather does not consist simply of a series of perfect anticyclones and depressions following one another along a fixed track. The systems may be of almost any shape and they affect the direction of movement of one another; a depression meeting an anticyclone alters course to pass round it, and when a depression is occluded, secondary disturbances are liable to form on its warm side and rotate round it. Such variations and the weather that is likely to accompany them cannot be predicted by a single observer. But the professional meteorologist receives simultaneous weather reports from a large number of ships and places spread over a wide area, and also from satellites, and is therefore able to draw a synoptic chart (weather map); the isobars on this chart show the position, size, shape, and depth of the various weather systems in the area covered. By comparing the most recent synoptic chart with earlier ones, it is possible for the meteorologist to see in what directions movements are taking place, and to predict what weather may be expected in the near future.

Most countries have meteorological offices, and the forecasts they produce and the reports they collect are generally broadcast by national radio stations, and often by coastal and coastguard radio stations. For most of Europe the radio frequencies used and times of forecasts will be found in *Reed's Nautical Almanac*, but for other parts of the world the appropriate volume of *Admiralty List of Radio Signals*, or *World Radio Handbook*, may have to be consulted, though the information can often be obtained from local sources which are less bulky and easier to use. Sometimes the wind strength is given in Beaufort numbers (see following page), sometimes in knots, and in some countries there is a move afoot to give it in kilometres per hour, or metres per second, and already some broadcasts give visibility in kilometres. Such changes are not likely to please the seaman who thinks and works in nautical miles and knots.

The American time-broadcasting stations WWV and WWVH (see pages 315 and 317) give brief but important weather information, such as the positions of tropical revolving storms, thunder storms, and fog, for the Atlantic and Pacific oceans respectively; at the time of proof-reading (January 1981) WWV starts at 8 minutes after each hour and WWVH at 48 minutes after each hour.

There are around the coasts of the British Isles a number of storm-signal stations. These display the following signals when an atmospheric disturbance is in existence which will probably cause a wind of force 8 Beaufort scale, or more, in the area to which the warning applies: by day a cone hung point down for a gale with any south in it, and point up for a gale with any north in it; by night three red or three white lights in the form of a triangle, point down for a southerly, or point up for a northerly gale. In the USA weather warnings are displayed by flags: one red pennant for small craft warning, wind up to 33 knots; two red pennants for gale warning, wind 34–48 knots; one square red flag with a black centre for whole gale warning, wind 49–63 knots; two square red flags with black centres for hurricane warning, wind 64 knots and above. Lists of storm-signal stations will be found in the appropriate *Pilot*. Some information about ocean weather and tropical revolving storms will be found in Chapter 21.

Beaufort scale of wind force

Beaufort Number	Speed in knots*	Description	Height of sea metres	feet†	Deep sea criteria
0	less than 1	Calm	—		Sea mirror-smooth
1	1–3	Light air	0·08	¼	Small wavelets like scales, no crests.
2	4–6	Light breeze	0·15	½	Small wavelets still short but more pronounced. Crests glassy and do not break.
3	7–10	Gentle breeze	0·6	2	Large wavelets, Crests begin to break. Foam is glassy.
4	11–16	Moderate breeze	1·0	3½	Small waves becoming longer; more frequent white horses.
5	17–21	Fresh breeze	1·8	6	Moderate waves, and longer; many white horses.
6	22–27	Strong breeze	2·9	9½	Large waves begin to form; white crests more extensive.
7	28–33	Near gale	4·1	13½	Sea heaps up; white foam blown in streaks.
8	34–40	Gale	5·5	18	Moderately high waves of greater length; crests begin to form spindrift. Foam blown in well-marked streaks.
9	41–47	Strong gale	7·0	23	High waves; dense streaks of foam. Crests begin to roll over.
10	48–55	Storm	8·8	29	Very high waves with long overhanging crests. Surface of sea becomes white with great patches of foam. Visibility affected.
11	56–63	Violent storm	11·3	37	Exceptionally high waves. Sea completely covered with foam.
	64+	Hurricane			The air is filled with spray and visibility seriously affected.

* Measured at a height of 10 metres (33 feet) above sea-level.
† In the open sea remote from land.

16

AIDS TO NAVIGATION

Charts – Chart instruments – Compass – Lead and echo-sounder – Patent log and speed indicator – Radio receiver – Radio direction-finder – Sextant – Binoculars – Lights, buoys, and beacons – Nautical almanacs and sailing directions

NAVIGATION has been defined as the science which enables a ship to be conducted from place to place in safety, and her position to be determined by observations of terrestrial or celestial objects, or by other methods. Pilotage might be defined as navigation near or within sight of land. Except when making a passage which will take him out of sight of land for some considerable time, the navigator will not have to rely on observation of celestial objects, though he may sometimes find a working knowledge of that branch of navigation (see Chapter 22) useful even on a short passage. Most of the methods used for finding a vessel's position by observations of terrestrial objects, or by dead reckoning, are simple to understand and call only for a slight knowledge of geometry and a little common sense; but before attempting to master them, the would-be navigator should understand the charts and instruments that he will be called upon to use. However, he need feel no alarm at the array of electronic equipment he sees in the cockpit and navigation space aboard many a modern yacht, for although such gear may be considered essential for winning races or keeping up with the Jones's the cruiser can manage very well without the help of most of this; so only the more important items will be touched on in this chapter.

Charts

Everyone knows that the earth is an almost perfect sphere rotating eastwards on its axis, that the equator is the great circle midway between the north and south poles, and that the poles must therefore be 90° from every point on the equator, the angle being measured from the centre of the earth. Any circle drawn round the earth parallel to the equator is known as a parallel of latitude, and its position is defined by the angle made at the centre of the earth between it and the equator; the angle is preceded or followed by the letter N or S to show whether it is in the northern or southern hemisphere. A place having a latitude of 45°N will therefore be situated on a circle parallel to the equator and half-way between the equator and the north pole. Any semicircle which joins the poles must cross the equator and all parallels of latitude at 90°; such a line is known as a meridian, and if we select a meridian which passes through some known place, all other meridians can be related to that place by the angles they make with its meridian. The meridian which passes through Greenwich observatory is used internationally as the zero meridian, and the longitude of any place is the angle between its meridian and the meridian of Greenwich measured along the equator east or west up to 180°. It may be of interest to recall that between 1450 and 1650 the meridian of the Azores was used as zero, and that the meridian of Greenwich was not used by all nations until the eighteenth century.

The difficulty of drawing a chart of part of the world's curved surface on a flat sheet of paper was overcome by the system known as Mercator projection, after the Dutch mathematician Gerard Mercator who invented it in 1580. On such a chart the meridians are laid down as parallel straight lines instead of converging on the poles, as they do on the earth, so that a degree of longitude, is kept the same size over the whole chart. This means that the chart is increasingly distorted as the pole is approached, and in order to preserve the correct proportion of length to breadth in every part of it, the parallels of latitude are laid down at increasing distances apart as they get nearer to the pole (Fig 61). One minute of arc ('), which is the 60th part of a degree (°), measured on the earth's surface, is one nautical mile of 6,080 feet (1,853 metres). So the minutes of latitude scale on the east and west margins of the chart can be used as a scale of nautical miles; but when using it for that purpose on a chart which covers a large area, the scale in the same latitude as the distance to be measured must be used, or there will be an error due to the lengthening of the minutes of latitude as the polar edge of the chart is approached. On large-scale charts, however, the difference in length of the minutes of latitude near the north and south extremes of the chart is so slight as to be of no practical importance. The longitude scale marked on the north and south margins of the chart must not be used as a scale of distance, because nowhere, except on the equator, does one minute of longitude equal one nautical mile.

All circles which bound the maximum circumference of the earth, that is, circles which have their centres at the centre of the earth, are known as great circles. All meridians are great circles, but of the parallels of latitude the equator is the only great circle. If a flat surface is laid to touch a globe at a certain point, all great circles projected on to it from the centre of the globe will appear as straight lines, and a chart constructed on that principle is called a gnomonic chart (Fig 60); here the meridians converge towards the pole, and all parallels of latitude, except the equator, appear as curves.

Any course represented by a straight line on a Mercator chart, except one which runs due north or south, is known as a rhumb line, and a vessel adhering to that course will reach her destination, but not by the shortest route. A rhumb line is, however, near enough for distances up to 300 or 400 miles, or in low latitudes, ie near the equator. The shortest distance between two points on the earth's surface is the arc of the great circle which passes through them, and it is in determining this course that the gnomonic chart is used.

Suppose, for example, we wish to determine the great-circle course from Bermuda to the Isles of Scilly. On the gnomonic chart of the North Atlantic we rule a straight line from Bermuda to Scilly, as has been done in Fig 60, and note the latitude in which this line crosses each of the six 10° meridians on the chart. (To enable this to be done easily, all the latitude and longitude lines on the chart, and there are many more of them than are shown in the figure, are marked at 1° intervals; but for the purpose of reproduction here these marks have had to be omitted.) We transfer these positions to the Mercator chart of the North Atlantic, and a curved line swept through them will be the great-circle course. But to follow that line exactly is impossible because it would involve a slight but continuous change of course. Therefore each position is joined to the next by a straight line, as has been done in Fig 61, and the course is altered at each position, ie at each 10° meridian, to keep to those lines.

It does not often happen that a sailing vessel can keep to a great-circle course, but in high-latitude sailing she should keep as closely as possible to it, weather and other circumstances permitting, because the higher the latitude the greater will be the saving in distance. But the chief use of the great-circle course is to show which is the most favourable tack in turning to windward, and in the absence of any special reason to the contrary, the vessel should

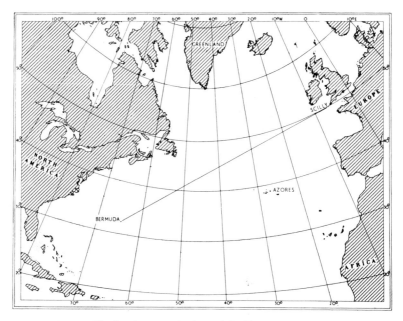

Fig 60   A gnomonic chart of the North Atlantic
on which Bermuda and Scilly have been joined by a straight line for the purpose of
ascertaining the great-circle course between them. (Based on Admiralty chart No 5095
with the permission of the Controller of HM Stationery Office and the Hydrographer of the
Navy.)

be put on the tack which brings her nearer to the great-circle course.

As a Mercator chart is drawn with the meridians running true north and south, to find what the true course is from one point to another one has only to join the points with a straight edge and measure with a protractor the angle made between that line and any meridian, if it does not cross a meridian it can be carried to the nearest one by means of a parallel ruler. Alternatively, if one wishes to lay off a known course from a certain point, one has only to measure the angle from one of the meridians and carry it with the parallel ruler to the point and draw it in. But to save the need for using a protractor for measuring angles, most charts have printed on them in one or more places a compass rose divided in degrees from 0 to 360, the circle being arranged so that the 0 is towards the top or north of the chart; one can then transfer the course with the parallel ruler direct to the centre of the rose and

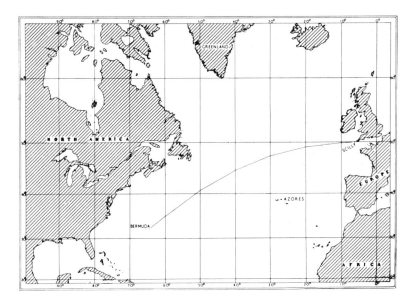

Fig 61   A Mercator chart of the North Atlantic
with the great circle course from Bermuda to Scilly drawn in. (Based on Admiralty chart
No 2059 with the permission of the Controller of HM Stationery Office and the Hydrographer of the Navy.)

read off the angle. On harbour, coastal, and narrow-water charts there is within the 360° circle often a second concentric circle tilted a little so that its north point (usually marked with a half fleur-de-lis or an arrow-head) points east or west of true north. Its degrees are numbered from 0 to 360, as in the outer circle. Within this circle there may be yet another concentric circle tilted the same amount as the other, and marked with the points and quarter points of the compass; but these are being dropped from some charts. The inner compass roses are tilted east or west of true north to the amount of the local magnetic variation (page 303), so that magnetic courses and bearings can be read direct from them without the need for any calculation.

Ocean charts, which cover large areas, and may have a scale as small as 1 : 21,000,000, cannot be provided with magnetic compass roses because the variation will be different in different parts of them; instead they have isogonic lines (lines of equal variation) drawn on them at one or two degree intervals, so that the navigator may know the variation in his area. Such charts, of course, are not suitable for use in the neighbourhood of land or shoals. A harbour plan might be drawn to the very large scale of 1:3,500, approximately 53 centimetres (21 inches) to 1 mile, though that is rare. Between these limits lie charts of several different scales, and in general the larger the scale the greater is the accuracy of the chart and the more detailed is the information given on it.

But a chart is far more than just a sheet of paper used for laying off courses and distances, for it gives a great deal of information essential for the navigator. The soundings (depths of water) may be given in fathoms, fathoms and feet, feet, or metres (see below), and it is always stated on the chart, usually beneath the title, what units are used. The datum to which the soundings have been reduced is also stated. This used to be low water ordinary spring tides (LWOS), but with most new charts it is lowest astronomical tides (LAT), a level below which no tide will fall except in exceptional circumstances. Against many of the soundings letters will be seen; these indicate the nature of the sea bed: M for mud, R for rock, St for stones, Wd for weed, etc. The figures on shoals or rocks which dry are underlined, and indicate the height above the datum level of the chart. Heights shown on the land or in brackets against small islands are above the level of high water at spring tides. A wealth of other information is also included on the chart: the position and character of navigation lights, fog signals, buoys, and beacons; the nature of the coast; important leading marks; information about tides and tidal streams, etc. All the signs and abbreviations used on British Admiralty (BA) charts will be found on chart 5011, a small book.

Great feats of seamanship, perseverance, and endurance were performed in the making of many of the early charts, for the work was done in the days of sail, and when there were no sounding instruments except the hand lead and line, no motor launches to do the inshore work, no radio signals with which to check the chronometers, and no refrigeration to keep the ships' companies supplied with fresh, health-giving food. Little is heard today of the men who performed this valuable service, and to most of us who use charts based on their surveys the only reminder is the credit line sometimes engraved beneath the title of the chart: 'Surveyed by Captain Fitzroy, RN, and the officers of HMS *Beagle, 1836.*' 'Compiled from the discoveries and surveys of Cook, Kotze,

Bellinghausen, Wilkes, and other navigators.' 'From the surveys of Captain H M Denham, RN, FRS, and the officers of HMS *Herald* and *Torch*, 1854–56.' Today, unfortunately for those who love charts and admire the men who made them, more and more of the credit lines are being dropped as new editions are printed, and their place taken by the unromantic statement: 'Compiled from the latest information in the Hydrographic Department.'

At one time BA charts covered the world, and it was considered they had no equal. Until the 1970s their soundings were mostly in fathoms, a fathom being a measure of 6 feet, ie what a man with arms outstretched can span. Today all BA charts, along with those published in other countries – but so far not in the USA though this will presumably happen soon – are being changed to the metric system, the metre of 3·28 feet being used instead of the fathom for soundings; when another but smaller figure a little lower down is shown adjacent to a sounding it is in decimetres, eg 12_4 indicates 12·4 metres. For drying heights and heights above high water metres are also used. So the present is a transition period, and it will be some time before all of the 3,300 BA charts can be changed; meanwhile caution needs to be exercised when reading a chart – one might float in one fathom but not in one metre. With the first of the BA metric charts came some other changes which were not to the liking of the yachtsman, and among these can be listed the following: total omission of information in some areas of a meduim scale chart which are covered by charts on a larger scale, compelling one to buy additional charts which perhaps may never be used, and lack of topographical and inshore information. These matters were taken up with the Hydrographic Office by the Royal Yachting Association, and it is likely that there will be some improvement as new editions are published. For cruising on the south coast of England and the east coast as far as the Wash, the Y series of charts published by Imray, Laurie, Norie & Wilson might well be considered, for they are small in size and contain extra information of value to yachtsmen. Stanford Maritime also publish charts for yachtsmen covering much the same ground.

Although there are in many ports at home and abroad agents for the sale of BA charts, often their stock is small and of only local coverage. I prefer to deal direct with one of the class A agents in the UK which maintain complete stocks, and correct them to the date of dispatch; for many years I have dealt with J D Potter Ltd of

145 Minories, London, EC3 and found their service prompt and efficient. On receipt of a roll of charts I open it as soon as possible and flatten each chart by rolling it the other way. With the help of the index chart in the appropriate *Pilot* (see page 330) – this is easier to use than the unwieldy *Catalogue of Admiralty Charts* – I arrange the charts in geographical order, ticking off on the index chart the number of each before stowing it away flat. If the short title printed on the back edge is not sufficiently descriptive, I add to it; for example '868, Five Fathom Hole and Murrays Anchorage'; to this I would add 'Bermuda'.

Since other countries are publishing more or all of their own charts, the navigator planning to go foreign would do well to obtain information about them; a class A agent should be able to supply this and obtain the charts for one, but if difficulty is experienced the following notes may help.

For cruising in US waters US charts are essential, and index charts showing the coverage may be obtained from Coast and Geodetic survey, Rockville, Maryland 20852. US charts on which the number is followed by the letters S-C contain additional information for small-craft, and often come in folders on which are printed tide tables for the year, times of weather forecasts, etc. They are not intended to be corrected, and new editions are published each year. Some of the abbreviations and symbols may be unfamiliar to the British yachtsman, but chart No 1 (a small booklet) lists all these and costs little. For some other parts of the world US charts are well worthwhile; for example, the

---

PLATE 35 (*facing*). *Top*: The saloon in *Rena*, the Vancils' floating home, has a pilot berth each side outboard of the settees, and the forecastle is used as a workshop, being fitted with a lathe and drill press. Cooking is done on a 110-volt electric stove. But that heavy displacement is not essential for gracious living is shown by the saloon, *bottom*, of the Sparkman & Stephens-designed and New Zealand-built ocean racer *Barnacle Bill*. She is of skeg and fin keel configuration with a displacement of 10,887 kilograms (24,000 pounds) and a LOA of 12·8 metres (42 feet), and has raced with success, including a Sydney–Hobart event. I met her cruising among the Society Islands in 1979 with her owners Jim and Donna Dicksen and their young family and others on board, and there appeared to be comfortable room for them all.

PLATE 36 (*overleaf*). *Left*: The world-girdling trimaran *Tryste II* (see pages 219–21) was built by Ernest and Val Haigh in a barn on Saltspring Island; I photographed her sailing gently in her native Canadian waters after she had completed a circuit of the Pacific in 1978. *Right*: Many blue-water voyages have been made in yachts of the popular Vertue class, which are now available in GRP. The most famous of the earlier ones, *Vertue XXXV*, is seen here well reefed and with No 2 headsail set just before Humphrey Barton, who later founded the Ocean Cruising Club, sailed her across the Atlantic by the intermediate route.

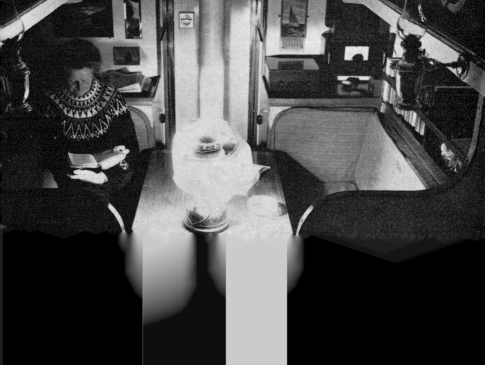

Galapagos Islands west of Panama, which extend over 2 degrees of latitude and $2\frac{1}{2}$ degrees of longitude, are covered by only one half-size BA chart, but the group is covered by a dozen US charts.

Canadian charts are in many respects similar to US charts, and for a few areas small-craft charts are published. Index charts showing the areas covered may be had from Canadian Hydrographic Service in Ottawa, and in Victoria BC. Again symbols and abbreviations may differ slightly from those used on BA charts, and Canadian chart No 1 lists these.

In both Australia and New Zealand some parts of the coasts are still covered by BA charts, but both countries are steadily extending the coverage with their own charts. Catalogues of these can be had from Navigation & Marine Services, 478 Collins Street, Sydney, NSW, and Marine Department Chart Agency, Stout Street, Wellington.

It is often stated that only the latest editions of charts should be used, but that is scarcely practicable for a wide-ranging cruising man who will build up a collection of charts over a period of years, or borrow from a friend or a club which has done so; the cost of replacing old charts with new ones when new editions appear would be considerable. But one must use some discretion. In rocky areas such as the west coast of Scotland or Brittany old charts will probably be safe to use so long as up-to-date information on lights and buoys is aboard; but in an area where sand or mud shoals abound, such as the Thames estuary or the Wash, changes in the channels and in the lights and buoys marking them

---

PLATE 37 (*overleaf*). The 9-metre (30-foot) heavy displacement sloop *Wanderer III* has made many long voyages, including three circumnavigations of the world; her best day's run was 169 miles, and once in the Indian Ocean she made good 440 miles in three consecutive days although she was floating below her designed LWL. The night photograph of her cosy saloon was taken by the light of the table pressure lamp alone. At the top each side can be seen the drip-catching handrails, and at their forward ends part of the two steel beams which strengthen the coachroof in way of the mast.

PLATE 38 (*facing*). Left: *Tarema*, one of the Trekka class (see pages 215–18), but with sloop instead of ketch rig, was built in Tasmania, and her present owner, Gary Adams, sailed her single-handed from Santa Barbara, California, to New Zealand. With a LOA of only 6·8 metres (20·8 feet) she is indeed a miniature though very able voyager. *Right: Manuiti II* is a larger yacht of similar type but without the tumble-home of the original design; the hull is that of a large dinghy with a fin keel added. In the ownership of Celia Reed she has cruised extensively from New Zealand, where she was built, among the islands of the South Pacific.

may take place, and an old chart might be unsafe to use. There is also the point that the datum for tide tables will be the same as the datum for the most up-to-date chart. Corrections affecting charts, known as *Notices to Mariners*, are published weekly and can be obtained from marine offices and chart agents. Most of the information contained in them is of direct interest only to large vessels, but they should be collected and looked through when preparing for a cruise, and any important changes and amendments which might affect the safe navigation of a small vessel should be noted on the charts. In 1979, however, the Hydrographic Department introduced the Small Craft Edition of *Notices* which contain only information of interest to yachtsmen; it covers the British Isles and European coast from the Gironde to the Elbe. It must be realized that when a chart has been replaced by a new edition the old one can no longer be corrected from this source. Some chart agents undertake the correction of valid charts for a fee.

Chart instruments (Plate 41)

The essentials are a parallel ruler for transferring courses or bearings to or from the compass rose, a pair of dividers for measuring distances, a protractor, and a pencil and rubber.

A three-sided pencil is better than a round or hexagonal one as it will not roll about the table quite so readily, and single-handed dividers are a little more convenient than the ordinary pattern as one hand is left free to manipulate the pencil or ruler.

Captain Field's improved-pattern parallel ruler made in transparent perspex is quite satisfactory, though a little care is needed to prevent it slipping when being worked in steps across the chart. Where a large and quite flat chart table is available, a roller parallel ruler is preferred by some as it is quicker to use and not so likely to slip.

In a small craft where the chart may have to be spread out on an uneven surface, such as a settee, a flexible course-setting protractor is better than a parallel ruler. To use it, place the centre of the protractor (there is a small hole in the middle of the pivot) over the end of the course and, holding it there, swing the arm to the centre of the nearest rose. Hold the arm and turn the protractor so that it agrees with the reading indicated by the arm on the rose, then hold the protractor from turning and swing the arm back to the course and read off on the protractor the course to steer.

A protractor will be needed for working on a chart which is not provided with a compass rose; a circular one marked in degrees from o to 360 is more convenient to use than the protractor engravings which most parallel rules possess. The Douglas protractor is an improvement on the common round one in several ways; it has a matt surface, on which pencil lines can be ruled and rubbed out afterwards, which is useful when laying off a position obtained by angles. In the USA the CNS-Nautech protractor is similar.

The station pointer (not shown) consists of a circular protractor marked in degrees and half-degrees, and has three arms from its centre, one being fixed and the others pivoted. It is not an important part of a yacht's navigational equipment, and on the rare occasions when it might be required, the Douglas protractor can be made to serve almost as well and is only a fraction of the cost.

Instruments are best kept in a fitted drawer or box to protect them from damage when not in use. If charts are kept flat, as they should be, there will be no need for weights to hold them down on the table, but spring clips are useful in preventing them from sliding off if the table is not provided with fiddles. A magnifying-glass, possibly incorporating a small bulb and dry battery in the handle, is a help when reading the small details on a chart.

The embryo navigator should avoid filling his yacht with a lot of clever-looking gadgets most of which would never be of any practical use to him, and he would do well to bear in mind the following passage from Captain Lecky's famous *Wrinkles in Practical Navigation* (George Philip):

... the navigator is deluged with any number of gimcrack methods, tables, diagrams and brazen instruments. Some of these latter are wonderful, and after a few weeks of study they can be made to do what a simple-minded person (not an inventor) would perhaps be stupid enough to think could be done equally well with the ordinary tools of the trade, and a few pencil figures on the helmet of the binnacle.

Compass

The magnetic compass usually consists of two or more magnetized needles attached to a circular card which is mounted on a pivot in a glass-topped brass bowl. The bowl is filled with fluid to damp down the movements of the card and keep it steady, and by reducing weight on the pivot decreases friction and wear; the bowl is slung in gimbals so that it will remain horizontal at all times. There are two kinds of fluid in common use: a mixture of alcohol and distilled water (the alcohol is to prevent freezing), and paraffin. If an air-bubble forms in the bowl it will make the compass difficult to read and may upset the balance of the card, so it should be removed by topping up with the correct fluid; some compasses are marked with the type of fluid used. The compass must be so arranged that its lubber line (the mark inside the bowl representing the ship's head, and by which one steers) is exactly forward of the centre of the card. When there is a wide gap

Fig 62   Points and quarter-points of the compass, north-east quadrant

between the edge of the card and the inside of the bowl, as there should be to reduce drag, the lubber line may consist of a thin wire almost touching the edge of the card, so as to reduce parallax to the minimum when the helmsman's eye is not directly abaft the compass.

The card may be marked with points and quarter points, or with degrees from o at north round clockwise to 360 again at north, and many compass cards are marked with both degrees and points, the degrees being on the outside. As there are 32 compass points in the circle of 360°, one point equals $11\frac{1}{4}$°, and a quarter-point, which is the smallest division shown on a card marked in that manner, equals just under 3°. Fig 62 shows the north-east quadrant and the names of the points and quarter-points. It should be noted that none of the by-points or quarter-points takes its name from a three-letter point: N by E is correct, not NNE by N; and NE by N¾N is correct, not NNE¼E.

Although quarter points are easier to see than degrees, and by night do not require so bright a light (which may dazzle the helmsman and prevent him from keeping a good lookout), the majority of people prefer to use degrees because this simplifies any calculations which may have to be made, such as allowing for variation when using a chart which has no magnetic compass rose, or when applying the deviation, and saves the trouble of converting degrees into points and vice versa.

Aboard a yacht with wheel steering, where the helmsman can place himself almost directly abaft the compass, the compass can be fitted with a prism to enlarge the lubber line and a portion of the card adjacent to it. But with tiller steering the helmsman will be to one side or the other of the centre fore-and-aft line, and then a compass fitted with a plastic dome magnifier (Plate 43*B*) will be better, and this is now the most commonly used type. However, some people prefer the grid type of steering compass (Plate 43*C*). In this the north-south diameter of the card is boldly marked with a line, wire, or some other straight device. On top of the bowl two parallel wires are fixed to a verge ring; this is engraved with degrees 0 to 360, and can be rotated on the bowl so that the course to be steered can be made to correspond with the lubber line. To steer that course the helmsman has only to keep the north-south line on the card parallel to the wires on top of the bowl, and as parallax need not be considered except in the circumstances mentioned below, such a compass can be placed anywhere within the helmsman's view. The north-south line and the wires can be treated with luminous composition so that no light is needed once the grid has been set. The disadvantages of the grid compass are that the ring has to be altered for every change of course, so the compass must be in an accessible position, and if the card is affected by dip (see page 307) a parallax error will occur unless the helmsman's eye is directly over the centre of the card. A grid compass made for use in aircraft is not suitable afloat as it has no markings on the card, and they are essential if bearings are to be taken, and to guard against a reciprocal course being steered by mistake.

The most important consideration when deciding on the position for the steering compass is that it should be placed where the helmsman can see it easily. When possible the best of all positions is immediately forward of the helm, and if the yacht is steered by wheel this will be on top of the wheel pedestal. In a small yacht a good position where it is safe from damage is beneath a pane of unbreakable glass or clear acrylic in the bridge deck, or if the compass is of the dome-top kind, recessed into the bridge deck. Sometimes it is placed just inside the cabin where it can be viewed through a port in the bulkhead, but as it will then usually have to be placed to one side of the companionway, it will be difficult to see on one tack. The practice of moving the compass from one side of the cockpit to the other each time the yacht stays or gybes is bad, for it may be subject to different deviation at the two positions.

If the steering compass is fitted in such a position that a clear view all round may be had from it, the instrument will be ideal for the purpose of taking bearings. A pair of sights will then be needed, and some compasses are provided by their makers with this facility, but for a compass without, it may be possible to make what is needed by glueing two vertical strips of brass, one with a hole in its top and the other with a V, opposite one another on a ring of thin hardboard to ship on the top of the bowl when bearings are to be taken (Plate 43D). But except in large yachts the compass cannot often be so placed. It may, however, still be used for taking bearings by putting the yacht's head on the object and reading the bearing at the lubber line, but that is inconvenient and sometimes impossible. Alternatively a pelorus (Plate 43A) may be used. This consists of a rotatable compass rose and a pair of sights pivoted on it; one could be improvised by cutting the rose from an old chart, mounting it on a wood base, and making a pair of sights for it as above. To use the pelorus, the card is set in relation to the ship's fore-and-aft line so that it corresponds to the course being steered. Then, while the ship is being kept steady on her course, the bearing is taken with the pelorus and will read as though taken with the compass. But except in a large craft it will be difficult to find a place for the pelorus where the operator can get his eye level with the sights, and only in smooth water will the helmsman be able to hold a sufficiently steady course for the instrument to be used accurately. So it may be more satisfactory to use a second compass, usually called the standard compass, if a suitable position for it can be found.

However, in the majority of wood or GRP yachts a hand bearing-compass (Plate 42B) is used for taking bearings, but care must be taken that it is not used within the magnetic influence of any iron or steel (even the wire earpieces of a pair of spectacles can affect it), and it is wise to test with a magnet any stainless steel rigging near which it might be used, for contrary to common belief that material often is magnetic. Such a compass cannot be used with accuracy in a steel or ferro-cement vessel.

The steering compass can be illuminated by electricity from the ship's supply without any adverse effect provided the twin wire system is used; the single wire system with earth return can set up a strong magnetic field. Ideally the circuit should include a dimming switch, but failing that, or perhaps as well, a coat of red nail varnish on the bulb will reduce dazzle, and for the same reason the inside of the bowl should be painted black and the lubber line white, as is now done with most compasses. Hand bearing-compasses may have dry-battery illumination, but some are provided with radioactive luminosity, which is said to last for 20 years.

Most people know that the north-seeking point of an undeviated magnetic compass points not to true north but to magnetic north, that the angle between these two 'norths' is known as variation, and that this varies from place to place and slowly changes over the years. Since the local variation is shown on nearly all charts, it should present no difficulty when courses or bearings are being laid off; but if the chart is so old that the accumulated annual change has over the period of years amounted to one degree or more it should be taken into consideration.

However, the compass may not point to correct magnetic north if it is under the influence of near-by ferrous metal or electrical equipment. The angular difference between correct magnetic north and north as indicated by such a compass is known as deviation. Whereas variation at any place is the same for all compasses and for all points of the compass no matter in which direction the ship is heading, deviation is different in different ships, and varies according to the direction of the ship's head because the metal which causes it is carried round the compass needles as the course is altered. Deviation is said to be east if the north point of the compass is pulled to the east of correct magnetic north, or west if the north point is pulled to the west; on some headings it may be considerable, on others nil.

Obviously it is sensible for the owner of any yacht to ascertain whether the compass has any deviation, and if so, how much and in which direction, and there are several ways in which this can be done. If the large-scale chart shows a buoy round which we may safely manœuvre, together with some conspicuous and clearly-defined object, such as a tower or a lighthouse situated a couple of miles from the buoy, we can with the parallel rule take the correct magnetic bearing of the object from the buoy direct off the chart. Then, sailing or motoring near the buoy, we steady the yacht with her head in turn on each of the four cardinal and the four inter-cardinal compass points, ie at each 45° mark, and take a bearing of the object. If the bearing remains the same throughout the whole swing of 360° the compass has no deviation; but if there is a difference between the correct magnetic bearing and the bearing taken by compass, that will be the deviation, west or east depending on whether the compass bearing is greater or less than the correct bearing, *for the point on which the yacht's head was lying at the time*. However, buoys do sometimes shift their positions, and, depending on the strength and direction of any tidal stream and on the scope of the mooring cable, a parallax error may occur; the nearer the object is the greater will this error be, and it will be aggravated if we do not remain very close to the buoy. A better plan, therefore, is to make use of a pair of leading marks, for preference a pair the bearing of which is given on the chart, noting that this will be given in degrees true and so must be converted to magnetic by applying the local variation. We can cross and recross the line on each 45° heading, watching the beacons as they close, and take our bearing of them at the moment they are exactly in line.

Mention was made earlier of the hand bearing-compass; that instrument can be used for checking the steering compass, but first a position must be found for it where it is not subject to deviation. Selecting what is likely to be a suitable place away from the other compass and ferrous metal, bearings are taken of a distant object while the yacht is being swung – any object will do and there is no need to know its bearing or its position on the chart. If the bearing remains constant throughout the 360° swing the compass has no deviation while being used at that place; if the bearing does not remain constant other places should be tried until one free of magnetic interference is found. Now, if the ship is swung again and simultaneous bearings of the object are taken with the hand bearing-compass and with the steering compass, any difference between them will be the deviation of the latter for the point on which the ship's head lay at the time.

If the horizon can be seen and the sky immediately above it is clear, there is a very simple way of using the sun to check the compass on a single heading; this is by taking an amplitude, ie a bearing of the sun at rising or setting. Because of refraction of the sun's rays the bearing should be taken when the sun's lower limb (edge) is half the sun's diameter above the horizon. *Reed's Nautical Almanac* (see page 329) and some other publications give a table which, when entered with the ship's latitude and the sun's declination (see page 447), both to the nearest whole degree, gives the sun's true bearing at rising and setting anywhere in the world between latitudes 66° north and south. The bearing taken from the table is converted to a correct magnetic bearing by applying the local variation, and any difference between this and the compass bearing of the sun will be the deviation for the point on which the ship's head was lying at the time.

Example: On passage between Mauritius and Durban, in latitude 22°S, and steering by compass 254°, a bearing of the sun was taken at setting. From *The Nautical Almanac* the declination of the sun to the nearest whole degree was 10°S; variation taken from the chart was 17°W. Required the deviation of the compass on the course being steered.

From amplitude table entered with lat 22°S and dec 10°S: sun's true bearing	259°
Variation	17°W
Correct magnetic bearing of sun	276°
Bearing of sun by compass	278
Deviation of compass	2°W

If a shadow pin (Plate 43*E*) can be erected temporarily in a vertical position in the centre of the glass top of the compass bowl, and provided the bowl is level and steady, the pin's shadow on the card will be the reciprocal of the sun's compass bearing. If this is corrected by adding or deducting 180°, is converted by applying the local variation, and is then compared with the true bearing obtained from the sight reduction tables when an observation of the sun is taken and worked for navigational purposes, the difference will of course be the deviation. But rarely is the sea smooth enough for a shadow pin to be used, though in port it might provide a useful check.

In yachts of wood or GRP construction deviation is not usually much of a problem, but if it exceeds about 3° on any heading it might be as well to get a professional compass adjuster to reduce or eliminate it by the positioning of one or more magnets near the compass; some internally-gimbaled compasses have such magnets, which can be moved, ready for this purpose in the binnacle. Then, unless some major change is made, such as installing a different engine or moving a steel fuel or water tank, one can usually forget all about deviation changes, though it would be prudent to swing ship occasionally. But with yachts of steel or ferro-cement construction the matter may not be at all simple, and I suggest that owners of such yachts should lose no convenient opportunity of checking their compasses in one or other of the ways outlined above, for vessels of such construction may change their magnetism to a surprising degree, perhaps when on a long passage on one heading, or when crossing the magnetic equator which, very roughly, coincides with the world's equator. On a recent north–south crossing of the Pacific the deviation of *Wanderer IV*'s compass (she is of steel construction) changed as much as 7°.

As well as the normal kind of deviation, a compass may be subject to heeling error, caused by ferrous metal (often an engine) swinging to one side beneath the compass as the vessel heels, and it is a tiresome error because it varies with the angle of heel. A compass adjuster can, with a heeling error instrument, discover if it exists, and may be able to reduce or eliminate it by placing a magnet vertically beneath the compass; it is said that this magnet should be reversed when crossing the magnetic equator. A point of interest is that in the northern hemisphere heeling error draws the north point of the compass towards the high side of the ship, so that a sailing vessel on courses with any north in them makes a better course to windward than is indicated by her compass, and the opposite on southerly courses.

While the yacht is being swung, the deviation (east or west) is written against each of the eight headings on a deviation card. When the deviation on some intermediate heading is required, it may be sufficiently accurate to interpolate if the deviation is small and is of the semicircular type in which it changes only once from east to west and back again in the 360° swing. But if the deviation is considerable and/or is quadrantal, ie changes from east to west and back again twice in the 360° swing, it should be plotted on a sheet of squared paper and a curve drawn; from this the deviation for every compass point, or every 10° mark, can be measured and the rest of the deviation card filled in. The card will be consulted whenever a compass course or bearing is to be converted to correct magnetic, or vice versa.

This conversion (Fig 63) is a simple matter, a small addition or subtraction, which on any cruise may have to be done several times a day, yet it is surprisingly easy to apply it the wrong way. Easterly deviation and variation are usually given the + sign, and westerly the − sign. If we remember this together with the couplet

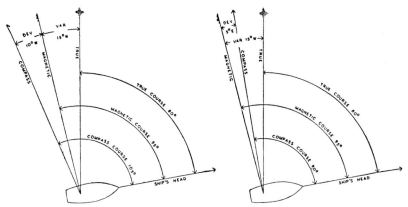

Fig 63   Applying variation and deviation. On the left both are westerly, on the right variation is westerly and deviation is easterly

Claud Worth composed and published in his excellent book *Yacht Navigation and Voyaging* (Potter) the business should be foolproof:

> 'Compass to true: the signs will do.
> True to worse; the signs reverse.'

Thus, to find the true course or bearing corresponding to a course steered or bearing observed by compass, leave the signs as they are, adding if easterly, deducting if westerly. The same applies when finding the correct magnetic course or bearing from a course or bearing from a compass which has deviation. Regarding the second line of the couplet, it is easy to imagine a correct magnetic course or bearing to be worse than a true one, and a course or bearing from a deviated compass to be worse than a correct magnetic one; the signs are therefore reversed, easterly variation or deviation being deducted, and westerly added.

Since the magnetic poles are buried deep in the earth, the compass card is tilted out of the horizontal plane as either pole is approached. If the compass card were free to dip fully it would at latitude 50° north or south register an angle from the horizontal of more than 60°, while at the equator it would show no dip at all. But a properly designed compass is so constructed that its card cannot move very far out of the horizontal, nor can dip cause it to foul the inner side of the bowl; but dip may make the card sluggish. If one is intending to sail from the northern into the southern hemisphere, it might be as well to discuss the matter with one's compass maker, because some compasses made in the northern hemisphere have weights attached to their south-seeking parts so as to offset some of the dip in the northern hemisphere, and such weights naturally aggravate dip in the southern hemisphere. For world-wide use the counterweights should be omitted unless one is prepared to change the magnetic assembly on crossing the equator.

A yacht with an auxiliary engine should be swung with and without the engine running, for when it is running magnetic fields may be created by its electrical equipment, or the different positions of a steel gear- or clutch-lever may cause deviation; two deviation cards will then be made, one for use under sail alone, the other for when the engine is running. Once a deviation card has been made out no alterations should be made to ferrous metal gear or fittings, and no iron or steel objects, or any magnetic equipment, such as radios, tape-players, photo-electric exposure meters, or even beer- or soft-drink cans (the latter are often highly magnetic) should be permitted near the compass.

Lead and echo-sounder

The sounding lead is one of the simplest and cheapest of navigational aids, and every yacht should have one of about 3 kilograms (6½ pounds) on a 25-metre (14-fathom) line, even though she may be fitted with an echo-sounder, for the latter may not always be in proper working order, nor may it always give a reading when the sea-bed is soft. The traditional lead had a recess in its bottom into which a little tallow (arming) was pressed to bring up a sample of the sea-bed, so that the position might perhaps be identified not only by depth as shown on the chart, but by the nature of the bottom, which the chart might also show; but if it is unlikely that a sample will be needed by the yacht navigator, the lead might with advantage have a round bottom so that it will sink more quickly. The line should be no thicker than is required for comfortable handling, perhaps 6 millimetres (¼ inch), or it will offer unnecessary resistance to its passage through the water; if terylene is used it should be of the braided type as 3-strand line kinks too readily, and the marks will then need to be sewn to it instead of being tucked in; it can conveniently be kept wound on a flat piece of wood with a deep V cut in each end.

As the fathom vanishes from the charts, along with it goes the traditional method of marking the leadline, and the Hydrographer of the Navy has introduced the following metric markings for leadlines which are still used in survey work, mainly for the calibration of echo-sounders:

1, 11, and 21 metres	one strip of leather
2, 12, and 22 metres	two strips of leather
3, 13, and 23 metres	blue bunting
4, 14, and 24 metres	green and white bunting
5, 15, and 25 metres	white bunting
6, 16, and 26 metres	green bunting
7, 17, and 27 metres	red bunting
8, 18, and 28 metres	blue and white bunting
9, 19, and 29 metres	red and white bunting
10 metres	leather with a hole in it
20 metres	leather with a hole in it and 2 strips of leather
30 metres	leather with a hole in it and 3 strips of leather
40 metres	leather with a hole in it and 4 strips of leather
50 metres	leather with a hole in it and 5 strips of leather

It will be noticed that some of the traditional marking materials, such as calico, serge, and cord, which could be identified in the dark by the touch of fingers or lips, have been abandoned; blue bunting feels just the same as red bunting.

Soundings are taken from the weather side, the leadsman holding the loosely coiled line in one hand while he swings the lead on a short scope of line in the other to and fro once or twice so that it may gather momentum; then he casts it as far ahead as he can so that it may have reached the bottom by the time the yacht passes over it; as she does so he hauls in the slack and bounces the lead on the bottom to make sure the line is up-and-down and he has an accurate sounding, and that if the lead is armed it will bring up a sample of the bottom. With the yacht moving this can of course only be done in shallow water; at other times it will be necessary to bring her head to wind and lose way, or even heave-to. A yacht which does much sailing in shallow waters might well have a long, weighted, marked bamboo, which is quicker to handle than a leadline.

However, the majority of yachts are now fitted with echo-sounders (depth-finders). Such an instrument is more than just a convenience, for it takes soundings with greater average accuracy and at vastly greater speed and frequency than ever a leadsman can, providing on a calibrated dial or strip of paper a continuous indication or recording of the depth of water regardless of the speed at which the vessel is travelling; this is of value for position-finding purposes, and when beating to windward in narrow waters when it is all too easy to run aground between casts of the lead.

The principle of the echo-sounder is based on the fact that sound travels through water at an almost constant speed, approximately 1,463 metres (4,800 feet) per second. If therefore a pulse or burst of sound waves is sent out from some point on the hull below water, and the time it takes to reach the sea-bed and echo back to the vessel is measured, the depth of water between that point and the sea-bed can be calculated. All of this the echo-sounder does automatically once it has been switched on. From the main housing, which contains the controls, an impulse of electric oscillations is sent to the transducer (a small disk of barium titanate in a plastic case which protrudes through a hole in the vessel's skin) where it is converted into an ultra-sonic sound wave, the pitch of which is far above the range in which the human ear is sensitive. The wave travels to the sea-bed, is echoed back and picked up by the same transducer, which now acting as a microphone converts it into an electric impulse. This is amplified, and in one of three ways is made to record the distance between transducer and sea-bed.

In large ships this is done by a fast-moving electric pen, which in running repeatedly across a strip of specially prepared paper in synchronism with the impulses, perforates it with a spark each time an echo is received. The paper is moved slowly by an electric motor, so drawing out the perforations to form a continuous line, the distance of which from the edge of the paper is a measure of the depth. A permanent record of this nature is valuable for surveying purposes, and is useful for fixing by the line of soundings method, but it is not often needed by the yachtsman. More compact instruments indicate the depth by means of a small neon light mounted at the end of an arm which, driven by an accurately governed electric motor, revolves at a constant speed. This lamp flashes each time it receives an electric pulse, thus giving one flash as the wave goes out and another as it returns. The operation is repeated so fast that the flashes are seen as continuous light, one opposite the zero mark on a scale arranged close to the revolving arm, and the other indicating the depth. Disadvantages of this type are that in bright light it is sometimes difficult to read, and power consumption may be high owing to the demands of the motor. In the third type the depth is indicated by means of a milliammeter which moves a pointer on a dial, and this can be read easily.

Most echo-sounders have some provision for adjusting the pointer or the neon light so that one can read direct from the scale the depth of water not beneath the transducer but beneath the keel, or from the surface of the sea; most seamen prefer the latter because soundings can then be compared with the soundings on the chart after only one allowance has been made for the rise of tide above chart datum.

The current needed to run an echo-sounder may come from the yacht's supply or, with some models, from dry cells housed within the instrument. If this is of the pointer type the consumption is tiny, and may be as little as 20 milliamps; small hearing-aid batteries can be used, and a set of these will last for up to one year with normal use, provided that the instrument with batteries in position is protected from the humid conditions commonly met with afloat. This, incidentally, is done with all Brookes & Gatehouse instruments, each case being nylon-sheathed and provided with a screw-in container holding indicator silica gel, a desiccating agent which can be rejuvenated again and again by heating to expel the moisture it has absorbed. On board I use silica gel for keeping all photographic apparatus and materials dry.

A yacht cannot always accommodate a single beam wide enough to 'illuminate' the sea-bed immediately below her, for when the transducer is on the windward side and the yacht is heeled the keel will obtrude into the vertical line from the transducer and cut off the sound-waves in that direction. No one wants to bore a hole through his keel, stem, or deadwood, so in 1959 Richard Gatehouse hit on the obvious (but until then untried) method of using two beams, one from a transducer in each bilge, each having a beam width of 40° and an angle of divergence of 15° to 20° from the vertical centre line (Fig 64). The lee transducer is selected by an automatic gravity-controlled switch. It has been found that to avoid air bubbles the transducers are best placed at a distance of from half to three-quarters of the waterline length from forward.

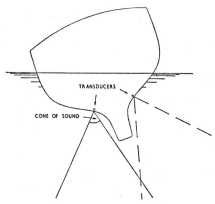

Fig 64   Twin transducer arrangement for the echo-sounder

A GRP yacht with a single skin, as opposed to a sandwich skin, need not have a hole bored for the transducer. If a small box or cylinder is bonded to the inside of the hull and is filled with water, the transducer can be submerged in this and the sound waves will be transmitted through the skin.

Patent log and speed indicator

Distance travelled at sea is recorded in nautical miles, but speed is recorded in knots, one knot being one nautical mile sailed in one hour. As a knot is a measure of speed it is incorrect to speak of a distance of so many knots, and it is equally incorrect to speak of a speed of so many knots per hour. The word knot is derived from the old log-ship method of ascertaining speed at sea which worked as follows. A wooden quadrant, weighted so as to float upright, was attached by a three-legged span to a line. Two legs of the span were securely fixed, but the third was held by a wooden pin driven only lightly into place. The quadrant was dropped over the stern where, so long as there was not much strain on the line, it would remain upright and almost stationary in the water while the ship sailed away from it. The line was marked with a knot at every 15 metres (50 feet), and the number of knots that ran out over the stern in 30 seconds was the speed of the vessel in nautical miles per hour. A jerk on the line pulled out the pin and allowed the quadrant to be hauled aboard without difficulty.

Such a method gave a reasonable idea of the distance sailed only so long as the vessel continued to sail at the same speed; obviously it is much more satisfactory to record the actual distance sailed, and for this a patent log, of which there are several kinds, is used. The older type consists of a distance-recording instrument mounted on an outrigger which is shipped into a shoe secured to the rail near the stern (Plate 44D); a rotator towing astern on a plaited line causes, through a train of gearwheels, hands to indicate the distance sailed in miles on the instrument's dial. The length of line required depends on the height of the instrument above water and the maximum speed of the vessel, and the maker's recommendations should be followed. Walker's Excelsior IV log, for example, requires about 21 metres (70 feet) of line for speeds up to 8 knots, provided the instrument is not more than 1·8 metres (6 feet) above water. For speeds in excess of 7 knots a weight is provided to be threaded on and secured to the line 60 centimetres (2 feet) ahead of the rotator. With too short a line the rotator does not sink deep enough and therefore under-registers; too long a line causes excessive drag but more regular registration. This type of log tends to under-register at slow speeds and when running before a heavy sea. Trials ought to be made, but rarely are, over a measured distance (charts show sets of beacons erected along the coasts which may be used for this purpose), a run both ways being made so that the tidal streams will cancel out; any error can then be noted, or further runs made while experimenting with different lengths of line. Care needs to be taken of the rotator, for if its fins are the slightest bit bent it will not record properly, and as rotators are sometimes taken by large fish, it is as well to carry a spare; it is said that a black-painted rotator is less likely to suffer this fate, but as I towed one unpainted rotator for some 60,000 miles before it was taken by a shark, I doubt whether there is much in this. When hauling in the rotator the inboard end of the line should be unhooked and paid out astern to prevent the line being tangled up by the turns that the rotator will still be putting into it.

The newer type of patent log is electronic, and consists of a tiny impeller which protrudes a short distance through the skin of the vessel, and at least one of these, that used with the Brookes & Gatehouse Harrier log, can be drawn inboard for cleaning without any water entering the hull. The impeller is connected electrically with the main instrument, which may have its own internal dry batteries, or run off the yacht's supply, and there the distance sailed through the water is recorded by moving figures similar to those in a car's speedometer. In the same instrument (or a repeater) a pointer indicates the speed in knots on a scale. Clearly such an instrument, always in position ready for use, is the more convenient type of patent log, and, although the speed indicator is not needed for the purpose of navigation, it is of value in showing instantly what effect a change of sails or trim of sheets has on the speed of the vessel. The accuracy of this instrument will depend largely on the positioning of the impeller in a place where an undisturbed flow of water may reach it on all points of sailing, and this is usually forward of the ballast keel (perhaps one quarter of the L W L from the forefoot) and as close as possible to the centre line; but in this matter the advice of the maker should be followed. Usually a calibrated control is provided, and once this has been adjusted during trials over a measured mile, it is claimed that accuracy will be maintained within plus or minus $1\frac{1}{2}$ miles in every 100 miles sailed, which is better than can be expected from the older (and cheaper) type of log, though the latter is preferred by many voyaging people because it is simple and robust and calls for no electricity. However, mention should be made of the Stowe log (Plate 44A) which combines features of both the above types. A small rotator, of which only the aft end is free to spin, is towed on a 9-metre (30-foot) insulated electric cable from any convenient position on either side of the yacht, but unlike the Walker log the cable does not rotate. The control box to which it is secured contains a small 9-volt dry cell battery, a large dial on which speeds of up to 10 knots are indicated by a pointer, and figures (with push-button reset) recording distance up to 999·9 sea miles. This instrument has the advantage over most other electric logs that no hole need be bored in the yacht's hull, and throughout a recent long voyage I found that it recorded distance run with remarkable accuracy.

Speed in small craft is deceptive and is frequently over-estimated. So if the patent log should fail during a passage, the speed ought to be checked occasionally by means of the Dutch-man's log. This consists of throwing overboard a float, such as a chip of wood, and timing it over a measured distance between two stations aboard. The time must be taken carefully and the greater the distance between the stations and the slower the speed the more accurate will the result be. Divide 3,600 (the number of seconds in an hour) by the time in seconds taken by the float to cover the distance, and multiply the result by the distance in feet between the stations. This gives the number of feet sailed in one hour, so to get the speed in knots divide by 6,080 (the number of feet in a nautical mile).

Radio receiver

Except for getting time signals the ordinary radio receiving set can hardly be regarded as an aid to navigation, but it is of value in obtaining weather forecasts as well as news and entertainment. The cruising yacht will need a receiver provided (as most are) with the medium-wave broadcast band, which extends approximately from 550 to 180 metres, ie from 540 to 1,650 kilocycles per second; since a cycle per second is known as a Hertz, the abbreviation used is kHz, and for a megacycle per second is mHz. The broadcast band can be used up to a distance of about 322 kilometres (200 miles) from a station, but if the receiver is intended for the British market it will probably have also the long-wave broadcast band – 150 to 225 kHz – enabling the BBC Radio 4 programme on 1500 metres (200 kHz) and a few continental stations to be received perhaps up to a distance of 644 kilometres (400 miles). The radio receiving requirements for the foreign-going yacht differ in that she will find the long-wave broadcast band of little value outside European waters, and she will need a set capable of receiving not only medium-wave stations when cruising coastwise abroad, but also stations broadcasting on the short-wave bands, because only short-wave signals are capable of being received with certainty at great distances.

Aboard a British yacht probably the BBC World Service and WWV (see below) will be the services most often required, and if the set is to be capable of being tuned to all of the twenty-odd frequencies on which the former service is broadcast, and the five on which the latter is broadcast, it will need to cover the short-wave bands from 2·5 to 22 mHz. A great many stations of all nationalities broadcast very close to one another on most sections of the short-wave bands, and their number continues to increase; so if anything approaching satisfactory reception is to be had (it is far from perfect even in the best conditions) a set with selective tuning by micrometer, and widely-spaced, clearly marked scales or digital readout is essential. When trying out a set on the short-wave bands, it should be remembered that a short-wave station is surrounded by a skip area, perhaps with a radius of 500 to 1,000 miles, within which signals from that station cannot normally be received.

A more or less vertical wire not less than 4·5 metres (15 feet) nor more than 15 metres (50 feet) long makes as good an aerial as any for a receiving set, so possibly a shroud will be used. Unless this is in direct metallic contact with the sea, as by a chainplate, it need not be insulated in a wood or GRP yacht with a wood mast. If, however, the mast and/or the hull is of metal or ferro-cement, the shroud must be insulated, and this may be done by fitting nylon-coated thimbles at the splices, or nylon bushes on the clevis pins. Good contact must be made where the lead-in wire joins the shroud, and this can be ensured by tinning with solder a little of the bared lead-in and seizing it with tinned copper wire to the shroud, the join then being parcelled with insulating tape, served with twine, and varnished. If the set calls for an earth (ground) this may be done by taking the earth wire to a keel bolt or other submerged fitting. With a transistorized receiver there should be no risk in doing this, but in the past damage was done to yachts by current leaks from the older types of set fitted with high-tension batteries.

As has already been mentioned above, the BBC World Service is broadcast on more than twenty frequencies, but not on all of them at the same time. The frequencies used by the station, and the choice of the most suitable one by the receiver, depend to some extent on the time of day, the geographical area at which the programme is directed, and the position of the receiving ship. Since the radius of the skip area is proportional to frequency, when on approaching a station the signals fade, they may be restored by switching to a lower frequency. Darkness and winter time favour the lower frequencies; daylight and summer time the higher ones; generally the best reception is had when the whole radio path is in darkness, but I have often noticed that signals are strongest when the ship is on or near the meridian of the station, and that a station which is not audible at any other time may come in clearly during twilight. A list of the frequencies on which the BBC World Service is broadcast, together with their times of use, and a schedule giving the weekly pattern of the month's programmes, is published a month in advance in a pamphlet with the title *London Calling*; this is obtainable from the BBC, and sometimes can be had from British consulates. It does not list the times when time signals are broadcast, but these often precede the news.

However, the most convenient and reliable means of obtaining time signals, which are so desirable for accurate navigation, is from station WWV.

This is situated at Fort Collins, Colorado, USA; it broadcasts almost continuously day and night on 2·5, 5, 10, 15, and 20 mHz, and sends out a pulse similar to the tick of a clock at 1-second intervals. In addition a whistling tone is emitted for the first 45 seconds of each minute. In the final 15 seconds a male voice gives 'universal coordinated time', which is the same as Greenwich mean time, and the moment the whistling tone returns is that time, correct to one-tenth of a second. A similar station located at Maui, Hawaii, provides the same service, but the voice is female, and precedes the male voice. Depending on one's geographical position and on radio conditions, sometimes one voice is heard, sometimes the other, and often both are heard for WWV and WWVH broadcast on identical frequencies.

During three world voyages my wife and I managed always to get time signals when required, no matter where we might be. In the North and South Atlantic, when out of range of local stations, we used either the BBC or WWV, and in the Pacific WWVH. In the Indian Ocean we were not always able to receive WWV or WWVH, and only picked up the BBC as Africa was approached, but we managed now and then to get time signals from Singapore and Colombo. Everywhere it is possible to hear some English-speaking station, but to obtain a time signal from it may entail hours of profitless listening unless one happens to have local knowledge; even then it may be found that programme changes are made, and the Sunday programme is likely to differ from that broadcast on weekdays. A comprehensive worldwide coverage of short-wave, medium-wave, and long-wave stations will be found in *World Radio TV Handbook* (Billboard Publications).

More and more yachts are being fitted with radio telephones, and although such equipment might be the means of saving life, it should be used with discretion and never allowed to take the place of constant vigilance and good seamanship. In many instances if the money spent on buying and installing the set, and the time taken learning to use it, had been devoted instead to the careful preparation of the yacht and her gear, the need to radio for help would not have arisen. The numerous mayday calls give the cruising yacht a bad public image, and unless they are reduced may cause bureaucratic restrictions to be imposed on our freedom. Most radio telephone equipment can be used also as domestic receivers, and many of them can be used as direction-finding sets by the addition of a rotating loop or ferrite rod aerial (see below); thus some of the original high cost may be offset. With all radio receiving sets headphones are desirable, not only for excluding ship noises when signals are weak, but so as to avoid disturbing other members of the crew, and it should always be remembered that much of the pleasure of others is spoilt by the thoughtless people who turn the volume of their radio sets up too high in quiet anchorages. The users of ship/shore radio equipment should be alert to the fact that, when they are transmitting, their signals may cause so much interference that people near-by afloat and ashore are unable to listen to programmes on any of the short-wave bands.

Radio direction-finder

There are several systems whereby radio can be used as an aid to navigation, eg radar, decca, loran-C, and radio direction-finding (RD/F). Of these RD/F is the most widely used in small craft because of its comparative low cost, small size, and minimal consumption of electricity.

For RD/F a sensitive receiving set linked to a directional aerial of special design is needed. By means of this bearings can be obtained of one or more of the large number of marine radio beacons which transmit signals from points on many coasts, and from some aeronautical beacons; such bearings can be laid down on the chart to fix a ship's position in exactly the same way as compass bearings of visible objects are used. The method has the advantage that it works just as well in foggy weather as in clear. On the chart marine radio beacons are circled in magenta and have the letters RC against them; aeronautical beacons are also circled and have Aero RC printed against them.

An aerial in the form of a loop is directional, and if it is turned on its vertical axis there will be two points 180° apart where the signal to which the set is tuned will lose volume and fade away. Such fade-away points are known as nulls, and they occur when the plane of the loop is at right angles to the direction of the transmitting beacon. The size of such an aerial can be greatly reduced if it is formed round the circumference of a ferrite rod; the nulls will still occur when the plane of the loop is at right angles to the beacon while the rod will be in line with the beacon (Fig 65). The rod type of aerial is the type most widely used with RD/F sets for small craft.

All nautical radio beacons and many aeronautical ones which can be useful to shipping are listed for all parts of the world with their characteristics in *The Admiralty List of Radio Signals*, Vol II, together with chartlets showing their positions. But this is a confusing and awkward book to use, and if one's cruising will be confined to the waters which lie between Italy and the entrance to the Baltic, all the necessary information will be found clearly set out and easy to use in *Reed's Nautical Almanac*. Alternatively the information for some areas may be had from special charts. For the east coast of the US and Great Lakes all RD/F information will be found in *Radio Publication* 117A, and for the west coast in *Radio Publication* 117B.

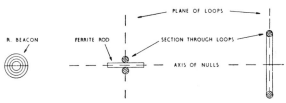

Fig 65   Radio direction-finding aerials
The null occurs when the plane of the loop is at right-angles to the radio beacon.

Most marine radio beacons transmit for one minute in every six minutes day and night, but a few transmit in fog or by night only. Each beacon broadcasts on a certain fixed frequency within the limits 160–415 kHz, and has its own identification signal which it transmits in Morse several times at the beginning and at the end of each transmission, the intervening time being occupied by one long dash or series of dashes. Start Point, for example, has a frequency of 298·8 kHz and a range of 50 miles, and transmits for one minute in every six, commencing at one minute past the hour. Its characteristic is as follows:

SP (... . ——.) 4 times	19·6 seconds	
Long dash (———)	25·0	,,
SP (... .——.) twice	9·6	,,
Silent	305·8	,,
	360·0	,, (6 min)

The effective range, outside which it is not wise to use a beacon by night, may be anything between 5 and 200 miles, but for the majority of British beacons is 50 miles. Air beacons have a greater range, and most of them broadcast continuously instead of only for one minute in every six. They are therefore much easier for the unskilled operator to use, but bearings of any that are not situated right on the coast should be treated with suspicion (see below). The listed range is rather an arbitrary quantity. There is no objection to using a beacon by day at ranges beyond the listed value, provided one realizes that the error increases progressively with the range. With some sets one can obtain well-defined nulls at distances of twice the listed range. In many localities from two to six nautical beacons are grouped together, all broadcasting on a common frequency, one immediately after the other in a set order; eg Start Point, which was mentioned above, is No 2 in the Channel west group, which it shares with Eddystone (No 1), Casquets (No 3), Roches d'Ouvres (No 4), Ile Vierge (No 5), and Lizard (No 6). So having been tuned to one, the set need not again be tuned, it being necessary only to swing the aerial to each station in the group in turn to pick it up and obtain the null.

All RD/F sets work on the same principle, but the actual manner of taking the bearing varies. In one type the revolving aerial is mounted on top of the set and has a pointer moving over a bearing plate, ie a disk free to pivot on its centre against a lubber line and engraved with degrees, 0–360. When the operator has obtained a null the helmsman tells him what course the ship's head was on at that moment; the bearing plate is then turned so that that course is against the lubber line, and the figure read beneath the aerial's pointer will be the magnetic bearing of the beacon. With the other type of set, the aerial, which must be of the ferrite rod type, is separate from the set but is linked to it with a cable and is mounted on a hand bearing-compass. The operator pivots the combined aerial and compass on its vertical axis until he has obtained the null, when he can immediately read off the magnetic bearing himself without any reference to the ship's head. Both types have their advocates; my own preference is for the hand-held aerial such as the Brookes & Gatehouse Heron linked to the same firm's Homer receiving set (Plate 42A). I believe this to be the more accurate system because the operation is independent of the ship's head, while the error caused by tilting the axis of the loop (which is inevitable when the aerial is mounted on the set and the ship is heeled) is avoided as the operator automatically holds it vertical.

As two nulls, 180° apart, are obtainable from one beacon, the operator might not know in certain rare circumstances – such, for example, as when visibility is poor and the beacon is situated aboard a buoy or a light-vessel – which is the correct bearing. The Heron, and some other equipment, incorporate a sense-finder which resolves this ambiguity. For a description of this and the working instructions for any set the maker's instruction book should be consulted.

The newcomer to sailing is inclined to believe that once he has invested in a RD/F set all his navigational problems will be ended. But this is far from being true. The aerial (and the compass if it is hand-held) are subject to errors; certain rules must be observed when selecting beacons; and some considerable skill, obtainable only by practice, is necessary when handling the instrument; even then large errors may, and often do, occur.

The metal-work of a yacht, no matter whether it is ferrous or not, can cause RD/F errors. Aboard a steel or ferro-cement yacht it may be possible to find a position on deck where the aerial is free from interference, though this is unlikely, and it is probable that special equipment employing two crossed fixed loop aerials at the masthead will have to be used. In a wood or GRP yacht the aerial can be used below deck so long as it is kept 1·8 metres (6 feet) away from a 12-metre (40-foot) metal mast and 0·9 metre (3 feet) away from metal beams, tanks, etc. The most likely cause of error will be a closed loop, such as is sometimes produced by guardrails running right round the deck; or by shrouds, mast fitting, chain plates, and steel deck beams connecting the chain plates all being in metallic contact. A closed loop must be broken by insulating some part of it. To find out whether the aerial and/or compass (if this is hand-held) are subject to error, it is necessary to swing the ship slowly through 360° while radio bearings are taken of a beacon, which, of course, need not be within sight. If all are the same there is no error, if they differ another position should be tried; but if a place completely free from error cannot be found, it will be necessary to swing ship and make out a deviation card just as is done for a steering compass. The necessary correction, according to the bearing of the beacon relative to the ship's head, will then be applied in the usual way when taking bearings.

If a bearing plate type of set is used, the helmsman must endeavour to have the ship sailing on a steady course without yawing at the time the bearing is taken; in my opinion this is the major weakness of this type of set.

When selecting a beacon one should try to choose one such that the line between ship and beacon passes only over water; if it does pass over land it should not cross the coast at a narrow angle or run parallel to the coast, neither should it pass within half a mile of high ground; bearings should not be taken between evening twilight and dawn at distances beyond the listed range. Coastal refraction errors very seldom exceed 3°. They are 'safe' in that they place the fix inshore of the ship's position. Night-effect errors can be more serious, but their presence is usually indicated by a badly defined null and fading of the signal strength.

Having selected a suitable beacon, it is found not by trial and error but by setting the tuning controls on both set and aerial to the frequency of the beacon, then a fine adjustment is made so as to produce a clear musical note when the beacon is transmitting. Best results will be got by using noise-excluding headphones rather than a loudspeaker; for use with the hand-held type of instrument they must be non-magnetic, then, provided they are not within 15 centimetres (6 inches) of the compass, they will not affect it. A knowledge of Morse is not essential for identifying a beacon, but it is a help as some beacons transmit their identification letters quite fast; it should, however, be noted that some of the newer sets require no tuning, the frequency of the desired beacon being dialled on a keyboard. Having identified the beacon and tuned in to your satisfaction, rotate the aerial on its vertical axis to find the null. If this were only a degree or two in width, obtaining a bearing would be a simple matter, but often the null is 10° or more in width. It is then necessary to rotate the aerial to and fro, noting the bearings each side of the null at which the signal is of equal strength, the angle between them being bisected (by interpolation) to obtain the bearing of the beacon. The only way to perfect this act is by practice, but I have noticed that young people are better at it than older ones, possibly because of their quicker reactions, but more likely because of their keener hearing. Some sets incorporate a null meter, ie a scale with a pointer to indicate the null visually.

The selection of beacons most suitable for giving a good fix, and the method of laying down bearings on the chart, are described on pages 342 ff., but mention should be made of 'homing', ie turning the yacht to bring the beacon nearly on the bow and keeping it like that until it is sighted. This, for example, might be done if the beacon is on a light-vessel, but one should remember that Nantucket light-vessel was run down and sunk by a ship 'homing' on her by radio.

Sextant

The sextant is a precision instrument used by the navigator for measuring angles. In offshore navigation it is used for measuring the altitude of a celestial body, ie the angle between the body and the horizon, thus enabling a position line to be obtained. In coastwise navigation the instrument may be used for finding the distance off by measuring the vertical angle of a terrestrial object, the height of which is known; or to provide a fix by measuring the horizontal angles between three objects the positions of which are indicated on the chart.

A description of the sextant and its use in astronomical navigation will be found in Chapter 22, but a word should be said here about one of the errors to which it is subject, as it has a bearing on the use of the instrument in coastal navigation. When the sextant is set at zero (micrometer or vernier also at zero, of course) the index and horizon glasses should be parallel to one another so that the direct and reflected images of a distant object, such as a star or the horizon, exactly coincide. If on making that test they do not coincide, move the tangent screw or micrometer head until they do, then read the sextant, and that reading will be the index error (IE). If this reading is on the arc, that is, to the left of zero, all angles measured with the sextant will be that much too great, and the IE must be deducted from all sextant readings to obtain true readings. If the IE is to the right of zero, that is, off the arc, it must be added to all sextant readings. When reading an angle off the arc, the vernier or micrometer must be read backwards. Unless the IE is more than about 3' it is best left uncorrected, for harm may be done by frequent or inexpert tampering with the adjusting screws, but it should be checked frequently. However, when using the sextant to measure a very small angle such as that made between the lantern of a lighthouse and the horizon, it is advisable to take two readings; in one bring the reflected image of the lantern down in the usual way until it is in line with the horizon seen through the clear part of the horizon glass, then read the sextant; in the other look directly at the lantern through the clear part of the horizon glass, and bring the reflected image of the horizon up into line with it, then read the sextant again. The first reading will be on the arc and the other off it, so if they are added together and divided by two, a correct reading will be obtained without having to take the index error into account.

Binoculars

A good pair of binoculars adds much to the pleasure and interest of any cruise, and is essential for picking up and identifying buoys and other navigational marks. Two figures are commonly used in the description of binoculars, such as 8 × 40, 7 × 50, etc; the first figure indicates the magnification, and the second the diameter of the object glass in millimetres. A magnification of 7 × means that an object 700 units away will appear as though only 100 units distant. The size of the object glasses largely governs the amount of light transmitted, so the larger they are the more efficient is the instrument on a dull day or at night. The greater the magnification of a binocular the more difficult it is to hold steady, and of two binoculars of different powers but with object glasses of the same size, the more powerful one will pass less light. For these reasons binoculars for use at sea in small craft should not normally exceed a power of 7 ×, but the larger the object glasses are the better. Centre focusing, whereby both eyepieces are moved simultaneously, is quicker and more convenient than individual eyepiece focusing, but the latter type of instrument is more robust and less likely to suffer from prolonged exposure to damp.

When light passes from air to glass or glass to air, about 5 per cent is lost by reflection, and not only is this reflected light wasted but it interferes with the brilliance of the image. The coating or blooming of a lens, which consists of depositing on its surfaces a transparent film of a lower refractive index than that of the glass, reduces the amount of light reflected to about 2 per cent, thus giving greater luminosity and a more brilliant image, both of which are particularly valuable for night work. All modern binoculars have coated lenses, and these appear purple or amber when seen by reflected light. As binoculars ought to be treated with care, it is a good plan to have two pairs, one for yourself and an older one for your friends to leave lying about.

Lights, buoys, and beacons

The coasts of the British Isles are provided with a fine system of lighthouses, light-vessels, and lighted and unlighted buoys and beacons to assist the navigator, to warn him of dangers, and to lead him through the deep-water channels into port. Other countries have similar aids to navigation, often excellent, sometimes indifferent.

A full description of nearly every light, buoy, and beacon in UK and adjacent European waters will be found in *Reed's Nautical Almanac*; they are also shown on large-scale charts and harbour plans, but a medium- or small-scale chart will only show the more important lights, so outside home waters (unless one carries a full set of charts) the appropriate volumes of *Admiralty List of Lights* and *Pilots* will be needed. The former give details of all lights exhibited from the shore and from light-vessels, but include only buoys with a light elevation of 8 metres (26 feet) or more; the characteristics of other buoys will be found in the *Pilots*.

The *geographical range* of a light is the theoretical distance at which it could be seen limited only by the curvature of the earth, the elevation of the light, and the height of eye of the observer, and does not take into consideration the power of the light. Until 1972 this was the range given on charts, and was for a height of eye of 4·6 metres (15 feet), and many charts still have it. *Luminous range* is the maximum distance at which a light can be seen as determined by the intensity of the light; it takes no account of elevation, height of eye, or curvature of the earth. *Nominal range* is the luminous range when the meteorological visibility is 10 miles or more. Some countries, including the UK, give the luminous range on charts and in light lists, others give the nominal range, but the yachtsman with his low height of eye is likely to be more interested in the geographical range. He can obtain this figure by entering the table in the light list with the elevation of the light (measured from high water mark) and with his height of eye; but if the light is of low power (the intensity in candelas is given for many lights in the light list) it may not be visible at the geographical range even in clear weather. It should also be remembered that a light with a great elevation may often be hidden in cloud although visibility at sea-level may be good.

The range should not be confused with the loom of a light, the glow in the sky which, on a dark night when visibility is exceptionally good and the sky is clouded over, can sometimes be seen and timed from a distance of 60 miles or more. The arc of visibility, unless the light is visible all round, is usually shown on medium- and large-scale charts by dotted lines, as also are any sectors which may be of different colours. This information is also given in degrees true in the light list, but it must be understood that such bearings are given as though taken from the vessel, not from the light. If, therefore, the light list states that a light sector extends from 0° to 90°, it does not mean that the light shows over the north-east quadrant on the chart, but that it will be seen only from a vessel in the south-west quadrant. If this sector is not shown on the chart and we wish to insert it, we must rule our dotted lines from the light in the directions 180° and 270°.

All lights are white unless otherwise stated on the chart or in the light list, and each may have any one of the following characteristics, no matter whether it is white, red, green, or orange, or has sectors of different colours.

Fixed (F). A continuous steady light.

Flashing (Fl). Showing a single flash at regular intervals, the duration of light always being less than that of darkness.

Fixed and Flashing (FFl). A steady light with at regular intervals a flash of increased brilliance.

Quick Flashing (QkFl). Flashing continuously more than 60 times a minute.

Interrupted Quick Flashing (IntQkFl). Flashing at a rate of more than 60 a minute with a total eclipse at regular intervals.

Group Flashing (GpFl). At regular intervals two or more flashes in a group.

Fixed and Group Flashing (FGpFl). A steady light with two or more brilliant flashes in a group.

Group Interrupted Quick Flashing (GpIntQkFl). Group of quick flashes separated by relatively long periods of total eclipse.

Occulting (Occ). A steady light with at regular intervals a total eclipse, the duration of darkness being less than the duration of light.

Group Occulting (GpOcc). At regular intervals two or more eclipses in a group.

Isophase (Iso). Duration of light and darkness are equal.

Alternating (Alt). A light which alters its colour when seen from any one place; not to be confused with a light which has coloured sectors.

Some air navigation lights near the coast are included on the charts and in the lists. These usually exhibit groups of long and short flashes representing one or more letters in the Morse code; the letters are given in brackets alongside the other details.

Light lists and charts (depending on their scale) also include particulars of the fog signals made in thick weather by lighthouses and light-vessels – explosives, nautophone, siren, bell, etc.

In 1977 work was started to change the system of buoyage in UK and some European waters to the International Association of Lighthouse Authorities (IALA) system, and the job was planned to take about three years. This system is a combination of the lateral and cardinal systems. The lateral system marks channels and approaches to ports. When sailing with the flood or into harbour, red can (flat top) buoys with can top marks and red lights (if any) are to be left on the port hand; green conical (pointed top) buoys with cone topmarks and green lights (if any) are to be left on the starboard hand. An isolated danger with clear water all round it may be marked with a black and red pillar buoy, having a topmark of two spheres, and a white group flash (2) light. Safe water marks, such as landfall and mid-channel buoys, may be spherical or pillar, painted in red and white vertical stripes, and having a single sphere topmark, and the light (if any) will be white. One might have thought that with such an expensive operation as a change of buoyage system, the lights prescribed for each situation would be standardized, but this is not so; for example, the light on the above safe water buoy may have one of three characteristics: isophase, occulting, or long flash every 10 seconds.

The cardinal system is used to indicate the safe side on which to pass a danger, or to draw attention to a feature in a channel, such as a bend, a junction, or the end of a shoal. For this system pillar buoys painted black and orange are used; each has two cone topmarks, and by their arrangement these indicate in which quadrant, from the danger, the buoy lies: north quadrant – points up; south quadrant – points down; west quadrant – points together; east quadrant – bases together. The first two are easy to remember; for the others I find the Royal Yachting Association's mnemonic a help: 'Western women are wasp-waisted whereas eastern are elegantly enlarged equatorially.' But here again the characters of the lights, all of which are white, can differ from buoy to buoy even though the buoys may be serving identical purposes and I refer the reader to *Reed*'s or the appropriate *Pilot*, in which the buoyage systems are shown in colour and the light characteristics are given, or, of course, to the latest large-scale chart.

It should be noted that the old method of marking wrecks with green buoys and green lights is not used in the IALA system, a wreck being marked exactly the same as any other navigational danger.

Whether countries outside Europe will change to the IALA system is not known, but so far as Canada and the USA are concerned it is unlikely, as their systems are already simple and excellent. But the European yachtsman must be on his guard when sailing in their waters, for the colours of buoys and the colours of their lights are the opposite to those of the IALA system to which he is accustomed; on approaching a Canadian or US harbour, black can buoys with white or green lights must be left to port, and red conical buoys with red lights left to starboard. A way to remember this is 'Red right returning, black right out'. However, it is likely that in US waters black buoys may be changed to green if the experiments carried out by the coastguard in 1980 show that colour to be more suitable.

Some care should be exercised when navigating by buoys, for in exposed positions in heavy weather they may break adrift or drag their moorings, and although their automatic lights are remarkably reliable, it is possible for them to get out of order. Black paint is apt to turn red with rust in time, while bird droppings may make a black or red buoy look as though it is striped or chequered from a distance. Therefore in daylight the shape and the topmark are the only things that can be relied upon or that really matter. (Sometimes from a distance a bird, a light, or a radar reflector may be mistaken for a topmark.) The position of a buoy on a chart is shown by a tiny circle drawn on the waterline of the buoy; and lights, whether on buoys, light-vessels, or lighthouses, are indicated with a dab of magenta ink.

Beacons, or day-marks as they are often called, may be of any size, shape, or colour, and will be found marked on large-scale charts. Two beacons kept in line are often used to lead through a channel or to clear some sunken danger. If any difficulty is experienced in deciding which way to go to close a pair of leading or

---

PLATE 39 (*facing*). Aboard a ketch or yawl a mizzen staysail (which is not hanked to a stay as its name suggests) is a valuable light-weather sail and sometimes will draw when the heavier working sails will not. Normally it is tacked down to windward of the mainsail, sets to leeward of the main backstay (to the legs of which a radar reflector is here secured) and is sheeted to the end of the mizzen boom.

PLATE 40 (*overleaf*). *A.* A jib-headed topsail rigged with a leader being sent aloft. The leader can be seen threaded through the thimble seized to the luff of the sail at the mitre. *B.* The topsail nearly mastheaded. Notice in these two pictures that a strain is kept on the sheet to prevent the flogging sail taking a turn with it round the end of the gaff. *C.* The sail is set, the tack has been hardened down and the leader set taut to keep the luff close to the mast. Like all good topsails, this one is a little smaller than the space it has to fill, and its head and foot are of equal length. *D.* The upper part of the luff of *Dyarchy*'s topsail runs in a groove along the topmast.

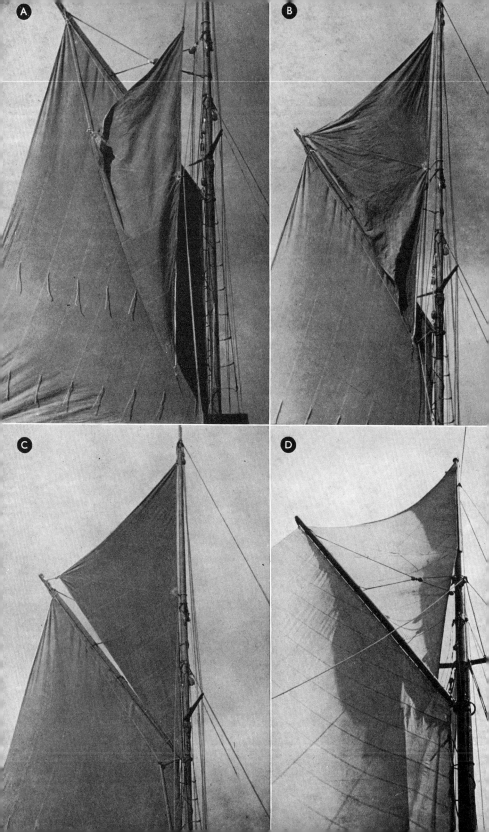

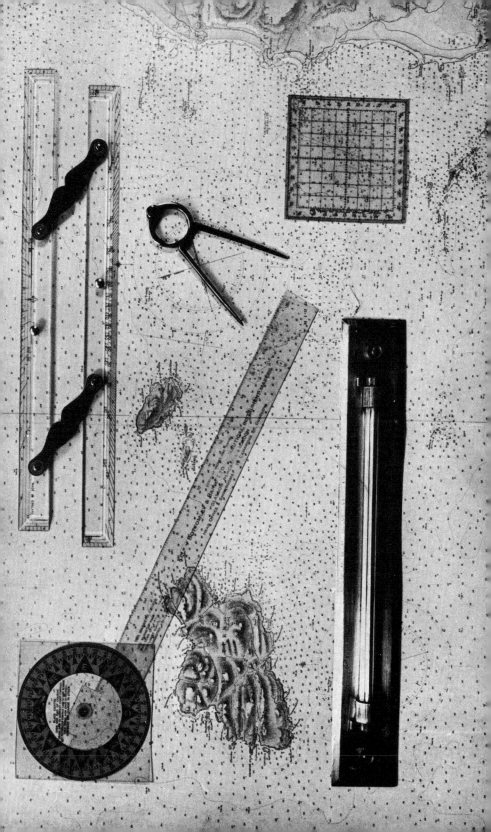

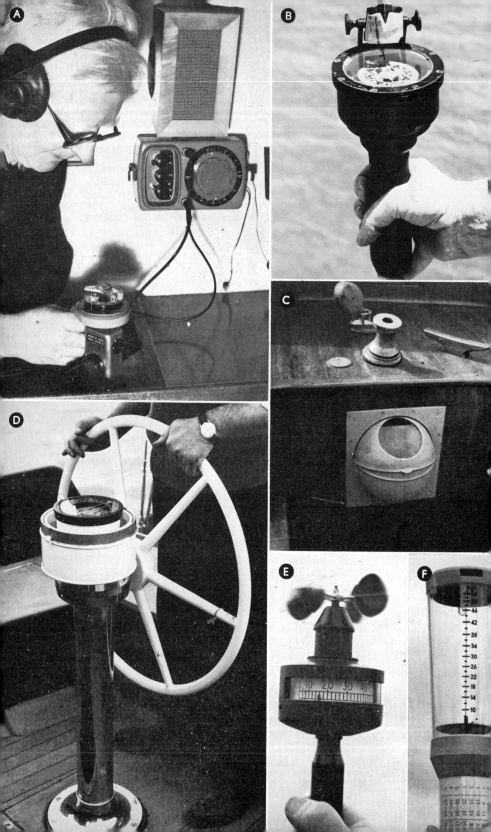

clearing marks, imagine a line drawn seawards through the marks, then alter course so as to get on that line.

Nautical almanacs and sailing directions

Nautical almanacs, which are annual publications, contain tabulated data which are essential for the purpose of astronomical navigation. *The Nautical Almanac*, published jointly by Britain and the USA, provides this in the most convenient form, but contains nothing else. *Reed's Nautical Almanac* and *Brown's Nautical Almanac* also give these data; the former does so in a more condensed and not such a convenient form, though it is quite adequate if only an occasional celestial observation is to be taken; but both contain such a wealth of other information for use particularly in British and European waters – tide tables and constants, lights, buoys, and radio beacons – that one or other of them is almost essential for the cruiser in that area. Both are excellent, but my preference is for *Reed*'s, to which some references have already been made. However, when cruising elsewhere one will need to have on board instead (or as well) the appropriate volumes of *The Admiralty List of Lights*, *The Admiralty Tide Tables*, and if radio direction finding is to be used, *The Admiralty List of Radio Signals*, Vol II.

Ocean Passages for the World, a large volume compiled by the Hydrographic Department of the Admiralty, contains a description of the winds, currents, and weather for all the oceans. It also gives details of the recommended routes between major points of departure and arrival for all oceans at different seasons for power-driven vessels and for sailing ships. A pocket at the back of the book contains current and wind diagrams, and charts showing the recommended routes. Although this book cannot be regarded

---

PLATE 41 (*overleaf*). Chart instruments. *Top left*: Course setting protractor. *Top right*: Field's improved parallel ruler made of perspex. *Middle right*: Single-handed dividers. *Bottom left*: Roller parallel ruler. This heavy brass instrument is historic in that it was orginally owned by Claud Worth, and then was used by Admiral Goldsmith on his long voyages. *Bottom right*: Douglas protractor.

PLATE 42 (*facing*). *A*. Using radio direction-finding equipment with hand-held aerial and compass to obtain a bearing of a radio beacon. *B*. For taking a bearing of an object within sight, a hand bearing-compass with magnifying prism is commonly used in yachts of wood or GRP construction, but not in those built of steel or ferro-cement. *C*. A binnacle let partly into the forward cockpit bulkhead, where the helmsman can see it easily. *D*. With wheel steering the ideal position for the compass is immediately forward of the wheel on the pedestal, where it may be high enough for taking bearings and perhaps be free from deviation. *E*. A hand-held anemometer. *F*. A ventimeter.

as essential it is of considerable value when a voyage is being planned, because it contains between one pair of covers most of the relevant information.

The other forms of sailing directions consist of written descriptions and instructions for the navigation of coastal waters, and are published by the appropriate authorities of most maritime nations. Such volumes, which are published for all parts of the world by the British Hydrographic Department, are known as *Pilots* (*The Bay of Biscay Pilot, The Red Sea Pilot,* etc). Each contains a detailed description of the coast, the dangers, the harbours, and the weather and, as has already been mentioned, only in the *Pilots* (and on large-scale charts) will be found the characteristics of the buoys outside home waters. But these books are written for large ships, and often ignore the smaller places which a yacht might wish to visit; for cruising in Canadian and US waters the sailing directions published in those countries are to be preferred, for they do give much information of value to the visiting yacht, though in some instances it is planned to remove this and publish it in separate volumes. Nevertheless, reading the *Pilots* encourages one to study the charts with greater care, and the views of the coasts which they contain may sometimes be of assistance in identifying a doubtful landfall or picking up leading marks. Also, should the navigator lack a chart of some place he wishes to call at, he may be able to draw one from the information in the *Pilot*. An example of this is given by Miles Smeeton in his book *Sunrise to Windward* (Nautical):

We were navigating on a tracing of the general chart of the Nicobars, but I had drawn a chart of the harbour from the *Pilot* on a plotting diagram, using a blown-up scale ... I felt I knew it all well, almost as if I was a native, as a result of the laboured drawings that I had made during the passage. Lights go out and beacons decay, buoys change colour and are missing, but the land remains the same and the sailing directions are usually given with reference to a recognizable landmark.

A yearly supplement of corrections and additions is published for each *Pilot* (available free from chart agents), and when this grows inconveniently large the volume is withdrawn and a new edition is published. Incidentally, some of the older, outdated ones, are repositories of fascinating sea lore.

There are also many books of sailing directions written for yachtsmen by yachtsmen, one of the earliest being Adlard Coles's *Creeks and Harbours of the Solent*. They are too numerous to be listed here, and new ones appear frequently; but two excellent examples are the volumes covering the coasts of Ireland and the west coast of Scotland, compiled by members of, and published by, the Irish Cruising Club and the Clyde Cruising Club respectively. Such specialized books are usually stocked by chart agents and chandlers, and they provide much valuable information which is not available elsewhere. Well written accounts of cruises made by experienced sailing people, such, for example, as appear in *Roving Commissions* (the annual journal of the Royal Cruising Club), provide much local knowledge and expertise.

17

TIDES

Finding the times of high and low water – Finding the
depth of water – Tidal streams

A TIDE is the periodic vertical rise and fall of the level of the sea caused by the attraction of the sun and moon. These bodies attract the part of the earth's surface which is nearest to them with greater force than they do its centre or its opposite surface, so that the water of the oceans is drawn up in a hump beneath them; but centrifugal force restores equilibrium by producing a similar hump on the opposite side of the earth. High water therefore occurs simultaneously at places which have a difference of longitude of 180°, while in between those places and at 90° to them there will be low water. So it will be seen that there should be two high and two low waters at any place for each revolution of the earth, but owing to the motion of the moon in her orbit it takes a little more than 24 hours, or one complete revolution of the earth, to bring a given meridian back beneath the moon. Each tide will be about 54 minutes later than the corresponding one on the previous day, successive tides being 12 hours 27 minutes apart; but this is only an average, and the actual interval will vary according to the phase of the moon.

The tide-raising power of the moon is about $2\frac{1}{2}$ times greater than that of the sun because, although she is smaller, she is very much nearer to the earth. When the sun and moon are in line with one another and the earth, no matter whether the moon is between the sun and the earth or on the opposite side of the earth, their united forces combine to raise higher tides than at other times; these are known as spring tides though they have no connection with that season of the year, the word coming from the Nordic and meaning 'to swell', and they occur when the moon is full and new (at full and change) which happens at intervals of just under 15 days. A spring tide not only rises higher than other tides but falls lower, so it has a greater range; but the range at springs varies a little according to the changing distance of the earth from sun and moon; the highest tides occur at the equinoxes in March and September.

Gradually, as the sun and moon get out of line with one another and the earth, the range of the tide becomes less until sun and moon are at 90° to one another, as viewed from the earth. Their tide-raising forces are then pulling against one another, and although the tide still rises beneath the moon and on the opposite side of the earth, it does not rise so high or fall so low as at other times because of the counter-attraction of the sun. Such tides are known as neap tides, from a Norse word meaning 'scarcity'. Tides are said to be taking off when changing from springs to neaps, and coming on or making when changing from neaps to springs; the change takes about 7½ days.

The moon in her passage round the earth does not draw after her the hump of water which has been raised by her attraction, but is all the time engaged in raising the water which is vertically beneath her. The tidal wave is therefore an oscillation of the water, not a horizontal bodily movement of the water from one place to another. This oscillation is similar to the fluttering of a flag in which waves run along the bunting, but the bunting itself does not move along with them. But the tidal wave is not free to travel unrestricted round the world, and as it approaches land or shoal water it becomes slower, steeper, and higher, and the range of the tide becomes greater. Part of the main tidal wave sweeping round the Southern Ocean strikes the east coast of Africa, is raised in height and is deflected towards the Cape. From there it travels northward up the whole length of the Atlantic. About 2 days after leaving the Cape this wave reaches the British Isles where it combines with the true tides, so that the highest tides in the British Isles are usually 2 days after full and change of the moon. If there is a strait through a land barrier, the water as it rises in height will pour through the strait by force of gravity and thus produce a tidal stream on the flood. This is an actual forward movement of the water; anything floating in the stream will therefore be carried along with it. As the crest of the wave passes, there is usually an interval of slack water before the ebb stream starts to run back the opposite way. When a tidal wave passes into a gulf which narrows towards its head, it is compressed and retarded by contact with the land so that it becomes steeper, gravity overcomes friction, and a tidal stream flows up the gulf and back again.

The configuration of the land has a marked effect upon the range of the tide, the time of high water, and the strength and time of turning of the tidal stream. For example, the spring rise at Portland is 2 metres (6¾ feet), while at Tréguier, on the opposite side of the English Channel, it is 9·7 metres (32 feet), and the stream in the Channel is so retarded as to cause high water at Dover when it is low water at the Lizard; in West Bay the stream rarely exceeds 1 knot, yet off Portland, the eastern extremity of that bay, it attains a rate of more than 6 knots.

Although the yachtsman need not understand the causes of the tides, it is essential that he should be able to find the time of high water at any place together with the rise, so that he may judge what depth of water there will be. A knowledge of the speed and direction of the tidal stream will also be of importance to him. If, for example, the speed of a yacht in light weather is 2 knots and she has a 2-knot tidal stream against her, clearly she will remain stationary; but if the navigator works the tides as he should, he will take advantage where possible of the fair stream, and his yacht will be making good 4 knots over the ground.

Finding the times of high and low water

Daily tidal predictions for many ports all over the world are given in the volumes of *Admiralty Tide Tables*, also in tide tables published by the hydrographic offices of other countries, and these are often to be preferred as they give data for more ports in the areas covered. Such publications give the time, usually together with the height, of each high water throughout the year for a number of standard ports, and often give the time and height of low water also.

Secondary ports are those for which no daily data are provided. Those in the neighbourhood of each standard port are listed in geographical order, and the time difference in hours and/or minutes between the time of high water at the secondary port and at the standard port is given together with the height difference in metres and/or feet. Thus it is possible to find the time and height of high water at a secondary port on any day of the year. Suppose we wish to find the time and height of the morning high water at St Malo on 8 October 1979. Looking up St Malo in the list of secondary ports we find that the relevant standard port is St Helier, Jersey, that the time difference is −0h 20m, and the height difference is +0·9 metre. Turning now to the tide table for St Helier, we find that on that day the morning high water is at 0748 and the predicted height is 11·8 metres. Deducting 0020 from 0748 we get 0728, the time of high water at St Malo; and adding 0·9 metre to 11·8 metres we find that its height will be 12·7 metres.

To find the time of low water at a secondary port for which no low water difference is given, we apply to the high water time the duration of mean rise, if it is listed with the secondary port information. If it is not listed we can obtain an approximation of the time of low water by applying 6¼ hours to the time of high water.

But it should be remembered that the times of high and low water at any place, and the height of the tide, may vary considerably from the predicted times and heights owing to the strength and direction of the wind, and the height of the barometer; such meteorological factors can affect the tide at a place many miles away. A fall of 34 millibars (1 inch) of the barometer might cause the tide to rise 0·3 metre (1 foot) above normal, and even further if the fall is sudden.

Finding the depth of water (Fig 66)

Chart datum is the fixed plane below which all depths (soundings) are measured. Parts of the sea bed which may be uncovered when the tide falls are also measured from chart datum, and their heights above it are given on the chart in figures which are underlined. Until 1972 the datum used for BA charts was, as was mentioned in Chapter 16, low water ordinary spring tides (LWOS); but a new and lower datum, called lowest astronomical tide (LAT), a level below which the tide seldom falls, is being introduced as charts are revised, and tide tables are being altered accordingly. The rise of a tide is the height of high water of that tide above chart datum. The range of a tide is the difference in height between high and low water of that tide, and must not be confused with rise. Mean tide level is half way between high and low water of any tide, and it remains constant at any place for all tides.

A tide does not rise an equal amount for each hour of the flood or drop an equal amount for each hour of the ebb. In a place facing to deep water, in the first and sixth hours the tide rises approximately one-twelfth of its range, in the second and fifth hours two-twelfths, and in the third and fourth hours three-twelfths. To find the depth of water at a given place and time, we must first find the range of the tide on that day by looking up in the tide table the heights of high and low water, and deduct the latter from the former; if we then divide the range into twelve parts and, using the above twelfths rule, deduct what is necessary from the high water height, depending on how many hours are lacking of high water, we shall get an approximate idea of the depth. But this became a tiresome operation as the foot and the inch were phased out, and it is far quicker to use a rise and fall table, such as is published in *Reed's*.

The figure obtained when calculating the depth of water over a bar or shoal should be treated with caution, for the heights given in tide tables are only predictions, and as already mentioned

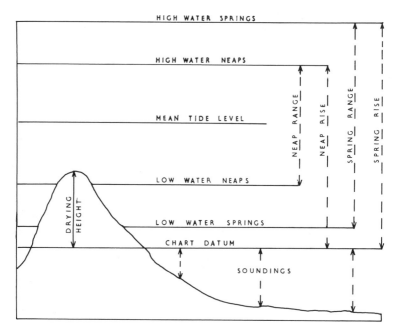

Fig 66   Tidal terms

meteorological conditions may affect the rise of tide; one should also consider how much water there will be when the vessel drops into the trough of the sea or swell.

Tidal streams

It is a common mistake to suppose that tidal streams (the horizontal movements of the sea) change their direction at the same time as high and low water by the shore; this in fact they rarely do. Particulars of the streams will be found in the *Pilots*, but these tend to be lengthy and not always easy to follow. Information is also given on charts, sometimes with arrows, but more often capital letters enclosed in diamond-shaped borders are printed in various positions, and the tidal stream information for those positions is tabulated elsewhere on the chart; the directions of the streams for each hour before and after and at high water at some standard ports are given in degrees true together with the speed in knots and tenths. If the chart is one which is often in use, it may be found more convenient to draw arrows showing the directions of the streams at each lettered position, and to write the average speeds alongside them. For the British Isles, however, tidal stream atlases are available; they are easier to use for one can obtain the required information at a glance. Such atlases contain twelve charts for each area covered, each chart showing by means of arrows the directions of the streams for a different hour while the tide is rising or falling at a standard port. Figures against the arrows indicate the speed in knots; when only one figure is given it refers to the spring rate, when two are given the higher is the spring rate and the lower the neap rate. On a date between springs and neaps an estimate will have to be made.

Meteorological conditions have a considerable effect on the speed and time of change of the tidal streams, so the information available from charts, sailing directions, and tidal atlases should be used with caution, especially in thick weather. It should also be remembered that there is usually an inset or indraught into any deep bay on both flood and ebb. In certain places and at certain states of the tide there may be an eddy behind a rock or island or close to the shore, ie a stream running in the opposite direction to the main stream. A notable example is the Goulet de Brest where one may see fishermen working the eddy close along the southern shore when entering to avoid the sluicing ebb in mid-stream.

A tidal stream is usually stronger within 2 or 3 miles of the shore than farther out, except in a deeply indented bay where there may be very little stream, and the stream always runs more strongly through narrow channels and off prominent headlands, where it may cause a tide rip or race. Tide races such as those found in the Pentland Firth and Raz de Sein, and off Portland Bill, may be dangerous to small craft even in quiet weather, but in heavy weather the terrible fury of the broken water with the seas heaping up on one another and running from all directions, is such that small vessels may be seriously endangered. Ripples or overfalls may be caused by the stream running over a shallow patch surrounded by deep water; these as well as the tide races are usually shown on the chart and every endeavour should be made to avoid them in heavy weather.

Unlike a tidal stream, a current (page 405) is not produced by astronomical conditions and does not therefore change direction every few hours; it is the result of various meteorological conditions, and is a permanent or semi-permanent onward movement of the water. The direction in which a vessel is moved by a tidal stream or a current over a period of time is known as the 'set', and the distance she is moved as the 'drift'. In the UK we consider there is no such thing as a tidal current; but this term is widely used for a tidal stream in Canadian and US waters even in official publications.

18

PILOTAGE

WHEN leaving port a yacht will usually be navigated by buoys or other fixed marks, and in clear weather this presents little difficulty; but unless the buoys are close together, it is as well when steering from one to another to note the compass bearing of the next buoy and compare it with the bearing on the chart, for if there are other channels in the vicinity it is surprisingly easy to steer for a wrong buoy unless this precaution is taken; check each buoy by its name or number as it is passed so that there will be no doubt as to the yacht's position in the event of the weather suddenly coming in thick, and note by the ripples round the buoy the direction in which the tide is setting. When beating in thick weather through a channel which has gently shoaling banks each side, the lead or echo-sounder will give good warning when it is time to go about, but if one bank is steep and the other shoals gently, keep to the gently shoaling side and work in short tacks along it. When the wind is fair through a channel and the weather is thick, it is not advisable to attempt to steer a middle course, for if the lead or echo-sounder should show the water to be shoaling, it might not be possible to tell which side of the channel is being approached; either keep to one side in a moderate depth of water, or zigzag a couple of points each side of the course so that when the soundings shoal you will know on which side of the channel you are.

Setting the course

As soon as the yacht has got clear of the harbour or the channel of approach, fix her position by cross bearings or one of the other methods to be described later. Mark the position on the chart with a cross or a dot surrounded by a small circle, and from it rule the course to the destination or to give a sufficient berth to any headland or other obstruction which has to be rounded to reach the destination. Carry the line with the parallel ruler to the magnetic compass rose on the chart to find the course to steer, correcting it if necessary for leeway and deviation, and for any accumulated change in variation if the chart is very old. Put the yacht on the course, set the patent log at zero, and note the time.

Some people use a proper log-book with separate columns for wind force and direction, patent log reading, course, deviation etc; others find a note-pad on which to jot these things adequate. I prefer to put the information on the chart straight away so that I can see my vessel's position in relation to her surroundings at any moment without having to work up the dead reckoning from notes. (Dead reckoning is a contraction of deduced reckoning, and is abbreviated to DR.) My log-book, which I write up each evening, or more often when on passage, is in the form of a journal which contains a mention of anything of interest that has happened.

There are certain factors in navigation, such as tidal stream and leeway, which cannot be known exactly, so the DR may not always be correct, though there are admittedly many occasions when the errors cancel out. The careful navigator therefore takes every opportunity of fixing his vessel's position, and by comparing such fixes with his DR positions he learns the extent of his errors and may be able to reduce them or allow for them on future occasions; the experience so gained in fine weather gives him greater confidence in his ability when visibility is reduced by rain or fog. But no matter how skilful he may be, he can never be quite certain of the accuracy of his DR, so he sets a course that will take him a little to windward of his destination, or if the passage happens to be a dead run, then a little to one side of it. If the weather is clear he will make his landfall, fix his position, and alter course as necessary when still some distance off, and the extra distance sailed by having kept to windward of the direct course will be very small. But if the weather is thick he may not be able to identify his position on sighting the land, but he will know which way to turn to reach his destination. This elementary but seaman-like rule may have to be broken when there are dangers close to windward of the direct course.

Allowing for leeway and tidal stream

The amount of leeway made depends on the type of yacht, the point of sailing, and the condition of wind and sea. An approximate estimate can be made by judging the angle between the wake or the log-line and the fore-and-aft line of the yacht. When sailing close-hauled, and when turning to windward, the leeway should be allowed for when laying off on the chart the course made good; but when sailing free the leeway should be allowed for when deciding on the course to steer. Suppose, for example, we wish to make good a course of 270° with the wind on the starboard side and on that point of sailing the yacht makes 4° of leeway. If we were to steer 270° we would only make good a course of 266°; so instead we steer 274° and will then make good the desired course.

The chart or the atlas of tidal streams will tell us in which direction the stream is setting and will give an approximate estimate of its speed. If the stream is running directly with or against the yacht, no allowance will have to be made for it when setting the course; but when from time to time the DR position is marked on the chart, the distance the tide has carried the yacht forward or held her back since her last position was plotted will be added to or deducted from the distance recorded by the log.

If, however, the stream is not setting directly along the course, the procedure when plotting the position will be a little different. Suppose that since the last position marked on the chart, A on the left of Fig 67, a south-west course (allowing for leeway) has been steered, that in 2 hours a distance of 10 miles has been recorded by the log and that during that time the stream has been running west at an average rate of 2 knots. Mark off along the course from A the distance sailed, AB, 10 miles. From B draw a line west to represent the direction in which the stream has been running, and mark off along it the total distance the tide has run in 2 hours, BC, 4 miles. Then C will be the position of the yacht and she will have been moving along the pecked line AC.

When the streams run with equal strength for an equal length of time on both flood and ebb, it is possible that, having regard to the distance to be covered by the yacht, and her speed, they may cancel out; one should then make no allowance for the tide by steering first to one side of the course and then to the other side of it, or the total distance sailed will be increased; steer the correct magnetic course just as though there were no tide. But if the yacht is expected to make the passage in one tide or part of a tide, or in an uneven number of tides, or if the course will take her close to some danger, an allowance must be made for the stream when deciding on the course to steer. Draw on the chart the direct course from the point of departure to the destination, AB on the right of Fig 67. From any point C on that line lay off a line in the opposite direction to that in which the tidal stream is running. In this instance the stream is running west, so we lay off the tide line in an easterly direction from C, and mark off along it to any convenient scale, the distance it will run in 1 hour, CD, 2 miles. Using the same scale, set the dividers to the distance the yacht is expected to sail in 1 hour, say 5 miles. With one leg of the dividers at D, swing the other round until it cuts the original line AB at E. Join DE and carry that line with the parallel ruler to the nearest compass rose and read off the course to steer, correcting it if necessary for leeway and deviation. By steering that course the

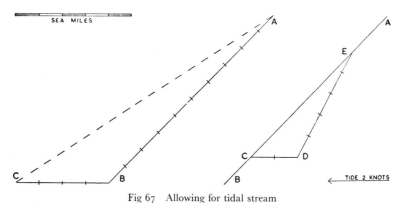

Fig 67   Allowing for tidal stream

Left, plotting the course made good; right, plotting the course to steer.

yacht will be kept moving along the line AB so long as she continues to travel at the same speed and the direction and rate of the tidal stream remain constant; but as soon as either of those factors changes a fresh tidal stream (or current) triangle should be drawn to obtain the new course to steer.

Position lines

The method most often used aboard yachts for fixing the position when within sight of land is by compass bearings. When the bearing of some object, the position of which is shown on the chart, has been taken, the edge of the parallel ruler is placed on that bearing on the magnetic compass rose on the chart; the ruler is then worked across the chart until its edge is on the object, and a line is drawn seaward from the object. This is a position line somewhere on which the yacht must be situated. If there is within sight at the same time a second object the position of which is also shown on the chart, a second position line can be obtained; where the two lines cross one another should therefore be the yacht's position. A third position line, if there is a third object available, will act as a check. But it is rare for the three lines to cross at one point; more often they form a triangle, which is known to seamen as a 'cocked hat'; if this is small the position is assumed to lie within it; if it is large an error has been made in the taking or laying down of the bearings, and one should try again.

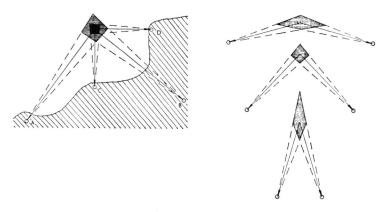

Fig 68   Cross bearings

On the left is shown the effect of distance on the accuracy of bearings, and on the right the effect of angle.

If there is a choice of objects, two considerations should be kept in mind when deciding which to use. The nearer an object is to the observer the more accurate will be the position line resulting from a bearing of it, and the nearer the two position lines are to crossing one another at an angle of 90° the more accurate will the resulting fix be. The left-hand drawing in Fig 68 shows the effect of distance. Here there are four objects; A and B are each 5 miles distant and C and D are each $2\frac{1}{2}$ miles distant. A bearing of each object has been taken and laid down as a solid line, and provided this has been done with absolute accuracy, the position will be at the intersection of these lines. But in practice such accuracy is not possible, so let us suppose the bearings have an error of up to 5° each side of the correct bearings. The lines marking the boundaries of error are shown dashed. It will be seen that the black quadrilateral resulting from bearings of the two close objects is much smaller than the shaded quadrilateral resulting from bearings of the more distant objects.

The effect of the angle that cross bearings make with one another is shown on the right of Fig 68. Here again let us assume that there may be an error of 5° each side of the correct bearings, and so that the effect of distance shall not enter into the matter, each pair of objects is placed the same distance from the ship's position. In the centre of the figure the bearings cross at 90°, and the quadrilateral resulting from the 5° errors each way is small and compact. At the top and bottom of the figure where the bearings cross at obtuse and acute angles respectively, it will be seen that the resulting quadrilaterals are larger than that produced by bearings crossing at 90°, and are considerably elongated, the margin of error therefore being greatly increased.

For the best results, therefore, one should take bearings of the nearest objects so situated that the position lines obtained from them cross at as near 90° as possible; and if three objects are available, it will be seen from the above that the most probable position within the cocked hat will be biased from the centre of the triangle towards the bearing of the nearer object; and if all three objects are equidistant, the position will be biased towards the shortest side of the triangle.

The method of obtaining bearings by means of a radio direction-finding set, the errors to which they may be liable, and the choice of the most suitable beacons have been described on pages 320–2. Such bearings are made use of in exactly the same way as bearings of visible objects, and the same rules for finding the most probable position within the cocked hat apply.

It often happens that there are not within sight or within effective radio range at the same time two objects or beacons of which bearings can be taken, but the opportunity of obtaining one position line should not be neglected even though it may be impossible to judge the ship's position on it. Take the bearing, draw the line, move the DR position to the nearest point on it and continue the DR from there. Later, after the first object has been lost to sight or has gone out of radio range, another object of which a bearing can be taken may appear. Carry the first line forward with the parallel ruler and draw it through the DR position at the time the second bearing was taken. Draw the new position line (the bearing of the second object) on the chart and where that line crosses the carried-forward line will be the position of the ship.

EXAMPLE (Fig 69). When making a passage one autumn from Cornwall towards the Needles in a yacht without a radio direction-finding set, we had had a slow passage across West Bay with light winds and in poor visibility, and were uncertain of our position when in the neighbourhood of Portland. At 2315 we could see the light on Portland Bill in a temporary clearing and got a bearing of it, 332° magnetic, but were unable to judge its distance. The patent log was read, the bearing was laid down on the chart, and the DR position moved to the nearest point on that line, DR1,

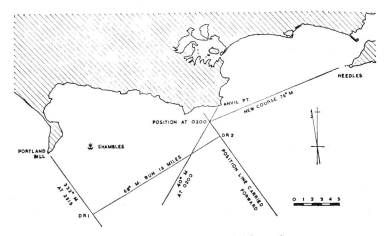

Fig 69   A position line carried forward

A method of obtaining a fix from bearings of two objects which are not in sight or within effective radio range at the same time.

from which point a fresh course was laid for the Needles, 68°. Soon the light was obscured again by rain as the wind freshened, and we did not see the Shambles or anything else until 0200, when we picked up the flash of Anvil Point bearing 40° magnetic. Again the log was read, the DR was brought up to date, having regard to the course and distance (16 miles) made good from DR1, and was marked on the chart, DR2. The first position line, obtained off Portland, was then brought forward with the parallel ruler and drawn through DR2; where the line cut the second position line (the bearing of Anvil light) was therefore our position at 0200, and as this placed us closer inshore than we had believed ourselves to be, the course for the Needles was altered accordingly to 76°. Had we neglected to take the single bearing of Portland light when the opportunity offered, our distance off at Anvil Point would have been uncertain, and our approach to the Needles an anxious one, for by then conditions had worsened considerably.

The sextant is a more accurate instrument than the compass for measuring angles; when, therefore, two objects marked on the chart are within sight but are so situated that position lines obtained by compass bearings would cut at too acute or obtuse an

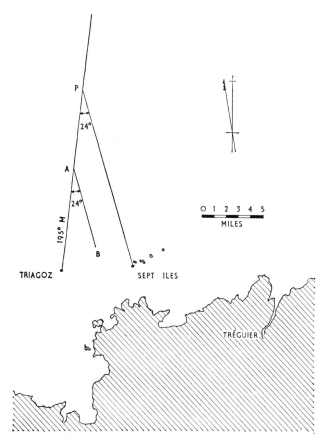

Fig 70   Fixing the position by one bearing and a horizontal angle

angle to be accurate, measure the angle between them with a sextant and take a compass bearing of one of them. Lay off the bearing on the chart, and on the same side of it as the other object, and from any point on the line lay off the observed angle with a protractor. Carry this line with the parallel ruler to the second object, and where it cuts the line of bearing of the first object will be the yacht's position. If preferred the chart rose may be used instead of a protractor. It is, however, very difficult to obtain a horizontal angle between two objects in daylight if there is much motion, for the direct and reflected objects cannot easily be kept in view for a sufficient time to enable them to be recognized and made to coincide. Yet it is fairly easy to measure the horizontal angle between two lights at night and I have found this method of obtaining a fix useful on several occasions.

EXAMPLE (Fig 70). Bound towards Tréguier on the Brittany coast from the nor'-west we made our landfall at night, raising the light of Triagoz and Sept Iles within half an hour of each other. The angle between them was too acute for cross bearings to have given an accurate fix, so a compass bearing was taken of Triagoz, 195° magnetic, and ruled on the chart. With the sextant the angle between the two lights was then measured, 24°. From any point (*A* in the figure) on the line of bearing, the angle of 24° was laid off with the protractor, and the resulting line (*A–B* in the figure), carried with the parallel ruler so that it passed through Sept Iles light; where it cut the line of bearing (*P* in the figure) was our position. We were then able to correct the course so that we fetched the Tréguier leading lights by the most direct route.

When there are three objects in sight and all of them are shown on the chart, the position can be fixed with great accuracy by measuring with the sextant the angle between the first and second and the second and third; the arms of a station pointer are then separated to those angles and clamped in position, and the instrument is moved about the chart until the edge of each arm passes through each object; the pivot of the arms will then be at the ship's position, and that position can be pricked on the chart through the small hole at the centre of the pivot. There is only one position on the chart where the station pointer can be placed so that its three arms coincide with the three objects, except in the situation where the three objects and the ship all happen to be on or near the circumference of the same circle, as is shown in Fig 71; in this event the method is useless because the centre of the station pointer can be moved over a wide arc of the circle while its arms remain in contact with the objects.

The horizontal angle method of obtaining a fix is rarely used in yachts because of the difficulty of measuring the angles (except between lights) from an unsteady platform, but it is the most accurate of all methods, and is therefore the best to use when fixing the position in relation to shore objects for the purpose of swinging the compass. A station pointer is not essential as a Douglas protractor can be made to do the job almost as well.

Using the matt side of the protractor, lay off with a pencil from its centre the angles measured with the sextant, but in the opposite direction to that in which they were measured, using the italic figures which are engraved anti-clockwise round the edge. Then capsize the protractor so that the lines are in contact with the chart. This avoids parallax which might be caused by the thickness of the protractor.

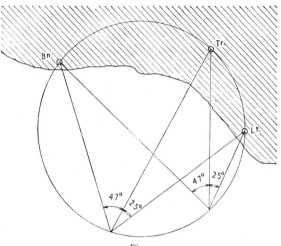

Fig 71

A fix by horizontal angles cannot be obtained when, as shown here, the three objects and the ship are all on or near the circumference of the same circle.

There are two methods of obtaining single position lines independent of the compass or the radio which may be worth mentioning here. Occasionally a series of soundings taken at regular and known distances apart may be made to serve. Reduce them to chart datum and lay them off on a piece of tracing paper on the same scale as that on which the chart is drawn, and on the same course as that on which the yacht has been sailing, and rule a meridian on it. Place the tracing paper on the chart and keeping its meridian parallel to the meridians on the chart, move it about until the soundings agree with those on the chart. But before accepting such a position line the chart must be examined to ascertain whether there is some other position in which the series of soundings might agree. This, however, does not rule the echo-sounder out as a valuable aid to navigation, for there are occasions when one may use it in waters where isolated dangers do not exist to approach a contour of soundings, and work along that contour until the channel one is seeking is found. But only a study of the chart will show whether this may be done with safety. Ferries keep closely to certain tracks. If one of these vessels is sighted and the service on which she is operating is known, her track may serve as a position line; but in using this it is as well to remember the man who followed a Thames barge, supposing her skipper to know his local waters well, only to discover that she was being beached in order to load sand.

Finding the distance off

When only one object is within sight, a compass bearing of it will give a position line; but if we can determine the distance of the object from the yacht and lay it off along the position line, we shall obtain a fix.

Distance at sea is deceptive and a measurement made by eye is apt to be influenced by the height of the land and to some extent by the clearness of the atmosphere. If, when looking at the shore with the naked eye or through binoculars, the land and sea are seen to meet at a clear unbroken line, the shore is beyond the horizon; if an irregular line is seen with small waves breaking on the beach, the shore is nearer than the horizon. By increasing or reducing the height of one's eye until the waves on the shore are just visible, and then measuring the height of the eye above sea level, the distance off can be obtained from the following table.

Height of eye		Distance of horizon		
0·9 metres	3 feet	2	sea miles	
1·5 ,,	5 ,,	2½ ,,	,,	
2·1 ,,	7 ,,	3 ,,	,,	
2·7 ,,	9 ,,	3½ ,,	,,	
3·6 ,,	12 ,,	4 ,,	,,	
4·5 ,,	15 ,,	4½ ,,	,,	
5·8 ,,	19 ,,	5 ,,	,,	
7·0 ,,	23 ,,	5½ ,,	,,	
8·5 ,,	28 ,,	6 ,,	,,	

When at night a light is seen just dipping on the horizon, its distance off can be obtained from a table in the *List of Lights*. The table is entered with the height of the light (obtained from the chart or the *List of Lights*) and the height of the observer's eye; but unless it is high-water springs at the time, one should add to the height of the light what the water level lacks of high-water springs, for heights on charts are always given above the level of high-water springs. When the sea is smooth the dipping of a light is quite sharp and easy to determine; if the observer is standing when it is first seen it will disappear when he sits down.

Sometimes a single sounding may give the distance off with a fair degree of accuracy, especially if the lead is armed to bring up a sample of the bottom; a glance at the chart will indicate whether or not this will help.

The best of all methods of finding the distance off in the day time when only a single object is available and its height is known, is by means of a vertical sextant angle. Measure the angle to the nearest minute of arc from the waterline to the top of the object, or to the centre of the lantern if the object is a lighthouse. Add to the height of the object what the tide lacks of high-water springs; with this figure and the vertical sextant angle (which should be read on and off the arc, page 323) enter the table, which is given in most volumes of nautical tables, and in *Reed's*, and read the number of sea miles and tenths the object is distant. A compass bearing completes the fix. This method may be used with a close approach to accuracy even for a hill the foot of which lies below the horizon, provided that the distance from the ship to the apex of the hill is not more than double the distance from the ship to the horizon.

One of the most difficult problems of pilotage is the need to pass a certain distance off a light at night when there is nothing but that one light visible, and one has to pass between the light and some unlit danger. When cruising north in *Wanderer III* inside Australia's Great Barrier Reef we sometimes had to pass by night between two reefs or low, mangrove-covered islands separated from one another by a passage two miles or less in width. In each of these instances only one of the reefs or islands had a light, so it was a matter of the utmost importance to pass the light the correct distance off; if we passed too close to it we might go ashore on the fringing reef, which usually extended some little distance from the light structure, while if we left it too far off we might strike the unlit reef on the far side of the channel. It was in these instances that an element of chance, or lack of control of the situation, crept in, something which in my opinion should play no part in the safe conduct of a vessel from one place to another, but I know of no simple, foolproof, and accurate solution to this particular problem. A rangefinder, if such an instrument suitable for use aboard small yachts were available, might serve the purpose, but we had to make do with that old textbook makeshift known as 'doubling the angle on the bow'.

This consists of steering a steady course, in our case towards what we hoped would prove to be the middle of the channel, and noting the distance run by log during the time taken for the angle between the light and the course to double itself. If there is no current, tidal stream, leeway, or steering error, the distance recorded by the log while the angle is being doubled is the distance off the light at the moment the angle is doubled; but if there are corrections to make for tidal stream, current, or leeway, it is of course the distance made good that equals the distance off.

One night we were approaching the two-mile-wide channel between Cairncross and Bushy Islets, two of the many low islets which lie within the Great Barrier Reef. The course was 355° magnetic, the south-east trade wind was on the quarter, and the night was dark. Neither of the islets was visible, and the only thing to be seen was the flashing light on Cairncross. We wished to fix our position so as to be able to lay a course to pass midway between the islets. When (at A in Fig 72) the light bore approximately two points on the starboard bow, we took a bearing of it and read the log. The bearing was 20° magnetic, and as we were steering 355° magnetic the angle on the bow was 25°. The log read 41 miles. We continued to watch the bearing of the light, and as soon as the angle on the bow had doubled, ie when the light bore 45° magnetic (at B in the figure) we again read the log; it registered $42\frac{3}{4}$ miles. At that moment our distance from the light was equal to the distance we had run from point A, ie $1\frac{3}{4}$ miles. Therefore, by laying off on the chart the bearing of the light and marking off along it a distance of $1\frac{3}{4}$ miles, we had fixed our position and could set a new course for the centre of the channel.

This method of fixing the position has two weaknesses. One is that as the increase of angle is small (only 25° in the example) the fix is subject to the usual errors associated with acute or obtuse angles. The other weakness is that as the distance run while the angle is being doubled may differ from that given by the log because of unknown tidal stream, etc, the fix may be considerably in error.

The 'four-point' bearing is similar and consists of noting the log reading when the object bears four points (45°) on the bow, and again when the object is abeam (90°); the distance run between the bearings is then equal to the distance from the object when it is abeam. But as the position is not obtained until the object is abeam, the method is not of much value.

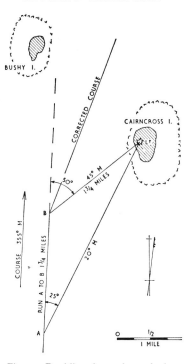

Fig 72   Doubling the angle on the bow
A not very reliable method of finding the distance off, but often the only available one at
night.

A coastal passage.

It is a good plan to obtain the charts some time before setting out
so that they may be studied at leisure and one may become so
familiar with them that any information required can be looked
up without delay. Sufficient general and large-scale charts, not
only of the waters in which the passage will be made, but of any
coasts and harbours which the yacht might be compelled to
approach, should be on board, there should also be a small-scale
passage chart including on one sheet the point of departure and
the destination, or several charts, each including two headlands or
other turning-points, for although it is, of course, possible to
transfer the position from one large-scale chart to the next, or to
obtain the course to steer from the traverse table or calculator,
such methods do not allow one to see the yacht's position in
relation to her surroundings at any time or to take in visually the

situation as a whole. The skipper should lay off in advance the courses that will have to be steered and try to decide what action he would take in the event of heavy weather or fog, so that he may be prepared for any eventuality and will be able to meet it calmly when it comes.

When it has been decided to sail on a certain day the start ought not to be postponed unless the weather is quite unsuitable, for a delay is bad for the morale of the yacht's company. If the port or anchorage in which the yacht lies is one to which it would be possible to return at any time, it will be worth while to go and have a look at the conditions outside, and they will frequently be found to be not so bad as was supposed. It would, however, be unseamanlike to start in thick weather in any vessel, or in a strong head-wind if the yacht is small, but a moderate head-wind should not be a reasonable excuse for delay, for the wind might be fair a short distance farther on.

It may be necessary to have a fair tide to help one out of harbour, but where the harbour can be left at any time owing to a strong, fair wind or a weak tidal stream, or it is decided to use the engine, it may in some instances be best to leave with a foul tide so as to have a fair one later at some more important part of the passage, perhaps off a prominent headland or in a narrow channel. Every opportunity should be taken of working the tides to advantage. Remembering that the streams run with greatest strength off headlands, but are comparatively slack in bays, it may be desirable to stand off-shore to avoid a foul tide off a headland and then to stand in to the slack water of the bay beyond, a manœuvre which will usually be found of greatest advantage when turning to windward. Most benefit from a fair tide will be got by keeping close to the headlands, but that should be done with caution where there are tide races or overfalls.

When the destination or the next point to be rounded lies dead to windward, it will not pay to deviate far from the direct course unless a change in the direction of the wind is anticipated, or there is some other factor, such as a favourable tide or smoother water, to be taken into consideration. Choose the most favourable tack and sail on it until it becomes the less favourable one by about 5°. Then it will be time to go about and sail on the other tack until that becomes the less favourable one by about 5°, the yacht thus keeping within an area 5° each side of the direct course. The reason for this is simply that by keeping near the direct course any change in the direction of the wind will make one tack more favourable than the other, and unless she is already on that tack the yacht will at once be put about to take advantage of the wind change.

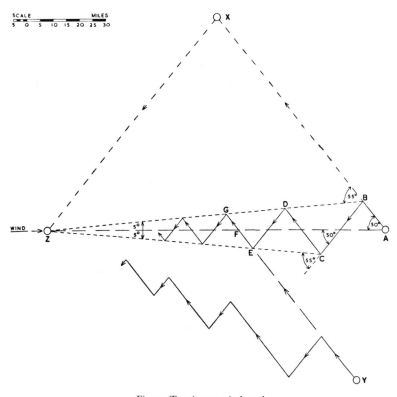

Fig 73 Turning to windward

Unless a certain change in the direction of the wind is anticipated, a yacht situated at *A* should not deviate far each side of the direct course to her objective. A yacht situated at *Y* should also get to leeward of her objective and work towards it in short tacks. Any change in the direction of the wind will then favour her.

In Fig 73 a yacht situated at *A* is bound to windward for destination *Z*, the wind blowing in the direction *ZA*. Let us suppose that, allowing for leeway, the yacht is able to make good a course 50° to the true wind. Starting off on the port tack she sails to *B*, from which point the destination *Z* bears 55° on the weather bow. Putting about she sails on the starboard tack until, at *C, Z* again bears 55° on the weather bow, and so on. If there were no possibility of a change of wind she could, if her skipper chose, reach *Z* in two long tacks, putting about once only at *X*. But it is not wise to gamble on the wind remaining steady, especially when there is nothing to be gained thereby, and suppose that when the yacht reached X the wind did change, backing $45°$, Z would be dead to windward of her again and she would be at a great disadvantage compared with a yacht which had kept close to the direct course and which would then be able to fetch Z on one tack. If, instead of backing, the wind were to veer $45°$, the yacht at X would, of course, be able to fetch Z on a broad reach while the other yacht would only be able to lay close-hauled for Z, but the yacht at X would have a much greater distance to sail, as may be seen in the figure.

A yacht situated at Y, also bound for the same destination and being the same distance from it, will have an advantage over the yacht at A. Two courses will be open to her; she may beat in long and short tacks and not deviate far from her direct course, or she may sail on the port tack until at G she brings Z to bear $55°$ on her weather bow, and then continue in equal tacks along the same course as the yacht from A. Either way she will sail an equal number of miles, but she will have an advantage over the yacht from A equal to the difference between the distance $ABCDEF$ and YF, and no matter what changes the wind may subsequently make, she will retain her lead over the yacht from A. But if she keeps near her own original direct course to Z she will have the same advantage as before over the yacht from A provided the wind remains constant in direction, but if the wind veers she will be badly placed in comparison with the yacht from A.

From the above it will be seen that, disregarding tide, smooth water, etc, a yacht bound for a destination to windward of her, no matter where her starting point may be, should sail on the most favourable tack until that becomes the unfavourable tack by say, $5°$, then she should continue working towards her destination in tacks which extend $5°$ each side of the direct course. (Obviously the tacks will become progressively shorter as the destination is approached, and the $5°$ rule will be abandoned when they become inconveniently short.) But if a change of wind can be forecast with some degree of certainty, she should stand more to that side of her course from which the wind is expected to come; if the wind is going to veer she should stand to the right of her course, but not so far as to permit the change of wind when it comes to enable her to fetch her destination with sheets more than just started.

When the destination lies exactly to leeward it may not pay to steer direct for it because, when running dead before the wind, the yacht will roll, the mainsail will chafe on the lee shrouds, and the headsail will not draw. By letting her come up a little so as to have the wind on the quarter instead of right aft, these troubles may be reduced or eliminated. Also she will sail faster, and that in turn will bring the apparent wind more on the beam, helping her to go faster still. Obviously a greater distance will have to be sailed to reach the destination, and tacking to leeward will be done, ie after a time with the wind on one quarter the yacht will be gybed and sailed for a time with it on the other quarter. Whether the extra speed will make up for or exceed the extra distance sailed will depend on the angle of the wind and the type of yacht; one of light displacement that quickly picks up speed, such as a multi-hull, is more likely to gain an advantage than a slower type of heavy displacement, but even the latter will benefit so far as improved comfort and reduction of chafe are concerned, and of course the risk of an unpremeditated gybe will be eliminated; a yawl or ketch might benefit more than a cutter or sloop because of the blanketing effect of the mizzen on the mainsail when running dead.

If a yacht running at 4 knots alters course so as to bring the wind 20° on the quarter and tacks to leeward, she will have to increase her speed by about $\frac{1}{4}$ knot if she is to reach the destination in the same time as she would take when running dead. If she were to bring the wind 40° on the quarter, and this is a much more likely angle if the headsail is to draw, she will need to increase her speed by about $1\frac{1}{4}$ knots.

Some people make a great labour of their coastal passages by attempting to accomplish them in daylight. Unless the passage is a short one, a very early start may have to be made; but even then, owing to a failing breeze the destination may not be reached until after dark, which will add to the difficulties of entering port and berthing. I therefore consider that unless the passage is so short that it can be made with certainty in daylight, it is better to leave in the evening and make a night passage, thus arriving in daylight. Provided that the shipping lanes are avoided and that there are no unlighted buoys or dangers on or close to the course, a night passage is no more difficult or hazardous than one made in daylight, and in fine weather close along the coast one is likely to have a fair off-shore breeze.

If the yacht's company is inexperienced it would be prudent to hand any large light-weather sails at dusk and to spend the hours of darkness under easy sail, but a competent skipper who is sure of himself, his crew, and his gear will not hesitate to carry as much canvas as his vessel requires by day or night, and he will then make a fast and satisfying passage.

With the intention of reaching the chosen cruising ground as quickly as possible, harbours on the way are best avoided unless there is some special reason for entering them, and if it is necessary to bring up to wait for a fair tide or for a strong head wind to moderate, it would be better to do so in an open roadstead under the lee of a headland, so that as soon as conditions are favourable the yacht may be got under way and put on her course with the minimum delay. When bringing up for the night in an open roadstead, preparations should be made for clearing out quickly if the wind should come on-shore. A safe course to clear all dangers should be laid off on the chart, and everything be made ready on deck, halyards cleared, sheets rove, and headsails bent on, but unless the weather is very unsettled it should not be necessary to reef the mainsail. Lying to the bower anchor alone with a sufficient scope of cable and with the riding light burning brightly, one may turn in to sleep with an easy mind, for the noise and the motion will wake one if the wind should come fresh on-shore in plenty of time to set sail and get away before the sea rises sufficiently to make that difficult. If waiting only for the turn of the tide an alarm clock can be set to rouse one at the right time.

Making a harbour and berthing

At the end of the passage little difficulty should be experienced in finding the harbour entrance in clear weather. The opening in the coast line may be obvious, or the entrance may be located in relation to some conspicuous mark or feature of the coast. But to enter a strange harbour and bring up in a good berth is often quite an undertaking. Even the most experienced of us may then suffer in some degree from 'harbour panic', for although we may, and should, have a harbour plan, we cannot be quite sure what we will find on entering. We may have difficulty in identifying leading or clearing marks, an unexpected tidal stream or eddy may set us towards some danger, or the harbour, if it is small, may be so congested with other craft as to make manœuvring difficult.

Before attempting to enter a strange harbour the sailing directions should be read and the plan studied in conjunction with them, so that one may visualize what the place will look like in reality. Remembering that the plan can only show the harbour in two dimensions, the height of the surrounding land and of any conspicuous or useful objects which will assist one to fix the yacht's position or keep her clear of dangers, should be noted. But such features are not always easy to identify; a small island, for example, which on the plan appears conspicuous, may be so low as to pass unnoticed, or it may be so close to the shore as to be indistinguishable from its background; while the 'Red House, Conspic' may now be part of a housing estate. We must determine the state of the tide and in which direction the stream will be setting. It is important to take in the scale of the plan; some plans are on a very large scale, and unless that fact is realized before entering the harbour there may be trouble owing to lack of space in which to manœuvre.

If the harbour is large one may go boldly in under all plain sail and select a berth at leisure, checking the depth before bringing up unless the plan shows that to be unnecessary. But if the place is obviously small, one must try to decide in advance what action will have to be taken immediately the yacht is inside. An anchor should be cleared ready to let go at a moment's notice, and if the harbour is an artificial one in which it is necessary to lie alongside a quay or other craft, or to moor between posts or buoys, we must have fenders and mooring lines ready. If the latter are too heavy to be thrown to a helper ashore or in another vessel, there should be a light heaving line to throw first. To help it carry, this sometimes has a large knot, known as a monkey's fist, worked in at its heaving end. The line is separated into two loose coils, one for each hand; that in the right hand is thrown first, and as it goes should take along some of the other coil. Practice is needed to throw a line any distance. Halyards should be cleared so that sail can be lowered quickly when required. But if the place is likely to be crowded it will be more seamanlike to hand sail outside and go in cautiously under power.

Most commercial ports provide a pilotage service, but except in the Panama and Suez canals, and a few other places where pilotage is compulsory for all vessels, it is rare indeed for a yacht to take a pilot, the owner preferring to find his own way in. But if a pilot is employed it is as well to remember that (except in the above mentioned canals where his orders must be obeyed) he is on board only in an advisory capacity, and that though he may be experienced in the handling of large vessels he may know very little about the behaviour of small ones.

When lying alongside a quay for a short time in quiet weather, it may be sufficient to have only one line ashore from the bow and one from the stern, each being taken a good distance along the quay so that they will be less affected by changes in the level of water. Never tie a line to a bollard: use a bowline, and, if someone else's line is already on the bollard, pass the loop of your bowline up through his loop from beneath before dropping it over the bollard; then either line can be cast off without interfering with the other. If there is any scend, tidal stream, or wash from passing craft, or if the yacht is to remain alongside for any length of time, springs (mentioned on page 253) will be needed as well. One spring is made fast at the bow and is taken to a bollard on the quay abreast or abaft the stern (this is the fore spring); the other is made fast at the stern and is taken to the quay abreast or forward of the bow (this is the after spring). The springs will prevent the yacht from ranging ahead and astern and will hold her in, and parallel to the quay. But unless the bollards are set well back from the edge of the quay, the springs will bear heavily on topside or guardrail stanchions. They may then be made fast not at bow and stern but amidships when they will be just as effective in preventing fore-and-aft movement, but will not hold the yacht parallel to the quay; so breastropes, one from the bow and one from the stern, each made fast to the nearest point on the quay, will have to be used, and because of their short length they will need frequent adjustment if there is much range of tide. If one is berthed along-side another vessel, unless she is very large, it will not be fair, or perhaps even safe, to lie to her shore lines; the newcomer should run out his own bow and stern lines to the quay or posts as soon as he can, and so share the strain with her.

If, at her berth beside the quay, the yacht will take the ground as the tide falls, unless she is of the bilge keel type precautions must be taken to ensure her listing inwards. The anchor chain may be ranged along the side deck nearest the quay, or, better still, a halyard may be taken ashore and a strain put on it just before the yacht grounds. But if she has to be left unattended, a halyard may be led through a block which is secured to a bollard on the quay by a rope of such a length that the block is just outside the edge of the quay; then if the halyard is set up taut the block will put a constant sideways pull on it, sliding up and down as the yacht falls or rises with the tide; the halyard will require no attention.

Fenders will be needed between the yacht and the quay, or her neighbour, to prevent damage to the topside or its paint. The most satisfactory and long-lasting fender is, in my opinion, the pneumatic kind of the sort to which lanyards can be secured at both ends (Plate 63D), but since injury has been caused by a valve blowing out when under great pressure, it is wise so to arrange the fender that the valve is not uppermost. At least four fenders should be carried, but many of those one sees in yachts are too small, and it is hardly an exaggeration to say that they cannot be too large; a diameter of 13 centimetres (5 inches) should be regarded as the minimum no matter how small the yacht may be. Stowage may present a problem, but there is often some waste space up under the side and stern decks round the cockpit, and if loops of shock-cord are fastened there to screw-eyes, the fenders can be tucked into them in that otherwise unusable space. Fenders may need to be hung vertically when going alongside, but often they are best arranged in a horizontal position once headway has been lost, for if the springs are properly arranged there will be only an up-and-down movement to be catered for. Many quays are faced with vertical balks of timber, or are of sheet piling, against which it is impossible to keep fenders in place; a spar or plank (a fender board – Plate 64B) perhaps 1·5 metres (5 feet) long, should then be slung horizontally over the side to take the chafe, with the fenders placed between it and the topside.

When going alongside another sailing vessel an eye should be cast aloft to see that crosstrees do not touch, for this can easily happen when the crew of a small yacht move to one side of her to handle lines and fenders. When finally tied up the yachts should be so arranged that their masts are staggered.

Pilotage among coral

Some corals, singly or in small colonies, are found in all oceans even in cold water, but the reef-building corals can live only in clear water the temperature of which seldom drops below 21 °C

PLATE 43 (*facing*). A. When the compass is badly placed for taking bearings a pelorus may be used, but the helmsman then must hold a steady course. B. A compass with a dome magnifying top which much increases the apparent size of the card markings and the lubber line. C. A grid compass is the easiest type of all to steer by, and if its grid is luminous no light will be required at night. D. Home-made sights for taking bearings with the steering compass when it is high enough for that purpose. E. A home-made shadow pin used for finding the deviation from a bearing of the sun, but it can only be used in smooth water.

PLATE 44 (*overleaf*). A. The Stowe log and speed indicator is worked by a rotator towed on an electric cable, and only its after end spins; its small size may be seen at B, where it can be compared with the rotator C of the Walker mechanical log (a favourite with many voyaging people because it requires no electricity) which is shown at D.

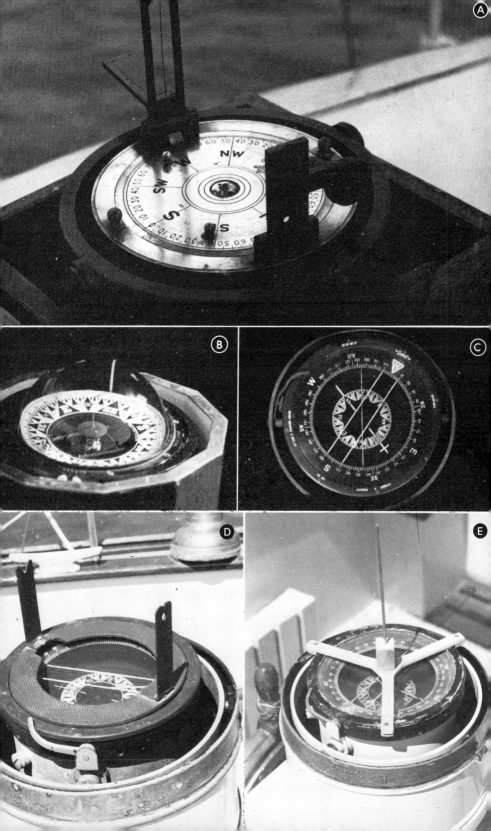

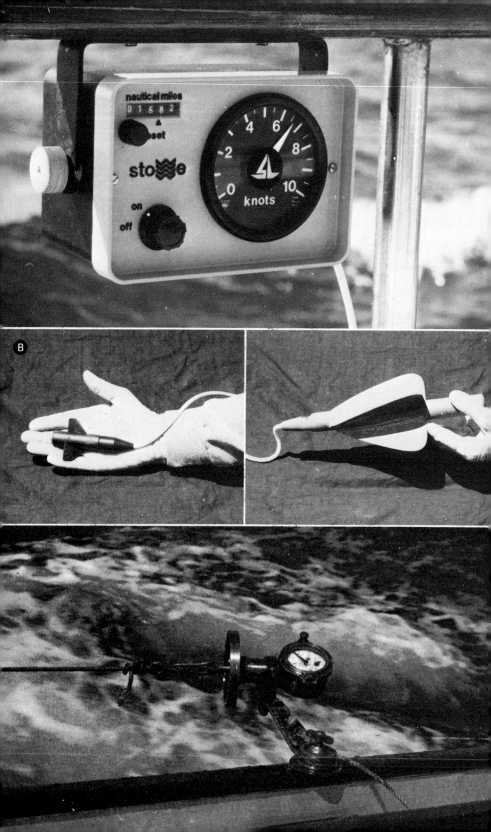

(70°F). They are therefore mostly restricted to a belt a little wider than the tropical zone, but due to warm currents they may thrive elsewhere, as, for example, around Bermuda, because of the Gulf Stream. Most coral reefs will be found on the windward sides of continents and islands, ie on their eastern sides, having regard to the direction of the trade winds; but they may also be found on the lee side of an island if a current carries there the plankton on which they feed.

The first essential in coral waters is vigilance. No opportunity of fixing or confirming the ship's position, or of obtaining a single position line, should be neglected, and all possible forethought and cunning must be brought into use, changing course, or heaving-to, so as to avoid getting into a dangerous position in darkness or bad visibility. Fog in coral waters is almost unheard of, but rain can reduce visibility to a few yards and last for a long time, though generally one has warning of its approach. The coral-encumbered waters in some parts of the world have not been surveyed in detail, and even where a thorough and detailed survey has been made, the charts in time become inaccurate because of the growth of coral; incidentally, coral never grows above the surface of the sea, though blocks of dead coral may be thrown by the breakers up on to a reef. Successful pilotage in such waters is therefore often dependent on the eye, and provided that conditions are right, this does not present any great difficulty, and confidence is gained with practice.

A barrier reef may front a coastline, as along the east coast of Australia, or encircle an island or group of islands, as in the Society Islands, leaving a channel or a lagoon between it and the land. An atoll comprises one or more coral islands of little elevation situated on a strip or ring of coral reef embracing a

PLATE 45 (*overleaf*). Ashore on Foulness Sand. With the wind rising, the glass falling, night coming on, and five hours to wait before his yacht will float again, the skipper with no echo-sounder regrets that he failed to use his lead when beating up for the mouth of the River Crouch. This 7-metre (23-foot) gaff cutter, *Wanderer II*, later sailed to Vancouver by way of Pacific islands.

PLATE 46 (*facing*). With her central cockpit, poop deck, and great cabin, and her colour scheme of red boot-top, white topsides, and vivid blue topstrake, the 15·4-metre (50·5-foot) ketch *Yankee* is a striking vessel. Irving Johnson wanted a ship capable of crossing oceans and climbing mountains (by way of the European canals), and got Olin Stephens to draw the final plans from which a steel hull with a beam of 4·7 metres (15·4 feet) – limited by the width of canal locks – and draught, with tandem centreboards up, of 1·4 metres (4·5 feet), was built of steel in Holland. *Bottom*: The great cabin with its athwartships bunk under the stern windows. Irving is on the left, and his wife Exy on the right.

lagoon. Such reefs as the above frequently rise steeply without warning from a depth of 1,829 metres (1,000 fathoms) or more, and on them the sea breaks with a fury that has to be seen to be believed. Usually the swell produced by gales in the southern part of the Pacific and Indian Ocean causes heavier breakers on the leeward side of a reef than the trade wind causes on the weather side; when approaching a reef down wind by night, which is an exceedingly dangerous thing to do and has been the cause of many wrecks, the breakers cannot easily be distinguished from the harmless crests caused by a fresh wind until they are too close for avoiding action to be taken, nor can their roar be heard up wind above the noises of the ship. The pass through a barrier reef is generally opposite a valley in the land, but the pass of an atoll (not all atolls have passes) is generally on the lee side of the lagoon, and as that may be the only exit for the surplus water thrown by the breakers over the reef into the lagoon, there is frequently a strong out-running current.

The lagoon, or the channel, protected by a coral reef, may be free of dangers, it may have isolated dangers, or it may contain a maze of reefs and coral heads. Reefs are always more plainly seen from aloft than from on deck, and when the sun is high rather than when it is low; also, the sun should be abaft the observer's beam, and the water rippled by a breeze; if there is no wind, nothing can be seen but the reflection of the sky. The wearing of polarizing spectacles is strongly recommended because they minimize light reflected from the surface of the water. Given the right conditions, the scene from aloft is very beautiful, and the depth of water can be judged by the colour. Approaching a channel, lagoon, or bank from the deep blue – almost mauve – of the ocean off soundings, the colour changes abruptly to a light blue when the depth over a clear bottom is 18–27 metres (10–15 fathoms); but if the bottom there is rocky, the colour will be dark green. As the depth decreases so the colour changes, and in 7–9 metres (4–5 fathoms) over a sand bottom it will be light green, in 2·7–3·6 metres (1½–2 fathoms) pale green, and in less than 1·8 metres (1 fathom) the water is almost colourless, indeed, in the Bahamas this is known as 'white water'. On a sand bottom coral heads show up clearly as black, brown, or yellow patches, but if the bottom is grassy they will be hard to see. A pale mauve or russet colour means there is very little water. My wife and I did not find pilotage by eye in the Pacific and the Indian Ocean particularly difficult, and in most of the lagoons we visited it was possible to sail round any apparent dangers; but when such dangers have to be crossed, as on some parts of the Bahama banks, skill in judging the depth by colour to within a few centimetres may be needed, and it is said that to acquire this skill may take 18 months or more.

Perhaps a mention should be made here of vigias, although they are not necessarily of coral formation. A vigia is a reported shoal, the existence or exact locality of which is doubtful. The Pacific abounds in these, for although many have been disproved by laborious search, sufficient remain marked on the charts to be a source of anxiety to the navigator.

19

MANAGEMENT IN HEAVY WEATHER

Waves – Steering in heavy weather – Procedure in gale conditions – Storm sails
– Bilge pumps

EVERYONE who has read the small-boat classics by Joshua Slocum, R T McMullen, and J C Voss, and the more modern wirters such as Peter Pye, Peter Haward, Hal Roth, and Bob Griffith, to mention but a few, must surely be convinced that a decked yacht of good design, strongly built and soundly rigged, will survive a severe gale no matter how small she may be, provided that she is in deep water, has sufficient searoom under her lee, and is properly handled. It is therefore more often lack of confidence in themselves than in their yachts which causes many sailors to worry when making a passage for fear that bad weather may overtake them. That anxiety, from which I have suffered, does a lot to spoil the pleasure of a cruise, and fortunate is he who early in his sailing career encounters and successfully weathers a hard blow. No one who has done so can honestly say that he has enjoyed it, nor would he readily seek to repeat the experience, but in no other way can he gain confidence in his ability as a seaman and prove to his own satisfaction the truth of R L Stevenson's words:

It is a commonplace that we cannot answer for ourselves until we have been tried. But it is not so common a reflection, and surely more consoling, that we usually find ourselves a great deal braver and better than we thought. I believe this is everyone's experience.... I wish sincerely, for it would have saved me much trouble, there had been someone to put me in good heart about life when I was younger; to tell me how dangers are most portentous on a distant sight, and how the good in a man's spirit will not suffer itself to be overlaid and rarely or never deserts him in the hour of need.

From time to time accounts appear in the press of disasters which have befallen yachts; but they should be kept in correct perspective, and it should be remembered that for each one many hundreds of successful cruises and voyages, which have not appeared in print, have been accomplished without mishap. A study of the disasters shows that the majority of them can be traced to failure not of the yachts or their crews, but of some part of their equipment, and that there was no time to effect repairs, or no gear with which to do so. We should not be discouraged by such examples; rather, we should learn from them that the sea cannot be trifled with, that the worst must always be anticipated and prepared for, that no yacht can be regarded as seaworthy unless every item of her gear is sound and strong, and that spares for every contingency are carried. These are matters not of great expense but of painstaking care and attention to detail, as I hope has been shown in Part I of this book.

Waves

When the wind blows along the surface of the sea it causes the sea to oscillate, the oscillations, known as waves or seas, moving forward in the direction in which the wind is blowing. The water in a wave does not move forward in a horizontal direction any more than does a bunting of a flag which is rippling in the breeze; apart from a rotary motion of the water particles (forward at the crest and backward in the trough), the surface of the water only rises and falls, and a vessel small enough to accommodate herself to the waves, and lying stationary or moving only slowly, will lift up and down with them. The advancing face of a wave is steeper than its back. In a moderate breeze a small vertical wall of water, known as a crest, forms on the top of the wave, and this, being a part of the wave, oscillates with it. But the pressure of the wind may cause the crest to overbalance and fall forward; the water of which it is composed does then move forward and may sweep across the deck of a small vessel lying within its path. Breaking crests are generally harmless, but if they are large, as they are in strong winds, they may do some damage.

The speed of waves depends largely on the speed of the wind which causes them, though 25 knots appears to be the maximum; so it will be realized that it is impossible for a sailing vessel to keep ahead of the waves by carrying a press of sail in a gale, though in certain circumstances she may occasionally surf-ride for a short time and travel on the crest at the same speed as the wave. The relationship between the height of waves in feet and the wind velocity in miles per hour is given by the US Hydrographic Office as approximately 1 to 2; a wind of 50 miles per hour should therefore raise 25-foot (7·6-metre) waves. The length, measured from crest to crest, is given as approximately twenty times the height; the length of waves 25 feet (7·6 metres) high would therefore be 500 feet (152 metres). These figures apply only in open water where the fetch, the distance from the weather shore or the point where the wind commenced to blow, is a thousand miles or more. When the wind drops the sea will not immediately become calm; the waves will lose height but their strength from crest to crest will remain the same, and they will continue travelling perhaps for several hundred miles as a long and slowly dropping swell, or until they meet a wind from another direction. There is always some swell running in the open sea, though it may be so gentle as scarcely to be noticed by a small craft.

From the limited information available it appears that in the open sea waves rarely exceed a vertical height form trough to crest of 50 feet (15 metres), and then only in very heavy gales; in soundings, ie where the depth of water is less than 100 fathoms (183 metres) the height of the waves is less. Close to the west coast of Ireland and the Hebrides waves 35 feet (10·7 metres) in height with a length from crest to crest of 100 yards (91 metres) have been measured, but in the English Channel and North Sea a height of from 15 to 20 feet (4·6 to 6 metres) is probably the maximum, and such waves are exceptional there.

It has often been observed that at intervals there is a succession of higher, or shorter and steeper waves. These may constitute a danger in heavy weather, as may the freak sea very occasionally caused by one wave being superimposed on another, for in certain circumstances this could overwhelm a small vessel or seriously damage a large one; but the chance of encountering one of these is slight, except perhaps in high southern latitudes or in the Agulhas Current off South Africa.

Afloat it is difficult to estimate the height of waves; the only practical method is for someone to climb the rigging to a point from which his eye sees the crest in line with the horizon when the vessel is in the trough, and then to measure the height of his eye above the vessel's waterline. But at a time when the sea is high enough to be interesting, one will probably be too occupied or too anxious to do this. Therefore the height is usually guessed at, and what follows here may give some idea as to why it is commonly exaggerated. In 1861 William Froude showed that aboard a vessel afloat in a swell or a seaway the direction of 'down', as indicated by a plumb bob, is not always at right angles to the plane of the horizon, as it is on land, but due to a combination of acceleration and gravity the plumb bob takes up a position at right angles to the surface of the sea on which the vessel is floating at the moment.

The balancing mechanism of the human ear, which on land indicates 'down' as toward the centre of the earth, and 'level' as at right angles to 'down', when at sea agrees with the plumb bob – unless the horizon happens to be visible all round, when the eye may correct the ear – and the new but temporary direction of 'down' is accepted together with a new and temporary 'level'. In Fig 74 the proportion of length to height of the waves has been much exaggerated to make the matter clearer; the direction of 'down' as registered by both plumb bob and human observer aboard the yacht is in the direction of the arrow, and to the observer 'level' is at right angles to 'down'; his eye, measuring from that plane, therefore judges the overtaking wave to be very much higher and steeper than it really is. The height of waves is, however, not of direct importance to a small vessel, beyond the fact that her sails may be becalmed when she is in the trough; it is their steepness and the size of their crests that matter to her.

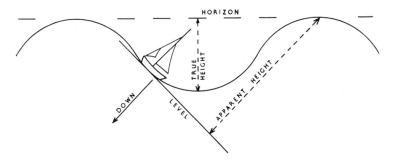

Fig 74   Height of waves

If a wave becomes too steep, as may happen in a great gale, or when it encounters a shoal or tidal stream, or is interfered with by the wake of a fast-moving vessel, the wave, instead of being merely a disturbance passing through water, becomes a bodily forward movement of water rushing onward at a greater speed than the basic wave. This is a breaking sea, something very different from a breaking crest (with which the landsman often confuses it), and consisting as it may of thousands of tons of forward- and downward-moving water, may capsize or smash a vessel which is lying in its path. The prudent seaman will therefore take care to avoid all areas where waves might break, and will handle his vessel in such a manner that her wake does not disturb the overtaking waves.

When bad weather overtakes a yacht which is making a coastal passage, her skipper will have to decide whether to seek shelter or to remain at sea and ride it out there. With the glass falling and the seas growing heavier hour by hour, the urge to run for harbour is strong; but if that harbour is on a lee shore and has a bar at its entrance, or if the tide will be running out of it at the time the yacht would arrive there, it will not be safe to attempt to run for it; more Breton fishing vessels have been lost in that way than in any other. Only if the lee-shore harbour entrance is deep, or is well protected by off-lying shoals which can be avoided, or by an adjacent headland, or, of course, if the harbour is to windward, should the decision to seek shelter be made; but it is as well to bear in mind that rain and spume may reduce the visibility and make the approach more difficult. If the skipper decides to remain at sea, he should get well away from the coast while he is still able to do so in order to have sufficient room under his lee in which to heave-to or lie a-hull, if the weather becomes so bad as to make that necessary; but in nine cases out of ten off the British coasts in summer, the wind will not reach such a force, and a few hours later he will be glad he decided not to waste time by seeking shelter.

There will, of course, be no choice of action, apart from a possible alteration of course to avoid the centre of a depression, if the yacht is making an open-water passage; neither should there be undue anxiety on the part of her skipper, for the open sea does not ask the impossible of any man or well-found craft except in storm conditions which are rare; it is the proximity of land or of shoals that constitutes a danger. So the yacht will continue sailing as long as it is safe for her to do so.

Perhaps it would not be out of place to mention here the mental attitude of a yacht's company which, for the first time, is over-taken by a severe gale at sea. If the crew are in good physical condition, the onset of a gale may at first give them a feeling of exhilaration, and for some hours they may actually enjoy the contest against wind and sea; but unless the duration of the blow is short, the time will certainly come when they will grow weary of the ceaseless tumult. The continuous violent motion, the stinging sheets of spindrift driving constantly across the deck, and the trembling shudder of the yacht as a crest hits her, all have their effect. But it is the roar of the wind in the rigging – rising in the squalls to a high-pitched scream – that is perhaps the most potent factor in producing a feeling of listlessness and utter weariness. It is at such a time, and more especially if some of the crew are seasick, that thoughts are apt to dwell longingly on the nearest port to leeward, if there is one within reasonable distance. I have no wish to induce a feeling of alarm in the mind of anyone starting a cruising career, but I suggest that it may help if the beginner will think out for himself beforehand what conditions may really be like in a small vessel after a good many hours of severe handling by the elements. He will then be on his guard against any feeling of panic that might arise through exhaustion, whether physical or mental, which might lead him against his better judgement to advocate some foolish course of action, such as running for a difficult harbour, when he knows in reality that the proper course is to face it out at sea. Older hands know the capabilities and limitations of themselves and their ships. The beginner will acquire confidence in himself and his ship after his first real brush with the elements, but I am sure that he will find it a great help if he has prepared himself in advance for the devilish caterwauling of the wind in the rigging that hour after hour will try to unnerve him.

Steering in heavy weather

If the yacht is sailing close-hauled when the wind freshens, it is unlikely that her skipper will continue to drive her beyond the point where that ceases to be safe. As the wind increases she will become hard pressed, her motion will grow violent and her lee deck will get buried, so that sail will be reduced in good time for the sake of comfort. The inexperienced are more likely to err by reducing sail too much, so that the vessel does not handle properly, and as a result may think that the weather is worse than it really is. It has often been said that the helmsman, on seeing a particularly high or steep sea approaching, should luff and take it nearly bows on with reduced speed. As, however, this cannot be done at night because one cannot then see the condition of the individual seas, I do not consider there can be any good reason for doing it in daytime.

In a freshening wind and a rising sea it may not be possible to continue sailing on a reach so long as might be done if close-hauled, for the crests will break against the weather side, driving over the deck and into the sails, and a small yacht might even be thrown on her beam-ends by the force of the impact. Here again it is unlikely that the skipper will continue on his course after it has become dangerous to do so, though in daylight by luffing or bearing away for the worst seas, or by sailing close-hauled for a time and then running with the wind on the quarter, he may be able to make good the course a little longer if there is some particular reason for doing so.

It is when running before a freshening gale and a heavy sea that good judgement is needed in deciding how long it is safe to continue at speed. The forward lift and surge as the advancing face of each sea raises the yacht up, the breathless rush on the summit in a smother of foam, and the quieter moments as she slides down its back into the trough beyond, only to be lifted once again and hurried on her way by the next overtaking sea – that is something so wonderfully exhilarating that once experienced it is never forgotten, and nobody aboard will wish to miss a moment of such glorious sailing by reducing speed before so doing becomes necessary. But as the wind increases and the seas grow larger and have bigger crests, it will be found that the yacht remains for a longer period on or near the top of each, and becomes less easy to steer, and as her stern lifts to the crest she may show a strong inclination to broach-to, ie round up broadside to wind and sea. This is caused partly by the unbalanced nature of the sails (this may be reduced or overcome by carrying a small spinnaker), but mainly by the fact that the stern, being near or on the crest, is pushed forward by the forward motion of the water there, while the bow, down in the trough, into which it may be buried deep, is held back by the water which, as has been mentioned earlier, is moving the opposite way. This should be taken as a warning that it is time to reduce sail, and if that is done it will be found that the yacht becomes easy to steer again, and that each crest passes quickly and harmlessly beneath her. But if the wind continues to freshen, steering will again become heavy and a further reduction of sail will have to be made. There may come a time when it is impossible to reduce sail further by reefing, or when reducing sail no longer has the desired effect, and when the seas immediately astern look steeper and more threatening and have higher crests than those elsewhere. If the yacht is kept running hard under such conditions, her wake may cause the following sea to break, or she may broach-to in spite of the helmsman's efforts. In either event the consequences could be disastrous; the hatches and skylights might be stove in, or the yacht be rolled over on her beam ends. Miles Smeeton in *Once is Enough* (Hart-Davis) tells us what such a dreadful experience is like.

A large yacht of good hull form may be able to continue running in safety long after her smaller sister has had to reduce speed, but the small, well-balanced modern yacht of moderate displacement can be kept going in circumstances which twenty years ago would have been considered disastrous, as has been shown again and again by the ocean racing fleets, which today hardly ever stop sailing because of stress of weather. Erroll Bruce, skipper of the 11-metre (36-foot) sloop *Belmore* in a transatlantic race wrote:

The thrill was exhilarating as she hurtled through the seas at a speed I had never known before.... It was like galloping an over-fresh horse down a rough slope, with the stirrups lost and the way ahead hidden beneath the curve of the steepening gradient. Riding *Belmore* on a wave face, the tiller was no more effective than tugging at the bit of the runaway horse.... She sometimes dashed on, wave-riding uncontrollably for thirty seconds at a time before the wave-crest overtook, and the feel of control came back to the tiller.

While admiring such courage, this is not a feat that many cruising people would wish to emulate, for most cruising yachts cannot be driven like that in safety because even if they are of a suitable type few carry a sufficiently skilled or strong crew capable of carrying on in such an exciting, and exhausting, manner.

Procedure in gale conditions

It would be foolish to attempt to lay down rules for the management of yachts in gale conditions, for so much will depend on the size and type of craft, her situation at the time, the strength and experience of her crew, and the particular conditions of wind and sea. The following notes, which are based largely on my own experiences in yachts of 7 to 15 metres (23 to 49 feet), should therefore be regarded only as suggestions.

There are four ways of dealing with gales. The yacht may be hove-to under sail; she may lie a-hull, ie be left to look after herself with no sail set; she may run before it under reduced sail or bare poles, perhaps with drag ropes out astern; or she may lie to a sea-anchor.

To heave-to, sail is reduced as necessary, and usually the headsail is backed so that it counteracts the forward drive of the mainsail (or mizzen), and the helm is lashed down (Fig 75). This reduces the speed through the water so that the yacht makes little headway. She should then yield easily to the oncoming seas and ride up over them without harm. In practice the term 'heaving-to' is used rather loosely to cover varying degrees of lying-to. For example, if the yacht is bound to windward, and more especially if there is land in proximity to leeward, the skipper will be unwilling to yield more ground than necessary; therefore at the onset of a gale he may content himself with hauling the clew of his headsail just aweather of the mast and keeping his vessel fore-reaching at perhaps $1\frac{1}{2}$ or 2 knots, and making about 4 points (45°) leeway. But as the wind and sea increase, he will take more way off by hauling the headsail clew more aweather, perhaps making a further reduction in the after canvas, and by lashing the helm further down.

In heaving-to, as when under way, each yacht will be found to have her own peculiarities, and one can only discover by experiment what combination and trim of sails, and what amount of helm suit her best. Some, such as the 7·6-metre (25-foot) *Cardinal Vertue*, and the 9-metre (30-foot) *Wanderer III* of similar type, lie-to best without a headsail and under the close-reefed mainsail or the trysail only. A vessel lying-to under trysail is said to be lying a-try. Yachts with a good length of keel generally lie-to quietly, looking after themselves and giving their crews a rest in comparative comfort; others, mostly small craft of easily driven type, will not lie-to well in a strong wind, but persist in forging ahead too fast. If a yacht cannot be made to lie-to quietly, but ranges about so much that one moment she is beam on to the wind and the next moment has her mainsail a-shake, either she is not a suitable type for heaving-to or the wind and sea are too much for her.

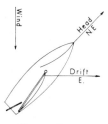

Fig 75   Hove-to.

With the wind approaching force 9 it is probable that the time has come to lie a-hull, ie stripped of all sail. Here again different craft behave differently, but with the helm lashed down many will lie beam on or quarter on to the wind and make a little headway and a great deal of leeway. The leeway creates a slick – a smooth patch, such as is caused by oil – to windward, and this has some protective qualities, the crests of advancing seas being reduced on meeting it. Presumably a shoal-draught yacht, by drifting faster to leeward, will leave a more effective slick than one of deep draught. If, however, the yacht makes much headway, as may happen with a fast type, or one with more windage forward than aft, the slick will be left away on the weather quarter and will then not offer proper protection. I have heard it said that yachts lying a-hull roll violently; but this has not been my experience except when persisted in after the worst of the gale was over. I have found that provided the wind is strong enough its pressure on mast and rigging reduces rolling in the same way as when acting on a sail, and that although the vessel may roll, she does not roll to windward of the vertical.

It is possible that a yacht might lie a-hull in a force 10 wind, but this is a storm, and if it persists for any length of time conditions will become very grave, and, in my opinion, the only safe course then will be to run before it under bare poles. In that end-on position the hull offers the smallest target to the elements, and as there is headway, the rudder is not subjected to unnatural strains. Running before it is, of course, the action that would be taken anyway if the yacht's course was down wind at the time the gale started, and has the merit that all the time miles are being made good in the desired direction; this is important for morale because few things are more disheartening than being stopped at sea due to stress of weather, unless one is in urgent need of a rest. But running calls for a strong and alert helmsman, for in the conditions now under discussion it is, in my view, imperative that the yacht be kept stern on, or nearly so, to each overtaking sea, otherwise the risk of her broaching-to will be greatly increased. The feel of the wind on the helmsman's neck and ears will be his best guide, but he must be on his guard against a sudden shift of wind, especially at night, and should not depend entirely on the compass.

If, even under bare poles, the yacht is considered to be running too fast for safety, ie hanging on the crests almost out of control for long periods, and with the seas astern and on the quarters looking particularly steep and dangerous, her speed may be reduced by using drag ropes. The longest and thickest rope there is with its ends made fast one on each quarter, may be paid out over the stern so that it drags in a bight, or single ropes with bundles of fenders or lifebelts, or indeed anything that will offer resistance and act as a brake, can be used. An example of this procedure is given by William Robinson in his book *To the Great Southern Sea* (Peter Davies), when his 20-metre (66-foot) brigantine *Varua* was running before what he so aptly called the 'ultimate' gale in high latitudes in the South Pacific. It is said that drag ropes have a smoothing effect on the overtaking seas and help the steering, but David Lewis does not agree. He reported that when weathering a 45-knot gale in *Cardinal Vertue* he streamed a 37-metre (20-fathom) rope in a bight astern and attempted to steer before the wind, but the yacht became unmanageable, persistently running across the seas and repeatedly broaching-to. The rope hindered steering, and each large sea swept it alongside. However, the slightly larger 9·5-metre (31-foot) sloop *Samuel Pepys*, when running in a hurricane-force wind in the North Atlantic under bare poles, streamed 73 metres (40 fathoms) of 28-millimetre nylon rope in a bight and two separate 23-millimetre hemp ropes each of 36 metres (20 fathoms). These drags reduced her speed to 3 knots and cut a smoother track through the seas which gave protection so long as she was kept exactly stern on, but an attempt to move out of the path of the storm by bringing the wind on the quarter at once resulted in heavy water coming aboard. The seas were estimated to exceed a height of 9 metres (30 feet) with a length of 122 metres (400 feet). The yacht was steered with little physical effort but with considerable nervous strain throughout the storm, and she suffered no damage.

The first of the well-known *Tzu Hang* disasters (see page 108) occurred when she was running at an estimated speed of 4 knots before a very heavy sea, a little to the east and south of the position where *Varua* encountered her great storm, but not during the same year. She was under bare poles at the time with one rope towing from the stern, and was being steered dead before the seas. The sea that caused the damage was phenomenally high and steep, but was not breaking or showing signs of being about to break. *Tzu Hang* was upended on her bows until she reached a position a little beyond the vertical, and was then rolled over sideways by her ballast keel. It seems reasonable to wonder whether the disaster might have been averted if the yacht's speed had been reduced further by putting out more drags; for after her masts had been swept away, thus reducing her windage so that she was moving only slowly, she was not again upended or further damaged, although the gale continued; but probably the sea was a freak from which no small vessel could have escaped unharmed, for no others like it were seen before or after. John Guzzwell, who was aboard at the time, suggested that the phenomenally high and steep sea may have been caused by a shoal, and Robinson firmly believed that *Varua* did pass over a shoal during her ultimate storm. Although no shoals are shown on the chart of the area, one must accept the fact that they could well exist between the widely scattered soundings. *Tzu Hang*'s second incident occurred after she had been refitted in Chile and had reached latitude 48°S, longitude 82°W on her second attempt to round the Horn. She was lying a-hull at the time in a full gale during which some of the seas had a great weight of broken water on their advancing faces. One of these caught *Tzu Hang* broadside on and rolled her completely over, dismasting her.

The seas in the forties and fifties of south latitude, driven unimpeded by the great westerly gales with a fetch of thousands of miles, are probably the heaviest in the world, and only a very brave man or woman – Beryl Smeeton was the driving force which launched *Tzu Hang*'s second attempt on the Horn – with the springs of adventure strong in him would venture to take a small vessel there.

In 1966 something happened to shake the long-accepted theory of small craft management in heavy weather. The Frenchman Bernard Moitessier and his wife sailed their 12-metre (40-foot) ketch *Joshua* (Plate 28 *bottom*) non-stop from Moorea, Society Islands, to Alicante, Spain, a distance of 14,216 miles, in 126 days. Moitessier had made a study of the behaviour of small craft in heavy weather, and when he was overtaken by a great gale between latitudes 43° and 45° S, ran before it with 5 warps weighted with iron pigs towing astern. These apparently had no effect on the yacht's speed, but they prevented her answering her helm correctly – by then the vane gear had been disconnected and steering was being done by hand. One great breaker caught *Joshua* on the quarter, instead of dead aft as Moitessier had intended, and this gave him the idea for the unusual technique which he then adopted. In a letter to a friend he wrote:

> ... it was this alone which saved the masts, otherwise the boat would have plunged forward and downward where the undertow was fiercest. In a flash I grasped the technique of Vito Dumas [the Argentinian who had sailed his 31-foot ketch *Lehg II* single-handed south of the three stormy capes]: to keep moving at about 5 knots, running full or nearly full [dead before it?] with as little canvas as possible [a small storm staysail], and just before the arrival of each roller to give a touch of helm and luff to take the roller at an angle of 15–20°. This trick made the boat skid, so that, as she planed, she heeled on to her beam. Thus she could not pitch-pole nor be thrown on to her beam-ends, as the sea was taken somewhat on the quarter. Directly I realised this – and none too soon – I cut away my hawsers and *Joshua* was no longer in danger.

A year after this event I took part in a *Yachting World* forum, in which four of us, including my old friend Adlard Coles – perhaps the most widely experienced British ocean-racing man of the day, and whose book, *Heavy Weather Sailing*, had recently been published – discussed yacht management in heavy weather. Naturally the Moitessier method cropped up, and we all found it rather startling. Adlard said he had never dared to try it, but he repeated what he had already written: in his opinion the best method of survival a small yacht has in storm conditions is to run before it under as much sail as she can stand up to, even though she may be laid flat on the water at times; but he added that he shrank from recommending this because if it proved wrong it could lead to loss of life.

Bob Griffiths advocates taking the seas on the quarter and did so in winds of 80 knots while circumnavigating Antarctica in the 16-metre (52-foot) *Awahnee*; but unlike Moitessier he found it best to tow a lot of drags, including a spinnaker boom and several anchors and chains, which had the same effect as a sea-anchor. He kept the sea on the quarter all the time because that helped to reduce speed and rolling.

Much has been written about the sea-anchor, often a conical- or pyramid-shaped canvas bag with its mouth held open by a metal hoop or crossbars, which when streamed on a warp acts as a brake on a vessel's speed through the water. I have used sea-anchors on several occasions, and in common with others have found them unsatisfactory except in certain peculiar circumstances such as are mentioned below. The widely held belief that if streamed from the bow a sea-anchor will hold a yacht's head to the wind, has been disproved so often that one wonders how it survives. No matter how large the sea-anchor may be the yacht will range about even if a riding sail is set aft, and although she may at times come head to wind for a little while she will soon fall off one way or the other and lie beam on. Also she will make sternway and impose a great strain on her rudder. I am convinced that in any normal type of yacht (this excludes the double-ended ship's lifeboat or a canoe such as Voss's *Tilikum*), if a sea-anchor is to be effective in holding her end on to the wind, which surely is its function, it must be streamed from the stern. It is not then fighting against the yacht's natural inclination to turn away from the wind, and, with headway instead of sternway, the rudder is safe. But a self-draining cockpit is essential, and the companionway must be as waterproof as possible and stronger than many are.

I have lain like that safely, but others have not been so fortunate, and it is debatable whether it is wise to attempt to hold the yacht so firmly against the advancing seas. I am of the opinion that it is not, and that it will be safer to continue running and to use drags if necessary to keep the speed within safe bounds. However, circumstances can arise when for survival it is essential to reduce the drift to leeward to the minimum, as, for example, when a danger – land, a shoal, a tide race – lies in that direction. I once used a sea-anchor for that purpose when near the Tonga Islands, and it so reduced our speed (to $1\frac{1}{2}$ knots) that it was safe to steer a little across the wind, and thus go clear of a small island and a reef which lay under our lee. That we could not have done in safety travelling at $5\frac{1}{2}$ knots under bare poles; even if we had dragged all the ropes we had aboard astern I am sure our speed could not have been reduced to the same degree. I have also been glad of a sea-anchor on another occasion when conditions were too wild to permit lying a-hull, and I had suffered an injury, leaving my wife to manage alone. The sea-anchor then kept us stern-on to the sea without the need for a helmsman. But it is only in situations such as these that I would now contemplate its use. Incidentally, if it is to be of any use at all, both it and its gear need to be as strong as it is possible to contrive; the strains are very great and chafe is persistent.

A small quantity of oil correctly applied appears to have a remarkable calming effect on the free waves of the open ocean, but is reported to have little effect on surf once the dissolution of the wave form has begun. Almost any form of oil except paraffin will do, but the heavier it is and the warmer the water the greater will be its effect. The recommended method of distributing oil is from canvas bags capable of holding about 2·25 litres (half a gallon) and these are towed on lines long enough to allow them to float just clear of the hull. They must first be pricked in several places with a sail-needle so that the oil may escape slowly; repricking may be necessary from time to time owing to the oil emulsifying. In *Varua*'s ultimate gale oil was used from two bags each side and was also pumped steadily from the heads. Robinson said he did not know how much good it did, but he thought the seas broke less frequently at the ship than at a little distance. I imagine that anyone who has ever lain in a gale, as I have done, in the sludge pumped out by a tanker, would refrain from using oil except as a survival measure, for the surface water picked up by the wind carries it all over the ship, and the resulting mess is indescribable, besides being dangerous because it is so slippery.

In prolonged storm conditions in the open sea, I believe that size is the final factor deciding between survival and disaster, a good large yacht having a better chance than a good small one. By this I mean that there undoubtedly are seas so steep and violently breaking, particularly in the high latitudes of the southern hemisphere, that the smaller yacht, of under 15 metres (50 feet) perhaps, may be overwhelmed by them no matter what steps her crew have taken for her safety, and that to take a small craft through such areas asks for some luck and calls for a great deal of courage. But such violence is not likely to be encountered in the normal course of cruising and voyaging so long as hurricane areas are avoided during the danger months.

Storm sails

Before the widespread use of terylene for sailmaking, if a mainsail was to be efficient in moderate weather it could not be made of sufficiently strong cloth to be used unharmed in heavy weather, so a trysail, a strong triangular sail of small size and roped all round, was set in its place then. Today a cruiser with a terylene mainsail does not have this same need for a trysail, as her mainsail, when it is reefed as necessary, should be capable of standing unharmed in any weight of wind in which the yacht can show any sail at all provided it is not allowed to flog. Nevertheless a trysail may be desirable as a standby for use in the event of the mainsail being torn, or to be used if the mainsail cannot be reefed sufficiently for use in the stronger winds. Also, as a trysail is set without a boom, when running or reaching the yacht is relieved of the strains imposed by the boom-end plunging into the sea.

Before setting the trysail the main boom with the mainsail stowed on it should be secured on the boom gallows; if there is no gallows, its after end ought to be got down on to the quarter if possible, and lashed there, but before attempting this, the slides on the lower part of the luff must be cut adrift or the sail will be pulled out of shape, or the track torn off the mast.

Aboard *Wanderer III* the trysail was sometimes carried for long periods, once for 14 consecutive days in the Indian Ocean, during one of which the yacht made a day's run of 150 miles under that 7-square-metre (75-square-foot) sail alone. I am sure that the simpler the heavy-weather gear is the better, for it will be brought into use under difficult conditions, and perhaps in the dark when the sense of feel is more valuable than that of sight. Therefore the trysail should, in my view, be hoisted on the main halyard, not on a special halyard of its own, and not on a separate track. In a gale it is difficult to feed slides into a track, but they must be used for that portion of the luff which will be above the crosstrees when the sail is set; for the rest of the luff a lacing is much to be preferred. Some yachts have on the lower part of the mast a short length of duplicate track into which the trysail slides can be fed while the mainsail is still set, and perhaps before the onset of bad weather. Then, when the mainsail has been lowered, a switch (something like the points of a railway line) is shifted and as the trysail is hoisted its slides will run into and up the main track above the stowed mainsail slides (Plate 23D). I have tried trysail sheets rigged as tackles, but found the upper blocks dangerous while the sail was being set and when gybing, and prefer to use single part sheets taken each through a block on the quarter and thence forward to a tackle lying on deck or to a headsail sheet winch. If the sheets chafe on the stowed mainsail the latter must be protected; indeed, an inspection for chafe should be carried out during a gale, for the lead of some of the gear may be different then and damage might result unnoticed.

The spitfire jib and/or storm staysail, which complete the set of heavy-weather sails for a single-mast rig, are, of course, strong headsails of small size. It is advisable to have them cut in such a way, or to fit them with tack pendants of such a length, that they may be correctly sheeted with the ordinary working headsail sheets.

It is a great mistake to have heavy-weather sails made of very heavy cloth, as this will make them stiff and difficult to handle and to stow away.

Bilge pumps

An efficient bilge pump installed where it can be worked comfortably in all conditions (not in a cockpit locker where water might enter while it is being used), is an essential fitting, for in the event of the yacht taking heavy water below or springing a leak, her safety and that of her people will depend on it; and when deciding on the position for the outlet, one should bear in mind that the greater the lift the harder will be the work; so the discharge, which should be fitted with a cock to prevent water syphoning back, ought to be close to the waterline.

A common old-fashioned type of pump consists of a vertical cylinder within which slides a plunger worked in an inconvenient way by pulling it up and pushing it down. The plunger and the lower end of the cylinder are fitted with one-way valves, and these need to be easy of access for cleaning. A hand-lever mounted on a vertical support, like the old village pump, makes working this type of pump easier.

The only merit of the semi-rotary pump is that it can be installed without difficulty in a suitable position, but it is easily put out of action by a foreign body. If it is mounted athwartships the leeward valve is inclined to hang open when the yacht is heeled, and the pump then works at only half its normal capacity, or fails to work at all. To avoid the need for priming a cock may be fitted immediately below the pump, to be closed after use, or the suction pipe may be bent round over the top of the pump to form a trap which will always retain some water.

The diaphragm pump is much to be preferred to any other hand-type, for its flexible diaphragm has a long life, its large simple valves are not easily put out of action, and it does not require priming. Like the semi-rotary, this pump may easily be fitted in any suitable position on deck or below, and is operated by a lever working in a vertical or a horizontal plane. Two well-known pumps of this type are the Munster Simms Whale Gusher, and the Henderson. There are several models of each, and the maximum capacity with 38-millimetre (1½-inch) id pipe is up to 113 litres (25 gallons) per minute; but it has to be remembered that the volume of water one man can deliver is between 45 and 90 litres (10 and 20 gallons) per minute, depending on his degree of panic and the position of the pump.

Many auxiliary engines have, or can be fitted with, a pulley at the forward end of the crankshaft. A bilge pump of the neoprene flexible impeller type (Jabsco) might with advantage be belt-driven off this for use in a real emergency; such a pump can be had with a clutch incorporated, but failing that a jockey pulley on a pivoted arm can be used to tension the belt when the pump is to be used. This type of pump with 2·5-centimetre (1-inch) diameter ports, and turning at 1,500 revolutions per minute can deliver about 90 litres (20 gallons) per minute to a height of 3 metres (10 feet) but it must not be run dry or the impeller will be ruined. There are many electric bilge pumps, but I would not rely on such in an emergency.

The lower end of the suction pipe for any bilge pump needs to be provided with a strainer to prevent foreign matter being sucked up and putting the pump out of action. A piece of wire gauze across the end of the pipe is not satisfactory as its small area soon becomes clogged. The pipe should be led into a strum-box of generous size, the lower side of the box being perforated with

small holes and raised on short legs so that it is about 13 millimetres ($\frac{1}{2}$ inch) off the bilge. The pipe must be flexible and free so
that its lower end, together with the strum-box, can easily be lifted
clear of the bilge for cleaning; it is not sufficient just to be able to
reach the strum-box where it is, for in the event of the yacht taking
dangerously heavy water below or springing a serious leak, the
bilge will certainly get fouled with debris, such as paper labels
washed off cans of food, and quick and frequent cleaning of the
pump suction will then be vital. A flat-floored yacht ought to have
two suction pipes, each fitted with a cock, leading from opposite
wings of the bilge, so that the pump may draw from the lee side
when the yacht is heeled, for a small quantity of bilge water in
such a yacht will all too readily invade the sole and the lower
lockers.

20

SELF-STEERING

Steering line and twin sails – Wind-vane gear – Automatic pilot

THE need for a yacht with a small crew, or one making a long passage, to be able to steer herself, is no longer of such importance as it used to be since wind-vane gears have been perfected and generally do the job better, so the matter need be touched on only briefly here; but it should be emphasized that with any form of self-steering in use a proper lookout must be kept, except perhaps in the empty wastes of the wide oceans away from recognized shipping lanes.

Steering line and twin sails

A yacht of well-balanced hull form, and carrying a little weather helm, should be capable of steering herself close-hauled in a steady wind with the helm lashed up a little, but if the wind freshens she will luff, and if it eases she will bear away. This may perhaps be overcome by balancing the sails, by hardening in the headsail or easing or reefing the main or mizzen, until the yacht does not carry any helm, when the helm may be left free. But rarely will a yacht steer herself for more than a few minutes with the wind abeam or on the quarter, unless some arrangement is made for a headsail to control the helm. For this the headsail (perhaps the staysail, or a small sail set especially for the purpose) will best be rigged with its foot on a boom, and instead of trimming the sheet on the lee side in the usual manner, a steering line will be rigged on the windward side, leading from the end of the boom through a block to windward, then aft and through a second block there to the tiller, to which it will be secured. A length of elastic shock-cord will be rigged on the lee side of the tiller. Fig 76 shows the arrangement, but the elastic might with advantage be taken through a block to a winch for ease of adjustment. Suppose we wish the yacht to steer with the wind abaft the port beam; we put her on the course and adjust steering line and elastic until she steers herself. If she should luff, the wind pressure on the headsail will increase, and as the sail moves to leeward it will increase the strain on the steering line and pull the helm up to put her back on course; if she should bear away to starboard, the wind pressure on the headsail will decrease and allow the elastic to pull the helm to leeward to put her back on the course. This is probably the simplest of the many variations that have been tried, and it was used with some success by *Viking*, *Kurun*, and *Solace* during their circumnavigations, and more recently by Tony Skidmore in the 7·3-metre (24-foot) cutter *Mona Sally* on a single-handed 17,000-mile voyage from England to British Columbia. Success with self-steering depends much on experiment and ingenuity, of which the following is a typical example.

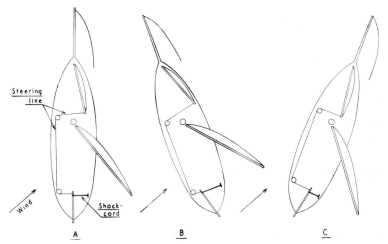

Fig 76   A common self-steering arrangement when the wind is on the quarter

The staysail controls the tiller by a steering line against the pull of the shock-cord. *A*: On course. *B*: When the yacht luffs, the tiller is automatically pulled to windward by the steering line, and when she bears away, *C*; the tiller is pulled to leeward by the shock-cord.

In *Speedwell of Hong Kong*, one of the 7·6-metre (25-foot) Vertue class, when the wind fell light and was more or less abeam, John Goodwin, who was something of a driver, found it was possible to carry mainsail, genoa, and spinnaker all at the same time, and he discovered that the latter, on its 4·2-metre (14-foot) boom, did not interfere with the set of the genoa. The total sail area of this rig was 59 square metres (640 square feet), which is a remarkable amount for so small a vessel; a Vertue normally carries a maximum of 29 square metres (314 square feet) and is not considered to be under-canvassed. Self-steering was achieved in the following manner. The spinnaker after guy was led aft to a whip, one end of which passed through a quarter block and was made fast to the tiller, while the other went to the weather headsail sheet winch so that it could be adjusted easily. Heavy elastic secured to the tiller was adjusted by the lee headsail sheet winch to achieve balance (Fig 77). If the yacht luffed, the spinnaker exerted a greater pull than the elastic, and the tiller was moved to windward; if she bore away the elastic exerted a greater pull than the spinnaker, and the tiller was moved to leeward until she returned to the course.

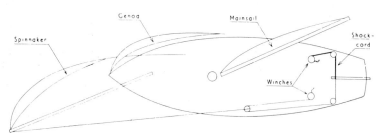

Fig 77   Self-steering arrangement used by John Goodwin in *Speedwell of Hong Kong*

Such arrangements as outlined above will probably not work with the wind more than 45° abaft the beam, for the headsail will then be starved of wind in the lee of the mainsail; the twin rig, with which two sails of equal area are set each on a boom of its own forward of the mast, will then have to be used, unless tacking to leeward is resorted to (page 356). Such a rig was probably first used for an ocean passage in *Imogen* in 1930, and many variations followed: with some the sails were hanked to twin stays, as in *Beyond* (Plate 49), in others they were set flying; some had the booms pivoted aloft, others low down on the mast or at the stemhead. Usually the braces, the ropes which control the fore-and-aft trim of the booms, were led through blocks to the tiller, or to a drum on the steering wheel, and worked in much the same manner as the steering line described above, ie if the yacht sheered to port, the port sail received more wind pressure than the starboard sail, and therefore pulled on the helm to return the yacht to her course.

The disadvantages of such a rig are that it will work properly only when the wind is aft or nearly so, therefore an alteration of course (or of wind direction) will call for the lee sail to be handed and the mainsail to be set in its place; also, with no fore-and-aft sail to steady her, the yacht rolls with abandon. A big advantage of the rig is that as the sails are set forward of the mast they cannot chafe on the shrouds like the mainsail does. Many trade wind crossings of the North Atlantic have been made under twins or boomed-out headsails, and some yachts still use the rig; but it has largely been replaced by the wind-vane gear which does the job far better, and is effective on all points of sailing.

Wind-vane gear

Probably Marin-Marie was the first to make use of a wind-vane steering gear, when in 1936 he made a west to east crossing of the Atlantic in the power yacht *Arielle*; next came *Buttercup* in 1955, going the other way under sail, but it was not until the advent of the single-handed transatlantic races that vane gears really came into their own. Much of the pioneering work was done by H G 'Blondie' Hasler, who gained experience with one of his own design on four single-handed Atlantic crossings in *Jester* for a total of 12,000 miles, during which the yacht was steered by hand for less than 50 miles.

The theory of the vane gear is easy to understand, it is the geometry and the engineering that present the problems. If a vane (usually a sheet of plywood, but occasionally of metal or even of cloth) is free to rotate about its vertical axis, it will take up a position end-on to the wind just like a weathercock. If, with the yacht on her course, such a vane is locked to the rudder and the yacht then alters course, the new direction of wind will turn the vane to the head-to-wind position, and in doing so will move the rudder to bring the yacht back on her course. But a rudder needs to be large as it has to be used for manœuvring, and to have sufficient power to move it the vane needs to be of great size. Francis Chichester had such a vane in *Gipsy Moth III*, but it needed to be so large for use in moderate winds, 4·2 square metres (45 square feet), that it required reefing in strong winds, and because of its size it had to be partly furled before the yacht could be gybed. But if an auxiliary rudder is arranged right aft, it can, because of the extra leverage it exerts there and the fact that it will not be needed for manœuvring, perhaps be of a size small enough for a vane of reasonable area to turn, and so will keep a small, well-balanced yacht on her course, though it may need some help from the main rudder, which can be given a bias one way or the other with the tiller line or elastic.

However, something more powerful than this is needed for a larger yacht or one that is not well balanced, and two devices have come to the fore, both depending for power on the water flowing past; they are the trim tab and the servo rudder (or pendulum) (Fig 78). The trim tab is a flap of small area (about one-fifth of the area of the rudder) hinged to the trailing edge of the rudder. The tab is linked to the vane, and when the vane turns it in one direction it imparts a considerable turning force to the rudder in

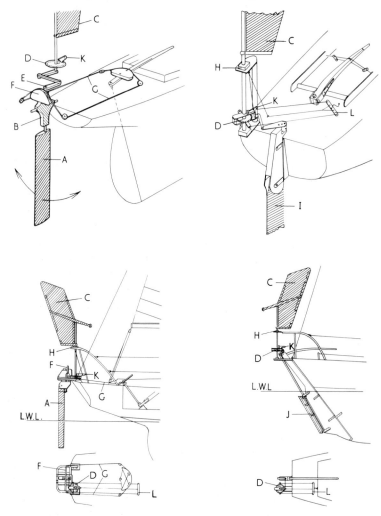

Fig 78   Early Hasler wind-vane gears

Top left and bottom left: Pendulum-servo. *Top right*: Auxiliary rudder. *Bottom right*: Trim tab.
A = blade; B = servo box; C = vane; D = toothed wheel; E = servo tiller; F = quadrant; G = steering lines; H = vane-shaft upper bearing; I = auxiliary rudder; J = trim tab; K = latch; L = brownstick. NB: the modern trend is to pivot the vane horizontally.

the opposite direction, so long as water is flowing past. We had such a gear, designed by Blondie, in *Wanderer III* for her circuit of the North Atlantic; it worked very well in most conditions, and my wife and I found the business of crossing oceans much less arduous than before, as it was at last possible for us to get all the sleep we needed; after a 26-day crossing from Tenerife to Barbados, during which we steered by hand only for an hour or two at each end, we arrived fresher and more relaxed than we ever had in the past. The De Ridder gear (Plate 50*B*) steers with its own rudder and uses a trim tab to turn it, but this is mounted not directly on the rudder, but on arms projecting aft from the rudder, and therefore has a more powerful turning moment. A normal trim tab can only be used with an outboard rudder, ie aboard a yacht with a transom or a lifeboat stern, unless some complicated engineering is done on the rudder.

The servo rudder gear has a vertical blade in the water, and this is connected to the vane in such a manner that when the vane turns it turns the blade out of the fore-and-aft line; the blade is also free to swing athwartships, pendulum fashion. When the blade is turned, the water flowing past it causes it to swing upward, and it is this powerful force, transmitted by steering lines rigged to the tiller, or to a drum on the steering wheel, that steers the yacht by means of her main rudder. Such gears have proved their worth on many long voyages, and *Wanderer IV* has used one of this type (an Aries, Plate 50*C* and *D*, made by Marine Vane Gears at Cowes, IW) with great success for some 40,000 miles.

The vane which pivots on a vertical axis has largely been replaced by the horizontally-hinged type; this has a balance weight so that it stands upright when head to wind, but as soon as the wind comes on one side of it, it leans over in the opposite direction. It is more powerful than the other type, and is more sensitive to small changes in wind direction. With either type means must be provided for linking it to trim tab, or servo rudder, in such a way that its relation to tab or rudder can be altered for a change of course or a change of wind, or be disconnected quickly when steering is to be taken over by a human helmsman. This may be done by means of a toothed wheel and pawl, or pawls, sometimes spring-loaded, lines from the arrangement leading to a position near the helm, as with the Aries gear. The brownstick (after Neville Brown who invented it) is simple and effective and was used with some of the earlier Hasler gears. The stick, a 30-centimetre (12-inch) piece of wood has a hole at its centre and one at each end to which light lines are secured. The middle line operates a latch engaging with a toothed wheel on the vane shaft, the others lead to the ends of a steering yoke. A pull on the stick disengages the vane, and by keeping tension on the lines and moving the stick in a horizontal plane about its own centre, steering by hand can be done through trim tab or servo rudder. On releasing the stick the latch falls into place and the vane resumes steering.

With the servo rudder some form of safety device is desirable, so that if the blade strikes an obstruction (a balk of timber or a turtle) it will not suffer damage. This may comprise a spring-loaded catch, which will release itself when the blade is hit and allow the blade to come to a horizontal position, or a coupling which will break and can be joined up again with new fastenings may be used.

Most professionally made vane gears are efficient, but they all need to be assisted in their work by the balancing of sails so far as that is possible. For example, it is expecting rather a lot of a vane to steer when the yacht is running before a fresh wind under mainsail only; a headsail or a spinnaker should then be boomed out on the opposite side to achieve some sort of balance.

Vane gears call for little maintenance, but when bushes and washers are of nylon it may be found that after a few years the gear stiffens up, for nylon tends to swell; as it is essential that every moving part be free, the nylon fittings will then have to be filed or renewed.

Automatic pilot

The automatic pilot is an electric device used for steering a vessel on a compass course. It usually consists of four units: heading unit, reversable steering motor, clutch, and control unit. The heading unit contains a gimbaled magnetic compass with a small light over it and two photo-electric cells beneath, and it can be rotated by the steering motor; the same motor can turn the steering wheel or push or pull the tiller when the clutch is engaged by hand; the control unit contains the on–off switch, fuses, and the electronic brain which controls everything. With the unit switched on, but with the clutch disengaged, the vessel is put on the desired course, and the motor runs to rotate the heading unit until the photo-electric cells are lined up and an equal amount of light falls on each through holes in the compass card. When the motor has done that it stops running, and the clutch can be engaged to connect the motor to the steering wheel or tiller. If the vessel should go off course, the heading unit moves in relation to the magnetic compass assembly within it, and the two photo-electric cells are no longer evenly illuminated; this situation sends a signal to excite circuits in the control unit, which start the motor running in the correct direction to turn the wheel or move the tiller to bring the vessel back on to her course. When she is back on course and the cells are evenly illuminated once more the control unit switches off the motor.

In common with most electronic equipment for yachts, improvements to auto-pilots continue to be made, and I under-stand a model can now be had fitted with a vane sensor, so that it can be linked not to a compass but to wind direction, thus eliminating the risk of a gybe when running dead before a wind which changes direction, and overcoming heeling error difficulties in steel or ferro-cement vessels. An auto-pilot may be of value even aboard a yacht fitted with efficient vane gear, for it removes the drudgery of steering when under power in a calm; also, when all hands are needed on the foredeck to change headsails or set or take in a spinnaker, a vane gear may not be able to hold the course because it is overpowered by a temporary but grossly unbalanced sail plan – the auto-pilot will then look after the steering.

PART III

VOYAGING

PLATE 47 (*facing*). A heavy swell is often the forerunner of bad weather. *Top*: The Nicholson ketch *Grockle*, with genoa and mizzen staysail set, finds little wind off the coast of Portugal. *Bottom*: *Wanderer III* runs at 4 knots under bare poles in a Caribbean gale while on passage between Bequia and the Panama Canal, usually a windy area when the winter trade is fully established.

PLATE 48 (*overleaf*). The American 11-metre (36-foot) centreboard cutter *Altair* (Charles and Chris Grey), leaving San Juan, Puerto Rico, in a steep swell which, *middle*, often hid her hull from my view and, *bottom*, broke angrily on the ramparts of El Morro beside the narrow harbour mouth.

21

PLANNING AND PRACTICE

*Wind systems of the world – Seasonal winds – Tropical revolving storms –
Currents – Pilot charts – Time and route planning – Provisioning – Self-
dependence – Vigilance – Welfare – At anchor – Single-handed cruising*

CONTRARY to a common belief among laymen, a successful voyage in a sailing yacht is not a haphazard undertaking, commencing at any moment convenient to owner and crew and leading
wherever the wind may blow. Certainly a number of voyages have
been started in such a casual manner, but few of them were carried
through to a successful conclusion.

Like any other worthwhile undertaking a voyage needs planning, and it is probable that the greater the care with which this is
done the greater will be the success of the voyage. The two chief
considerations are to avoid dangerously bad weather, notably the
great storms known variously as hurricanes, cyclones, or
typhoons, to which certain areas of the oceans are subject at
certain times of year; and to take advantage of fair winds, in which
it will sometimes be found that the longer way round is the quicker
in the end, as well as being kinder to ship and crew.

The basis of planning is to be in the right place at the right time,
but first one must decide how long can be allowed before one must
be home again, or at some specified place, and even the fortunate
few who can start on a voyage with no fixed time of return must lay
their plans with care.

PLATE 49 (*overleaf*). Twin running sails are not so often seen now that wind-vane gears
have been perfected. *Beyond*'s 70 square metres (750 square foot) twins gave her a speed of
7½ knots in a force 5 wind, and I took this picture of her from the pilot launch as she bustled
along off Viti Levu, Fiji, during her world voyage.

PLATE 50 (*facing*). *A*. A Hasler trim-tab gear with vertically-pivoted vane; here it is
mounted on a small platform on the boomkin, and is coupled to the trim-tab shaft with a
link. *B*. The De Ridder gear steers with its own rudder, which is moved by a trim-tab on
long arms to increase leverage. *C*. An Aries gear with its servo blade hinged up in port to
avoid damage; the little wood bracket in which it is housed is the owner's addition. *D*. The
Aries, like most modern gears, has a horizontally-pivoted vane, which is more powerful and
sensitive than one with a vertical axis.

Usually those who intend to make a voyage have had the idea in mind for some time, or at least have taken an intelligent interest in the subject, and have read some of the published accounts of other small-ship voyages. Such reading is a great help, not only in providing a realistic picture of the conditions likely to be encountered and the difficulties that will have to be overcome, but in deciding which ports or places are worth visiting, and which are best avoided. Such reading may form the basis of the plan; but alone it is not enough, for some understanding of the wind systems of the oceans is needed, together with the detailed information and advice which is to be found in certain textbooks and charts.

Wind systems of the world

A description of the winds and weather of all oceans will be found in *Ocean Passages for the World* and the appropriate *Pilots*; but the following brief outline should serve as a sufficient introduction to the subject to enable the reader to understand the general principles and make the best use of the pilot charts (see page 407 and front endpaper), which provide in a simple and clear manner the essential information needed when a voyage is being planned. Some of the matter in the following sections is based on information obtained from *Ocean Passages* and the *Admiralty Navigation Manual*, Vol I, with permission of the Controller of HM Stationery Office.

If all parts of the earth's surface had the same temperature, the atmospheric pressure at the surface would everywhere be the same, and there would be no wind. The primary cause of wind is a difference of temperature, which in turn is responsible for differences of atmospheric pressure. As was mentioned in Chapter 15, warm air rises and cooler air flows to take its place; also air tends to flow from an area of high pressure to an area of lower pressure.

Between the latitudes of 20° and 40°, both north and south, there are belts of relatively high pressure over the oceans; on each side of these belts the pressure is relatively low. The belt of nearly uniform low pressure in the neighbourhood of the equator is known as the doldrums, a region of calms, light variable winds, and intermittent heavy rains; its average width varies between 200 and 300 miles. If there were no other wind-creating factors, and if the earth was stationary, wind would blow on the surface from the high-pressure belts to the low-pressure belts, the winds being north and south, and the displaced air returning high up in the contrary direction. But the earth is rotating on its axis in an easterly direction, and this movement causes any mass of air which is being drawn towards a low-pressure centre to be deflected to the right in the northern hemisphere, so that a circulation is set up in an anti-clockwise direction about the centre. Around a centre of high pressure a clockwise circulation is set up in the northern hemisphere. In the southern hemisphere these directions are reversed. Therefore the winds on the equatorial

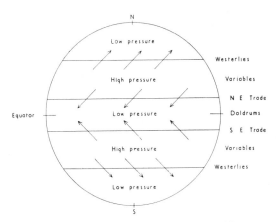

Fig 79   Pressure and wind belts of the world

sides of the high-pressure belts, blowing towards the doldrums, do so from a north-east and south-east direction, Fig 79. It was because of the steady assistance these winds gave to the trade of sailing ships that they became known as trade winds, and so far as is possible a sailing yacht's route should be planned to make the best use of them.

Normally the trade winds do not blow with gale force, and the weather within their belts is mostly fine and clear with a pleasantly warm temperature, while the barometer remains steady, except for the diurnal rise and fall, which results from the atmospheric pressure waves with a period of 12 hours which sweep regularly round the earth from east to west. These waves are at their maximum in the tropics, and the pressure rises from approximately 0400 to 1000 hours, then falls until 1600 hours, after which it rises again until 2200 hours. If this diurnal rise and fall ceases, or if there is a marked upward or downward trend of the glass, the presence of a tropical disturbance may be suspected.

The trade-wind belts of both hemispheres, and therefore the zone of doldrums that lies between them, move bodily north and south during the year, following in a small measure the declinational path of the sun, which ranges from 23° 27' N (Tropic of Cancer) to 23° 27' S (Tropic of Capricorn).

The south-east trade wind of the Pacific is not so constant or steady as are the trade winds of the other oceans. Only during the months of June, July, and August is there a continuous belt of south-east wind blowing steadily across the ocean. During the rest of the year there is a space 600 miles wide and extending diagonally across the belt in which the wind is unsteady in force and direction, and is often punctuated by calms.

On the polar sides of the trade-wind belts there are regions in which calms and light or moderate variable winds are encountered; these extend approximately between latitudes 25° and 35°, both north and south, and correspond more or less with the high-pressure belts. They are known as the variables of Cancer and Capricorn respectively, and are often referred to as the Horse Latitudes, because sailing-ships becalmed for long periods there sometimes had to jettison their cargoes of livestock to conserve the freshwater supply. On the polar sides of latitude 35° in each hemisphere, the westerly direction of the wind becomes more and more definite as the latitude increases. The forties of south latitude, where these westerly winds commonly reach gale force and blow continuously from the same direction for several days at a time, are known as the Roaring Forties. In the corresponding latitude of the northern hemisphere, namely, in the more restricted areas of the North Atlantic and North Pacific, the westerly winds are generally lighter and more variable in direction, due to the presence of large land masses, and to the succession of low-pressure formations, known as depressions, which were described in Chapter 15.

The above main wind systems, together with the seasonal variations which are described in the following section, are shown diagrammatically in Figs 80–3, each figure covering 3 months of the year.

Seasonal winds

In certain parts of some oceans seasonal winds are experienced. Such winds, which blow steadily from one direction for several months, and then, after a short pause, become reversed and blow as steadily from the opposite direction for the remainder of the

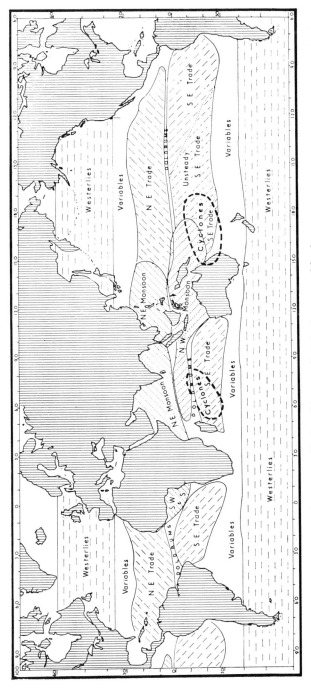

Fig 80   Diagram of winds, January to March

Off the coast of north-west Australia willy-willies blow during these months and until
April.

(Figs 80–3 are based on the former Admiralty Diagram of Oceanic Winds with the
permission of the Controller of HM Stationery Office and the Hydrographer of the Navy.)

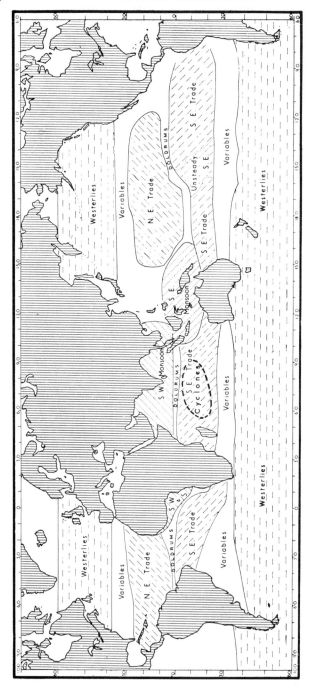

Fig 81 Diagram of winds, April to June

The cyclone season in the western part of the South Pacific finishes in April. The south-
west monsoon starts in May.

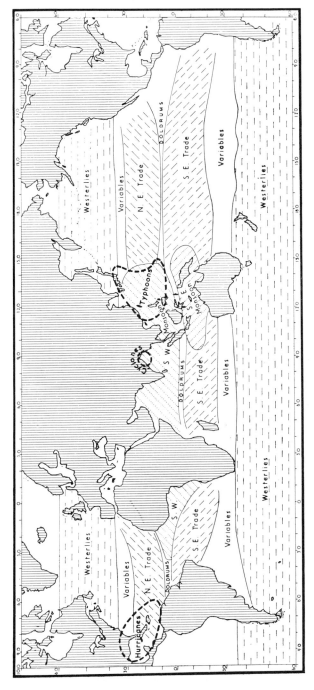

Fig 82   Diagram of winds, July to September
Pamperos blow in the River Plate during these months.

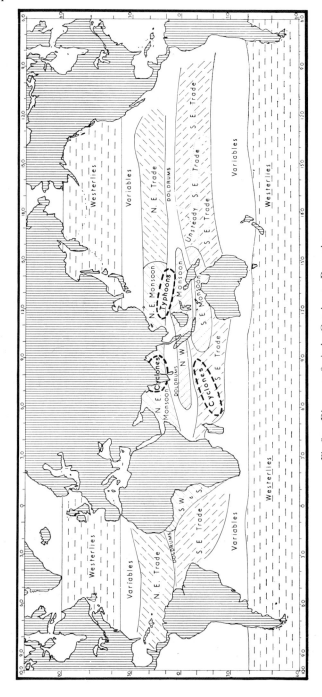

Fig 83   Diagram of winds, October to December

West Indian hurricanes may be experienced until mid-November. The north-west monsoon starts in November. The cyclone season in the western South Pacific, and willy-willies off the north-west coast of Australia, start in December.

year, are known as monsoons, from an Arabic word signifying 'seasons'.

During the summer the great land mass of Asia becomes heated, and in the winter months is cooled, relative to the temperature of the sea along its southern and eastern coasts. Sea water does not absorb or release heat as rapidly as land, and in spite of large alterations in the temperature of the air, remains at about the same temperature all the year round. During the summer months, therefore, a great region of heated air is established over Asia, and the area becomes one of low pressure relative to that of the cooler air over the sea. While these conditions prevail, there is an anti-clockwise circulation of air around this part of the continent, and this is felt as a south-west wind in the northern part of the Indian Ocean and in the China Sea. But during the winter months the conditions are reversed, and there is then a large high pressure area over the cooler land, and low pressure over the warmer sea, producing a clockwise movement of air, which is felt as a north-east wind over the same waters. These two winds are known as the south-west and north-east monsoons.

Monsoons also occur in northern Australian waters, and extend in a comparatively narrow band westward from Australia across the Indian Ocean, filling the space between the equator and the northern limit of the south-east trade wind. In this case a north-west or north monsoon blows during the southern summer, and a south-east wind – known either as monsoon or trade wind – blows for the rest of the year, ie from April to October.

The approximate seasons of the monsoons are:

> SW monsoon – May to September.
> NE monsoon – October to March.
> NW monsoon – November to March.

Over the full length of the Red Sea the prevailing wind is NNW from June to September; but from October to April a SSE wind prevails in the southern part while the NNW wind continues in the northern part. Between them lies a calm belt.

On the south-east coast of South America, south of about 15°S, the SE trade wind does not reach the coast, and during the southern summer a NE monsoon blows along the coast as far as the River Plate; during the winter the winds there are SW and SE. Violent SW gales, known as pamperos, are experienced in the vicinity of the River Plate from July to September.

The SE trade wind does not extend into the Gulf of Guinea on the west coast of Africa; there the prevailing wind throughout the year is south or south-west. Between June and September this wind extends as a monsoon in a narrow belt westward from the African coast towards South America, and occupies the region between the equator and the southern limit of the NE trade wind as far as longitude 32°W.

There are some other seasonal winds, but these are not usually given the name monsoon.

In the vicinity of Cape Horn the prevailing wind is westerly, and gales from between south and north-west occur at all seasons. Off the Cape of Good Hope south-east winds are common in the summer, and westerly in the winter. Gales from between north-west and south-west are most common in June and July, but they may occur at any time of year.

Tropical revolving storms

The strongest winds at sea are encountered in tropical revolving storms, when they may attain a speed of 100 knots or more, and raise a huge sea which could overwhelm a small vessel, particularly if the centre, or eye, of the storm passes over her. These storms are so named because they originate in the tropics, and the wind blows round an area in which the lowest pressure is in the centre. The direction of rotation is anti-clockwise in the northern hemisphere and clockwise in the southern hemisphere. The wind does not revolve round the low-pressure centre in concentric circles, but has a spiral movement in towards the centre of the disturbance; see Fig 84.

These storms occur for the most part at the western sides of the oceans, though they are also experienced in the Bay of Bengal, and off the north-west coast of Australia, while some Atlantic hurricanes have started near the Cape Verde Islands; they are unknown in the South Atlantic. Usually they form between latitudes 10° and 20° either side of the equator, and in addition to their circular motion they have a forward movement. At first this is in a westerly direction, but frequently the storms recurve, turning to the north or north-east in the northern hemisphere, and to the south or south-east in the southern hemisphere; they lessen in intensity and increase in area and speed as they leave the tropics, and may then travel for long distances, bringing destructive gales of great strength to places far removed from their origin. It is, for example, not uncommon for hurricanes originating near the American coast to travel across the Atlantic to the coast of Europe.

A vessel lying in the track of the centre, or eye, of the storm will be in particular danger, for the wind will remain constant in direction until the eye reaches her when, after a short calm, it will blow with great violence from the opposite direction and raise a

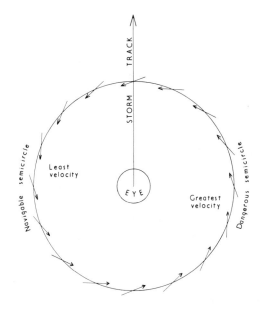

Fig 84   Tropical revolving storm, northern hemisphere

wickedly steep and confused sea. In the northern hemisphere the right hand is the dangerous semicircle, for a vessel caught in this will tend to be blown towards the track of the centre, or the storm may recurve and its centre pass over her; also she will encounter a greater wind velocity than would be found in the left-hand, or navigable, semicircle, for the storm may be travelling at anything between 5 and 50 knots, and where the wind is blowing in the same general direction as the eye is travelling the two velocities combine. In the left, or navigable, semicircle the velocities are subtractive.

One of the most obvious and important considerations when planning a voyage will be to ensure that the vessel will not find herself in an area subject to tropical storms during the danger months, or if she has to pass through an area which is never entirely free from them, that she does so during the months of reduced risk.

Tropical revolving storms are most frequent during the late summer or early autumn of their hemisphere, being comparatively rare in the northern hemisphere from mid-November to mid-June, and in the southern hemisphere from mid-May to mid-November. But in the Arabian Sea they are most likely to occur in October–November and May–June, ie at the change of the monsoon. Out-of-season storms occur from time to time, and in the Western North Pacific no month is entirely safe.

According to location the storms have different names; they occur in different parts of the world as follows:

Western North Atlantic. Hurricanes may blow here from June to mid-November. They are most frequent during August, September, and October when the trade wind is feeble, and they generally curve to the northward by the Bahamas and between the American coast and Bermuda. Some pass to the Gulf of Mexico, others curve well out into the Atlantic east of Bermuda.

Western North Pacific. Typhoons may blow here during all months of the year, and are most frequent from July to October; in the China Sea October is the worst month. They generally move in a west or north-west direction at first, then curve north or north-east.

Eastern North Pacific. Hurricanes blow from mid-June to end of October, and are most frequent in September.

Western South Pacific. Cyclones blow from December to April, but are most common from January to March.

Bay of Bengal. Cyclones blow from May to December, but are most frequent during September.

Arabian Sea. Cyclones blow from April to January and are most frequent during June, October, and November. They rarely blow in August.

North-West Australia. Willy-willies blow from December to April.

Southern Indian Ocean. Cyclones blow from October to June and are most frequent from December to April.

More detailed information regarding tropical revolving storms in any area, together with the rules for avoiding them, will be found in the relevant *Pilot*.

Currents

As was noted in Chapter 17, a current is a permanent or semi-permanent movement of water; it should not be confused with a tidal stream, which depends on the movements of celestial bodies and is subject to hourly changes.

Currents may be caused by differences of specific gravity, such as result from variations in temperature and salinity; but the major cause is wind. When wind blows over water, friction causes the surface particles of the water to move in the same direction as the wind, and these particles act on those below them so that a current is created. Such a current, while it is still under the influence of the wind that created it, is known as a drift current. Permanent winds, such as the trade winds, create drift currents, but these do not follow the exact direction of the wind because the rotation of the earth has a similar effect on them to its effect on wind; in the northern hemisphere this causes a current to flow to the right of the direction towards which the wind is blowing, and in the southern hemisphere to the left. Having regard to the general wind systems of the world, it will be realized that ocean currents north of the equator tend to flow in a clockwise direction, and those south of the equator in an anti-clockwise direction. Ocean currents not under the influence of the parent wind may be caused by the following: (1) The momentum of a drift current which carries water into regions where it is no longer under the influence of the wind that created it. (2) The deflection of a drift current by land or shallow water, so that it sweeps on under its own momentum in a new direction. (3) The replacement, in the form of a counter or compensating current, of water carried away by the primary current.

The currents of the North Atlantic (Fig 85) may be taken as a fair example of ocean currents in general. The north-east trade wind, blowing almost continually, creates the west-flowing North Equatorial Current, which has a rate of from 10 to 40 miles a day. Some of the surface water displaced by this current, together with some from the South Equatorial Current (created by the south-east trade wind), returns to the east along the narrow doldrum belt where there is no wind to hinder it or set up a drift current; this is known as the Equatorial Counter Current, and has a rate of from 10 to 30 miles a day. But the bulk of the North Equatorial Current presses on along the north coast of South America, and passes through the openings between the West Indies to pile up with a rise of level in the Caribbean Sea. The only escape for this water is between the Yucatan Peninsula and Cuba, and thence through the gully separating Florida from the shallow Bahama Banks; the current taking that route is known as the Gulf Stream, but that is a misnomer, for it does not originate in the Gulf of

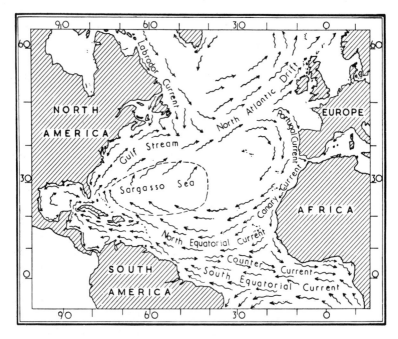

Fig 85   Currents of the North Atlantic

(Based on Admiralty chart No 5310 with the permission of the Controller of HM Stationery Office and the Hydrographer of the Navy.)

Mexico, indeed, no water goes into that Gulf as there is no exit from it. The Gulf Stream, a band of warm and very salt water some 40 miles wide, flowing at a rate of up to 100 miles a day, and in narrow bands within the Stream sometimes at a greatly increased rate – it is said that a speed of 9 knots has been recorded – sweeps along the eastern coast of North America to the New-foundland Banks, where it meets the cold Labrador Current and is deflected to the east. No doubt it would lose its impetus there were it not for the westerly winds which continue the easterly drift; this is sometimes called the Gulf Stream, but it is more commonly known as the North Atlantic Drift; it has a rate of from 10 to 25 miles a day. In the neighbourhood of the Azores it divides, one part setting north-east to the arctic regions, the other turning down the eastern side of the ocean, where inshore it is known first as the Portugal Current, and then as the Canary Current. Eventually it swings to the south-west and west as the North Equatorial Current, thus completing the cycle.

This great clockwise circulation of the surface waters of the North Atlantic revolves round a large area where there is little or no current; flotsam comes to rest there, together with a quantity of Sargassum weed, from which the area got the name Sargasso Sea, a place said to be so stagnant that it gave rise to legends of ships held fast until they rotted.

The other oceans, except the northern part of the Indian Ocean where the currents are affected by the monsoons, have similar circular current systems, clockwise in the northern hemisphere, anti-clockwise in the southern hemisphere. They also have their named currents, as, for example, the warm Agulhas Current of the Indian Ocean, which flows south-west along the south-east coast of Africa; and the Benguella and Humboldt Currents of the South Atlantic and South Pacific, both of which are cold and flow up the west coasts of South Africa and South America respectively.

There is much yet to be learnt about ocean currents, and the navigator should remember that they are variable both in strength and direction. Even when a trade wind has been blowing steadily for many days, the surface drift may be in any direction, and may vary as much as sixteen points from one day to the next; indeed, I have sometimes found the least current when the trade wind is blowing with strength and constancy. Although the more powerful currents, such as the Gulf Stream and the Agulhas Current, keep a more constant direction, considerable variations in strength do occur. Current arrows on charts should therefore be regarded only as an approximate indication of the general trend, and no reliance should be placed on them or the rate written against them when a landfall has to be made under difficult conditions.

Pilot charts

US pilot charts are fascinating documents, showing as they do practically everything that the mariner needs to know when planning an ocean voyage. By a simple system of colours and symbols they indicate the average strength and direction of the winds and currents, and the percentages of calms and gales that have been encountered in all navigable parts of each ocean at different times of year. A set of such charts for the area in which the voyage is to be made is the most essential requisite when planning that voyage.

The originator of the pilot charts was Matthew Fontaine Maury, a lieutenant in the US Navy, who started collecting material for them in the early part of the nineteenth century by persuading mariners of all nations to fill in the special log-books with which he provided them. Some idea of the immensity of the task may be gained, for example, from the fact that the meteorological data of the April pilot chart for the North Atlantic are based on more than 4 million observations, and that is only one chart of a set of twelve for that ocean.

Pilot charts are published by the US Navy Oceanographic Office, and can be obtained through British chart agents if advance notice is given. They are published as follows: Monthly for the North Atlantic; quarterly (December–February, etc) for the South Atlantic; monthly for the North Pacific; quarterly for the South Pacific; monthly for the Indian Ocean. They are continually being amended as fresh information is obtained. A full-size reproduction of a portion of one of the North Atlantic charts will be found in the prelims.

Four colours are used for the symbols; blue, green, red, and orange. The chart is divided by pecked and solid black lines into 5° rectangles. In the centre of each rectangle is a small blue circle. The figure in that circle indicates the percentage of calms and light airs that has been experienced within the rectangle during the month for which the chart is valid by the observers who have supplied data. The blue arrows flying towards the circle fly with the wind, and indicate the direction of the wind (concentrated on eight points of the compass) which has been experienced within the rectangle. The length of each wind arrow, measured against a scale in a corner of the chart, expresses the percentage of wind from that particular point. When, as sometimes happens in trade-wind areas, the percentage of wind from one point is so great that the arrow would be inconveniently long, the arrow is broken and the percentage in figures is inserted, as may be seen in the lower part of the endpaper. The number of feathers on each arrow indicates the average force of that wind expressed by the Beaufort scale (page 288). The average percentages of all available ships' observations in which gales (winds of force 8 and above) were reported in each 5° rectangle are shown in figures on a small inset chart. The direction of currents is shown by green arrows, and the figures printed in green against some of these arrows express the speed of the currents in knots and tenths, but see below.

The tracks of some representative storms which occurred during the month (or quarter) in the past are shown in solid red lines, with the dates of their positions at Greenwich noon. The maximum and minimum limits of ice, and the extreme limit of icebergs, are also shown in red, and the percentage of fog in dotted blue lines.

With these essentials before him, the navigator can plan his passages to the best advantage, seeing where winds and currents are likely to be most favourable and where they are adverse, and what the risk may be of encountering a great storm, gales, fog, or ice. But when he puts his plans into practice and finds himself out in the ocean, he must not be disappointed if he encounters conditions different from those shown on the chart, but should remind himself that the symbols can only represent the average of many observations taken in the past, and that no efforts of man to reduce nature to a formula are ever entirely successful. This fact was realized as long ago as 1740, when Anson set out on his famous voyage. In his book, *A Voyage Round the World*, he comments that during the passage from Madeira to St Catherine's Island, Brazil, the trade winds did not blow as expected or as had been experienced by earlier navigators; but he then continues:

> I mention not these particulars with a view to cavilling at the received accounts of these trade winds, which I doubt not are in general sufficiently accurate; but I thought it a matter worthy of public notice that such deviations from the established rules do sometimes take place.

In addition to the information which has already been mentioned, the pilot charts contain certain other matter that is of value and interest to the navigator. Lines of equal magnetic variation (at intervals of one degree) for the year stated are shown by orange lines, and the rate of annual change in the variation is shown, also in orange, in a small inset chart. The normal atmospheric temperatures are shown by dotted red isotherms, the positions of ocean station vessels are shown by bold red circles, and the normal atmospheric pressure is shown in blue isobars on an inset chart. The dashed red lines, and the large letters *B* and *D* in the reproduction, are connected with the division of the chart into hydrolant areas for the purposes of correction, and do not concern us.

Finally, pilot charts show a number of regular shipping routes with distances, but one is naturally sorry to discover that in new editions the sailing-ship routes, which from the yachtsman's point of view formed such an interesting and valuable feature of earlier charts, have been omitted. As changes are made from time to time, it may be found on comparing the above description with a pilot chart that some of the colours differ, also that the rate of the currents may be given in miles per day instead of in knots.

British routeing charts provide much of the above information, some of it in a more detailed form, but in my view the symbols are not so easy to read.

Time and route planning

As has already been mentioned, the essentials when planning a voyage are to make the greatest use of fair winds and avoid dangerously bad weather by choosing a suitable course and being in the right place at the right time. Therefore, the destination having been decided on, one will study *Ocean Passages* and/or the pilot charts, to obtain as much information as possible about the winds and weather between the point of departure and the destination, and make brief notes. Possibly an area in which tropical revolving storms occur will be the most serious consideration round which the plan will begin to grow, and from the safe months for that area one will work backwards and forwards.

To illustrate this, let us take a simple example and suppose that we wish to make a round trip from the English Channel to the West Indies and back by way of Bermuda, a voyage which is often made by British yachts.

From a previous section in this chapter we have seen that the West Indies hurricane season extends from June to November, but it is generally considered that the last half of November is safe. Although navigation among the islands is possible during the hurricane months – indeed, a number of yachts have safely made the West Indies during the summer months – the risk is one which a prudent seaman will do his best to avoid. So here is the first time factor: we should not arrive at the West Indies area before mid-November, and we ought not to remain there after May.

From the chart of the world showing sailing-ship routes, or from the text of *Ocean Passages*, it is obvious that the shortest route (great circle course, see page 291) from the English Channel to the West Indies is not practicable for a sailing vessel, because she would probably have headwinds for a great part of the way; a glance at the pilot charts of the North Atlantic will confirm this. The passage recommended is by the southern route, ie down the eastern side of the ocean until the north-east trade wind is picked up, and then curving away to the westward. This route passes close to the Madeiras and Canaries, either or both of which will make convenient stopping places for refreshment. By measuring on the Atlantic chart, we find that the distance by the recommended route from the Canaries to Barbados, the nearest of the West Indies, is about 2,700 miles. How long will that passage take? I have usually planned on the assumption that my vessel will average 100 miles a day in the trade winds and have not often found that to be far wrong. Others have taken anything between eighteen and forty-four days for this passage, so perhaps we will do it in twenty-five days, and as we do not wish to arrive at the West Indies before 15 November, we should not leave the Canaries before 21 October.

The Canaries lie about 1,500 miles from Falmouth, and if we decide to sail there direct, the passage might take us something between twelve and twenty-five days, depending largely on the weather we encounter while crossing the Bay of Biscay. If we take the larger and very pessimistic figure, and allow ourselves a week at the Canaries, we should leave Falmouth not later than 19 September. But if we look at the pilot charts for September and October, we shall find that the north or north-east wind, known as the Portuguese trade wind, which predominates during the summer from Cape Finisterre to the southward, is becoming variable, and that the proportion of south-west winds is increasing; also we shall find that the percentage of gales is rising. If time permits, it will therefore be better to leave the Channel earlier, say in August, and put the time to good advantage at Madeira and the Canaries.

As we have already seen, we may cruise safely among the West Indies until May, but by June we should be on passage to Bermuda. We may leave earlier if we wish, but up to March the pilot charts show a high proportion of gales in the Bermuda area. The passage to Bermuda, about 800 miles from Nassau, will be in the variables, but the charts show that in May and June winds with a southerly component predominate.

From Bermuda to the English Channel we should get a large proportion of fair winds if we follow the great circle course; but in deciding on the course to steer, we should bear in mind that in the

Atlantic the farther north one goes the stronger are the winds likely to be; also that the great circle course passes within the line marking the extreme limit of ice off Newfoundland, and into an area where 10 to 15 per cent of fog may be expected. The majority of cruising yachts therefore take a more southerly course to keep in a pleasanter weather area, and some call for refreshment at the Azores; but in the neighbourhood of those islands in the summer there is a considerable chance of falling in with north-east winds, which will compel one to stand away to the north or north-north-west to seek the westerlies of higher latitudes. June, July, and August are good months for making the crossing, the smallest percentage of gales being in July. The crossing may take thirty to forty days, so if we leave Bermuda on 1 July, we should be in the Channel during the first half of August.

The planning of a voyage which is to extend across more than one ocean is naturally a more complicated and lengthy business. The method employed by Tom Worth when planning *Beyond*'s voyage round the world was as follows. He mounted the world chart showing sailing-ship routes on a piece of soft wallboard, and glued the names of the months (cut from a calendar) to the heads of drawing pins. Having roughly pencilled in the proposed route, he read *Ocean Passages* and stuck the drawing pins of the best months for each area into the chart. Then he consulted the pilot charts, measured distances, and computed the possible time it would take to sail from one place to another, and the pins were gradually moved. He spent about 300 hours at it, and at the end simply had a list of ports and approximate dates; but it was a valuable list, and much had been learnt in the making of it.

Although a small-scale chart of the ocean or oceans in which one intends to voyage is of value when planning, it will not be necessary at that stage to buy all the coastal charts and harbour plans that one may think will be needed during the voyage. Indeed, if cost is a major consideration, it will be better to plan the route in some detail before buying them so as to avoid spending money on charts of coasts which one may discover, on studying the *Pilots* and pilot charts, are best avoided. And while it is, of course, important to have all the necessary charts some time before sailing day so that they may be studied and arranged in a suitable order, the longer their purchase can be delayed the less correcting will have to be done, for agents supply charts corrected in most respects to the date of dispatch. It is as well to refrain from ordering very large-scale harbour plans until the general and approach sheets have been studied, for it often happens that the latter give sufficient detail to enable ports to be made by a small vessel in safety. But I would advise the navigator not to be too parsimonious, particularly in buying charts which cover coasts or islands near his proposed route, for he may well find it desirable to make some changes to his plans during the voyage, and the probability then will be that the only way of obtaining missing charts will be to have them sent out from home.

It is important to allow oneself a reasonable length of time in a port or on a coast at the end of a stage, otherwise an unexpectedly long passage could upset the time plan for the following passages. If a passage takes the expected time, one has the full allotted time in port; but if the passage is a slow one, the time in port will be reduced to permit departure on the planned date.

Provisioning by Susan Hiscock

It is not possible to give precise information about provisioning for a voyage as much will depend on the tastes and appetites of the crew, the amount of stowage space, the types and qualities of the provisions available at the port of call, and costs; some years ago I kept a record of all that two of us consumed in one week, and when compiling the provision list for our first long passage, multiplied that quantity of food by the number of weeks we expected to be at sea (reckoning an average of 100 miles a day), and then allowed something extra for emergencies. Having notes of how this worked out was useful for subsequent voyages, but there were occasions when the quantity we wished to take was limited by space and the desire not to put too much weight on board. The notes that follow are not intended for the comparatively few yachts that have seagoing refrigeration.

If space is available and one is in a place with reliable suppliers it is worth while buying a large supply of dry stores, staples such as flour, oatmeal, pastas, rice, etc. When displayed for sale in remoter places these stores are often kept in open sacks and contain weevils. They are best stowed in strong plastic bags secured with elastic bands, for even if there are no drips or leaks the atmosphere is often humid on board and paper bags soon split as their contents swell with moisture and turn mouldy.

Perhaps the majority of voyagers when they leave their home port head for warmer waters, partly to take advantage of fair winds but also for the enjoyment of warmth and sunshine; so, if we want to maintain a palatable and varied diet we must guard our stores and preserve our independence of the shore.

Potatoes and onions will keep for months, depending on when they were harvested, if they are kept in a dark but dry and well-ventilated place. Hard white cabbage is good for a month and crisps up a coleslaw even if most of the other ingredients are canned; carrots and celery are long lasting. Hard apples and green tomatoes will often be good for three weeks, but if either have a small black hole they probably contain a creature which will rapidly turn them bad. Bananas bought green on the stem should be stowed where they will not be bruised or excessively burnt by sun and salt – quite a problem in a small boat; once they start to ripen, perhaps after two weeks, there will be a surfeit for a few days. Fruit and vegetables in plastic bags will rot.

In hot climates I wash all fruit and vegetables that are to be eaten unpeeled or uncooked in water to which a few crystals of permanganate of potash have been added, and avoid eating lettuce where dysentry is common.

Citrus fruits, bought not fully ripe and wrapped in wax paper, will keep a month, lemons will last three months. Really fresh eggs will be good for three weeks but if wanted to keep longer, they should be covered with a thin film of vaseline as soon as possible. I keep eggs in boxes holding twelve and turn the boxes every few days, and do not throw away the boxes which will be of value in the many places where eggs are sold loose.

Concentrated thick soups in cans or packets are good; of the many canned meats available the ones I prefer are corned beef, braised or stewed beef, ox tongue, and spam. I avoid ready-made stews as they are mostly vegetable and do not taste of much, and find it is better to make a stew on board with a tin of stewed beef and fresh onions and any other vegetables I have. Tuna and sardines (Portuguese or Spanish) are the most popular canned fish. Cans of ham weighing over a kilo (2 pounds) will not keep for long. There is no doubt that sterilized bottled meat is superior to canned and all manner of meats or chicken or fish can be used. Aboard *Wanderer IV* I process steak and kidney, using preserving jars 10 centimetres high × 9 centimetres diameter (4 × 3½ inches); each jar will take nearly 475 grams (1 pound) of meat. I cut the meat (blade steak does well) in large chunks, and the kidney in small, and layer into the bottles to within 2 centimetres (¾ inch) of the top, adding no water. With the lids screwed on lightly I place them in a pressure-cooker with plenty of water but keep this below the tops of the bottles by 2 centimetres ($\frac{3}{4}$ inch), bringing to pressure slowly and pressurizing for 90 minutes. If the jars are packed too tightly in the cooker they may crack. Some cookers will hold two tiers of bottles enabling a large quantity to be pressurized at the same time. The metal screw band of the top may be removed when the bottles are cool. At sea, with the addition of onions, etc, this is a quick, easy meal to prepare, and originally tough meat will be tender without losing its flavour. The cook in a short-handed yacht needs to have a repertoire of quick hot meals as there are few things more disheartening than to be cold and tired *and* hungry.

Ashore, bread and butter are two items we are apt to take for granted but after a week at sea they are luxuries. Canned butter may be excellent, but one needs to be sure the stock is fresh as it does not have a canned life of more than six to twelve months. For a long passage it is therefore worth salting fresh butter which will then keep for several months. Buy firm, salted butter, sterilize some glass jars (jam jars will do), and when they are cool press in the butter with a knife to within 1 centimetre (0·4 inch) of top and fill up with dry salt and screw on the lids. Some margarines keep well and remain firmer than butter in hot climates.

White or brown bread will keep for ten days in an airy place, either in a paper bag or wrapped in a cloth; an air-tight container will encourage mildew. There are many excellent crispbreads with which to fill in when there is no bread, but fresh bread can be made on board with either soda or yeast, and although a loaf using the latter is more trouble to prepare, it is more like the real thing. Dried yeast can be had in vacuum packed jars or foil packets but has a limited life of perhaps 6 to 9 months. Every sea-going baker has a special recipe but I use the following simple one:

> 500 grams (1 pound), or three cups,
>   of flour (white or wholemeal)
> Salt
> Teaspoonful sugar
> Teaspoonful dry yeast pellets
> Tablespoonful corn oil
> $1\frac{1}{2}$–2 cups water

For the yeast to work in the dough the temperature is best at 30 °C (86 °F), so I have the ingredients and mixing bowl (actually a saucepan) ready warmed and am prepared to keep them warm while the dough is rising – inside a plastic bag in the sunshine is sometimes enough. Dissolving sugar and yeast in half a cup of warm water, I let it stand for fifteen minutes, then stir and add to the flour, plus about another cup of warm water to which the oil has been added. The dough needs to be fairly wet or it will not be elastic when kneaded with floury fingers – err on the wet side as it is easy to knead in dry flour; I knead for five minutes, replace in the bowl, cover and allow to rise and double its size, which takes a minimum of forty-five minutes. Then I knead again and place in a greased baking tin approximately 24 × 14 × 7 centimetres ($9\frac{1}{2}$ × $5\frac{1}{2}$ × $2\frac{3}{4}$ inches) and allow to rise once more before baking for forty-five minutes at 180 °C (356 °F). Most yacht ovens will take two loaves this size.

I try to have a supply of little luxuries for night watches, such as slab chocolate, sweets, nuts and dried fruit, or whatever is our fancy and was available at our last port of call. For a fresh flavour it is worthwhile to sprout some mung beans or alfalfa: just cover the bottom of a glass jar with seeds, fasten a piece of fine netting over the top with an elastic band, and cover the seeds with water for twelve hours. Then drain them dry, and at about eight hourly periods rinse them with fresh water, but do not leave any water in the jar or they will rot. When the shoots are 2–3 centimetres (1 inch) long they are ready to eat in a salad, sandwich, stew, or whatever. In the tropics they are ready in about three days.

The late Tom Worth wrote the following note on fishing for the first edition of *Voyaging Under Sail*:

For one as unskilled in sea fishing as myself, it would be unwise to depend on catching fish [for the pot] in the Atlantic; in the Pacific there is a good chance of catching good fish near the coasts or islands, but not offshore. Off European coasts perhaps the best tackle is the ordinary mackerel line with spinner; say 12 feet of gut, a lead of about 3 lb. and 100 feet of $\frac{1}{8}$-inch diameter line. In the Pacific we used various coloured feather lures, 2 to 6 inches long and weighing 1 to 4 ounces, 15 feet of wire leader with a breaking strain of 150 lb., and 100 feet of $\frac{1}{4}$-inch diameter hemp line. A piece of shock-absorbing rubber was looped in the standing end of the line to take the shock if a big fish struck. We caught a fair amount of fish, mostly Spanish mackerel, and members of the bonito family up to about 15 lb., and occasionally up to 40 lb. The gear was broken by bigger fish several times. A rod is of no practical value, and is not a great deal of fun because you never know what you will catch. The cheapest place for fishing gear is in the Panama Canal Zone. *Dictionary of Fishes* by Rube Allyn, published by the Great Outdoors Association, St. Petersburg, Florida, is of great interest in identifying strange fish. We never hesitated to eat any fish that really looked like a fish should look, even if we could not name it, and we suffered no ill effects. Occasionally we caught some odd-shaped, ugly-looking fish which we would not touch.

Two other wild-life books of special interest to the voyager are: *Birds of the Ocean* by W B Alexander (Putnam), and *Giant Fishes, Whales and Dolphins* by J R Norman and F C Fraser (Putnam).

Self-dependence

As there is no longer any commerce done under sail, many of the ocean routes likely to be followed by a sailing yacht are empty of shipping. These routes are, of course, crossed in places by power-vessel routes, but although there are a lot of them, one should bear in mind that on some there may be no more than a ship every few months or so, and that as the bridge of a ship will be visible in clear weather up to a distance of between 5 and 10 miles, depending on its height, one may see nothing when crossing a route.

During *Wanderer III*'s first world voyage only three ships were sighted, and throughout *Omoo*'s crossing of three oceans only two were seen. On more recent voyages, those of *Wanderer IV* between 1968 and 1978, we did see a few more ships, even though with auto-pilot or wind-vane steering we did not keep quite such a good lookout as we had in the past. On the first of her two Atlantic crossings between Canaries and West Indies two ships were sighted, and on the second crossing we saw one ship and three yachts. Between Panama and Marquesas (4,000 miles) we saw only one ship after clearing the Gulf of Panama. In the Indian Ocean between Christmas Island and Durban (4,400 miles) we saw two ships, and between Cape Town and Horta (4,500 miles) we met one ship on the equator and saw two others as we neared our destination. On a recent 7,000-mile voyage north in the Pacific we sighted four ships and one yacht. All the above sightings were made at times when no land could be seen, but with land in sight there was often a great deal of shipping. Clearly little reliance should therefore be placed on receiving any assistance when away from the land, and when one sets out it must be with the understanding that no matter what may happen – failure of gear, injury or illness, lack of stores or water, or the urgent need for a check on the position – the yacht's company must rely entirely on its own resources. I believe most people suffer from a feeling of apprehension before the start of any venture in the successful conclusion of which they have to depend on themselves; and which is usually aggravated by the knowledge that they will be out of touch with the rest of mankind for a time. This feeling becomes less strong as experience is gained, and it may be of some comfort to know that it usually dies soon after the land has dropped astern.

Vigilance

Good seamanship implies constant vigilance. In a time of stress, such as during bad weather, or when executing a difficult manœuvre or piece of pilotage, most people are keyed up to their best endeavours, are alert and quick to react in an emergency; but when all is going well, particularly when difficulties have recently been overcome, or when a passage is nearing its end, there is a risk that vigilance may be relaxed or that one will become over-confident – that is a dangerous moment, and it is then that the vessel is most likely to get into trouble. The perfect seaman will not let that happen, but we are not all perfect, no matter how experienced we may be, as the following examples will show.

I almost wrecked *Wanderer III* on a rocky Panamanian shore where a big sea, driven by the north-east trade wind, was breaking heavily, simply because I was lacking in vigilance. The ten-day crossing of the Caribbean from Antigua had been a rough one and my wife and I were glad when the lights of Cristobal/Colon lifted ahead, and we could see bright among them a powerful flashing light. Tired and relaxed, the passage nearly completed and port just ahead, I omitted to check the period of that light with the *List of Lights*, and steered for it, taking for granted that it was the 18-mile light on the end of the breakwater. It was only my wife's alert lookout and common sense that averted disaster, for it was she who realized, just in time, that the light was an air-beacon some distance inland. I learnt from this how important it is when I am tired to place no trust in my judgement and to check every item, no matter how obvious it may appear.

My shame at that unseamanlike approach to Central America was reduced a little when I learnt that even a fine seaman like Tom Worth can also be guilty of negligence, as is shown by an incident which occurred when he and his wife in *Beyond* had crossed the Indian Ocean and were sailing up the African coast bound for Aden. They were never certain of their position off that almost featureless coast except at noon, but one evening at dusk they knew that Hafum Peninsula – which sticks out about 15 miles and is joined to the shore by a low beach – lay fairly close ahead. There is a light on its end, the only one for hundreds of miles. Tom saw a headland which could be Hafum, and set a course to pass outside it, thinking it could be positively identified by its light later on, and that in any case the brilliant moon would be up in a couple of hours. Nearly two hours later he noticed that the swell was confused, and then he suddenly saw breakers very close ahead. He immediately altered course to starboard, and *Beyond* just – but only just – sailed clear of the lee shore.

What had happened then became obvious. Before dusk, unsuspected mist had obscured Hafum; the headland sighted was not Hafum but a part of the mainland, and the ship had almost been wrecked on the low connecting beach. Describing this incident in the *Royal Cruising Club Journal*, Tom wrote: 'The lesson is, of course, either to keep out to sea and rely on celestial navigation, or keep inshore and pay *very* close attention to business all the time. I hope I never let such a thing happen again as I would not deserve to be so lucky a second time.'

Another great sailing man, Peter Pye, nearly lost his 8·8-metre (29-foot) converted fishing boat *Moonraker* (Plate 57) during a West Indies cruise. When sailing among the Bahamas one day, Peter had just completed a difficult piece of pilotage and manœuvring when passing through a narrow cut against a tide race, and, pleased with the success of this, he was, to quote from his book *Red Mains'l* (Herbert Jenkins), 'relaxed and off guard', as *Moonraker* sailed in towards the anchorage at Royal Island Harbour at about high water. From the chart he knew that two rocks lay there, one large, the other small, and he supposed both of them to be above water. Two rocks were sighted, and although these looked rather closer together than they should be, he was not very concerned, as there was no need to go close to them. The headsails had been handed preparatory to anchoring, but the old ship was still sailing fast when she struck, and with such force that her stern rose 0·6 metre (2 feet).

Peter then realized that the 'two' rocks he had seen were in reality one, its pinnacles separated by shallow water at high tide, while the second rock, which his ship had struck, was covered at high water, a fact which a study of the chart should have revealed. Fortunately there were two motor boats in the harbour; with one of them towing from ahead and the other pulling from abeam with a rope made fast to *Moonraker*'s mast so as to heel her farther and thus reduce her draught, she was got safely off.

The above three incidents will suffice to show the danger that is attendant on relaxation or over-confidence in conditions believed to be straightforward and easy. But there is another danger, also due to the human element, which must be guarded against. This arises when land is close, and the ship's company, mentally and physically exhausted by a long-drawn-out voyage, or a continuance of bad weather, are eager for a night of undisturbed sleep in a quiet harbour, and an end to their present wretchedness, and their one thought, to the exclusion of all else, is bent to that end. Against their better judgement they carry on running towards the land in worsening weather and poor visibility, from a position which may be doubtful, when good seamanship would counsel that the only prudent action is to keep a good offing and remain at sea until conditions have improved, or at least until such time as the position has been verified. This is highly dangerous and may lead to complete loss of control of the situation, for the sea will grow more confused as land is approached, and even though the danger may at last have been realized, it will probably be too late then to round up and heave-to, or attempt to regain an offing.

The 13·7-metre (45-foot) ketch *Omoo*, when nearing the end of her circumnavigation, during which there had been no bad landfalls or narrow escapes, nor any suggestion of anything but the highest order of seamanship, found herself in such a situation. She had left Ascension on 9 April bound for the Azores, had crossed the equator in about 20°W longitude, and soon after found the north-east trade wind through which she punched close-hauled. But the trade died 600 miles before it should have done, and thereafter calms, light headwinds, and squalls were experienced, and the passage grew more lengthy than had been expected by Louis Van de Wiele, who had said when at the Cape: 'The Atlantic is before us again, and from now on it's a piece of cake.' The squalls were the cause of much sail-drill, for the cotton sails had become rotten and could not be risked in strong winds; the more palatable stores had been consumed, though there was no real shortage of food or water, and the ship's company were suffering from boils, enteritis, and cramp in the legs. When eventually a fair wind made, it soon hardened into a gale from west-south-west, and rain reduced visibility. The chronometer had received a knock, and its rate, no longer certain, could not be checked because the radio battery was exhausted, so the ship's position was uncertain.

In the circumstances a choice of two safe actions lay before *Omoo*'s skipper: to heave-to and wait for better weather before closing with the land, or to abandon the idea of calling at the

Azores, and alter course accordingly. But he took neither of these, for he and his companions were tired with the long passage and the frequent sail-shifting, the uninteresting diet, the cold and wet after their time in the tropics, and their one desire was to have done with it all and reach the comforts of the land; so they held on under reduced sail, hoping to make the harbour of Horta on the island of Fayal. The gale increased, rising to force 10, and the seas, which were estimated at 9 metres (30 feet) in height, grew steeper and became confused, while visibility was as little as a quarter of a mile at times. Apparently the gravity of the situation did not sufficiently impress itself on Louis until it was too late to do anything about it; indeed, control of the situation had almost been lost – lifebelts had been got ready and the ship's papers put in a watertight bag – when soon after dawn on the fortieth day at sea, land was sighted less than a mile ahead. This proved to be the south-west corner of Pico, an island to the eastward of Fayal and one which has no harbour. Fortunately the wind was drawing along the island's southern shore, and *Omoo* ran with it, thus narrowly escaping shipwreck.

It is not in any derogatory sense that I have referred to this incident here, for I have the highest regard for Louis. But that so experienced a seaman could make so obvious an error because his judgement was warped by mental and physical fatigue surely emphasizes the grave danger attending that state, and the need for all of us to be aware of it so that we may be on our guard.

Welfare

When making a passage which will last for more than a few hours the physical well-being of everyone on board is of the first importance, for unless they obtain sufficient food and sleep they will become mentally and physically tired.

The motion of a small yacht, particularly in heavy weather, may make the preparation and cooking of elaborate meals impossible, but unless the galley is so arranged and equipped that even in the worst of weather ready-prepared food can be heated up, the yacht cannot be regarded as seaworthy. It should be possible to boil a kettle of water and make a hot drink of coffee, cocoa, or tea, warm up a tin of soup or a stew which has been prepared beforehand, and do a little simple cooking such as scrambling eggs, the yacht being hove-to for the purpose if necessary. The position and equipment of the galley has been discussed in

Chapter 3, but it is in most instances not so much a lack of cooking facilities as seasickness that prevents the preparation and eating of sufficient nourishing food.

Most people suffer in some degree from seasickness; a few unfortunates become completely incapacitated, but the majority get their sea legs after a day or two, though they may have to go through the process each time they sail in open water. Of itself seasickness weakens one, but even the squeamish feeling without actual vomiting causes one to feel lethargic and disinclined for work, particularly in the galley.

Motion-sickness pills have a remarkable effect in warding off seasickness; they do not, however, work well for everyone, and they tend to cause drowsiness, but Stugeron tablets are very highly spoken of. A few suggestions to those who, in spite of pills, are prone to seasickness may not be out of place. Though it should be realized that it is the balancing canals of the ears rather than the state of the stomach that are responsible, it may be as well to go easy on fats, alcohol, and red meat before putting to sea so as to give one's stomach a chance to clear itself of acidity. It helps to remain on deck as much as possible so that the eye can be kept on the horizon; to eat and drink plenty, to keep warm and dry and fully occupied – many a crew member has been saved from sickness in the nick of time by taking over the steering. The sufferer will probably feel a little better after vomiting; but to avoid nauseating others this should be done neatly and with as little fuss as possible over the lee side. If someone is laid up in his bunk with seasickness, give him a supply of stout brown-paper bags; they are tidier than a basin and less likely to upset whoever has to dispose of them.

Sound sleep is so important that one must be prepared to make some sacrifice of speed if necessary. If the watch below is frequently roused out to make or take in sail, or, because of hard driving, the motion and the noise are excessive, there will be a general lack of sound sleep; this at first may show itself in frayed tempers and poor appetites, and finally will lead to loss of efficiency. I do not advocate shortening sail for the night as a matter of course, for such action will make night sailing dull and spoil each day's run and the pleasure to be had from swift and efficient passage-making; but judgement should be used to ensure, so far as is possible, that sail-handling is done only at the change of watches. Even then in a short-handed yacht there may come a time when her people show signs of suffering from lack of a long, undisturbed sleep, and if the yacht has no self-steering arrangements it will be wise to heave-to and let all hands have a night in their bunks. The resulting cheerfulness and increased efficiency which will inevitably follow will be worth the miles sacrificed.

With a ship's company of three, watchkeeping presents no problems. With three-hour spells on deck each will get six hours below, and then what is lacking of the required seven or eight hours' sleep can be made up in the daytime, preferably in the afternoon. The watchkeepers may be shifted forward one watch each night so that each in turn gets the pleasant and the less enjoyable watches, but many people prefer to stick to the same watches and grow accustomed to them. If the yacht is near the shore or in the neighbourhood of dangers, the skipper may decide not to stand a watch, but to remain free to attend to the navigation and get what sleep he can between whiles. There is little point in setting watches throughout the daylight hours unless it is discovered that a member of the crew would otherwise fail to take his share of watchkeeping; one would not wish to spoil the pleasure of a cruise or voyage by making and enforcing many rules, for the happiest ships are those in which everyone does without thought a little more than his just share of all the work.

A light sleeper's rest can be spoilt by unnecessary noise, particularly if it is intermittent; the loose bottle or can of food rolling in the locker, the clinking of plates in the pantry, the slapping of an idle headsail sheet upon the deck. During the afternoon sleep, which is an important part of the routine when night watches are kept, bright light should be subdued as much as possible, and the tinkerbell, caused by a shaft of sunlight from a deck- or port-light, flashing to and fro across the cabin as the vessel rolls, should be extinguished with a curtain or perhaps a piece of cardboard held in place with a small plastic suction cup.

Only aboard a large vessel is anyone likely to make a habit of sleeping on deck at sea, but in port in the tropics when the cabin may be uncomfortably hot, the deck or cockpit may be the most popular place; the essentials then will be a flat space of sufficient area without obstructions, in a position where the awning gives complete shelter from dew or rain; an inflatable mattress with a small foot-operated pump incorporated, such as is sold for beach use, may be found convenient.

Every effort should be made to keep warm and dry, and if the weather calls for it there should be no hesitation about lighting the saloon stove. A paraffin-burning riding light placed in the well of the cockpit, and it and the helmsman's knees covered with a sailbag, will do much to keep him warm and contented during a cold night watch, particularly in the chilly hours just before dawn.

There is a great variety of yachting clothing available. The so-called 'sailing jacket' with a zip-fastened front may be convenient when working on deck, but most are too short to protect the lower part of the back from chill. It is the wind more than the temperature that saps body heat, and waterproof clothing (oilskins, foul-weather gear) offers the best protection, but it need not be thick or heavy. I favour a short waterproof jacket worn with waterproof trousers; but the jacket must have a belt or line at the waist, otherwise when one bends over the wind will blow under and lift it, and spray or rain will get in. The suit must be of generous size so that it can be worn over plenty of clothes, and the trousers should have wide legs with elastic at their ends so that they may be pulled on over sea-boots. Most of the waterproof jackets one sees today have hoods attached, and although these prevent water from trickling down the back of the neck, they restrict hearing and peripheral vision, and do not provide protection for the face and eyes like the old-fashioned sou'wester does. A small towel wrapped round the neck should stop water entering there. Boots, even short ones, are clumsy, but most people wear them in cold, wet weather. They, and deck-shoes, should have non-slip soles, and ought not to be worn ashore or they will pick up grit and carry it aboard. In warm weather I prefer to go barefoot, for I can then tell whether or not I have a sure foothold, and usually find I have one better than any footwear provides.

PLATE 51 (*facing*). The contrasts of voyaging. For more than twenty lonely days *Wanderer IV* had been hard on the wind sailing north from Hilo on the last leg of a voyage from New Zealand toward British Columbia. The spray flew, the motion was wild, and the days grew longer – and colder. Later, in a quiet, pine-ringed anchorage at Prevost Island, she had the pleasure of the company of her old Canadian friend *Tryste II*, who had, only the year before, also sailed 'up' from 'down under'.

PLATE 52 (*overleaf*). *Top*: Waiting for wind in the doldrums, the region of calms, light airs, and heavy rains, which lies between the trade wind belts. *Bottom*: With dorsal and tail fin breaking surface, a shark swims close alongside as the yacht lies without steerage way; the little striped pilot fish, *bottom left*, which usually accompanies it, sometimes changes over to a yacht, and may then remain in company with her for many hundreds of miles.

At anchor

The chief aim at the end of a passage, particularly if it has been a long, difficult, or rough one, is to reach a comfortable and secure anchorage, so that for a time vigilance may be relaxed and one can rest with an easy mind. But some caution needs to be exercised when entering foreign naval or commercial ports by night, for although one may be using up-to-date charts and sailing directions, it is possible that changes have been made either to the buoyage or the harbour works, but of which no notice has yet reached the hydrographic offices of other countries. On my only visit to the Cape Verde Islands I nearly got wrecked on an unmarked, submerged breakwater, which was at the time under construction at Porto Grand, but of which neither chart nor *Pilot* gave any hint. Navies, including our own, are in the habit of laying moorings with enormous unlighted buoys in waters through which a yacht may wish to pass, and because most towns are today so brilliantly lighted, it may be impossible to see such dangerous obstructions or even the navigational lights against the blinding glare. There is also the risk of some illuminated advertisement sign ashore being mistaken for a navigational light. For example, Port Elizabeth in South Africa used to have, and for all I know may still have, a red sign in the town with the same characteristic as, and a greater range than, the breakwater light; this confused me for a time. It is for such reasons as these that I prefer to find my way in the dark into some natural and unlighted anchorage rather than risk the dangerous trap of a man-made or man-improved one.

When choosing an anchorage the chart or the *Pilot*, or the

PLATE 53 (*overleaf*). *Top*: The Plath vernier sextant which I used throughout *Wanderer III*'s first long voyage. Key: *A* frame, *B* arc, *C* leg, *D* handle, *E* rising piece, *F* telescope, *G* horizon glass, *H* index bar, *I* index glass, *J* release, *K* tangent screw, *L* microscope, *M* index shades, *N* horizon shades. *Bottom*: The Husun micrometer sextant I used on subsequent voyages. Key: *O* micrometer head, *P* electric light, *Q* Wollaston prism, *R* stellar lenticular, *S* bubble horizon attachment, *T* prism monocular, *U* bubble control knob, *V* electric light for bubble.

PLATE 54 (*facing*). *A*. A sextant box stowed on a sideboard where, after it has been pulled forward, *B*, the lid can be opened and the sextant is instantly available. *C*. Tangent screw and vernier of the old type of sextant. *D*. The arc and micrometer of a modern sextant is clearer and easier to read; here the reading is $46° \, 42'$. *E*. A small vernier adjoining the micrometer head permits the instrument to be read to 10 seconds of arc, if desired; the reading here is $45° \, 34' \, 40''$.

account of some trustworthy sailor who has been there, will be the surest guide. Though it would be unwise to ignore local advice which might warn one of some unsuspected danger, such as foul ground, or a risk of theft, an anchorage recommended contrary to the advice given in the *Pilot*, or by one's own common sense, should be avoided. This may appear obvious, but the temptation to act on it may be great if it offers certain advantages, such as cleanliness, access to a good landing place, or conveniently shallow water.

The schooner *Lang Syne*, having sailed without mishap across the Pacific, through the labyrinth of the Great Barrier Reef, among the Indonesian Islands and across the Indian Ocean, was wrecked at Zanzibar because for once her competent owners, Bill and Phyllis Crowe, acted on local advice when choosing an anchorage. Before following this advice they questioned the lack of protection from an onshore wind, but were assured that there was no need to worry as there would be no such thing at that time of year; it was not until later that they read the sailing directions and learnt that although the south-west monsoon, bringing heavy rains and winds, is said to set in about March, the seasons are so uncertain and subject to such variation that no reliance can be placed on them. One evening a few days after *Lang Syne*'s arrival, the wind did come suddenly onshore, the engine failed to start, and before sail could be set she was driven on to the sand and coral beach and suffered severe damage. She was refloated by her owners unaided, and they displayed fine seamanship and perseverance at a time when a tug which was sent to their assistance considered it too dangerous to help; they repaired the schooner themselves and completed their circumnavigation.

But in some places the *only* anchorages are exposed and deep. The lagoons of many of the Pacific islands, for example, are large enough to give a fetch of several miles, so that a strong wind can raise a considerable sea, and they are often between 18 and 36·5 metres (10 and 20 fathoms) deep, while the anchorages at some other islands which have no lagoons are frequently much deeper. It is therefore imperative for the visiting yacht to have adequate ground tackle, and for her skipper's peace of mind it is desirable that this should be a little heavier than is normally specified for use in home waters.

The nature of the bottom in recognized anchorages is often indicated on the chart or mentioned in the *Pilot*. The following should if possible be avoided: cinders, coral, ooze, rock, shingle, stones, and weed; sand is sometimes only a thin covering to smooth rock, and may afford no hold for the anchor.

As was mentioned earlier, using a rope instead of a chain cable is asking for trouble, and there are many instances of rope cables parting due to chafe, and of yachts anchored with them dragging. On their world voyage in *Viking* Sten and Brita Holmdahl had to anchor twice during contrary tides when approaching Darwin on the north coast of Australia. On each occasion the rope cable parted, and they lost both their anchors. At the conclusion of her voyage the yacht was bought by Joe Pachernegg, who renamed her *Sunrise*, and started off on a single-handed trip. He anchored, using rope cable, off the north-west coast of Santa Cruz, one of the Galapagos islands, where she blew ashore in the night and was a total loss. Joe endured great hardship during his four-day walk across the island to the settlement at Academy Bay, drinking the blood of goats he managed to shoot, as he was unable to find any water.

To reduce rolling in an anchorage subject to swell roll-damping gear (a flopper-stopper) can be improvised (Plate 16*A* and *B*). This may consist of a triangular piece of plywood, with a weight to act as ballast at its centre and another weight at one corner; a line from each corner is taken to a shackle to make a three-legged sling, and the whole affair is suspended below water from the end of the spinnaker boom rigged out one side. When the yacht rolls toward the damper the strain comes off the sling, and the weight at the corner causes the plywood to dive; when the yacht rolls the other way the triangle on its sling resumes a horizontal posture, and by offering strong resistance to being pulled up through the water damps the roll. I understand that *Widgee*'s gear, which is shown in the Plate, was effective although the wood triangle measured only 25 centimetres (10 inches) along each side, but one I made for the 15-metre (49-foot) *Wanderer IV* measuring 61 centimetres (2 feet) along each side could have been larger with advantage.

Single-handed cruising

Sailing alone is not to everyone's taste, but there is nothing like it for giving one confidence in oneself and one's ship, and a complete feeling of independence. That it is not so dangerous as is commonly supposed is shown by the large number of transatlantic single-handed races in which few losses or failures have occurred, and the other oceans have been crossed many times by single-handed cruising people. Of course this is largely due to the perfection of wind-vane steering gears (Chapter 20), but in one respect it is an unethical occupation, for it is the duty of all ships to keep a proper lookout, and a wind-vane gear or an auto-pilot keeps no lookout while the lone sailor sleeps. I would be worried if I had to make a west to east crossing of the North Atlantic while one of these east to west races was in progress.

Some years ago I often sailed alone in European waters, and I always tried to make my coastal passages in hops sufficiently short so that I needed no sleep, ie distances that could be covered in twenty-four hours or so. When doing this the important thing is to make preparations in advance, not only preparing the yacht and her gear so that nothing is likely to go wrong, but in laying off courses, measuring distances, noting times when tidal streams are due to turn, writing down the characteristics, ranges, and sectors of any lights that would (or should) be sighted on the passage, and by preparing food and drink (putting it in a thermos flask, perhaps) so that if one has to remain on deck because of bad weather or, more likely, because of congestion of shipping, one can remain there contented and alert, and well prepared for all eventualities.

22

NAVIGATION

Course and distance – The sextant – Taking sights – Star recognition – Time – Astronomical navigation – Working sights – The calculator – Making a landfall

THERE should be no mystery or any great difficulty connected with the navigation of a vessel from one place to another across a wide stretch of sea, for setting the course, keeping the dead reckoning up to date, and fixing the position by observations of celestial bodies, calls for nothing more than simple arithmetic, a little geometry, and some dexterity in handling the sextant. There are many ways of working sights to obtain position lines, but only those which I have found to be simple and practical are described in this chapter, because the navigator of the small ocean-going yacht usually has plenty of other things to attend to and will probably wish to reduce to the minimum the time spent at the chart table without sacrificing reasonable accuracy.

Course and distance

By means of the traverse table, or a calculator, it is possible to find the course and distance between two points on the earth's surface if their latitudes and longitudes are known; or, given the course and distance made good from a known position, to find the new position. But I would advise the beginner to take his courses and distances from, and to mark his positions on, the chart. For that purpose he will need an ocean chart such that his point of departure and his destination, or turning point, are both on one sheet. He will mark his noon positions on this chart and thus be able to see the situation of his vessel in relation to her surroundings at any time. But so that a large part or the whole of an ocean can be included on one sheet, such charts have to be drawn to a very small scale, perhaps 1:8,000,000 or 1:21,000,000, when 1° (60 miles) may measure as little as 5 millimetres (3/16 inch). A pencil line may then be a mile or more in thickness, and obviously it will not be possible to do any accurate drawing on such a small-scale chart, and distances measured on it will be only approximate.

To overcome this difficulty plotting sheets are available. These are blank Mercator charts for different latitudes, and are on a sufficiently large scale to enable plotting to be done on them; but I prefer to use a Baker's position line chart, as the one sheet can be used in any latitude. This is published by Norie & Wilson, and can be obtained from chart agents. It comprises a sheet of paper 66 by 46 centimetres (26 by 18 inches) with a scale of longitude marked along its north and south margins. On folding flaps at each side are latitude scales in proportion with the scale of longitude, from 0° to 40° on the west side and 40° to 60° on the east. Such a chart is shown in Fig 98, pages 468–9, but for convenience in reproduction the latitude scales have been detached from the chart and placed on the facing page. An explanation of the drawing shown on this chart will be given later.

The longitude on the Baker's chart remains constant, as on a Mercator chart, but all measurements of latitude (or distance) are taken from the latitude scale, using the scale marked with the latitude in which the vessel lies, or in which the work is to be done. In other words, by using the appropriate latitude scale, one uses the Baker's chart as a blank Mercator chart for any desired latitude between 0° and 60° north or south; the large circle marked in degrees enables courses and bearings to be laid down with the parallel ruler. If a 'B' pencil is used for drawing, the work can be rubbed out easily and the chart used over and over again; indeed, when only a small-scale ocean chart is available, the Baker's chart will be in daily use, and because the work is done diagrammatically, instead of in figures (as with the calculator or traverse table) any serious error should at once be obvious.

The sextant

As was mentioned in Chapter 16, the sextant is an instrument used by seamen for measuring vertical or horizontal angles. It is most commonly used for taking an observation (or sight), ie measuring the vertical angle between the visible horizon and a celestial body – sun, moon, planet, or star – and this is the use that should be kept in mind when reading the following description.

As may be seen in Plate 53, the sextant consists of a rigid frame *A* in the shape of a segment of a circle, with divisions engraved along its arc *B*. On the under side of the frame are three legs *C*, on which the sextant stands when not in use, together with the handle *D*, by which it is held in a vertical plane when an observation is being taken. At one side of the frame is the telescope *F* and *T*, which usually can be raised or lowered within small limits on the rising piece E, and at the opposite side of the frame is the horizon glass G, which is half clear glass and half mirror. Pivoted at the apex of the frame is the index bar H; this has a mirror, known as the index glass I, fixed to it immediately over the pivot; movement of the index bar therefore pivots the index glass about its own axis. At the other end of the index bar, where it swings along the arc, provision is made for reading the angle that the one mirror makes with the other. At its extremity the index bar has a quick release clamp J, with which it may be held firmly at any point along the arc. There a tangent screw K, or a micrometer head O turns a wormwheel, which engages with teeth on the under side of the arc, and is used for making the delicate final adjustment when taking a sight.

The optical law on which the construction of the sextant is based is this: if a ray of light from an object is reflected twice at the surface of two plane mirrors, and the final reflection is brought into line with some other object, the angle between the planes of the mirrors is half the angle subtended by the objects observed. If, therefore, we look directly at the horizon through the clear half of the horizon glass, and move the index bar until the image of a star is reflected from the index glass into the silvered half of the horizon glass so that it appears to touch the horizon, and then back to our eye at the telescope, the angle shown by the index bar on the arc would, if the latter were engraved with degrees, be half the angle between the star and the horizon. For this reason, and to avoid the need to double the angle read on the arc to obtain the true angle between star and horizon, the divisions engraved on the arc and numbered as degrees are in reality the size of half degrees.

The arcs of most sextants are engraved up to $120°$, ie one-third of a circle, but because the degree markings are half-size, the arc is in fact only one-sixth of a circle; hence the term sextant. But many sextants, especially the older ones, have their arcs engraved beyond $120°$, sometimes up to $150°$. This is to facilitate the measuring of horizontal angles (page 346) but is of no value for celestial navigation. The arc of every sextant is engraved for $5°$ or $10°$ to the right of the zero mark. The reason for this was explained on page 323.

The radius is usually 18 centimetres (7 inches), and the weight between 1·4 and 2 kilograms (3 and $4\frac{1}{2}$ pounds). A heavy instrument may perhaps be held more steadily when the wind is fresh or the motion jerky, but unless the observation is quickly made the observer's hand may grow unsteady. I do not consider small size is desirable, except in a very small yacht where it may be impossible to arrange a convenient stowage place for a full-size instrument, the box for which will measure about 30·5 centimetres (1 foot) square and 14 centimetres (5½ inches) high. The box is best kept in a readily accessible position so that the sextant can be lifted quickly from it, otherwise the opportunity for getting a sight on a cloudy day when the sun shows only momentarily may be lost. I keep mine on a sideboard where it is a snug fit between the sideboard fiddle and a strip of wood screwed to the sideboard; the box has only to be pulled away from the bulkhead, its lid opened and lodged against the bulkhead, and the sextant can at once be lifted out (Plate 54A and B).

All sextants work on the same principle, and all serve the same purpose, but the more expensive instruments do it with greater accuracy, and possess features which make it possible to take an observation and read the angle with greater ease and speed. There are many excellent sextants to be bought cheaply second-hand, and I would advise a beginner to buy one of these. Later, when he has gained experience, he will be in a better position to decide what refinements he would like and which would be of little value to him, and can choose the sextant which best suits his needs and his pocket.

It is not practicable to engrave the arc with minutes of arc for they would be impossibly close together. Yet the sextant can be read to the nearest minute, and with a degree of accuracy greater than that, if desired. With most this is done by micrometer, but older ones make use of a vernier, and since some readers may buy this type because of its lower cost, it will be described briefly here.

A vernier is a small-scale auxiliary arc attached to the lower part of the index bar and sliding in contact with the arc. It contains one more division than the number of divisions on a similar length of the arc, and it makes use of the fact that the human eye is able to judge easily whether a line is continuous or whether it has a break in it. A simplified vernier, together with a part of the arc adjoining it, is shown in Fig 86. From this it will be seen that the arc is engraved in degrees, every fifth degree being numbered. Each degree is divided into six equal parts with shorter lines, each of these parts therefore equals 10 minutes ('). To make the counting of these small divisions easier, the 30' mark is a little longer than the 10', 20', 40', and 50' marks. To read the angle measured by the sextant, swing the little microscope (L), which is pivoted on the index bar, over the vernier, and note where the zero mark of the vernier (often engraved with an arrow head) cuts the arc. In the figure this is to the left of the 31° mark, and between it and the first of the small 10' marks; so the sextant reads 31°+ something less than 10'. Now swing the microscope slowly to the left and note which of the numbered lines on the vernier is coincident with any line on the arc. In the figure this is the line numbered 5. The vernier therefore reads 5', and this added to the 31° read on the arc makes a total reading of 31°5'. However, when looking at a vernier on the sextant you will note that each of its big divisions is divided into six equal parts, enabling the angle to be read to one-sixth of a

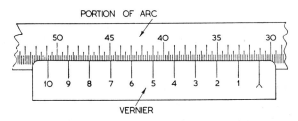

Fig 86 A simplified sextant vernier

minute, ie to 10 seconds (″) of arc; for the sake of clarity these small divisions have not been included in the figure, and in fact such accuracy of reading is not of great value in yacht navigation, because one cannot take an observation if there is any motion with an accuracy greater than 1'.

If the engravings on arc and vernier are clearly defined – a touch of lamp black mixed with light oil will help to make them bolder – no difficulty should be experienced in reading the angle measured provided the light is good. But a micrometer (all modern sextants have this refinement) makes reading much easier. Here the ordinary tangent screw, with which the final adjustment is made when taking a sight, is replaced by a larger wheel which is engraved with 60 equal parts, that number of divisions exactly filling its circumference. The wormwheel it actuates, and the teeth with which this engages on the under side of the arc, are so cut that one complete revolution of the micrometer head moves the index bar exactly 1 degree. The arc of a micrometer sextant is engraved with whole degrees only, and an arrow, known as the index, is engraved on the index bar. In Plate 54D, which is a close-up view of a micrometer and part of the arc, it will be seen that the index points to between 46 and 47, so the sextant reads 46° and something more. Adjoining the micrometer head will be seen another arrow which points almost at the mark 42; the micrometer therefore reads 42′, and the total reading of the sextant is 46° 42′. However, if desired the reading may be got to the nearest 10″ by using the vernier adjoining the micrometer head. In Plate 54 *E* the fourth of its lines is coincidental with a mark on the micrometer, so the vernier reads 40″, and the total reading is 45° 34′ 40″. With this sextant, as with most modern ones, a small light is provided to illuminate a part of the arc and the micrometer (*P* in Plate 53), so that when star sights are being taken the observer can read the sextant without losing his night vision; the battery for the light is usually housed in the hollow handle.

Most sextants used to be provided with two or more telescopes, high power for sun or moon, low power for stars, and it was possible to adjust the optical axis within small limits so as to include more or less of the silvered half of the horizon glass. But a modern trend is to provide one telescope only and to fit it permanently in position. This is a retrograde step, for a choice of telescopes is an undoubted advantage, and for those who prefer to take star sights with both eyes open and without using a telescope, the inability to unship the telescope is a serious handicap.

There are on the market plastic sextants which have the merit of low cost. Naturally they do not have the large mirrors or high-quality optics of more expensive instruments, and some have been known to change shape with changes of temperature. Nevertheless some people seem to manage well enough with them.

The bubble sextant enjoyed a period of popularity in the 1950s when ex-RAF instruments came on the market at very attractive prices; since, as the name implies, the instrument makes use of a free-floating bubble instead of the visible horizon, it would appear to offer great advantages, notably the ability to observe stars during the hours of darkness, or the sun when mist obscures the horizon. M W G Webster, an experienced navigator, made some trials of a bubble sextant fitted with averaging mechanism, and his findings, which were published in *Yachting Monthly*, were as follows: On a calm sea the error was + or − 3′; when the sea was slight with a height of 0·9 metre (*3* feet) the error was + or − 6′; with waves above 1·2 metres (4 feet) the results were too unreliable to be of use. This will not surprise the reader who has taken a look at Fig 74 and the accompanying text on page 367, and he will appreciate that in anything of a seaway great errors could arise unless the sight is taken at a moment when the vessel is truly level in the trough or on the crest; but without the help of a visible horizon one could never tell her attitude. A bubble horizon attachment is shown shipped on the Husan Sextant in Plate 53, but I rarely used it.

The reflected image of the sun is too bright to be viewed through the telescope by the naked eye, and an attempt to do so could result in permanent eye damage. A set of (usually) four coloured glass shades of different densities, known as the index shades (M in Plate 53) is therefore fitted on the sextant frame in such a position that whichever is needed, according to the power of the sun, can be turned up into position between the index glass and the horizon glass. Sometimes, when the sun shines from a thinly clouded sky and appears indistinct and woolly, a correct choice of index shade will make it clear-cut so that a satisfactory observation can be taken. It is important to remember that with some sextants all the index shades have to be turned up into the working position before the instrument can be shipped in its box; failure to do this can cause a shade to break, or its frame to be bent. Similar shades, usually three in number (N in the Plate) known as horizon shades, can be turned up in front of the horizon glass to reduce sun glare on the sea. On a few instruments the index and horizon shades are replaced by polarizing filters, with which the power of the sun, or the reflection off the sea, can be reduced as necessary by rotating one element of each filter. On occasions when fast-moving cloud is continually altering the power of the sun, these may be of some assistance because they are quicker to use.

The sextant is subject to certain errors. Those which are known as non-adjustable errors occur in manufacture, and with a good instrument should be insignificant. There are four adjustable errors, which the owner can correct himself if he wishes. A description of them and their cure will be found in Captain O M Watts's excellent little book, *The Sextant Simplified* (Thomas Reed), but index error (IE) should be checked frequently; the method of doing this and allowing for it has already been described on page 323.

Taking sights

Lift the sextant from its box with your left hand, grasping it not by the index bar or arc, but by the frame, and transfer it to your right hand, holding it by the handle so that the plane of the frame is vertical; all adjustments will be done with your left hand.

If you are not familiar with the sextant, you should practise taking sights of the sun before attempting other bodies, and you will find the following method the easiest to start with. Turn up into the operative position a medium index and horizon shade, press the quick-release clamp and swing the index bar back so that the sextant reads approximately zero. Holding the sextant in the vertical plane, tilt it up and look directly at the sun through the telescope, and you will see the direct and reflected images of the sun superimposed, or nearly superimposed, on one another. Alter the index shade if necessary to prevent eye strain and to make the reflected image clear and sharply defined. Now separate the direct and reflected images by moving the index bar slowly away from you, at the same time slowly lowering the sextant to follow the reflected image down until the horizon comes into view through the clear portion of the horizon glass. Release your finger pressure on the clamp, and make the final adjustment with the tangent screw, or micrometer head, until the lower rim of the sun (the lower limb) just touches the horizon. The reading on the sextant will be the angle between the visible horizon and the lower limb of the sun. This is known as the observed altitude, and for practical use will have to be corrected, as described on page 448, to obtain the true altitude.

Once you have accustomed yourself to the use of the sextant, you will probably not use this method except, perhaps, for observing stars. Instead you will turn what you consider to be the most suitable index shade into position, not using an horizon shade unless the sun is low and there is much light reflected from the sea. Looking through the telescope and the clear half of the horizon glass directly at the horizon immediately beneath the sun, you will swing the index bar slowly to and fro until you pick up the reflected image of the sun near the horizon, and then proceed to make contact as before. This is the quicker and more commonly used method.

At the moment when contact is made between the reflected image and the horizon, it is essential that the sextant be exactly vertical, or the angle measured will be too great. To ensure that the sextant is vertical, swing it a few degrees out of the vertical from side to side, pendulum fashion, with the index glass as centre. The image will then be seen to lift from the horizon, as shown in Fig 87A, describing the lower part of a circle, and the final adjustment must be so made that the lower limb just kisses the horizon at the bottom of its swing. This is not so difficult as it sounds, and becomes almost automatic with practice. If the lower limb is obscured by stationary cloud, or when observing the moon and its lower limb is not illuminated, the upper limb will be observed (Fig 87*B*). It is important then to remember, when correcting such a sight to obtain the true altitude, that semi-diameter must be deducted, not added. If it is essential to take a

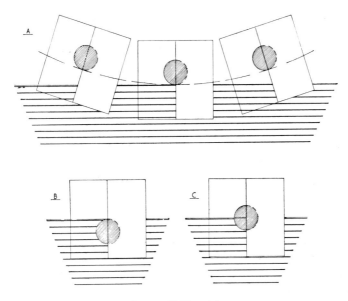

Fig 87   Taking sights

A: Swinging the sextant pendulum fashion to ensure that it is vertical when contact is made. *B*: Observing the upper limb. *C*: When the body is indistinct, it should be bisected by the horizon.

sight when the body is indistinct, a more accurate result may be had if it is brought down so that it is bisected by the horizon (Fig 87*C*). In such an event no correction will be made for semi-diameter.

The common method I have described for observing the sun or moon cannot be used for observing a star because of the risk of picking up the wrong star in the index glass. There are, however, three other methods that can be used. One of these is the same as I have already recommended the beginner to use when practising observations of the sun, ie to look direct at the star with the index bar at zero, then to move the bar slowly away to separate the direct and reflected images, lowering the sextant at the same time and following the reflected image down until it touches the horizon. But there is a risk with this method that one may lose sight of the reflected image on the way down and pick up some other star. In rough weather a better method is to find out in advance what the approximate altitude and azimuth of the star will be (see page 470), set that altitude on the sextant, and then sweep the horizon in the azimuth direction and the star will appear on or near the horizon. The third method may be even more useful. This consists of taking the horizon up to the star, and as the horizon is a continuous black line, it is easy to see it when it arrives at the star. Proceed as follows. Set the index bar at zero; reverse the position of the sextant, holding it by the handle in the *left* hand so that the arc is uppermost. Look directly at the star through the telescope, and with your right hand release the index bar and move it slowly away from you, keeping the star in sight through the clear half of the horizon glass until the reflected image of the horizon arrives near it. Clamp the index bar, reverse the sextant to its normal position, and make the final adjustment to bring the star to the horizon. As a star is such a tiny point of light there is no question of observing its upper or lower limb.

There are two accessories that can be fitted to a sextant to make the observation of stars easier. One of these, the Wollaston prism, has the property of doubling the image so that two stars are seen close together one above the other; the index bar is moved until the images are equidistant from the horizon, one above it and one below, and this is of some assistance when the horizon is indistinct. The other accessory, the stella lenticular, has the property of elongating the image of a star, so that it appears as a fine horizontal streak of light. This obviates the need to swing the sextant pendulum fashion to ensure that it is vertical at the time of contact, for one can see immediately whether the streak of light coincides exactly with the horizon, or whether it is at a small angle. Either or both of these accessories, which look like colourless shades, may be pivoted on the fitting to which the index shades are attached (*Q* and *R* in Plate 53), and are turned up for use in the same way.

When taking sights the observer needs a position from which he can see the horizon and the body clear of interference from sails and rigging, yet this must be a place where he can wedge himself so that both arms are free, and the upper part of his body can swing at the hips and thus keep vertical no matter how much motion there may be. The small yacht offers little choice of position; often the companionway will be the only possible place, and one may have to slow the yacht down or alter course to ease the motion and avoid drenching the sextant with spray.

The ability to measure accurately the altitude of a celestial body from a small vessel in rough weather can only be got with practice. One has to bring the reflected image down until it kisses the horizon only at the moment when the vessel is perched on the top of the highest sea then running. Between such moments the reflected image of the body will be seen well below the horizon. In such conditions it is a help if the observer can place himself in a higher position, but this is not often possible. It is sometimes said that one should add to the height of eye half the height of the sea running at the time; but this is incorrect because the horizon is made up of seas of the same height as those affecting the observer, except on the occasion of a single freak sea.

Many navigators are of the opinion that it is not sufficient to take a single observation, but that several should be taken and plotted on squared paper against their times; any that are badly off a straight line ruled among them should be discarded, and the remainder, together with their times, averaged. Of course these people are right, for as Michael Richey, Director of the Royal Institute of Navigation, has pointed out to me, the error in a series of sights will vary as the square root of the number of observations, so the mean of a number of sights taken in poor conditions stands a very good chance of achieving an acceptable accuracy. Nevertheless, the physical difficulties may be considerable. On deck in wind and spray when the sea is rough one's arm and eye soon tire, and finding the mean of a set of altitudes and times can lead to such inaccuracies as to defeat the project, but the use of a calculator should much reduce that risk. Normally I take only one observation, and usually can judge whether or not it was a good one.

It is an excellent plan to practise taking sights from a known position so as to gain confidence and discover if there is any personal error. If the embryo navigator does not live near the sea, he might practise with an artificial horizon, but cannot do so if the altitude of the body exceeds about 50°. In its best form the artificial horizon consists of a shallow bath of mercury shielded from the wind, but heavy oil in a baking dish will serve. The observer arranges himself in such a position that he can see the sun and its reflections in the oil. Pointing the sextant down so that the reflection of the sun in the oil can be seen through the clear half of the horizon glass, he brings the image of the sun down until its lower limb touches the upper limb of the reflection. The angle read off the sextant must then be halved, and to it all corrections, except that for dip, must be applied before the sight is worked.

Star recognition

Although this is too large a subject to be dealt with properly here, a few words about it might not be out of place; but the newcomer to navigation need not think that he must master it before he can progress further because, as will be seen later, if Volume I of *Sight Reduction Tables for Air Navigation* is used, it is not essential to be able to identify any of the stars. Nevertheless the ability to recognize some of the brighter ones will be of use at times, and will add much to the pleasure and interest of a voyage.

As children most of us were taught how to recognize one or two of the more obvious constellations, though a fertile imagination was required to picture the objects some of them are supposed to portray; Orion, for example, although he has shoulders, feet, and a belt, has no arms or head; but at least the Plough, which is also known as the Big Dipper, or as Charles's Wain, does look to my eye something like a plough. With the help of the Plough and Orion it is possible to identify at least half of the stars most useful to the navigator, but as Orion is not visible in the northern summer or southern winter, because he is then on the same side of the earth as the sun, the newcomer to star recognition would obviously be well advised to learn his way about the night sky during the other half of the year; in mid-December, for example, Orion crosses the meridian at midnight.

There are various aids to star recognition: star globes (very expensive), star finders, and star maps such as appear in nautical almanacs. Many years ago when I first started taking an interest in astronomical navigation, I made the primitive little star maps which, now drawn a bit better, are reproduced in Figs 88 and 89, to help me find my way about the night sky and enable me to put a name to such stars as I wished to use. Fortunately these were few, for although nautical almanacs list about 60, only 22 could be used with the tables I was using, and that number is sufficient for all practical purposes. In Fig 88, northern celestial hemisphere, I have shown 15 of them, though 3 of these belong in the southern celestial hemisphere as they have south declination (see page 442). All 15 cannot, of course, be seen at any one time because of the rotation of the earth. Their names are in capitals. I have added a few other stars of lesser magnitude and importance to help with the description which follows, and their names are in lower case. I have sketched in with solid lines some of the constellation shapes,

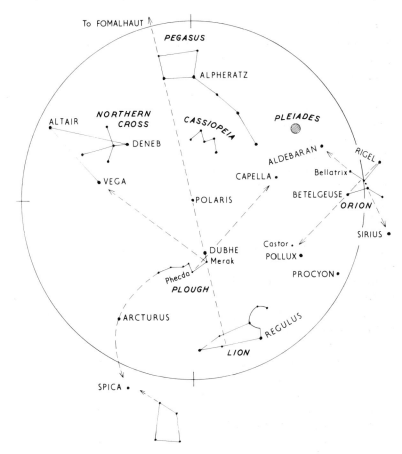

Fig 88 Northern stars

and their names are in italic capitals. The three types of lettering used in the Figures are also used in the text of the following paragraphs. Leading or identification lines are dashed.

POLARIS lies very nearly at the celestial north pole, and a line from Merak through DUBHE – the 'pointers' at the fore end of the *PLOUGH* – leads to it, and if that line is continued beyond

POLARIS it goes past the constellation of *CASSIOPEIA* (this is like a sprawling **W**) to one side of the square of *PEGASUS*, in which ALPHERATZ, of second magnitude, is the only useful star. The same line, if projected the opposite side of the *PLOUGH*,

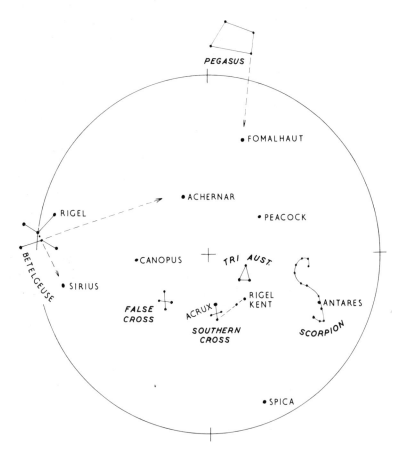

Fig 89   Southern stars

cuts through the rump of the *LION*, and REGULUS lies at the fore-paws of that animal. Some people cannot see a lion there at all, but recognize a sickle where the lion's head should be; then REGULUS lies at the handle end. A line drawn from the fore end of the *PLOUGH*, bisecting the angle made by DUBHE, Merak and Phecda, leads to VEGA, which is one of the three bright but widely separated stars marking the extremities of a big **V**. The star at the apex of this **V** is ALTAIR, and at the third extremity lies DENEB. This last is easy to identify as being the brightest star in the *SWAN* or *NORTHERN CROSS* (some call this constellation the *KITE*). Returning to the *PLOUGH*, if the curve of the handle is lengthened backwards in a generous sweep, it passes through ARCTURUS to SPICA. Near SPICA four stars form a gaff-headed sail, and the peak of the gaff points to SPICA. One final line from the *PLOUGH*, if drawn from Phecda to pass midway between DUBHE and Merak, leads to CAPELLA.

ORION with his glorious bodyguard is the finest spectacle in the night sky. BETELGEUSE and Bellatrix mark his broad shoulders; his narrow waist is spanned by a sloping sword belt, and one of his feet is marked by RIGEL. The slope of his belt, if continued downwards, leads to *SIRIUS*, the brightest star in the sky, though not so bright as the planets Venus and Jupiter. The star at the lower end of the belt in line with Bellatrix points to reddish ALDEBARAN, which lies half-way between *ORION* and the *PLEIADES*, a clearly defined patch of stars which is a useful skymark. Incidentally, the star at the upper end of *ORION*'s belt rises due east and sets due west of an observer anywhere in the world. A line from Bellatrix through BETELGEUSE goes close to PROCYON, while a line from RIGEL through BETELGEUSE points out POLLUX, which lies with its twin Castor nearly half-way between *ORION* and the *PLOUGH*.

The southern celestial hemisphere is not so generously provided with easily recognizable constellations, and contains only 10 of our 22 required stars. In Fig 89 these are shown together with one, BETELGEUSE, which belongs in the northern hemisphere. The best-known constellation in the southern sky is the *SOUTHERN CROSS*, and although this is not so prominent as its reputation would have one believe, a northerner's first sight of it always produces a thrill. It lies in the same quarter of the sky as the *PLOUGH*, with its longest arm, at the end of which is ACRUX, pointing towards the south celestial pole, and very close to it is a small, starless patch of black sky known to seamen as the 'coal sack'. Two bright stars point towards the *SOUTHERN CROSS* from the side, the one farthest away being RIGEL KENT, close to which lies a small triangle, *TRIANGULUS AUSTRALIS*. On the opposite side of the *SOUTHERN CROSS* to the triangle lies the *FALSE CROSS*, which as its name implies has often been mistaken for the real one when seen between clouds. CANOPUS, the second brightest star, stands alone between SIRIUS, the

brightest of them all, and the celestial pole. A line from
BETELGEUSE through the lower end of *ORION*'s belt goes close
to ACHERNAR, far down to the south and in complete isolation.
The two outer stars of the square of *PEGASUS*, which as we have
seen in Fig 88 point to POLARIS, lead in the opposite direction
to FOMALHAUT. PEACOCK, nearly half-way between
FOMALHAUT and RIGEL KENT is only a second-magnitude
star, but there are no others of the same magnitude near by. An
equal distance from RIGEL KENT, but with much smaller declination, is reddish ANTARES, the brightest star in the unmistak-
able *SCORPION*.

It will be seen that I have failed to discover many worthwhile
leading lines for stars in the southern celestial hemisphere, but my
attempts to do so, during which I grew more familiar with the
night sky, helped to pass many a watch pleasantly.

A bright star which cannot be identified is probably a planet.
Four of these can at times be used for navigation, but as their
positions in relation to the stars change, they can best be found by
consulting a nautical almanac. If, however, movement is detectable, the object is almost certainly a space-craft or satellite; one
cloudy night I took an observation of one of these instead of
CANOPUS, and only realized my mistake when I saw it overtake
a star.

Time

To obtain a position line (PL) – sometimes called a line of position
(LOP) – from an observation of a celestial body – except when
obtaining the latitude from a meridian altitude of the sun, or from
an observation of Polaris – one must know the Greenwich mean
time (GMT) at the moment the observation was taken. An error
of one minute in time can cause an error of up to 15 miles on the
earth's surface, 4 seconds an error of one mile.

For keeping GMT a chronometer, an accurate clockwork
timepiece compensated for changes of temperature and slung in
gimbals to keep it level, was used, but today its place has largely
been taken by the quartz crystal clock running off a dry cell, and
although this is subject to errors caused by changes of temperature, for which allowance can be made if the maker's instructions
are followed, it keeps remarkably good time. However, a wristwatch may serve the navigator well enough, for since time signals
are now so easy to get almost anywhere in the world (see page
316), the need for an accurate timepiece is not so important as it

was in the past. For some years I have been using a Rolex GMT-Master self-winding wristwatch. Apart from being a fairly good time-keeper, this watch has the advantage that in addition to the hour, minute, and second hands, it has a fourth hand which takes 24 hours to make one revolution, and an outer bezel, marked in the 24-hour notation, which can be moved one hour each time the hour is changed on passing from one time zone to another. From this watch I can therefore read instantly in any part of the world not only zone time but GMT.

The gaining or losing rate of the navigator's timepiece – let us call it the chronometer from now on whatever its type may be – does not matter; the important point is that the chronometer should keep a steady rate, and that the daily rate of loss or gain be known, then in the event of a breakdown of the radio receiver one will know how much to add or deduct day by day to obtain GMT.

It is easiest if the navigator has an assistant to read the time or start a stopwatch when he calls out at the moment he has got his sight; but if he is single-handed he can do it for himself with fair accuracy if he practises counting seconds: 'one thousand, two thousand . . .' and counts them until he is able to reach and read the chronometer. Alternatively he might find a digital watch more convenient.

Zone Time (ZT) is the system which enables all vessels and people within certain defined limits of longitude to keep the same time. For this purpose the world is divided into 24 zones, each of which covers $15°$ of longitude. In each zone the time differs by one hour from that of the neighbouring zones. The meridian of Greenwich is in the centre of Zone O, which therefore extends from $7\frac{1}{2}°$E to $7\frac{1}{2}°$W. The zones lying to the eastward are numbered in sequence with a negative $(-)$ prefix, those lying to the westward are similarly numbered with a positive $(+)$ prefix. The 12th zone is divided centrally by the 180th meridian, and both prefixes appear in this zone, their position depending on the date line, which is modified in places so as to include all islands of one group on one side or the other of it. As a vessel sails to the westward, local noon, ie the moment the sun reaches its maximum altitude, will become increasingly later, and in 60°W, for example (West Indies), will occur at approximately 1600 GMT. This would appear to be inconvenient only because we are accustomed to the clock indicating 1200 in the middle of the day; but if we stop at a port in that area (Zone +4) it will be awkward to keep in step with the inhabitants, whose watches will be four hours slow on ours. So it is convenient for the voyager to keep ZT, and although there is no need for him slavishly to follow the time habits of the other inhabitants of the zone he happens to be in, there is, as Churchill once pointed out, a time called 'stomach time', which at sea agrees fairly well with ZT. So, when passing from one zone to another it is usual to alter the ship's clocks accordingly, but the chronometer should, of course, be left untouched to register approximate GMT. If the clocks of a vessel making a circumnavigation west-about from the meridian of Greenwich are shifted to ZT in each zone, clearly they will be 12 hours slow on GMT by the time she arrives in Zone 12, and 24 hours slow on arriving back at the Greenwich meridian. Therefore, on crossing the date line from east to west the date must be changed ahead so as to skip a day, thus making a six-day week; if crossing from west to east a day must be added, and of course these rules apply to any crossing of the date line from far or near. A small chart, BA No 5006a, shows the time zones of the world, and indicates in what countries or parts of countries ZT is not adhered to. A list of all countries showing the time they keep will be found in *The Nautical Almanac* together with information about summer (or daylight saving) time. However, in large countries which extend over several time zones (Australia, Canada, USA, and USSR) the zone boundaries are modified to some extent to conform with state or other internal boundaries. In the USA the times kept in these are spoken of not by zone number but by name: Zone +5 keeps Eastern Standard Time (sometimes known as Atlantic Time); Zone +6 keeps Central Standard Time; Zone +7 keeps Mountain Standard Time; and Zone +8 Pacific Standard Time.

Astronomical navigation

For working any observation of a celestial body so as to obtain a position line, a nautical almanac is essential, and as was mentioned earlier, I recommend the deep-sea navigator to use *The Nautical Almanac* (HM Stationery Office and US Government Printing Office), which is referred to hereafter as the *NA*. In 1958 the layouts of this and the *American Nautical Almanac* were changed so that, under the same title, both are identical in content. Like most almanacs, the *NA* is valid for one year, starting on 1 January, but it contains instructions enabling it to be used, though with some inconvenience, for sun and star sights for the following year, to provide for the navigator who finds himself at the end of the year in a part of the world where a new almanac cannot be obtained. The *NA* contains instructions for its use, and these will not be repeated here.

Before attempting to explain briefly how a position line is obtained and drawn, I must define some of the terms that have to be used.

Dead reckoning (DR). The account kept of a vessel's position, having regard to the course and distance made good since her position was last fixed by observations of terrestrial or celestial objects.

The *Geographical position* (GP) of a celestial body is the point on the earth's surface immediately beneath the body, ie where a line joining the centre of the body to the centre of the earth would cut the earth's surface.

Declination (Dec) is the angular distance of a body measured north or south of the equator from the centre of the earth. Dec therefore corresponds to the body's geographical latitude (Fig 90).

The *Greenwich hour angle* (GHA) of a body is the angular distance of its meridian measured westward from the meridian of Greenwich (Fig 91). The Dec and GHA of the bodies used for navigation can be obtained for any moment of GMT for any day of the year from the nautical almanac. In other words it is possible to ascertain from the almanac a body's GP at the moment of observation.

The *Local hour angle* (LHA) of a body is the angular distance of its meridian measured westward from the observer's meridian. It is obtained from the GHA of the body by subtracting the observer's west longitude or adding his east longitude (Fig 91).

The *Rational Horizon* is a plane through the earth's centre at right angles to a line joining the earth's centre to the observer's zenith.

The *Zenith* of a place is the point in the sky directly overhead.

The *Zenith distance* (ZD) of a body from any place is the angular distance between the body and the zenith of the place, or it may be taken as the angle measured at the centre of the earth between the GPs of the body and the place (Fig 92).

The *True altitude* of a body is the angle between its centre and the rational horizon as measured from the centre of the earth (Fig 92). An observer obtains this angle as follows. With his sextant he measures the angle between the body and the visible horizon, and corrects for index error. Then, turning to the altitude correction tables inside the front cover of the *NA* (inside the back cover if the body is the moon) he enters the table headed 'Dip' with his height of eye and the table headed 'Sun' or 'Star' with the sextant

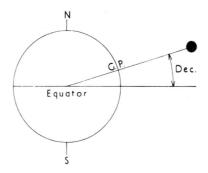

Fig 90   The declination of a body corresponds to the body's geographical latitude

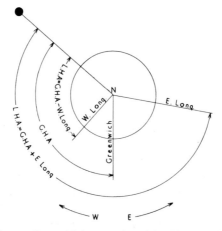

Fig 91   Greenwich hour angle and local hour angle

reading, and thus obtains two corrections which have to be applied according to their signs to the sextant reading to obtain the true altitude. These corrections allow for refraction (bending of light rays in the earth's atmosphere), dip (the effect of using the visible instead of the rational horizon), and in the case of the sun for semi-diameter (the lower limb was observed, but the angle required is to the centre).

The *Azimuth* of a body is its true bearing, measured east or west from the elevated (nearest) pole.

If we know a body's GP (Dec and GHA) and our distance from that position (ZD), we must be situated at some point on the circumference of a circle drawn on the surface of the earth with the body's GP as centre and the ZD as radius. But it is not possible to draw such a large circle on the chart, so the procedure is to calculate what the ZD would be from some position close to our

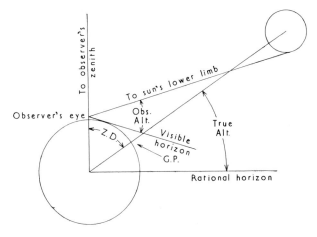

Fig 92 Observed and true altitude

real position. It used to be the practice to use the DR position for this purpose, but modern tables require something a little different, which will be mentioned later. We can obtain the body's azimuth from tables, and this we draw through the position which we have chosen and marked on the chart. From calculations we know what the ZD would be if we had measured it from that position, and from the observation we have taken we know what the ZD is at our real position. The difference between these two ZDs is known as the intercept and shows us how far wrong the assumed position is in one direction. Modern practice is to use not the calculated and true ZDs, but the calculated and true altitudes. Along the azimuth we measure off the intercept from the assumed position, either towards or away from the body according to which of the altitudes is the greater, and through that point rule a line at right angles to the azimuth. This line is part of the circumference of the big circle mentioned above, having the body's GP as centre and the observed ZD as radius; but as only a very small part of this circle is being drawn on the chart, it can be drawn as a straight line without error, and we must be situated at some point on it.

From this it will be clear that all can ever be obtained from any single observation of a body is a position line at right angles to the azimuth of the body. But if we can obtain simultaneous position lines from two bodies, the azimuths of which differ by about 40 degrees or more, our position will be fixed at their point of intersection as shown in solid lines in Fig 93. It is for this reason that

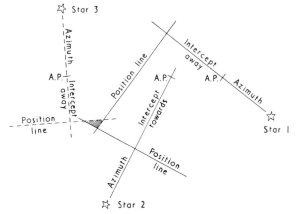

Fig 93 A fix by two position lines (solid) with a third (dashed) as a check
(AP=assumed position.)

star sights may result in greater accuracy than sun sights. It is usual to take three star sights as close together in time as possible, the third one, shown dotted in Fig 93, acting as a check. Ideally the resulting position lines should intersect at one point, but more often they form a triangle, the seaman's 'cocked hat', which is shaded in the figure. This should be small, when the position is presumed to be at the centre of it. If it is large an error in taking, timing, or working one or more of the sights has been made.

If only a single body, usually the sun, is being observed, one must of course wait until its azimuth has changed before obtaining a second PL. Where the first PL – brought forward with the parallel ruler along the course made good and to the extent of the distance run since the first observation was taken – cuts the second PL, is regarded as the vessel's position. An example of this is shown in Fig 94. But unsuspected deviation of the compass, indifferent steering, an inaccurate patent log, or a current of unknown strength and/or direction, will affect the accuracy of the final position, so the shorter the time that elapses between taking the two sights the better. It is commonly thought that PLs should, like those got from compass bearings, cross one another as near as possible at right angles to minimize any errors that might have occurred when taking the sights; but in fact an angle of cut of 50° is almost as good as one of 90°, and 40° is acceptable.

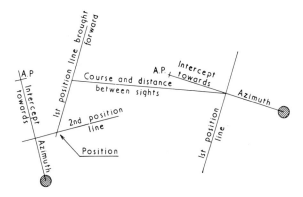

Fig 94   Position obtained by carrying forward one position line to cross another obtained from a sight taken later

My own practice is to take an observation of the sun in the forenoon, obtain the latitude from a meridian altitude sight at noon, and then carry forward the first position line as described above. This has the advantage that all the navigation work can be completed at noon, which is the traditional time of day for marking the position on the chart, measuring the day's run, and making any needed alteration to the course; if the vessel is well away from the land nothing further need then be done until the following morning. I make use of stars only when the sun has not shone during the day, or when I am getting anxious about a landfall, or some danger that must be avoided, for the period of twilight so often occurs at awkward times, when a meal is being prepared or eaten, or when the watch below is still asleep, and in the tropics twilight is brief. When I do have to use the stars I prefer to take the sights at dawn rather than at dusk, because I can then more easily recognize the constellations while the sky is still dark and choose such stars as are most likely to be of use. But if *SRT*, Vol I, is used (see page 470) this reason is not valid.

Even though it may not be possible to obtain a fix, the opportunity for getting a single PL should not be neglected, particularly when one is near the land, for such a line can often be of great value then. An example of this occurred in my early days when on passage from Ushant towards La Coruña on the north-west coast

Fig 95   A position line corresponding with the course

of Spain. The sky was overcast and visibility was perhaps only 5 miles as the coast was approached with a fresh north wind. The DR position was a little to the west of the direct course for Cabo Prior, on which it was intended to make a landfall. At about 1030 I got an observation of the sun through a momentary thinning of the overcast, and on drawing the resulting PL on the chart, found that by a happy chance it cleared Cabo Prior by 2 miles (Fig 95). Course was therefore altered to run confidently along that line, and in the afternoon the cape was sighted fine on the port bow. This taught me the value of a single PL, and I realized that in such a situation a sight should, when possible, be taken when the body is on the beam so that the resulting PL will be parallel to the course being steered at the time.

Working sights

The simplest and most popular method of obtaining the latitude is by observing the meridian altitude of the sun. This is commonly known as a 'noon lat'. As at the moment of observation the sun will be on the observer's meridian, the position line obtained will be a parallel of latitude. The observation therefore is independent of a knowledge of GMT. As the sun will bear true north or south at noon, a compass bearing of it, corrected for variation and deviation, will give a rough idea as to when the time for observation is approaching. But unless the compass is particularly well situated and is provided with an azimuth mirror, such a bearing may be impossible to take, particularly if the sun's altitude is considerable, and time and trouble will be saved if we make use of GMT and work out in advance the time of the sun's meridian passage.

As the sun moves 15 degrees to the westward in one hour (one degree in 4 minutes), we can convert arc into time by dividing by 15, or more conveniently by consulting the 'Conversion of Arc to Time' table in the NA. If we work out the probable DR longitude at noon and convert it into time, and add it to 1200 if we are in west longitude, or deduct it if in east longitude, we would obtain the time of the sun's passage across the ship's meridian, provided the sun kept precisely to GMT in its movements. But only occasionally does the sun cross the meridian of Greenwich at 1200 GMT, and it may be as much as 20 minutes fast or slow. We must therefore ascertain the time it does cross the Greenwich meridian on the day we wish to take our sight. This information, in hours and minutes, is given in the NA, where under the heading 'Mer. Pass.' it will be found at the foot of each right-hand page. To obtain the GMT of the sun's passage across the ship's meridian, we convert the DR noon longitude into time, and add it to the sun's meridian passage time if the longitude is west, deduct it if east.

Example. On 31 October, in DR longitude 15°45′ W; required the GMT of the sun's passage across the ship's meridian.

From conversion table in the NA   15°45′ = 1h 3m
Sun's mer. pass. at Greenwich on 31 Oct
     from daily page in the NA   + 11h 44m
                                       12h 47m

If we are certain of our longitude, and therefore of the time of noon, we can go on deck and take our observation at the predicted time, but it is customary to go up a little earlier while the sun is still ascending; adjusting the tangent screw or micrometer head as necessary, we keep the reflected sun's lower limb just kissing the

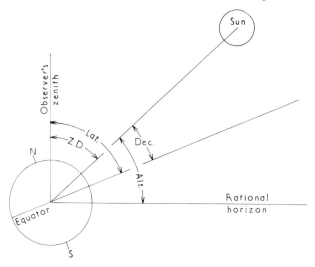

Fig 96
When latitude and declination are of the same name, the sum of the zenith distance and the declination gives the latitude

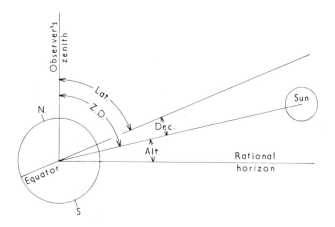

Fig 97
When latitude and declination are of contrary names, the difference between zenith distance and declination gives the latitude

horizon, until the sun rises no higher and appears to maintain a steady altitude for a little while before commencing its downward path. To work the sight, read the sextant and apply the index error to obtain the observed altitude. Convert this to true altitude by applying the two corrections from the *NA*, the 'Sun' table being entered with the observed altitude, and the 'Dip' table with the height of eye. Subtract the true altitude from 90° to obtain the ZD. Obtain from the *NA* the Dec of the sun at the date and GMT of the sight, and write it beneath the ZD. If the latitude and the Dec are of the same name, that is, both north or both south, add the ZD and the Dec together to obtain the latitude (Fig 96); if they are of contrary names, that is one is north and the other south, their difference will give the latitude (Fig 97).

Example. On 5 July, in the mouth of the English Channel in DR lat 49°32′N, long 5°49′W, the meridian altitude of the sun was observed. The sextant read 63°02′; IE was −2′, and HE 1·8 metres (6 feet). Required the latitude.

Sextant	63°02′
IE	−2′
Observed altitude	63°00′
Correction for sun	+15′·5
„ „ dip (HE 1·8 metres (6 feet)	−2′·5
True altitude	63°13′
	90
ZD	26°47′
Dec at time of sight from *NA*	22°49′N
Latitude	49°36′N

As Dec and latitude were the same name (both north in this example) Dec and ZD were added to obtain the latitude.

Example. On 9 September, when on passage from Suva, Fiji, towards Russell, New Zealand, and in DR lat 28°16′S, long 174°E, the meridian altitude of the sun was observed. The sextant read 56°05′; IE −2′, HE 1·8 metres (6 feet). Required the latitude.

Obs Alt	56°05′
Total correction	+11′
True Alt	56°16′
	90
ZD	33°44′
Dec	5°31′N
Latitude	28°13′S

Here Dec and latitude were of different names, so the difference between ZD and Dec gave the latitude.

There is one other variation of this problem, and it only affects navigators in low latitudes. If, when in the northern hemisphere, the Dec is also north but is greater than the latitude, then the sun is to the north of the observer, and the difference between Dec and ZD will give the latitude. Of course a similar thing applies in the southern hemisphere.

Example. On 9 February when on passage from Panama towards the Marquesas Islands, and in DR lat 3°55′S, long 98°05′W, the meridian passage of the sun was observed; the sextant read 79°04′; IE −2′, HE 1·8 metres (6 feet). Required the latitude.

Obs Alt	79°04′
Total correction	+11′
True Alt	79°15′
	90
ZD	10°45′
Dec	14°35′S
Latitude	3°50′S

When the sun passes nearly overhead at noon, ie when its Dec is almost the same as the observer's latitude, it is difficult to observe from a small vessel at sea. But on such occasions there is a way,

---

PLATE 55 (*facing*). Landfalls. *Top*: Depending on their height, the tops of the palms growing on an atoll may lift above the horizon when 10 to 15 miles away, and there will probably be no more than the usual trade wind clouds sailing over the low land and its lagoon – Takaroa, one of the Tuamotu, or Dangerous Archipelago, in the South Pacific. *Middle*: Cloud streaming away like smoke, could be seen to leeward of Rodriguez, 396 metres (1,300 feet) high, when the island was well out of sight. *Bottom*: Landfall on San Miguel, Azores. '. . . as we approached it took shape, the volcanic peaks, the dark green areas of trees, a patchwork of tiny fields . . . gathered colour and substance'.

PLATE 56 (*overleaf*). *Top*: Many small cruisers have been built to the designs of the late T Harrison Butler (who was an eye surgeon), but few of them can have travelled so far as *D'Vara*. She was built at Fremantle, Australia, by Blue and Dot Bradfield, who then sailed her to England and beyond. Here she is seen beating gamely up the Gulf of Suez under her wishbone ketch rig, which was not a part of the original HB design, but of which Blue spoke highly. *Bottom*: The American ketch *Adios*, in which Tom Steele twice circled the globe, seen here lying alongside at Aden shortly before setting off up the Red Sea. Designed by John Hanna she is a typical 'Tahiti ketch' 9·7 metres (32 feet) LOA, carrying a single headsail set from the end of a long bowsprit, and with no inner forestay. Among other equipment she had on her long voyages was a washing machine and a motor cycle.

known as very high altitude sights, of obtaining not only the latitude but also the longitude at around noon, and it is one of the most delightfully simple and satisfactory navigational procedures available for obtaining a fix. To do it take a timed sight about 5 or 6 minutes before predicted noon, and mark on the plotting diagram the GP of the sun (Dec and GHA) at that moment. Correct the sextant reading in the usual manner and deduct from 90 to obtain the ZD. With the GP as centre and ZD as radius sweep an arc. Take a similar sight shortly after noon, and treat it in a similar manner, then where the two arcs cut was the ship's position at noon; but as the arcs cut in two places, one must know whether the sun passed north or south of the position at noon. A useful check would, of course, be a noon latitude sight, if it was possible to obtain one. With luck the circumnavigator may have several opportunities for taking such sights, others less fortunate may never get the chance.

It has often been said that the ship's longitude, as well as her latitude, can be obtained at noon simply by noting the GMT as the sun crosses the meridian, and converting this into arc; but since the sun appears to hang stationary for a while on reaching its maximum altitude, it is not possible to take the time of transit with sufficient accuracy, bearing in mind that an error of one minute can cause an error in longitude of up to 15 miles. I consider it is best to ignore this and some other 'simple' methods that get renewed publicity from time to time, and to use traditional and

---

PLATE 57 (*overleaf*). The gaff cutter *Moonraker*, a converted Looe fishing boat, in which the late Peter Pye and his wife Anne cruised widely and made great voyages in the North and South Atlantic and in the Pacific. 'She looks like a box and sails like a witch,' Peter once said of her. She was subsequently housed at the Exeter Maritime Museum. At sea the table was unshipped and cooking was done on a Primus stove hidden in a locker on the starboard side, part of the door of which can be seen at the extreme right of the picture. A wood-burning stove is in the corner behind the table and was much in use during a cruise to Finland.

PLATE 58 (*facing*). Joshua Slocum was the first to sail round the world single-handed, and did so in the beamy, shoal-draught 11·2-metre (37-foot) *Spray*. Several replicas of this famous vessel have been built in the USA, and one of the best of them is *Scud* (*top*), built by her owners George and Mary Maynard, and sailed by them twice across the Atlantic, then out to Fiji and beyond. Like the original, *Scud* has no engine. *Bottom*: The first yacht to sail round the world south of the three stormy capes was the 12·8-metre (42-foot) ketch *Saoirse* in the capable hands of her Irish designer/owner Conor O'Brien. He made the east-about voyage in 1922–5, and when I met him was much interested in square rig; but the old ship, under her present owner Eric Ruck, has reverted to orthodox ketch rig, and is here seen with a bone in her teeth in Falmouth Harbour.

well proved methods of obtaining PLs, such as the one outlined below; but first let us consider the use of Polaris (if we are in the northern hemisphere) for the purpose of obtaining the latitude.

If this star were situated exactly over the north pole its true altitude would equal the observer's latitude. In fact it lies about one degree from the celestial pole, round which it circles, and some simple corrections, obtained from the *NA* and applied to the true altitude, will give the observer's latitude. To enter the tables some knowledge of GMT is required, but the time within a few minutes is sufficient; an error of as much as 15 minutes would only cause an error of 2 or 3 miles.

As Polaris is only a moderately bright star, it is frequently invisible to the naked eye in the evening until the night has become too dark to permit the horizon to be seen clearly. The procedure, therefore, is to clamp the index bar of the sextant at the DR latitude, and while the night is still light enough for the horizon to be seen, sweep the horizon with the sextant in the direction of true north, when the star will usually be seen through the telescope near the horizon; the final adjustment to bring it to the horizon can then be made. Note the approximate GMT of the sight, read the sextant, apply the index error and the corrections for dip and refraction, using the correction table for stars. Find in the *NA* what the GHA of Aries was for the date, hour, and nearest minute of the GMT of the sight, and write it down. (Aries is a point in the sky to which all the stars can be related.) Beneath the GHA of Aries write the assumed longitude, and subtract it if it is west, add it if it is east, to obtain the local hour angle (LHA) of Aries. Turn to the Polaris tables in the *NA*. These have to be entered in three places, as explained at the foot of the tables, with the LHA of Aries, the DR latitude, and the month. Add the three corrections so obtained to the true altitude, *deduct one degree*, and the result is the latitude.

Example. On 15 January, when on passage in the Red Sea from Port Sudan towards Suez, and in DR lat 23°29′N, long 37°13′E, an observation of Polaris was taken at 15h 48m GMT; the observed altitude (correction for index error having been made) was 24°33′; HE 1·5 metres (5 feet) Required the latitude.

GHA Aries at 15h	339°34'·8
Increment for 48m	12 00
	351°35'
Assumed longitude	+37 25'E
	389°
	−360
LHA Aries	29°
Observed altitude	24°33'
Correction for dip and refraction	−4'
True alt	24°29'
Correction for LHA Aries	+4'·1
,, ,, latitude	−0'·6
,, ,, month	+0'·8
	24°34'
	−1°
Latitude	23°34'N

For the working of all sights other than meridian altitude and Polaris sights, some books of tables will be needed in addition to the nautical almanac. Tables which reduce the work to the minimum and eliminate the use of logarithms in solving the spherical triangles, which occur in most navigational problems, have been available to the yachtsman for some years. Unlike the nautical almanac, these do not alter from year to year, and once the navigator has bought the volumes he needs they will, with the exception noted on page 470, last him for the rest of his life.

The handy sized and very clearly printed *Astronomical Navigation Tables*, which have been used successfully by many ocean-going yachtsmen, are no longer in print, their place having been taken by the publication known as *Sight Reduction Tables for Air Navigation* (the US equivalent is HO 249), referred to hereafter as *SRT*, and two pages from it are reproduced on pages 462 and 463. Volume II is for use with any celestial body with a declination of up to 29°, and for latitudes 0° to 39°, north or south; Volume III, with the same limit of declination, is for latitudes 40° to 89°, north or south. These are the tables to which reference is made in this section. Although they were devised for use in air navigation they are equally suitable for surface navigation, and it should not be thought that they can only be used with the *Air Almanac*; on the contrary, the yacht navigator would do better to use the *NA*, one volume of which covers the whole year, whereas three volumes of the *Air Almanac* are needed for the same period. *SRT* Volume I is for selected stars only.

Tables of Computed Altitude and Azimuth (HD 486) do the same job as *SRT*, but with a greater accuracy which is not required by the yacht navigator. They are not quite so easy to use, and they are more bulky and more expensive.

As was explained in the section on astronomical navigation, if at any moment we know from a sight we have taken the altitude of a body from some position close to us, and we know the body's altitude from our own position, the difference between the two altitudes is our distance in one direction from that place, the resulting position line being drawn at right angles to the azimuth of the body. *SRT* make it unnecessary for us to calculate the altitude at that place, for they tell us straight away what the altitude and azimuth of any body with a declination of up to 29° is for every whole degree of latitude from 89° N to 89° S, and for every whole degree of LHA.

From this it will be apparent that we cannot make use of the DR position, except in the very unlikely event of the latitude being in whole degrees and the longitude being such that when it is applied to the GHA of the body the resulting LHA is also in whole degrees. It therefore becomes necessary to assume a position such that the latitude is in whole degrees, and the longitude is a figure such that when applied to the GHA (added if east, subtracted if west) it gives a LHA in whole degrees. Naturally we will assume a position as close as possible to DR position, otherwise the intercept might be inconveniently long.

Suppose, for example, the DR latitude is 48° 45′ N, the DR longitude 22° 36′ W, and the GHA of the body 323° 50′. The nearest whole degree of latitude is 49° N, so that must be used as the assumed latitude. As west longitude has to be deducted from GHA to obtain the LHA, the assumed longitude will have to be 22° 50′ W, so that the minutes of arc cancel out and leave LHA in whole degrees, as below:

GHA	323° 50′
Assumed West longitude	−22° 50′
LHA	301° 00′

To take another example: if the DR position is latitude 54° 26′ N, longitude 3° 21′ E, and the GHA of the body is 294° 46′; the assumed latitude will have to be 54° N, and the assumed longitude 3° 14′ E, as below:

GHA	294° 46′
Assumed East longitude	+3° 14′
LHA	298° 00′

In certain circumstances it is possible for the LHA to exceed 360°; 360 must then be deducted from it as in the working of the Polaris sight on page 459. If the assumed west longitude is greater than the GHA, the LHA will be a minus quantity; 360 must then be added to it.

Having arranged an assumed position such that SRT can be entered with it, the appropriate volume is opened at the page headed with the assumed latitude. It will be noticed that some pages are headed 'Declination *same* name as latitude', and others 'Declination *contrary* name to latitude'; one must, of course, use the correctly labelled page. From the reproduction of a page of SRT on the following page, it will be seen that it is divided into vertical columns, one for each whole degree of declination, the declination figures being boldly printed at top and bottom. Degrees of LHA are printed down the sides. Entering the table with the whole degree of declination numerically less than that of the body at the time of the sight, and with the LHA, three sets of figures will be found in a row; from left to right these are Hc, d, and Z. Hc stands for height calculated, ie the altitude of the body calculated for the assumed position. The d figure (the difference in Hc for one degree difference in declination), prefixed by a plus or minus sign, enables a correction to be made to the Hc figure to allow for the minutes of declination, as explained below. The Z figure is the azimuth. This is given in degrees from the elevated (nearest) pole, and must be named east or west according to whether the body has not yet crossed the observer's meridian, or has crossed it. If preferred, it may be converted to a true bearing, ie expressed in degrees (0–360 clockwise from true north) by following the rules printed on each page of SRT.

The d figure is used as follows for correcting Hc for the minutes of declination. Suppose, for example, the body's declination at the time of the sight was 29° 33′, and the d figure was +45. Turn to the correction table at the end of SRT (this is reproduced on page 463), and entering it across the top with the d figure, 45, and down the side with the minutes of declination, 33, the figure 25 will be found. This is the correction in minutes of arc, and as the d figure was prefixed by a + sign, 25′ must be added to the Hc figure to correct it for those 33′ of declination.

To demonstrate the simplicity of SRT, an example of a sun sight showing all the work that is needed is given on page 464 and it is followed by a brief explanation of each step to show how or where the figures were obtained.

CRUISING UNDER SAIL

DECLINATION (15°-29°) SAME NAME AS LATITUDE

LHA	15° Hc d Z	16° Hc d Z	17° Hc d Z	18° Hc d Z	19° Hc d Z	20° Hc d Z	21° Hc d Z	22° Hc d Z
0	61 00 +60 180	62 00 +60 180	63 00 +60 180	64 00 +60 180	65 00 +60 180	66 00 +60 180	67 00 +60 180	68 00 +60 180
1	60 59 60 178	61 59 60 178	62 59 60 178	63 59 60 178	64 59 60 178	65 59 60 178	66 59 60 178	67 59 60 178
2	60 57 60 176	61 57 60 176	62 57 60 176	63 57 60 176	64 57 60 176	65 57 59 175	66 57 60 175	67 56 59 175
3	60 53 58 174	61 53 59 174	62 53 58 174	63 53 59 174	64 53 59 173	65 52 60 173	66 52 59 173	67 52 59 173
4	60 48 58 172	61 48 59 172	62 47 58 172	63 47 58 171	64 47 59 171	65 46 59 171	66 46 59 171	67 45 58 170
5	60 41 +60 170	61 41 +59 170	62 40 +60 170	63 40 +59 169	64 39 +59 169	65 38 +60 169	66 38 +59 169	67 37 +59 168
6	60 33 60 168	61 33 59 168	62 32 59 168	63 31 59 167	64 30 59 167	65 29 59 167	66 28 59 166	67 27 59 166
7	60 24 58 166	61 23 59 166	62 22 59 165	63 21 58 165	64 19 59 165	65 18 59 164	66 17 58 164	67 15 59 163
8	60 13 58 164	61 11 59 164	62 10 59 163	63 09 58 163	64 07 58 163	65 05 59 162	66 04 58 162	67 02 58 161
9	60 00 58 162	61 58 58 162	61 57 58 162	62 57 58 162	64 55 58 161	64 53 58 161	65 49 58 161	66 47 58 160
10	59 47 +58 160	60 45 +58 160	61 43 +57 160	62 40 +58 159	63 38 +58 158	64 36 +58 158	65 33 +57 158	66 30 +57 155
11	59 32 59 159	60 29 58 158	61 27 57 158	62 24 57 158	63 21 58 157	64 18 58 157	65 15 57 155	66 12 56 154
12	59 15 58 157	60 13 57 156	61 10 57 156	62 07 57 156	63 04 57 155	64 00 56 154	64 57 56 154	65 53 57 154
13	58 58 57 155	59 55 56 155	60 51 57 155	61 48 56 153	62 44 56 153	63 40 56 152	64 36 56 152	65 32 56 151
14	58 39 56 153	59 35 57 153	60 32 56 152	61 28 55 151	62 23 56 150	63 19 55 150	64 14 55 149	65 09 54 148
15	58 19 +56 152	59 15 +56 151	60 11 +55 149	61 06 +55 149	62 01 +55 148	62 56 +55 148	63 51 +54 147	64 45 +54 146
16	57 58 55 150	58 53 54 149	59 49 55 148	60 44 54 148	61 38 55 147	62 33 54 146	63 27 53 145	64 20 53 145
17	57 36 55 148	58 31 54 147	59 25 55 147	60 20 54 146	61 14 54 145	62 08 53 144	63 01 53 143	63 54 52 143
18	57 13 54 147	58 07 54 146	59 01 54 145	59 55 54 144	60 49 53 143	61 42 53 142	62 35 52 142	63 28 52 140
19	56 48 54 145	57 42 54 144	58 36 53 143	59 29 53 142	60 22 53 142	61 15 52 140	62 07 52 140	62 59 51 138
20	56 23 +53 143	57 16 +54 143	58 10 +53 142	59 03 +52 141	59 55 +52 140	60 47 +52 139	61 39 +51 138	62 30 +50 137
21	55 57 52 142	56 50 52 141	57 42 53 140	58 35 52 139	59 27 52 138	60 18 51 137	61 10 50 136	62 00 50 135
22	55 29 53 140	56 22 52 139	57 14 52 139	58 06 51 138	58 57 51 137	59 48 51 136	60 39 50 135	61 29 49 133
23	55 01 53 139	55 54 51 138	56 45 52 137	57 37 51 136	58 28 50 135	59 18 50 134	60 08 49 133	60 57 49 132
24	54 33 53 137	55 24 51 136	56 15 51 135	57 06 50 135	57 57 49 134	58 46 50 133	59 36 48 131	60 24 48 130
25	54 03 +51 136	54 54 +51 135	55 45 +50 134	56 35 +49 133	57 24 +49 132	58 14 +49 131	59 03 +48 130	59 51 +47 129
26	53 33 53 134	54 24 51 134	55 14 51 133	56 03 50 132	56 53 51 132	57 41 48 130	58 29 48 129	59 17 47 127
27	53 01 51 133	53 52 49 132	54 41 50 131	55 31 48 130	56 19 49 129	57 08 47 128	57 55 47 127	58 42 47 126
28	52 30 49 132	53 19 50 131	54 09 48 130	54 57 49 129	55 46 48 128	56 33 48 127	57 22 46 126	58 09 45 125
29	51 57 49 130	52 48 49 130	53 37 49 129	54 24 47 128	55 13 47 127	56 01 46 125	56 48 46 124	57 35 45 123
30	51 24 +49 129	52 13 +48 128	53 01 +48 127	53 50 +47 126	54 39 +47 125	55 23 +46 124	56 09 +46 123	56 55 +45 122
31	50 50 49 128	51 39 47 127	52 27 47 126	53 14 47 125	54 02 46 124	54 47 46 123	55 33 45 122	56 18 44 121
32	50 16 48 127	51 04 48 125	51 52 46 125	52 38 47 124	53 25 46 123	54 11 45 122	54 56 44 121	55 40 44 119
33	49 41 48 125	50 29 47 124	51 16 46 124	52 04 45 123	52 49 45 122	53 34 45 121	54 19 44 119	55 03 44 118
34	49 06 47 124	49 53 47 124	50 40 46 123	51 25 46 122	52 11 45 121	52 56 44 120	53 40 44 119	54 24 43 118
35	48 30 +47 123	49 17 +46 122	50 03 +46 122	50 49 +45 120	51 34 +44 119	52 18 +44 118	53 02 +44 117	53 46 +42 116
36	47 54 46 122	48 40 46 121	49 26 45 120	50 11 45 119	50 56 44 118	51 40 44 117	52 24 43 116	53 07 42 115
37	47 18 46 121	48 03 45 120	48 48 45 119	49 33 44 118	50 17 44 117	51 01 43 116	51 45 42 115	52 27 42 114
38	46 40 45 120	47 25 45 119	48 11 44 118	48 55 44 117	49 39 43 116	50 23 42 115	51 05 42 114	51 48 41 113
39	46 02 45 119	46 47 44 117	47 32 44 117	48 16 44 116	49 00 43 115	49 43 42 113	50 26 41 113	51 08 41 112
40	45 24 +45 118	46 09 +45 117	46 54 +43 116	47 37 +44 115	48 21 +43 114	49 04 +42 113	49 46 +41 112	50 27 +41 111
41	44 46 44 117	45 31 44 116	46 15 43 115	46 59 44 114	47 43 42 113	48 25 42 112	49 07 41 111	49 48 40 110
42	44 07 44 116	44 51 44 115	45 35 44 114	46 19 42 113	47 02 42 112	47 44 41 111	48 25 41 110	49 06 40 109
43	43 28 44 115	44 12 44 114	44 56 43 113	45 39 42 112	46 21 42 111	47 03 41 110	47 44 40 109	48 25 40 108
44	42 49 44 114	43 33 43 113	44 16 42 112	44 58 41 111	45 41 41 110	46 21 41 109	47 02 40 108	47 41 39 107
45	42 09 +43 113	42 53 +43 112	43 35 +42 111	44 18 +42 110	45 00 +41 109	45 41 +41 108	46 22 +40 107	47 02 +40 106
46	41 29 43 112	42 12 42 111	42 55 42 110	43 37 41 109	44 18 41 108	45 00 40 107	45 40 40 106	46 21 39 105
47	40 49 43 111	41 32 42 110	42 15 41 109	42 56 41 108	43 38 40 107	44 19 40 106	44 59 39 105	45 39 39 104
48	40 09 41 110	40 51 42 109	41 33 41 108	42 15 40 107	42 56 40 106	43 37 39 105	44 18 39 104	44 58 38 103
49	39 28 41 109	40 11 42 108	40 53 40 107	41 34 41 106	42 15 40 105	42 57 39 104	43 36 39 103	44 16 38 102
50	38 47 +42 108	39 29 +40 107	40 11 +40 106	40 53 +40 105	41 34 +40 104	42 14 +40 104	42 54 +38 102	43 34 +38 101
51	38 06 42 107	38 48 41 107	39 30 40 106	40 11 40 105	40 52 39 103	41 33 39 103	42 13 39 102	42 52 38 101
52	37 25 42 107	38 07 39 106	38 48 40 105	39 29 39 104	40 10 40 103	40 50 38 102	41 29 38 101	42 08 38 100
53	36 43 42 106	37 25 40 105	38 06 39 104	38 48 39 103	39 28 39 102	40 07 38 101	40 47 38 100	41 26 37 99
54	36 02 41 105	36 43 40 104	37 25 39 103	38 05 38 103	38 45 40 102	39 25 39 100	40 04 38 99	40 43 36 98
55	35 20 +41 104	36 01 +40 103	36 42 +39 103	37 23 +40 102	38 04 +39 101	38 43 +38 100	39 22 +38 99	40 00 +38 98
56	34 38 41 103	35 19 41 103	36 00 40 102	36 40 40 101	37 20 40 100	38 00 39 99	38 39 38 99	39 17 38 98
57	33 56 41 103	34 37 40 102	35 18 39 101	35 58 39 100	36 38 38 99	37 18 38 99	37 56 38 98	38 35 37 97
58	33 14 41 102	33 55 40 101	34 36 39 100	35 16 38 100	35 56 38 99	36 35 38 98	37 14 38 97	37 52 37 96
59	32 31 41 101	33 12 41 100	33 53 40 100	34 33 39 99	35 12 39 98	35 51 38 97	36 30 38 96	37 08 37 95
60	31 49 +41 100	32 30 +40 99	33 10 +39 99	33 50 +39 98	34 29 +39 97	35 08 +38 96	35 46 +38 95	36 24 +37 95
61	31 07 40 99	31 47 40 99	32 27 39 98	33 07 38 97	33 46 39 96	34 25 38 96	35 03 38 95	35 41 37 94
62	30 24 40 99	31 04 40 98	31 44 39 97	32 23 39 96	33 02 38 96	33 41 38 95	34 19 37 94	34 56 37 93
63	29 42 40 98	30 22 39 97	31 01 39 96	31 40 39 96	32 19 38 95	32 57 38 94	33 35 37 93	34 12 37 92
64	28 58 41 97	29 39 39 96	30 19 39 96	30 58 38 95	31 37 38 94	32 16 37 94	32 53 37 93	33 30 37 92
65	28 16 +40 96	28 57 +39 96	29 36 +39 95	30 15 +39 94	30 54 +38 93	31 33 +37 93	32 10 +37 92	32 47 +37 91
66	27 33 40 96	28 13 40 95	28 53 39 94	29 32 38 94	30 11 38 93	30 49 38 92	31 27 37 91	32 04 36 91
67	26 50 40 95	27 30 39 94	28 09 39 93	28 48 39 93	29 27 37 92	30 04 38 91	30 42 37 91	31 20 36 90
68	26 07 40 94	26 47 39 94	27 26 38 93	28 05 38 92	28 43 38 91	29 21 37 91	29 59 36 90	30 35 37 89
69	25 24 40 93	26 04 39 93	26 43 40 92	27 23 38 91	28 02 37 91	28 41 36 90	29 17 37 89	29 54 36 89

LHA	23° Hc d Z	24° Hc d Z	25° Hc d Z	26° Hc d Z	27° Hc d Z	28° Hc d Z	29° Hc d Z	LHA
0	69 00 +60 180	70 00 +60 180	71 00 +60 180	72 00 +60 180	73 00 +60 180	74 00 +60 180	75 00 +60 180	360
1	68 59 60 178	69 59 59 177	70 59 59 177	71 59 60 177	72 59 59 177	73 59 60 177	74 59 60 177	359
2	68 58 60 175	69 58 59 175	70 58 59 175	71 56 59 174	72 56 59 174	73 55 60 174	74 55 59 173	358
3	68 51 60 173	69 51 59 173	70 50 59 172	71 50 59 172	72 49 58 172	73 49 60 171	74 49 59 171	357
4	68 44 59 170	69 44 59 170	70 43 59 169	71 43 59 169	72 42 59 168	73 41 59 168	74 40 59 167	356
5	68 35 +59 167	69 35 +59 167	70 34 +59 166	71 33 +59 166	72 32 +58 165	73 30 +58 163	74 29 +58 163	355
6	68 26 58 167	69 25 58 166	70 23 58 166	71 21 59 165	72 20 58 165	73 18 57 161	74 15 58 160	354
7	68 14 59 165	69 13 59 164	70 10 57 163	71 08 57 160	72 05 57 159	73 03 57 158	74 00 57 157	353
8	68 01 58 161	68 59 57 160	69 57 58 159	70 55 57 159	71 52 57 158	72 46 56 157	73 45 56 156	352
9	66 44 60 160	67 42 59 168	69 42 55 157	70 39 56 156	71 35 59 157	72 42 57 168	73 40 59 167	351
10	67 27 +56 155	68 23 +57 155	69 20 +54 154	70 16 +55 155	70 50 +54 149	71 44 +54 148	72 38 +52 146	350
11	67 08 56 154	68 04 56 152	69 00 55 154	69 55 55 150	70 50 54 149	71 44 54 148	72 38 52 146	349
12	66 48 55 152	67 44 55 151	66 38 55 149	69 34 53 148	70 28 52 147	71 02 52 144	72 13 51 144	348
13	66 27 56 151	67 23 54 150	69 00 54 150	69 55 55 150	70 54 52 147	72 02 53 147	71 02 50 143	347
14	66 03 54 147	66 57 54 146	67 51 53 145	68 44 52 143	69 36 52 142	70 28 50 140	71 18 50 139	346
15	64 45 +54 146	66 32 +53 145	66 58 +52 142	68 17 +52 142	66 09 +50 140	67 59 +50 138	70 49 +49 136	345
16	64 20 53 145	65 13 53 143	66 06 52 142	66 58 51 142	67 49 50 139	68 40 50 138	69 30 49 136	344
17	65 39 54 145	66 33 54 145	66 51 51 145	68 44 49 145	69 36 49 142	70 54 48 139	71 46 51 141	343
18	63 32 53 144	64 25 52 143	65 18 52 141	66 10 50 139	67 02 50 137	67 53 48 135	68 44 48 134	342
19	63 50 53 145	66 41 54 144	65 30 53 143	67 08 47 145	67 55 47 134	68 42 45 130	68 42 45 128	341
20	62 30 +50 137	63 21 +50 135	64 11 +49 134	65 00 +48 133	65 48 +47 131	66 35 +47 130	67 22 +46 127	340
21	62 00 50 135	62 51 49 134	63 40 49 133	64 29 48 131	65 16 47 130	66 03 45 127	66 48 45 127	339
22	62 09 49 140	63 06 48 133	63 55 48 131	64 59 47 133	65 48 43 130	66 55 42 130	67 45 43 127	338
23	61 12 48 129	62 00 48 128	62 48 46 126	63 35 46 125	64 22 46 125	65 07 43 122	65 53 43 122	337
24	60 24 48 130	61 12 48 129	62 00 48 128	62 46 46 126	63 32 45 125	64 17 44 123	65 00 43 122	336
25	59 51 +47 129	60 38 +47 128	61 25 +45 126	62 11 +45 125	62 56 +44 123	63 41 +43 122	64 24 +43 120	335
26	59 17 47 127	60 04 46 126	60 51 45 125	61 36 44 123	62 20 44 122	63 04 43 120	63 46 41 118	334
27	58 42 47 126	59 29 45 125	60 14 45 123	60 59 43 122	61 42 43 120	62 25 42 119	63 06 39 117	333
28	58 09 45 125	58 54 45 123	59 39 43 122	60 22 43 120	61 05 43 119	61 48 40 117	62 28 40 115	332
29	57 35 45 123	58 20 43 121	59 03 43 120	59 46 42 119	60 28 41 117	61 09 40 115	61 49 39 113	331
30	56 55 +45 122	57 40 +44 121	58 24 +43 119	59 07 +42 118	59 49 +41 116	60 31 +40 114	61 11 +39 113	330
31	56 18 44 121	57 02 43 119	57 45 42 118	58 28 42 116	59 10 40 115	59 50 40 113	60 30 37 111	329
32	55 40 44 119	56 24 43 118	57 07 41 117	57 50 41 115	58 31 40 113	59 11 39 112	59 51 38 110	328
33	55 03 44 118	55 46 41 117	56 28 42 115	57 10 40 114	57 50 40 112	58 31 39 111	59 10 37 109	327
34	54 24 43 118	55 07 42 115	55 50 41 114	56 31 40 113	57 12 39 111	57 52 38 110	58 31 37 108	326
35	53 46 +42 116	54 28 +42 114	55 10 +41 113	55 51 +40 112	56 32 +39 111	57 11 +38 109	57 49 +38 108	325
36	53 07 42 115	53 49 41 113	54 30 41 112	55 11 40 111	55 51 39 109	56 30 38 108	57 08 37 107	324
37	52 27 42 114	53 09 41 113	53 50 40 111	54 30 39 110	55 09 38 109	55 48 37 107	56 25 36 106	323
38	51 48 41 113	52 29 40 112	53 09 40 110	53 49 39 109	54 28 38 108	55 06 37 106	55 43 36 105	322
39	51 08 41 112	51 49 40 111	52 29 39 109	53 08 39 108	53 46 38 107	54 24 37 105	55 01 36 104	321
40	50 27 +41 111	51 08 +39 110	51 47 +39 108	52 26 +38 107	53 04 +37 106	53 41 +37 105	54 18 +35 103	320
41	49 48 40 110	50 28 39 108	51 07 39 107	51 45 38 106	52 23 37 105	53 00 36 104	53 36 36 102	319
42	49 06 40 109	49 46 38 107	50 24 38 106	51 02 37 105	51 39 37 104	52 16 36 103	52 52 35 101	318
43	48 25 40 108	49 05 38 107	49 43 38 105	50 21 37 104	50 58 36 103	51 34 36 102	52 10 35 100	317
44	47 41 39 107	48 20 39 106	48 59 38 104	49 37 37 103	50 14 37 102	50 51 36 101	51 27 35 100	316
45	47 02 +40 106	47 42 +38 105	48 20 +37 104	48 57 +37 103	49 34 +36 102	50 10 +35 100	50 45 +35 99	315
46	46 21 39 105	47 00 38 104	47 38 37 103	48 15 37 102	48 52 36 101	49 28 35 100	50 03 35 98	314
47	45 39 39 104	46 18 37 103	46 55 37 102	47 32 37 101	48 09 36 100	48 45 35 99	49 20 35 98	313
48	44 58 38 103	45 36 38 102	46 14 37 101	46 51 36 100	47 27 35 99	48 02 35 98	48 37 34 97	312
49	44 16 38 102	44 54 37 101	45 31 37 100	46 08 36 99	46 44 35 98	47 19 34 97	47 53 34 96	311
50	43 34 +38 101	44 12 +37 100	44 49 +36 99	45 25 +36 98	46 01 +35 97	46 36 +35 96	47 11 +33 95	310
51	42 52 38 101	43 30 36 100	44 06 36 98	44 42 36 97	45 18 34 96	45 52 35 95	46 27 33 94	309
52	42 08 38 100	42 46 37 99	43 23 35 98	43 58 36 97	44 34 34 95	45 08 34 94	45 42 34 93	308
53	41 26 37 99	42 03 36 98	42 39 36 97	43 15 35 96	43 50 34 95	44 24 34 94	44 58 33 92	307
54	40 43 36 98	41 19 37 97	41 56 35 96	42 31 35 95	43 06 34 94	43 40 34 93	44 13 33 92	306
55	40 00 +38 98	40 38 +35 97	41 13 +35 95	41 48 +34 94	42 22 +34 93	42 56 +33 92	43 29 +33 91	305
56	39 17 38 98	39 53 35 96	40 28 35 95	41 03 34 94	41 37 34 93	42 11 33 92	42 44 32 91	304
57	38 35 37 97	39 11 35 95	39 46 34 94	40 20 34 93	40 54 33 92	41 27 33 91	42 00 32 90	303
58	37 52 37 96	38 28 35 95	39 03 34 94	39 37 34 93	40 11 33 91	40 44 32 90	41 16 32 89	302
59	37 08 37 95	37 45 35 94	38 20 34 93	38 54 33 92	39 27 33 91	40 00 32 90	40 32 32 89	301
60	36 24 +37 95	37 01 +35 93	37 36 +34 92	38 10 +33 91	38 43 +33 90	39 16 +32 89	39 48 +31 88	300
61	35 41 37 94	36 18 34 93	36 52 34 92	37 26 33 91	37 59 33 90	38 32 31 89	39 03 32 87	299
62	34 56 37 93	35 33 35 92	36 08 34 91	36 42 33 90	37 15 33 89	37 48 31 88	38 19 31 87	298
63	34 12 37 92	34 49 34 91	35 23 34 90	35 57 33 90	36 30 32 89	37 02 32 88	37 34 31 86	297
64	33 30 37 92	34 07 34 91	34 41 33 90	35 14 32 89	35 46 32 88	36 18 31 87	36 49 31 86	296
65	32 47 +37 91	33 24 +34 90	33 58 +33 89	34 31 +33 88	35 04 +32 87	35 36 +31 86	36 07 +31 85	295
66	32 04 36 91	32 40 34 90	33 14 33 89	33 47 32 88	34 19 32 87	34 51 31 86	35 22 31 85	294
67	31 20 36 90	31 56 34 89	32 30 32 88	33 02 32 87	33 34 32 86	34 06 31 85	34 37 30 84	293
68	30 35 37 89	31 12 34 89	31 46 32 88	32 18 32 87	32 50 31 86	33 21 31 85	33 52 30 84	292
69	29 54 36 89	30 27 34 88	31 01 32 87	31 34 32 86	32 06 31 85	32 37 30 84	33 07 30 83	291

DECLINATION (15°-29°) SAME NAME AS LATITUDE

LAT 44°

Table 5   Correction to tabulated altitude for minutes of declination

These tables, reduced, are taken from *Sight Reduction Tables for Air Navigation* with the permission of the Controller of **HM** Stationery Office.

Example. On 28 June, in DR lat 43° 48′ N, long 20° 45′ W the sun was observed in the forenoon at 10h 24m 47s GMT. The observed altitude was 47° 38′, and HE 1·5 metres (5 feet). Required the assumed position, the intercept, and the azimuth.

Obs Alt	47° 38′	Sun's GHA at 10h	329° 14′·4
Sun Corr	+15′·1	Increment for 24m 47s	+6° 11′·8
Dip	−2′·3		
		GHA	335° 26′
True Alt	47° 51′	Assumed longitude	−20° 26′ W
		LHA	315°

Assumed latitude 44°N	Dec 23° 18′ N	Same name.
	d+39	Z105 = N 105°E
Hc	47° 42′·	
d corr	+12′	
Calc Alt	47° 54′	
True Alt	47° 51′	
Intercept	3′	away

Obs Alt. The observed altitude is the angle measured between the visible horizon and the sun's lower limb, index error of the sextant having been allowed for when reading the instrument.

Sun Corr. The correction for semi-diameter and refraction, taken from near the front of the *NA*, the table being entered with the observed altitude.

Dip. The correction necessary because the visible, not the rational, horizon was used. The dip table is near the front of the *NA*, and was entered with the height of the observer's eye above the sea, which was 1·5 metres (5 feet).

True Alt. The altitude between the rational horizon and the sun's centre. Note that although decimals of a minute of arc are included in the corrections for refraction and semi-diameter, the true altitude is written to the nearest whole minute only, because Hc is given for the nearest whole minute only in *SRT*. The same applies when taking the GHA and Dec from the *NA*.

Sun's GHA at 10h. Obtained from the appropriate daily page (28 June) in the *NA*.

Increment for 24m 47s. Obtained from the increments table headed 24m, found on the coloured pages near the end of the *NA*, and entered with 47 seconds.

GHA. The angular distance of the meridian of the sun measured westward from the meridian of Greenwich at the GMT of the sight, ie at 10h 24m 47s on 28 June.

Assumed longitude. This is as near as possible to the DR longitude, but is such that when subtracted from the GHA the seconds cancel out.

LHA. The local hour angle, ie the angular distance of the sun's meridian measured westward from the assumed longitude; it is obtained by subtracting west longitude from, or adding east longitude to, the GHA of the body.

Assumed latitude. The whole degree of latitude nearest to the DR latitude.

Dec. The declination (angular distance of the sun north or south of the equator) at the GMT of the sight is obtained to the nearest minute of arc from the daily page of the *NA*.

Same name. A reminder that as latitude and declination are both north, a page in *SRT* headed '*Same* name' must be used.

Hc. Height calculated is obtained from *SRT* by entering the table headed 'Lat 44°, declination *same* name as latitude', with Dec 23° and LHA 315°. (This table is reproduced on page 462.)

d. This is found in the same column and next to the Hc figure. It will be used to correct Hc for the 18' of declination. Note that it is given a + sign in the table.

Z, the azimuth, is given in the same column and same line as the Hc and *d* figures. This sight was taken in the northern hemisphere and in the forenoon, so the sun's bearing must be reckoned from north (the elevated pole) in an easterly direction, N 105°E.

d Corr. The correction for minutes of declination is obtained from Table 5 in *SRT*, which is reproduced on page 463. The table is entered across the top with *d* 39, and down the side with the minutes of declination, 18, and gives a correction of 12'. As *d* had a + sign, the correction must be added to the Hc figure.

Calc alt. The altitude of the sun calculated for the assumed position at the time of the sight, and corrected for the minutes of declination.

Intercept. The difference between the calculated altitude at the assumed position and the true altitude at the observer's position, ie the distance the position line must be moved away from the assumed position along the azimuth either towards or away from the sun according to the following rule: If the calc alt is the greater, the intercept must be measured away from the body; if the observed altitude is the greater the intercept must be measured towards the body. An easy way to remember this rule is by means of the word GOAT – greater observed altitude towards.

Here is another example of a sun sight, taken during the afternoon of 6 September when nearing the island of Rodriguez in the Indian Ocean. It differs from the previous example only in the following respects. As the assumed longitude was east, it had to be *added* to the GHA to obtain the LHA, and as the LHA exceeded 360°, 360 had to be taken from it; as latitude was south and declination was north, a page in *SRT* headed 'Declination *contrary* name to latitude' had to be used.

At 9h 44m 31s GMT on 6 September in DR lat 19°23′ S, long 64°40′ E, the observed altitude of the sun was 49°37′; HE 1·5 metres (5 feet). Required the intercept and azimuth.

Obs Alt	49° 37′	Sun's GHA at 9h	315° 22′·3
Sun Corr	+15′·2	Increment for 44m 31s	11° 07′·8
Dip	−2′·3		
		GHA	326° 30′
True Alt	49° 50′	Assumed longitude	+64° 30′ E
			391°
			−360°
	LHA		31°

Assumed latitude	19°S	Dec 6° 34′ N Contrary names
Hc	50° 32′	d−39 Z 126 = S 126°W or 306°
d corr	−22′	
Calc Alt	50° 10′	
True Alt	49° 50′	
Intercept	20′	away

Figure 98 (following pages) is a reproduction of Baker's position line chart, and on it is shown the plotting done during a typical 24-hour period in which two observations of the sun were taken. The yacht was on passage between Cape Town and St Helena, and her noon position on 25 March was 25°37' S, 6°26' E. The central parallel on the chart was therefore named 25°S, and the meridian towards the east side was named 6°E. Using the longitude scale at top or bottom of the chart, and the latitude scale labelled 25–6° on one of the folding flaps (in the figure this can be identified by the arrows and letter S) the position was marked (*NP 25 Mar*). From that position the course steered (310° true) was laid down with the parallel ruler, using the circle marked in 360°, and the distance run by patent log until the first observation was taken on 26 March was marked on it (*DR*). The sight was worked, the assumed position (*AP*) for that sight was marked on the chart, the azimuth (*AZ*) was drawn through it, and the intercept (*Int*) measured along it. Through that point the position line (*PL*) was drawn at right angles to the azimuth. The yacht continued on her course, and at local noon an observation was taken and the resulting latitude, 24°24' S, was laid down on the chart. The distance run by log between the two sights was stepped off along the course that had been steered from the point where the first position line cut the course, and is marked *DR2*. The first position line was brought forward with the parallel ruler and drawn through *DR2*, and where it (*PL2*) cut the noon latitude was the noon position (*NP 26 Mar*). The day's run, (the distance sailed between the two noon positions) was measured, and as it exceeded the distance recorded by the log the presence of a favourable current was suspected. Finally the noon position was transferred to the chart of the South Atlantic, so that the course to the destination could be checked and altered if necessary.

In practice the above abbreviations are of course not used, nor do I use the Baker's chart exactly as it is, for I find its scale inconveniently large for my purpose as I like to be able to have more than two noon positions on it at any one time. I therefore halve the latitude and longitude scales, and change the figures so that 5' becomes 10', 10' becomes 20', etc.

The working of a planet sight is identical with that of a sun sight, except that the correction to the sextant reading must be taken from the table in the *NA* headed 'Stars and Planets'.

A star sight is similar except that as the GHA of the individual stars is not given in the *NA* because there are so many of them, it

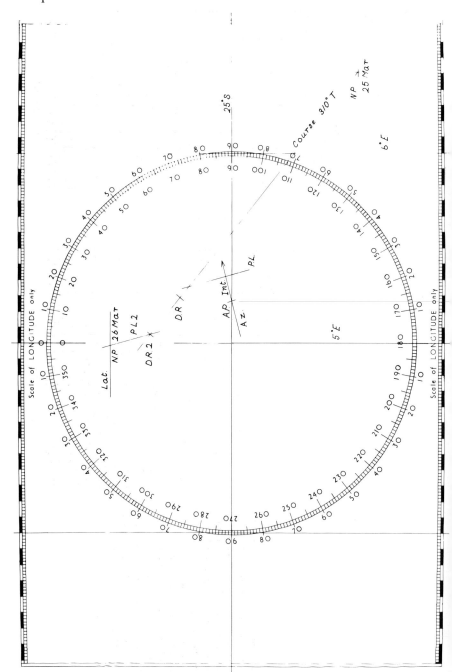

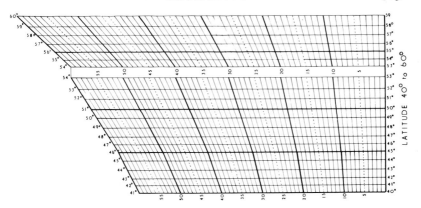

Scale of MILES or MINUTES of LATITUDE

LATITUDE 40° to 60°

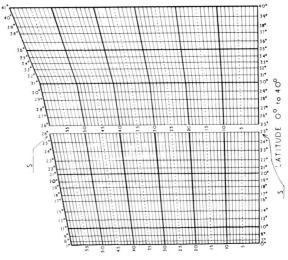

LATITUDE 0° to 40°

Fig 98   Baker's position line chart
The upper part shows the chart with
a day's work drawn on it; the lower
part shows the latitude scales, which
normally are printed on folding
flaps at the west and east edges of
the chart. In use the longitude scale
remains constant, while the scale of
latitude and distance for the latitude
in which the ship lies is always used,
thus making the chart into a blank
Mercator chart for any latitude from
0° to 60°. (Reproduced by courtesy
of Imray, Laurie, Norie & Wilson.)

must be calculated. The *NA* gives the GHA of Aries, to which, as was mentioned earlier, the stars can be related; it also gives the siderial hour angle (SHA) of all the navigational stars. SHA is the angular distance of the meridian of the star measured westward from the meridian of Aries, and this, like a star's declination, does not change appreciably throughout the year. To obtain the GHA of a star, add together the GHA of Aries and the SHA of the star. The LHA of the star can then be obtained in the same way as for the sun, and Volume II or III of *SRT* can be entered in the usual manner, provided the star's declination does not exceed 29°.

However, if the navigator intends to make much use of star sights he may decide to obtain a copy of *SRT* Volume I, which is devoted entirely to stars and has certain advantages, but unlike *SRT* Volumes II and III, which never become out of date, Volume I needs to be recomputed after approximately 5 years, and then a new edition is published. Its method of use is different, for instead of being entered with the assumed latitude and the declination and LHA of the observed star, it is entered with the assumed latitude and LHA of Aries; when it at once indicates which 6 of the 34 stars tabulated may be used for navigation from the ship's position at the chosen time. For each entry of assumed latitude and LHA of Aries, the Hc (altitude) and Z (azimuth) of the 6 selected stars will be found in adjoining columns on the same page. Before taking any sights one should first consult the tables to find what stars can be used. This is done by making in advance an approximate determination of the LHA of Aries at the intended GMT of the observations, using the DR and the *NA*. With the information so obtained, the tables are entered, and the navigator can make his selection of 3 of the 6 available listed stars, noting for each the Hc and Z. From this it will be understood that Volume I serves also as a star finder for a limited number of stars. In making his selection from the 6 stars available, the navigator will be guided by considerations of magnitude (apparent brightness) and azimuth, choosing as far as possible stars easily seen and evenly spaced around him so that the resulting 'cocked hat' may be approximately in the form of an equilateral triangle. At twilight he will set his sextant to Hc of the first star, sweep the horizon in the direction indicated by the azimuth, pick up the star in the telescope, make contact, and note the time in the usual way, repeating the procedure with the other two stars. The LHA of Aries at the GMT of each sight is then obtained from the *NA*, and with these figures and the assumed latitude the volume of tables is again entered to obtain the Hc and Z of each star, these figures of course being needed for working and plotting the three observations. The need to enter the tables in advance, and again after the sights have been taken, may seem to be a complication, but in practice much time is saved in identifying and observing and, particularly in the tropics, where twilight is brief, the results will be more certain.

As a navigational body the moon is of particular value when she can be seen at the same time as the sun, and when her azimuth differs from that of the sun by about 40° or more, for simultaneous observations of both bodies will then provide a fix. It is often thought that a moon sight is difficult to work, and this may be due to Lecky's remark: '... so many petty and vexatious corrections which spin the calculations out to a weary length'. But since he wrote his classic *Wrinkles in Practical Navigation* (George Philip) the matter has been much simplified, so that to obtain the true altitude from the sextant reading calls for little more correction than is needed for any other body. The only additional correction is for horizontal parallax. This is the error caused by the fact that the sight is taken from the surface of the globe, but the angle required is from the earth's centre; with the far distant sun this is so small (never more than 9″) that it is disregarded, but the moon is so close that horizontal parallax, which varies with her changing distance from us and with her altitude, has to be taken into consideration. On each daily page of the *NA* the horizontal parallax is given for each hour; with this figure and with the apparent altitude (sextant reading corrected for index error and dip) we enter the altitude correction table for the moon near the back of the *NA*, and there obtain two corrections which must be added to the apparent altitude; the lower part of the table has separate columns for observations of the upper and the lower limb; if the upper limb is observed, as of course it must be if the lower limb is not illuminated, 30′ must be deducted from the total correction. There is no need to memorize the procedure, for instructions are given at the foot of the correction table.

The calculator

For some time navigators have been using electronic calculators. In the beginning they were employed to do the simple arithmetic, and later for solving the spherical triangle, but since this could be done simply and quickly by tables such as *SRT*, and as the *NA* still had to be consulted to obtain the Dec and GHA, their advantages were in my view not very great. However, calculators are now available which, when entered with the year, date, and GMT, give the Dec of the sun and the GHA of both sun and Aries, and are able to continue providing this information for many years to come. A calculator of this type is a great help in speeding up the working of a sight, but it is expensive and far from fool-proof, we do not yet know how well it can withstand the damp environment aboard a small craft, and it depends on dry-cells or rechargeable batteries for its operation. No doubt improvements will continue to be made, but even so the navigator would be wise still to carry tables and almanac and be proficient in their use, to guard against a failure of the instrument; and, of course, the basic accuracy of any position line obtained from an observation of a celestial body will continue to depend, as it always has, on the navigator's ability with the sextant.

Making a landfall

When the time approaches to make a landfall, the only sights that really matter are the last pair the navigator has taken, and if he was satisfied with them and made no error in their working, and was certain of the GMT, the landfall should be a good one, that is, the right piece of land should appear ahead at the estimated time. This is the common experience of most of us. Nevertheless there will be a feeling of excitement aboard as the time draws near for the land to lift above the horizon, or materialize through the haze, for the thrill of making the land, especially after one has been for many days out of sight of it, never grows stale. But the navigator will feel more tense than his shipmates, for the responsibility is his, and it is probable that he will start looking too early, and perhaps a little anxiously, for land, especially if the landfall is to be on a low and featureless coast, or a comparatively small island which he is fearful of missing, when it might be necessary to sail on a great distance to find a larger target. Such a happening has occurred on many occasions in the past, when, before the advent of radio, the navigator had no means of telling that his chronometer had changed its rate, and that his longitude was therefore badly in error. The risk of that happening today is small; but if for some reason GMT is not known, the navigator can resort to latitude sailing, that is, get on to the latitude of the intended landfall some distance east or west of it, and sail along that latitude, checking with meridian altitude sights (which are independent of GMT) until he reaches his objective, just as his forefathers did before the advent of the chronometer.

A landfall on a high island should present no problem if the weather is clear, for the land will be visible a long way off. Even before it is visible there will probably be signs of it, such as the appearance of land birds, or an accumulation of cloud standing above it, or perhaps a cloud trail driven by the wind streaming away like smoke for many miles to leeward. I have seen this on several occasions, but it was most marked to leeward of the 396-metre- (1,300-foot) high island of Rodriguez, where it could clearly be seen while the island was well out of sight (Plate 55 *middle*). But one must not always expect the land to be cloud-capped, or to be able to see high land at a great distance, even though visibility may appear to be excellent, a lesson I learnt when making the island of San Miguel, one of the Azores. The day was bright and sunny with a blue sea and sky and a sharp horizon, and I guessed the visibility to be very good. The island rises to 1,097 metres (3,600 feet), and at o600 it was by account less than 40 miles away, so I expected to sight it soon. But the morning wore on with an empty horizon, and although terns visited us, and my wife, who is a non-smoker, could smell pines and flowers, we had no sight of land or of any cloud in the sky to suggest the proximity of land; and not until we had sailed to within 15 miles of it did the island appear faintly through its unsuspected shroud of mist, which was the same colour as the sky. Then slowly, as we approached, it took shape (Plate 55, *bottom*); the volcanic peaks, the dark green areas of trees, a patchwork of tiny fields, and clusters of whitewashed dwellings hanging on the slopes, gathered colour and substance.

If a landfall has to be made on a small, low island, there may be no intimation of the island's nearness, for it may be lacking in bird life, and it will probably have no cloud cap, though if it lies beside or within a lagoon there is just a chance that light reflected from the shallows may tint the atmosphere above with a green hue – I have seen this phenomenon several times among the Tuamotu, and once on approaching South Caicos in the Bahamas. Because of the island's low elevation any palms growing on it will be visible from the deck of a yacht only 10 to 15 miles off (Plate 55, *top*) depending on their height. Every opportunity should be taken of fixing the position, but if one is uncertain of the position in one direction, then the island should be approached on a line of which one is more certain. A lookout should be kept from aloft, because of the increased distance seen with the extra height of eye.

23

IN PORT

ALTHOUGH we may have been looking forward to the occasion with mounting enthusiasm, we will probably find that the transition from the sea to a foreign city at the conclusion of a long passage is at first far from enjoyable. It is likely that we will be tired, and a little dazed by the noise, the heat, the smell, and the multitude of strange faces after the silence and emptiness of the sea, and would like more than anything else just then to be left in peace for a little while to relax and clean up and adjust ourselves to the change; but inevitably there will be officials to deal with and paperwork to do.

Port officials

The first stop in a foreign country must be at a port of entry (such ports are usually listed in the relevant *Pilot*) where health, customs, and immigration officials are stationed. On approaching the land and entering the port the overseas yacht should wear her national colours (ensign) and a courtesy ensign (see page 507), and in a conspicuous place she must fly international code flag 'Q', a square yellow flag which means: 'My ship is healthy and I request free pratique' ie permission to land. If the quarantine anchorage shown on the chart is too exposed or remote, as it usually is, bring up in a conspicuous place, or ask of the pilot cutter (if there is one) or of some other yacht what the local procedure is, or perhaps make a radio call. In most countries it is illegal to land before someone has come off to grant pratique; sometimes this will be the port doctor, but often a customs officer will do it. If, however, after waiting for several hours no official has appeared, the skipper alone should land and call at the port office or custom-house. To avoid paying overtime charges it is not wise to enter a port of entry on weekends or public holidays (the *NA* lists the latter), or between 1700 and 0800 hours.

Port officers will wish to see the certificate of registry, the clearance from the last port, and the passports of all on board sometimes together with vaccination certificates; only once (at Cristobal) have I been asked for a deratting exemption certificate, and as I did not have one I had to pay $13 to get it, but had I known at the time, I could have obtained one for nothing at Barbados. Questions will mainly concern the following: is the yacht carrying items subject to duty, notably spirits, tobacco, cameras, and electronic equipment (these may have to be listed with their serial numbers), and has she any firearms aboard (the police may wish to hold them); but above all else does she possess any drugs? Only in Fiji and New Zealand has a yacht of mine been searched, and then it appeared to be done more to impress than in the expectation of finding undeclared, prohibited goods. Immigration will be concerned that the yacht's people do not overstay the allotted time, which in some countries may be limited to a few weeks. But even if one is allowed to stay indefinitely the yacht will probably be subject to import duty, ranging from 10 to 60 per cent of her original cost, or a value put on her, if she stays longer than the stipulated time of perhaps one year.

However, there would be little point in listing here the various requirements for yachts calling at countries I have visited, for not only are they liable to change but may vary from one port to another in the same country. In the interest of those who follow after, every attempt should be made to comply with the regulations and every facility be given to the officials. In my experience it is rare to encounter discourteous or dishonest ones, and if they are welcomed aboard with a smile and a little hospitality, any small difficulties can usually be resolved. A particularly tiresome restriction imposed in some countries is that the yacht must enter and clear at every port she touches, so one should enquire of the Chief of Customs – preferably in advance of arrival, for sometimes local officials deny knowledge of it – if a cruising permit can be issued; this document, which permits the yacht to go where she will without further paperwork, can be had in the USA and in Australia.

Before leaving port a visit should be paid to the port office to settle any port or other dues; although dues are now levied in many British harbours, it is rare for a yacht to be charged anything outside European waters unless, of course, she occupies a mooring or a marina berth. Probably a visit will have to be paid to immigration and customs, passports will be stamped, and an outward clearance issued. It may be possible to obtain duty-free stores, notably wines, spirits, and tobacco, on which there will be a great saving. In most countries this is not allowed for yachts of less than 40 register tons; nevertheless it is sometimes permitted, though I have found in recent years increasing reluctance to grant the privilege. If customs sanction a shipment of duty-free stores, a locker must be available in which they can be stowed and sealed until such time as the yacht has put to sea; again depending on local attitude, the stores may be re-sealed on arrival in another country, or perhaps one may be permitted to use them *on board*.

Mail and money

Practically everyone has to make some arrangements for collecting mail, and it will be best if all mail goes to a bank or the office of some firm in one's home country, where there will always be someone to attend to it, whereas a friend may fall ill or go away on holiday or business. Brief forwarding instructions can then be sent from time to time, a number of strategic ports being selected. I have had mail sent in care of consulates, yacht clubs, and banks, and found the latter the most reliable. I always wrote some time in advance saying approximately when I expected to arrive, asking if the bank would be kind enough to hold mail for me, and offering to pay any fees or expenses incurred. I was never refused or charged, but I have heard of British consulates declining to accept mail for yachts. Perhaps yacht clubs are the least responsible, for often all the mail is left in a public place for every new arrival to sort through; but this at least means that one is expected, and one can gain some idea of what other yachts are on the way. Some post-offices will not hold mail for more than a short time before returning it to the sender, and nobody is personally responsible for seeing that it is handed over or forwarded after one has left. The yacht's name is important, especially on parcels, for apart from helping to identify one, it may make the difference between having to pay duty or not. Gear for a yacht in transit if sent out from home, should be allowed to be shipped duty-free; nevertheless duty (or a bribe) may have to be paid. When collecting mail one's passport should be shown as proof of identity.

Probably the best way of carrying money is in the form of travellers' cheques, which will be cashed by banks or tourist agencies, or sometimes by hotels or shops, in the countries endorsed on them, or in any country if stamped 'world wide'. A letter of credit has little merit as money can only be drawn on it at a bank. When staying in a country for several months I open a banking account, which greatly simplifies all money transactions; nevertheless some cash in a universally respected currency (eg US dollars) kept in a secret place on board, is convenient and can be of great value in an emergency.

In the past many voyagers earned their living and expenses as they went by working at their trade – doctor, dentist, diesel or electrical engineer, schoolteacher, or shipwright – but for this to be done legally today a work permit may be required in most places and that will be hard or impossible to obtain.

Hospitality

My wife and I have never made use of letters of introduction, as we consider they place their recipients in the awkward position of feeling they must offer some hospitality no matter how inconvenient that may be. Indeed, such letters proved to be unnecessary, for the spontaneous friendship and hospitality extended by English-speaking and some other strangers to us during our voyages was remarkable, and I believe this to be the common and delightful experience of most little-ship voyagers. Some respectable clothes suitable for wear in hot weather are essential, and these are best of the permanently pressed kind, but unless they are washed or cleaned before being stowed away after use they will become fusty, and in warm weather may grow mildew.

One of the chief difficulties of accepting hospitality ashore in some places, especially at night, is guarding the yacht against thieves. Of course a riding light should be left burning and it should be possible to lock her up, but even so she may be broken into, or gear may be stolen from on deck. One will perhaps be warned if there is much risk (usually the smaller the place the smaller the risk), and the only solution then will be to employ a watchman or a guard dog, though an alarm system might be a deterrent even if nobody answers it.

There is little one can do to return shore hospitality, except to invite one's hosts on board for drinks, and this does seem to be appreciated. For such an occasion it is important that the berth be a quiet one, otherwise the motion may upset the guests and spoil the party, and it is best for the yacht to lie alongside so that the guests may come and go without dinghy work. If there is duty-free drink aboard and customs have not locked it up, such a party need not be a very expensive affair in spite of the large quantity sometimes consumed. Perhaps it might not be out of place to give here the recipe for the famous rum-punch of the Caribbean: 'One of sour, two of sweet, three of strong, and four of weak.' In practice this means the juice of one lime, two heaped teaspoonfuls of sugar, three ounces of rum, and plenty of water or ice; a little nutmeg should be grated to float on top. Ice can often be had easily enough in hot places, and if there is no refrigerator or ice-box on board, there should be a large thermos flask with a wide neck in which to collect a supply of cubes from the shore; but a warm hand must not be thrust into the cold flask or the glass may shatter.

Perhaps a photograph of the yacht may serve as a mark of appreciation to people who have been kind, or, for a yacht club, the burgee of one's own club; but certainly a letter of thanks should be sent later, old-fashioned though the idea may seem, and personally I feel that a stereotyped circular letter lacks the personal touch.

Pest control

If in the tropics a yacht spends much time alongside, pests of one kind or another are bound to get aboard, and at a commercial wharf the infestation of cockroaches and copra fly can become appalling. I recall one evening visiting a large yacht which had spent some years in the Pacific, and when I switched on a light in the galley the whole place – bulkheads, deckhead, and deck – appeared to move; all were alive with cockroaches. But this kind of thing need not happen if the yacht lies at anchor and some care is taken when loading stores. Cardboard cartons should not be permitted on board (they may contain not only roaches but roach eggs), all vegetables should be picked over and egg boxes searched before they go below, and stems of bananas should be submerged in the sea for a few minutes. The occasional cockroach which gets through these defences, and they are a hardy breed, can probably be killed by spraying or swatting, but if there is an infestation all lockers and places where the creatures could live and breed should be sprayed frequently with a 5 per cent solution of Chlordane in paraffin, or with one of the numerous insecticides. I have known ants come off from the shore along mooring lines for quite some distance and live on board for many months, so perhaps a short length of each line should be treated with insecticide. Only twice have we had rats aboard (a cat is good insurance against this) and never any mice, centipedes, or snakes, but there are places such as the rivers in the Guianas and in northern Australia where, according to the *Pilot*, there is a risk of snakes getting aboard by way of the anchor cable unless this is fitted with a rat guard, a metal cone with the apex pointing inboard.

The farther a vessel lies from the shore the less will she be troubled by insects, but sooner or later the foreign-going yacht will need insect screens to protect her people from flies and/or mosquitoes, and in this connection it should not be thought that insects are a bother only in hot places; indeed, my wife and I rarely found screens essential until we visited Maine, but we did at times, notably in the northern part of Australia and in New Caledonia, use mosquito netting over our bunks at night in *Wanderer III*. For this we had wide pieces of netting rather longer than the bunks, and fastened them with clothes-pegs to the hand-rails on the coachroof coamings above the bunks, from which they hung down to touch the cabin sole. They were easy to rig and quite effective provided insects were not trapped inside them. But I now feel sure that it is better to exclude insects from the entire accom-modation, as we do in *Wanderer IV*, by fitting portable screens of plastic netting to all external doors, hatches, vents, and opening ports; we sometimes find that if these are shipped at sundown they can be removed when we turn in after the lights, which tend to attract insects, have been extinguished, thus allowing a freer flow of air during the night.

But there are occasions when screens are needed in the daytime, as, for example, at Nukuhiva, Marquesas Islands, where the *nono* – a small black sand-fly with a bite which sometimes becomes septic – is particularly troublesome, also against sand-flies of a larger but equally intolerable type in Fiordland, New Zealand. As screens reduce the flow of air, they need to be easy to ship and unship; the screen in the main companionway should therefore be hinged for ease of passage, and if there is a cat aboard the screen should be provided with a two-way cat-flap (Plate 8*A*). Opening ports are easily provided with removable screens in the following manner. Cut a length of stiff wire (welding rod serves well) a little greater than the circumference or perimeter of the inside of the port, and bend it in such a way that it has to be compressed a little to be sprung into position; turn its ends out at right angles to provide finger grips, and tie them loosely together so that they cannot spring far apart. Then sew the netting to the wire. To ship the screen, hold it by the protruding ends of wire, squeeze them together to reduce the size of the screen, insert it into the port recess, and then release (Plate 8*E*). Some small insects, such as the 'noseeums' of the Bahamas, can penetrate mosquito screens unless these are treated with paraffin or insecticide.

Sometimes one may not suspect the presence of mosquitoes until it is too late to ship the screens. Then one will be glad to have a supply of mosquito coils. These come in boxes usually holding half-a-dozen, together with a little metal stand, and are available world-wide. A coil is rigged up on the stand on a saucer to catch the ash, and its outer end is lighted. The coil will smoulder for many hours, giving off a smell, harmless to humans and not unpleasant, which mosquitoes detest. On the hot, still, humid nights when a single mosquito can ruin one's sleep, the use of one of these coils may be preferable to shipping the screens. A supply of the ointments and liquids used to keep insects off one's skin should certainly be carried, otherwise shore excursions in some places, and life in the open at sundown, will be a misery. Nevertheless it is a wise precaution in areas where mosquito-carried malaria is prevalent to take anti-malarial pills, one or more a week according to the instructions; but the latter should be noted carefully, for it may be found that to be effective the course of pills must be started two weeks before arrival in the area and continued for up to eight weeks after leaving.

Pets

I have no experience of dogs as shipmates, but some I have met gave the impression that for them life afloat was not much fun. However, there are, as was mentioned earlier, places where a dog would be of value in discouraging unwelcome visitors. Many long-distance voyaging yachts have carried dogs of the smaller breeds, and in each the dog learnt to use a part of the deck as heads, and this was sluiced with seawater.

Most cats appear to be as content afloat as they are ashore if they start the life young. Some people consider they are of no practical use except for catching vermin, but they can be good company and affectionate, and they help to keep up morale by their indifference to bad weather or anxious situations. When visiting the shore they often pick up fleas, and we used to get ours to wear an anti-flea collar, which drugs the fleas so that they can be popped with a pair of small tweezers. For the cat's heads we started with the traditional sand-box, but soon abandoned it as damp paws carried the sand everywhere. The Carrs in *Havfruen III*, who had two Siamese aboard, advised us to try wood planings; this, which can be got at any boatyard or timber mill, was an improvement, but we failed to train our cat to use a small basin like the Carrs' cats did, for he was a powerful digger and flung the planings all over the forepeak. So we rigged him up with a shallow plastic container to hold the planings in the bottom of a high-sided bread-bin. No doubt each cat has its particular likes and dislikes regarding food, though most enjoy fresh fish. Ours could not keep down for more than a few minutes most of the cat foods sold in cans, but he approved of all raw pieces of fresh chicken and meat, and of the canned foods for humans preferred tuna (in water, not oil), and if there was nothing better around would share with us an occasional can of corned beef. There are available packets of pea-size crisp biscuits, which at times are popular, and a raw yolk of egg (uncooked white of egg is indigestible) is of value when other fresh food is not available, and is relished by some felines.

Today quarantine regulations make the carrying of dogs, cats, or birds very difficult, for in many countries there is a compulsory quarantine period of up to twelve months, irrespective of the time taken on the last passage, or an assurance that the animal has had no contact with the shore for a long time, and I understand that in at least one country, Malta, all animals are destroyed on arrival. The quarantine period is too long for any pet to be separated from the people with whom it has affectionately shared the confines of a small vessel, but in some countries (New Zealand is one) the quarantine period may be spent aboard the yacht. It would certainly be wise to have one's pet inoculated against rabies, and to have a vet's certificate to prove it.

Yacht clubs

There are in many parts of the world a great number of yacht and sailing clubs, but the majority are mainly concerned with racing and social events and may have little appeal to cruising and voyaging people. However, there are some notable exceptions which do much to encourage cruising, the individual members helping one another and promoting the well-being of the club and the sport by exchanging ideas, information, and charts, each member being prepared to give to the club a little more than he expects to get out of it.

The Royal Cruising Club has a limited and exclusive membership and is something like a big family. It awards trophies to its members for their cruises, and its Seamanship Medal for an outstanding performance by anyone. The club publishes port information sheets for most European coasts; it also publishes the *Royal Cruising Club Journal*, a well-produced annual containing accounts of members' cruises, which is available to the public under the title *Roving Commissions*. The Cruising Association has probably the finest nautical library in the UK housed in its St

Katherine's Dock headquarters. The Little Ship Club, with a fine club house on the Thames in the heart of London, provides, among much else, instruction in seamanship and navigation. The Ocean Cruising Club, founded by Humphrey Barton, is young and, as its name implies, has long-distance sailors as members, and each must have made a passage of 1,000 miles before being proposed. The general interests of the sport, particularly where governmental interference is concerned, are guarded by the Royal Yachting Association, but much of its energy is absorbed by racing matters.

The Cruising Club of America is perhaps best known overseas for its rules under which some of the more important ocean races are sailed, yet, like the RCC, it has as members many famous cruising people, and although its membership is not limited, it is exclusive. The Blue Water Medal of the CCA (Plate 64*E*) is awarded annually 'for the year's most meritorious example of seamanship, the recipient to be selected from among the amateurs of all the nations'. This large bronze medal was struck in 1925, and is generally regarded among the voyaging fraternity as the premier and most coveted award. Mention must also be made of the American-run Seven Seas Cruising Association. Membership of this is limited to those who live continuously aboard their yachts, but anyone who wishes to subscribe may receive the monthly *Bulletin*, the contents of which are letters written by active cruising members (and subscribers) scattered all over the world, and these, after a little sifting, provide a wealth of up-to-date information which is not available elsewhere.

The voyager will find along his route some clubs which will offer him help and hospitality. Notable among them are the Panama Canal Yacht Club at Cristobal at the north end of the canal, and the Balboa YC at the south end; the Royal Suva in Fiji; the Royal Akarana at Auckland, NZ; The Cruising YC of Australia at Sydney; The Point and the Royal Natal, both at Durban, and the Royal Cape at Cape Town. All have fine club houses and some have hauling-out facilities which may be available to the visitor. Some clubs are now finding it difficult to continue offering their hospitality to the ever-increasing number of voyagers, and I feel we should treat their kindness as something remarkable and precious, as indeed it is, and not abuse it by outstaying our welcome.

PART IV

Miscellanea

24

SAFETY

Guardrails and harness—Lifebuoys—Man overboard—Fire—A medical note—Abandoning ship

MOST worthwhile sports have some element of risk, and cruising and voyaging are not exceptions; but the risk is small, and count-less sailing yachts make coastal cruises and offshore passages each year without anyone being lost or injured. Safety involves pains-taking preparation, seamanlike execution, and above all personal care in every action that is taken, coupled with a strong feeling of the need for self-dependence – in other words, prevention is infinitely better than cure. In my view insufficient emphasis has been placed on this, and far too much attention has been given in recent years to safety and survival equipment, and rescue. I hope that preparation and seamanship have been covered in sufficient detail in earlier chapters, but since unforeseen emergencies may occur, some of the means of avoiding them or dealing with them are outlined here.

Guardrails and harness

Falling or being washed overboard is the greatest risk to which the sailor is exposed. In heavy weather the sense of self-preservation makes most people act on the old maxim 'one hand for yourself and one for the ship', so the risk of going overboard is likely to be greater in moderate weather when a moment's carelessness or a sudden unexpected lurch catching one off guard may send one headlong over the side. Guardrails rigged along each side of the deck greatly reduce the risk, but they must be rugged and strong, capable of being jumped on without ill effect. It is obvious that the height of guardrails must be the same in any size of yacht, yet rails only 46 centimetres (18 inches) high, which are just right for tripping one overboard, are often fitted in small craft. They should never be less than 76 centimetres (30 inches) above the deck. The stanchions are usually made of 29-millimetre ($1\frac{1}{8}$-inch) diameter stainless or alloy tube, the guardrail, preferably of plastic-covered wire, passing through holes at their upper ends. If naked wire is used and it is not of the same material as the stanchions, the holes in the latter should be bushed with short lengths of plastic tube to prevent galvanic action. The wires are best set up taut with rigging screws, and if there is an opening in the guardrail, such as for a gangway or for getting the dinghy aboard, it can be secured with a Senhouse slip, sometimes called a pelican hook (Plate 60*A* and *B*), this is released by knocking or sliding back a small link, and as the slip has the mechanical advantage of a short lever, it will set the guardrail up reasonably tight. Usually a second guardrail is rove through the stanchions half way down to give additional security. When anyone lurches against the guardrail the stanchions exert great leverage on the sockets into which their lower ends are shipped, particularly if the wires are not set up taut; the sockets must therefore be strongly fastened with bolts passing through the covering boards, and if the yacht has bulwarks, the sockets might with advantage be of the type that can be fastened to them as well as to the deck to give additional support. If the deck is of metal the fittings should be of the male type welded to it, and this is the strongest of all methods of attachment. Sockets, stanchions, fastenings, and retaining pins should all be of the same or of compatible metals. It is common practice to rig a weathercloth on the guardrails each side of the cockpit to give some protection there, and very snug they can make it. But I have on one occasion had the stanchions bent a long way inboard when a heavy crest burst against the weathercloth, and on another occasion in a wood yacht the sockets were torn out of the deck. It might therefore be advisable to use marline instead of synthetic line for the lacing or lashings so that it will give way before damage can be done.

Most yachts have a metal railing, known as a pulpit, round the bows at the same height as the guardrails, and to which the latter are secured. If the yacht has a platform or bipod bowsprit it is best to have the pulpit embracing it, and problems with the headsail will not arise provided the headstay is within it and the sail is not cut with too low a foot. A similar railing, to which Jack Laurent Giles gave the name pushpit, usually runs round the stern. If the guardrails are strong people should be able to get about on deck safely provided there are plenty of strong handholds, and that the deck, if not of bare wood, has been made non-slip by non-skid paint, adhesive strips, or other means.

However, it is now common for anyone on deck to wear a safety harness, such as was first devised and made by Peter Haward after one of his crew had been lost overboard. It comprises a set of webbing straps embracing chest and shoulders, with a lanyard having a carbine hook at its end to be attached temporarily to any strong point, and if the wearer should fall overboard he will be towed right way up. But to have to shift the carbine hook from place to place as the harness-wearer moves about the deck defeats the object; therefore it is common practice to arrange a taut rope along each side of the deck for the yacht's full length, so that a crew member can clip on before leaving the security of the cockpit, and remain secure as he moves about; but a harness takes time to put on and hampers free movement. It is as well for a helmsman standing a night watch to take a turn with a rope's end round himself and belay it to windward, or to wear a clipped-on harness, to prevent him falling or being thrown to leeward if he should doze. A single-hander needs to be particularly careful at all times, for if he should go overboard there will be no hope of rescue, and even if he is wearing a clipped-on harness he may well find it impossible to climb back on board.

Lifebuoys

There should be within the helmsman's reach a lifebuoy carried in such a manner that it can instantly be thrown to a person who has gone overboard. It might lie in chocks on hatch or coachroof, or hang in a canvas pocket on the guardrail, but it must not be lashed as delay in releasing it could be fatal. Usually such buoys are made of cellular plastic covered in nylon or terylene, and bright orange is the best colour. If the buoy is circular, the inside diameter should be not less than 61 centimetres (24 inches), but the horseshoe shape is much to be preferred, when the opening should be not less than 30 centimetres (1 foot) across; with this a man can get his chest within and his arms over it so that he floats high. But at sea something in addition to this is required, for the man overboard with his low height of eye cannot readily see the lifebuoy lying awash unless it is close to him, and in anything of a seaway those on board will have difficulty in keeping his head (or the buoy) in view. Therefore many yachts carry a danbuoy, which consists of a bamboo or alloy pole 3·6 metres (12 feet) or so in length with a weight at its lower end, a plastic buoy on its axis, and a large orange flag at its top (Plate 60C). This is secured with a short length of line to a lifebuoy, and both are thrown overboard together, when the flag will more clearly indicate the position. Such buoys are mandatory for ocean racing, but a point sometimes overlooked is that the buoy, with the lifebuoy in tow, may blow down wind faster than one can swim, so unless it can be let go up wind of the man overboard it may, unless provided with some form of sea-anchor, be of no value, and the yacht heading back to the flag will find that the lost man has failed to reach it. Even if buoy and man have made contact neither can be seen at night unless one or the other can show a light. Lights available for this purpose are of two kinds. One contains dry cells and a gravity-actuated switch; when on board it is hung upside down, but it is so ballasted that when it is in the water it floats right way up and the light comes on. The other type derives its current from a water-activated cell, and lights up when submerged. The former has the merit that its condition can be ascertained at any time by turning it right way up for a moment. With this set-up we have three things to throw overboard: danbuoy, lifebuoy, and light, and if we add, as some do, a sea-anchor, shark-repellent, and a whistle, the chance of a tangle becomes almost a certainty. Many therefore consider that it is wise for every crew member to wear a lifejacket with light and whistle permanently attached; I do not agree because this is too restrictive of movement, and psychologically it is the wrong approach. The all-important thing is to hold on tight and *never* fall overboard.

Man overboard

This is a fearful situation which calls for immediate and faultless action, for the man's life will depend on the skill and judgement of the helmsman. A lifebuoy should be thrown to him instantly, all hands should be called, and one of them detailed to watch the lost man (or the lifebuoy light), pointing constantly to him with outstretched arm, and never for a moment letting him out of sight no matter what may happen on board. At night disorientation, the bewilderment caused by change of wind and course, on the part of

---

PLATE 59 (*facing*). A liferaft inflating itself. As this was being done ashore for inspection and maintenance, the raft had first been removed from its GRP canister to avoid risk of damage to the latter when the CO_2 was released.

PLATE 60 (*overleaf*). A. A guardrail at the gangway can most conveniently be secured with a Senhouse slip. B. It is instantly released by knocking back the small link. C. A dan buoy secured to a lifebuoy, but it may blow to leeward faster than a man overboard can swim. D. A burgee sewn to a piece of stiff wire which is free to rotate on the stick; the halyard is made fast with two clove hitches. E. A windsock at the masthead is cheaper and lasts longer than a flag and gives a steadier indication of wind direction.

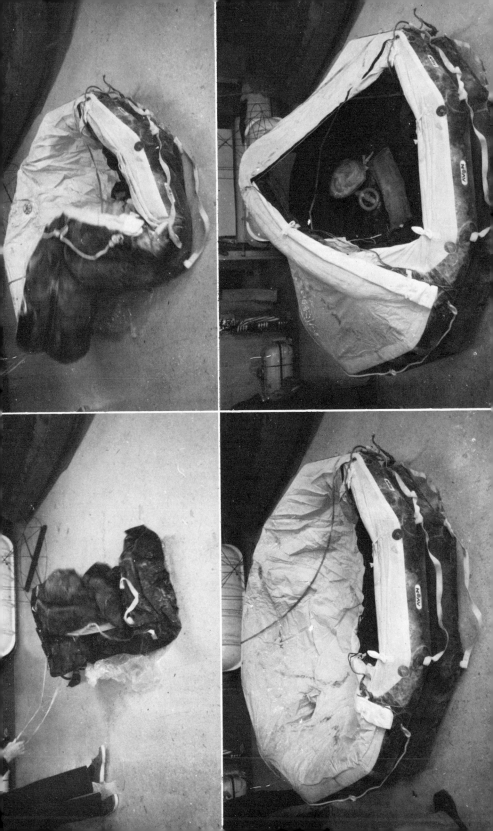

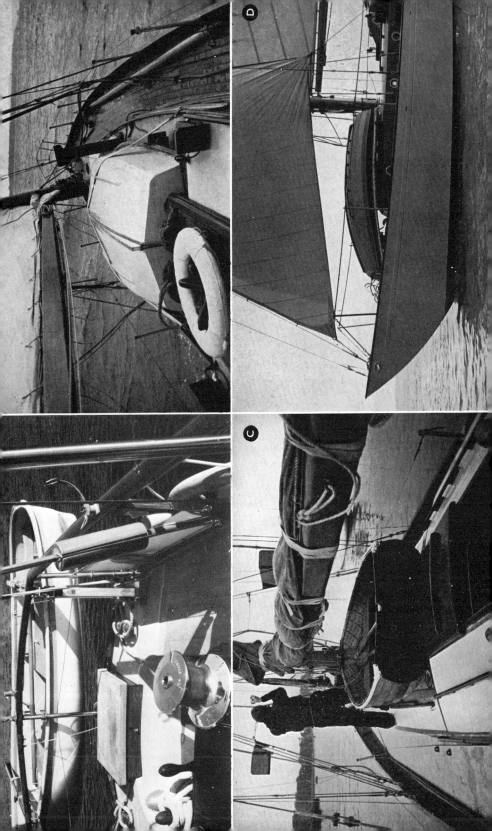

those roused from sleep, is likely to be a hazard. No attempt at rescue by small dinghy should be made.

Most of us have been taught that the yacht must be gybed, so as to reach the man in the shortest possible time no matter what point of sailing she is on, but there are exceptions. If she has the wind abeam or forward of the beam she should be gybed at once, for luffing will take her to windward of the man and waste time. With the wind on the quarter, one has the choice of gybing and coming round to the man in a circle as before, or bearing away, then tacking and bearing away again a little before shooting up head to wind. By gybing we will reach him in the shortest time, but we will have to decide whether it is safe to gybe all-standing in the conditions then prevailing, for there may be no time to get in the sheet and set up the runner, and damage to the gear at such a moment could be disastrous. But if the yacht is running dead there is nothing to be gained by gybing, and therefore no point in risking damage; the man will be reached just as quickly by luffing and tacking. Indeed, some maintain that it is never right to gybe, and that no matter what point of sailing she is on the yacht should at once be put on a reach with the apparent wind abeam, then tacked, and reached back.

If the yacht has an engine that can be quickly started and has power enough to drive her against whatever wind and sea there may be, one may decide to manœuvre under power, but if sail is then taken in one must remember that any sheets or other ropes left trailing overside in the emergency are likely to foul the propeller and put the engine out of action; also that a turning propeller is lethal to anyone in the water near it.

Ideally we would pick our man up while stopped and head to

PLATE 61 (*overleaf*). A rigid dinghy ought not to be towed except perhaps for short distances in sheltered water, for she will cause considerable drag and there is risk of her being lost. In a yacht of 12 metres (40 feet) or more she might be carried in davits over the stern *A*, though this could rule out the use of a wind-vane gear. On deck amidships is usually the best place, either capsized *B* or right way up *C*. If there is not room there the foredeck may be the only alternative *D*, but there the dinghy will obstruct the forehatch and be much in the way when sails or ground tackle are being handled.

PLATE 62 (*facing*). *A*. A derrick with tackle being used to hoist a heavy dinghy aboard. The bilge keels of this dinghy are made in the form of handrails. *B*. A light dinghy, such as this 2·1 metre (7-foot) alloy pram, needs no derrick and can easily be held clear of the side while being lifted with the main halyard. *C*. The Duckling dinghy, with her round and buoyant bows, makes a fine sailing tender to a yacht large enough to carry her. With sliding gunter rig the spars are short enough to stow inboard. *D*. A GRP dinghy, also with gunter rig, and with built-in buoyancy.

wind, but once she has lost headway the yacht will not remain like that, so we must decide whether we are going to pick him up over the windward or the leeward side. If we decide on the windward side and fail to get him at the first attempt, time will be lost while we gather way and try again. The lee side has the advantage that we will drift down on him, and that side may be the lower; but if we do not get him aboard smartly the yacht may drift over him, sinking him, and/or causing injury. I believe we should make our choice in this matter in advance of the event, and stick to it, so that we have a clear action in mind.

Getting the man back on board will probably prove to be the most difficult part of the whole affair. Most yachts carry an accommodation (or boarding) ladder, often provided with one or more steps below the waterline for convenience when bathing; if the man is in good heart and is uninjured, he may be able, with assistance from on deck, for his waterlogged clothes will much increase his weight, to climb up this, or a couple of bowlines to act as steps might be arranged. But if he is in a weak state some other means of recovering him will have to be organized. Many have been suggested, but I believe the most likely to succeed, and without doing serious injury, is as follows. Hank the luff of the smallest headsail to the guardrail on the chosen rescue side, and bend a halyard to its clew and let it go overboard. Get the man into the bunt of the sail, even if someone has to go into the water to assist. Then, by hauling on the halyard which can be taken to a winch, it should be possible to parbuckle him up and inboard. In cold water speed of rescue is important if hypothermia (lowered deep-body temperature which can result in death) is to be avoided. An average adult male in clothes but without flotation, and if holding still (not swimming) may survive in water at 10 °C (50 °F) for $1\frac{1}{2}$–2 hours; a woman or a child does not last so long. The yacht is unlikely to have electric blankets or other quick means for heating someone suffering from hypothermia, so the patient should be stripped of wet clothes and tucked into a bunk under blankets with a naked crew member in the closest embrace.

Fire

Before the use of petrol (gasoline) and liquid petroleum gas became common, the risk of fire or explosion aboard yachts was small, a flare-up of a paraffin pressure stove being the worst situation that was likely to arise. The precautions to be taken with gas have been described on page 48, but it is not always realized that a cupful of petrol spilt in the bilge has the same potential explosive power as 2·2 kilograms (5 pounds) of dynamite; the vapour formed by evaporation of petrol is heavier than air. Every precaution should therefore be taken to prevent leakage of fuel from carburettor, taps, and faulty unions, and when filling the tank. A high-sided drip-tray covered with wire gauze should be fitted beneath the carburettor, and a second much larger tray with a well at its lower end from which oil or fuel can be removed by a sponge or a syringe, be fitted beneath any type of engine. The filler for the tank and the air-vent should be on deck, and a gravity feed tank must have an *accessible* shut-off cock. There is not so much risk of fire from diesel fuel as it does not vapourize at low temperatures.

Any fire must have three things in order that it may burn: a supply of fuel, oxygen, and sufficient heat; if any one of the three is removed the fire must go out. There are three classes of fire, A, B, and C. A – general combustables, eg wood, paper, clothing. B – inflammable liquids and gasses, eg petrol, paraffin, paint. C – energized electrical equipment.

Water in sufficient quantity is effective on class A fires, and acts by removing heat in the form of steam, but must not be used on class B fires (except in the case of alcohol), for the burning oil will float on the water and spread the fire. Nor should it be used on class C fires, but they should only be of concern if high-voltage electricity is involved, when the essential act is to isolate the source to prevent electric shock, after which the fire can be treated as class A.

Most fire extinguishers act by blanketing and denying the fire the oxygen it needs; the contents of the extinguisher should therefore be aimed not at the flames but at the base of the fire. The most suitable type for general use aboard a yacht is the kind in which dry chemical powder (similar to baking soda) is held under pressure, or is pressurized at the moment of use by the puncturing of a small internal cylinder of carbon dioxide (CO_2); the powder comes out of the nozzle as a fine, white fog. This is excellent for class B and C fires, but is not suitable for deep-seated class A fires, such as among sails or in upholstery, for which water is preferable. Extinguishers of the above type, holding about 1·3 kilograms (3 pounds) of powder, and having a minimum discharge time of about 10 seconds, are the best sort to have; but since the powder may consolidate (tapping the container occasionally with a block of wood may prevent this), or the container lose pressure (some have a gauge to show the pressure) it is wise to have it recharged about once a year. Powder extinguishers should not be exposed to temperatures exceeding 60 °C (140 °F) and therefore ought not to be kept close to a cooking-stove or cabin-heater.

Carbon dioxide, which is not toxic but does not support life, is very effective in cooling and smothering all classes of fire, but only in confined places; however, the container is heavy, and the operator should be prepared for the loud noise made during discharge. The halogenated agents, such as carbon tetrachloride, are highly effective, but are so toxic as to be extremely dangerous to life if used in a confined space. A small fire might be smothered with a towel or blanket.

The rules for fire-fighting are: don't delay for a moment, get close, and aim low.

A medical note

Advice and instruction for tending the sick or injured at sea when medical help cannot be had, is too large, complex, and controversial a subject to be included in a book such as this; but it does appear that people who cruise or voyage are in general a healthy lot, perhaps more subject to injury than illness.

Nevertheless it should be remembered that a voyaging yacht and her people must be prepared to rely on their own resources for everything once the land has been dropped; even though the yacht may have ship/shore radio (and many have not) she may still be out of touch, and the 'call the doctor' philosophy of most medical books and articles is unhelpful.

So the skipper or a member of the crew should familiarize himself with first aid, and make himself responsible for the medical stores and their use; he would be well advised before leaving to discuss with a doctor the medical requirements, and obtain prescriptions where needed together with a covering note from the doctor stating why drugs are being carried, otherwise difficulties may arise with port officials.

The yacht's library should include one or other (more than one may confuse the neophyte) of the following books: *Reed's Nautical Almanac*, in which there are some useful and practical first aid notes; the *Red Cross First Aid Manual*; *First Aid for the Yachtsman* by Haworth (Adlard Coles). The American yachtsman will probably do best with *The Ship's Medicine Chest and Medical Aid at Sea*, which is obtainable either from The Superintendent of Documents, US Government Printing Office, Washington DC 20402, or from the

Government Printing Office, 194 Federal Building, 915 Second Avenue, Seattle, Washington 98174.

My friend Don Boots, an American doctor, who, with his wife and family, made a splendid circumnavigation in their 14-metre (46-foot) sloop *Spencerian*, while in New Zealand wrote some medical notes for the benefit of fellow voyagers, and I quote here his final sentences: 'In the treatment of illness and injury at sea, do what you can to make the patient comfortable in a position of safety. Treat what appears you must. Be patient and have faith . . . the body will generally heal itself.'

Abandoning ship

The decision to abandon a badly damaged or leaking ship has occasionally been made too readily, and there are instances of yachts, abandoned in a panic, being found still afloat many days later and towed into port. While she remains afloat, even though almost waterlogged, the yacht will provide some measure of shelter and security for her people, and she will offer a much better target for a rescuing ship or a searching plane than will a liferaft or dinghy. It takes a lot of water to sink a yacht, and pluck and determination, instead of hurried abandoning, may succeed in stemming the inrush of water so that bailing or pumping may keep the level down. There are many fine examples of this, among which that of single-handed Bill King in *Galway Blazer II* is outstanding. The 12·8-metre (42-foot), cold-moulded mahogany yacht was holed by some large creature, probably a great white shark, when 200 miles SSW of Cape Leeuwin, the SW extremity of Australia. Bill immediately put the yacht on the other tack so as to raise the damaged area above the water. Between bouts of pumping he managed to stuff the hole from inboard with sponge rubber and towels, fothered the wound with part of a sail, and fitted shores, wedges, and lashings within. The repair took several days, during which *Galway Blazer* made a lot of unwanted southing, for the wind was force 5, and sail had to be kept on her to keep her heeled; but when the job had been completed she was put about and sailed 600 miles to Fremantle, and eventually completed her circumnavigation.

This incident brings to mind the widely discussed question of the risk of damage being inflicted by whales, a subject which gained much publicity through the books written by Dougal Robertson and the Baileys, though it appears from the latter that the mortal blow that sank *Auralyn* in 50 minutes was inflicted by a whale which had been badly injured. On our voyages my wife and I have on numerous occasions fallen in with whales of various kinds, including sperm whales and killers. Often they were curious, but never belligerent; no doubt these mammals are highly intelligent, and the thought of meeting them does not seriously worry us. Nevertheless, there could be some risk of colliding with a sleeping whale by night, as happened to Peter and Ann Pye in *Moonraker*, but surely the chance of striking a waterlogged container, a balk of timber, or some other object lost or thrown overboard from a ship is much greater. Of other creatures we feel less sure, for *Wanderer III* was once attacked by a spearfish in the Atlantic doldrums, and such attacks were not uncommon in the days of wooden ships. It may be of interest to note that in the Tasman Sea three yachts recently damaged or sunk by whales [*sic*] were of the short keel, separate skeg and rudder configuration; whether this was pure chance, or whether that shape has sex appeal or just makes a convenient scratching place, who can tell?

Many yachts carry liferafts. By means of an internal cylinder of CO_2 all inflate themselves (including the canopy) automatically (Plate 59) when, on being thrown overboard the painter/inflating line is jerked. There are several makes, and they may be contained in GRP canisters or in valises; the former may be stowed on deck, but the latter should be protected from the weather in a readily accessible deck or cockpit locker. A 4-man raft is the smallest size made; in its canister it weighs about 31 kilograms (70 pounds), and when inflated has an outside diameter of 1·8 metres (6 feet). Some makers offer as an extra a double inflatable floor to provide insulation, and this would seem to be highly desirable. Contained within the raft are paddles, bailer, sea-anchor, knife, torch, flares, etc; but an emergency pack can also be included; this might have a little water and food, fishing tackle, first-aid kit, etc. But unless one can expect to reach land or be rescued quickly, additional equipment will be needed, and most voyaging people therefore keep a 'grab bag' in a handy place, as well as some plastic water containers ready but not quite full so that they will float on being tossed overboard. The bag might contain extra clothing (protection against the sun may be just as important as protection against cold and wet), additional first-aid materials including sunburn cream and seasick pills (most people suffer from motion sickness in a raft), sun glasses, foghorn and mirror, extra rockets and flares, more food, automatic distress transmitting radio, and perhaps a sextant and tables, though these last may be only of psychological value, since a raft cannot be propelled for more than a very short distance, and that with difficulty.

It would appear from the experience of survivors that the yacht's dinghy complete with oars and rowlocks should be taken along too, with buckets tied to it for bailing; indeed, without its help some people would never have survived, for any kind of dinghy is more robust than a raft, which has to be of thin material so that it can be stowed away in a small space. If survival in raft or dinghy is to be taken seriously for more than just a few hours, the owner must give the matter some careful consideration, and to gain an idea of what may be involved he could not do better than study Dougal Robertson's *Survive the Savage Sea* (Penguin), and Maurice and Maralyn Bailey's *117 Days Adrift* (W H Allen). The books make sobering reading, and I think the most important matter to emerge from both is a need for the will to survive. It is said that if one can endure the first 48 hours of being cast adrift there is a strong chance of survival, no matter how long eventual rescue may take.

As the fabric of the liferaft can become weak or perished, perhaps due to corrosion of torch batteries or CO_2 cylinder, the raft should be serviced once a year. This is expensive, and operators of integrity (sometimes at an airport) are not to be found everywhere; it is said that an owner can undertake the job himself, but he will need a new, filled gas cylinder, repair materials, proper adhesive for re-sealing the canisters, French chalk, and probably the use of a vacuum cleaner for removing all the CO_2 before the raft can be folded and repacked. Demonstrations of liferaft inflation, sometimes given at boat shows, are of considerable value.

25

THE DINGHY

THE dinghy is an essential item of equipment, her main function being to act as ferry between the yacht and the shore, but except with a large yacht she is bound to be a compromise, for she should be large enough to carry the complete crew safely in moderately sheltered water, and strong enough to hold her own when lying in the huddle of craft which crowd the landing places at every yachting centre; yet she should be light enough to carry or pull up or down a beach and small enough to stow on deck.

Types of dinghy

Dinghies may be rigid or inflatable. Of the former there are three main types: those with pointed or rounded bows and transom sterns; prams, which have transoms at both ends; and flatties, which may have ends of either shape, but have flat bottoms and hard chines. Of these the dinghy with a pointed or rounded bow is the most pleasant to row, but size for size is usually the heavier and more expensive. The pram is a good weight-carrier and is lighter and cheaper, but is inclined to be wet in a headsea because of the spray thrown up by the forward transom. Any dinghy should have a flat floor, ie the bottom should not rise from the keel at an angle, but should be horizontal until the turn of the bilge commences (Fig 99). Such a section makes a boat stiff, while a round or barrel section makes her crank. It is here that the flattie scores, for it has great stability; it is also easier for the amateur to build, but has little grip on the water and is difficult to row straight unless provided with a skeg.

Round-bilge wood dinghies may be of clinker or carvel construction, or of moulded ply. The former is the heavier but is easier to build, while the lands (the exposed overlapping edges of the planks) provide a little extra buoyancy. Dinghies may also be built of alloy, but the most widely used material today is GRP; neither requires much maintenance and both are lighter, strength for strength, than those built of wood.

With any dinghy, except one of alloy, bilge keels will be needed to protect the skin when being dragged up or down a beach; they are usually in the form of narrow strips of hardwood, but can with advantage be made in the form of grab-rails (Plate 62A), which will be found convenient when the dinghy is capsized on deck, but increase drag when the dinghy is under way. Buoyancy bags or blocks, secured to the rising, one or more each side, or fastened beneath the thwarts, enable a waterlogged wood dinghy to float a little higher and be baled out; for a metal or GRP dinghy they are essential, otherwise the dinghy will sink if it fills.

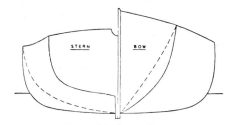

Fig 99 Dinghy sections
The pecked lines show weak sections which will make a dinghy crank.

Except in smooth water a 2-metre (7-foot) dinghy is the smallest that can carry two people, but one of 2·4 or 2·7 metres (8 or 9 feet) is much to be preferred. Sometimes a very small dinghy has a fore-and-aft seat instead of thwarts so that the oarsman may correct the trim according to the weight of his load by shifting his own weight, but this weakens a dinghy to some extent.

Rowlocks should have lanyards spliced round their necks (not through the holes at their lower ends), and hitched to the rising or thwarts; one pair of rowlocks can then be used in any of the alternative rowing positions. Self-stowing rowlocks have the advantage that they cannot be lost or stolen, but a separate pair will have to be provided for each rowing position, and means provided (possibly pieces of elastic) to hold them in the out-of-action position when the dinghy is to be capsized. A notch in the transom, or a socket there to take a rowlock, is essential so that the dinghy can be sculled, or a kedge cable underrun. The gunwale of a rigid dinghy will need to be fitted with a fender to prevent damage to the yacht's topsides, or to the dinghy itself when left alongside a quay or among other boats. Rubber fendering of several types can be had, but if this is not available a length of rope seized at 61-centimetre (2-foot) intervals to the gunwale, and resting on a narrow wood ledge, will serve.

Oars ought to be as long as possible, provided they will lie within the dinghy when not in use, and they need to be well balanced otherwise the oarsman will have to bear down heavily on their looms when feathering, which is tiring and wasteful of energy. Where an oar ships in its rowlock it is customary to protect it with leather tacked on, but plastic is frequently used now and is often incorporated with an 'up river' button, a protrusion to hold the oar from slipping outboard.

The inflatable dinghy, such as the Avon, made of tough rubberized fabric, and inflated by a foot pump or, in an emergency, by a bottle of CO_2, has achieved great popularity; this is chiefly because of its light weight, which enables it to be carried up the shore or taken aboard with ease, and if space on deck is limited it can be partly or entirely deflated. It is stiff, buoyant, and seaworthy, but is not a pleasure to row, and in a fresh headwind calls for an outboard motor if satisfactory progress is to be made; also it is liable to be blown upside down in a gale if it has no load aboard. Usually the rowlocks are of rubber permanently attached; burden boards, which I regard as highly desirable, are provided as an extra as, usually, is a bracket for an outboard; no fender is required.

Towing and stowing (Plate 61)

Except for short distances in smooth water it is not wise to tow a rigid dinghy, for it will reduce the speed of the yacht, especially when turning to windward, and there will be some risk of the dinghy filling or being lost. Every effort should therefore be made to stow the dinghy on deck, but if it must be towed the tow-rope should be secured to a ring or eye low down on the bow. Drag can be slightly reduced by having the rope of such a length that the dinghy rides on the advancing face of one of the yacht's stern waves, but with a following sea it may be necessary to veer at least 27 metres (15 fathoms) or the dinghy may run up and ram the yacht. This tendency might be checked by towing a length of rope from the dinghy's stern, but of course this will increase the drag. To prevent an inflatable dinghy from capsizing while under tow, the bow can be lifted and secured on the yacht's stern.

The best position for the rigid dinghy on board is amidships, even though a skylight may then be covered and the saloon made dark. I favour a capsized attitude, but if carried right side up the dinghy must be provided with a drain, the bung being left out, otherwise rain or spray will accumulate. Where the presence of a doghouse or other obstruction precludes the amidships position, the dinghy is sometimes carried on the foredeck; but here it is much in the way when sails are to be handled or anchor work be done, and probably the forehatch will be obstructed. Rigid dinghies are therefore being increasingly carried in davits over the stern, a position which has a lot to recommend it in a large yacht, the lifting and lowering being done easily with tackles or small winches, but in a small yacht the extra windage right aft may make steering difficult in strong quartering winds, and the dinghy will have to be short or there will be a risk of its bow or stern touching the water when the yacht is heeled. A disadvantage of the arrangement is that a wind-vane steering gear cannot normally be used.

A light dinghy can be hauled aboard bows first over the rail, which should be protected by a brass strip or wood shoe 0·6 metre (2 feet) long, but of course the guardrails must first be disconnected at that point. I prefer to use a masthead halyard to lift the dinghy up and over the guardrails, the painter having been made fast at bow and stern to make a sling and the halyard secured to it at the point of balance (Plate 62B); but a second hand is needed to bear out on the dinghy to keep it clear of the side, and to help capsize it on deck. For a big or heavy dinghy I think the best thing to use is a short spar rigged from mast or rail as a derrick, a halyard serving as topping lift, with a tackle of sufficient power at the spar's outer end (Plate 62A). To turn a heavy dinghy over without injury to deck fittings is not easy, and I would stow it right way up.

Handling

Much pleasure can be had from skilful dinghy handling, and although this can only be acquired by practice, a few hints for the beginner might not be out of place here. Before setting off make sure there is a bailer aboard, and bail out if necessary, for no boat will handle well if there is water in her, and if there is much she will be unstable; bailing can often be done most conveniently from the bow. A shammy-leather or sponge-cloth is excellent for wiping dry the thwarts. See that the painter is made fast forward, and is coiled down with its end on top within reach, and that there is an anchor aboard – a four-arm grapnel is convenient, for it can be folded flat on withdrawing a pin from the shank, but a CQR has much greater holding power. There should also be a stern-line for use when making fast fore-and-aft, for slinging the kedge anchor if it has to be laid out, for towing, and to act as a safety line for an outboard motor in the event of one being used.

When rowing do not attempt to take long 'up-river' strokes, for if the water is rough you may catch a crab, ie fail to reach the water with the blades of your oars and fall over backwards; take short, but not jerky, strokes. Feathering (turning the oars on their axies between the strokes so that their blades are parallel to the water) is a natural action of the wrists as the looms (handles) are pushed forward, and by reducing the wind-pressure on the blades, makes rowing easier. But if the blades are not turned quite flat, a strong headwind may lift a light pair of oars out of the rowlocks. Brace your feet firmly against a thwart or stretcher (an athwartships bar fixed to the burden boards) or you will be unable to put much weight on the oars. Unless you have a passenger who will guide you by word or an inclination of the head, keep a good lookout over your shoulder, and by watching a shore mark seen over the stern, or the rows of oar puddles left in the dinghy's wake, try to steer a straight course. When rowing against the tide, keep close to the shore as the stream is usually slacker there and you may even find a favourable eddy to help you; but avoid very shallow water or progress will be retarded by suction.

When going alongside a yacht which is free to swing head to wind or tide, you should do so in such a way that when the dinghy has lost way she will be pointing in the same direction as the yacht (Plate 63). Steer as though to hit the yacht a little abaft amidships (or abaft the accommodation ladder if one is rigged) and at an angle of about 45°. Then when you have reached a position such that the dinghy will carry her way for the rest of the distance, stop rowing and unship the oar which is nearest to the yacht. If you have a passenger in the sternsheets, place the oar with its blade forward to avoid wetting him or the thwart on which he is sitting; unless the oar is heavy this can be done by bearing sharply down on the loom, which will cause it to jump out of the rowlock; a turn of the wrist will then toss it inboard (this cannot be done with the rubber rowlocks fitted to most inflatable dinghies, when the oar must be pulled free); when shipping an oar with its blade forward allow yourself plenty of room or the blade may strike the yacht's side. Just before the dinghy reaches the yacht, backwater with the other oar, ie put its blade in the water and hold or push the loom; the oar blade will then act as a brake and the dinghy will slew round, and if you have judged correctly will bring up neatly alongside with all way lost. Unship the other oar, unship both rowlocks, and hold on while your passenger disembarks, then get aboard the yacht, stream the dinghy astern of her, and make fast the painter. Should the yacht be moored fore-and-aft, go along-side bows to tide. If an accommodation ladder is rigged, the traditional position for it is on the starboard side.

When going alongside in a dinghy driven by an outboard motor a modification has to be made to the above procedure. The majority of outboards used with dinghies are not provided with clutches or astern gears, and steering is achieved by swivelling the motor together with its propeller, so as soon as the motor is stopped one has no directional control. Therefore when under power you must not approach the yacht or the landing at an angle, but must go alongside parallel to, and very close to, the yacht or landing, so that after the motor has been stopped and the dinghy has lost way, a hand may be put out to hold her. Incidentally, if you have no passenger or other load, your weight and that of the motor at the stern will put the dinghy down by the stern and she will not go well. An extension to the tiller (a piece of a broom handle serves well) permitting you to sit amidships will greatly improve matters.

When the wind and the tide are opposed, a dinghy lying astern and having little grip on the water will often blow up over the tide and bump her parent ship, causing some irritation, especially at night. The best way of preventing this is to take her aboard; alternatively the spinnaker boom may be rigged out on the beam, and the dinghy's bows hauled out to the end of it, a line being taken from her stern to the yacht's quarter; but if there is any sea, the dinghy will snatch and jerk on her lines, just as she will if she is secured alongside. A bucket on a short lanyard, secured not to the dinghy's stern but to her painter close to the bow, will prevent bumping to some extent, for the tide will get a grip on the bucket and hold the dinghy off so that only her stern can blow round.

When leaving a dinghy at a landing place used by others, put her on a long painter so that she can be pushed out of the way when other people wish to land, otherwise they will have to scramble through her; and make sure the oars are properly stowed inboard, and that the rowlocks (if removable) are un-shipped, so that there is nothing that the painters of other craft can foul.

If a dinghy which is too heavy to be carried down a hard that runs across soft mud, much wear and tear will be avoided if she is launched into the mud and dragged down that; but so that her bows shall not be pulled into the hard, make fast the painter to a thwart or other fitting nearly amidships, and she should then slide parallel to the hard. An inflatable should be carried, not dragged, when ashore or the fabric may get cut by sharp objects.

Fig 100 *A* and *B* shows two ways in which a more or less permanent outhaul might be rigged at the home port. The hypotenuse mooring, shown at *C* in the figure, is sometimes useful when landing at steps where the dinghy is to be left without inconveniencing others who may wish to use the landing. It can also be employed to keep a dinghy afloat off a beach.

To scull is (in the seaman's language) to propel a boat by means of a single oar worked over the stern; this is often convenient for a short trip in a crowded place and may be of value in the event of a rowlock being lost or an oar broken. Thrust the oar into the water at an angle of about $45°$, place it in the half-round sculling notch in the transom and start to scull immediately or the blade will float to the surface. It is easier to start sculling if the dinghy has no headway. Move the handle of the oar from side to side, and your wrists, which should be well under it, will automatically turn the blade through a small angle so that on each stroke it tends to be forced down towards the stern; but the pull of your arms and the grip of the sculling notch will prevent it from doing so and the dinghy will move forward instead, though some of the effort will be wasted in trying to depress the stern. Make the turn from one stroke to the next quickly or the blade will tend to float. It is easier to learn to scull with a long oar in a long boat with a good length of keel.

If there is much surf running, landing on a beach calls for considerable skill and entails some risk to the boat and the people in her. The average yacht's dinghy, short and beamy as she usually is and probably lacking in freeboard, is unsuitable for beach work, so it is wise to avoid exposed beaches except in case of absolute necessity. If the dinghy has a transom stern, she should be turned before reaching the breakers – which from seaward never look so dangerous as they really are – and backed in stern first. She must be kept bows on to the overtaking seas, and in order that they may pass her as quickly as possible, the oarsman should pull away from the shore as each goes by, and then continue backing in until the next one approaches. The tendency of a breaking crest on meeting the end of a boat is to drive it shorewards, but as the other end of the boat is probably in static water, or in water moving the other way, there is some risk of the boat being thrown end over end; if, however, she is allowed to turn at an angle to the crest, she is almost certain to be rolled over on her side. As soon as she touches the bottom her crew should leap out and hold her against the backwash, then on the next sea run her

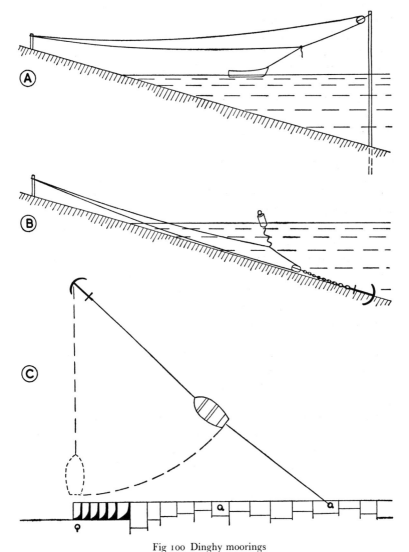

Fig 100 Dinghy moorings

A outhaul with post; *B* outhaul with anchor and buoy; *C* hypotenuse mooring.

right up the beach. A long and able boat with a skilled crew may be able to make a safe landing through heavy surf, or even leave a beach under such conditions, as the old pulling boats of the Royal National Lifeboat Institution have done on countless occasions, but they often made use of a hauling-off line to an anchor laid out beyond the surf.

The sailing dinghy (Plate 62 C and D)

The pleasure of cruising can be much increased if the yacht's dinghy is able to sail, for not only is the ferry work between the yacht and the shore made more entertaining, but sometimes a good anchorage has near-by creeks and backwaters which are well worth exploring.

Many of the standard dinghies on the market are designed for sailing, but almost any dinghy with a length of 2·5 metres (8 feet) or more can be made to sail in some fashion provided she is not inherently tender and has sufficient freeboard, but she will need to be fitted with a leeboard or centreboard to provide the necessary lateral resistance. For lightness and simplicity, a centreboard should be a wooden dagger board, ie one which has no pivot and is shipped vertically into its case, and the case should be provided with a lid to prevent water splashing up when the board is not in use. The rudder also does much to reduce leeway, so it should be of good depth; its lower pintle ought to be a little longer than the upper one so that the rudder may be shipped easily, only one pintle at a time then having to be guided into its gudgeon.

Simplicity and the need to be able to stow the spars within the dinghy are the major points to be kept in mind when planning the rig. If the mast is so tall or so weak as to require more than a single shroud a side for its support, the bother of rigging it will not be considered worthwhile for sailing a short distance, and unless the spars can be stowed within the dinghy they will be vulnerable or a nuisance when she is left among other boats at a pier or quay. If the thwart through which the mast passes, and its step, are strong, a short mast may need no other support, though the fall of the halyard can be taken through a lead at the stem so as to act as a forestay. Because of its short mast the sliding gunter rig (Plate 62 C and D) is particularly suitable, and on the wind it is a little more efficient than the lug. The gear can be very simple and cheap; wooden jaws on the boom, for example, serve quite well as a gooseneck, a tack line from them to a cleat on the mast just below will prevent them from pulling away during a gybe; and a piece of rope passing through a hole in each quarter knee or the gunwale capping, and having a figure-of-eight knot at each end, makes a cheap and satisfactory horse to carry the standing end of the mainsheet over the tiller.

26

FLAGS AND SIGNALS

Ensigns and burgees—Positions for flags—Dressing ship—Visual signalling—Distress sigals

THERE are few regulations regarding the use of flags in yachts, and they mainly concern the wearing of special ensigns. But there are certain customs based on naval practice which many civilians respect, and as some uniformity in the flying of flags is desirable, these customs are described in the following sections together with such of the regulations as apply to yachts. As few things look more slovenly than dirty, faded, or tattered flags, it is worth some trouble and a little expense to ensure they look crisp and bright by washing, repairing, or renewing them when necessary. It is obvious that a tiny yacht does not call for tiny flags, for her flags should be visible and easily read at a considerable distance or they will be of no value.

Ensigns and burgees

All British-owned yachts are classed as merchant vessels, and are therefore entitled to wear the red ensign, which is the flag of the Merchant Service, but if a yacht is to wear a special ensign (see below) she must be registered as a British ship. Any British-owned yacht can be registered no matter how small she may be, and she should be registered if she is going foreign. With a new yacht there is no difficulty; application is made to the Registrar of Shipping at the chosen port of registry, and approval obtained for the name selected, which must not be the same as that of any other ship of British registry; on payment of a fee she will then be measured, her official number and register tonnage will be carved in the main beam or other approved position, and a certificate of registry will be issued; this is evidence of the flag she is entitled to wear, establishes her identity, and is prima facie evidence of ownership. There may be difficulties in getting an old yacht registered unless a builder's certificate is available together with a bill of sale recording each occasion when she changed hands.

The white ensign is worn only by HM ships, and yachts belonging to members of the Royal Yacht Squadron, but the right to use the blue ensign has been granted by the Admiralty to certain yacht clubs; the blue ensign is sometimes defaced by having a club's particular emblem in the fly, and some clubs use the red ensign similarly defaced. A member of one of these privileged clubs may obtain an individual warrant permitting his yacht to wear the special ensign provided the following rules are observed:

The owner must be a British subject and his yacht must be registered as a British vessel. A warrant is obtained through the secretary of the privileged club, and it should be carried aboard at all times; in the event of the yacht changing hands or the owner ceasing to be a member of the club, the warrant must be surrendered. If the owner belongs to two or more privileged clubs, and wishes his yacht to be able to wear the special ensign of any of them, he must obtain a separate warrant through each club. A special ensign may only be worn when the owner is aboard or, although ashore, is near by and in effective control of his yacht, and it must not be worn unless the burgee of the club is flown at the same time. A warrant will not be issued for a houseboat or a yacht used for commercial purposes. The union flag must not be flown afloat except in the royal yacht and ships of the navy, where it is used as a jack, ie at a staff in the bows when at anchor. However, the pilot jack (the union flag with a broad white border) may be flown at the jack staff of a registered yacht in port if the owner wishes, but this is rarely done.

At one time permission to wear a special ensign was regarded as a mark of honour, but so many clubs are now privileged that special ensigns are seen more often than plain red ones, and it is doubtful if they carry with them any special advantage; indeed, in some foreign countries they are not understood, and it may be preferable for a yacht to wear the plain red ensign, which is understood everywhere.

It is the accepted custom for any vessel visiting a foreign port to wear a courtesy ensign, ie a small merchant ensign of that country; in a few countries this is insisted on, and failure to comply may result in a fine being imposed. It should be noted that the merchant ensign is not always the same as the national flag; eg in Britain the visitor should wear the red ensign, not the union flag; in Mexico, Belgium, and Venezuela (to mention only three countries) the merchant ensign does not carry the emblem or coat-of-arms of the national flag, and the Australian and New Zealand merchant ensigns are red, not the blue of the national flags. Incidentally, it has become a custom in some circles, and a pleasant one I think, for a yacht to wear in a string the ensigns of all the countries she has visited on the day she returns to her home port from a cruise or voyage, and perhaps on some other special occasion in the same year, such as the annual meet or rally of the owner's club.

Every yacht club has its own burgee, usually a pennant (triangular flag) bearing a special design, and all members may fly the burgee whether their yachts are registered or not. The senior flag-officer (usually known as the commodore) flies instead of a pennant a flag with two tails (a swallow-tail or broad pennant) bearing the same design; the vice-commodore's flag is similar but has one ball in the upper corner of the hoist; the rear-commodore's flag has two balls.

In addition to the burgee (instead of it when racing) an owner may fly his distinguishing flag. This is nearly always a square flag bearing the owner's special emblem or design.

Positions for flags

A yacht when at anchor or in port should wear the ensign at the ensign staff aft, and it is now agreed that when at sea that also is the correct position, except aboard a gaff-rigged yacht, where the peak of the aftermost gaff (the traditional place) is regarded as the preferable position. If the ketch or yawl cannot carry an ensign staff when under way, because of the mizzen boom and sheet, she may wear the ensign at the mizzen masthead. With the short booms of today the bermudian cutter or sloop can usually carry an ensign staff when under way, but if she cannot, the ensign will have to be worn two-thirds up the leech of the mainsail, which is not an ideal position as the flag will eddy round to leeward of the sail, and it gives the impression of being at half mast. The courtesy ensign should be flown at the main starboard crosstree and hoisted close up to it.

The burgee ought to be flown at the main masthead, but if this is too cluttered with wind-speed and direction sensors and/or a whip aerial, there will be no alternative but to fly it at a crosstree. With a single mast rig the distinguishing flag (if there is one) will also have to go there, but the schooner can carry it at the fore masthead, and the ketch or yawl at the mizzen. One sometimes sees a yacht flying the burgees of two clubs at the same time, but as the foremast, mizzen, and crosstrees are regarded as being inferior positions to the mainmast, and the port crosstree inferior to the starboard one, obviously one of the burgees must be flown in a degraded position. The owner thus has the invidious task of deciding which of his clubs is the senior, and some hard feelings among fellow members will be avoided if he decides to show allegiance only to one club at a time, preferably the local one. However, the Royal Yachting Association and the Royal Cruising Club have partly overcome this difficulty by providing membership flags. These are rectangular, and although each bears the club device it cannot be mistaken for a burgee. Such a flag, flown at a crosstree, indicates to all who may be concerned that the owner is a member of that association or club, but at the moment feels he should fly the burgee of some other club. It is customary for a flag-officer to fly his broad pennant at all times, no matter whether he is a member of the local club or not.

In British and most overseas waters colours should be made, ie ensigns and other flags hoisted, at 0800 from 25 March to 20 September, inclusive, and at 0900 for the rest of the year; they should be lowered at sunset or at 2100, whichever is the earlier. This is a naval custom, and although there is no compulsion for the yachtsman to adhere to it, any keen owner who likes everything to be ship-shape and Bristol fashion will take a pride in attending to this small matter, and will, I think, agree with me that it is very pleasing when all the ensigns in an anchorage go up or come down together, the time being taken from a naval vessel, a yacht club, or the senior flag-officer present. At sea the burgee will probably be kept flying day and night as a wind-vane, though the ensign will only be worn when meeting other vessels, but yachtsmen are divided as to whether or not the burgee should be lowered at sunset in port. In common with many I regard it as a commissioning pennant to be kept flying all the time when on a cruise and when the owner is living aboard. One reason for lowering it is to save wear, but this is of less importance now that flags can be made of a long-lasting mixture of wool and nylon. Flags entirely of nylon are also available but they make an irritating noise.

The ensign (not the burgee) should be dipped as a mark of respect when passing a man-of-war or the yacht of a flag-officer of one's own club. This is done by lowering it slowly two-thirds of the way down from its normal position, keeping it there until the salute has been acknowledged by a similar dip, and then hoisting it close up again. In a naval harbour, or when meeting a squadron or flotilla at sea, one dips only to the senior ship, not to each. On a day of national or private mourning, the ensign is hoisted right up, then lowered to half mast position for the rest of the day, again being hoisted fully up before being lowered for the night.

Makers usually fit a short rope with a wood toggle at the upper end and an eye at the lower end of the hoists of most flags. This serves well for an ensign, for the halyard can have a small eye at one of its ends into which the toggle can be inserted; the other end of the halyard may have a toggle to fit into the loop at the lower end of the flag rope, but is more commonly secured with a sheet bend. A burgee which is to be flown at the masthead should, however, never be secured to the halyard in that manner for it would then be below the truck and get twisted round the mast. It is essential that it be flown above the truck and any gear that clutters the masthead, on a stick of its own; a bamboo cane serves very well. Remove the toggle and rope from the burgee and sew its hoist to a piece of stiff wire; bend each end of the wire over at 90° and form an eye with each, the lower one to be a loose fit round the stick, the upper one to rest on top of the stick which may be fitted with a washer to increase its area and reduce friction; the upper eye is held to the stick with a screw driven not quite home. The wire with the burgee attached will then be free to revolve on the stick, and the burgee will always fly clear. Knot the ends of the halyard together and secure the halyard to the stick by means of two clove hitches (Plate 60D). A metal mast, or one of wood on which the topmast fitting is in the form of a cap, does not have the traditional truck, the function of which is to carry a sheave for a flag halyard and prevent rain entering; but if one is fitted it is better pointed than flat to discourage seagulls from perching on it. On a long passage I prefer to have a wind-sock at the masthead rather than a burgee (Plate 60E), for it gives a steadier indication of wind direction, has a long life, and is cheap to replace. It can be made of thin nylon with its mouth sewn to a ring of light wire with eyes formed in it to fit the burgee stick on which it is free to swivel; the apex end must have a hole for steadying purposes.

Dressing ship

On special occasions, such as the Sovereign's birthday, regattas, etc, yachts which have a set of international code signalling flags (see facing page) may be dressed overall. The flags are strung together in no special order, but are arranged so that the square flags and the pennants are evenly spaced and the colours well contrasted. The flags should extend from stemhead or bowsprit end to the masthead, or all mastheads if the yacht has more than one, then down to the taffrail or boomkin; a pilot jack, if available, is hung beneath the end of the bowsprit. No club burgee, distinguishing flag or ensign should be included in the line, but such flags should be flown in their usual places. In addition, especially if the occasion is a national rather than a local one, an ensign may be worn at each masthead as well as at the ensign staff, but the club burgee should not then be flown above the ensign at the main. When dressing ship abroad the ensign of that country should be at the main masthead. Sailing vessels are not dressed overall when under way; they wear instead on these special occasions an ensign at each masthead. Yachts are dressed at the time colours are made.

Visual signalling

The three methods of visual signalling used at sea are by international code flags, Morse code, and semaphore.

A set of international code flags consists of one for each letter of the alphabet, ten numeral flags, three substitute flags for repeating a letter or number which is to appear more than once in the same hoist, and the answering pennant; 40 in all. *The International Code of Signals* is printed in nine languages, and it includes almost everything of importance that one ship might wish to say to another, each sentence being represented by a different hoist of the code flags; it contains instructions for signalling. Few yachts carry code flags large enough to be of any use except for the purpose of dressing ship; 61 centimetres (24 inches) hoist by 77 centimetres (30 inches) fly is none too large, and the cost of such flags and the stowage space they require is considerable. However, messages in international code may be sent by flashing lamp, using the Morse code for each letter, though it is more usual for words in clear language to be spelt out letter by letter, and this is the form of signalling most likely to be used by yachts.

Figure 101 shows the symbols of the Morse code, and it will be seen that each letter and number is represented by dots and dashes. The length of a dash is equivalent to three dots; the space of time between any two elements of a symbol is equivalent to one dot; between two complete symbols is equivalent to three dots, and between two words or groups is equivalent to seven dots. It is easy to learn to send messages by Morse code, but much practice is needed to read it even if it is being sent very slowly. Morse signals may be sent by sound (foghorn, siren, radio, etc), by flag (moving a flag in a wide sweep for a dash and a short sweep for a dot), or by lamp. The Aldis lamp is the instrument most widely used by day or by night, and the dots and dashes are made not by switching the light on and off but by pulling a trigger which moves a reflector; however, its powerful beam is narrow, and although the lamp is fitted with sights, difficulty will be experienced in

ALPHABET					
A	- —	J	- — — —	S	- - -
B	— - - -	K	— - —	T	—
C	— - — -	L	- — - -	U	- - —
D	— - -	M	— —	V	- - - —
E	-	N	— -	W	- — —
F	- - — -	O	— — —	X	— - - —
G	— — -	P	- — — -	Y	— - — —
H	- - - -	Q	— — - —	Z	— — - -
I	- -	R	- — -	STOP	- - - - - -

NUMERALS			
1	- — — — —	6	— - - - -
2	- - — — —	7	— — - - -
3	- - - — —	8	— — — - -
4	- - - - —	9	— — — — -
5	- - - - -	0	— — — — —

Fig 101   Morse code

keeping it accurately trained when there is much motion. So for short-range signalling by night a masthead light fitted with a Morse key, or even a common torch, may be preferred, but it is useless to attempt to send at high speed with these because of the time taken for the bulb to light up and die out; but that may be no bad thing, for a common fault of the amateur signaller is to try to send too quickly.

A ship or a shore station is called up by flashing AA AA until answered by a series of Ts. The message is then commenced, and as each word of it is received, the receiver will acknowledge it with a single T. If he does not send T, he has not received the word, and it must be repeated. If he sends W instead of T, he means: 'I am unable to read your message owing to your light not being properly trained, or light burning badly'. AR without a break (· — · — ·) indicates that the message has been completed.

Semaphore signals are made by a signalman holding a pair of flags on short poles one in each hand, and forming the letters by positioning the flags; but the range is short and it is rarely used today.

Distress signals

When a vessel is in distress and requires assistance, the following are some of the signals to be used or displayed either separately or together:

Firing of a gun or other explosive at intervals of about one minute.

Rockets or shells throwing red stars fired one at a time at short intervals.

Red flares, or any flames, such as can be made by burning paraffin-soaked clothes.

A smoke signal giving off orange smoke.

The international code signal NC.

The Morse signal SOS (· · · — — — · · ·) made by light, foghorn, whistle, or radio.

A continuous sounding of any fog-signal apparatus.

The distance signal, ie any square flag having either above or below it a ball or anything resembling a ball.

Arms outstretched raised and lowered slowly and repeatedly.

The ensign flown upside down in any conspicuous position.

The best way for a yacht in distress to attract attention to herself by night and probably by day, especially if she has no radio transmitter, is with pyrotechnics. Considerable advances have been made in this field, so that even the smallest of craft can carry in a waterproof container what may in extreme circumstances be the means of saving the lives of her people. The signal which may be seen from the greatest distance is the parachute flare, the cylindrical container of which may measure as little as 25 centimetres (10 inches) by 5 centimetres (2 inches). With this a rocket sends a red flare to a height in excess of 304 metres (1,000 feet), where it is ejected and falls slowly for about 40 seconds, suspended by a parachute. This is visible up to 35 miles on a clear night, or 6 or 7 miles by day, and is for use when land or assistance is out of sight. Obviously such a flare will be of no use when there is low cloud; then, or if help is within sight, a red star signal, which throws red stars to a height of about 61 metres (200 feet), should be used. When help is nearby, hand-held red flares or orange smoke signals can be used to indicate one's position. It should be remembered that red is the colour for distress, while white or green is intended only for drawing attention to oneself if, for example, there is grave risk of collision. There are other means of indicating distress, such as the Verey pistol and the Miniflare, which shoot cartridges, but a firearms certificate is required for either.

If pyrotechnics are kept dry they should work properly for at least three years after their date of manufacture, which is usually stamped on them. After that they will work, and without risk to the operator, but with reduced efficiency, and should then be replaced with new. As different makes may have different firing instructions, and as one cannot read the small print in the dark, it would be wise to get familiar with them, and occasionally when in a place where it could not possibly be mistaken for a call for assistance, fire one just to find out how it does work; but to avoid burning oneself or the ship, fire it from the leeward side, and be prepared for burning dross falling out on deck or feet.

For fog signals see page 277; for storm signals see page 387.

27

MAINTENANCE

In the past it was customary for yachts to be laid up for the winter either ashore or in mud-berths, with masts removed and decks and topsides protected from the weather by covers rigged on strongbacks; this gave wood yachts a chance to dry out and made fitting out easier. But now that so many yachts are built of GRP and have alloy masts and stainless steel rigging, and the use of safe and convenient marinas has become widespread, an increasing number of owners keep their yachts afloat right through the year; some even keep them permanently in commission to enjoy the peace of uncrowded winter anchorages, and with a cabin heater installed winter cruising can at times be very pleasant, and the sense of snug content heightened.

The remarks that follow are not intended to cover the wide subject of maintenance, but it is hoped that some of the points touched on may serve as reminders or suggestions.

It is often thought that a GRP yacht will come to no harm if kept permanently afloat, but apparently this is not so. There have been many cases of osmosis, a blistering of the gel coat caused by water permeating it until eventually the blisters burst, and if this is not attended to delamination of the glass fibre can occur. It is suggested that osmosis is less likely if the yacht is taken out of the water from time to time, or is allowed to dry out between tides. If a hard beach is available, and provided the yacht has a sufficient length of straight keel, it might be arranged for her to stand there on legs during the winter, being moored all-fours, ie with a line from each bow to the shore, and an anchor out on each quarter. A simple arrangement for legs is to have two steel tubes or ballasted balks of timber fitted with wood feet at their lower ends, each being somewhat longer than the distance from the ground to the deck in way of the main rigging; the upper end of each leg is fitted with a luff tackle, the lower block being secured to a chain-plate or other strong point at the yacht's side. The tackles can be adjusted when the yacht first takes the ground so that she stands upright with all her weight resting on the keel, and of course each leg must be held firmly in a vertical position with guys fore and aft. If the yacht is to be taken right out of the water a boatyard will probably be employed to haul her out on a railway, and then with skids and jacks strike her over, ie move her off the rails so that others may use them. This can be an expensive operation, it does the yacht no good, and one may not be able to have her launched when desired as others may be in the way. In my view it is better to use a yard which has a travel-lift. This straddles a berth into which the yacht is brought, two straps are passed beneath her, and with these the lift raises her out of the water, and under its own power transports her to her winter resting place and lowers her there. This is quick and convenient. Unless a yacht has all inside ballast, which would first have to be removed, she cannot be careened (hove down on to her beam ends while afloat), so one or other of the above three methods may have to be used at other times when the yacht's bottom needs scrubbing and antifouling, unless there is a scrubbing berth handy. This may comprise a pier or wall against which to lean as the tide falls, or in some places stout piles are provided against which to lean, and bearers for the keel to stand on. But before using such a berth it should be examined at low water to make sure that the bearers are long enough if the yacht has considerable beam, and closely enough spaced so that at least two of them will take the keel if this is short; also the tides should be considered to avoid getting neaped.

There have been instances of yachts left on moorings during a cold spell being damaged (some were sunk) by a sheet of thin ice moving on the tide. If this risk seems likely, a plank or hurdle should be secured on each bow in way of the boot-top to part and deflect the ice.

With stainless rigging I would leave the mast standing, but would unreeve the running rigging, and I would only unstep one of wood if it was in need of scraping before painting or varnishing, and if there is any brightwork (varnished wood) on deck I would endeavour to cover as much of it as possible to protect it from rain and frost. I would take ashore bedding, books, and anything likely to suffer from damp, such as electronic equipment, and unless I planned to run the engine frequently I would protect it with inhibiting oil, drain off the cooling water (from the heads, too) and take the battery ashore for periodic charging.

It is said with some truth that successful fitting out begins with efficient laying up. So it is wise to clean the yacht thoroughly, including all lockers and the bilge, clean and lubricate all moving parts, and attend to any alterations, additions, or repairs before the rush of spring work starts. And when fitting out does begin I find it best to start at the top, ie with mast and rigging, and then to attend to the deck before working on the topsides; the final job will be to antifoul the bottom.

It takes some practice to become a good painter able to produce a gleaming surface free from brush marks, but no painter can do a good job unless the surface is well prepared, and it is this that takes much time and labour. A GRP yacht ought not to need painting for the first few years of her life; all that she should require is cleaning and polishing with the special products available for the purpose. But in time discoloration, which no amount of rubbing will remove, may occur together with cracks that will need filling. Wet and dry (W/D) paper is very effective in preparing a surface for painting, and has the merit that it creates no dust, but if it is used on gel coat it will produce a slightly shiny surface to which paint will not adhere, and the surface will have to be gone over again with the paper used dry. However, because of osmosis it is questionable if builders of GRP yachts will continue to use gel coat; already some are relying instead on special paints, particularly for underwater surfaces.

Before starting a major painting operation on GRP, or indeed on a yacht of any other material if about to do such work for the first time, it will be wise to study the literature provided (usually free) by one or other of the major marine paint-makers, or seek advice from a builder or yard with experience.

As I am familiar with the painting of wood yachts, I am astonished that so many owners burn off the paint so often. In the 17 years that I owned one wood yacht it was necessary to burn off the topsides only once, for the paint was not allowed to build up in thickness over the years; each time before the annual painting the surface was worked on with a stripping block and water, or with W/D paper, to reduce the thickness of paint and get a smooth surface. However, if old paint is in bad condition with blisters, opening seams, or damage, it may have to be removed down to the bare wood and a complete painting specification, of priming, filling, undercoating, and topcoating carried out. For burning off, a paraffin-burning blow-lamp is to be preferred to one burning LPG as its flame is less likely to blow out or to blow away from the work. With the lamp in your left hand and scraper in your right (unless you are left-handed) start to burn off at the top right-hand corner of the work. As the flame plays on it the paint will bubble and soften so that it can easily be removed with the scraper, which must follow the flame closely or the paint will cool and harden again; watch that the hot paint does not drop on your feet. While the scraper is at work the flame will be playing on a fresh surface below or to the left, and it must be kept on the move so that it does not char the wood. Do not burn off more than can be rubbed down and primed that day, as bare wood should not be left exposed for long. A steel vessel cannot be burnt off because the steel dissipates the heat too quickly and the paint on the inside of the plating will be destroyed; of course paint remover, which is applied by brush and left for a few minutes to soften the paint, can be used; but if the area is large sand-blasting will be the only practical method of dealing with it and, apart from the dreadful mess it makes, this is to be preferred because in a single operation it not only removes paint but prepares the steel for re-painting. A blow-lamp must not be used on GRP, which is inflammable, nor should ordinary paint remover be employed, but I understand a special remover for use on this material is available from International Paints. If anti-fouling paint has to be removed it is not wise to burn it off even if the yacht is built of wood, because materials injurious to health are then produced, nor should the paint be removed by dry sanding as the dust produced is harmful. W/D paper used wet or paint remover should be used.

For painting yachts most people now use two-pot polyurethanes, for these have greater durability, which is quite remarkable in some instances, and lower water permeability than traditional oil-base paints; the maker's recommendations and instructions must faithfully be followed, and such paints should not be applied over oil-base paints without first experimenting on a small area as crazing may result. A disadvantage of two-pot paint is that the base and the hardener need to be mixed shortly before use, and if rain then sets in or one has mixed up too much, the paint will be wasted for it has a pot life of only a few hours; also brushes (or sprayers or rollers, if used) must be washed in special solvent, which is expensive, and they must be completely cleaned of paint immediately after use or they will set up hard. Polyurethane varnish is also available, but I have had better service from the oil-base kind, and I have learnt that the former must not be applied over the latter or it will not adhere properly.

For a yacht to look smart the cutting-in of any paint line, such as that at the boot-top, needs to be cleanly and sharply done; with patience this can be achieved with a bead of paint on one corner of the brush, working up from below, not down from above. Much time will be saved, however, and a more professional job will result if masking tape is used, but this must be removed soon after the painting is finished or it will stick on hard and have to be scraped off – it will come off best if the end being held is led sharply back to lie parallel with the bit still adhering.

Good quality brushes are worth their higher cost as they do not shed their bristles. If a brush used with oil-base paint is squeezed out it may be kept immersed in water between coats, and later can be washed in paraffin or turpentine when the whole job is completed; a brush used with oil-base varnish will keep in good condition for a month or so in a mixture of turpentine and linseed oil; but, as was mentioned above, a brush used with polyurethane paint or varnish must be completely cleaned in the proper solvent immediately after use. Sometimes one needs only a dab or two of paint to touch up a blemish; for this I find a short length of terylene rope, bound close to its teased-out end with insulating tape, makes an adequate brush which can be disposed of after use instead of having to be cleaned. I have had no practical experience with the spraying-on of paint, but except perhaps on a very large area I doubt if it is worthwhile because of all the masking and general protection from wind-blown paint that must first be done, and the risk to one's neighbour. But I have used rollers for applying antifouling paint; they did just as good a job as brushes, and more quickly.

The maintenance of a yacht is a never-ending occupation and it should be a pleasant and satisfying one provided a little is done at a time as and when it is needed, but neglect will in the end add immensely to the task.

GLOSSARY OF NAUTICAL TERMS
USED IN THIS BOOK

Aback. A sail is aback when sheeted to windward, or when the wind comes on what should be its lee side.

Abaft. Nearer the stern than some other object mentioned.

Abeam. At right angles to the fore-and-aft line amidships.

Aboard. On board or in a vessel.

About. A vessel is said to go, come, or put about when she stays from one tack to the other.

Accommodation ladder. A ladder or flight of steps enabling one to climb up the topside from a dinghy to a vessel's deck.

Accommodation plan. A drawing showing the internal arrangements of a vessel.

Aft. Towards the stern; behind.

Aground. When the keel rests on the bottom.

Ahead. In front of, in the direction of the bows.

A-hull. Lying without any sail set in a gale.

Aloft. Up above; up the mast or in the rigging.

Amidships. The middle part of a vessel; sometimes refers to the fore-and-aft line, eg put the helm amidships, ie neither to port nor starboard.

Anemometer. An instrument for measuring the strength of the wind.

Apron. A strengthening piece behind the stem.

Archboard. That part of a counter stern at the extreme end to which the skin and deck are fastened.

Arming. Tallow held in the recess of a sounding lead to bring up a sample of the sea bed.

Ashore. The same as aground.

Astern. Behind; in the direction of the stern.

Athwart. Across; the opposite to fore-and-aft.

PLATE 63 (*facing*). *A.* When taking a dinghy alongside, approach at an angle of about 45°. *B.* When she will just carry her way to the yacht, stop rowing, ship with its blade forward the oar which is nearest the yacht, then, *C*, hold or back water with the other oar and the dinghy will slew round and come alongside with all way lost. *D.* The accommodation ladder is traditionally rigged on the starboard side. As this simple rope-stropped ladder is hung by its ropes it can be lowered for use when bathing. Pneumatic fenders of the type seen here can also be suspended horizontally if additional lanyards are rove through the lower eyes.

PLATE 64 (*overleaf*). *A. Wanderer III* (Gisel Ahlers from Germany) arrives at the Marquesas with patches of weed on her topsides to tell of her 38-day passage from Balboa. *B.* When lying alongside piles where fenders will not stay in place a fender board is the thing to use. *C.* If the fall of the topping lift is rove through fairleads it cannot swing and foul the ends of the crosstrees, and if the falls of idle halyards are flipped into thumb-cleats on the crosstrees they cannot tap the mast. *D.* Though an Aquavalve is rather clumsy it does ensure that water cannot reach the engine through the exhaust pipe. *E.* The award most coveted by the voyaging fraternity – the Blue Water Medal of the Cruising Club of America.

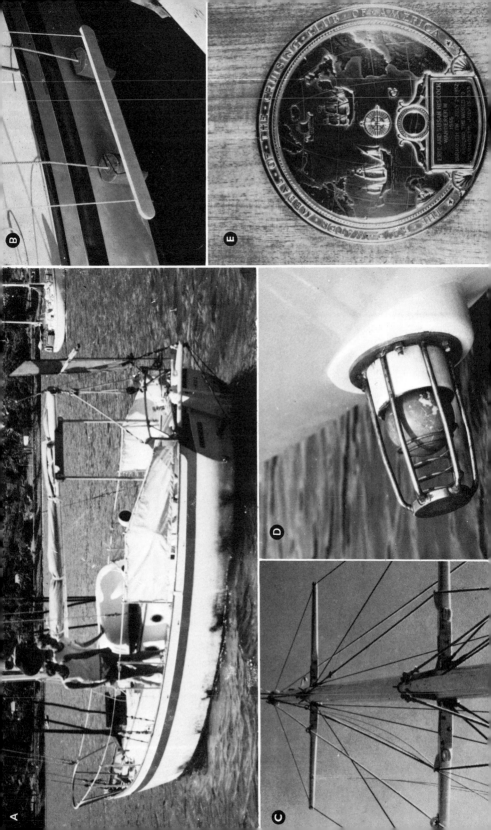

A-try. Lying under the trysail in a gale.

Auto-pilot. An electric device controlling the helm to steer a compass course.

Awash. Just washed over by water.

Aweather. To windward; towards the weather side.

Awning. Canvas spread above the deck as a protection against sun or rain.

Back, to. To sheet the clew of a sail to windward. The wind is said to back when it changes its direction anti-clockwise in either hemisphere.

Backstay. A wire-rope support leading aft from a mast to prevent it from bending forward.

Back water, to. To stop the progress of a dinghy by pushing on the looms of the oars.

Back-wind, to. One sail is said to back-wind another when it throws wind on to the other's lee side.

Baggy-wrinkle. Chafing gear made from old rope.

Ballast. Weight carried low down in a vessel's bilge or on her keel to give her stability.

Balloon jib. A large, light-weather headsail set in place of the working jib; generally used for reaching, but rarely seen today.

Bar. A shoal at the mouth of a river or harbour.

Batten. A flexible strip of wood, metal, or plastics inserted in a pocket on the leech of a sail to extend the roach and/or prevent curling or flapping.

Beacon. A landmark built on a shoal or ashore as a warning, steering, or recognition mark.

Beam. The extreme breadth of a vessel. Also a transverse member supporting the deck. A vessel is said to be on her beam ends when she is heeled excessively so that her masts are horizontal. Anything which lies outside a vessel on an imaginary line drawn from amidships at right angles to the fore-and-aft line is said to be on the beam or abeam.

Bear away, to. To turn a vessel away from the wind.

Bearers. Supports for an engine, cabin sole, etc.

Bearing. The direction of an object expressed as an angle in degrees or compass points from the vessel's meridian, or, sometimes, from the direction of the bow, stern, or beam.

Beat, to. To make progress to windward by a zigzag course with the wind first on one bow and then on the other.

Becalmed. A vessel is said to be becalmed when there is no wind and the sails hang limp and lifeless.

Becket. An eye or loop made with a wire or fibre rope. Also a metal fitting on a block to which a rope is secured.

Bee-block. A wooden chock on the side of a boom near its after end, to take the standing part of a reef pendant.

Belay, to. To make fast or secure a rope on a cleat, pin, etc.

Belly. The fullness or draught of a sail.

Bend, to. To fasten, eg one rope to another, or to some other object, a sail to its spars, etc.

Beneaped. See *Neaped.*

Bermudian sail. A triangular fore-and-aft sail without a gaff or yard, set on the aft side of a mast.

Berth. A sleeping-place on board. Also the place ashore, in a dock, or at an anchorage, occupied by a vessel. To berth a vessel is to put her into such a place.

Bight. A bend or loop in a rope. Also a bay.

Bilge. The curve of a vessel's bottom where it merges into the side. Also the space in a vessel beneath the sole.

Bilge keel. A wood or metal plate fastened to the bilge of a shoal-draught vessel to reduce leeway and to enable her to stand upright on the shore. Also a· rubbing piece to prevent chafe on a dinghy's bottom.

Binnacle. The case in which a compass is fixed.

Bitter end. The last (inboard) link of the anchor cable, or the inboard end of a rope.

Bitts. Posts fitted in the foredeck to take the heel of the bowsprit and to which the anchor cable is made fast.

Blade. The flat part of an oar, rudder, or propeller.

Block. A device for changing the lead of a rope with the minimum of friction. A landlubber's pulley.

Board. A tack or leg to windward when beating.

Boathook. A pole with a hook at one end used for picking up a mooring buoy, holding on to a dinghy, etc.

Boatswain's (bosun's) stores. Spare rigging materials carried on board.

Bobstay. A chain, wire, or rod, supporting a bowsprit or boomkin against upward pull.

Body plan. A drawing which shows the shape of the athwartships sections of a vessel.

Bollard. A post, usually on a pier or quay, to which mooring or warping lines are made fast. Also a metal fitting, often with two heads, on a vessel's deck at the bow or quarter to which mooring lines are secured.

Boltrope. A rope sewn along the edge of a sail to strengthen it and take the strain off the cloth.

Boom. A horizontal spar for extending the foot of a sail.

Boomkin. A spar projecting from the stern to take a backstay or sheet.

Boot-top. That part of a vessel's side at the waterline where the bottom meets the topsides.

Bosun's chair. A wood or canvas seat in which a person is hoisted aloft.

Bower. The principal anchor, which is generally used with a chain cable, as opposed to a kedge, which is lighter, and may be used with a rope cable.

Bows. The sides of the fore part of a vessel, from the stem to the midship section. Also used for the whole fore part of a vessel.

Bowse down, to. To haul down taut.

Bowsprit. A spar on which the jib is set, projecting from the bow.

Brace. A rope by means of which the yard of a squaresail is controlled in a horizontal plane. The term is sometimes used for the after guy of a spinnaker boom.

Brail. A rope which encircles a sail for the purpose of gathering it in to the mast.

Breaker. A sea which is breaking, ie the water of which is in forward motion. Also a container for fresh water.

Breasthook. A knee binding a pair of shelves, stringers, or gunwales to one another and to the stem.

Breast rope. A rope from bow or stern made fast to the nearest point of a quay, pier, or another vessel, when lying alongside.

Bridge deck. The deck, often lower than the main deck, between cockpit and companionway.

Brightwork. Woodwork which is kept varnished.

Bring up, to. To anchor.

Broach-to, to. To slew round in spite of the helm when running before a strong wind or heavy sea so that the wind is brought abeam.

Bulkhead. A partition below deck separating one part of a vessel from another.

Bulldog grip. A screw-fitting for temporarily clamping two parts of wire rope side by side.

Bull rope. A rope leading from the bowsprit end to a mooring buoy which is too large to be taken aboard, to keep the buoy from bumping the stem when wind and tide are opposed.

Bull's eye. A round, hardwood thimble used for altering the lead of a rope.

Bulwarks. A solid protection built round the edges of a deck to prevent people or gear from being washed overboard.

Bunk. A sleeping-berth.

Bunkboard. A bulwark of wood or canvas to prevent a sleeper from being thrown out of his bunk by the motion of a vessel.

Bunt. The middle part of a sail.

Buoy. A float.

Buoyancy bags or tanks. Air containers fitted in a dinghy to give additional buoyancy should she become waterlogged.

Burden boards. The floor boards in the bottom of a dinghy which distribute the weight of the load in her.

Burgee. A triangular flag flown at a yacht's main masthead to show to which yacht club her owner belongs.

Burton. A tackle sometimes used for lifting the anchor aboard.

Butt. Where two planks, plates, or other members touch one another end to end.

By the lee. Running with the wind on the same side as the boom.

Cable. A chain, or fibre or wire rope, by means of which a vessel rides to her anchor. Also a measure of distance, one tenth of a nautical mile (200 yards).

Camber. The athwartships curve of the deck.

Canoe stern. A stern with a pointed end projecting beyond the rudder stock.

Capstan. A mechanical appliance with a vertical barrel to give increased power when hauling on a rope or chain.

Carline. A fore-and-aft member at the side of a coach-roof, hatch, or skylight, to which the ends of the half-beams and the coaming are secured.

Carry away, to. To break or lose any spar or part of the rigging.

Carvel. A method of building in which the skin-planks lie flush with one another and present a smooth surface.

Cast, to. To turn a vessel's head on to the chosen tack when getting under way. Also to take a sounding with the lead.

Cast off, to. To let go; undo.

Catamaran. A vessel with two hulls parallel to one another.

Catenary. The curve or sag of the cable between a vessel and her anchor.

Cat rig. A fore-and-aft rig with one mast right forward and only one sail.

Cat the anchor, to. To secure it for sea.

Catspaw. A light puff of wind.

Caulk, to. To drive strands of cotton into a seam to make it watertight.

Ceiling. The lining inside a vessel which prevents anything from coming in contact with her skin.

Centreboard. A hinged or sliding vertical plate or board which can be lowered through a slot in the keel of a shoal-draught yacht, or dinghy, to provide lateral resistance.

Centre of effort. The centre of gravity of a sail or sail plan regarded as a plane figure.

Centre of lateral resistance. The centre of gravity of a plane figure, the outline of which corresponds to a vessel's underwater profile.

Chafe, to. To rub, or damage by rubbing.

Chafing gear. Anything which is used to prevent chafe.

Chain plate. A metal strap on the side of a vessel to which the lower end of a shroud, backstay, etc, is secured.

Channels. Ledges sometimes built out from the sides of a vessel to increase the spread of the shrouds.

Chine. The angle where the topside joins the bottom in a flat- or V-bottomed vessel.

Chronometer. An accurate clock used in navigation.

Claw off, to. To beat away from a lee shore.

Cleat. A fitting to which a rope may be secured without making a hitch.

Clevis. The double end of a tang or other fitting in which a pin engages to hold an item of standing rigging.

Clew. The lower after corner of a fore-and-aft sail.

Clinker. A method of building in which the edges of the skin-planks overlap one another.

Clipper bow. A bow in which the stem has a forward curve and the sides much flare. Also known as schooner bow or fiddle head.

Close-hauled. A vessel is said to be close-hauled when she is sailing as close to the wind as she can with advantage, and her sails are trimmed more nearly fore-and-aft than on any other point of sailing.

Closing. A pair of leading or clearing marks are said to be closing when a vessel approaches their line, so that they draw closer together. A vessel is said to close with another or with the shore when she is approaching them.

Cloth. A strip of canvas used in sail making.

Coach-roof. A part of the deck raised to give increased head-room.

Coaming. The side of a coach-roof, hatch, cockpit, etc, extending above deck level.

Cocked hat. A triangle formed by three bearings, or astronomical position lines, when they are drawn on the chart.

Cockpit. The well near the stern or amidships from which a small vessel is steered.

Companionway. The entry from deck or cockpit to the accommodation.

Compass point. A division of the compass card; the thirty-second part of a circle, ie $11\frac{1}{4}°$.

Compass rose. A circle, marked like a compass card, printed on a chart.

Composite. A method of building with iron framing and wooden skin.

Contlines. The spiral spaces between the strands of a rope.

Counter. A stern which extends beyond the rudder stock and terminates in an archboard or small transom.

Course. The direction in which a vessel is sailing, measured in degrees or compass points from her meridian.

Courtesy ensign. The mercantile ensign of the country being visited, worn at the starboard crosstree.

Covering board. The outermost part of the deck, which covers the heads of the frames.

Crank. Said of a vessel which heels too readily. The same as tender.

Cranse iron. The metal cap or band at the bowsprit end to which the shrouds, topmast stay, and bobstay are secured.

Cringle. A rope eye formed on the outside of the boltrope of a sail and fitted with a metal thimble.

Crosstrees. A wood or metal strut fitted to a mast to spread a shroud so that it makes a greater angle with the mast; sometimes known as a spreader.

Crown. The part of an anchor where the arms join the shank.

Cuddy. A small cabin, usually in a day boat.

Cutter. A fore-and-aft rigged vessel with one mast, a mainsail, and two headsails (staysail and jib).

Davit. A small crane used for hoisting a boat or large anchor aboard.

Deadeye. A disk of wood with three holes through which a lanyard is rove for setting up the rigging.

Deadlight. A metal cover which can be clamped over the glass of a port-light.

Dead reckoning (DR). The account kept of a vessel's position at sea, having regard to the course made good and the distance run over the ground.

Deadwood. A strengthening member binding the keel to the sternpost.

Deckhead. The under surface of the deck.

Deck light. A piece of glass let flush into a deck.

Declination. The angle between a celestial body and the equinoctial, as measured from the centre of the earth.

Derrick. A spar rigged with a tackle for lifting anything.

Deviation. An error of the compass caused by the proximity of ferrous metal; it varies with the direction in which the vessel is heading.

Dip. The difference between the sensible horizon and the visible horizon. A light is said to dip when it drops below the horizon. Also the deflection of a compass card from the horizontal.

Dip, to. To dip an ensign is to lower and rehoist it as a salute.

Displacement. The weight of a vessel.

Doghouse. An erection, usually provided with windows, built on deck over the companionway.

Dolphin striker. A spar at the stem to spread the bobstay.

Downhaul. A rope used for pulling down a sail.

Down helm, to. To put the tiller to leeward so as to bring the vessel's head towards the wind.

Drag, to. An anchor is said to drag when it fails to hold the vessel in position.

Drags. Ropes or other gear towed from the stern to slow a vessel running in heavy weather.

Draught. The depth of water required to float a vessel.

Draw, to. A sail is said to draw when the wind fills it. To let draw is to let go the weather sheet of a sail and haul in the lee one, so that the sail may drive the vessel ahead.

Dress, to. To dress a mast is to put on its standing and running rigging. To dress a vessel is to run a string of code flags from stem to stern over the mastheads.

Drift. The distance between the blocks of a tackle. Also the distance a vessel is moved by a tidal stream or a current.

Drift, to. To move with the tide, or current.

Ease, to. To slacken.

Ebb. The withdrawal of a tide.

Echo-sounder. An electronic instrument for measuring depth of water by the time taken for a sound wave to echo from the sea bed.

Eddy. A circular movement of water; or a stream running in the opposite direction to the main tidal stream.

Ensign. A maritime flag worn by a vessel to show her nationality.

Eye. A closed loop in a rope.

Fairlead. A fitting through which a rope is passed to alter the direction of its lead or to keep it clear of other gear.

Fall. The hauling part of a rope.

Fall off, to. A vessel is said to fall off when she shows a tendency to bear away from the wind.

False keel. An addition to the main keel, usually to fill in the space at the after end of the ballast keel.

Fathom. A nautical measure; 6 feet (1·8 metres).

Feather, to. To turn the blade of an oar horizontal above the water, or the blades of a propeller so that they offer no resistance to a vessel's movement through the water.

Fender. A pneumatic, or rubber, or other cushion used to prevent damage when one vessel lies alongside another or a quay.

Fetch, to. When a vessel is able to reach her objective without tacking she is said to fetch it. Also the distance a wind has been blowing over open water.

Fid. A large spike, usually of wood. Also a short metal bar passing through a hole in a spar or other object to hold it in position.

Fiddle block. A block having two sheaves in the same plane, one of them larger than the other.

Fiddle head. Another name for a clipper bow.

Fiddles. Strips of wood or metal fitted to a table, stove, etc, to prevent the contents from sliding off.

Fife-rail. A rail in which belaying pins are inserted. Also called a pinrail.

Fit out, to. To overhaul a vessel after she has been laid up.

Fix, to. To find a vessel's position by observations of celestial or terrestrial objects, or by radio bearings.

Flake down, to. To arrange a rope on deck in large figure-of-eight turns so that it will run out freely without kinking.

Flare. The outward curve or slope of a vessel's side. Also a pyrotechnic used for attracting attention.

Flattie. A dinghy with a flat bottom and chines.

Floor. A transverse member of wood, metal, or GRP, binding a pair of frames or timbers to one another and to the keel.

Fluke. The pointed part of an anchor which bites into the ground.

Fly. The horizontal length of a flag.

Foot. The lower edge of a sail.

Fore. In front; opposite to aft.

Fore-and-aft. In the direction of a line drawn from stem to stern, ie parallel to the keel.

Forecastle. That part of the accommodation which is beneath the foredeck.

Forefoot. That part of the bow which is between the load waterline and the fore end of the keel.

Forepeak. The triangular space in the extreme bow below deck, but now often used to mean the forecastle.

Fore-reach, to. To make headway when hove-to.

Foresail. The fore-and-aft sail set on the aft side of a schooner's foremast.

Fore-staysail. The fore-and-aft triangular sail which is set hanked to the forestay. Generally abbreviated to staysail.

Fother, to. To stop a leak by hauling a padded sail over it from outboard.

Foul. The sea bed is said to be foul when there are rocks or chains which might foul the anchor. An anchor is said to be foul when its fluke catches on such an obstruction; it is also foul when its cable gets round the fluke. A vessel's bottom is foul when weed or barnacles have grown on it.

Foul berth. To anchor too close to another vessel is to give her a foul berth.

Foul hawse. When the anchor cables have become crossed or twisted.

Frame. A rib of a vessel.

Frapping. The bracing together of ropes or lines to increase their tension by taking crosswise turns. Halyards are said to be frapped when held in to the mast by spiral turns of one of their number.

Free. Not close-hauled.

Freeboard. The height of a vessel's side above the water.

Full-and-by. Sailing close-hauled and steering by the wind, not by compass or mark.

Full and change. Full and new moon.

Gaff. The spar to which the head of a quadrilateral mainsail, foresail, or mizzen is bent.

Gaff jaws. The fitting at the inboard end of a gaff which slides on the mast.

Gaff sail. A quadrilateral sail fitted with a gaff.

Galley. A sea-going kitchen.

Gallows. A permanent framework on which the boom rests when the sail is lowered.

Galvanize, to. To coat iron or steel with zinc to protect it from corrosion.

Gammon iron. The ring which holds a bowsprit to the stemhead.

Garboard. The skin-plank which lies next to the keel.

Genoa. A large triangular headsail which alone fills the entire fore triangle and often extends abaft the shrouds.

Gimbals. An arrangement of concentric rings and pivots for keeping a compass, lamp, etc, level against the movements of a vessel at sea.

Gipsy. A wheel on a windlass with recesses to hold the links of a chain cable.

Girt, to. A rope leading across the lee side of a sail and making a hard ridge in it is said to girt the sail.

Gooseneck. The universal joint which holds the boom to the mast.

Grapnel. A small anchor with four or more arms.

Great circle. The shortest distance between two points on the earth's surface.

Gripe, to. A vessel is said to gripe when she carries excessive weather helm and shows a strong inclination to round up into the wind.

Gripes. The lashings which hold a dinghy on deck or to the vessel's side when lifted in davits.

Grommet. A ring made of rope. Also an eye made in the edge or corner of a sail inside the boltrope.

Guardrail. A railing, usually of wire, supported by stanchions, to prevent a person from falling overboard.

Gudgeon. A metal eye on the after side of a sternpost into which the rudder pintle ships.

Gunter. A fore-and-aft rig used for small craft. Instead of a gaff the mainsail has a yard which continues the line of the mast.

Gunwale. The upper edge of a boat's side.

Guy. A steadying rope attached to a spar.

Gybe, to. When running, to bring the wind from one quarter to the other so that the boom swings across.

Half-beam. A deck beam which does not extend right across a vessel but stops short at a carline.

Halyard. A rope used for hoisting a sail or flag.

Hand, to. To lower, take in, or stow a sail.

Handsomely. The opposite of hasty; gradually or moderately but not necessarily slowly.

Handy-billy. A tackle used temporarily to give extra power on a rope.

Hang off, to. To hold one rope temporarily with another while something is done with the end or bight of the first rope.

Hank. A clip used to hold the luff of a sail to a stay. A sail which is held to a stay by hanks is said to be hanked on.

Hard. A landing-place, usually artificial, where the foreshore is firm.

Harden in, to. To haul in a sheet so as to flatten a sail.

Hard up, hard down. Putting the helm as far as possible to windward or to leeward, respectively.

Hatch. An opening in the deck provided with a cover.

Haul, to. To pull.

Hawse hole. A hole in the bulwarks or topside through which the anchor cable runs.

Hawser-laid rope. A three-strand rope with a right-handed lay.

Head. The bow. Also the top edge or corner of a sail.

Headboard. A piece of wood or aluminium sewn to the head of a bermudian sail or spinnaker to increase the area of the sail slightly, to distribute the load on it, and prevent it from twisting.

Head-room. The distance inside a vessel between the sole and the deckhead.

Heads. A seaman's latrine. The wc.

Headsail. A sail, nearly always triangular, set forward of the fore- or mainmast.

Headstay. A rope supporting a mast forward.

Headway. The forward movement of a vessel through the water.

Head wind. A wind which prevents a vessel from laying the desired course, compelling her to beat.

Heart. A strand in the middle of a rope.

Heave-to. To trim the sails and helm in such a manner that the vessel lies almost stationary.

Heaving-line. A light rope, often with a small weight at one end, used for making connection between a vessel and the shore or some other vessel so that a stronger rope may be hauled across.

Heel. The after end of a keel or the lower or inboard end of a spar.

Heel, to. To lay over or list out of the upright.

Heeling error. Deviation of the compass caused by near-by ferrous metal changing its relative position when a vessel heels.

Helm. The tiller or wheel used for steering.

Highfield lever. A mechanical appliance used for setting up and letting go a runner or some other part of the rigging.

Hitch. A method of making a rope fast to some object. Sometimes a short tack is called a hitch.

Hog-backed. Said of a vessel which has been strained so that her sheer is convex instead of concave. Some craft are built like that.

Hoist. The vertical edge or measurement of a sail or flag.

Hoist, to. To haul aloft.

Hold, to. To stop the progress of a boat by holding the blades of the oars steady in the water. An anchor is said to hold when it gets a good grip of the bottom and does not drag.

Hood-end. The end of a plank where it fits into the rabbet cut in stem or sternpost.

Horn timber. The fore-and-aft member at the bottom of a counter.

Horse. A bar or rope on which the sheet of a sail may travel athwartships.

Hounds. Chocks on a mast on which the eyes of the lower rigging are seated.

Hove down. A vessel is said to be hove down when heeled excessively.

Huffler. A longshoreman whose job it is to take the lines of vessels about to berth.

Hull. The body of a vessel exclusive of her masts and gear.

HWF&C. High water at full and change of the moon.

HWOS. High water ordinary spring tides.

In. One is said to be in a vessel, not on her.

Initial stability. The resistance a vessel offers to being heeled, due to the shape of her hull and not to the effect of her ballast.

Inshore. Close to or towards the land.

Irons. A vessel is said to be in irons when attempting to come about she hangs stationary head to wind, and will not pay off on either tack.

Jackstay. A rope holding the luff of a sail (usually a topsail) close to the mast.

Jackyard. A short yard to extend the foot of a topsail beyond the end of the gaff.

Jib. The foremost headsail.

Jib-headed. Said of any sail the upper part of which terminates in a point.

Jib-topsail. A light-weather jib set hanked to the topmost stay.

Jumper stay. A stay which runs over a spreader (jumper strut) at the fore side of a mast; used to keep the upper part of a mast straight.

Jury rig. A makeshift or substitute rig, such as may be arranged when masts or gear have carried away. Often used to denote that a vessel does not carry sufficient canvas in her ordinary rig.

Kedge. An anchor smaller than the bower, often used with a fibre cable instead of a chain. Used for hauling a vessel off when she has gone aground and to prevent her from fouling her bower.

Keel. The fore-and-aft member on which the whole structure of a vessel is built.

Ketch. A two-masted, fore-and-aft rigged vessel with the mizzen mast stepped forward of the sternpost.

Kevel. A type of cleat made by bolting a piece of wood across two bulwark stanchions.

King-plank. The centre-plank of a deck.

Knee. A piece of timber or metal with two arms, used for strengthening certain parts of a vessel. A hanging knee is one arranged in a vertical plane, a lodging knee in a horizontal plane.

Knot. A measure of speed; 1 nautical mile (6,080 feet) per hour.

Lands. The overlapping parts of the planks in a clinker-built boat.

Lanyard. A short rope, especially one used for setting up a shroud or some other part of the rigging.

Lash, to. To bind or secure with rope.

Latitude. Distance north or south of the equator expressed in degrees and minutes of arc.

Lay. Of a rope, the direction in which the strands are twisted together.

Lay, to. A vessel is said to lay her course when she can sail in the desired direction without tacking.

Lay up, to. To dismantle a vessel and berth her for the winter.

Lazy jack. A rope passing from one topping lift, down beneath the boom, and up to the other topping lift, to gather in the sail as it is lowered.

LBP. Length between perpendiculars, that is, from the fore side of the stem to the after side of the sternpost, on deck.

Lead. A weight on a marked line, used for taking soundings.

Leader. A rope with an eye at its upper end which is free to slide on the topmast; it is used to keep the luff of a topsail close to the mast.

Leading edge. The forward part or luff of a sail.

Leading marks. Two objects which when kept in line lead one through a channel or clear of a danger.

Lee. The side opposite to that on which the wind is blowing.

Leeboard. A board which can be lowered on the lee side of a shoal-draught vessel to provide lateral resistance.

Leech. The aftermost part of a sail.

Lee helm. A vessel is said to carry lee helm when she has a tendency to turn her bow away from the wind and the helm has to be kept to leeward to prevent her from doing so.

Lee shore. A shore under a vessel's lee; one towards which the wind tends to drive her.

Leeway. The amount of sideways movement made through the water by a vessel, that is, the difference between the course steered and the course made good, assuming there to be no tidal stream.

Leg. A piece of wood or metal secured to a vessel's side to keep her upright on a hard when the tide leaves her. When beating to windward a tack is sometimes known as a leg.

Let go, to. To undo or cast off a rope. To drop the anchor.

Lifeline. A line secured to a person as a safety precaution when working on deck or aloft.

Limber holes. Holes in or beneath the floors to enable bilge water to run down to the bilge-pump suction.

Lines. The shape of a vessel, as shown in a set of drawings comprising body plan, sheer plan, and half-breadth plan.

List, to. To heel over out of the vertical.

LOA. Length over all, ie the extreme length of the hull, but not including a projection such as bowsprit or boomkin.

Locker. A stowage place or cupboard.

Log. An instrument for recording distance sailed through the water.

Log-book. A book which contains a record of a voyage or cruise.

Long in the jaw. A rope is said to have become long in the jaw when it has stretched considerably and the spiral of the strands is less steep.

Longitude. Distance east or west of the meridian of Greenwich, expressed in degrees and minutes of arc.

Longshoreman. A waterman who makes his living near the shore.

Loom. That part of an oar which is inboard of the rowlock.

Lubber line. The mark on the compass bowl which corresponds with the vessel's head.

Luff. The forward part of a sail.

Luff, to. To put the helm down and bring the vessel's head closer to or into the wind.

Luff rope. The boltrope sewn to the luff of a sail.

Lug. A quadrilateral fore-and-aft sail, the head of which is secured to a yard slung on and projecting a short distance forward of the mast.

LWL. Load waterline. The line on the hull which is reached by the water when a vessel is trimmed to float as the designer intended.

LWOS. Low water ordinary spring tides.

Lying-to. The same as heaving-to.

Mainsail. The fore-and-aft sail set on the aft side of the mainmast.

Make fast, to. To secure or belay a rope.

Man-rope. A steadying rope, to provide a handhold when climbing up an accommodation ladder.

Marina. A harbour for yachts in which they are berthed alongside and so can be boarded from the shore.

Marl, to. To take turns with small line at frequent intervals round some object, each turn being half-hitched.

Marline. Tarred twine made up of two loosely laid-up strands of hemp.

Marlinespike. A pointed instrument for opening up the strands of a rope and for tightening up or loosening the pins of shackles.

Martingale. A device to prevent a spar lifting. Also known as kicking strap.

Mast step. The slotted member on the top of the keel or floors, or on the deck, into which the lower end of a mast is shipped.

Masthead. The top of a mast.

Meridian. A true north-and-south line.

Miss stays, to. A vessel is said to miss stays when she fails to come about and falls back on the old tack.

Mitre. A seam each side of which the cloths of a sail run in different directions.

Mizzen. The fore-and-aft sail set on the aft side of the mizzen mast.

Mizzen mast. The aftermost mast in a ketch or yawl.

Mizzen staysail. A triangular sail set from the mizzen masthead to the deck forward of that mast.

Moor, to. To make a vessel fast alongside a quay, or between two posts or buoys, or to anchor her with two anchors so that she lies between them.

Mould loft. The place in which a vessel's lines are laid down full size so that the various members of her construction may be measured for and cut to shape.

Moulding. The dimension of a piece of wood between its curved surfaces.

Mouse, to. To take turns with twine or marline round sister hooks to prevent them from opening, or across the open part of a hook so that it cannot become unhooked.

Navel pipe. A fitting in the deck through which the anchor cable passes to the cable locker.

Neap tide. A tide which occurs between full and new moon and has a smaller range than a spring tide.

Neaped, or *beneaped*. A vessel is said to be neaped when she has run aground at high water and the tides are taking off so that the following tide fails to float her.

Nip. A sharp bend in a rope, such as where it passes over a sheave or through a fairlead.

Null. The silent part of the arc when taking the bearing of a radio beacon.

Offing. Position at a distance from the shore.

Offsets. Measurements supplied by a designer in order that the builder may lay down a vessel's lines in the mould loft.

Off the wind. Not close-hauled.

On the wind. Sailing close-hauled.

Open hawse. When each anchor cable leads from the bow direct to its anchor without crossing or being twisted up with the other.

Open up, to. A wood vessel is said to open up when her planks shrink and her seams are no longer watertight.

Opening. A pair of leading or clearing marks are said to be opening when, as the vessel leaves their line, they appear to draw further apart.

Outhaul. The gear used for hauling a sail out along a spar, or a dinghy from the shore.

Overhang. That part of a vessel at bow or stern which extends beyond her LWL.

Painter. The rope attached to a dinghy's bow by which she is made fast.

Palm. A fitting worn on a sailmaker's hand for thrusting the needle through the sailcloth. Also the flat part of the fluke of an anchor.

Parbuckle, to. To roll any cylindrical object upwards by passing a rope beneath it, making one end fast, and hauling on the other.

Parcel, to. To bind canvas or insulating tape round a rope in a spiral manner to keep water out.

Parrel. A fitting to keep the jaws of a gaff to the mast.

Partners. A framework or pad which supports the mast where it passes through the deck.

Patent log. An instrument for recording distance sailed.

Patent sheave. A sheave with roller bearings.

Pawl. A stop or catch which holds a moving object against movement in one direction, as in a winch or windlass.

Pay, to. To run marine glue into a seam after it has been caulked.

Pay off, to. When a vessel's head falls to leeward she is said to pay off.

Pay out, to. To ease away or slack out.

Peak. The upper after corner of a gaff-headed sail. Also the upper end of a gaff.

Pelorus. A compass card without magnets, fitted with sighting vanes and used for taking bearings.

Pendant. A hanging rope, such as a reef pendant, which hangs from the reef cringle on the leech; by means of the pendant the cringle is hauled down to the boom.

Pennant. A pointed flag.

Permanent backstay. A backstay which is cleared by the boom end and therefore does not have to be cast off when tacking or gybing.

Pinrail. A rack in which belaying pins are fixed.

Pintle. The fitting on a rudder which ships into a gudgeon so as to form a hinge.

Poop. A deck higher than the main deck at the after end of a vessel.

Poop, to. An overtaking sea is said to poop a vessel when it breaks aboard over her stern.

Port. The left-hand side of a vessel when looking forward.

Portlight. A small pane of glass, sometimes made to open, fitted in a topside or coaming.

Port tack. A vessel is on the port tack when the wind is blowing over her port side.

Position line. A line on some point of which a vessel lies.

Pram. A dinghy with a transom at bow and stern.

Preformed rope. Wire rope of which each strand is set to the linear shape it will assume in the rope before being laid up. Such rope shows no tendency to unlay.

Preventer. Another name for backstay.

Profile. The shape of a vessel as seen from the side.

Puddle. Circular ripples made by the blade of an oar as it leaves the water.

Pump-well. The lowest part of the bilge from which the bilge-pump sucks.

Purchase. A rope and blocks used for increasing power. Also called a tackle.

Quarter badge. A shaped chock of wood protecting the upper corner of a transom.

Quarters. The points on each side of a vessel which lie midway between her midship section and her stern; but the word is frequently used to indicate the whole of each side from amidships to stern, thus corresponding to the bows, which lie forward of amidships.

Rabbet. A groove cut in keel, stem, sternpost, etc, to receive the edge or end of a plank.

Racking seizing. A seizing made with figure-of-eight turns.

Radio beacon. A broadcasting station which sends out a signal so that bearings of it may be obtained with a radio set.

Rail. A narrow member fitted to the edge of a deck or top of the bulwarks.

Rake. The fore-and-aft inclination of a mast, sternpost, etc, out of the perpendicular.

Range. The difference in level between high and low water of a tide.

Range, to. A vessel is said to range about when she does not lie steadily at anchor or hove-to. To range a cable is to lay it on deck before anchoring.

Ratlines. Horizontal ropes seized to a pair of shrouds to form a ladder in the rigging.

Rat tail. A reduction of a rope to a fine point, as the termination of a boltrope.

Reach. A point of sailing with the wind abeam or forward of the beam, but not so far forward as to make the vessel close-hauled.

Reef, to. To reduce the area of sail by tying or rolling up a part of it.

Reeve, to. To pass a rope through a block, fairlead, or a hole of any kind.

Render, to. To run or slide freely; of a rope.

Rhumb line. A line crossing all meridians at the same angle.

Riding light. A lantern hung up in the fore part of a vessel at anchor showing a white light all round.

Rigging screw. A fitting with threaded ends screwing into a common body; used for setting up the rigging.

Rising. A fore-and-aft member supporting the ends of the thwarts inside a dinghy's timbers.

Roach. The outward curve sometimes given to the leech of a sail.

Round up, to, or *round to,* to. To bring a vessel head to wind from a run or a reach.

Rowlock. A crutch into which an oar is shipped when rowing.

Rudder stock. The part of a rudder which is closest to the sternpost.

Rudder trunk. A housing in the counter through which the rudder stock passes.

Run. The upward sweep of a vessel's bottom from the point of greatest beam to the stern.

Run, to. To sail before the wind.

Runner. A movable stay to support the mast from aft against the pull of a headsail or the thrust of the gaff jaws.

Running by the lee. Running with the wind on the same quarter as the boom.

Running rigging. Sheets, halyards, topping lifts, etc, by means of which sails are hoisted, trimmed, and controlled, as opposed to standing rigging which is a fixture.

Sag, to. When the luff of a headsail curves to leeward instead of being straight it is said to sag. A vessel making excessive leeway is said to sag away.

Samson post. A strong post in the foredeck to which the anchor cable is secured; also sometimes fitted at the stern or on the quarter for use when mooring fore-and-aft or towing.

Sawn frame. A wood rib which is sawn to shape as opposed to a timber which is bent to shape. Also called a grown frame.

Scantlings. The dimensions of the members used in the construction of a vessel.

Schooner. A fore-and-aft rigged vessel having two or more masts, the mainmast being as tall as or taller than the foremast.

Schooner bow. Another name for a clipper bow or fiddle head.

Scope. The length of cable by which a vessel is anchored.

Score. A groove to take a rope, such as on the circumference of a sheave or on the shell of a rope-stropped block.

Screen. The board to which a sidelight is fixed to prevent it from showing on the opposite bow.

Scull, to. To propel a boat by working one oar from side to side over the stern.

Scupper. A hole in the bulwarks to allow water to drain from the deck.

Sea. A wave.

Sea-anchor. A conical canvas bag or other contrivance for reducing the speed of a vessel to the minimum in heavy weather.

Seacock. A valve in a pipe passing through the skin-planking to prevent sea-water from entering.

Seam. Of a sail, the stitching which holds two cloths together. In yacht building, the space between two planks.

Section. The shape of a vessel if she were cut through in any place. But unless otherwise defined, a section is taken to mean an athwartships section.

Seizing. A binding together of two ropes or two parts of the same rope.

Senhouse slip. A kind of hinged hook moused with a link; by knocking back the link the hook can be opened so as to release its hold even though the strain on it may be great.

Serve, to. To bind a rope tightly with twine or wire as a protection.

Serving board, or *mallet.* The tool used for putting on a serving.

Set. The direction in which a vessel is moved by a current or tidal stream.

Set, to. To hoist or make sail.

Set flying. Said of a sail, the luff of which is not secured to a mast or hanked to a stay.

Set up, to. To tighten.

Sew, to. A vessel aground is said to have sewed by as much as the tide has left her, ie the amount the tide will have to rise to float her.

Sextant. An instrument for measuring vertical or horizontal angles.

Shackle. A metal U-shaped fitting with an eye in each of its arms through which a pin is screwed or driven. Also a length, 15 fathoms (27·5 metres), of chain.

Shake out, to. To let out a reef.

Shank. The part of an anchor which joins the arms to the ring.

Sharpie. A vessel with hard chines instead of round bilges.

Sheave. The wheel in a block or spar over which a rope runs.

Sheer. The curve of the gunwale or top strake in a vertical plane.

Sheer, to. To move a vessel at anchor in a tideway to port or starboard of her anchor by putting the helm over. A vessel which does not lie steadily to her anchor but ranges from side to side is said to sheer about.

Sheer plan. A drawing showing the shape of a vessel as viewed from the side. Also called a profile drawing.

Sheerstrake. The uppermost part of the topside.

Sheet. A rope by means of which a sail is trimmed, secured either to its clew or boom.

Shelf. A longitudinal member to which the ends of the deck beams are secured.

Shell. The outer casing of a block.

Shifting backstay. A backstay which can be set up or let go according to whether it is to windward or leeward.

Ship, to. To put a thing in its proper position for working. A vessel is said to ship a sea when a sea invades the deck.

Shroud. A wire rope giving athwartships support to a mast, bowsprit, or boomkin.

Skin. The outer covering of the hull.

Slack water. A short period at the turn of the tide when there is no tidal stream.

Slick. The comparatively smooth patch which is left to windward on the surface of the sea when a vessel is driven broadside to leeward by the wind.

Slip. A sloping hard fitted with rails or skids, used for hauling a vessel out of the water.

Slip, to. To haul a vessel out. Also to let go the anchor cable instead of weighing the anchor.

Sloop. A fore-and-aft rigged vessel similar to a cutter, but having one instead of two headsails.

Snap shackle. A shackle which has a hinged bar instead of a screw pin.

Snatch block. A block with an opening in one side of the shell so that a rope may be inserted without reeving it.

Snub, to. A vessel at anchor is said to snub when her bows lift to a sea and the cable is pulled taut with a jerk.

Snugged down. Well reefed; under a small or comfortable area of sail.

Soft eye. An eye made at the end of a rope, but not round a thimble.

Sole. The saloon or cabin floor.

Sound, to. To measure the depth of water with a leadline or other means.

Sounding. A measurement of the depth of water, as marked on charts.

Span. A rope or chain, both ends of which are secured some distance apart to the same object, such as a spar or boat, for the purpose of lifting.

Spinnaker. A triangular sail set with its boom on the opposite side to the mainsail when a vessel is running.

Spitfire jib. A very small jib used in heavy weather.

Splice. A method of joining ropes or forming eyes at their ends by interlacing the strands.

Spline. A thin strip of wood fitted in a seam in place of stopping.

Spreader. A wood or metal strut on a mast to give the rigging more spread. Usually called a crosstree.

Spring. A rope to prevent a vessel secured alongside from moving forward or aft.

Spring tides. Tides at full and change, which have a greater range than neap tides.

Spritsail. A quadrilateral sail, the peak of which is extended by a spar (sprit) from tack to peak.

Sprung. A mast or spar is said to be sprung when it is dangerously cracked or split.

Squaresail. A sail set from a yard slung athwartships on the fore side of a mast.

Stanchion. A support for bulwarks, guardrails, etc.

Stand off and on, to. To sail away from and then towards something, usually while waiting.

Standing part. That part of a rope which is made fast and not hauled upon.

Standing rigging. Shrouds, stays, etc, which support the mast or some other spar, and are not handled in the sailing of the vessel.

Starboard. The right-hand side of a vessel when facing forward.

Starboard tack. A vessel is on the starboard tack when sailing with the wind blowing on her starboard side.

Station pointer. A protractor with movable arms used for fixing the position on the chart after the horizontal angles between three objects have been measured.

Stay. A wire rope giving fore-and-aft support to a mast.

Stay, to. A vessel is said to stay when she goes about from one tack to the other by turning head to wind.

Staysail. A triangular fore-and-aft sail set hanked to a stay.

Steerage way. A vessel has steerage way when she is moving through the water with sufficient speed to answer her helm.

Stem. The member to which the skin is secured at the fore end of a vessel.

Stern board. When a vessel in irons moves astern fast enough to answer her helm so that she can be made to pay off on one tack or the other, she is said to make a stern board.

Sternpost. The member to which the under-water skin is secured at the stern and on which the rudder is usually hung.

Sternsheets. That part of an open boat which lies abaft the aftermost rowing thwart.

Stiff. A vessel is said to be stiff when she does not heel readily. The opposite to crank or tender.

Stock. The bar of an anchor which passes through a hole in the shank, or across the crown, and lies at right angles to the arms.

Stopper knot. A knot worked on the end of a rope to prevent it from unreeving through an eye, block, cringle, etc.

Stopping. Putty worked into a seam after caulking.

Stops. Separate lashings holding the head or foot of a sail to its spars. Also turns of easily broken twine with which a sail may be tied when it is to be set in readiness to be broken out later by a pull on the sheet.

Stopwater. A wooden plug driven into a small hole bored across a join which cannot be caulked, to make it watertight.

Strand. Wires or yarns twisted together in rope-making.

Stranded. A rope is said to be stranded when one of its strands is broken.

Stretcher. A crossbar in the bottom of a dinghy against which the oarsman braces his feet.

Strike over, to. To move a vessel off the cradle or slip on which she has been hauled up.

Stringer. A longitudinal strengthening member secured on the inner side of the frames or timbers of a vessel.

Strongback. A portable wood or metal bar used for supporting the ridge of a winter cover, or reinforcing a door or hatch.

Strop. An iron or rope band used for securing rigging or a block to a mast or spar.

Strum box. A strainer on the end of a bilge-pump suction to prevent foreign matter from choking the pump.

Studding sail. A narrow, light-weather sail set at the outer edge of a squaresail.

Stud-link chain. Chain in which each link has a crossbar to prevent the sides from pulling together.

Swallow tail. A flag with two tails flown at the masthead instead of a burgee by the Flag-officer of a yacht club.

Sweep. A long oar.

Swell. Long, easy waves, the crests of which do not break.

Swig, to. To tighten a rope by holding its fall round a cleat or pin while the standing part is pulled on at right angles, the slack then being taken up round the cleat or pin.

Swing, to. A vessel at anchor is said to swing when she turns at the change of the tide or wind. To swing a vessel is to turn her head to all points of the compass in turn when checking or adjusting the compass.

Tabernacle. The housing on deck for the heel and pivot of a lowering mast.

Tabling. Strengthening pieces of cloth sewn along the edges of a sail.

Tack. The lower forward corner of a fore-and-aft sail. Also a point of sailing as close to the wind as a vessel will go with advantage.

Tack, to. To beat or work to windward in a zigzag manner, close-hauled first on one tack, then on the other.

Tack tackle. A purchase applied to the tack of a fore-and-aft sail to get its luff taut.

Tackle. A purchase formed by the combination of a rope with two or more blocks to give increased power.

Taffrail. The rail across or round the stern.

Tail. A short rope attached to a block to enable it to be temporarily secured to anything.

Take in, to. To hand or stow a sail.

Take off, to. Tides are said to be taking off when changing from springs to neaps.

Take up, to. A wood vessel is said to take up when immersion in the sea causes her planks to swell so that her seams no longer leak.

Tang. A metal fitting screwed or bolted to a mast or spar for the attachment of rigging.

Taut. Stretched tight.

Tender. Easily heeled; the opposite of stiff. A yacht's dinghy is sometimes called her tender.

Thimble. A round or heart-shaped metal eye or ring, with a score on its outer surface so that a rope may be taken round it and spliced or seized, the thimble protecting the eye from chafe and distortion.

Throat. The upper forward corner of a gaff sail.

Thumb cleat. A triangular piece of wood secured to a spar or crosstree to keep some part of the rigging in place.

Thwart. An athwartships seat in a dinghy.

Tier. A strip of canvas or short length of rope used for securing a sail when it is stowed. Sometimes called a gasket.

Tie rod. A rod with head and nut binding the carline of a coach-roof, etc to the shelf so that the side deck cannot open and leak.

Tight. A vessel which does not leak is said to be tight.

Tiller. A wood or metal bar secured to the rudder head, by means of which a vessel is steered.

Timber. A wood rib which has been bent rather than sawn to shape.

Toggle. A short piece of wood to pass through the eye in the end of a rope to hold it without making a bend and in such a way that it can be cast off quickly. Also a universal joint fitted to a rigging screw to prevent lateral strain.

Topmast. The upper part of a mast; with gaff rig sometimes a separate spar.

Topping lift. A rope supporting the after or outboard end of a boom.

Topsail. A triangular fore-and-aft sail set above a gaff-headed sail.

Topside. That part of a vessel's side which is above water when she is afloat but not heeled.

Track. A grooved metal rail on which sail slides run.

Trail boards. Decorative fore-and-aft members with gilded carving arranged one each side of a clipper bow.

Transducer. A fitting in a vessel's bottom by which sound waves are sent and received in connection with an echo-sounder.

Transom. A flat or slightly curved stern above the LWL.

Traveller. A ring or other fitting which can be hauled out along a spar to take the tack or clew of a sail.

Triatic stay. A rope connecting two mastheads.

Trim. The angle the fore-and-aft line of a vessel makes with the water when she is afloat.

Trim, to. To sheet a sail so that it draws to the best advantage.

Trimaran. A vessel with a float at each side to keep her upright.

Trough. A valley between two seas.

Truck. A wooden cap at the masthead or topmasthead which has holes or a sheave for the burgee halyard.

Trysail. A small, strong sail sometimes set in place of the mainsail in heavy weather.

Tumble-home. The inward curve that the sides of some vessels have above the load waterline.

Turn to windward, to. To beat, tack, or work to windward, steering a zigzag course.

Turn up, to. To belay or make fast a rope on a cleat or pin.

Unbend, to. To remove a sail from its spars and other gear.

Under bare poles. Under way but with no sail set.

Under-run, to. A method of weighing a kedge anchor by hauling the dinghy along the cable (which slides in the sculling notch) until the dinghy is directly over the kedge.

Under way. A vessel is said to be under way when she is moving through the water.

Unreeve, to. To pull a rope out of a block, sheave, eye, etc.

Unship, to. To remove something from its proper or working position.

Up and down. An anchor cable is said to be up and down when it has been hauled in until it is vertical and any further hauling will break the anchor out.

Up helm. The act of putting the helm to windward so as to make a vessel bear away.

Vang. A rope controlling the upper end of a sprit or gaff.

Variation. The difference between true and magnetic north at any place.

Veer, to. To pay out anchor cable. The wind is said to veer when it changes its direction clockwise in either hemisphere.

Wake. The path of disturbed water left astern of a moving vessel.

Warp. Originally a strong rope by means of which a vessel was moved in or out of dock. The fibre rope attached to a kedge anchor is often known as a kedge warp.

Washboards. Planks which slide vertically into grooves in a companionway to prevent water from entering.

Waterlines. Horizontal sections of a vessel's hull at and below the LWL.

Way. The movement of a vessel through the water.

Wear, to. The act of putting a vessel about on to the other tack by turning her away from the wind and gybing instead of staying.

Weather, to. A vessel is said to weather something when she is able to pass to windward of it without tacking.

Weatherly. Said of a vessel which is capable of sailing close to the wind.

Weather shore. A shore to windward of a vessel; therefore one which offers shelter.

Weather side. The side of a vessel on which the wind is blowing.

Weigh, to. The act of raising the anchor from the bottom.

Well. Another name for a cockpit. Also that part of the bilge from which a bilge pump sucks.

Whip. A purchase in which only one block is used.

Whip, to. To bind the end of a rope with twine to prevent it from unlaying.

Whiskers. Crosstrees from the bows to spread the bowsprit shrouds.

Winch. A mechanical appliance consisting of a drum on an axle, a pawl, and a crank handle with or without gearing, to give increased power when hauling on a rope.

Windlass. A type of winch fitted with a gipsy, for hauling chain cable.

Wind-vane gear. A device controlling the helm to steer a course in relation to wind direction.

Windward side. The same as weather side.

Wishbone. A spar in two halves like a wishbone, between which a sail is hoisted, the wishbone extending its clew.

Working sails. Sails which are used in most kinds of weather: mainsail, foresail, staysail, jib, and mizzen; sometimes referred to as 'the lowers'.

Worm, to. To fill in the contlines of a rope before parcelling and serving.

Yankee. A large triangular headsail used in light or moderate winds and set on the fore topmast stay. Unlike a genoa it does not fill the whole fore triangle, but is set in combination with the working staysail.

Yard. A spar to which a topsail or squaresail is bent.

Yarn. Fibres which are twisted together to form the strand of a rope.

Yaw, to. A vessel which will not hold a steady course, but swings from side to side of it, is said to yaw.

Yawl. A fore-and-aft rigged vessel with two masts, main and mizzen, the mizzen being stepped abaft the sternpost.

INDEX

(Figures in italics refer to Plates and the relevant captions)

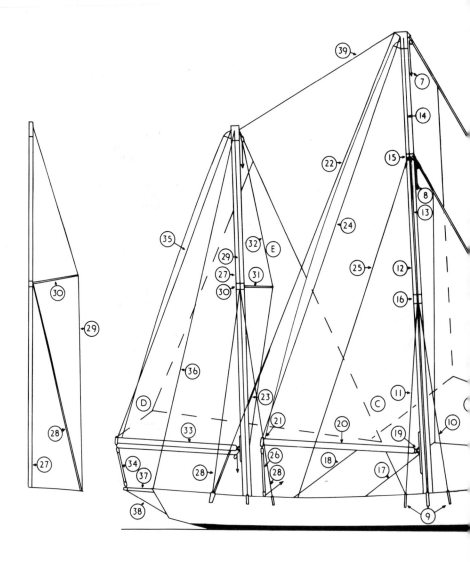

Fig 102   Standing and running rigging of a ketch (not to scale)

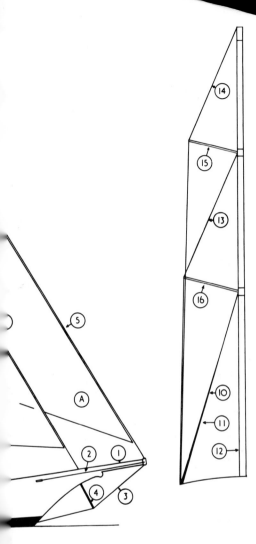

Spars and
Rigging

1 Bowsprit
2 Bowsprit shroud
3 Bowsprit bobstay
4 Dolphin striker
5 Topmast or
  masthead stay
6 Forestay
7 Jib halyard
8 Staysail halyard
9 Chain-plates
10 Forward lower
   shroud
11 After lower
   shroud
12 Mainmast
13 Intermediate or
   cap shroud
14 Topmast or
   masthead shroud
15 Upper crosstree
   or spreader
16 Lower crosstree
   or spreader
17 Staysail sheet
18 Jib sheet
19 **Main gooseneck**
   and roller reefing
   gear
20 Main boom
21 Swivel band
22 Backstay
23 Backstay legs
24 Topping lift
25 Runner
26 Mainsheet
27 Mizzen mast
28 Mizzen lower
   shrouds
29 Mizzen topmast
   shroud
30 Mizzen crosstree
31 Mizzen jumper
   strut
32 Mizzen jumper
   stay
33 Mizzen boom
34 Mizzen sheet
35 Mizzen topping
   lift
36 Mizzen runner
37 Boomkin
38 Boomkin bobstay
39 Triatic stay

Sails

A Jib
B Staysail
C Mainsail
D Mizzen
E Mizzen staysail